BUSINESS REPORT WRITING
Second Edition

BUSINESS REPORT WRITING

Second Edition

Joel P. Bowman
Bernadine P. Branchaw

Department of Business Information Systems
Western Michigan University

THE DRYDEN PRESS

Chicago   New York   San Francisco
Philadelphia   Montreal   Toronto
London   Sydney   Tokyo

Acquisitions Editor: Mary Fischer
Developmental Editor: Deborah Acker/Joanne Smith
Project Editor: Karen Steib
Design Director: Alan Wendt
Production Manager: Barb Bahnsen
Permissions Editor: Cindy Lombardo
Director of Editing, Design, and Production: Jane
 Perkins
Text Designer: Image House, Inc., Stuart Paterson
Copy Editor: Jean Berry
Compositor: University Graphics, Inc.
Text Type: 10/12 ITC Garamond Light

Library of Congress Cataloging-in-Publication Data

Bowman, Joel P.
 Business report writing.

 Includes index.
 1. Business report writing.   I. Branchaw, Bernadine P.
II. Title.
HF5719.B68   1988   808′.066651   87-15438
ISBN 0-03-013244-4

Printed in the United States of America
890-016-987654321
Copyright © 1988, 1984 by The Dryden Press, a division of Holt,
Rinehart and Winston, Inc.

Address orders:
111 Fifth Avenue
New York, NY 10003

Address editorial correspondence:
One Salt Creek Lane
Hinsdale, IL 60521

The Dryden Press
Holt, Rinehart and Winston
Saunders College Publishing

P R E F A C E

With every passing year, our culture is becoming more communication intensive—communication is playing an increasingly important role in our daily lives, influencing both our business and our social relationships. Business reports are more important now than they ever have been before. Since we wrote the first edition of *Business Report Writing,* business operations have become more complex, office technology has changed, and the demands on report writers are greater.

NEW EDITION

Although our general approach to report writing and our philosophy of communication remain unchanged, this new edition of *Business Report Writing* reflects the changes currently taking place in the practical world of business reports. Those who are now entering the job market can anticipate writing many more reports than those who entered even 10 years ago. Furthermore, they will be expected to write better reports more quickly in spite of the need to consider and include more data in each report. Fortunately, new computer technology will help, and this book will help readers take advantage of that technology.

We also attempt to prepare readers for anticipated changes. Throughout the book, we stress a problem-solving approach to report writing and focus on the unchanging commonalities of report writing situations: the relationship between reader and writer, the ethical obligations of communicators, the use of language to convey meanings, and the need for objective information in the decision-making process. Because changes in method are certain, report writers need a firm foundation in principles so that they can adapt as required by circumstances. *Business Report Writing* provides that kind of foundation.

SPECIAL FEATURES

This new edition contains several new features to improve its usefulness to students, teachers, and practitioners.

- *Marginal Questions.* In place of traditional marginal comments, we have used questions to encourage increased reader participation in understanding the material. These questions not only help students think about the material being discussed but also may serve as quiz or discussion questions.

- *Chapter Overviews and Summaries.* Each chapter begins with an overview of content to help orient readers to chapter material in a more interesting way than that provided by typical "learning objectives" found in most textbooks. Each chapter concludes with a comprehensive summary to reinforce the most important learning points.

- *Real-World Examples, Problems, and Cases.* All examples, problems, and cases have been taken directly from or adapted from real report writing problems, cases, and situations encountered by people working in business, industry, or government.

- *Current Information on Computer Applications.* We provide a thorough introduction to computer-based communication practices and to the uses of computer technology in report writing.

- *The Cultural Context of Reports.* Because reports are always written in a specific cultural context that includes the nationalities of reader and writer, the ethical dimensions of the situation, and a public relations dimension, we discuss the ramifications of these factors.

- *Business Statistics.* Because of the increasing complexity of business decisions, business report writers increasingly need to use statistics in analyzing data and drawing conclusions. In Appendix A, we provide a brief overview of the most important applications of statistics.

- *New Problems.* Appendix B contains a wide assortment of problems for both short and long reports. Data are provided for some; others require both secondary and primary research.

ORGANIZATION

We have organized the book for ease of use. We believe the book to be the most flexible work currently available for teaching—and learning—report writing. Part I provides the foundation for understanding the nature and functions of business reports (Chapters 1 and 2).

Part II covers the writing process, especially as it applies to business reports. Chapter 3 covers basic writing principles. Chapters 4 and 5 discuss the writing process, including the collaborative writing that those assigned to committees will be required to do and the development of writing strategies appropriate for business reports.

Part III provides an overview of report conventions and techniques, including classification of reports (Chapter 6), form and appearance (Chapter 7), and common types of reports (Chapter 8).

Part IV introduces report research and the presentation of data. Chapter 9 covers planning, from brainstorming to outlining. Chapter 10 covers secondary research, including online database retrieval. Chapter 11 discusses methods of documentation. Chapter 12 introduces primary research. Chapters 13, 14, and 15 cover surveys, analysis and interpretation of data, and use of graphic aids in presenting data.

Part V covers formal reports, including organization (Chapter 16) and presentation (Chapter 17).

Part VI discusses special applications. Oral reports and presentations (Chapter 18), the use of computers in report writing (Chapter 19), and the cultural context of reports (Chapter 20) complete the coverage of business reports.

The appendixes present statistical information (Appendix A), additional problems (Appendix B), and job application materials (Appendix C).

Each chapter includes an overview, a list of topics, a summary, review and discussion questions, and problems or cases as appropriate.

TEACHERS, STUDENTS, AND PRACTITIONERS

This book has three distinct and very different groups of readers, each of which has a special set of needs. We believe that we have done a good job of addressing those needs. For teachers, we have organized the material in the way it is most often taught and have provided a wide array of instructional aids. As a whole, the book covers all aspects of report writing, yet each chapter is complete in itself so that instructors may omit chapters if necessary to meet the requirements of their semester, quarter, or term without diminishing student comprehension of the topics actually covered.

Teachers will also find the *Instructor's Manual* especially helpful because it contains answers to the review and discussion questions, sample student reports, exam questions and answers, and numerous transparency masters.

Students will appreciate the numerous examples and clear explanations that will enable them to apply the techniques in a wide variety of situations. We provide step-by-step instructions and checklists where such guidelines are useful, and where they are not, we show students how to analyze problems and provide clear explanations of their analysis. Students will appreciate the way in which *Business Report Writing* answers the questions they most often have about reports.

Students and practitioners will appreciate the thorough index and numerous topic headings. We recognize that one of the most useful functions of a book on report writing is the service it can provide as a reference tool. People who are actually in the process of writing a report need to be able to look up answers to their how-to questions quickly and easily. We have designed the book so that it will serve well not only as an orientation to and source of information about report writing but also as a handbook or guide for those who need to look up answers to specific questions as they prepare reports.

The extended coverage of designing questionnaires, interpreting data, drawing conclusions, and using computers to write reports and prepare graphic aids will be especially helpful, as will the many samples of the most common types of reports. The index, lists of chapter topics, marginal questions, numerous examples, and checklists will help report writers with the very practical matter of finding solutions to their specific report writing problems—and finding them quickly and easily.

We believe that whether you are teaching business report writing, studying report writing, or currently writing real business reports, you will find *Business Report Writing* both readable and helpful.

ACKNOWLEDGMENTS

Many people have contributed their time and talent to make this edition of *Business Report Writing* a better book than it might have been otherwise. Our views of communication in general and of report writing in particular have been strongly influenced as a result of our membership and participation in The Association for Business Communication. As a result of presentations by and the research of our colleagues in the Association, we have incurred debts too numerous to mention.

Our reviewers were especially helpful and deserve special mention for their valuable comments and suggestions. We would like to thank Marian C. Crawford of the University of Arkansas at Little Rock, Stephen G. Driggers of Auburn University, Robert D. Gieselman of the University of Illinois—Urbana, Florence B. Grunkemeyer of Ball State University, Robert B. Mitchell of the University of Arkansas at Little Rock, Kevin F. Mulcahy of California State University—Northridge, Charles L. Snowden of Sinclair Community College, Skaidrite Stelzer of The University of Toledo, and Daniel J. Sundahl of Hillsdale College for their useful suggestions. We have also received assistance from Mary Fischer, Deborah Acker, Joanne Smith, and Karen Steib of The Dryden Press, the copy editor Jean Berry, and the designer Stuart Paterson.

We are grateful to our friends in business, industry, and government who have provided the many examples used throughout the book, and we are indebted to our editors at Dryden for their assistance and attention to detail.

Our students also have helped us make this second edition a better book in both major and minor ways. By asking astute questions, casting a critical eye on our illustrations and explanations, offering suggestions, and pursuing and insisting on excellence, our students have encouraged us to produce a better book.

To the best of our abilities, we have incorporated the best of the suggestions offered by those who helped. We believe that the result will greatly facilitate the process of writing business reports.

Joel P. Bowman
Bernadine P. Branchaw

Kalamazoo, Michigan

CONTENTS

CHAPTER 4
The Characteristics of Functional Writing   67

CHAPTER 5
The Process of Writing   99

PART III   Report Conventions and Techniques   131

CHAPTER 6
Classification of Reports   133

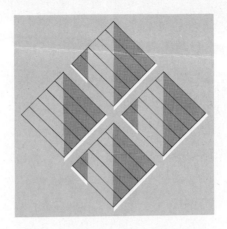

Report Writers and Readers

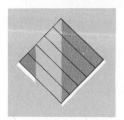

Report Writing at Work

"Submit a proposal."
"I need your findings in report form."
"It's your turn to do the annual report."
Sooner or later you will have to write a report—a report on which your business future will probably depend. Although this book will not eliminate all the stress that accompanies the task of preparing reports, it will certainly make your job easier by showing what to include and how to include it. This chapter introduces the basic concepts.

Topics

Who Reports to Whom—and Why
The Communication Process
Functional Writing in Business, Industry, and Government
Definition of a Report
Importance of Report Writing
A Good Report

Everyone in business, industry, and government submits reports on a regular basis. Some of these reports are oral; some are written. Some are informal; some are formal. Every organization needs reports to coordinate activities, to provide a record of events, and to serve as a basis for managerial decisions. Although different organizations have different reporting procedures and responsibilities, *every* job in *every* organization requires reports of one sort or another.

WHO REPORTS TO WHOM—AND WHY

Reports are the principal means by which members of an organization communicate with each other about job-related matters. Oral reports are exchanged daily about a wide variety of business concerns—ranging from the number of boxes of paper clips on hand to the status of billion-dollar investments. Written reports are also prepared on a regular basis. These range from brief, informal memos dashed off by hand to formal documents thousands of pages long and bound in volumes.

Reports and the Organizational Hierarchy

Reports usually go *up* the chain of command in an organization. Those who are working on specific tasks submit reports to those higher in the organizational hierarchy. The recipients of the reports use them to make decisions and perhaps as the source of information that becomes part of new reports to be sent on to higher management. When reports are exchanged between persons of equal rank, they are still used to provide information necessary for decision making. As a rule, reports are distributed *down* the chain of command only as a means of disseminating information.

Which direction do reports normally go in the chain of command? When might they go in the opposite direction?

As reports go up the chain of command, the information may receive different treatment or emphasis at each level of the decision-making process. For example, a line worker may report to his or her supervisor that a top-drive press has developed a vibration.

Worker: Listen to this, Jack. Something's wrong. It may be the main bearing.

Supervisor: You're right, Nancy. I'll get on the horn and schedule maintenance as soon as possible. Meanwhile, shut this one down and use the one-point.

At the next level, Jack would report to *his* supervisor.

Jack: We've had a breakdown on line five. It may be the main bearing on the two-point top-drive press. When can we schedule maintenance? We'll need to hustle to maintain schedule on the Berman project.

Section Supervisor: I'll schedule the crew as soon as possible. Isn't this about the third breakdown this quarter for that press?

Jack: Actually, it's the fourth. Once we were able to repair it ourselves. We had only an hour's downtime. We really should be thinking about replacing it.

Exhibit 1.1   Reports and the Organizational Hierarchy

Annual report

Primarily informa-
tional reports—
reporting decisions
and the results of
decisions

Informational and
analytical reports
based primarily on
information pro-
vided by lower-
level management

Informational, in-
terpretive, and
analytical reports

Primarily informa-
tional reports,
many using
printed forms

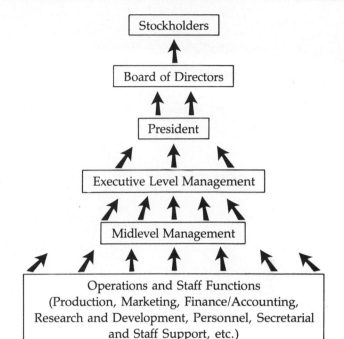

Depending on the circumstances, the section supervisor might need to report the problem immediately and orally to the plant manager, or she or he might wait until the end of the week, month, or quarter to send a written report. The problem could be discussed in an urgent memo, an activities report, a justification report (requesting a new press), or an equipment report.

How may the reporting of information change as it goes up the chain of command?

In fact, this problem might be mentioned at this and higher levels of management. It could be included in (1) a planning report, (2) a financial report, (3) a letter to the press manufacturer, (4) a progress report on a new press, or even (5) the firm's annual report to stockholders. As Exhibit 1.1 indicates, at each level of the hierarchy, information is condensed and consolidated before being transmitted to the next level. Although some critical reports may be transmitted without change from lower levels all the way to the top, most are not. As a result of the natural tendency of employees to emphasize the positive when reporting to their supervisors, negative information may be subordinated or even omitted as reports go up the chain of command. In our hypothetical example, the information about the bad drill press might not reach the appropriate decision maker in time for the company to maintain the schedule on the Berman project.

Exhibit 1.2   Model of the Communication Process

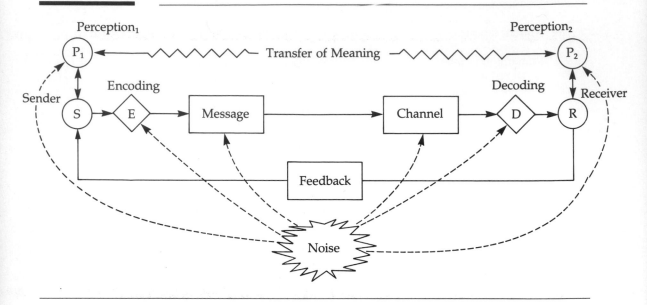

Reports and Business Decisions

Regardless of how well or poorly facts are conveyed, business decisions depend on a flow of information that often takes the form of oral and written reports. Most of this book will concentrate on written reports because they usually require more extensive research and preparation. Oral reports are covered in Chapter 18.

THE COMMUNICATION PROCESS

What is the definition of communication?

The process controlling the flow of information in business is not different from that controlling the flow of information in any complex relationship. By definition, communication is the successful transfer of meaning from a sender to a receiver. The process begins with a **perception** in the mind of a **sender.** This perception is the impetus for a **message.** The sender **encodes** a **message** and selects a **channel** that will convey the message to a **receiver,** who **decodes** the message into a new perception. **Feedback** indicates to the sender how well the meaning has been transferred. **Noise**—anything that interferes with the transfer of meaning—can occur at any point in the communication process. The goal of this process is the **transfer of meaning.** Each of these variables influences the communication process, as Exhibit 1.2 illustrates.

Although the exhibit suggests that each factor operates separately from the others, in actuality the factors are interdependent and essen-

Exhibit 1.3   **The Role of Communication in Business Organizations**

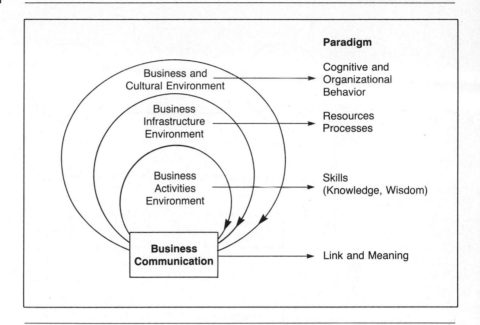

Source: Developed by Andrew S. Targowski and Joel P. Bowman, Western Michigan University, Kalamazoo, MI.

tially take place simultaneously. The sender, for example, may be watching the receiver for signs of feedback while she or he is in the process of sending a message. Thus, the sender may be in effect sending and receiving messages simultaneously.

Communication and Organizational Activities

What is the difference between qualitative and quantitative corporate aims?

The communication process occurs within a framework of assumptions held by the sender and receiver that add to or detract from the meaning each perceives in a given message. Exhibit 1.3 illustrates the role communication plays in organizing and regulating organizational activities within the larger environments of business and culture, and Exhibit 1.4 illustrates the network of aims within an organization. Communication links each element of the network and provides an interpretation of meanings inherent in a given situation.

Communication and Frames of Reference

Why do frames of reference differ within the same organization?

No one communicates in a vacuum. The sender and receiver both bring a history of experiences, preconceptions, and expectations to the communication situation. As a rule, the greater the differences in previous experiences, preconceptions, and expectations, the greater the diffi-

Exhibit 1.4   ## Network of Aims within an Organization

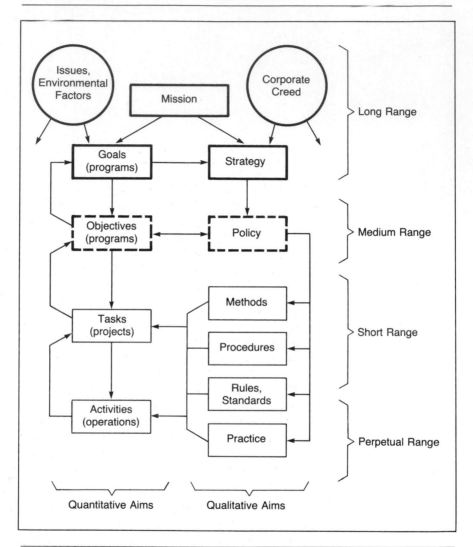

Source: Developed by Andrew S. Targowski and Joel P. Bowman, Western Michigan University, Kalamazoo, MI.

culty sender and receiver will have communicating. People from different cultures—even different corporate cultures—may have difficulty understanding one another. Even within the same organization, however, differences are present. For example, those lower in the organizational hierarchy tend to be more concerned with short-range tasks and activities and consequently focus primarily on methods, procedures, and rules for their frames of reference. Those higher in the hierarchy tend to be more concerned with the mission of the organization and focus primarily on goals and strategy. The effectiveness of communication between such a sender and receiver will depend at least partially on how well each understands the frame of reference of the other.

Exhibit 1.1 makes the communication process seem simple and straightforward. This is far from the case. The model illustrated in Exhibit 1.1 is concerned primarily with the physical transmission of a message from sender to receiver. A sender and receiver are linked not only by the physical mechanism they use to communicate but also by their associated frames of reference, which provide them with their respective interpretations of the messages sent and received. Imagine the communication difficulties that could result from the following business situation:

> The chief executive officer of your organization, ABC Company, decides that ABC needs to begin marketing its products in Japan. After some preliminary research, an appropriate Japanese outlet is identified, an appointment is arranged, and you are elected to fly to Japan to meet with the representative of the Japanese organization. You speak no Japanese; the Japanese speaks little or no English. The CEO expects you to make a quick deal, whereas it is clear to you that the Japanese expects to establish a good personal understanding before conducting business. What do you report to your CEO, and how do you go about it? What do you say to the Japanese?

The example includes three very different frames of reference: the CEO's, yours, and that of your Japanese counterpart. Your communication in this situation would be effective to the extent that you were able to reconcile the differences among these divergent views.

Because we spend so much time sending and receiving messages, we tend to take communication for granted. Such an attitude has led to countless costly business mistakes, of which the following are typical:

- A Midwest company shipped ten boxcars of the wrong paint to a California factory because a shipping clerk received an incorrect order.
- A sales manager went to the wrong hotel and missed the opportunity to present her organization's product to a group of prospective buyers.
- The president of a major corporation asked for and received a number of concessions from unionized employees and then awarded large bonuses to himself and his management team, causing an expensive wildcat strike.

Communication and Problem Solving

Although good communication does not automatically solve all problems, no problem can be solved without it. Good communication simply helps the people involved in a situation to understand one another. Once they understand each other, they are in a better position to make the best decisions from their respective frames of reference.

Business reports play an important role in this process. They have evolved over the years to help ensure that the appropriate people receive the information needed to make the appropriate decision at the appropriate time. For this reason, they are often referred to as **functional writing.**

Why is the writing of business reports called functional writing?

FUNCTIONAL WRITING IN BUSINESS, INDUSTRY, AND GOVERNMENT

Reports generally have their inception in a need. Somebody needs information on which to base a decision; or somebody wants management to make a decision and reports the information to the appropriate person. Whether the report is reader initiated or writer initiated, reports are written to help management make decisions.

Purposes of Reports

What are the four most common functions of reports?

Although the content of reports may vary from organization to organization depending on the nature of products and services, all reports are functional writing; that is, each report has a particular function or purpose to perform. The following functions are the most common:

1. Serve as a permanent record. Organizations require records for a variety of reasons. Reports concerning income and expenditures, for example, may be required for tax purposes. Other major reasons organizations need permanent records are to avoid duplication of effort at a later date and to profit from successes and failures in a wide variety of areas.

2. Provide specialized information. As mentioned previously, reports usually convey information from those with specialized knowledge to those with more generalized responsibilities. Because of special training, experience, or proximity to matters of organizational importance, a report writer is able to observe, describe, and interpret events or problems for those making organizational decisions.

3. Evaluate problems, possibilities, and people. The specialized information provided in reports allows decision makers to see how the particular parts of a problem fit into the larger organizational whole. Reports can present the advantages and disadvantages of various possibilities, allowing decision makers to select the best possibility from a number of alternatives.

   Reports help managers evaluate people in two ways: First, supervisors use reports to provide a record of their evaluations of subordinates; and second, managers use written reports to help evaluate the performance of report writers. Written reports, in fact, are one of management's chief evaluative tools because they reveal the writer's organizational ability, judgment, clarity of thought, and ability to express himself or herself.

4. Help in decision making. The report writer needs to be certain to provide the kind of information that will assist the decision-making process. The writer should know what the reader already knows about the topic of the report to avoid emphasizing an aspect of the topic with which the reader is already familiar. The writer should discover what the reader *needs* to know: Are the reader's main concerns financial, technical, organizational, or political?

The writer also needs to anticipate questions the reader may have while reading the report. Those questions will usually take the form of one of the following:

What forms will the reader's questions usually take?

What: action do I need to take? is the next step? are my responsibilities? caused the problem? changes will be required?

Why: should I act? should the company invest in this project? should I permit the writer to act?

How: will I benefit from this? will the company benefit from this? will the project be accomplished? much investment will be required? soon will we need to start? long will it take to finish?

Who: will benefit from this? will be affected by this? should act on this? needs to know more about this?

Most managers in business, industry, and government cannot directly observe materials, personnel, events, and other factors that will influence their decisions. When managers (1) are too far away from an operation to observe it directly, (2) lack the time to observe it directly, or (3) lack the technical expertise to observe it accurately, they must rely on the reports of others. Persons who are in a position to make accurate, reliable, and objective observations write reports for the benefit of a person or persons who will make decisions about the observations.

Reports and Organizational Objectives

An organization is any group of people working together to achieve a common purpose. The coordination of activity this requires is made possible by communication. Communication in general and reports in particular help organizations meet the routine and special objectives necessary to reach long-term goals. Routine and special objectives can be classed as maintenance, task, or human depending on the way in which they contribute to the overall goal. Maintenance objectives are those that help an organization maintain its existence by solving regular, recurring problems. Task objectives are made necessary by special circumstances, events, or managerial decisions. Human objectives are usually satisfied by writer-initiated reports, often proposals suggesting an improvement in the writer's area of expertise.

What type of
reports meet
maintenance
objectives?

Maintenance Objectives Maintenance objectives require routine reports written as a regular part of a job. Every week, for example, a sales representative will submit a report on the previous week's sales. Many maintenance reports are *periodic reports* because they are prepared according to a regular time interval (weekly, monthly, quarterly, annually, or even hourly under some circumstances). Reports written to meet maintenance objectives monitor and regulate the sustenance of the organization. Because these reports are written on a regular, recurring basis, most companies use printed forms or specific guidelines to facilitate presenting facts quickly and easily in the desired form.

What type of
reports meet task
objectives?

Task Objectives Organizations must also solve special problems and meet special objectives. Task reports are often necessary to meet these needs. They can be as simple as a one-line memo or as complex as a long, formal report requiring months of research. Because task reports deal with special circumstances, they are prepared on a one-time basis without the aid of printed forms or specific guidelines. Report writers have only general guidelines to help them prepare task reports.

You might, for example, be assigned the task of selecting a site for your organization's new world headquarters building; or you may be responsible for determining the market potential of a new product or service; or perhaps you will need to determine the effectiveness of your organization's public relations efforts. Whatever the problem, as the one assigned the task, you would be responsible for determining the appropriate form and content for the report.

What types of
reports meet
human objectives?

Human Objectives People who deal with certain operations on a regular basis are often able to foresee problems and suggest improvements. Management can encourage employees to make full use of their creativity and expertise by providing them the opportunity to submit reports anticipating problems or recommending improvements in procedures, products, processes, or services. Reports of this kind are not an assigned part of a job but may be rewarded (with a percentage of the first year's savings, perhaps).

Proposals, justification reports, and even brief notes dropped into a suggestion box all help an organization meet its need to encourage the full productivity of its employees. Organizations usually establish specific guidelines for such reports and suggestions to simplify their evaluation.

DEFINITION OF A REPORT

What is the
definition of a
report?

The word *report* covers an extremely wide range of communication activities in modern organizations. As we will use the term in this book, **a report is an organized presentation of information to a specific audience for the purpose of helping an organization achieve an objective.**

What are the
characteristics of
reports?

Reports are more than the communication of random data. Because someone in the organization will use the information to help achieve an objective, it is important that the information be organized in a way that will facilitate its use. One of the characteristics that distinguishes reports from routine oral exchanges of information and most casual, written messages is the care given to organizing the presentation of information. The presentation may be either written or oral and may include a wide variety of graphic aids (written reports) or visual aids (oral presentations) as well.

Reports are almost always prepared for a select reader or group of readers who will use the information as a basis for making decisions about organizational matters. In addition, reports are usually assigned to those persons who are in the best position to organize, interpret, and analyze the required information. Because those responsible for making the decisions need accurate, reliable, and impartial information, another characteristic of reports is that they should be based on objective, factual data rather than on unsupported opinions. As noted previously, reports help managers achieve a wide variety of organizational objectives, including maintenance, task, and human objectives. However they are defined, reports play a vital function in both routine and special operations in every organization.

IMPORTANCE OF REPORT WRITING

Why have reports
assumed a central
role in modern
organizational life?

Reports have assumed their central role in modern organizational life because they have long demonstrated their ability to provide essential information in usable form. A 1980–1981 study of newly promoted executives revealed that business communication, including report writing, was the single most useful area of study for those wishing to work in general managerial positions.[1] Reports and other written communications have always been important to business, and studies of business people consistently show that they rank communication, and especially written communication—letters, memos, and reports—as their single most important activity.[2]

How are business
reports used to
avoid information
overload?

Reports play an important part in almost every decision made in business, industry, and government. The history of report writing reveals steadily increasing use of written reports of all types. The current need for clear, concise reports is being fueled by what many researchers are calling the **information age.** Most managers now receive far more information than they can digest, a phenomenon known as **informa-**

---

[1]H. W. Hildebrandt et al., "An Executive Appraisal of Courses Which Best Prepare One for General Management," *The Journal of Business Communication,* 19:1 (Winter 1982): 5–15.
[2]See, for example, "Accreditation Research Project, Report on Phase I," *AACSB Bulletin* 15:2 (Winter 1980): 21.

tion overload. Business reports have become one of management's most important ways of regulating the flow of information. Reports allow managers to request the information they require for decision making and to ignore the superfluous.

Why is information called the critical resource?

In previous times, agriculture, capital, or manufacturing capacity formed the basis for decisions in business, industry, and government. Today, the critical resource has become information.[3] Having the right information at the right time is frequently more important than the availability of other resources. Because the need for information is increasing daily, the need for more—and more effective—reports can only increase in the future.

History of Reports

Written reports are as old as written history. In fact, early governmental and business reports provide much of our information about ancient civilizations. Even before recorded history, oral reports were serving their primary function of providing military and other leaders with the information they needed to make decisions. With the advent of writing, written reports began to supplement the oral reporting. The abilities of writing to transcend distance, to transcend time, and to permit the careful consideration and controlled use of language were responsible for the growing importance of written reports. With the Industrial Revolution and the development of complex, modern organizations, the need for clear, concise reports increased greatly.

Current Usage

How do managers use reports?

Reports allow managers to

1. Make decisions about operations they are unable to supervise directly due to constraints of distance or time.
2. Understand and make decisions about technical operations being supervised by specialists.
3. Retain information in easily accessible form for future use.
4. Evaluate the technical and communication skills of those preparing the reports.

Because of their general utility, reports are often seen as an essential step in any planning process. If anything, reports are more likely to be required when not needed than they are to be needed and not required.

---

[3]See John Naisbitt, *Megatrends.* New York: Warner Books, 1984. Especially p. 6.

For reports to be their most useful, they must be controlled in both number and content. Managers need to ensure that routine reports continue to provide essential information and that task reports are assigned only to meet real organizational needs.

Why do managers need task reports?

Managers need task reports primarily to answer one or more of the following questions.

Can We?   Before undertaking any project, management needs to know if it is possible for the organization to do it. Current technology, for example, might not permit the completion of a particular project. Some projects may be possible for one organization but not for another because of the new capital, resources, or technology involved.

Should We?   Once the feasibility of a project has been demonstrated, the next question is whether it should be undertaken. Will the expected benefits exceed the costs involved? The benefits and costs may not always be profits and monetary expenditures. Safety, public relations, and environmental impact are but a few of the concerns managers must consider.

Which Way Is Best?   Once management decides that a project is possible and worthwhile, it needs to determine which means of achieving the objective will provide the greatest return for the least investment.

Future Possibilities

Whatever changes take place in communication technology over the next several years, it is certain that oral and written reports will continue to play a vital role. Technological advances will undoubtedly influence reporting policies and procedures. Computers will automatically gather, collate, and transmit important data to appropriate personnel. They will also perform many of the analytical functions report writers must now perform themselves.

What new challenges can report writers expect in the 1990s?

As technology advances, another change report writers will face will be the increasing need to prepare technical reports for nontechnical audiences. Specialists will be writing reports for managers who have only a limited knowledge of the various areas of specialization within their areas of responsibility.

Along with preparing increasingly specialized reports for general audiences, report writers will be faced with the additional challenge of writing increasingly concise reports. Over the past several years, the average length of reports has been shrinking, and this trend is likely to continue as long as organizations put a premium on managerial time.

These changes will all put increased demands on report writers, who will continue to be responsible for the flow of information that makes organizational decision making possible.

A GOOD REPORT

What are the characteristics of a good report?

Regardless of the changes that new technologies will bring about, good reports have always displayed—and will continue to display—the same characteristics. A good report is

1. Timely. It arrives on or before it is due and contains up-to-date information.
2. Well-written. It is clear, concise, interesting; it is free from errors in grammar, mechanics, and content; and it is helpful.
3. Well-organized. It is designed to be read selectively, so that a reader can pay attention only to those parts necessary.
4. Attractive. It is clearly labeled and assembled so that it will arrive in good condition, and designed for easy readability.
5. Cost-effective. It is designed to solve a problem for the organization that will make the investment in the report worthwhile.

What type of information ensures a reliable report?

A good report anticipates the reader's questions and provides answers. To help the reader make the right decision, the writer should provide reliable answers to those questions.

To ensure the reliability of your reports, check all data for accuracy, impartiality, and completeness. **Accurate** information conforms to the truth and is free from error. **Impartial** information is fair and objective. It presents all sides of critical issues so that the reader can see how you reached your conclusions and is free and able to draw different conclusions when the information may be interpreted in more than one way. **Complete** information gives the reader everything he or she needs to make the best decision.

What are the reasons for providing only necessary documentation?

Although the main function of reports is to provide information that will help a manager make a decision, reports can often provide a record that will protect the writer. Some organizational communication books go so far as to recommend that employees should document every idea, telephone call, conversation, and action with a memo or longer report. We believe that excessive written documentation is dysfunctional. The paper avalanche that results from excessive documentation helps no one and, in fact, interferes with the acceptance of significant reports.

In report writing, as in all of life, importance and emphasis are indicated by contrast; without valleys there would be no mountains. When an employee attempts to document everything, each document loses importance. Reports written by an employee who writes only a few will be read much more carefully than those written by employees who report every telephone call.

Why is timing often a factor in report writing?

Sometimes *not* writing is the best way a writer can help her or his supervisor. Does the reader really *need* the information? Does the reader have the resources or ability to act on the recommendation? Does the reader have the time to act on the recommendation?

Organizational life is complex. Budgets are cut, crises can occur at any time, and organizational objectives can change quickly as a result of outside influences. How well will the information you intend to present fit in with the current organizational situation? Managers are slow to accept suggestions for larger expenditures in times of decreasing budgets and for any new actions in times of crisis. The timing of reports, as well as their content, should take the reader's needs into account.

In the chapters that follow, we will show you how to produce well-written, well-organized, and attractive reports to meet the needs of business, industry, and government. We will also provide guidelines to help you gauge both the possible cost-effectiveness of a report and general time requirements for each step of the report-writing process.

SUMMARY

Reports are the principal means by which members of an organization communicate with each other about job-related matters. Reports usually go *up* the chain of command in an organization, as individuals at lower levels provide information to those responsible for making decisions.

Communication is the successful transfer of meaning from a sender to a receiver. The goal of this process is the transfer of meaning. The process occurs within a framework of assumptions held by the sender and receiver that add to or detract from the meaning each perceives in a given message. Business reports play an important role in this process. They ensure that the appropriate people receive the information needed to make the appropriate decision at the appropriate time.

Reports are necessary when managers are too far away from an operation to observe it directly, lack the time to observe it directly, or lack the technical expertise to observe it accurately. Reports help management achieve maintenance, task, and human organizational objectives by providing the routine or special information needed for managerial decisions.

A report is an organized presentation of information to a specific audience for the purpose of helping an organization achieve an objective. Reports have assumed their central role in modern organizational life because they have demonstrated their ability to provide essential information in usable form. A good report is timely, well written, well organized, attractive, and cost-effective.

EXERCISES

Review and Discussion Questions

1. What are the variables in the communication process? How does each influence the process as a whole?

2. What is meant by "no one communicates in a vacuum"?

3. What are the most common functions of reports?

4. What is the relationship between reports and organizational objectives?

5. What is a report?

6. What are the characteristics of reports?

7. What do reports allow managers to do?

8. What three questions do task reports answer?

9. What changes are likely to take place in report procedures in the next several years?

10. Why have reports assumed a central role in modern organizational life?

Problems and Applications

Present the following in written or oral form as your instructor directs.

1. Based on the information presented in this chapter, what would you say are the differences between reports and term papers?

2. Interview three or four people who work in business, industry, or government and list their oral and written reports. Describe how the reports they prepare relate to their job functions.

3. If you were a district sales manager responsible for sales representatives in 17 Midwestern cities, what reports would you expect to receive from your staff and why? What reports would you expect to prepare for your supervisor? Why?

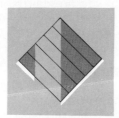

The Reader-Writer Relationship

What you do *before* you write will have a major influence on how successful your final report turns out to be. As a writer, your main goal will be to help the reader solve a problem or make a decision. To do that, you will need to learn your readers' needs and focus your attention on those needs. This chapter introduces the principal questions for understanding your purpose and analyzing your audience.

Topics

What Is Your Purpose?
Who Are Your Readers?
What Do Your Readers Need to Know?
What Do Your Readers Already Know?
What Action Is Required?
How Will Your Readers Feel About Your Message?
What Are Your Readers' Organizational Roles?

Reports are written to accomplish a specific purpose and, further, reports are designed to accomplish it by working through someone else. For these reasons, the reader or readers of a report are of central importance. As a report writer, you will need to ask yourself several questions to help you present the information in a way that will facilitate any action the reader may need to take.

WHAT IS YOUR PURPOSE?

Before beginning work on any report, a writer needs to determine how the report will be used and what action should occur as a result. Each of the basic organizational objectives—maintenance, task, and human—may require written reports. In addition to these general objectives of reports, each report will also have at least one of three specific objectives:

1. To inform
2. To analyze
3. To recommend

What may happen if you do not know the purpose of your report?

A report writer may wish (or be required) to provide information, to interpret that information for the reader, to analyze the information and reach conclusions about what the information means, or to do all of these and make recommendations based on the analysis of information. A writer needs to know which of these purposes is appropriate for a particular report. To inform only when analysis and recommendations are required is to be incomplete. To analyze and recommend when the reader wants information only is to be presumptuous.

Why must you rely on objective evidence?

One purpose reports do *not* have is to persuade. Although a report writer may need to use persuasive techniques to ensure a fair reception for unpopular ideas, the purposes of such reports remain to inform, analyze, and recommend. Even when a report writer desires upper management to make a specific decision, he or she has the obligation to present all the information in an accurate, impartial, and complete manner. Managers need sound evidence on which to base their decisions, and a report writer should allow the objective evidence to constitute the entire effort to persuade.

WHO ARE YOUR READERS?

Who is the primary audience for your report? Who might a secondary audience be?

As a rule, specialists write reports for generalists. Field sales representatives, for example, have specific, detailed knowledge of their territories. Regional sales managers know something about each of the territories in their regions, but their knowledge is less specific and detailed than that of the representatives. The vice president of sales would know still less about any one territory and would be more concerned with general sales figures and projections.

The situation is more complicated when the report writer needs to report on a technical process to an audience unfamiliar with the field. In many instances, the person addressed may not prove to be the actual audience for the report. The person addressed may forward the entire report to someone higher in the organization, and that person may not be familiar with the situation or expect the report. Or the report may be reviewed by a series of people, each of whom has the power to disapprove the recommendation but only one of whom has the authority to approve it.

How do the frames of reference of the audience affect the purpose of the reports?

Regardless of the report situation, writers should begin by considering the purpose of the report in relation to the readers' needs, desires, and frames of reference. Managers with financial or accounting backgrounds, for example, may be primarily interested in the financial details of the situation. Operations managers, on the other hand, may be concerned with procedures. Although general reports should be written to satisfy the needs of the primary decision maker, the needs of the secondary audience should not be overlooked.

The initial **audience analysis** should determine who has the authority to make a decision as a result of the report and who else might be affected by its content. Once the primary and secondary audiences for the report have been identified, the report writer can begin to develop a plan for meeting their specific needs.

WHAT DO YOUR READERS NEED TO KNOW?

Why must reports be written with the decision maker in mind?

As a report writer, your principal obligation will be to meet the needs of the person who will take action as a result of your report. Your supervisor, or the person to whom your report is addressed, may not be that person. He or she will act as a result of the report and thus needs accurate and complete information on which to base a decision. For many task reports, the decision maker will need to know

1. The nature of the problem
2. The causes of the problem
3. Possible solutions to the problem
   a. Costs for the solutions
   b. Advantages of the solutions
   c. Disadvantages of the solutions
   d. Possible long-term results of the solutions
4. Recommended solution and supporting reasons

One of the problems decision makers face in many organizations is that report writers often distort information as it goes up the chain of command. As mentioned in Chapter 1, at each level report writers tend to minimize problems and to magnify accomplishments, because naturally no one likes to give the boss bad news. Without accurate and complete information, however, the decision maker cannot possibly solve potential problems before they become major concerns.

How may information become distorted on the way to the decision maker?

A friend of ours in the packaging business told us about such a problem that occurred in one of the plants where he had worked. An operator of a critical piece of machinery told his foreman that the equipment was "on its last legs" and that it needed to be replaced. The foreman told the section supervisor that the machine would need to be replaced "soon," and the supervisor reported to the plant manager that "they needed to think about replacing" the aging equipment. The problem was presented in one sentence in the plant manager's 30-page, monthly report to the vice president. The vice president did not mention it at all in his report to the president. Shortly thereafter, the equipment broke down so completely that it was unrepairable, and the entire plant had to close for more than six weeks while a new piece of equipment was ordered, shipped, and installed. The company lost millions of dollars worth of business.

The reader of your report will need to know anything that will influence the success of the organization. The reader, however, will probably be more concerned with the *whats* and the *whys* than with the *hows*. The decision maker needs to know *what* needs to be done by *when* and for what reason. The specific *hows* are usually left to be decided by those working directly with the problem.

What information do decision makers want in a report?

Because managerial decision makers have general responsibilities for a number of specific areas, they want the necessary information reported in a way that facilitates the decision-making process. Report writers should provide:

1. A quick overview of the problem, including the main point and recommendation.
2. Complete facts, including costs, advantages, disadvantages, and results of any action.
3. Clear writing presented in readable format.
4. Separation of facts, inferences based on fact, and opinion.
5. Constructive suggestions.

How should the information be organized?

As a rule, managers expect to find this material quickly and easily without reading the entire report. For this reason, all but the briefest reports should include a summarizing abstract that covers all the critical points, an introduction that describes the problem and its background in general terms (rather than specific or technical terms), and specific conclusions and appropriate recommendations. Most managers will *not* read the body of the report unless they have a special interest in the subject, they have been directly involved in the project, the problem is especially urgent, or they are skeptical of the conclusions or recommendations.

Because the reader's time is valuable, reports need to make the organizational pattern clear, predictable, and easy to follow. For this reason, writers often use headings, itemized lists, and a variety of graphic aids to present information in a way that will enable the reader to determine quickly which parts require close attention and which can be skimmed.

WHAT DO YOUR READERS ALREADY KNOW?

Why is it important to control emphasis and subordination?

Reports written at someone's request or as a routine part of the job fit into an existing communication context. In these cases, you will have a good idea of what your reader already knows. When you initiate a report, your reader will obviously require a more comprehensive introduction to the problem and the purpose of the report.

Whether your readers expect the report or not, what they already know will influence the content of your report. No one likes to be told things he or she already knows. For that reason, you should avoid mentioning facts your reader already knows unless they are an essential part of the report. When facts already known to the reader are essential, subordinate them to some new, important piece of information with which the reader is not yet familiar.

Change this: Our company installed the new computer system in December 19xx. Since that time we have discovered . . .

To this: Since December 19xx, when we installed the new computer system, we have discovered . . .

Also subordinate any necessary information your reader *should* know but may not remember.

Change this: We currently have a capital investment of $2.7 million in the Hawthorne plant alone.

To this: The $2.7 million capital investment in the Hawthorne plant may now be fully depreciated over the next three years.

In general, it is better to assume that your reader knows little than to assume that he or she knows too much. Your reader will forgive you more readily for telling more than he or she wants to know than for omitting details required to understand the situation and make a decision. See Chapter 4 for a discussion of emphasis and subordination.

WHAT ACTION IS REQUIRED?

Why is it important to anticipate questions?

The ultimate objective of every report is some kind of action. Even the most routine informational memo contains data that will eventually contribute to a decision. A report writer needs to see that information from the perspective of the reader. The reader's main questions are always going to be, "What action will I have to take as a result of this report?'' and "How will the organization benefit as a result of the action?''

Whenever you are writing a report, you will need to anticipate those questions even if you have not been authorized to suggest possible courses of action. When you have the opportunity to make recommendations, state them clearly and explicitly, explaining the advantages and disadvantages of each possible alternative.

When it is obvious that no action is possible, do not bother to complete and submit a report unless the purpose of the report is to determine whether action is possible. You can avoid unnecessary communication—and the time and effort it takes to write a report—if you will attempt to place the action you are recommending within the larger context of the organization. If your department has been ordered to trim its budget by 20 percent and your company has instituted a hiring freeze, a report suggesting the hiring of additional support personnel— no matter how well written—will not be well received. Similarly, if your organization is facing an immediate crisis, reports that can wait, should wait.

HOW WILL YOUR READERS FEEL ABOUT YOUR MESSAGE?

When should information be presented deductively? Inductively?

Even though your reader may need bad news to make a good decision, no one will enjoy learning that the organization has a problem. Your reader will especially resist recommendations that will require spending significant amounts of either time or money. A reader will also resist conclusions and recommendations that run counter to his or her own theories and vested interests.

How the reader is likely to feel about your message will influence the way in which you should organize the material. When your reader will welcome your recommendation and conclusions, present your information *deductively,* with the most important point (the action recommended) first. When you suspect that your reader will resent or resist your conclusions and recommendations, present the information *inductively,* with the main evidence presented before the specific recommendation. When your message will contain information the reader will consider negative, inductive order of presentation will help ensure an objective reading of your report. Report organization is covered in Chapter 16.

WHAT ARE YOUR READERS' ORGANIZATIONAL ROLES?

Why are organizational roles important to the report writer?

One of the most critical factors in the reader-writer relationship is the role each plays within the organization. New employees in particular may forget that, as relatively junior employees, they will usually be preparing reports for their superiors, and these superiors are responsible for current policies and practices that new employees may be prone to criticize. As a result, new employees may offend and alienate the very people they need to impress to ensure a successful career.

An acquaintance of ours, for example, went to work for an insurance agency following his graduation. During his first few weeks on the job, he noticed that the form letters being used by the agency violated many of the rules of effective communication. Wishing to impress his boss with his superior skills, he wrote a report detailing the problems with the letters and proposing new, improved versions. He submitted the report, expecting a commendation and early promotion, but he was surprised and more than a little disappointed when he failed to pass his six-month probationary period. In his haste to correct what he perceived as a problem he forgot that his boss, as the head of the agency, had probably written the letters of which he was critical.

Before you write any report, consider the reader's role in the organization and the role you yourself are playing. Given those roles, what is appropriate for you to request, recommend, or criticize? Remember that your boss may have a vested interest in current policies and practices, and he or she may perceive a criticism or alternative recommendations as an attack on his or her authority.

SUMMARY

In addition to the basic organizational objectives—maintenance, task, and human—each report will also have at least one of three specific objectives: to inform, to analyze, to recommend. Once the primary and secondary audiences have been identified, the report writer can develop a plan for meeting their specific needs by answering these questions: What do my readers need to know? What do my readers already know? What action is required? How will my readers feel about my message? What are my readers' organizational roles?

EXERCISES

Review and Discussion Questions

1. What are typical report objectives?
2. Under what circumstances should a report writer use persuasive techniques?
3. What are some examples of maintenance, task, and human reports?
4. Who is the ultimate reader of a report?
5. Under what circumstances will the ultimate reader be different from the person addressed?
6. What does a typical report reader need to know?
7. In what ways does information become distorted as it goes up the organizational chain of command?

8. Why should the writer provide the reader with a general, nontechnical overview of the situation?

9. How should the writer handle necessary information with which the reader is already familiar?

10. How do the reader's feelings about the message influence the presentation of information?

Problems and Applications

1. Select a company discussed in a recent issue of *Forbes, Business Week,* or *Fortune,* and
   a. Write a brief summary of the article, making sure to include a description of any problems the company faced, the decisions made or required, and any results.
   b. List possible report subjects, writers, and readers who would have contributed to the decision-making process for company management.

2. You are the field representative for a major pharmaceutical company. Yesterday, when you called on a hospital in your territory, you were told by the hospital's chief of internal medicine that your company's new drug developed to treat glaucoma may have pernicious side effects. Of the seven patients using the drug, five have developed liver and kidney complications. You know that the company spent nearly five years and several millions of dollars developing the drug and that the FDA approved its use only after extensive and closely monitored tests. What do you report, to whom, and how do you present the information? Write a short paper explaining and justifying your choices.

3. Find three articles describing what managers want in the reports they receive and prepare a brief summary of their contents. Note especially the similarities and differences in what the articles say managers want.

4. Interview a business manager responsible for preparing and receiving reports and ask him or her what is essential for a good report. Write a summary of his or her comments. If your instructor requests, compare the manager's opinions with those stated in the articles used for Question 3 above.

5. Obtain an actual business report (or, if your instructor permits, use one of the samples presented in this text) and
   a. Identify the objective or objectives.
   b. Identify the ultimate reader.
   c. Identify the information necessary to make the report effective.
   d. Specify information that would have helped the reader but was not included in the report.
   e. Evaluate the report.

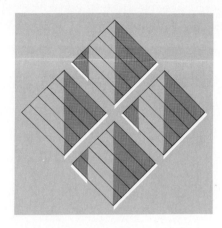

Functional Writing

C H A P T E R 3

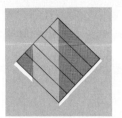

The Principles of Writing

Is it *who,* or is it *whom?*
Is it *lay,* or is it *lie?*
Should it be a comma or a semicolon?
Every time a writer has to stop and ask a question of this kind, the process of writing comes to a halt. Ignorance of the ways in which the English language should be used is one of the main impediments to writing quickly and easily. This chapter provides a brief overview of the most important aspects and common problems of English usage.

Topics

Understanding the Parts of Speech
Building Sentences
Using Words Correctly
Using Sentences Correctly
Avoiding Common Sentence Errors
Paragraphing
Avoiding Other Common Difficulties
Using Punctuation Correctly

Regardless of your occupation, writing—reports, letters, documentations, procedures—will play an important role in your career. To be comfortable submitting copies of your materials for the review of others, you will need to feel confident of your ability to use English correctly. The guide we present here is not meant to serve as a substitute for a complete handbook of English usage. It is designed to be a quick and handy reference to the common problems of usage you encounter while writing reports. Those who write regularly on the job will probably want to invest in one or more of the English handbooks and guides to writing style listed at the end of the chapter.

Although it is not an exciting subject for most people, grammar is an essential component of effective communication. The rules of grammar have, in fact, been established for precisely that reason: When we all follow the same grammatical rules, it is easier for us to understand each other. Fortunately, you do not have to be an expert to use language well. Grammar is quite simple when you concentrate on the few absolute essentials you will need to communicate effectively. Any objections you may have to grammar are probably a result of its sometimes arbitrary nature. Certain grammatical rules cannot be logically explained but must simply be accepted.

UNDERSTANDING THE PARTS OF SPEECH

The words we use to express grammatical principles are merely symbols for concepts we have about the ways language functions. To be able to discuss the concepts, we need a common terminology. One important part of this terminology concerns the components of language—the parts of speech—and how they function in sentences.

Part of Speech	Function
Noun	Names something
Pronoun	Takes the place of a noun
Verb	Expresses action
Adjective	Modifies a noun or pronoun
Adverb	Modifies a verb, adjective, or another adverb
Conjunction	Joins one element to another
Preposition	Shows relationship
Interjection	Expresses strong feeling

Nouns

A noun names a person, place, thing, or idea. In sentences, nouns can function as subjects, direct objects, indirect objects, objects of prepositions, subject complements, and appositives. **Proper nouns** name particular persons, places, or things; they are usually capitalized. Examples of proper nouns include *Abraham Lincoln; Washington, D.C.;* and *Blue Ridge Mountains.* **Common nouns** name persons, places, or things that are not specific, such as *man, woman, city, state, chair, desk, profits,* and *losses.*

Common nouns may be classified as **abstract** or **concrete.** Abstract nouns refer to intangible things—things that cannot be seen, heard, touched, tasted, or smelled. Abstract nouns refer to qualities or ideas, such as *goodness, freedom, democracy,* and *capitalism.* Concrete nouns refer to tangible things—things that can be seen, heard, touched, tasted, or smelled—such as *chair, noise, skin, fur, apple, smoke,* and *fumes.*

What is meant by the ladder of abstraction?

Abstract and concrete are, of course, matters of degree rather than absolutes. Most nouns are abstract or concrete only in relation to other nouns. The word *dog,* for example, is less concrete than a specific breed, *English setter,* and less abstract than the word *mammal.* This concept is often referred to as the **ladder of abstraction.**

Pronouns

A pronoun is a word that takes the place of a noun. The noun for which a pronoun stands is its **antecedent.**

Personal pronouns refer to the person speaking, the person spoken to, or the person spoken about.

	Singular	**Plural**
Person speaking:	I went.	We went.
Person spoken to:	You went.	You (all) went.
Person spoken about:	He went.	They went.

Which relative pronoun is best to use when referring to people?

Relative pronouns introduce subordinate clauses by referring to antecedents in the main clause. *Who, whom, which,* and *that* are relative pronouns.

Dolores Powers is an executive who works hard.

In this example *who* is a relative pronoun that introduces the subordinate clause; it refers to the antecedent, *executive,* in the main clause.

Use *that* to introduce essential noun clauses (those that define or restrict a preceding term). Use *which* to introduce nonessential noun clauses (those that describe rather than define or limit).

Correct: This is the kind of book that causes arguments.

Correct: This book, which has caused many arguments, has been on the best-seller list for 25 weeks.

See the section on restrictive and nonrestrictive phrases and clauses later in this chapter.

What is an indirect question? A direct question?

Interrogative pronouns start direct or indirect questions. *Who, whom, what, which,* and *whose* are interrogative pronouns. (Do not confuse *whose* with the contraction *who's,* which stands for *who is.*)

Direct question: Whose account is this?

Indirect question: I wonder what stock we should purchase.

Demonstrative pronouns point out particular persons or things. *This, these, that,* and *those* are demonstrative pronouns. *This* (singular) and *these* (plural) refer to objects that are near. *That* (singular) and *those* (plural) refer to objects that are distant.

Singular: This is mine.   That is hers.

Plural: These are mine.   Those are hers.

What is wrong with "these kind"?

Indefinite pronouns refer to groups of persons or to things in general. Some indefinite pronouns are

all	everything
any	neither
anybody	most
anyone	much
anything	none
each	several
either	some
every	somebody
everybody	someone
everyone	something

How is the nominative case used? The objective case? Reflexive? Possessive?

Case   Pronouns have different cases, depending on the role they play in a clause. When the pronoun is acting as the subject of a verb, it is the *nominative* case (because it *names* the subject of a verb). When the pronoun receives the action of a verb or is the object of a preposition, it is in the *objective* case. When a pronoun refers to a noun or pronoun earlier in the sentence, it is in the *reflexive* case. When it expresses ownership, the pronoun is in the *possessive* case.

Nominative Case	Objective Case	Reflexive Case	Possessive Case
I	me	myself	my/mine
you	you	yourself	your/yours
he/she	him/her	himself/herself	his/her
it	it	itself	its
we	us	ourselves	our/ours
you	you	yourselves	your/yours
they	them	themselves	their/theirs

What is grammatically wrong with "me and my RC"?

Incorrect: *Me* and Carl prepared the work schedules.

Correct: Carl and *I* prepared the work schedules.

Incorrect: Just between you and *I,* Susan Crowfoot will be our new president.

Correct: Just between you and *me,* Susan Crowfoot will be our new president.

Incorrect: Give a copy of the report to her and *myself.*

Correct: Give a copy of the report to her and *me.*

Incorrect: *Them* and *us* designed the brochure for the seminar.

Correct: *They* and *we* designed the brochure for the seminar.

Incorrect: It was *me* who called yesterday.

Correct: It was *I* who called yesterday.

Incorrect: She believes that Darrell or *him* submitted the plan.

Correct: She believes that Darrell or *he* submitted the plan.

Incorrect: Is this book *her's?*

Correct: Is this book *hers?*

Incorrect: Everyone liked *them* acting.

Correct: Everyone liked *their* acting.

Incorrect: For *me,* I prefer the longer weekend.

Correct: For *myself,* I prefer the longer weekend.

Incorrect: A man like *yourself* should know better.

Correct: A man like *you* should know better.

Compound personal pronouns are those in the reflexive case, the "self" pronouns (myself, yourself, himself, herself, itself, ourselves, yourselves, themselves). They are used to direct the action of the verb back to the subject.

Sherry bought *herself* a new desk.

They satisfied *themselves* by buying 100 shares of IBM stock.

They are also used when you want to emphasize a noun or pronoun already expressed.

I *myself* shall do the job.

The manager conducted the workshop *herself.*

Mr. Rousch *himself* told us the news.

How is the reflexive case most often misused?

Do not use a compound personal pronoun unless the noun or pronoun to which it refers is stated in the sentence.

Incorrect: Give the papers to Joan and *myself.*

Correct: Give the papers to Joan and *me.*

Incorrect: A person (any person) such as *yourself* should recognize the importance of deadlines.

Correct: A person like *you* should recognize the importance of deadlines.

Verbs

A verb is a word that expresses action or being. A verb is essential to complete the meaning of any sentence. A **transitive** verb needs an object to complete its meaning; an **intransitive** verb does not need an object to complete its meaning.

Transitive: David completed the project.
Intransitive: Mary Ann sat.

Some verbs are both transitive and intransitive.

Transitive: Fred sells stocks.
Intransitive: Fred sells frequently.

What is a linking verb?

An intransitive verb has no object, but it may have a **complement** (discussed later in this chapter under "Sentences"). An intransitive verb that joins a subject to its complement is called a **linking** verb. Common linking verbs are *be, seem, appear,* and verbs describing the senses, such as *feel, taste,* and *look.*

Profits seemed high.

Profits are good.

The pie tastes wonderful.

When is a verb in the active voice? The passive voice?

Voice   If the subject of the sentence does the action that the verb describes, the verb is in the **active voice**. If the subject of the sentence receives the action, the verb is in the **passive voice**.

Active voice: Edward prepared the sales report.
Passive voice: The sales report was prepared by Edward.

In active voice sentences the subject of the sentence always performs the action. Passive voice sentences use the verb "to be" and the past participle of an action verb so that the subject receives the action.

Active voice: The *manager decided* to buy a new desk.
Passive voice: It *was decided by* the manager to buy a new desk.
Passive voice: It *was decided* to buy a new desk.

Tense   The simple tenses (past, present, and future) are easier to understand than the compound tenses. Use them when possible, but make sure that the verbs used for each event accurately depict the time appropriate for the event. See "Progression of Verb Tenses" later in this chapter.

Adjectives

Adjectives are words that modify nouns or pronouns. In the following sentence, *short-term* modifies *profits.*

Short-term profits increased.

When is the
positive degree of
comparison used
for an adjective?
The comparative
degree? The
superlative degree?

Adjectives have three degrees of comparison—*positive, comparative,* and *superlative.* Use the positive degree when the word modified is not being compared with anything else. Use the comparative degree when comparing two things; use the superlative degree when comparing more than two things.

Generally, add the suffix *-er* to form the comparative degree, and add *-est* to one-syllable adjectives to form the superlative degree. For adjectives of more than two syllables, add the words *more* (for comparative) or *most* (for superlative). For negatives, add *less* (for comparative) or *least* (for superlative). Two-syllable adjectives may take either form to show the comparative or superlative degree.

Positive	Comparative	Superlative
bright	brighter	brightest
angry	angrier	angriest
	more angry	most angry
appreciative	more appreciative	most appreciative

Some adjectives have irregular forms of comparison.

Positive	Comparative	Superlative
bad	worse	worst
good	better	best

What name is given
to adjectives that
cannot be
compared? Are
negative
comparisons
permitted?

Other adjectives cannot be compared; they are absolutes. *Round, square, perfect,* and *unique* are absolute adjectives.

Incorrect: It was the *most unique* party I had ever attended.

Correct: The party was *unique!* (Unique means one of a kind.)

Negative comparisons of absolutes are always correct:

Correct: The party was *almost* unique.

Correct: The report was *nearly* perfect.

Adverbs

Adverbs are words that modify verbs, adjectives, or other adverbs. They give information about *when, where, how,* or *how much.* Most adverbs end in *-ly.*

Profits increased rapidly.

Often adverbs can be moved from place to place in a sentence without changing the meaning of the sentence. When the sentence contains more than one word that could be modified by the adverb, however, confusion may result.

The profits that had declined sharply rose the next day.

What is the rule for the positioning of limiting adverbs?

In this example, we cannot tell whether the profits "declined sharply" or "sharply rose." **Limiting adverbs** (*only, nearly, almost, just,* and *hardly*) must immediately precede the word they modify.

Only profits declined 18 percent. (Nothing else declined.)

Profits *only* declined 18 percent. (Profits did not plummet.)

Profits declined *only* 18 percent. (Profits did not decline 20 percent.)

Conjunctions

What type of conjunction joins elements of equal rank? Unequal rank? Joins matched pairs?

A conjunction is a word that connects words, phrases, or clauses. Conjunctions are classified as **coordinate, correlative,** and **subordinate.** Coordinate conjunctions—*and, but, or, for, not*—join elements of equal rank.

Both the executives and their secretaries planned the program.

Correlative conjunctions connect matched pairs. Some correlative conjunctions are *either . . . or; neither . . . nor; both . . . and; not only . . . but also.*

The bank will have its grand opening on either Monday or Wednesday.

Subordinate conjunctions connect elements that are not of equal rank. Some subordinate conjunctions are

after	since
although	so
as	unless
because	when
if	while

After we save enough money, we will buy a new car.

Prepositions

A preposition is a word that shows a relationship of one word in the sentence—its object—to some other word in the sentence. Common prepositions are the following:

about	for
between	into
by	over
down	to
during	toward

This book is *about* communication.

Evelena is the president *of* Permanent Press Inc.

Interjections

An interjection is a word that expresses strong emotion and is generally isolated from the rest of the sentence.

> Wow, did you see that?

> Ouch! You hurt me.

BUILDING SENTENCES

What is the definition of a sentence?

Parts of speech are used to build sentences, the basic units of communication. A sentence is a group of words that expresses a complete thought and contains a *subject* and a *predicate* (verb).

> Profits (subject) increased (predicate).

In addition to the two essential parts—the subject and the predicate—sentences contain other elements that modify or complete those parts. These elements are *complements, phrases,* and *clauses.*

Subject and Predicate

The subject of a sentence is that part about which something is being said. Subjects can be simple or compound.

Simple: *Jessica* works in marketing.
Compound: *Jessica* and *Jerome* work in marketing.

The predicate of a sentence is that part that says something about the subject. Predicates can be simple or compound.

Simple: Norman *reads.*
Compound: Norman *reads* and *writes.*

Complements

A complement is a word that completes the meaning of the subject and the verb. Complements are of three kinds: direct objects, indirect objects, and subject complements. A **direct object** is a word that receives the action of a transitive verb. Direct objects answer the question *what* or *whom.*

> Patricia sold *trucks.* (what?)

> Alfonso loved *Olga.* (whom?)

In a sentence with both direct and indirect objects, which is first? What question does each answer?

An **indirect object** always precedes the direct object; it answers the question *to whom, for whom, to what,* or *for what.*

Patricia sold *Joshua* a truck. (to whom?)

Patricia bought *Joshua* a truck. (for whom?)

I gave the *tire* a kick. (to what?)

Reggie bought the *company* a plane. (for what?)

A **subject complement** is a noun, pronoun, or adjective that renames or describes the subject. Two kinds of subject complements are the predicate nominative (a noun or pronoun) and the predicate adjective. A **predicate nominative** is a noun or pronoun that follows a linking verb and renames the subject.

Joshua is the *buyer.* (noun)

It is *he.* (pronoun)

A **predicate adjective** is an adjective that follows a linking verb and describes the subject.

Margarite is *intelligent.*

Phrases

What is a phrase?

A phrase is a group of related words that do not express a complete thought. A phrase may contain a subject or a predicate but not both. Phrases may be either prepositional or verbal; both modify other parts of the sentence.

A **prepositional phrase** is a phrase beginning with a preposition and modifying other words in the sentence.

The cover *of the book* is red.

The book sold *for $5.*

What is a verbal?

A **verbal phrase** begins with a **verbal**—a verb used as a noun, adjective, or adverb. Three kinds of verbal phrases are gerund phrases, infinitive phrases, and participial phrases.

Gerund phrase: *Dictating letters* is not an easy task.
Infinitive phrase: *To become president* was her ambition.
Participial phrase: *Having dictated letters all morning,* the executive was tired.

Do not confuse gerund phrases with participial phrases. Gerund phrases act as nouns; participial phrases act as adjectives.

Gerund phrase: *Making a profit* is necessary to stay in business.
Participial phrase: *Making a profit,* I stayed in business.

Clauses

How is a clause defined?

A clause is a group of words that contains a subject and a verb. Clauses are either main or subordinate. A **main clause** contains a subject and a verb and expresses a complete thought; it is a *simple sentence* (discussed later under "Kinds of Sentences"). A **subordinate clause** contains a subject and a verb but does not express a complete thought; it needs the main clause to make its meaning complete.

Main clause: *Profits increased rapidly* before the Christmas holidays.

Subordinate clause: *After our profits increased,* we bought additional property.

Uses of Phrases and Clauses

Phrases and clauses are used in sentences as nouns, adjectives, and adverbs. When a phrase or clause modifies a verb, adverb, or adjective, it is an adverb phrase or clause.

> Profits increased *in the afternoon.* (adverb phrase)

> *Because sales increased,* profits rose. (adverb clause)

When a phrase or clause modifies a noun or pronoun, it is an adjective phrase or clause.

> Profits *on the sales of cars* increased. (adjective phrase)

> Profits, *which had been low,* increased. (adjective clause)

When a phrase or clause is used as a noun, it is a noun phrase or clause.

> Our company makes *cars.* (noun)

> Our company makes *whatever you want.* (noun clause)

> *After the meeting* would be the best time. (noun phrase)

> *Making profits on cars* is easy. (gerund phrase)

> *To make a profit on a car* is easy. (infinitive phrase)

What is the difference between a restrictive clause and a nonrestrictive clause?

Phrases and clauses may be restrictive or nonrestrictive. A **restrictive** phrase or clause is one that is essential to the meaning of the sentence. A **nonrestrictive** phrase or clause is not essential to the meaning of the sentence.

Restrictive: The man *who is director of research* conducted the seminar.

Nonrestrictive: A. W. Wells, *who is director of research,* conducted the seminar.

USING WORDS CORRECTLY

Reports are more likely to be well received when the writer has avoided common usage problems such as the following:.

Adjective/Adverb Confusion

Adjectives modify nouns and pronouns. Adverbs modify verbs, adjectives, and other verbs. They cannot be used interchangeably.

Wrong: He always writes *concise.* (adjective in place of an adverb)
Right: He always writes *concisely.* (adverb used correctly)
Right: He always writes *concise* memos. (adjective used correctly)

Some sentences change meaning depending on whether an adjective or adverb is used:

> I feel *bad.* (adjective meaning "I do not feel well.")

> I feel *badly.* (adverb meaning "My sense of touch is impaired.")

When is it wrong to use badly*?*

Many adjectives become adverbs by the addition of *-ly,* and many others have the same form whether serving as an adjective or an adverb. When in doubt, check a dictionary.

Among/Between

When is it wrong to use between*?*

Use *among* for groups of more than two. Use *between* when comparing two persons or things.

Wrong: *Between* the three of us . . .
Right: *Between* you and me . . .
Right: *Among* the three of us . . .

Amount/Number

When is it wrong to use amount*?*

Use *amount* for quantities that cannot be counted. Use *number* to refer to items that can be counted.

Right: The *amount* of gasoline purchased . . .
Right: The *number* of gallons of gasoline . . .

As to

As to is an indefinite way of saying *about, of,* or *whether.* Avoid it when possible.

Indefinite: The instructions were not clear *as to* assembly procedures.
Better: The instructions were not clear *about* assembly procedures.

Center on

Because the verb *center* means "to gather to a point," it should be followed by *in, on,* or *at* and not by *about* or *around*.

Wrong: The problems *center about* managerial communication style.

Right: The problems *center on* managerial communication style.

Compose/Comprise

When is *comprise* incorrect?

Both compose and comprise refer to the relationship between a whole and its parts. *Compose* is used to refer to the parts that make up the whole. *Comprise* is used to refer to the whole that includes the parts. *Comprise* is not used with the prepositon *of.*

Right: The new soft drink was *composed* of secret ingredients.

Right: The organization *comprises* six divisions.

Contact

Contact is best used as a noun meaning the act or state of touching. As a verb, *contact* should usually be replaced by a more exact substitute, such as *write, call,* or *visit.*

Imprecise: Please *contact* me when I can help again.

Better: Please *call* me when I can help again.

Divided into/Composed of

Something can be *divided into* parts, and it can be *composed of* parts, but meanings are not interchangeable.

Right: I *divided* the orange *into* sections.

Right: The orange is *composed of* skin, juice, pulp, and seeds.

Different from

Although some authorities accept *different than* in comparative constructions, *different from* is usually preferred.[1]

Poor: This is *different than* that.

Better: This is *different from* that.

Done

Done is not an acceptable substitute for *finished* or *complete. Done* can be used to mean "sufficiently cooked."

---

[1]Theodore M. Bernstein, *The Careful Writer: A Modern Guide to English Usage* (New York: Atheneum, 1980) 139–141.

Wrong: The project is *done.*
Right: The project is *complete.*
Right: The hamburgers are *done.*

Enthuse

What does the
dictionary say
about *enthuse?*

Enthuse is not an acceptable substitute for *enthusiasm* or *enthusiastic.*

Wrong: Alicia was *enthused* about her promotion.
Right: Alicia was *enthusiastic* about her promotion.

Etc.

When is it safe to
use *etc.?*

Et cetera, abbreviated *etc.,* means "and other things of the same kind."
Use *etc.* only when the items included will be clear to your reader.

Wrong: Remove the shop equipment: the drill press, the lathe, *etc.*
Right: Count by even numbers: 2, 4, 6, 8, *etc.*

Foreseeable Future

How much of the future can be foreseen? If something is a prediction,
say so.

Wrong: We will have no difficulties in the *foreseeable future.*
Right: I predict no future difficulties.

Have Got

Have got is a particularly inelegant redundancy.

Wrong: *Have* you *got* a new model on the market yet?
Right: *Do* you *have* a new model on the market yet?

Hopefully

Do not use *hopefully* as a substitute for *I hope.*

Wrong: *Hopefully,* it won't rain.
Right: *I hope* (or she hopes or they hope) it won't rain.

Impact

Do not use *impact* as a verb.

Wrong: Will that *impact* on this department?
Right: What *impact* (noun) will that have on this department?
Right: Will that *influence* this department?

-ize

The suffix *-ize* is suitable for use with some words: *burglarize, hospitalize, computerize*. When used to form words for which adequate substitutes already exist, however, the new *-ize* word reveals a poor vocabulary. If in doubt, consult a dictionary.

Not This	But This
Finalize	Complete
Prioritize	Rank
Solidize	Solidify

Less/Fewer

When is *fewer* correct?

Use *less* for quantities than cannot be counted. Use *fewer* to refer to items that can be counted.

Right: We've had *less* success than they have had.

Right: We had *fewer* sales this month than they had.

Needless to Say

If it is needles to say something, don't say it. If you do need to say it but it may be obvious to your reader, find a less obtrusive way of subordinating it.

That/Who

Although *that* can be either a demonstrative pronoun or a relative pronoun in referring to people, it is usually better to use *who* as a relative pronoun when referring to people.

Wrong: He is the man *that* sold me the car.

Right: *That* man sold me the car. (demonstrative pronoun)

Right: He is the man *who* sold me the car. (relative pronoun)

Right: Here is the house *that* she told me about. (relative pronoun)

Thanking in Advance

To thank someone in advance is presumptuous because it implies that the person has no choice but to do as you have asked. It also suggests that you are too lazy to write a second note to thank the person after he or she has helped.

Wrong: I *thank you in advance* for your cooperation.

Right: I would appreciate your cooperation. (Thank the reader *after* she or he has cooperated.)

-wise

As a suffix, *wise* means "to be knowledgeable about" (pennywise, worldlywise) or "in the manner of" (clockwise, otherwise). Do not use *-wise* to mean "about the matter of."

Wrong: *Qualitywise,* this procedure is superior.

Right: This procedure results in superior quality.

Wrong: The new company will add a lot to the community *jobwise.*

Right: The new company will provide a number of new jobs in the community.

USING SENTENCES CORRECTLY

Sentences are the basic building blocks of thought. Words themselves convey an image or a concept, but until we know the context in which a word will be used, we cannot assign it specific meaning. The word *effect,* for example, can be either a noun or a verb, depending on how it is used.

Kinds of Sentences

Sentences are simple, complex, compound, or compound–complex. A **simple sentence** contains one subject and one verb.

> The bridge collapsed.

What is a simple sentence? Compound sentence? Complex sentence?

A **complex sentence** contains one independent clause (can stand alone as a sentence) and one dependent (subordinate) clause.

> Because it was poorly designed (dependent clause),

> the bridge collapsed (independent clause).

> The bridge collapsed because it was poorly designed.

Complex sentences are useful to control emphasis in a sentence, because readers pay more attention to information presented in the independent clause than they do to information in the dependent clause.

> After reviewing the data, *I concluded that the bridge was poorly designed* (main point).

> Because the bridge collapsed, *we reviewed our procedures for conducting stress tests* (main point).

A **compound sentence** contains two independent clauses (simple sentences) joined by a coordinating conjunction. Compound sentences are useful for linking or contrasting ideas of equal importance.

The bridge collapsed, and we had no insurance.

The bridge collapsed, but no one was injured.

Compound-complex sentences contain two independent clauses and one or more dependent clauses. Compound-complex sentences are useful for showing the relationships among ideas.

When the bridge collapsed (dependent clause), we had no insurance (independent clause), but no one was injured (independent clause).

Purposes of Sentences

What is a declarative sentence? Interrogative sentence? Imperative? Exclamatory?

In addition to being classified according to type, sentences are classified according to their purpose: declarative, interrogative, imperative, or exclamatory. Most sentences are **declarative**—they make an assertion or statement about something.

Our third-quarter profits are up 39 percent.

Interrogative sentences ask questions.

What was our sales volume this quarter?

Imperative sentences give orders.

Bring me the file on Ehrle.

Exclamatory sentences express strong feelings.

Think of the college graduate who can't make an oral presentation!

Control of Sentences

An effective writer combines sentence kind and purpose to achieve a particular effect. The parts of the sentence should combine into a unified, logical whole so that each part has a specific job to do and makes a specific contribution to the complete thought. The ideas in a sentence should be related, and that relationship should be clear to the reader.

Unrelated: Qualified forecasters anticipate a substantial increase in business investment by fall, and the market value of gold is at an all-time high.

Related: Qualified forecasters anticipate a substantial increase in business investment by fall, and productivity should increase as a result of the new capital investment.

Transition   Elements in sentences are joined by conjunctions, conjunctive adverbs, subordinating adverbial conjunctions, or simple adverbs. These elements serve to control sentences by showing the relationships between the parts of the sentence.

Conjunctions	Simple Adverbs	Conjunctive Adverbs	Subordinating Adverbs
and	better	also	after
but	beyond	anyway	although
or	here	besides	as
for	suddenly	consequently	because
nor	then	finally	before
so	worse	furthermore	if
yet		hence	once
		however	since
		incidentally	that
		indeed	though
		instead	till
		likewise	unless
		meanwhile	until
		moreover	when
		nevertheless	whenever
		next	where
		otherwise	wherever
		still	while
		then	
		therefore	
		thus	

These words, and many other words and phrases, show relationships between parts:

What kinds of relationships are possible between elements in a sentence?

Addition: and, also

Comparison: similarly, likewise

Contrast: but, however

Cause and effect: hence, therefore

Summary: in brief, for example

Exemplification: in brief, for example

Time or place: first, second, now, later, here, there

Variety   In addition to controlling the relationships between sentences and sentence parts, writers need to control the kinds of sentences used to achieve variety. Variation in sentence pattern helps make writing interesting. Just as a report composed of all simple sentences would obviously make for dull reading, a report with too many complex or compound sentences would be uninteresting, though the reason would not be so obvious.

Which two sentence variations are overused by beginning writers?

The two most common problems writers have are beginning too many sentences with subordinate clauses and joining too many simple sentences with conjunctions to form long series of compound sentences.

Change this: *Because annual sales figures indicate a need for improved market strategy,* Morgan Corporation should hire an outside consultant to review current practices and to recommend changes. *Although outside consultants have been used in the past with little success,* the right consultant could make a significant contribution to our market strategy. *After reviewing the proposals submitted by three leading consulting companies,* I have concluded that Lissakers, Inc. has the most to offer.

(Three complex sentences beginning with subordinate clauses.)

To this: Because annual sales figures indicate a need for improved market strategy, Morgan Corporation should hire an outside consultant to review current practices and to recommend changes. The right consultant could make a significant contribution to our market strategy, and the problems we've experienced in the past with outside consultants can be overcome. I recommend that we accept the proposal submitted by Lissakers, Inc.

(One complex, one compound, and one simple sentence.)

Change this: Word processing equipment is proliferating, *and* the office of the future has already arrived. The cost of computing power has been dropping rapidly, *and* now almost any company can afford one or more desktop computers capable of processing, storing, and retrieving documents. The new equipment promises to reduce costs and increase productivity, *but* many executives resist using it because they feel that the terminal's keyboard is more suitable for their secretaries than for them.

(Three compound sentences.)

To this: Word processing equipment is proliferating. As a result of the rapid drop in the cost of computing power, the office of the future has already arrived. Now almost any company can afford one or more desktop computers capable of processing, storing, and retrieving documents. Although the new equipment promises to reduce costs and increase productivity, many executives resist using it. They feel that the terminal's keyboard is more suitable for their secretaries than for them.

(Three simple sentences, two complex sentences.)

AVOIDING COMMON SENTENCE ERRORS

What are the purposes of grammatical rules?

The most common errors in written reports occur within sentences. While grammarians do not always agree on the correct use of language, a few rules are universally accepted and should be considered absolutes. The most important grammatical rules have been established because they contribute to clarity and the logical communication of ideas.

Subject-Verb Agreement (Agr)

A verb must agree with its subject in person and number.

Incorrect: Five members of the team *was* selected to attend.

Correct: Five members of the team *were* selected to attend.

Incorrect: The team *are* attending.

Correct: The team *is* attending.

Because irregular verbs change forms with changes in person and are the verbs used most frequently, they usually present little difficulty.

	Singular	**Plural**
1st person:	I go	We go
2d person:	You go	You go
3d person:	He, she, it *goes*	They go

	Singular	**Plural**
1st person:	I run	We run
2d person:	You run	You run
3d person:	He, she, it *runs*	They run

	Singular	**Plural**
1st person:	I am	We are
2d person:	You are	You are
3d person:	He, she, it *is*	They are

When does subject-verb agreement present a problem to the writer?

Agreement in number causes problems when writers are uncertain whether a subject is singular or plural and when subjects and verbs are separated by an intervening phrase or clause.

Singular: *Bill has* written the report. *It is* now being typed. *He thinks* it will please the Director.

Plural: *Bill and John have* written their reports. *They are* now being typed. *They think* that the reports will please the Director.

Sometimes agreement is influenced by the connective element used. When two elements are connected by *and,* the verb is usually plural. When the elements are connected by *with, or, together with,* or *as well as,* the verb is often singular.

Singular: This report, *along with* the four others submitted, *is* necessary to understand the problem.

Plural: This report *and* the four others submitted *are* necessary to understand the problem.

Why do collective nouns cause problems?

Collective nouns can also cause problems. Collective nouns are words that name a group of objects, persons, or acts. They require singular verbs and pronouns when the entire group is intended and plural verbs and pronouns when individual units. of the group are meant. Typical collective nouns are

army	gang
athletics	group
audience	herd
class	jury
committee	majority
company	mankind
contents	number

couple	offspring
crowd	politics
dozen	public
faculty	remainder
family	team

The *committee* (singular) *has* (singular) decided to table the motion.

The *company* (singular) *is* (singular) moving to Hastings.

Some collective nouns always take plural verbs.

The *police were* helpful in pointing out our need for increased security.

The *people need* to know.

The *cattle were* sold at auction.

But: The entire *herd was* sold at auction.

Intervening phrases or clauses can also cause problems.

The marble *statue,* having stood in Florence for 600 years, *was* moved to Dallas to grace the entry of Canoil, Inc.

After undergoing 32 hours of training, the new *managers*—each of whom must successfully complete the business presentation course—*are* required to write summaries of the management training program.

Pronoun-Antecedent Agreement (Ref)

A pronoun must have a clear and logical antecedent with which it agrees in person, number, and gender. Because pronouns derive their meaning from the nouns—or previous pronouns—to which they refer, accurate pronoun references are essential to clear writing.

Margaret thought that everyone would approve of *her* report.
(*Margaret* is the antecedent of *her.*)

The *company* will succeed if all *its* employees work together.
(*Company* is the antecedent of *its.*)

The Board *members* voted "No" on the proposal because *they* felt that the project would be too expensive.
(Board *members* is the antecedent of *they.*)

What are the three rules governing pronoun-antecedent agreement?

The rules governing pronoun-antecedent agreement are essentially the same as those governing subject-verb agreement: (1) plural antecedents require plural pronouns, and (2) singular antecedents require singular pronouns. In addition, masculine antecedents require masculine pronouns, while feminine and neuter antecedents require feminine and neuter pronouns respectively.

> *Fred* forgot *his* notes.

> *Alice* forgot *her* notes.

> The *notebook* was not in *its* proper place.

How may sentences be rewritten to avoid sexist language?

Indefinite pronouns, which almost always require singular pronouns, take their gender from the antecedent. When the gender is unknown, writers should be careful to avoid sexist language.

> *Everyone* in the Women's Division won *her* game.

> *Everyone* in the Men's Division won *his* game.

> *Each* of the engineers completed *his* or *her* report on time.

> A *manager* needs to make *her* or *his* decisions quickly.

When possible, use plural constructions to avoid the awkwardness of repeating he/she constructions.[2]

> *All* the engineers completed *their* reports on time.

> *Managers* need to make *their* decisions quickly.

Collective nouns may be either singular or plural and require either singular or plural pronouns, depending on meaning.

> The *committee* accepted *its* new responsibility graciously.

> The *audience* left *their* seats before the presentation was complete.

Sentence Fragments (Frag)

What are sentence fragments? When can they be used for special effect?

Most written English requires complete sentences. A complete sentence consists of at least one subject and one verb and expresses a complete thought. A complete sentence makes sense when standing alone. A sentence fragment, on the other hand, is an incomplete part of a sen-

---

[2]For more information on techniques for avoiding sexist language, see Judy Pickens, ed., *Without Bias: A Guidebook for Nondiscriminatory Communication,* 2d ed. (New York: John Wiley & Sons, 1982), sponsored by the International Association of Business Communicators.

tence, which may be missing a subject or a verb or may depend on some other element to complete its thought.

Fragments may result from punctuating subordinate clauses, verbal phrases, prepositional phrases, or appositives as sentences.

Fragment: Because they had missed the meeting.

Sentence: Because they had missed the meeting, they failed to note the changes in specifications on the working drawings.

Fragment: During rush hour traffic.

Sentence: During rush hour traffic, the traffic signal follows a predetermined two-minute sequence.

Fragment: After complete reconstruction

Sentence: The building will be ready for occupancy only after complete reconstruction.

Fragment: Who reports directly to the Vice-President of Finance.

Sentence: All expenditures must be approved by the Operations Manager, who reports directly to the Vice-President of Finance.

Failure to write in complete sentences is usually considered a serious error. Unless used carefully for special effect (primarily in fiction and direct mail advertising), fragments suggest carelessness or a lack of knowledge about sentence structure. Because a complete sentence is necessary to express a complete thought, ideas expressed in fragments are unclear and difficult to follow.

Run-on Sentences (RO)

What are the three ways to separate sentences?

Run-on sentences are two or more sentences with insufficient separation. Sentences may be separated by a period, a semicolon, or a comma and a conjunction.

Run-on: Profits increased by 47 percent in the fourth quarter the press was very quick to report the gain.

Corrected: Profits increased by 47 percent in the fourth quarter. The press was very quick to report the gain.

Or: Profits increased by 47 percent in the fourth quarter; the press was very quick to report the gain.

Or: Profits increased by 47 percent in the fourth quarter, and the press was very quick to report the gain.

What are two common causes of run-on sentences?

While not so serious a detractor from clarity as is a fragment, a run-on sentence also suggests carelessness or failure to understand sentence structure.

Run-on sentences often result from a writer's failure to use a comma in addition to a conjunction.

Run-on: The press overlooked the 44 percent increase in capital investment and only one side of the story appeared in print.

Corrected: The press overlooked the 44 percent increase in capital investment, and only one side of the story appeared in print.

Another common cause of run-on sentences is punctuating for a conjunctive adverb (however, besides, therefore, consequently, etc.) as though it were a conjunction.

Run-on: The press doesn't deliberately distort the facts, however a built-in bias against business may influence the selective perception of some reporters.

Corrected: The press doesn't deliberately distort the facts; however, a built-in bias against business may influence the selective perception of some reporters.

Or (even better):   The press doesn't deliberately distort the facts; a built-in bias against business, however, may influence the selective perception of some reporters.

Comma Splice (CS)

A comma splice results when two sentences are joined by a comma only.

Comma Splice: Raw material substitutions are not permitted, impurities must be below the 0.04 percent level specified.

Corrected: Raw material substitutions are not permitted. Impurities must be below the 0.04 percent level specified.

Misplaced and Dangling Modifiers (Mod)

Prepositional phrases, subordinate clauses, participial phrases, infinitive phrases, adverbs, and adjectives all add meaning and precision to sentences by modifying the more general meaning provided by the subject and verb. A modifier (word or phrase) is misplaced when it seems to modify something it logically cannot, or when the reader cannot be certain what the writer meant.

What is the difference between misplaced modifiers and dangling modifiers?

A dangling modifier is one that cannot logically modify any word in the sentence. In general, modifiers should be placed directly before or after the word or words they modify.

Misplaced modifier: No one I know would eat a steak in a restaurant that was not cooked the way she or he wanted it.

Correct: No one I know would eat a steak that was not cooked the way he or she wanted it in a restaurant.

Better: No one I know would eat an improperly cooked steak in a restaurant.

Dangling Modifier: Driving over the bridge, the structural defects were clearly visible.

Correct: Driving over the bridge, I could clearly see the structural defects.

Shifts (Shift) and Parallel Construction (// cst)

To be clear, a sentence must be consistent. Shifts in person, number, verb tense or mood, or voice detract from clarity.

Shift: One (3d person) should never forget your (2d person) reader's needs. (shift in person)

Correct: Never forget your reader's needs.

Correct: One should never forget the reader's needs.

Shift: A person (singular) should prepare their (plural) reports carefully. (shift in number)

Correct: A person should prepare his/her reports carefully.

Shift: I would go. Will you? (shift in mood)

Correct: I would go. Would you?

Corect: I will go. Will you?

Shift: I have considered your proposal, and it has been decided to postpone any action until the end of the month. (shift in voice)

Correct: I have considered your proposal, and I have decided (or simply "and decided") to postpone any action until the end of the month.

Why do shifts confuse readers? Why is nonparallel construction confusing?

Just as shifts tend to confuse readers by altering perspectives in mid-sentence, an absence of parallelism confuses readers by presenting similar concepts in uncoordinated grammatical form. Parallel grammatical structure is required for clarity whenever similar elements are joined by coordinating conjunctions or correlative conjunctions, arranged in a list, compared, or contrasted.

Faulty: We met our production quota and also affirmative action.

Parallel: We met our production quota and also satisfied affirmative action guidelines.

Faulty: New employees need to learn how to write reports and oral presentations as well.

Parallel: New employees need to learn how to write reports and to make oral presentations as well.

Faulty: Not only was I interested in his ideas but also his manner of presenting them.

Parallel: I was interested in not only his ideas but also his manner of presenting them.

Faulty: The new word processing center will alleviate the problems we've been having with the shortage of secretaries, the backlog of correspondence, and losing documents.

Parallel: The new word processing center will alleviate the problems we've been having with the shortage of secretaries, the backlog of correspondence, and the loss of documents.

Faulty: It is better to rely on market research than making wild guesses.

Parallel: It is better to rely on market research than to make wild guesses.

PARAGRAPHING

Writing clear, grammatically correct sentences is the single greatest obstacle for most writers, and most problems with writing occur at the sentence level. Effective writing, however, requires not only that sentences be clear, correct, and effective, but also that sentences be connected into larger units that are also clear and effective.

In connecting sentences to form paragraphs and paragraphs to form complete reports, the writer needs to provide clear and distinct statements about the topic being discussed and to organize material so that related ideas are close together.

Topic Sentences

How should other
sentences in a
paragraph relate to
the topic sentence?

In general, each paragraph should focus on one central idea, which should be expressed in a topic sentence. The remaining sentences in the paragraph should clarify, limit, or support the topic sentence.

Topic Sentence: Running a business is not easy.

Sentence of Limitation: As any business owner knows, money, employees, and customers are all sources of difficulty.

Sentence of Clarification: Because a business must make a profit, a businessperson constantly worries about the costs of staying in business.

Support Sentence: Equipment, raw materials, advertising, rent, insurance, and employees are all costs that must be considered in determining the cost of a product. (Rest of paragraph—or paragraphs—would describe the kinds of problems caused by employees and customers.)

Paragraph Organization

It is easier for the reader to follow a paragraph when the topic sentence is first. Placing the topic sentence in the initial position provides the reader with a road sign indicating the direction the paragraph will take. Such a paragraph is organized as follows:

Topic Sentence: Generalization

Sentence 2:   Support

Sentence 3:   Support

Sentence 4:   Support

Or, when the paragraph is longer and more complex:

Topic Sentence: Generalization

Sentence 2:   Clarification

Sentence 3:   Limitation

Sentence 4:   Support

Sentence 5:   Support

Sentence 6:   Limitation

Sentence 7:   Support

Sentence 8:   Support

Sentence 9:   Limitation

Sentence 10:   Support

What form of
paragraph
organization makes
the material easiest
for the reader to
follow? When
should it not be
used?

This is the most effective form of paragraph organization when the reader is willing to accept the generalization expressed or implied in the topic sentence.

When the reader is likely to reject the generalization in the topic sentence, however, the supporting sentences should precede the topic sentence.

Sentence 1:   Specific fact (support)

Sentence 2:   Specific fact

Sentence 3:   Minor conclusion (limitation)

Sentence 4:   Specific fact

Sentence 5:   Specific fact

Sentence 6:   Minor conclusion

Topic Sentence: General conclusion

Coherence and Transition

What are the principal ways of indicating relationships between sentences or paragraphs and of providing transition?

A paragraph or complete report is coherent when all the parts add up to a unified whole and the relationships among the thoughts are clear and easily discerned. Although the relationship between sentences— and between paragraphs—may be either explicit or implied, it must be sufficiently clear for the reader to follow without rereading. The principal ways of indicating relationships and providing transition are the following:

1. Repetition. The repetition of key words and ideas, or the use of pronouns to stand for key words and ideas, provides continuity. Repetition shows the reader that the same idea is still being discussed.

2. Cause and effect. When a writer can show that one event has caused another, such words as *because, thus, therefore, then,* and *as a result,* indicate a cause-effect relationship.

3. Comparison/contrast. Pointing out similarities *(like, similar to)* and differences *(although, however, on the other hand)* clarifies the relationship between two items or ideas. This is an effective way of providing transition.

4. Time and place. References to movement in time *(yesterday, today, tomorrow),* or movement in space *(here, there, above, below),* or a combination of the two *(meanwhile, in Detroit . . .)* are the most common transitional devices.

AVOIDING OTHER COMMON DIFFICULTIES

The careful report writer avoids awkward constructions and inconsistencies in the use of capital letters and numbers.

Awkward Expressions (Awk)

Occasionally a phrase, clause, or sentence will be awkward without having anything specifically wrong with it. Awkward phrasing, unnatural word order, or constructions that force the reader to read more than once to be sure of your meaning need revising.

Check placement of modifiers and recast to achieve a more direct word order (subject-verb-object).

Capitalization (Cap)

The following should be capitalized:

1. The first word in a sentence
2. The first word in a quoted sentence
3. Proper nouns and adjectives, including names of places (cities, counties, countries), races, languages, days of the week, months, companies, and historical events
4. The first word in each item of a vertical list
5. Words in titles, except articles *(a, the, an)* and short prepositions. Capitalize the first word of the title even if it is a short preposition
6. Abstract nouns when they are personified, refer to ideals, or stand for institutions (Good, Evil, the Church, the Company, our Department)

Do not capitalize:

1. Seasons of the year (summer, fall, winter, spring)
2. Directions (east, west, north, south). (But: capitalize regions—the East, the South—because they are places.)
3. The first word of items in a list contained within a paragraph
4. Subjects or fields of study (chemistry, accountancy, marketing), except for languages (Chinese, Russian, German, English)

Numbers

Use figures for:

1. Numbers above ten
2. Dates and time (with a.m. and p.m.)
3. Dimensions
4. Monetary sums (For whole amounts, omit the decimal and ciphers.)
5. Statistics and numbers with decimals
6. Series of more than two numbers
7. References to pages and chapters

Use words rather than figures:

1. To begin a sentence (Recast the sentence if the number is large.)
2. When use of a figure would confuse the reader, as with two numbers in sequence (two 2 × 4s)

Use figures or words for numbers between one and ten, depending on company style. Except in dates, phone numbers, and street addresses, use a comma to separate each group of three digits.

1988 (date)   62081 (street address)

1,988 (number)   62,081 (number)

Use cardinal figures (1, 3, 8,) when the day follows the month.

February 8   August 12

Use ordinal numbers (1st, 2d, 3d, 4th) when the day precedes the month.

We should have the contracts by the 15th of May.

Express dates in month-day-year sequence or day-month-year sequence.

American form for date: November 14, 1988
International form for date: 14 November 1988
Computer forms for date: 14 NOV 1988   1988 11 14

The international form, sometimes referred to as inverted form by Americans, is used virtually everywhere but in the United States. For this reason, many U.S. companies doing business abroad have adopted the international date form.

USING PUNCTUATION CORRECTLY

The usefulness of even the most accurate, complete, well-organized report will be lessened if poor punctuation alienates the reader or obscures the meaning. Only a few simple rules are needed to ensure clarity.

Ampersand &

Use the ampersand, a symbol for the word *and,* when it is part of the official name of an organization. Spell out the word *and* in other contexts; do not use an ampersand.

Peat, Marwick, Mitchell & Co. audits the books for us each year.

Apostrophe '

What are the two uses for the apostrophe?

Use the apostrophe to show possession.

boss's office   Pomaz' report   men's club

Dee and Bee's Shop

Use the apostrophe to form contractions.

don't   she'll   he'd   can't   it's

Do not use the apostrophe with personal pronouns.

yours   hers   his   its

Note: Be especially careful to avoid confusing *it's* (it is) with the personal pronoun *its*.

Its cost was too high.

It's time to order supplies.

Asterisk *

Use the asterisk to refer the reader to a footnote.

The increased cost would be $1,500 before taxes.*

*See Table 4.1.

Brackets [   ]

Use brackets to insert parenthetical expressions, remarks, or corrections into existing text. Brackets (as opposed to commas, dashes, or parentheses) indicate editorial insertions rather than textual commentary.

After the officers [Jack Hammon and Art Bellow] presented their report, the president proposed that it be approved.

Colon :

What two sentence constructions require a colon?

Use the colon before lists, enumerations, and such expressions as *the following, as follows,* and *these.*

The supervisor asked for the following three reports: Bell's report on telephone techniques, Schully's report on taxes, and Mostel's report on graphic aids.

Use a colon after a salutation when using mixed punctuation.

Dear Ms. Anderson: Ladies and Gentlemen:

Use the colon to separate hours and minutes.

3:15 p.m.   9:15 a.m.

Use the colon to indicate that the following statement amplifies a preceding clause.

Our new microcomputer has been successful: so successful that we are more than six months behind in deliveries.

Comma ,

Use a comma before a coordinating conjunction (*and, or, but,* or *for*) that connects two complete sentences.

> Our supervisor announced the new procedure, and the workers implemented it immediately.

Use a comma after introductory words, phrases, and clauses.

Words: Of course, we'll need to have the manuals before we can make the changes.

Phrases: To make the necessary repairs, we had to hire a technician.

Clauses: Whenever we hire new employees, we always explain their insurance benefits carefully.

Use a pair of commas to set off nonrestrictive clauses.

> After the meeting, which lasted two hours, we went to lunch.

Use a comma to separate items in a series.

> Business reports are used to inform, to convince, and to entertain.

Use a comma to set off parenthetical expressions.

> The newsletter, however, printed only half the story.

Use a comma to set off words that explain or identify preceding nouns.

> Sue Meyers, our office manager, announced the new procedures for filing documents.

Use a comma to separate two or more words that modify the same noun.

> The tall, distinguished-looking gentleman gave the invocation.

Use a comma to separate items in an address or a date.

> The meeting will be on Saturday, July 12, 1983, at 9 a.m.

> She worked for five years for Blaine Brothers, 265 N. Hampton Road, Canton, OH, and then for four years for Stewart & Clark, 630 East Monroe Street, Cincinnati, OH.

Use a comma to set off nouns of direct address.

> Barb, will you please answer the telephone?

Dash —

When are dashes used in report writing? When are diagonals used? Ellipsis marks?

Use a pair of dashes when commas do not provide sufficient separation.

> We strongly recommend that all employees—especially those hired in the last two months—seriously consider signing up for liability insurance.

Use a dash to show hesitation.

> She had one thing on her mind—getting promoted.

Diagonal /

Use a diagonal between letters in some abbreviations and expressions and between numerals in fractions.

> c/o Donaldson Brothers

> and/or

> 3/4   1 5/8

Ellipsis Marks . . .

Use ellipsis marks (three spaced periods with one space before and after each period) to show the omission of words from a quotation. When the omission occurs at the end of a sentence, use ellipses followed by a space and the closing punctuation mark for the sentence.

> The warranty says: "This warranty will remain in effect for all parts and labor . . . for one year from date of purchase."

Use ellipses in advertising material for emphasis.

> The handy XL-140 will . . . act as a sorter . . . an organizer . . . a work saver.

Exclamation Point !

What is a good rule of thumb for deciding when to use the exclamation point in business reports?

Use the exclamation point to express strong feelings.

> That's beautiful!   I don't believe a word of it!   No!

The exclamation point is rarely used in business writing.

Parentheses (   )

Use parentheses to set off nonessential expressions.

> Please call me (556-1389) when you have questions.

Use parentheses to set off references.

> Construction should begin April 1 (see contract for details).

Use parentheses for enumerated items presented within a paragraph.

The three major divisions are (1) introduction, (2) body, and (3) conclusion.

Period .

How does the reader know that a sentence is a polite request rather than a question?

Use a period at the end of a declarative sentence, an imperative statement, or a polite request.

> The reports should arrive by June 1.

> Let me know when you plan to leave.

> May we have your reply before 15 April.

Use a period after abbreviations and initials.

> a.m.   p.m.   B.A.   M.S.   Ph.D.   Tues.   Oct.   E. T. Brown

Use a period to indicate decimals.

> 1.5 percent   2.5 inches

Use periods after letters and numbers in outlines and in enumerated lists presented vertically.

1.	a.	I.
2.	b.	A.
3.	c.	B.
		II.

Use two spaces between the period and the material that follows.

Question Mark ?

Use a question mark after a direct question.

> Have you been able to reach Mr. Jorgenson?

Use a question mark with statements with questions.

> You did receive the material, didn't you?

> We'll sign the contract in June? (meant as a question)

> He'll receive $4,000 (?) a month. (expresses doubt)

Use a question mark after a series of questions. The question mark is followed by two spaces at the end of a sentence, but by one space within a sentence.

> Do they have offices in Detroit? Los Angeles? Boston?

Quotation Marks " "

Use quotation marks for direct quotations.

> Helen said, "The prices are effective immediately."

Use quotation marks for titles of articles, chapters of books, songs, and poems.

> Before you complete the assignment, check the article, "Working Together," by R. J. Rodosky.

> Chapter 2, "Elements of Effective Communication," is well written.

Which punctuation
marks go inside
quotation marks?
Which go outside?

Periods and commas go *inside* the quotation marks. All other punctuation goes *outside* unless it is part of the original quotation.

> He told us to read the article, "Marketing Strategies."

> Who wants to read "Marketing Strategies"?

> He asked, "Have you read the article, 'Marketing Strategies'?"

Semicolon ;

What are two
important uses for
the semicolon?

Use a semicolon to connect two complete sentences when a conjunction is omitted.

> They wrote the first book in three months; they wrote their second book in eight months.

Use a semicolon to separate items in a series containing commas.

> They visited offices in Syracuse, NY; Stillwater, OK; and Glendale, CA.

Underscore _____

Use the underscore for words italicized in print.

> It is not <u>what</u> you say, but <u>how</u> you say it.

Use the underscore for titles of literary and artistic works, such as books, long poems, magazines, newspapers, movies, television shows, plays, musicals, and operas.

> Our president regularly reads <u>The Wall Street Journal</u>.

> They enjoyed the film, <u>Star Trek IV</u>, which was filmed in the San Francisco Bay Area.

SUMMARY

A knowledge of grammar is essential for those who need to write quickly and easily. To be confident that the reports, letters, and other documents you produce are free from error, you will need to understand the parts of speech, to use words correctly, to use sentences correctly, to avoid common sentence errors, to paragraph appropriately, to avoid common difficulties, and to punctuate correctly.

EXERCISES

Review and Discussion Questions

1. What are the eight parts of speech? How are they used in sentences?
2. What are the differences between transitive and intransitive verbs?
3. What is the difference between a phrase and a clause?
4. What is meant by *agreement?*
5. What is meant by *parallelism?*
6. What are the differences between active and passive voice?
7. What are the differences among simple, complex, compound, and compound-complex sentences?
8. What is a topic sentence?
9. What is meant by *coherence?*
10. How can punctuation influence the meaning of a sentence? Give three examples.

Problems and Applications

1. Identify the errors in the following sentences, and correct the sentences:

   After entering data for more than five hours, her eyes began seeing spots.

   Whenever a manager makes a bad decision, they run the risk of losing their jobs.

   Because consumers has less financial resources than automobile dealers and feel justified in misrepresenting the quality of the cars they bring in for trade.

   The committee agreed to complete their share of the project by the end of the month, assuming that they had the required time, resources, and had access to the data from previous projects.

A new employee like yourself should know better than to challenge the authority of one's boss.

2. Write three sentences demonstrating the use of sentence structure to control emphasis.

3. Indicate whether the verbs in the following sentences are active or passive, and rewrite the sentence to change the voice of the verb.

The decision was made by the manager more than a month ago.

I mailed the first package to you yesterday and will mail the second early next week.

The office was cleaned thoroughly just last night.

He always said that preparation and organization were the keys to success.

Johnstown, Pennsylvania, has more than once been declared a disaster area because of flooding.

4. Write a short paragraph employing the principal ways of achieving transition between sentences. Indicate where you have used each method and why you selected that method for use in that place.

5. Select an article from a newspaper or magazine and analyze the first two or three paragraphs (depending on length) for the principles of writing employed. Note especially word and sentence usage, transitions, and punctuation. Submit the article (or a photocopy) along with your analysis.

Suggested Readings

Bernstein, Theodore M. *The Careful Writer: A Modern Guide to English Usage.* New York: Atheneum, 1980.

A thorough, entertaining, and authoritative guide to English usage arranged in alphabetical order for quick reference.

Branchaw, Bernadine P. *English Made Easy.* 2nd ed. New York: McGraw-Hill, 1986.

Complete coverage of the basics of English usage.

Branchaw, Bernadine P. and Joel P. Bowman. *SRA Reference Manual for Office Personnel.* Chicago: Science Research Associates, 1986.

An alphabetical guide to problems of English usage and composition. Covers all problems report writers are likely to encounter.

Flower, Linda. *Problem Solving Strategies for Writing.* New York: Harcourt Brace Jovanovich, 1981.

Good coverage of the writing process; emphasizes techniques for converting writer-based prose into reader-based prose and editing for clear organization.

Strunk, William Jr. and E. B. White. *The Elements of Style.* New York: Macmillan, 1959.

A classic guide to writing style and correctness. Everyone should own a copy of this short paperback.

Williams, Joseph M. *Style: Ten Lessons in Clarity and Grace.* 2nd ed. Glenview, IL: Scott, Foresman, 1984.

Deals with larger, more difficult issues than Bernstein or Strunk and White. Concentrates on sentence and paragraph construction.

Zinsser, William. *On Writing Well.* 3d ed. New York: Harper & Row, 1985.

Good coverage of techniques for solving common writing problems; contains useful hints for controlling emphasis and subordination.

C H A P T E R 4

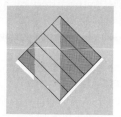

The Characteristics of Functional Writing

Although all writing—and all communication—is "functional" in that it serves a purpose, reports are functional in a special sense. Poetry, literature, and magazine articles, for example, are all written for a purpose: they communicate ideas that a writer considers important. Reports, however, are functional not only because they communicate ideas, but also because the reader will act based on the information communicated in the report. Readers of poetry or a magazine article *may* act as a result of reading, but a report is designed to help the reader decide on a course of action. For this reason, the process of preparing to write a report actually begins with developing a solid foundation of knowledge about the characteristics of functional writing. This chapter describes those characteristics.

Topics

Readability
Clarity
Courtesy
Conciseness
Confidence
Correctness
Conversational Tone
Style

What is
emphasized in
functional writing?

What does your reader want from a report? The chances are that your reader is an extremely busy person who will appreciate everything you can do to save his or her time. Certainly your reader will not expect or desire to be "entertained" by your report in the same way she or he would wish to be entertained by a novel. Report writing is functional writing, designed to communicate ideas quickly and easily to a reader who does not want to invest a great deal of time and effort understanding or interpreting your point. Functional writing has a businesslike style that puts the emphasis on the content—the ideas—rather than on the use of language itself.

The characteristics of functional writing are readability, clarity, courtesy, conciseness, confidence, correctness, and conversational tone. The style of functional writing may be either formal or informal, impersonal or personal, as long as it contains these characteristics.

READABILITY

Before the twentieth century, most writers were not concerned with readability. Few people could read and write, and those who could had more time to spend polishing their writing and more time to read carefully the writing they received from others. Following the Industrial Revolution in the late nineteenth and early twentieth centuries, the faster pace of business life required increased information flow.

Readability Formulas

By the 1940s, researchers were attempting to provide business writers with formulas to predict whether their letters and reports would communicate quickly and clearly to a given audience. Rudolf Flesch and Robert Gunning developed the best known of the readability formulas.[1]

Which is the most
widely used
readability
formula?

The formulas they developed are based primarily on sentence length and the number of words containing three or more syllables. Because the resulting figure corresponds with the educational level required to read a given writing sample, the Gunning Fog Index has become the most widely used formula.[2] Exhibit 4.1 describes the procedure for using the Fog Index.

Take, for example, the passage following the heading "Readability" excluding the heading "Readability Formulas" and concluding at the sentence beginning "Exhibit 4.1."

---

[1]Rudolf Flesch, *The Art of Plain Talk* (New York: Harper & Row, 1946); and Robert Gunning, *The Technique of Clear Writing* (New York: McGraw Hill, c. 1952, rev. ed., 1968).
[2]Gunning 39.

$$Total\ words = 172$$
$$Total\ sentences = 7$$
$$Polysyllabic\ words = 20$$
$$Average\ sentence\ length = 24.6$$
$$Percentage\ hard\ words = 12$$
$$(Average\ length + percentage) \times 0.4 = Readability\ level\ (years\ of\ education)$$
$$(24.6 + 12) \times 0.4 = 14.64$$
$$Reading\ level = 14.6\ (college\ sophomore)$$

What are the
shortcomings of
readability
formulas?

While the Fog Index and other readability formulas promise mathematical precision in gauging readability, they can at best provide a rough guideline. The formulas all require arbitrary mathematical manipulation to result in a usable figure. The Flesch formula uses constants; the Fog Index adds percentages and whole numbers and multiplies by a constant. There are other problems as well. The formulas do not, for example, take into account the need for polysyllabic technical terms that may be well known to the reader or the fact that some longer words are more familiar than their shorter equivalents. A long, well-constructed sentence is also easier to read than a short sentence with a modifier out of place.

Exhibit 4.1   Application of the Gunning Fog Index

How to Use Gunning's Fog Index

1. Using a sample of at least 100 words, determine the average number of words in a sentence by dividing the total number of words by the total number of sentences. Count each independent clause as a separate sentence. Example: "We should expand our current operations, and we should diversify as well." Count as *two* sentences.

2. Count the number of polysyllabic words (three syllables or more). Omit from this count proper nouns (primarily names of people and places), verbs containing three syllables as a result of the addition of "es" or "ed," and combinations of short, easy words ("insofar," "however," "undertake").

3. Determine the percentage of "hard" words by dividing the number of polysyllabic words by the total number of words in the passage.

4. Add the average number of words in a sentence to the percentage of polysyllabic words. Multiply the total by 0.4.

5. The resulting figure shows the readability of the passage in terms of the level of education (grade) required to read the passage.

EXAMPLE: A passage contains
     152 words
     11 sentences
     21 polysyllabic words
Average sentence length $= (152/11) = 13.8$.
Percentage of hard words $= (21/152) = 14\%$.
Average length + percentage $\times 0.4\ (13.8 + 14 \times 0.4) = 11.12$.
Reading level $= 11.12$ (11th grade).

Despite the shortcomings of the formulas, the Gunning Fog Index can help you write at a level suitable for your audience. A Fog Index of 10 to 12 is appropriate for most business reports, although readers trained in the subject matter of the report would be comfortable with material written at a higher level. The index also provides three important clues to readability.

1. Readability is as much a function of the reader as it is of the material. Materials suitable for one reader may be either too easy or too difficult for another.

2. Writing can be made easier to read by shortening the sentences and reducing the number of "hard" words.

3. Writing can be made more suitable for a well-educated audience by lengthening the sentences and using a larger number of polysyllabic words.

In applying these formulas, remember that people reading for business purposes do not want to "work" at reading. They expect reading to be easy so that they can concentrate on the work of making decisions. At the same time, however, no reader appreciates being patronized. A report with a Fog Index of 6 would be insulting to a college-educated manager.

Both Flesch and Gunning recognized that factors other than sentence length and word difficulty influence readability. Those factors are not so easy to evaluate using a formula. Diction, sentence structure and variety, paragraphing, specificity, voice, tense, figures of speech, and control of emphasis influence readability as much as sentence length and word difficulty.

Diction

Your choice of words will obviously affect the readability of your writing. To be readable, the word must be used correctly, be familiar to the reader, and denote and connote appropriate meanings in the context of your report.

The words selected to express an idea have a limited range of meanings. This range of meaning is what people have agreed a word should mean. The word itself has meaning only because the people who use it agree that it does. A dictionary, then, does not show you what a word *means* as much as it shows you how people *use* the word. The way in which people use words is known as diction. The dictionary is the report writer's best tool for using words in the way others expect them to be used. Exhibit 4.2 illustrates a dictionary entry.

How do dictionaries aid in word selection?

In addition, the other information provided by a dictionary, including the etymology (derivation and history) and the list of synonyms with abbreviated definitions and distinctions, helps writers select the exact word necessary to convey a particular meaning.

Exhibit 4.2   **Dictionary Entry**

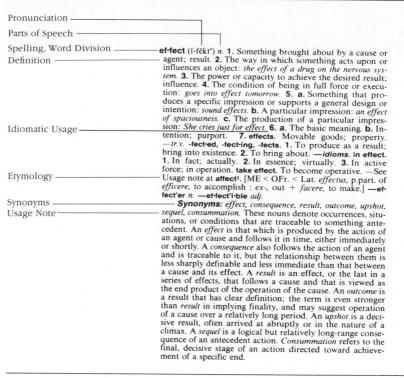

Pronunciation
Parts of Speech
Spelling, Word Division
Definition
Idiomatic Usage
Etymology
Synonyms
Usage Note

ef·fect (ĭ-fĕkt′) *n.* **1.** Something brought about by a cause or agent; result. **2.** The way in which something acts upon or influences an object: *the effect of a drug on the nervous system.* **3.** The power or capacity to achieve the desired result; influence. **4.** The condition of being in full force or execution: *goes into effect tomorrow.* **5. a.** Something that produces a specific impression or supports a general design or intention: *sound effects.* **b.** A particular impression: *an effect of spaciousness.* **c.** The production of a particular impression: *She cries just for effect.* **6. a.** The basic meaning. **b.** Intention; purport. **7. effects.** Movable goods; property. —*tr.v.* **-fect·ed, -fect·ing, -fects. 1.** To produce as a result; bring into existence. **2.** To bring about. —*idioms.* **in effect. 1.** In fact; actually. **2.** In essence; virtually. **3.** In active force; in operation. **take effect.** To become operative. —See Usage note at **affect¹.** [ME < OFr. < Lat. *effectus,* p.part. of *efficere,* to accomplish : *ex-,* out + *facere,* to make.] —**ef·fect′er** *n.* —**ef·fect′i·ble** *adj.*

Synonyms: *effect, consequence, result, outcome, upshot, sequel, consummation.* These nouns denote occurrences, situations, or conditions that are traceable to something antecedent. An *effect* is that which is produced by the action of an agent or cause and follows it in time, either immediately or shortly. A *consequence* also follows the action of an agent and is traceable to it, but the relationship between them is less sharply definable and less immediate than that between a cause and its effect. A *result* is an effect, or the last in a series of effects, that follows a cause and that is viewed as the end product of the operation of the cause. An *outcome* is a result that has clear definition; the term is even stronger than *result* in implying finality, and may suggest operation of a cause over a relatively long period. An *upshot* is a decisive result, often arrived at abruptly or in the nature of a climax. A *sequel* is a logical but relatively long-range consequence of an antecedent action. *Consummation* refers to the final, decisive stage of an action directed toward achievement of a specific end.

Regional, occupational, and educational differences, however, all contribute to different expectations about how a word should be used. The less familiar you are with a word, the greater your chances are of using the word incorrectly. Writers use words incorrectly for two reasons. First, they simply don't know what a word means (though they think they do). Second, they confuse one word with another similar word that has a different meaning.

The only way to prevent your own incorrect use of words is to build a large enough vocabulary so that you can express yourself with confidence. If you aren't absolutely certain how a word should be used, look it up. The larger your vocabulary, the easier you will find the process of writing. A large vocabulary not only gives you more words from which to select, but also increases your confidence in your speaking and writing. Any of the paperback books on vocabulary building would be a good place to start. You should also build your own list of words based on your reading. Your vocabulary and command of the language are two undisguisable indicators of your level of knowledge. Every time you speak, every time you write something, your audience will be evaluating you based on your use of the language.

What are two ways
to build
vocabulary?

You may, for example, have picked up an erroneous idea of how a word should be used because you've heard others use it incorrectly. *Unique* is an example. *Unique* is properly used to mean "one of a kind, without equal." For that reason, a solution to a problem (or anything else) cannot be "very unique," "really unique," or "most unique." Something can, however, be "truly unique" or "almost unique," although *truly* is redundant and *unusual* or *exceptional* conveys the meaning expressed in "almost unique" more clearly and with greater economy.

One area of difficulty is confusion caused by similar words with different meanings. Are you familiar with the different meanings of the following often confused words?

Affect/Effect

Affect: (verb)—to influence or change

Effect: (verb)—to bring about
     (noun)—a result or consequence

Appraise/Apprise

Appraise: to estimate

Apprise: to inform

Aggravate/Irritate

Aggravate: to make worse

Irritate: to provoke

As/Like

Why did
Shakespeare not
use the title *Like
You Like It?*

As: (conjunction, used to introduce a clause)—*as* I said

Like: (preposition)—a manager *like* you

Assure/Ensure/Insure

Assure: to promise (to a person)

Ensure: to guarantee or make certain

Insure: to protect against loss

Continual/Continuous

Continual: on a regular basis (but interrupted)

Continuous: without interruption

Distinterested/Uninterested

Disinterested: free of bias, impartial

Uninterested: indifferent, not interested

Imply/Infer

Imply: to suggest

Infer: to draw a conclusion

What is a malapropism?

Occasionally, the confusion between similar words with different meanings results in a humorous (though not to the report writer) **malapropism.**

Your speech was *superfluous!* (for *superb*)

Your report contained many *meretricious* ideas. (for meritorious)

In addition to making sure that you are using words in the way they are usually used, you need to ensure that you and your reader share a common vocabulary. While a dictionary provides a guide to the way words are used, no two people have identical conceptions of what a word means. When words are familiar—used often by most people—you can assume that your reader will attach similar meanings to the words.

What is the difference between jargon and slang?

Another main cause of difficulty is **jargon.** Jargon is the specialized, working vocabulary of a discipline. Computer specialists, for example, speak of *ROM, RAM, bits, bytes, bauds,* and *modems.* All these terms are legitimate and carry specific meanings—to those familiar with computers. They constitute a functional shorthand that speeds communication with those who understand the terms. They do not, however, communicate meaning to those not familiar with computers.

Do not confuse jargon with slang. Slang is excessively informal writing and is inappropriate in professional reports.

Slang: I didn't get it.

Better: I didn't understand it.
I didn't receive it.

Slang: Is the report done?

Better: Is the report complete?
Have you finished the report?

When is it safe to use technical terms?

Every discipline has its own jargon, and only a few outside the field ever are truly comfortable with it. This is one of the reasons that audience analysis is so important. Is your reader a specialist in your discipline? If so, you are safe in using technical terms, though you may wish to add some explanation for newer or less-used terminology. If not, you will need to avoid jargon when possible and explain all technical terms essential to the meaning of your report.

Also, as suggested by the readability formulas, short, familiar words usually communicate more clearly than long, less familiar words:

Difficult Word	Easy Word
ameliorate	improve
ascertain	find out
cognizant	aware
consummate	complete
effusive	enthusiastic
endeavor	try
exacerbate	make worse
excursion	trip
institute	start
interrogate	ask
jaundiced	hostile
lobscouse	stew
mandible	jaw
mordacious	biting, sarcastic
outré	improper
paraphrase	restate
sinecure	an office or charge that requires no work
transient	temporary

What do readers want?

Naturally, well-educated readers will have a well-developed vocabulary and will expect the writer to select the exact words to carry the precise meaning intended. Likewise, a technical audience will expect to encounter a technical vocabulary. Rather than the familiar but too general *done,* for example, most readers would prefer the more specific *completed* or *finished.* Even well-educated readers, however, will appreciate your reports more if they can read them quickly and easily. The short word, however, is not always more familiar, as the table below illustrates.

Short, Unfamiliar Words	Longer but Easier Words
berm	shoulder (of road)
cahier	notebook
fend	provide or turn aside
jibe	swing (verb)
quod	prison
thewy	muscular
vie	compete

Why must both denotation and connotation be considered when choosing a word?

To help ensure that your reports will be clear to your readers, select words that have not only the proper denotative (dictionary) meaning but also appropriate connotative (personal) meanings. The words *as soon as possible,* for example, may be interpreted either as "immediately" or as "when you can find the time." Just as beauty is in the eye of the beholder, the meaning of words is in the mind of the user. A *smell* may be an *aroma* to one and a *stench* to another, as the table below illustrates. The words *cheap* and *inexpensive,* for example, both denote low in cost. *Cheap* also implies low in quality, whereas *inexpensive* does not.

Consider the connotations of the following words:

automobile	antique	jeep	carriage
car	hot rod	lemon	hearse
compact	wheels	4 × 4	convertible
station wagon	taxi	vehicle	bug
heap	limousine	van	buggy
clunker	import		

Each of the words denotes a means of transportation, yet each carries a different set of associated meanings. To communicate effectively, a writer needs to select the word with the most appropriate connotations for the situation.

In some cases, words have connotations that many people would agree on. In other cases, the associated meanings of a word will vary greatly from person to person. How much would you have to pay for an *inexpensive* car? How much is a *significant* increase? We can eliminate confusion that might result from using words with too many possible interpretations by being specific. Words used to signify time and space are often subject to wide interpretation. How often, for example, is *often?* The meaning would vary both according to context and according to the user. *Occasionally, frequently, seldom, soon, long, short, far, near,* and many of the other words (like *many*) that we use *(regularly)* in conversation, should be defined in more specific terms in written reports.

Specificity

When you are specific, your reader automatically interprets your words in the same way you do. Specific words do not allow varied interpretations. Study the examples below.

General (Vague)	Specific
soon	January 23
significant increase	12 percent increase
high profits	A 57 percent markup
our product	The Clark CRT
improved morale	A 43 percent decrease in absenteeism
a majority	51 percent (or 93 percent)

Why is concrete language usually best?

Your writing will be more readable if you substitute concrete language for abstract words and expressions. Just as specific words provide exact facts, figures, details, and amounts; concrete language focuses on people doing things:

Abstract	Concrete
It was decided	I decided
Consideration was given	I considered
My analysis is that	I think that
Avoid contact with potentially lethal residue.	Don't touch. Contact may cause death
Attitudinal improvement is required before promotion	Jim has a bad attitude and shouldn't be promoted at this time.
The data are significant.	The data indicate a 14 percent increase.
We performed a number of experiments to test the hypothesis.	Forty-two experiments support the hypothesis.

When is general language preferable to specific details?

While specific language is usually easier to read and understand than general language, excessive use of specific details can be annoying. Don't say *Budweiser* when any beer will do; don't say *11:27* when *about 11:30* is close enough. When specific details are unimportant or obvious to the reader, you are better off using general language or omitting the detail completely.

Too specific: Grab your London Fog, and let's walk over to Persing's Place and have a pitcher of Budweiser.

Better: Let's go have a beer.

How specific you will need to be depends on your subject and on your audience's familiarity with it. Technical subjects usually require greater specificity than nontechnical subjects, and audiences familiar with a subject usually require fewer details. You will need to make your decisions about the appropriate level of specificity based on the needs of your subject and your analysis of the audience.

Sentence Structure

Sentence structure is another component of readability. In general, long sentences with a great deal of internal punctuation are more difficult to read than short sentences with fewer components. Simple sentences and compound sentences are the easiest to read. Complex sentences, which contain at least one subordinate clause, and compound-complex sentences are more difficult.

Why must sentence structure be varied?

As we mentioned in the section on readability formulas, however, simply using all short sentences will not result in readable writing. Variety in sentence length and type is necessary to maintain reader interest. Most ideas can be expressed in different types of sentences, so recast when necessary to achieve variety *and* to keep the *average* sentence length to about 17 words.

Too simple: I inspected the building sites. I found site *A* too hilly for our purpose. Site *B* is not zoned commercial at this time. Site *C* is zoned commercial. Site *C* is level, hard-packed ground suitable for our purposes. I recommend site *C*.
(six simple sentences)

Too complex: As a result of my inspection of the building sites, which revealed that site *A* is too hilly for our purposes, that site *B* is not zoned commercial at this time, and that site *C* is level, hard-packed ground and is zoned commercial, I recommend site *C*.
(one complex sentence)

Good variety: I recommend site *C*. My inspection of the sites revealed that *A* is too hilly, and *B* is not zoned commercial. Site *C* is level, hard-packed ground and is already zoned commercial.
(two simple sentences and one compound sentence)

What is the basic rule for placement of modifiers?

In addition to the need for a variety of sentence types (and, of course, the need to control choice of words and phrases within the sentences themselves), writers need to be concerned about the placement of modifying elements within sentences. In general, modifiers should be placed as close as possible to the word or phrase modified. This is most evident when the modifier is a single word. Note the way the meaning changes in the following sentences depending on the position of the modifier:

Only I will kiss her.

I will *only* kiss her.

I will kiss *only* her.

The same is true when a phrase or clause is used to modify. The meaning of the sentence will change, depending on the placement of the modifier:

With over four years' experience as a sales representative, Betty thought that Allen had management potential. (Betty has four years of experience.)

Betty thought that Allen, *with over four years of experience as a sales representative,* had management potential. (Allen has four years of experience.)

In general, phrases or clauses used as modifiers can be placed at the beginning or end of a sentence, or they can be *embedded* in the middle.

Beginning: *To complete the report,* you will need the March sales figures.

Middle: Our accountant, *who previously worked for Dynamic Innovations,* recommends immediate divestiture.

End: Purchasing the new computer system now would offer several advantages, *including increased production capacity.*

What is the advantage of placing modifiers at the beginning of the sentence? The disadvantage?

Each of these patterns has advantages and disadvantages. Placing the modifier at the beginning has the advantage of clarifying or qualifying the subject of the sentence for the reader. An opening modifier in essence provides the reader with the correct perspective with which to read the sentence: The reader is prepared for the *what* of the sentence because he or she already knows the *why*.

Because the company has lost over $40 million this year, we have decided to close the plant in Flint.

This sentence type has two disadvantages. The first is that writers sometimes forget that the introductory phrase or clause modifies the subject that follows, and a dangling modifier (see Chapter 3) may result:

Dangling: Arriving at work early, the report has to be completed for the 9:00 a.m. meeting.

Correct: Arriving at work early, he needed to complete the report for the 9:00 a.m. meeting.

The second difficulty occurs when the modifying phrase or clause is too long, causing the reader to wonder what the sentence is likely to be about. To ensure the effectiveness of sentences of this variety, keep the opening phrase or clause relatively brief and check to make sure that it correctly modifies the noun that follows.

Embedding the modifier in the middle of the sentence may be an effective way of combining sentences to make material more emphatic or more concise.

Two sentences: Robots are gaining popularity as a means of reducing production costs. Robots can perform repetitive tasks with fewer errors than people make.

Embedded: Robots, which can perform repetitive tasks with fewer errors than people make, are gaining popularity as a means of reducing production costs.

Two sentences: Susan was the best sales representative in the company this past year. She sold more than $4 million in new accounts alone.

Embedded: Susan, who sold more than $4 million in new accounts alone, was the best sales representative in the company this past year.

Embedded clauses are either restrictive or nonrestrictive depending on whether they are essential to the meaning of the sentence (see Chapter 3). An effective embedded sentence results in a more compact presentation of two ideas that would otherwise be presented in separate simple sentences.

Placing modifiers at the end of a sentence often results in the most logical construction: a *what* followed by a *why* or a *when*.

I am going downtown *because I need to buy a shirt.*

We will purchase new microcomputers *when the cost of the new technology drops.*

What is the advantage of placing modifiers at the end of the sentence? The disadvantage?

The principal disadvantage of this construction is that it may encourage writers to continue adding material and result in long-winded, rambling sentences.

The principal disadvantage of this construction is that it may encourage writers to continue adding material and result in long-winded, rambling sentences that go on and on, causing readers to become annoyed, and perhaps causing them to lose track of the original purpose of the sentence, which does not do either the reader or the writer any good (and so on).

Note also that changing the position of the modifier in the sentence may change the relative emphasis afforded the ideas presented in the sentence. (See the discussion of dependent and independent clauses in Chapter 3.)

I'll complete the report *when I receive complete data from Jim.*

When I receive complete data from Jim, I'll complete the report.

(The second sentence places greater emphasis on the need to receive complete data.)

The new computers will save us thousands of dollars every year *because they can automate many of our routine functions.*
Because they can automate many of our routine functions, the new computers will save us thousands of dollars every year.

(The second sentence places greater emphasis on automating routine functions.)

Paragraphing

Why is it important to vary the lengths of paragraphs?

Paragraphing is another factor that influences readability. As is true for sentences, long, involved paragraphs are more difficult to read than short paragraphs containing only a few ideas. Paragraph length is especially important in single-spaced material, where long paragraphs appear especially heavy and uninviting.

Variety is again the key. A series of short paragraphs, although easy to read, would seem choppy and simplistic. Report writers should strive for a mixture of paragraph lengths. The following rules will help:

1. Short paragraphs are more emphatic and receive more attention than long paragraphs.
2. Introductory paragraphs should be short (about 4 or 5 lines). Introductory paragraphs should put the material in an appropriate context (so the reader knows what you are doing) and introduce the material that follows.
3. Developmental paragraphs—which explain, analyze, and give examples—need to contain more information and can be longer. No paragraph, however, should run much longer than 15 lines.
4. Concluding paragraphs—which draw conclusions, make recommendations, or summarize—should also be short.
5. As a rule, the first sentence in a paragraph should introduce the main idea or *topic* of the paragraph. Other sentences in the paragraph limit, clarify (by explaining or illustrating), or support the idea introduced in the first sentence. (deductive structure)

6. When the first sentence does not contain the main idea of the paragraph, it should provide transition from the previous paragraph or give the reader a clear idea of where the paragraph will lead. When the first sentence does not contain the main idea of the paragraph, the last sentence should be the topic sentence. (inductive structure)

Voice

It is easier to read about people doing things than it is to read about ideas. For this reason, most sentences in business and technical reports should be in the active voice. The term **voice** refers to the relationship between the subject of the sentence and the action expressed in the verb. A sentence is in the **active voice** when the subject of the sentence performs the action. When the subject receives the action of the verb, the sentence is in the **passive voice.**

Active: The selection committee must make a final decision by June 7.
(The subject, *committee,* performs the action of the verb, *make.*)

Passive: A final decision must be made by the selection committee no later than June 7.
(The subject, *decision,* receives the action of the verb *made.*)

Why does using the active voice increase readability?

Active voice is more readable for two reasons. First, it gives the reader a clear picture of who is doing what. Second, the action moves forward, from the beginning of the sentence to the end. Sentences in the passive voice do not reveal the doer of the action until the end of the sentence. Sometimes, in fact, the doer of the action is omitted entirely from the sentence:

It was decided to purchase new equipment.

Who made the decision? The reader's opinion may be influenced by that missing piece of information. Neither technical subject matter nor a formal writing style require passive voice. In fact, passive voice is one of the main distractors from clarity in many technical and formal business reports. To form a clear idea of what the report is about, the reader needs to be able to identify *who* is doing (or has done) *what* to *whom* and for what reason. Active voice is the best way to make these relationships clear.

While most of your sentences should be in active voice, you can make good use of passive voice on two occasions: (1) when the performer of the action is immaterial or unknown, and (2) when your reader or other important person (though *not* yourself) has made a mistake.

Doer immaterial: This machine was overhauled just last month.

(It doesn't matter who did the overhauling, so the emphasis is rightly placed on what happened rather than on who did it.)

Doer unknown: The typewriter was stolen.

("Someone stole the typewriter" puts the emphasis on the *someone* rather than on the typewriter.)

Doer at fault: The engineering specifications should have been followed more closely.

(The active voice version, "The builder—or YOU—should have followed the engineering specifications more closely," is too accusatory.)

Tense

Verb tense is another factor that influences readability. The simple tenses are easier to read than the compound tenses. Likewise, the progression of tenses must be logical, giving the reader an accurate perception of when events took place. (For a review of tense formation and use, see Chapter 3.)

Figures of Speech

We tend to think in terms of generalization and differentiation; that is, we think in terms of similarities and differences. One of the easiest ways to learn something new, in fact, is to compare the new thing with something similar already known. A figure of speech is a word or words used in an imaginative way to compare two things that are not similar in a literal sense. The statement, "Because dogs and cats are both mammals, they have a number of physiological similarities," is a literal rather than an imaginative comparison, so the statement is not a figure of speech.

What are the principal figures of speech?

Figures of speech are often useful to help explain and to illustrate, but the items being compared must be similar in significant ways if the comparison is to be helpful. The principal figures of speech are simile, metaphor, analogy, hyperbole, metonymy, and personification.

Simile   A simile makes a comparison by simple assertion. It uses "like," "as," or "so" to equate two similar items:

> To be an effective sales representative, you must be *like* a tiger—aggressive.

> To be an effective sales representative, you must stalk your prospect *as* a tiger stalks its prey.

> As it is with tigers, *so* it is with sales representatives. To be effective, you must be aggressive.

The comparison in a simile must be figurative rather than literal. "Television is like radio in that both convert electronic transmissions into intelligible messages" is not a simile because what is said is exactly true for both items being compared. The statement, "Radio is like TV without a picture," however, *is* a simile because the resemblance described is figurative rather than literal.

What is a cliché?

Many clichés are based on overused similes: *red as a rose, go like a shot, nervous as a cat in a room full of rocking chairs.* Such expressions have become clichés because they originally provided effective illustrations of the ways in which two things were alike. The stronger the resemblance between the two items, the clearer the image the simile will give a reader.

A good simile can be useful because it labels the comparison for the reader (who can see exactly what you are comparing), and it uses a known quantity to describe an unknown.

Metaphor   A metaphor is more compact than a simile because it omits the labeling word, *like, as,* or *so.* A metaphor simply states that one thing *is* another:

Simile: An effective sales representative is like a tiger.

Metaphor: An effective sales representative is a tiger.

Simile: Radio is like TV without the picture.

Metaphor: Radio is TV without the picture.

Simile: Pollution spreads like cancer throughout the body of the lake.

Metaphor: The malignancy of pollution is evident throughout the lake.

Simile: Clear writing is like an arrow—it penetrates because it moves with force—straight and to the point.

Metaphor: Clear writing is an arrow moving with force—straight and to the point.

What may happen when metaphors are mixed?

Mixed metaphors can be a source of unintentional humor:

Mixed: His report ruffled the waters.

Better: His report muddied the waters.

Better: His report ruffled the boss's feathers.

While metaphors may be used occasionally in business and technical writing for dramatic impact, they are likely to mislead a reader because the comparisons are implied rather than stated explicity. A reader must be able not only to perceive the implied comparison, but also to determine the extent of the resemblance. For example, the following metaphor could be either figuratively or literally true:

The two-point press on line 4 is a real killer.

For this reason, metaphors in reports often require explanation.

Analogy   An analogy is simply an extended simile or metaphor, comparing the two items in several respects instead of just one. Like metaphors, analogies need to be used carefully. A bad analogy may lead the reader to a false conclusion:

Good sales representatives are like tigers. First, they stalk their prospects, pursuing them relentlessly. Then, they frighten them into submission. Finally, they pounce with the contract and secure a signature before the prospects know what's hit them.

Can analogies be used as proof? If not, what is their value?

Analogies, then, can be either true or false. A true analogy is one in which the resemblance is sufficiently complete and exact to provide a good illustration. A false analogy either misleads the reader into accepting a resemblance when there is none or uses the analogy to prove instead of to illustrate or explain.

Analogies are especially useful for explaining new concepts to a reader. You could, for example, easily explain television by using its similarities to radio. From a technical standpoint, the similarities would be significant. If you were writing to an advertiser making a decision about which medium to use to reach a particular audience, however, the differences would be more significant than the similarities.

The following examples illustrate the basic form of analogies, which usually state that *A* is to *B* as *C* is to *D.*

A vocal cord (A) produces sound (B) in much the same way a guitar string (C) produces sound (D)—by vibrating.

A transistor is like a gate. When it is open, electrons can pass through. When it is closed, they can't. By controlling the gate, we can control the flow of electrons from one side of the gate to the other.

Analogies are effective when used to define terms, explain processes, or illustrate. Analogies, however, are sometimes offered as proof. The Domino Theory, offered in support of America's military presence in Vietnam, compared the countries of Southeast Asia to a row of dominoes, implying that if the first fell to communism, all the others would follow. Such an analogy is useful as an illustration, but analogies do not prove that what is true in one case is necessarily true in another.

Does hyperbole have a place in report writing?

Hyperbole   Hyperbole is exaggeration, using a stronger word than accuracy requires for the purpose of emphasis: "I could sleep for a week," "I'm starving" (instead of hungry) and "Your suggestion is perfect" (instead of good or excellent), are examples of hyperbole. Hyperbole is often used with humorous intent:

A camel is a horse designed by a committee.

Our company is in such bad financial condition that three guys went broke just reading our annual report.

While the intent of hyperbole is to intensify an impression rather than to deceive, it is more appropriate in conversation and in informal writing than in report writing.

How may
metonymy confuse
readers?

Metonymy   When you substitute one word for another closely associated with it, you are using the figure of speech known as metonymy. If you say that your plant employs "4,000 *hands*" or that "two *heads* are better than one," you are using parts of the body to represent the whole. You might also say, "Our *plant* won the softball tournament," meaning that the plant's team won, which is using the whole to represent a part. Substituting *crown* for *king*, *bread* for *money*, *book* for *study*, or *pen* for *write* illustrates metonymy in which words frequently associated with particular ideas have come to stand for those ideas.

As with hyperbole, metonymy is not used often in formal business and technical writing, though it does have informal applications. The danger of using metonymy is that the reader might misinterpret your use of words. If your plant employs "4,000 hands," for example, does it employ 4,000 people or 2,000 people?

Is personification
acceptable in
business writing?

Personification   When the figure of speech assigns human qualities to nonhuman entities, it is known as personification. Pet projects or pieces of equipment may, for example, be referred to as *she:* "She's not acting quite right today." Personification is usually inappropriate in formal business and technical writing.

Poor: The generator prefers to warm up slowly.
(Obviously, a generator does not really have a preference. It should be warmed up slowly because it will last longer.)

Better: Allow the generator to warm up at 1500 rpm for 5 minutes to ensure complete oil circulation.

Poor: The company feels that the new computer is a good investment.
(The company cannot feel—or think or decide. Only people can feel.)

Better: Our manager feels (believes, thinks) that the new computer is a good investment.

Emphasis and Subordination

Not all ideas in a report will be of equal importance. For this reason, writers need to select the most important ideas for emphasis, while subordinating less important information. The basic rule of emphasis is that it is impossible to emphasize everything equally. Underlining every word in a book, for example, has the same effect as not underlining at all.

Remember that emphasis is a matter of contrast. Something can be emphasized only in relation to something else. Also, some things *should* be subordinated. When your reader will find part of your message negative or accusatory, for example, subordinate that part by placing it in the middle of a paragraph, putting the most negative concept in a subordinate clause and—especially when the reader has made a mistake—using passive voice.

Variety

As stated previously, your report will be more readable if you provide variety in word usage, sentence structure, and physical appearance. The following list is a summary of techniques for achieving variety in your writing:

1. Use synonyms, pronouns, or alternate phrasing to avoid repeating the same word frequently.

2. While short, simple sentences are the easiest to read, if all of your sentences are short, your writing will seem choppy and simplistic. Use a variety of sentence lengths. Try for an average sentence length of about 17 words, with no sentence exceeding about 40 words.

3. Use a mixture of sentence types (simple, compound, complex, compound-complex).

4. Make your report *look* easy to read by keeping most paragraphs short. In single-spaced material, first and last paragraphs should be about four lines long (*lines,* not sentences). Middle paragraphs should be about eight lines. The length of the paragraphs, however, should vary. An entire report of four-line paragraphs would appear choppy. A report consisting entirely of long paragraphs would appear heavy and uninviting. Paragraph length is less critical in double-spaced material, but following the same guidelines as for single-spaced material will help ensure visual variety.

CLARITY

What is the report writer's primary obligation to the reader?

Clarity is obviously an important factor in readability. Clarity is the transfer of thoughts from writer to reader without misunderstanding. A report writer's first obligation to the reader is to be clear. Grammatical correctness, logical structure, and specific transitional devices provide the basis for clear writing. These topics are covered in Chapter 3. In addition to the general tests for readability, clarity requires explicit use of language and complete coverage of ideas.

Explicit Statements

Because explicit statements provide the *who, what, when, why,* and *how,* they are easier to understand than implicit statements that omit one or more of those factors.

Implicit: You might find that wire too hot to handle.

Explicit: Don't touch that wire! It's carrying 10,000 volts.

Use implicit language only when an explicit statement would be too obvious or too accusatory.

Explicit (too obvious):   Currently, all of our frozen dinners are packaged in aluminum trays. Aluminum is not compatible with microwave ovens. (Reader would already know these things.)

Implicit: Because the aluminum trays our frozen dinners are packaged in are not compatible with microwave cooking, we should consider alternate methods of packaging.

Completeness

To be clear, a message also needs to be complete. After reading your report, the reader should have a clear understanding of each of the following:

1. **Your purpose.** Why did you write the report?
2. **Your methodology.** What procedures did you follow in gathering information?
3. **The significant facts.** What have you found out about the problem under investigation?
4. **Your conclusions and recommendations.** Who is to do what next, and when should it be done?

While different report writing situations will place different emphasis on these four factors, any report should answer all the reader's appropriate questions. A brief report of explanation, for example, might not contain a methodology, and a simple informational report would not contain conclusions and recommendations. A complete report contains everything necessary to answer questions that might occur to readers.

COURTESY

Why should reports be written from the readers' point of view?

A courteous message is written with the readers' point of view in mind. A courteous report, like a courteous person, is polite and cooperative. A courteous report explains even difficult situations in a way designed to help the readers act in the most reasonable way possible. Courtesy is achieved by using the you-attitude and through cooperation as equals.

You-Attitude

A simple definition of the you-attitude is putting your readers and their problems first. Think—and write—in terms of what a particular fact means to your readers rather than in terms of what it means to you.

Writer viewpoint: My department really needs the additional secretarial help because we are so far behind.

Reader viewpoint: With an additional secretary, my department could expedite work orders influencing the entire company.

Writer viewpoint: I am happy to present this report to you.

Reader viewpoint: The attached report shows you how ABC can save several thousand dollars a year.

Writer viewpoint: We have had 25 years of experience in providing organizations like yours with solutions to their telecommunications problems.

Reader viewpoint: Let us put our 25 years' experience in solving telecommunications problems to work for you.

Passive voice (see Chapter 3) may help avoid accusing the reader of having made a mistake:

Accusatory: You neglected to inform us of the accident in your March report.

Reader viewpoint: We should have been informed of the accident in the March report.

When you and your readers have conflicting interests, acknowledge your differences in an honest way. Your readers will expect you to have legitimate interests, and they will appreciate your recognizing their interests as well.

Writer viewpoint: We cannot possibly agree to a compromise on this issue.

Reader viewpoint: Thank you for letting us know how you feel about this issue, and although we are not able to accept the compromise you propose, we will be glad to continue discussion on other matters.

Cooperation as Equals

Although reports usually go up the chain of command—from the person making observations to the persons making decisions—reports should be free of both undue humility and condescension. The writer should present himself or herself as knowledgeable in the area under discussion without either amplifying or diminishing the reader's expertise.

Undue humility: I know you can't be bothered by all my department's problems,

Condescension: Here's another problem that would probably escape your attention unless I reported it.

Cooperative: I've discovered a problem you should know about.

CONCISENESS

What is the difference between brevity and conciseness?

Because no one has extra time to read wordy reports, conciseness is an important contributor to both clarity and courtesy. A concise message is usually clear, and it is courteous because it saves the reader's time.

Conciseness and brevity, however, are not synonymous. A concise message is as brief as possible without sacrificing clarity or courtesy. A brief message, on the other hand, may omit some of the details necessary for the reader to have a full understanding of the situation.

Focus on the Problem

The first step in achieving conciseness is to focus on the main problem by answering the following questions:

1. What does my reader most want to know? Answer this question as quickly as possible unless the reader will react negatively to the answer.

2. What details does my reader need to understand the situation? Provide these details in a logical order.

3. What action should my reader take? When appropriate, suggest any action your reader should take to solve the problem.

4. What details are necessary for an accurate record of the event or situation? Provide these details as unobtrusively as possible. Consider including them in a section specifically designed to review the history of the situation.

5. What does my reader know already? Omit details your reader already knows unless repetition of those details is necessary. To include details already known to your reader, deemphasize them by allocating them as little space as possible and by subordinating them to something of greater importance.

   Not this: Line 3 has never been able to match the production rate of our other six lines.

   But this: Because line 3 has never been able to match the production rate of our other lines, we should . . .

   Or this: Although line 3 . . .

6. What details are extraneous to the core of the problem? Avoid discussing details that will not influence the decision the reader needs to make.

Wordy Expressions

Many messages are too wordy simply because they contain tautologies (phrases containing needless repetition), redundancies, or simple repetition.

Wordy	Concise
first of all	first
needless to say	(omit)
square in shape	square
the color red	red
true facts	facts

Wordy	Concise
basic fundamentals	fundamentals
assembled together	assembled
join together	join
at all times	always
at the present time	now
in the nature of	like
until such time as	until
due to the fact that	because
in the event that	if
in the final analysis	finally
in order to	to
by means of	by
for the reason that	because
entirely complete	complete
new innovation	innovation
in the neighborhood of	about

In addition to avoiding these and similar expressions, you should also avoid repeating ideas. Make sure, for example, that your summaries actually summarize—state in abbreviated form—rather than merely repeat what you have already said.

CONFIDENCE

How does positive language affect readers?

An effective report displays confidence. As a writer, you need to express confidence in your abilities to observe accurately, present information well, and—when appropriate—decide on the best method of solving problems.

Your reader will react more favorably to what you are saying when you use positive language. Most ideas can be expressed in either a positive or a negative form:

Negative: Closed Saturday at noon.

Positive: Open until noon on Saturday.

The positive expression is always more appealing. Focus on what can be done rather than on what cannot be done. In general, avoid negative words, such as the following:

can't	bad	trouble
impossible	unfortunately	unable
unwilling	inferior	misfortune
failed	problem	misunderstand
claim	unlikely	loss

Also, avoid expressions that imply that you do not trust your reader:

> You claim . . .

> If what you say is true . . .

> Your request came as a surprise . . .

What undesirable
impressions may
negative language
give the reader?

Avoid expressions that imply that your report is inadequate and those that the reader will consider presumptuous.

> I *hope* that this report answers your questions.

> *Why not* give my suggestion a try?

> *If* this report hasn't answered your questions, do not hesitate to call me.

> You *must* act on this immediately.

> You *should* follow my suggestions.

> You *need* to consider the following alternatives.

Every now and then, however, you will need to make a forceful negative statement to avoid misleading your reader:

> Product *Y* has performed so poorly in the test market that we should halt production immediately.

Confidence does not mean a Pollyanna, everything-is-perfect approach to writing or management. It is rather a determination to *solve* problems instead of complaining about them. Occasionally negative language will help achieve a positive solution.

CORRECTNESS

Naturally, a report must present correct information if it is to be useful to the reader. Double-check all figures and statements for accuracy. Identify for your reader which statements are fact and which are opinion.

Your report will also be more effective if you use correct spelling, grammar, and mechanics. Correctness in these areas is not only an aid to readability and clarity, but also an indicator of a writer's care and attention to detail. Be sure to look up any words you are unsure of, review any punctuation rules that give you difficulty, and proofread carefully to eliminate simple mechanical errors. See Chapter 3 for a brief review.

CONVERSATIONAL TONE

How is the reader helped when a conversational tone is used?

Your reader should be able to understand you quickly and easily. A natural, inconspicuous, conversational writing style will help your reader focus on the most important aspect of your report—its contents. While some reports may need to contain complex technical or legal information, the bulk of the information in even the most complex report can be presented simply and clearly. When possible, use conversational words.

Conversational, however, does not mean "chatty." Many letters and memos contain language that is too informal for use in most reports. The conversational style needs to be adapted to the audience and the purpose of the report. If your style is too informal, your reader will conclude that you do not take the problem (or your reader) seriously. If your tone is too formal, your reader will conclude that you are cold and mechanistic in your thinking. The best approach is a balance that results from using simple, conversational language while avoiding slang, legalese, and business clichés.

Not This	But This
beg to advise	tell
please find enclosed	the enclosed booklet
in the final analysis	finally
a viable alternative	a possibility
in regard to	of, about
in order to utilize	to use
parameters (nontechnical)	limits, aspects
it is my conclusion that	I conclude
impact (as a verb)	influence

In addition to the absence of legalese and business clichés, conversational tone requires the kind of variety and emphasis normally present in oral communication. In conversation, we use our voices, gestures, and the exchange of information provided by questions and answers to keep the conversation from becoming monotonous. In written communication, we can use variety of sentence length and type, paragraph length, and vocabulary to make writing interesting.

STYLE

What is the advantage of informal style?

Functional writing may be either formal and impersonal or informal and personal. Many companies prefer reports written in one style or the other. Formal, impersonal style avoids the use of personal pronouns, uses longer sentences, and uses abstract nouns and technical terms not often used in conversational English. Informal, personal style is conversational English. It uses technical terms when required by context and uses personal pronouns where they would naturally be used in conversation.

Some people believe that the formal, impersonal style is more objective than the informal, personal style. We disagree. Objectivity is a result of the quality of the research, fairness in analyzing data, and accuracy in presentation. Compare the following examples:

Formal: The experimenter divided the subjects into two equal groups.

Informal: I divided the subjects into two equal groups.

Formal: The decision was made to terminate employees in ascending order of seniority.

Informal: I decided to lay off people according to their seniority.

Formal: A study of the relative merits of the two computer systems in question has led to the conclusion that System *A* is the superior system. System *A* is therefore recommended.

Informal: I recommend computer System A. After studying System *A* and System *B,* I concluded that *A* would be better for our purposes.

Informal, personal English is more readable and clearer. Formal, impersonal style forces the reader to ask *who* and *what* questions. It implies, rather than stating explicitly, who is performing what action. With formal style, readers have to stop and ask themselves, *who* is the experimenter, *who* is recommending.

Should you work for an organization that requires the formal style of writing, try to make your reports as lively and as readable as possible by using active instead of passive voice and by using nouns in the place of pronouns so that the person performing the action will be clear.

Not this: It was concluded that . . .

But this: The writer concluded that . . .

SUMMARY

Functional writing communicates ideas quickly and accurately without drawing attention to itself. Functional writing is designed to save the reader's time and energy. The characteristics of functional writing are readability, clarity, courtesy, conciseness, confidence, correctness, and conversational tone.

Readability formulas developed by Rudolf Flesch and Robert Gunning use sentence length and word difficulty to test readability. The Gunning Fog Index provides an indication of the amount of education required to read a passage. Diction—or word usage—also influences readability. In general, short familiar words with limited connotations are easier to read and understand. Report writers need to develop a good vocabulary so that they can be sure they are using words correctly. Specific language, sentence length and variety, and paragraph order and length also contribute to readability. Active voice, appropriate verb tenses, and appropriate use of figures of speech improve readability by making writing more interesting.

Readable writing also emphasizes important points and subordinates less important material. Emphasis and subordination result from contrast and variety in placement, proportion, language, and mechanics.

Clarity is the report writer's first obligation. The report must transfer ideas from writer to reader without misunderstanding. In addition to being readable, a clear report uses explicit language and provides complete details. Report writers also need to take the reader's point of view into account. This is known as courtesy. The you-attitude and a problem-solving, cooperative approach will ensure courtesy.

Good reports are concise, focusing on the problem and on possible solutions. Good reports are also confident, expressing ideas in positive terms. Avoid negative language, terms that imply that you do not trust your reader, and expressions that imply that your report is inadequate. Reports must be correct in form and content if they are to be effective. Conversational tone and an informal, personal style will contribute to the readability and overall effectiveness of a report as well.

EXERCISES

Review and Discussion Questions

1. In what way are reports functional writing?
2. What does the dictionary tell us about words?
3. What are the common ways words are misused?
4. What is the difference between a word's denotative meaning and its connotative meaning?
5. What are the main figures of speech, and what are their functions?
6. What is the difference between jargon and slang?
7. Why are specific words better than general words in most cases? When are general words preferred?
8. How does sentence structure contribute to readability?
9. How do paragraph length and development contribute to readability?
10. What are the differences between active and passive voice? When should each be used?
11. In what ways are similes and metaphors different?
12. When are analogies appropriate in business and technical reports?
13. What are the principal means of controlling emphasis and subordination in written material?
14. Why is explicit language better than implicit language in most situations? When is implicit language preferred?

15. What is the you-attitude?

16. How does a report writer achieve conciseness?

17. What kinds of negative expressions should report writers avoid?

18. Why should report writers avoid legalese and business clichés?

19. What are the differences between a formal, impersonal style and an informal, personal style?

20. Why is clarity a report writer's first obligation to the reader?

Problems

1. Select three sample short reports for analysis (or, if more convenient and your instructor permits, three articles from *Time, Newsweek, Forbes, Business Week, Fortune,* or another magazine or journal important for your planned career).
   a. On one report, identify each sentence as a topic sentence, sentence of clarification, sentence of limitation, or support sentence.
   b. On one report, identify all figures of speech, and describe how each functions within the sentence or paragraph.
   c. Apply the Gunning Fog Index to each of the three reports.
   d. Select the report that you consider the most readable of the three. Write a one- or two-page memo stating the reasons that the report you selected is the best.

2. List all the words you can think of that mean "to move by the power of one's feet" and provide the denotations and connotations for each word.

3. Use one of your own short reports or papers, and
   a. Apply the Gunning Fog Index.
   b. Identify topic sentences, sentences of clarification, sentences of limitations, and support sentences.
   c. Evaluate the variety in sentence length and type.
   d. Locate and explain any figures of speech.
   e. Discuss the effectiveness of the language from the standpoint of clarity, courtesy, conciseness, confidence, correctness, and conversational tone.

4. Rewrite the following sentences to improve their word usage. Indicate sentences in which all the words have been used correctly with a "C."
   a. Read Aburdene's letter carefully. His proposal seems deviant to me, perhaps even illegal.
   b. An effective mediator must be completely uninterested.
   c. Canvas the district to see how people intend to vote.
   d. Apprise me of your intentions as soon as you decide.
   e. Penrose selected the best cite for the new building.
   f. How will the new tax law effect our company?

g. Like he said, we all need to work together.

h. Sondra's solution to the problem was clearly the most unique.

i. Matty tells some very clever antidotes.

k. Her meretricious behavior earned her a quick promotion.

5. Rewrite the following sentences to eliminate clichés and mixed metaphors.

   a. If we acquire the company, we'll acquire it hook, line, and sinker.

   b. When I examined the data, the course of action was as clear as crystal.

   c. After two months of beating arround the bush, they have finally accepted our proposal.

   d. Even though the experiment was not fully successful, in the final analysis you can be proud of what you accomplished.

   e. Our new boss is as stubborn as a mule, so I am not at all convinced that we can pursuade him to go along with us on this.

   f. I want to burn the midnight oil until this project is complete.

   g. When the chips are down, you can count on his backing you to the hilt.

   h. We'll need to sift your proposal through the acid test of profitability.

   i. A horse of a different color would smell as sweet.

   k. His rocking the boat has really delayed our climbing the ladder of success.

6. Rewrite the following sentences to improve their you-attitude.

   a. I would like to thank you for your cooperation on this project.

   b. I have received your suggestion and will give it careful consideration.

   c. Our company has been in business for almost 100 years and has specialized in solving problems for companies like yours.

   d. You failed to complete Section 3 of the sales report, and I cannot issue your commission check until you finish the report.

   e. Because you have been a good customer, I am willing to allow you the 30-day extension on Phase 2.

   f. I am sending you the blueprints you requested by United Parcel. As I will send them today, they should arrive at your office by next Monday.

   g. You evidently entered the wrong formula in the computer program, as it gives an incorrect answer every time.

   h. I am a graduate of Midwest University with a degree in business management, and I have four years of part-time sales experience.

   i. I believe that our voice mail system is the best available, and you would be crazy not to install it.

     k. I would appreciate receiving the information about your telecommunications equipment by the first of the month so that I can complete figures for the report I need to submit to our Purchasing Agent by the 15th.

7. Rewrite the following sentences to make them clearer and more concise.

     a. As a way of beginning, I would like to briefly summarize the most important conclusions and recommendations contained in this report.

     b. We will have to arrive at a decision about our tax situation before the month of April.

     c. The meeting was postponed until later due to the fact that the chairman was out of town.

     d. Needless to say, we're delighted with the results of your most recent study.

     e. At the time of the present writing, we have no reason to anticipate continued growth of the target market, but we can perhaps effect a change in our advertising to help assist in the development of new markets.

     f. Here is your check in the amount of $534.

     g. The reason why we altered our policy is because of the need to increase employee satisfaction.

     h. As you know, we need to endeavor to complete a number of experiments to test our hypothesis before presenting the theory to our client.

     i. As a result of our recent significant increase in sales, it has been decided to provide a bonus for all employees sometime soon.

     j. First of all, allow me to congratulate you on the most unique advertising campaign I have ever seen.

     k. In order to write an effective report, it goes without saying that you need a firm foundation in the basic fundamentals of writing.

8. Rewrite the following sentences to eliminate negative expressions and improve the level of confidence.

     a. Why not give my idea a try? What do you have to lose?

     b. If you think that reorganization of the department is a good idea, I am willing to go along with you.

     c. If this proposal hasn't answered all your questions, do not hesitate to contact me at your earliest convenience.

     d. I hope that you can find the time to read at least the conclusions and recommendations in the attached report.

     e. Although sales for this last quarter have not been very encouraging, I am hopeful that the new advertising campaign will make it easier to call on new clients and that sales will improve.

     f. Unfortunately, we are unable to approve your proposal at this time, although we are willing to reconsider it next month, when we will have entered our new fiscal year.

     g. If what you say is true, I am unable to explain how so many bad widgets could have been shipped to you.

     h. You must comply with all the requirements of our request if we are to consider your proposal.

     i. Your request for an increased budget came as a suprise, and unfortunately I think that it would be more trouble than it is worth and simply can't agree to it.

     j. You have evidently misunderstood my suggestion, and you need to reread my original proposal to fully understand what I am saying.

     k. I hope that these exercises have been beneficial and that you have learned how to avoid unnecessary negative expressions.

9. Rewrite the following sentences to make their tone more conversational.

     a. Please find enclosed the data you requested detailing the sales figures for 1988.

     b. Please advise me posthaste on possible viable alternatives to our current procedures.

     c. I assume that you are cognizant of recent developments in the subject company.

     d. We need to finalize the interface between our company and theirs now that the merger has been formalized.

     e. How is the recently acquired computer system going to impact this department?

     f. It is my conclusion that a systematized approach is the only logical way to effect a training program for employee-types.

     g. While you are perusing the report, it should be noted that all monetary figures are expressed in 1980 dollars for purposes of calculating inflationary trends.

     h. Please be advised that we must complete the project within the specified time frame.

     i. This will acknowledge receipt of your check in regard to shipment of four (4) dozen thermostats.

     j. The decision was made as to video equipment purchases by the vice president of operations.

     k. As to which microcomputers would be superior for our company, a variety of systems were analyzed and compared, which led to the conclusion that virtually any moderately priced system with relatively comparable configuration would meet our needs for the foreseeable future.

10. Write a three-page memo explaining the advantages of the informal, personal style and encouraging its use.

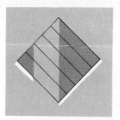

The Process of Writing

Although no two reports are identical, report writers face the same tasks repeatedly: planning, composing, revising, writing with others, and applying specific strategies to solving common writing problems. This chapter covers these routine activities of the process of writing.

Topics

Prewriting
Composing
Revising
Using Word Processing Equipment and Electronic Mail
Collaborative Writing
Solving Common Writing Problems

The process of writing a report actually begins long before a writer receives a specific assignment. Much of what we need to know for this process we take for granted: the English language, the subject of the problem, the readers, the environment in which the report will be written and read, and so on. Previous chapters have covered many of these aspects.

PREWRITING

What you do *before* writing will have a tremendous influence on the quality of the final product. Prewriting activities may, in fact, determine the relative success of the finished report. Before you actually begin writing any report (except for the most routine of informational reports), you will need to ask yourself several questions about your readers and the subject of the report. The most important of these are the following:

1. What do my readers already know about the subject?
   a. Have we communicated about this subject before?
   b. Are my readers familiar with the specialized language of the subject?
   c. Are my readers familiar with basic business terminology?
   d. Will my readers require a full explanation of the subject, a simplified explanation, or no explanation at all?
2. What do my readers want to know about the subject?
   a. Is the subject already important to my readers?
   b. Can knowing about the subject benefit my readers?
   c. Does my subject have built-in reader interest, or must I create interest in some way?
3. How do my readers feel about the subject?
   a. Do my readers have a positive, negative, or neutral view of the subject?
   b. What previous experience have my readers had with the subject that would influence their feelings about it?
   c. Are my feelings about the subject the same as my readers'?
4. How do my readers feel about me and my company (or my department)?
   a. Do my readers have a positive, negative, or neutral view of me and my company?
   b. What previous experience have my readers had with me or my company that would influence their feelings?
   c. Are my feelings about my readers the same as their feelings about me and my company?
5. How do my readers feel about other people, business, and life in general?
   a. Are my readers optimistic or pessimistic?

b. Do my readers tend to be accurate and precise in business dealings?

c. Are my readers generally willing to grant the benefit of the doubt?

When can the purpose of the report be determined?

You also need to clarify what you hope to achieve with the report. Although the purpose of the report cannot actually be determined until after the research is complete, you should know what questions you *hope* to answer in the report before you begin your research. As most of these questions are problem specific, we will cover them in Chapter 9. You also need to know your own biases about the subject. Do you favor a particular outcome? If so, you will need to guard against allowing your prejudices to influence the objectivity of your research and presentation of data. With these preliminary questions answered, you will be ready to begin planning the report (Chapter 9) and researching the problem (Chapters 10 and 12).

COMPOSING

After you have answered the preliminary questions about your reader and the purpose of your report and after you have conducted any required research, you will eventually reach the stage at which you are ready to begin composing the report. Even with pages of notes, writers often find it difficult to begin the process of writing. Understanding the causes of that hesitancy, commonly known as **writer's block,** and knowing the most effective means of overcoming it will greatly increase your ability to write quickly and easily.

What are the two major causes of writer's block?

The two major causes of writer's block are fear of making errors in grammar and mechanics and fear of making an unwarranted recommendation. You can guard against the first of these by being familiar with the fundamentals of English usage and having an English handbook available. You can help prevent the second by ensuring that your recommendation is appropriate and well supported by the data. At the same time, however, you will need to learn how to determine when you have gathered enough evidence on which to base conclusions and recommendations. How much evidence is necessary will naturally depend on the (1) nature of the decision, (2) amount of risk involved, and (3) cost of conducting additional research. Regardless of the report assignment, these factors can be plotted as an exponential curve, as Exhibit 5.1 illustrates.

How critical are the consequences of the decision to be made?

No matter how much time or money is spent researching a topic, 100 percent certainty about a decision is impossible to achieve. The degree of certainty required needs to be weighed against the cost of conducting the research. For some scientific and technical applications, for example, the cost of failure would be so high that virtually all available evidence should be considered before the final decision is made. When

Exhibit 5.1   Costs of Research

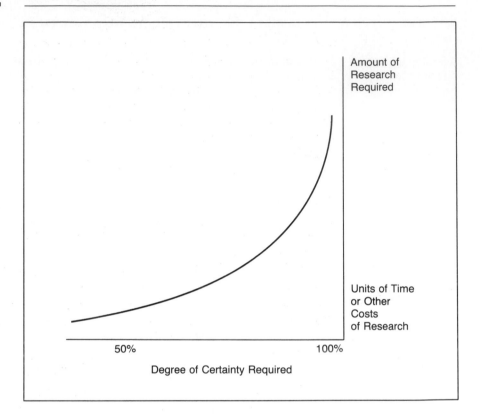

the consequences of a decision are not critical, much less evidence may be required. For example, think about the level of certainty you would want before making the final decision on the following:

- The best design for a part used in an artificial heart
- The best design for a computer used in the space shuttle
- The best location for a toxic waste dump
- The best location for a new manufacturing facility
- The best computer system to purchase for your company
- The best automobile to lease for your sales representatives
- The best method of training your employees to use your company's new computer system

Why are large tasks divided into smaller components?

Once you have determined the degree of certainty required and decided to begin the writing process, you still may face obstacles that will slow your progress. Because reports are usually longer and more complex than other kinds of writing, the sheer size of the task may be inhibiting. If this proves the case, use the techniques of **factoring** (Chapter 9) to divide the large task into smaller, more manageable components.

Another common cause of writer's block is the desire to produce a perfect rough draft. Attempting to write a perfect first sentence or paragraph before you begin the second virtually guarantees that writing will be a painful and slow process. If you constantly criticize your efforts to produce the report, the creative part of your brain will eventually stop producing new ideas.

The key is to remember that writing is a process calling for a variety of intellectual activities and that each of these activities requires time. In the course of producing a report, you will need to gather, evaluate, select, and organize data; draw appropriate conclusions; determine an appropriate structure and content for your presentation; create and arrange sentences and paragraphs; and evaluate and revise created materials. Because the process is so complex, we should not expect to be able to complete it satisfactorily the first time.

Why does the writing process almost always involve starts and stops?

Rather than proceeding smoothly from start to finish, the writing process is almost always recursive, including many stops and restarts along the way. Most writers will collect some information, write a few notes, collect more information, rewrite and add to the first notes, collect even more information, reconsider their original ideas, and revise and add to their notes.

This procedure will continue until the report—or a major section of it—is complete. At that point, the next step in the writing process, revising, begins.

REVISING

Although you may have been doing some revising during the composing process, most documents will require further revision before they can be considered finished. If time permits, let a document sit for a while before you attempt to revise it. A delay between composing and revising will help you approach the report with a fresh mind and to see it more objectively.

Are documents ever perfect? When is a revision complete?

In general, the less writing experience you have, the longer you should let the materials sit. Even when time is short, plan to spend at least some of that time revising. Just knowing that you can—and will—improve the report by revising it will make composing it easier. Remember, however, that no document is ever perfect, and if you continue to revise with the idea of achieving perfection, the cost of the report will eventually exceed its value to you and the organization. This curve is also an exponential curve, as shown in Exhibit 5.2. The exact curve would, of course, vary from person to person and from report to report, but the general shape would remain the same. The major improvements can be achieved quickly and easily. Once you have taken care of the major problems, subsequent improvements make less and less difference to the quality of the report while taking more and more time.

Cost-effectiveness is also influenced by any deadline you may have.

Exhibit 5.2   Revision Time and Improvement

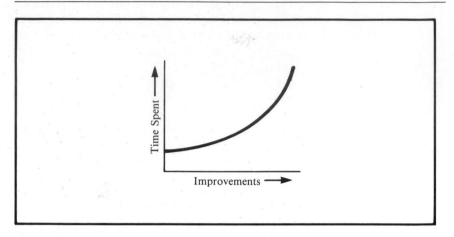

Many deadlines in business are absolutes. If a boss suggests that you have a report ready to go by the 12th, she or he may well mean that the report had better be ready, or else. Although you may be able to obtain an extension in some cases (especially when you can show that the person requesting the report will benefit from the delay), do not count on one. Be prepared to do the best job you can in the time available.

When you revise the report, you should, of course, watch for errors in spelling, grammar, and punctuation. Correct these errors whenever you see them. If you tell yourself that you will remember to fix them later, you run the risk of allowing them to slip through into the final report. In addition to providing the opportunity to correct surface errors of this variety, revising also allows you to improve a document by

- Deleting unnecessary materials so that the final report will be as concise as possible
- Adding materials you may have inadvertently omitted
- Changing wording to express your meaning more clearly, making sure that your diction is correct and that you have placed the emphasis where it belongs
- Rearranging elements of the report to achieve a more logical or effective presentation of your ideas

Deleting

Reports place a premium on conciseness. While editing, look for and eliminate redundancies, deadwood, and unnecessary repetition.

Redundant: *The color* red
Square *in shape*
A *bad* disaster

Today's *modern* computer systems
Postponed *until later*
At *the* present *time*
Revert *back*
Only this solution *alone*

Deadwood: This report deals with *the matter of* employee morale.
There is only one solution *that* is possible.
The following statistics *serve to* support my conclusions.
It was during this time *that* the company was founded.
The site *located* in Missouri . . .
The illustration *which is shown* on p. 27 of Appendix A illustrates . . .

Unnecessary repetition: *The problem of* improving employee morale is one of our most serious *problems.*
Our *facility* is going to be the largest *facility* of its kind in the world.
The results, as *computed* by our VAX 8650 mini *computer*, are as follows . . .
I will have to *repeat* the experiment *again.*

Verbiage of this variety obviously takes up space. You may discover, however, that even when you have eliminated all wordiness, you still need to condense your report to meet certain space requirements. Many companies and foundations, for example, place specific limits on the length of proposals they will consider.

When you do need to condense beyond the usual requirements of eliminating wordy expressions and unnecessary repetitions, you face essentially the same problem as you do when writing an abstract or executive summary. The following procedure will help you produce meaningful condensations:

To what can meaningful condensations be compared?

1. Content
   a. Find the topic sentence for each paragraph and make sure that it contains the most important idea (a general principle) in that paragraph.
   b. Find the most significant support for each topic sentence.
   c. Locate any other essential details in the report which were not included in a topic sentence or the main support sentence.
   d. Evaluate items in a, b, and c against your length requirements. Add details in order of their significance from the readers' point of view.

2. Style
   a. Subordinate ideas of secondary importance to those that have greater significance.

   Change this: Site A is bounded on the north by Ellinger's Bog. The bog is a breeding ground for mosquitoes but does not support significant wildlife. If we were to drain the bog, Site A would be ideal for the construction of our new plant.

   To this: Site A, which is bounded on the north by Ellinger's Bog, would be ideal for the construction of our new plant if we drain the bog and eliminate the mosquitoes' breeding ground.

b. Combine sentences by making one subject serve for two verbs or one verb do for two objects. Embed one sentence within another.

Change this: The Japanese system of management has resulted in continued high levels of productivity. It has also resulted in an unusually high level of employee morale.

To this: The Japanese system of management has resulted in continued high levels of productivity and an unusually high level of employee morale.

Change this: Line 4 has mechanical difficulties at least once a week. This has a detrimental effect on the morale of those who work on the line or depend on it for parts.

To this: The continual difficulties on line 4 have a detrimental effect on the morale of those who work on the line or depend on it for parts.

3. Appearance
   a. Single-space rather than double-space. Paragraph more often to increase white space.
   b. Decrease side margins.
   c. Eliminate one or two levels of headings.

Adding

What are the two most likely reasons for adding material to a report?

In most cases, editing problems are caused by the need to condense. The need to expand is usually the result of a failure to be complete in the first place. Because of the high value placed on conciseness in business and the professions, you will probably need to expand under two circumstances only. First, you may need to add details to provide further support for one of your conclusions. Second, you may need to expand to increase readability or clarity.

As you examine the first draft of your report, check to see whether you have supplied sufficient evidence to support all your conclusions. Are you making mental leaps from an item of evidence to a conclusion that your readers may not follow? If so, expand by adding the missing link. Provide all the details necessary to lead your readers from your beginning point to your conclusion.

Writing that is too condensed is often difficult to read, not only because it omits details that may be necessary for a full understanding, but also because it packs a great deal of information into each sentence. Just as we can combine sentences to condense information, we can break complicated (compound-complex and embedded) sentences into several simple sentences. Simple sentences require more space to express ideas, but they are easier to understand.

Changing

When should sentence structure be changed?

Sentence and paragraph structures may need changing to improve clarity or emphasis. To improve clarity, change passive-voice sentences to active and implicit statements to explicit. Check complex sentences to ensure that the appropriate element is in the subordinate clause. Compare the following sentences:

> Although sales were slow the first quarter, they were the highest in history the last half of the year. (subordinates slow sales)

> Sales were slow the first quarter although they were the highest in history the last half of the year. (subordinates highest sales in history)

Change verbs that you may have inadvertently converted to nouns back into verbs. This will make your writing more concise and more readable at the same time.

Change This	**To This**
I will make the *decision*	I will *decide*
Upon *resumption* of work	When work *resumes*
Begin the *writing* of the report	Begin *writing* the report
I made the *announcement* that	I *announced* that
His *performance* is not as good as it should be.	He has not *performed* as well as he should.

Watch especially to see whether forms of the verb *to be* have been used in combination with a noun when an action verb would be more appropriate.

Change this: The purpose of this report *is the presentation of* data concerning the efficacy of Procedure A.

To this: This report *presents* data concerning the efficacy of Procedure A.

Rearranging

When should you finalize the order of presentation?

The first draft may reveal that the tentative outline will not prove adequate for the final report. You may need to change your order of presentation from deductive to inductive, or you may find that factors you thought would be significant were not so important as factors you had not anticipated. Do not be afraid to scrap your original outline and to rearrange whole sections of your report. In fact, one of the questions you should ask yourself at the completion of each rough draft is whether other arrangements of the material are possible and whether any of the alternatives would improve your report.

Which positions in a unit provide emphasis? Subordination?

You might also need to rearrange portions of some sections to control emphasis or to provide better transition from one part to the next. Recall that the beginning and ends of units (whether sentences, paragraphs, or sections) are the parts to which the reader will pay closest attention. Rearrange material when necessary to place the important words and ideas at the beginnings and ends of units.

If you are working from handwritten or typed copy, you may wish to cut and paste to achieve the new arrangement. Simply cut the material out of one section and use paste, staples, or tape to paste it into its new location. When only a sentence or two requires moving, you may wish to encircle the sentence and draw an arrow to show its new location.

Editing Others and Being Edited

Different people have different ideas about how an idea should be expressed. When you begin working, you will find that your supervisors will edit your materials and request revisions before they will agree to "sign off" on them and send them forward. Once you have a few years of experience behind you, you will have the responsibility of ensuring that the work leaving your area of responsibility meets the standards it should.

How are writing style and reliability weighed in the editing process?

Whether you are being edited or are editing the work of others, you will need to remember that writing is an intensely personal activity. Writing style is an extension of a person's personality and thought processes, and editorial suggestions are frequently perceived as threats. Learning to produce reports that satisfy your supervisors and helping others improve their writing are a normal part of business life. Accept the comments of others as the legitimate expression of their perceptions. In most cases you will be able to revise your reports to meet your boss's expectations without drastically altering your own writing style. When you are doing the editing, attempt to suggest improvements without implying that the material is poorly planned or poorly written. Positive suggestions for changes will work better than critical remarks. The proofreaders' marks on the endsheet are an effective and convenient way of communicating about and commenting on written material.

In general, you should give your boss the kind of report she or he desires. Make sure, however, that any final report with your name on it is an objective and honest presentation of facts. Should your boss suggest that you make a change that would reduce the reliability of the report, you will need to discuss that change with your boss and perhaps a higher ranking officer in the company as well. You can never tell how far or to whom a report will go, and if the report contains mistakes, it will reflect badly on you. Naturally, you should never ask someone working for you to falsify information in a report or letter.

USING WORD PROCESSING EQUIPMENT AND ELECTRONIC MAIL

What is word processing? How is it different from composing on a typewriter?

Word processing (WP) equipment and electronic mail (EMAIL) greatly simplify the process of preparing and sending written communications. They are not, however, magically different from writing with pen and paper or composing on a typewriter. Words, sentences, and paragraphs still have to be put together, and that will remain your responsibility. What a word processor will do is amplify your ability to produce written material (whether good writing or bad) by automating many of the tasks that had to be performed manually before its advent.

What hardware and software are necessary for word processing?

Regardless of type or brand, WP equipment usually consists of a keyboard (for entering data—typing); a computer program, which allows the equipment to perform the word processing operations; a memory system for saving (storing) created materials (usually a magnetic disk); and a printer for producing a "typed" (or **hard**) copy of created materials. WP equipment may be **dedicated,** or designed specifically for word processing, or it may be a text editing program used with a microcomputer or minicomputer designed for general use.

In spite of their similarities, each word processor (or text editing program for microcomputers) is different, and you will have to read the manuals accompanying your equipment and program and experiment with using it if you are to realize its full potential. The techniques we suggest here will work with most of the equipment and programs currently on the market, but you may need to alter the procedure to achieve the same result. Expect to take some time to learn a WP program. Even those computers advertised as "user friendly" will require some study and trial-and-error experimentation. The investment of time, however, will be worth it.

Because they represent such an increase in efficiency over hand-drafted or dictated (even machine-dictated) letters, many organizations are beginning to require management personnel to produce their own documents using WP equipment. For people planning to enter management ranks this means two things: (1) you will need to know how to type, and (2) you—and you alone—will have full responsibility for the appearance, correctness, and content of your written work. In the very near future, only a few managers will have the luxury of secretaries or administrative assistants to help with written materials.

The Composition Process

How does using a word processor simplify the task of composing?

One of the main advantages of using a word processor is the ease with which material can be written, deleted, and moved. The writer is freed from worries about conserving time and energy while writing, allowing him or her to concentrate on developing an effective message. Material can be created and changed very quickly and easily.

Most WP keyboards are very fast, and typing on them is a pleasure. If you do not like what you have written, it is just as easy to delete material as it is to add it. You do not have to pull the sheet out, wad it up, and throw it away. You simply delete the material you do not want and save the rest.

Most WP equipment will also allow you to move blocks of information from one location to another with the press of a key or two. Would your third paragraph be better as the opening paragraph? Simply mark the paragraph and move it from one position to the other. The complete document, as corrected, can be reviewed for errors before it is printed. It is easier to review clean copy for errors than a marked-up manuscript. And should additional revision be required, only those few changes will need to be made before reprinting affected pages.

Form and Guide Letters

What are differences between form and guide letters? When should each be used?

As mentioned previously, business frequently uses form and guide letters to reduce the cost of preparing correspondence. WP equipment is especially useful for producing form and guide letters, memos, and reports. The user is able to prepare the basic document, save it (by following the instructions in the manual that accompanies the program), and change only those parts of the document necessary for a particular reader. Some WP programs will automatically insert new names, addresses, and specific information in a document before printing. With other programs, the operator must make the appropriate changes manually.

Special Features

What features are common to most word processing programs? What does each feature do?

Most word processing and text editing programs contain a number of special features to facilitate the writing and revising process. The following features are the most common and the most useful.

1. **Block move.** With a WP program, rearranging text is usually a matter of marking the beginning and end of the section to be moved and indicating the place to which it should be moved. The document will be reformatted automatically with the section in its new location.

2. **Editing.** Virtually all WP programs allow the user to insert and delete material by moving the **cursor** (position marker on screen) to the appropriate location and making the changes. The entire document will be automatically adjusted to accommodate the changes.

3. **Formatting.** WP programs and equipment vary in formatting options. Some programs do not, for example, display boldfaced and underlined text as it will appear, but instead mark the beginning and end of printing features with special characters. Some programs do not indicate where page breaks (divisions between pages) are going to occur, which makes avoiding **widows** (single lines appearing by themselves at the top or bottom of a page) difficult. Most WP programs allow the user to indicate where pages should end if the naturally occurring page breaks are awkward. Some programs will insert footnotes automatically at the bottom of the page on which the note occurs.

4. **Global search and replace.** Most WP programs allow the user to search a complete document for a specific term and, if necessary, replace it with another. This feature can help locate overused words. It also can be used to save time in the composition process and in preparing form documents. Suppose, for example, you need to prepare a form report for a number of companies in which you will mention the name of the addressed company several times. Simply prepare the original document with [company name] (or any convenient designation) in the places the name should occur, and before printing each copy of the report, initiate a global-search-and-replace command to replace all occurrences of [company name] with the appropriate company name.

   If you have a scientific document to prepare that includes several occurrences of a long, difficult-to-type formula, you could simply enter X at each point the formula should appear, and replace each occurrence of X with the formula after the document is complete, typing the formula once instead of many times. Or perhaps you have used a word incorrectly throughout the document or misspelled a word consistently. Simply replace all occurrences of the erroneous word with the correct one with one command.

5. **Mailing list programs.** Many WP programs come with (or have available) special supplements for maintaining mailing lists. The mailing list program can usually be used in combination with the WP program to produce individualized form letters.

6. **Programmable keys.** Many WP programs have a **glossary, macro,** or programmable-keys function that allows the user to define certain keys to represent text for insertion or formatting functions. By using this feature, an operator may call up a complete paragraph, complex scientific formula, or specific format with a simple keystroke or two.

7. **Spelling checkers.** Some WP programs come with (or have available) spelling checkers. The spelling checker will "read" through a document looking for misspelled words, stopping at those words it "recognizes" as misspelled and allowing the operator to make the required correction.

   If you use a spelling checker, remember that it is an *aid* to proofreading and not a substitute for it. The computer cannot read and understand content. It merely matches the words it finds against words in a dictionary and flags any word not found in the dictionary. This is a tremendous help in finding typographical errors and genuinely misspelled words. The computer cannot tell, however, when a key word has been omitted from a sentence, when the incorrect homonym has been used, when an apostrophe has been omitted, or when a correctly spelled word has been used incorrectly.

Some spelling checkers permit correction of the misspelled word when it is found. Others simply mark the word and require the user to correct it after the completion of the marking.

8. **Split screen.** Some WP programs will allow the user to view two or more parts of the document at once, which facilitates checking correlated parts for consistency.

9. **Top and bottom lines (headers and footers).** Most WP programs allow the user to insert special material automatically at the top and/or bottom line of each page. Top-line entries, for example, are useful for second (and following) page headings on letters and for running heads on reports. Most WP programs will automatically count pages and insert the appropriate number into either a top or bottom line.

10. **Wordwrap.** Most WP programs require a carriage return only when the writer wishes to begin a new paragraph. Within paragraphs, the text automatically continues to (*wraps* around to) the next line. Some WP programs give the writer the opportunity to hyphenate words at the ends of lines, but that option may defeat the automatic wordwrap.

Selecting a WP Program

If you already have a WP package, you will have to learn how to achieve the results you desire by working around any of the program's shortcomings. If you will have the opportunity to select or recommend a word processor or WP program for a microcomputer, read the manuals for different programs closely before you make your decision. Select on the basis of which program will make it easiest for you to accomplish the kinds of things you desire to do.

Electronic Mail

What is electronic mail? What are its advantages and disadvantages?

The term **electronic mail** refers to the sending and receiving of written documents using electronic media. The most common electronic medium for electronic mail is a computer network consisting of two or more computers or word processors connected by wire (either special wires or telephone lines) or radio transmission. Local-area networks (LANs) are now common in large organizations, and they are increasingly common in small and medium-sized organizations as well. Computer networks allow one person to compose a message at one computer, and through a series of commands, send it to another person at another computer—in another office in the same building, across the country, or around the world.

Electronic mail is not only much faster than traditional postal systems but also more economical. It also puts greater pressure on business communicators to be concise. Business people using electronic mail have a tendency to neglect the human objectives present in many communication situations because of the emphasis on speed and succinctness. If you are working with electronic mail, review your complete message in the same way you would a typed or hard copy before you send it. The psychological impact of a negative message, for example, can be as devastating electronically as it is when written on paper. The electronic message deserves every bit as much care as a paper message.

What are uploading and downloading?

Electronic mail frequently uses memo format. Also, most systems automatically record the name of the sender and the time that the message was sent. Messages may be prepared in advance using word processing software and **uploaded** (transmitted or sent) into the electronic mail system; or they may be prepared on-line, using the text editing program built into the electronic mail system. Messages waiting in an individual's mailbox can also be **downloaded** onto a disk (captured or saved) for later review and printing.

What are problems that may need to be overcome for electronic mail to be effective?

Electronic mail systems do not offer all the text editing or printing functions that word processing programs typically offer. Most, for example, do not provide wordwrap, so they require a carriage return at the end of each line. Most also will not accept printing commands, such as underline and boldface, because those commands do not employ standard characters. Users may indicate added emphasis by using solid capital letters, an asterisk before and after a word, or an underline mark before and after a word:

We must do it SOON.

We must do it *soon*.

We must do it _soon_.

Formatting may also pose problems in electronic mail. Some programs, for example, will not accept a blank line, so creating the appearance of a standard paragraph may be difficult. Some programs will accept blank spaces (which are indicated by a standard character) as a "line," and others may accept a period as a line. In other systems, however, you may have to use solid single spacing and simply indent to indicate a new paragraph.

Only by using a specific system can you learn its commands, advantages, and disadvantages. Each system is at least a little different from all others, but all are fast and economical, and they are increasing in number at a phenomenal rate.

COLLABORATIVE WRITING

In many ways, writing is a private process; it is an act of converting one's thoughts to words and making them available for public view. Because few people write quickly, easily, and without false starts and hesitations, most of us prefer to do our writing in private and allow others to see only the finished product—after we have eliminated the weaknesses and obvious errors.

In modern organizations, however, many reports are written in groups. If an issue is complex, a committee will be assigned the task of investigating the problem and recommending solutions. Group writing is often called **collaborative writing** because a number of people need to work together to produce a document acceptable to all.

For short documents, a committee may elect to meet, discuss the required document, and record ideas while someone takes notes. The entire group may contribute to composing and revising the document until everyone is reasonably satisfied with the result. For longer documents, individual committee members may receive specific research and writing assignments. To be successful in most organizations, you will need to be prepared to contribute to both kinds of collaborative writing.

When the group as a whole participates in the writing process, the main problem likely to occur is too much criticism too soon. If every idea presented is rejected immediately, group members will quickly stop offering suggestions. The best technique for overcoming this obstacle is known as **brainstorming.** Although brainstorming is usually a group problem-solving activity, you can follow the same procedure when working alone to help overcome writer's block. Whether you are working alone or in a group, successful brainstorming sessions employ the following steps.

1. Have all members of the group agree to the procedure.
2. Suggest and record as many ideas as possible without criticizing, analyzing, or otherwise evaluating the ideas.
3. Make sure that ideas are generated to cover the fundamental questions of who, what, where, when, why, and how.
4. When group members have run out of ideas, combine related concepts, eliminate duplicate ideas, and arrange suggestions in a logical order.
5. Discuss the advantages, disadvantages, and implications of each suggestion.
6. Reach consensus on the final version of the document or on the best solution to whatever problem is being discussed.

When committee members decide that the best approach to producing a report is to assign each member specific responsibilities, two problems may result. First, some group members may not complete their assignments on time (or their portions may be so poorly prepared as to be unacceptable). Second, the writing styles of the various portions may be so different that a complete revision of the entire report is mandatory.

Side notes:

What is collaborative writing?

What is brainstorming?

How are different writing styles combined?

The first of these difficulties is, of course, a common managerial problem, and the solution to it depends more on the manager's ability to structure rewards and punishments than on writing strategy.

Two solutions are possible for the second difficulty. The first is simply to assign the best writer in the group the task of revising. The second is to undertake the revision process as a group. Each of these approaches has advantages and disadvantages. Having the best writer undertake the revision will probably result in a better report, but the final version may not retain the original intent of the group, even if the entire group has the opportunity to review and approve the report. Working on the revision as a group helps guarantee that the final version represents the thinking of the group as a whole, but it can be a slow and painful process. Also, group members may hesitate to criticize the work of others, and so poor writing may go unrevised.

Whatever approach is favored by the group to which you belong, you should be responsible for alerting the group to the advantages and disadvantages of the approach, and you should make certain to contribute your fair share. Nothing will contribute to—or detract from—your reputation in an organization so much or so quickly as your participation in important group activities.

SOLVING COMMON WRITING PROBLEMS

In addition to the tasks involved in the writing process itself, writers repeatedly solve problems related to specific elements of the report: definitions, descriptions, classifications, introductions, summaries, conclusions, recommendations, and abstracts. Virtually every report requires the writer to solve one or more of these problems.

Definitions

Because definitions provide the basis for many discussions, they are an essential component of most reports. As a report writer, you will need to be concerned not only about *what* to define but also about *how* to define it.

What are the two purposes of definitions?

Definitions have two purposes: (1) they can clarify what something is for a reader not familiar with the subject, or (2) they can explain the subject in a way that goes beyond the needs of clarity. Both clarifying definitions and extended definitions provide meaning for unfamiliar terms and new meaning for familiar terms.

What to Define   Deciding what to define can present problems. A non-technical audience will need definitions of technical terms but will be confused if the terms are defined with equally technical language. A technical audience, on the other hand, would be insulted if you defined common technical terms or sacrificed precision by expressing a technical concept in nontechnical language.

Determining what to define will require an understanding of your readers and their backgrounds and expectations. In general, however, you should define the following:

1. **Familiar words used in an unfamiliar way.** When a common word has a technical or special meaning, let the reader know how the word is being used. (The word "apron," for example, has a variety of specialized meanings depending on the field. It can be part of a lathe, part of a runway, part of a stage, or part of a dock—all in addition to the common meaning familiar to chefs and backyard barbecuers.)

2. **Technical terms for which there are no nontechnical equivalents.** (The word *modem* is an example. It stands for "modulator-demodulator" and refers to a device for converting a computer output signal into a form suitable for transmission over telephone lines and the telephone signal back into the proper form for a computer.)

3. **Words whose meanings you wish to restrict.** Occasionally, you will need to let your reader know how you intend for a word to be used because several interpretations are possible. If you were writing a report on office conflict, you would need to define *conflict* for your reader. *Conflict* can mean either a fruitful discussion of differences or a pitched battle.

How to Define   The basic rule for defining those terms that require it is to keep the definition brief. When possible, clarify the meaning of the word by using a synonym or phrase in apposition to the word you wish to define.

> Before the furnace can be repaired, all *clinker* (residue) must be removed.

> The *moratory contract* (term), *which delays payment* (definition) until January 2, was necessary to prevent default on outstanding obligations.

How do informal and formal definitions differ?

When a simple word or phrase is insufficient to define a term, you can clarify the meaning of the word in a sentence. Sentence definitions can be either informal or formal depending on context and the needs of the reader. Informal definitions are usually incomplete, providing only enough knowledge of the term for the reader to understand its use in the one context. Formal definitions designate the class to which the term belongs and then provide the features that make the term different from the other members of the class.

Informal: The new operation will require ultraviolet filters to prevent damage to the *retina.* The retina is the light-sensitive lining of the inner eye. Damage would result in blindness.

Formal:	**Term**	**Class**	**Features**
	Stress is	any influence on a person	that tends to be mentally disruptive and results in physical or emotional distress.

Whether your sentence definition is informal or formal, be careful to avoid using the term to define itself, and avoid using *where* and *when* in defining a term.

Incorrect: Stress is any stressful situation.

Incorrect: Stress is when you feel physical or emotional distress.

What are extended definitions?

When the meaning of a term is a major element of the report, you will need to provide an extended or amplified definition. In many ways, for example, this book is an extended definition of the term *report.* A report on insurance coverage might need an extended definition of bodily injury, or a report on management techniques might require an extended definition of quality circles. An extended definition might include some of the following information.

Etymology   The history of the word may help to provide an understanding of its current meaning. Even when the etymology does not clarify current meaning, it may provide a starting point for a detailed analysis.

Background   What factors have influenced the development and current use of the term? The background may be related to the etymology of the term, but background also includes discovery, development, and application of the term being defined.

The etymology of the word *computer,* for example, would discuss its origins in the Latin word, *computare,* to reckon together. The background of the word would discuss the invention and development of electronic computers.

Illustrations   Examples and illustrations, whether verbal or graphic, are one of the best methods for clarifying the meaning of a term. Abstract terms, such as *liberal, conservative, morale,* and *efficiency,* can be clarified only by providing examples. Certain technical terms, too, can be understood only if the reader can *see* what the items looks like. What is a camshaft? How does one work? If you needed to define a camshaft, you would need to provide an illustration similar to that in Exhibit 5.3.

Descriptions and analyses   When the item or concept consists of several parts, each part should be described and explained. What does the item do? How does it work? How does it relate to the other parts and to the whole? Descriptions of mechanisms and processes, classifications, and interpretations are all important enough to merit separate discussion.

Exhibit 5.3   **Illustration**

Comparison and Contrast   How is the item or concept being defined similar to or different from other items or concepts with which the reader would already be familiar? When possible, do both:

> A is similar to B in that . . .

> A, however, differs because . . .

Because comparison and contrast is a form of analogy, you will need to focus on significant similarities and differences to convey an accurate impression.

Connotations   When a word has a particular set of associations, you may need to clarify the meaning the word has within the context of the report. Patriotism, for example, can be the "last refuge for a scoundrel" or "courageous self-sacrifice in defense of one's country."

Where to Place Definitions   When you have only a few terms that require definitions and you can define them briefly and simply, it is best to include the definitions in the text immediately following the term. Definitions within the text, however, interfere with readability when they are either long or numerous. Unless you are presenting an

When should definitions be placed in the text?

extended definition central to your discussion, consider placing definitions in a special section in the introduction, in footnotes, or in a glossary.

Introduction   When the terms are critical to understanding your report, include a list of technical terms requiring definitions in the introduction. Readers already familiar with the terms can skim the list to see whether you have attached special meaning to a term.

Footnotes   When some of your readers will understand all the terms used but others will not, footnotes are the best solution. Readers who are familiar with the terms may ignore them; readers who are not familiar with them will not have to flip forward (to a glossary) or backward (to the introduction) to find the definitions.

Glossary   Placement in the glossary is the least obtrusive method of providing definitions. It is also the method most likely to be ignored. When most of your readers will understand the terminology in the report and none of the terms is critical to understanding the purpose of the report, a glossary can be a useful aid to readers unsure of some meanings. Tell the reader early in the introduction that the glossary is available.

Descriptions and Classifications

Descriptions play an important role in many reports. Many problems—and their solutions—in modern business center on mechanisms or processes with which readers will be unfamiliar. The main challenges in writing descriptions are in providing information appropriate to the readers' needs and in using language that presents an accurate picture of the mechanism or process.

What are five things to consider when describing a mechanism?

Describing Mechanisms   In describing a mechanism, you have five things to consider: (1) what it is, (2) what it does, (3) how it does it, (4) what it looks like, and (5) why your reader needs to know.

Stating what a mechanism is, is primarily a matter of defining it. To what class does the mechanism belong, and what features differentiate it from other mechanisms in its class? A report on restaurant management, for example, might require descriptions of microwave ovens and food processors. How is a microwave different from other ovens? In what ways is a food processor different from other kitchen equipment?

Readers will also need to know the purpose of the mechanism. Obviously, the purpose and the definition are closely related. Saying what a microwave oven *is* requires a statement about what one *does*. The purpose can often be clarified by including the reporter's "serving men": *who* uses the mechanism, *when* is it used, *where* it is used, and *why*.

Accuracy is critical. A microwave oven, for example, is not simply used to cook or heat food—it is used to cook or heat food *quickly,* which may be an important fact for restaurant management.

How does the mechanism work? When the mechanism is of critical importance to the report, you should provide a complete analysis of the mechanism, including a description of each of its parts. This is especially true when the mechanism is new, unusual, or complicated. Photographs, cutaway and exploded drawings (which reveal the relationships of the parts to each other and to the whole), and flowcharts (which show how the action of one part influences another) may be necessary to clarify the way the mechanism works.

The description should also include information about the size of the mechanism. What are its size, weight, shape, color, material of composition, and finish? What is the physical relationship of the parts to the whole (as opposed to the mechanical relationships)? How does the mechanism fit into the surrounding environment?

How do purpose and audience affect descriptions?

Finally, all of the previous aspects must be considered in terms of how much readers know about the mechanism already and the use to which they will put the information. Are readers going to build, use, or make a business decision about the mechanism? A reader who wanted to build a microwave oven would obviously need to know more about it than someone who was simply going to use one, and a reader who was making a decision about whether to install one in a restaurant would be less concerned with how microwaves work than with how they influence food preparation and delivery.

Describing Processes   A process involves action over time. You may need to describe the action of a mechanism or the actions of people engaged in a particular activity. How does a television set transform the signal it receives into pictures and sound? How does one use a food processor?

What must the writer know to describe a process?

Describing processes requires chronological and spatial organizational patterns (see Chapter 16). To be able to understand the process, the reader will need to know

1. The purpose of the process
2. The nature of any equipment involved
3. The steps in the process
4. Any hazards or special precautions

The typical automobile owner's manual contains several descriptions of processes. After describing the features of the car and identifying all the important parts of the mechanism, the owner's manual describes the steps involved in starting the car, in changing a tire, in finding the problem when the car will not start, and perhaps other processes as well.

Descriptions of this sort require extensive graphic aids. Flowcharts, pictures of the mechanism or of a person performing the activity, and pictures featuring close-up details of important steps can contribute to reader understanding.

Again, a critical consideration is what your readers will do with the information. Are your readers going to perform the process, or do they simply need a basic understanding of the process to be able to make a decision about it? Suppose, for example, you are writing a report recommending that your company invest in an exercise room and equipment so that employees can maintain physical fitness before and after work and on their lunch breaks. You would need to describe the equipment required and the general ways in which it is used, but you would not give complete descriptions of how to use each piece of equipment.

Classifying Mechanisms and Processes   Classification is a system of defining a whole in terms of its parts. The division of a whole into parts needs to be logical and consistent. Functions, materials, locations, benefits, and disadvantages are common bases for classification in reports.

Classification is a useful form of presentation when you have several items to discuss and when these items have significant similarities and differences. Small computers, for example, could be classified according to size (micro or mini, amount of internal memory) or use (personal or business). Within each category, different computers would have features in common and differences that could lead to a basis for selecting one brand or model for a specific application.

Introductions

What are three objectives of an introduction?

In most cases, the introduction of the report proper will follow an abstract of the complete report. Nevertheless, an introduction, as the formal beginning of the report, must accomplish at least three objectives. First, it must place the report in a communication context that makes sense to the reader. Second, it must create interest in the topic. And third, it must give readers a good idea of what to expect in the rest of the report.

Context   You will recall from our previous discussion of emphasis that the beginning of any unit is a place of emphasis. Readers will pay close attention to an introduction and form opinions about the entire report based on the material you present first. This is true regardless of the length and formality of the report. Even in a short report of one or two pages, the introduction needs to orient readers to the topic, be interesting, and provide a guide to the material that follows.

Longer reports require a fuller introduction. Certain topics are traditionally included in introductions to complete analytical reports. Most of them are intended to contribute to one of the three main objectives.

Origin and History of the Report   Where did the idea of the report originate? Who authorized it, and what problem did he or she think that the report could help solve? Because answers to these questions are probably already known to readers, they are usually presented in a letter of authorization, letter of transmittal, or both. Even though readers for whom the report is written are familiar with this information, it should be included because it may have historical significance.

When the problem developed over time, it may prove useful to include a discussion of the history of the problem so that similar problems can be recognized more quickly in the future. Unless the history or development of the problem is of special significance, subordinate this information to something of more interest to the readers.

Subject and Purpose   Even if the origin and history are covered in the letters of authorization and transmittal, the first two or three sentences of the introduction should include a statement of what the report is about (subject) and the benefit to be gained (purpose—or objective, goal, or aim). The first sentence should give the reader a reason for reading the entire report.

When should the purpose of the report be stated explicitly?

The most common phrasing for the purpose statement is, "The purpose of this report is . . .". This phrasing is acceptable and will accomplish its objective, and many companies prefer such wording because it forces a writer to state a specific purpose. Through overuse, however, it has become both a little hackneyed and self-conscious. When possible, avoid drawing such obvious attention to your beginning. Below are some possibilities.

Hackneyed and Self-Conscious: The purpose of this report is to recommend sending our sales staff to the 3-day motivational seminar sponsored by the University of Illinois.

Better: Our sales staff could benefit by attending the 3-day motivational seminar sponsored by the University of Illinois.

Better: The 3-day motivational seminar sponsored by the University of Illinois would offer our sales staff the opportunity to improve their understanding of the relationship between motivation and sales.

Better: Sending our sales staff to the 3-day motivational seminar sponsored by the University of Illinois would result in a 12 to 15 percent increase in sales over the next 6 months.

Each of the "better" purpose statements above implies the purpose while emphasizing the benefit. Even when the report does not offer a benefit, the purpose can be implied rather than stated explicitly.

Explicit: The purpose of this report is to explore the risks of asbestos poisoning in our Millview Plant.

Implicit: The risk of asbestos poisoning continues to be a problem in our Millview Plant.

Explicit: The objective of this study is to determine the advantages and disadvantages of subcontracting the thermoplastic skylights for our modular houses.

Implicit: Subcontracting the production of the thermoplastic skylights for our modular houses would save us approximately $4,500 a year but would cost us 14 jobs and reduce worker morale.

In each case, the opening emphasizing the *idea* of the purpose, rather than the purpose itself, is a stronger, more interesting opening.

Definition of the Problem   The introduction should include a clear statement of the problem, including its scope and limits. See Chapter 9.

Research Methodology   Readers will need to know how you went about gathering data. Include both secondary and primary sources. When many secondary sources are important enough to include, consider adding a section on the review of the literature. Being specific about research methodology is especially critical when you have used experimental methods to collect information. The reader will use your descriptions of the research methodology to evaluate your conclusions and recommendations. See Chapters 10 and 12.

Limitations   Not every experiment turns out as expected. Lack of funds, lack of time, difficulties with sample size, or unexpected and unavoidable conditions might all contribute to a report's being not so complete or objective as you would like. Negative factors that influence the reliability of the report belong in the introduction.

Are limitations an excuse for a poor report?

Limitations, however, should not be used as an excuse for a poor report. Be specific about how the lack of funds hampered your investigation or about what you would do if you had more time. Make sure that the limitations really are limitations and not attempts to cover up a lack of preparation on your part.

Definitions   When definitions are included in the introduction, they may be placed in paragraph form where they occur naturally. This is the least obtrusive way to define terms when only a few terms require definition. If your list of terms is long, it is best to set a section of the introduction aside for listing the terms in alphabetic order and providing their definitions.

What is the purpose of including a report plan?

Report Plan   The report plan is the road map that tells readers where the report will take them. Because it gives them an overview of what they will encounter, the report plan helps readers concentrate on the content rather than on what the writer is going to include next.

As is true with the purpose statement, the report plan can be stated either explicitly or implicitly.

Explicit: This report is divided into five main sections: Possible Benefits, Potential Difficulties, Costs, Savings, and Adjustments.

Implicit: The five factors of most significance are the possible benefits, the potential difficulties, costs, savings, and the necessary adjustments to the new system.

Telling readers what to expect in the rest of the report is a well-accepted formula. In fact, one of the clichés of effective communication is, "Tell 'em what you're going to tell 'em; tell 'em; and then tell 'em what you've told 'em." The trick is to stress the principal ideas or areas of concern by repeating them without giving your readers the idea that you do not trust their ability to remember the important points. As with the problem statement, the report plan is best stated implicitly because an explicit statement is too obvious in most cases.

Techniques   Not all reports will require each of these elements. The length and content of the introduction should be relative to the length and content of the report as a whole. The following techniques always apply:

1. Do *not* use *Introduction* as a heading. The reader already knows that the beginning is the beginning.
2. A short introduction (no more than two paragraphs) may follow the title without a separate heading.
3. Longer introductions should begin directly after the title with a general statement emphasizing the benefits or significant ideas in the report. Place the first heading after the general statement. This heading should be general enough to include the rest of the items covered in the introduction. See Chapter 16 for more information about headings.

What is the maximum length for an introduction?

4. The length of the introduction should not exceed 5 percent of the report as a whole.
5. Subordinate the obvious to the significant. Do not say, "I developed a questionnaire to discover . . .". Instead, say "The questionnaire I developed concentrated on three main factors . . ."

Summaries, Conclusions, and Recommendations

Ending a report or section of a long report presents particular problems. The ending section (or sections) needs to clarify the significance of the report and, when appropriate, tell readers who should do what next. Also, the end of the report should imply that the report is finished and complete. The three ways to accomplish these objectives are summaries, conclusions, and recommendations.

Is new information ever included in a summary?

Summaries   Informational reports, which present findings only, often end with a summary listing the important findings. A summary is simply a brief restatement of the main points already presented. A summary, therefore, should never present new information. In extremely long reports, it may prove useful to summarize each main section before proceeding to the next. For specific techniques see the section on Abstracts.

What are the two
most common flaws
in conclusions?

Conclusions   Like summaries, the conclusion section of a report never contains new material. The conclusion should be a logical and objective result of the material presented previously. In addition to the need for logic and objectivity in drawing conclusions, writers need to ensure that they present conclusions clearly and label them as such. The two most common errors in writing conclusions are the failure to state who is doing the concluding and the tendency to present conclusions as facts rather than as inferences based on fact.

Poor: Based on these findings, it is concluded that . . .

Better (informal):   Based on these findings, I conclude that . . .

Better (formal):   Based on these findings, the experimenter concludes that . . .

Poor: For our purposes, television advertising obviously provides the best exposure for the investment.

Better: For these reasons, I conclude that television represents the best investment for our advertising dollar.

Depending on the number and distinctness of the conclusions, you may wish to place them in a tabulated list, which may be either numbered or unnumbered. When you have only two or three conclusions, setting them off by tabulation (indentation) may seem pretentious. When you have several conclusions, however, your reader will remember them better if you set them off in a special way. A numbered list implies a hierarchy (in which 1 is the most important) or an order (chronological or spatial) not implied by an unnumbered list. Items in an unnumbered list may be set off with asterisks (*), bullets (•), or hyphens(--).

Recommendations   When recommendations are called for, they almost always appear as the last section in the report. As they depend on the conclusions, they often appear in a combined section that proceeds directly from the conclusions to the recommendations. When more than one solution to a problem is possible, the alternatives may be mentioned before the recommendations.

Conclusion: As a result of my study of staff and equipment needs, I conclude that we need an additional 4,500 square feet of plant space.

Alternative: Although we have the room to expand, the age of our current facility is such that the cost of maintenance may soon exceed the cost of new construction.

Recommendation: For this reason, I recommend that we begin the search for a suitable construction site and begin planning for a new facility.

How should
complex
recommendations
be treated?

Unless the recommendations are self-explanatory, provide some explanation for them so that they do not seem too arbitrary. Also, if you have several recommendations, you may wish to tabulate them.

Reports written in deductive structure will, of course, have at least a brief mention of the major conclusions and recommendations in the initial position. In most reports, this opening section is not as thorough as the final section. When the complete conclusions and recommendations are presented first, a summary of the most important points is sufficient for ending the report.

Abstracts and Executive Summaries

An abstract (also known as synopsis, epitome, or precis) or an executive summary is a condensed version of the entire report. It is written after the report is complete and follows the same basic outline in both order and proportion as the entire report. A critical part of the report, it may be the only part to which readers pay close attention.

Unlike report summaries—which remind readers of what they have just read—abstracts and executive summaries help readers determine whether reading the entire report will prove helpful. Abstracts may be distributed in printed or electronic form to a far wider audience than the one that sees the report. For this reason, they should be prepared carefully. Because the results, conclusions, and recommendations are the most important part of the report, they may be afforded relatively more space than they have in the report proper.

After reading a summary, a manager ought to know the following:

1. The nature of the problem or hypothesis of investigation
2. The methodology and results of the investigation
3. The advantages and disadvantages of alternative solutions
4. The writer's conclusions and recommendations

What is a summarizing introduction?

Abstracts   Informal reports of five pages or less rarely require more than a summarizing introduction for an abstract, stating the main conclusion and recommendation and providing a brief overview, or forecast, of the rest of the report. The summarizing introduction tells the reader where the report is going (the final destination) and the way in which it will get there (the route). Having the destination and route in mind helps prevent the reader from losing track of the important points in the report.

Reports of between 5 and about 15 pages may incorporate an abstract into the letter or memo of transmittal. The first paragraph of the transmittal would transmit the report and clarify the authorization for the report. The middle paragraphs would provide the actual summary, and the final paragraph would conclude the letter. See Exhibit 5.4 for an example of a memo of transmittal.

What are the differences between descriptive language and summarizing language?

Abstracts are usually more helpful to the reader when they use summarizing language rather than descriptive language. Summarizing language tells the reader what the report says, whereas descriptive (topical) language—as in a table of contents—tells only what the report is about. In general, avoid descriptive language for abstracts.

Descriptive language: This report is about desalinization of ocean water.

Summarizing language: Desalinization of ocean water will become practical within the next decade.

Exhibit 5.4   **A Memo of Transmittal**

The first paragraph
is the *transmittal*,
indicating the
sending of the
report to the reader
and the
authorization for
the report.

The middle
paragraphs provide
the abstract of the
report, with
emphasis on
conclusions and
recommendations.

Letters and memos
of transmittal
traditionally end on
a positive, forward-
looking note.

MERCY HOSPITAL
ONE SILVER LANE • HOUSTON • TEXAS • 77251

September 9, 19xx

TO: Arron Toplinger

FROM: Mary Leubecker *ml*

REPORT ON GENERAL LEDGER SOFTWARE

Here is the report you authorized on the three software packages
I investigated to replace our current general ledger system.

The software package with the system most capable of meeting
Mercy's needs is the McCormack & Dodge G/L PLUS. Its variety of
applications and the quality of its performance offers a sound
investment at a reasonable price. The G/L PLUS is a completely
advanced computer software system, as you will see in the report.

The other software systems included ADS G/L Software and Wheaton
Systems' Oracle. Both are capable of handling almost any
hospital and its area of need, but the G/L PLUS offers the most
for the money.

You gave me quite an opportunity to see the latest in computer
technology by approving my request to attend the computer con-
ferences. I had the privilege of hearing guest speakers Tom
Peters, author of In Search of Excellence, and Commodore Grace
Hopper, Pioneer of COBOL.

Perhaps we can have lunch together soon to discuss some of the
highlights of the conventions. I thoroughly enjoyed this research
and hope to have a similar opportunity soon.

Usually an abstract should be about one-tenth as long as the entire document, but no longer than one page. The abstract, however, may be single-spaced (with double spacing between paragraphs) even when the report proper is double-spaced. Because the abstract should emphasize the important points, rely primarily on the ideas presented in the topic sentences in the various sections to provide the ideas for the abstract. Remember that readers need to know primarily what they should *do* as a result of the information presented in the report. You need to provide only enough of the *why* so that the *what* makes sense. If a reader wants more supporting details, he or she will read the entire report. Remember that the abstract may be used for an oral presentation.

What are the differences between an abstract and an executive summary?

Executive Summaries   In recent years, the three-to-five page executive summary has become popular, especially for long reports. An executive summary should emphasize important conclusions and recommendations and include the most important supporting evidence. An executive should be able to make an informed decision after reading the executive summary.

Executive summaries are, in fact, short reports, and they employ all the basic report-writing techniques, including headings and graphic aids. The principal difference between an executive summary and the more traditional one-page abstract is in the amount of supporting detail provided. Executive summaries are useful when the conclusions and recommendations are ambiguous and based on complex data or when the reader has a special need to be familiar with the contents of a long report.

SUMMARY

After you have answered the preliminary questions about your readers and the purpose of your report and after you have conducted any required research, you are ready to begin composing the report. Writers often find it difficult to begin this process because of writer's block. Writing is a process calling for a variety of intellectual activities. Producing a report calls for gathering, evaluating, selecting, and organizing data; drawing appropriate conclusions; determining an appropriate structure and content for presentation; creating and arranging sentences and paragraphs; and evaluating and revising created materials. Revising allows you to improve a document by deleting, adding, changing, and rearranging.

Word processing equipment and electronic mail simplify the process of preparing and sending written communications. Word processors facilitate composing and editing. They also aid in the use of form and guide materials for letters and reports. Different programs offer different features, and each offers certain advantages. Electronic mail is faster and more economical than traditional postal services and may be the best way to distribute short reports.

Group writing is often called collaborative writing because a number of people need to work together to produce a document acceptable to all. When the entire group participates in the writing process, the main problem likely to occur is too much criticism too soon.

In addition to the tasks involved in the writing process itself, report writers repeatedly solve certain kinds of specific writing problems involving definitions, descriptions, classifications, introductions, summaries, conclusions, recommendations, and abstracts.

EXERCISES

Review and Discussion Questions

1. What tasks are involved in the process of writing?
2. What are three causes of writer's block?
3. How does revising allow you to improve a document?
4. How can a word processor simplify the process of preparing and sending written communications?
5. Name ten special features of word processing and text editing programs that facilitate the writing and revising process.
6. What is electronic mail?
7. What are uploading and downloading?
8. What is collaborative writing?
9. What are the six steps in successful brainstorming?
10. What is an abstract?

PROBLEMS AND APPLICATIONS

1. Provide word, phrase, sentence, and extended definitions for three technical terms in your area of specialization.
2. Provide word, phrase, sentence, and extended definitions for the following terms: *modem, emulsifier, bobbin, encomium,* and *kata.*
3. Classify and describe one the of the following: lawn mowers, sewing machines, bicycles, fishing rods and reels, food processors, small computers, synthetic fuels.
4. Describe the process of developing, building, or using the mechanism you described in Problem 3.
5. For any of the longer reports you may have been assigned, submit your abstract, introduction, and appropriate summaries, conclusions, and recommendations.
6. Write an executive summary for the report used in Problem 5.
7. In groups of three to five, work with others to write a five- to seven-

page report on word processing equipment. Assume that a friend who writes technical manuals on a freelance basis has asked you to investigate word processing equipment for her and to make a recommendation. She can afford to spend about $8,000. Each person in the group should edit and submit a final version of the report.

8. Condense the report in Problem 7 to three pages.

9. Expand the report in Problem 7 to ten pages.

10. Your boss has asked you to prepare an executive summary of this report writing text. He wants to know whether this book will help with the reports he has to write.

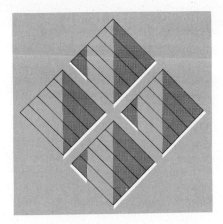

Report Conventions and Techniques

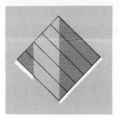

Classification of Reports

Just like people and companies, reports come in a variety of shapes and sizes. As a report writer, you will need to know how these shapes and sizes help a report achieve particular objectives. Each of the systems of classifying reports says something about how the report should be written, what it should contain, and how it will be used.

Topics

Classification by Function
Classification by Time Intervals
Classification by Length
Classification by Importance
Classification by Subject
Classification by Reader-Writer Relationship
Classification by Presentation

Why should writers
understand the
basic systems of
classification?

Because the myriad of businesses and organizations preparing reports have widely differing needs, no one system of classification has proved satisfactory for all. Report classifications vary from organization to organization depending on the purpose of the reports and the practices of the organization. Although the various systems of classification are not by any means standardized, being familiar with these systems will help you understand the purposes of and audiences for the common report types. In addition, familiarity with the basic systems of classification will help you understand how members of organizations think about, refer to, and file their reports.

The following are the generally accepted classifications:

1. Function
   a. Informational
   b. Interpretative
   c. Analytical

2. Time Intervals
   a. Periodic
   b. Progress
   c. Special

3. Length
   a. Short
   b. Long

4. Importance
   a. Routine
   b. Important
   c. Critical

5. Subject
   a. Accounting
   b. Engineering
   c. Financial
   d. Insurance
   e. Management
   f. Personnel
   g. Sales
   h. Tax
   i. And so forth (varies from organization to organization)

6. Reader-Writer Relationship
   a. Internal
   b. External

7. Presentation
   a. Written
   b. Oral

Wherever you work and whatever kind of reports you write, your reports will be more successful if you understand the reasons behind these systems of classification.

CLASSIFICATION BY FUNCTION

The basic classification of reports is by function—by what they do. Nearly every organization acknowledges and uses this system of classification. Reports can do three things. They can give information; they can give information and examine and interpret it; and they can give information, examine and interpret it, and draw conclusions and make recommendations. According to function, then, reports are informational, interpretive, or analytical.

Informational Reports

What are some common informational reports?

Informational reports simply provide the facts. They do not interpret or analyze the data, nor do they offer opinions, conclusions, or recommendations. Some common examples of informational reports are financial statements, sales reports, audit reports, and minutes of meetings. See Exhibit 6.1 for an illustration of an informational report.

Interpretive Reports

Interpretive reports (also called examination reports) not only provide the factual information, but also explain and interpret the information. They do not draw conclusions or make recommendations. Interpretive reports are usually written when the reader requests the interpretive information or when specialists in technical areas report to managers who are generalists. The addition of a single paragraph expands the informational report in Exhibit 6.1 into the interpretive report, Exhibit 6.2.

Analytical Reports

What are some typical analytical reports?

In addition to presenting information and interpreting it, analytical reports analyze the data, draw conclusions, and offer recommendations. Analytical reports may combine several informational reports so that conclusions and recommendations can be made for a solution to a complex problem.

All analytical reports begin as informational reports to which the writer adds interpretation and analysis. In theory *any* informational report could become an analytical report if the reader needed to have the writer interpret and analyze the data. In practice, only complex, nonroutine situations call for analytical reports. Typical examples would include attitudinal surveys, product surveys, and investigations of special problems. The author of the report in Exhibit 6.3 added expository data and personal recommendations to create an analytical report.

Exhibit 6.1   An Informational Report

heading[a]

"Here is/are"[b]

itemized list[c]

15 August 19xx

TO: Sonya Silverton, Sales Manager, District I

FROM: Martin Overloop, Sales Representative

SALES FOR WEEK ENDING 15 AUGUST

Here are the figures for last week's sales.

Calls	Sales	Amount
212	52	$18,792

The sales breakdown is as follows:

	Calls	Sales	Amount
Jewelry stores	15	18	$ 5,400
Clothing stores	14	15	5,022
Specialty shops	13	9	4,612
Record stores	70	4	1,400
Hardware stores	55	3	1,252
Miscellaneous small businesses	45	3	1,106
Total	212	52	$18,792

[a]The heading on a memo must contain the date, a "To" line, a "From" line, and a subject line. Note the use of the international form for the date.

[b]The words "Here is/are" are a usual beginning for letters and memos transmitting specific items of information (sales figures in this case) or enclosures.

[c]Use an itemized list (numbered or unnumbered) to increase the readability of a series of items, especially when the list includes numbers or monetary amounts.

Exhibit 6.2   An Interpretive Report

<table>
<tr><td>heading</td><td></td></tr>
</table>

heading

"Here is/are"

itemized list

interpretation[a]

---

15 August 19xx

TO: Sonya Silverton, Sales Manager, District I

FROM: Martin Overloop, Sales Representative ⁓⁓

SUBJECT: SALES FOR WEEK ENDING 15 AUGUST

Here are the figures for last week's sales.

Calls 212
Sales 52
Amount $18,792

The sales breakdown is as follows:

	Calls	Sales	Amount
Jewelry stores	15	18	$ 5,400
Clothing stores	14	15	5,022
Specialty shops	13	9	4,612
Record stores	70	4	1,400
Hardware stores	55	3	1,252
Miscellaneous small businesses	45	3	1,106
Total	212	52	$18,792

As the figures illustrate, jewelry stores, clothing stores, and
specialty shops account for 80 percent of the sales even though
they constitute only 20 percent of the calls.

---

[a]This paragraph *interprets* the important facts revealed by the preceding figures.

Exhibit 6.3   ## An Analytical Report

heading

"Here is/are"

itemized list

interpretation

conclusion[a]

recommendation[b]

15 August 19xx

TO: Sonya Silverton, Sales Manager, District I

FROM: Martin Overloop, Sales Representative ᴍᴼ

SALES FOR WEEK ENDING 15 AUGUST

Here are the figures for last week's sales.

	Calls	Sales	Amount
Jewelry stores	15	18	$ 5,400
Clothing stores	14	15	5,022
Specialty shops	13	9	4,612
Record stores	70	4	1,400
Hardware stores	55	3	1,252
Miscellaneous small businesses	45	3	1,106
Total	212	52	$18,792

As the figures illustrate, jewelry stores, clothing stores, and specialty shops account for 80 percent of the sales even though they constitute only 20 percent of the calls.

Increased need for security in jewelry, clothing, and specialty shops because of the increased value of gold and silver and increased shoplifting make our security systems necessary.

I recommend that in the future we concentrate sales calls on jewelry stores, clothing stores, and specialty shops. Sales personnel should call on other businesses only as time permits.

[a]*Conclusion* based on the preceding facts.

[b]*Recommendation* that naturally results from the preceding conclusion.

Exhibit 6.4   **A Periodic Report Form**

```
                        WEEKLY SALES REPORT


        Week of   _____

        Salesperson _____

        Store No. _____


        Day                Date                  Total Sales
        Monday         _____        _____

        Tuesday        _____        _____

        Wednesday      _____        _____

        Thursday       _____        _____

        Friday         _____        _____
```

CLASSIFICATION BY TIME INTERVALS

Another way to classify reports is by time intervals or by frequency of issue, schedule, or occurrence. Reports classified by time intervals are periodic, progress, and special.

Periodic Reports

What are examples of periodic reports?

Periodic reports are prepared regularly—daily, weekly, monthly, quarterly, or annually. Examples of periodic reports are the daily reports prepared by bank tellers, weekly reports prepared by sales representatives, monthly reports prepared by plant managers, quarterly reports prepared by auditors, and annual reports prepared by corporations for their stockholders.

Because of the availability of computers, many report writers use computers to help in preparing periodic reports. Also, many companies use standard forms for periodic reports so that all the report writer has to do is simply supply the missing facts and figures. Exhibit 6.4 illustrates a periodic report.

Progress Reports

Progress reports explain what has happened in the past on a project during a particular period of time and what can be expected in the future. Progress reports do not report on completed projects; they provide information about the status of the project. Because progress reports are submitted according to a predetermined time schedule—daily, weekly, monthly, or some other regular interval—they can be classified as time interval reports. Supervisors may request progress reports on continuing activities. For example, an academic department chairperson may request progress reports from faculty members who are working on special projects; a plant supervisor may request a progress report on the construction of a new plant; or a president of an organization may request progress reports from committee chairpersons.

What are the three divisions of a progress report?

Progress reports usually start with an initial report that gives the background of the project. Continuing reports state what has happened and what can be expected. Finally, the terminal report summarizes what has been accomplished. Progress reports generally have three divisions: (1) an introduction that gives the background or summarizes previous progress reports; (2) the heart of the report that details the progress for the particular time period of the report, possibly with tentative conclusions and recommendations; and (3) the summary, which may tell the reader what can be expected on the project or present the final conclusions and recommendations for the entire project. Exhibit 6.5 illustrates a progress report.

Special Reports

Exhibit 6.6 is an example of a special report. Special reports are generally prepared not on a regular but on a one-time basis. Special because they are not likely to be requested again, these reports are nonroutine. Most special reports help solve a specific problem or resolve a single incident. In some cases, a problem or event may require more than one special report. If an incident will require more than one report, the special report may be based on a series of progress reports that precede the concluding special report.

CLASSIFICATION BY LENGTH

Although reports are often classified by length, no precise criterion exists for what makes a long report long or a short report short.

Short Reports

How short can a short report be? How long?

Generally, reports ten pages or fewer are classified as short reports. Short reports can be very brief, even one or two words. Most business reports are short; they are usually informal and informational. They provide the requested information, such as the sales figures for the day, the total transactions for the week, or the traffic patterns for the month.

Exhibit 6.5   A Progress Report

November 2, 19xx

TO: Thomas R. Clarke, Chief of Police

FROM: Kimberly M. Dieterle *KmD*

PROGRESS REPORT--DATA MANAGEMENT STUDY

opening paragraph[a]

Here is a four-week progress report on the Data Management Study
I am conducting for the Louisville Police Department Records
Bureau. The information included in this progress report covers
the problem background, work accomplished, and work projection.

PROBLEM BACKGROUND

Each of the hundreds of thousands of reports that pass through
the Louisville Police Department (LPD) Records Bureau is handled
by many different people in various processing stages. A computerized system was installed two and one half years ago and is
working well. The changeover, however, has caused disorder, and
reports are being misplaced and lost. The clerks in the Records
Bureau are swamped with work because of this problem. Because
of the legal problems that could arise from the current situation,
the LPD would like to streamline the paper flow system within the
Records Bureau.

WORK ACCOMPLISHED

On September 29, 19xx, I met with Lt. Steven Harmon, who gave me
a tour of the Police Department and introduced me to Jill Nevens,
Supervisor Records Bureau. Lt. Harmon also supplied me with
blank copies of the various report forms and his Records Manual
on how to complete those forms. On October 11, 19xx, I talked
with Mrs. Nevens about what activities were performed in the
Records Bureau and read over a few completed reports. The next
day, October 12, I met again with Lt. Harmon to discuss my conversation with Mrs. Nevens. After speaking with Lt. Harmon, I
went to City Hall and briefly spoke with Mrs. Jeanne Hayden,
Human Resources Administrator. Mrs. Hayden has just completed
a similar study and was able to give me a copy of her report.

I have also designed a 17-item questionnaire that was tested
before distribution by Ms. Beth Evink, a Criminal Justice
major at Walsh College and a volunteer assistant to the Prose-
cuting Attorney for the City of Louisville. I distributed 15
questionnaires on October 22, 19xx. Ten questionnaires were
sent to the clerks in the Records Bureau, three to the secretaries in the Detective Bureau, and two to the secretaries in

---

[a]The opening paragraph tells the reader what the report is about and introduces the topics that will
be covered.

(*continued*)

Exhibit 6.5   *(continued)*

directives[b]

Thomas R. Clarke, Chief of Police   November 2, 19xx   2

the Police Patrol Division. Those 15 people are the only personnel directly connected with the paper-flow system. Twelve of
those questionnaires have been returned and are in the process
of being tallied. The remaining three questionnaires from the
Records Bureau are due next week.

WORK PROJECTION

In the next week, I expect to receive the three outstanding questionnaires from the LPD Records Bureau. A total tally will then
be completed. I also plan to further review Mrs. Hayden's report
and to set up an interview with her to discuss her findings.
Interviews will also be arranged with Mrs. Nevens, Supervisor
Records Bureau, and Lt. Harmon. Upon the completion of these
interviews, I will analyze the data gathered and make my recommendations. You should have the final report on December 2,
19xx.

[b]Progress reports (and many other reports as well) should end by telling the reader who is
responsible for taking what action next. When a specific date is appropriate, state it.

Source: Courtesy of Kimberly M. Dieterle.

Exhibit 6.6   A Special Report

typical
governmental
report[a]

City of Kalamazoo
Inter-Office
MEMO

To Honorable Mayor and City Commission   Date 12-2-xx

From Robert C. Bobb, City Manager *RCB*

Regarding Major and Local Street Improvements

Improvements in the City's infrastructure are critical to the
long-term well-being of this community. This memorandum outlines
my 19xx budget recommendation for the proposed major and local
street improvements.

Project Description

The proposed project provides for the reconstruction or resurfacing of approximately 10.86 miles of streets. The streets
include the worst major and local streets within the City as
determined by a survey of all streets performed by the Public
Works staff in 19xx. Some of these streets have virtually no
pavement structure other than a gravel surface or a badly
deteriorated sealcoat surface. For these we are recommending
a minimum 2" thick asphalt strip surface.

Other streets have no curb and gutter; their current pavement is
so deteriorated that an immediate repair and resurfacing is
warranted. Some streets have curbs and gutters which are still
relatively good, but the pavement itself requires resurfacing.
The fourth category within this proposal includes streets needing
the entire pavement, curb, and gutter replaced.

Street Ratings

During late 19xx and early 19xx, the Public Works staff rated all
the streets within the City. The system used is one developed by
the Michigan Department of Transportation (MDOT) for the state-
wide needs study. The two items used in our determination of
"worst streets" are surface condition and, where applicable,
curb condition. The proposed project includes those streets
with a surface rating of 5 or 4 or a curb rating of 3.

Surface condition is rated as follows:

    1--Excellent--No visible deterioration

    2--Good   --Some surface deterioration but less than 5%
                  of the road length being rated. Average
                  maintenance required.

[a]This is a typical governmental report. In this case, a city manager is submitting a recommendation
for a method of financing street repairs. Inductive order (see Chapter 2) is used because the city
commission might react negatively to the recommendation for a bond issue of more than $1 million.
The details in the central portion of the report have been omitted to save space.

(*continued*)

Exhibit 6.6   *(continued)*

Honorable Mayor and City Commission
December 2, 19xx
Page 2

3--Fair   --Surface deterioration on up to 25% of length
              being rated. May require above-average
              maintenance but considered reasonable when
              weighed against cost of total resurfacing.

4--Poor   --Deterioration on over 25% of surface. Requires
              excessive maintenance and warrants resurfacing
              soon.

5--Very Poor--Excessive deterioration beyond maintenance or
              no improvement exists. Warrants immediate
              resurface or reconstruction.

Curb condition is rated as follows:

1--Good--Curb is structurally sound and height is adequate
         for more than one resurfacing.

2--Fair--Curb could be spot repaired on less than 50% and
         adequate height exists for one resurfacing.

3--Poor--Structural condition is poor and warrants total
         replacement and inadequate height exists for
         resurfacing.

Kalamazoo Streets

The City of Kalamazoo contains approximately 250 miles of public
streets for which we are totally responsible for maintenance.
Of this total, 82 miles are classified as major streets and the
remaining 168 miles as local streets. In addition, the City
maintains approximately 12 miles of State trunkline under contract with MDOT.

A major street generally refers to a street carrying relatively
high traffic volumes and serving one of the following criteria:

1. Streets that provide extensions to State trunklines or
    County primary roads in facilitating through traffic.

2. Streets that provide an integral network to serve the
    traffic definitely created by industrial, commercial,
    educational, or other traffic-generating centers.

3. Streets that provide for the circulation of traffic in
    and around the central business district.

Exhibit 6.6   *(continued)*

Honorable Mayor and City Commission
December 2, 19xx
Page 3

4. Streets designated as truck routes.

5. Streets that collect traffic from an area served by an
   extensive network of local streets.

The City Engineer designates major and local streets subject to
and requiring certification by MDOT. The number of miles of
major and local streets, as well as population, is used by the
State in calculating the Michigan Transportation Funds (MTF)
revenues allocated to the City annually. The City's MTF revenues
have steadily decreased since 19xx when we received $2,091,495 as
compared to $1,764,254 in 19xx.

The life expectancy of a permanently paved street on an average
is 20 years, at which point the surface should receive some form
of preventative maintenance or resurfacing to preserve its integ-
rity. Streets that have never received permanent paving require
constant repair activity and eventually end up costing more than
it would have cost to pave the street permanently in the first
place. If a permanently paved street does not receive some form
of maintenance at the end of its 20-year life, it deteriorates
at an increased rate. It may then require total reconstruction
at a much higher cost than a mere resurfacing. If this philosophy is followed for the total system of 250 miles, we should be
resurfacing or providing a specific level of maintenance of a
minimum of 12 1/2 miles a year to protect the investment within
our infrastructure.

Local Streets Recommendations

I respectfully recommend that the City Commission finance the
local street improvements totalling $1,000,000 by issuing
$500,000 in MTF bonds and $500,000 in special assessment bonds.
Your conceptual approval of this approach is requested at this
time. Final approval would come with the approval of the appropriate resolutions.

That process is as follows:

a. Approval of a resolution authorizing the City Clerk to
   publish a notice of intent to specially assess 50% of these
   projects. This action triggers the 45-day referendum period.

b. During the 45-day referendum period three standard resolutions for the special assessment rolls would be considered by
   the City Commission along with the required public hearings.

(continued)

Exhibit 6.6   *(continued)*

Honorable Mayor and City Commission
December 2, 19xx
Page 6

c. If the assessment rolls are confirmed, and if there is not
   a referendum, the City Commission then considers the bond
   sale resolution. When that is approved, the bond sale
   process begins.

In terms of the special assessment impact on the average property
owner assuming a $500,000 special assessment bond issue or half
of the total project cost, property owners would be assessed an
average $8.50 per front foot. This is based upon a range of
$4.46 a front foot for the two-inch strip surface to $10.40 a
front foot for total reconstruction. For a property with front-
age of 60 feet, the cost for the improvement at $8.50 a front
foot would be $510 for over 15 years at 10%.

Regarding the MTF bond issue, the same process as the one
followed earlier this year applies. First, plans and specifications are submitted to MDOT and the Form 2020 is filed with the
State. Following MDOT approval, two resolutions are presented
to the City Commission, a bond resolution and a notice of sale
resolution. Following approval of these, the bond issue package
is presented to the Michigan Finance Commission.

In conclusion, I would like to stress that we are requesting
conceptual approval of the local street projects under the
recommended funding approach of $500,000 in MTF bonds and
$500,000 in special assessment bonds.

Furthermore, I recommend approval of the MTF bond issue for
major streets totalling $1,252,000.

I look forward to discussing these projects with you.

reference initial   r

copy notation   c   Sheryl L. Sculley
                          William Nelson
                          Robert Willard
                          Don Schmidt
                          LuAnn Stampfler

Source: Courtesy of Robert C. Bobb, City Manager, Kalamazoo, MI, November 1976 through January 1984.

Long Reports

Long reports generally exceed ten pages. Some can be very lengthy. Many businesses must prepare reports several volumes long to comply with governmental regulations, for example. Long reports are for the most part formal and analytical. They provide the reader with a complete analysis of the problem that may include many tables and figures. Exhibit 6.6 is an example of a long report (though we did not present the report in its entirety).

CLASSIFICATION BY IMPORTANCE

Reports can be routine, important, or critical. The content of the reports classified by importance is determined by how the content affects readers.

Routine Reports

Routine reports are those written on a regular basis to provide information that may become useful but is not of immediate importance. Because they are routine, these reports can be submitted on a prepared form. For example, supervisors who report the readings of various pieces of equipment in a plant may provide the information on a prepared form. Exhibit 6.7 illustrates a routine report.

Important Reports

How soon are important reports acted upon?

Important reports are those that need to be considered or acted upon within a short time. Circumstances will vary from organization to organization, but important reports often call for action within one to ten days. Exhibit 6.8 illustrates an important report.

Critical Reports

How soon do critical reports require action?

Critical reports are those that need to be acted upon immediately, generally within 24 to 48 hours. Again, these numbers are arbitrary. Exhibit 6.9 illustrates a critical report.

CLASSIFICATION BY SUBJECT

One of the most common methods for classifying reports is by subject matter—accounting, engineering, financial, insurance, management, personnel, sales, tax, and so forth. Each of these major divisions can be further subdivided. For example, audit, cost, inventory, and tax reports would be subdivisions under accounting. Exhibit 6.10 illustrates an accounting report.

Exhibit 6.7   A Routine Report

March 13, 19xx

TO: Staff

FROM: Roger Ballace, Principal

UPDATE REPORT ON HOME/SCHOOL COMPONENT

opening[a]

Consultations and Counseling

As of this date, March 12, 19xx, the Home/School Component has received 20 requests for service. Fourteen of the requests were from school staff and the other 6 were directly from parents. Six of these cases are in the evaluation state, 7 are in the implementation stage, 3 are in maintenance, and 4 are terminated. In 8 of these 20 cases, all performance objectives established have been met. Work is in progress on the other active cases.

Since February 15, ten parents have indicated a need for referral of information about community programs. All of the referrals have been made. Eight of the referrals have been followed up to ensure that the parents had called the community program office. Two referrals are in process.

Communication Systems

The daily note system has been implemented and is being used in all classrooms in the Program. Surveys have been conducted to determine the acceptance of the daily note system, and the results are favorable. In November, a questionnaire was sent to participating parents. The overall rating of home/school communication by all parents responding (on a five-point scale, 5 being excellent) was 3.2.

Another system has been developed to increase home/school communication. That is the use of report cards. Parents and school staff were interviewed for suggestions. It was determined that the report cards would best fit into the system as a means of providing parents with feedback following the regular reviews of their children's current educational program.

[a]Because the subject line is considered a title or a heading, most memos include a general introductory paragraph before introducing the first subdivision of the subject.

Exhibit 6.8   An Important Report

```
                    BIRMINGHAM VALLEY INTERMEDIATE SCHOOL DISTRICT
                               Bradley Avenue School


        December 15, 19xx

        TO:        Bradley School Staff

        FROM:      Brenda Owens, Principal

        SNOW DAY PROCEDURES

        The Birmingham Valley Intermediate School District's programs
        for students are open and in session whenever one or all of our
        constituent districts are open and transporting students to our
        program.

        When all nine of our constituent districts are closed, our
        programs at Bradley Avenue School, Youth Opportunities Unlimited,
        and Valley Center will also be closed to students.  Depending on
        the time that the closings occur, this announcement may or may
        not be heard on WBIR radio.

        In all cases, all BVISD full-time staff are expected to report,
        and programs at the Juvenile Home will be in session.  When
        weather conditions are severe, the Intermediate office will be
        closed, and the announcement will be made on WBIR radio that
        "no staff member needs to report."
```

Exhibit 6.9   A Critical Report

```
          April 14, 19xx



          TO:      Mike Lowery, Control Lab
          FROM:    Phil Bowden, Plant Superintendent  PB
          SUBJECT: GOLD PAINT #5764


          Gold paint #5764 is showing signs of degeneration at temperatures
          below 0°C.  I request immediate chemical analysis.
```

telegraphic style[a]

[a]Note the "telegram" sense of urgency conveyed by this brief request.

CLASSIFICATION BY READER-WRITER RELATIONSHIP

Still another means of classifying reports is by reader-writer relationship. Although they might be called by other names, reports may be classified as either internal or external depending on whether reader and writer work at the same company.

Internal Reports

Internal reports are those written for a reader by an individual in the same organization. They move vertically—generally up the chain of command from subordinate to supervisor—and horizontally between equals. Most internal reports use memo format. Exhibit 6.11 illustrates an internal report.

External Reports

When are external reports needed?

Reports submitted to an organization by an outsider are external. When management has a problem that cannot be solved internally—or when an organization does not have the expertise, equipment, or facilities to provide the required information—it seeks outside assistance. A professional consulting firm, for example, may be hired to do an extensive survey of corporate-wide records management systems. External reports are usually more formal than internal reports. When they are short, external reports often use letter format. Longer external reports usually receive formal treatment. Exhibit 6.12 illustrates an external letter report. For an example of an external formal report, see Chapter 17.

Exhibit 6.10   An Accounting Report

Foxley Accountants
500 Scott Street
Baltimore, MD 21204

February 2, 19xx

Board of Directors and Shareholders
Bixley Corporation
411 Petersen Drive
Omaha, NE 68144

Ladies and Gentlemen:

**short-form
auditor's report[a]**

We have examined the balance sheets of Bixley Corporation as of
December 31, 19xx, and December 31, 19xx, and the related statements of income and retained earnings and changes in financial
position for the years then ended. Our examinations were made
in accordance with generally accepted auditing standards and,
accordingly, included such tests of the accounting records and
such other auditing procedures as we considered necessary in the
circumstances.

In our opinion, the financial statements referred to above
present fairly the financial position of Bixley Corporation at
December 31, 19xx, and December 31, 19xx, and the results of
its operations and the changes in its financial position for
the years then ended, in conformity with generally accepted
accounting principles applied on a consistent basis.

Sincerely,

FOXLEY ACCOUNTANTS

signature block[b]

Bruce Pickard

Bruce Pickard, Accountant

[a]The language of this short-form auditor's report has evolved over time and is clear to most people who rely on the report for financial information.

[b]The use of the company name makes this a "legal" signature block, which indicates that the company, not the writer, has the legal responsibility for the contents of the letter. Most companies now prefer to assume that responsibility in other ways because the company name makes the letter appear too formal.

Exhibit 6.11   An Internal Report

March 1, 19xx

TO: William Bohn, Director of Sales

FROM: Diane Chapman, Manager, Hartford Sales District *DC*

MONTHLY REPORT FOR HARTFORD SALES DISTRICT

<u>Summary</u>

The sales figures for February increased 15 percent. Two additional sales representatives were hired to help with sales.
Sales for next month look promising.

<u>Office Staff</u>

Elizabeth Denomme, the office secretary, submitted her resigna-
tion effective March 15. Ms. Denomme is moving to St. Louis
because of her husband's recent promotion. Susan Oldford,
Ms. Denomme's assistant, will be the new office secretary.
We'll be hiring an assistant for Ms. Oldford within the next
month.

Exhibit 6.12   An External Letter Report

Connecticut State

Department of Highways and Transportation
Hartford, CT 06101

July 1, 19xx

Mr. Craig Ackerson
City Road Commissioner
City Hall
Bridgeport, CT 06611

Dear Mr. Ackerson:

transmittal function[a]

As you requested in your letter of May 10, we conducted a study on the technical, environmental, and economic aspects of highway deicing salts. Here is our report.

informational purpose[b]

Summary

Since the early 1960s, deicing salts have been extensively used as a method of snow and ice removal. In recent years many adverse environmental and economic impacts have been found to result from the use of deicing salts. The impacts include damage to roadside vegetation; contamination of surface water and groundwater supplies; disruption of aquatic ecosystems; and the corrosion of automobiles, highway structures, and the underground utilities. It has been estimated that the cost and application of deicing salts and the resulting damage amounts to close to $3 billion annually.

Technical, Environmental, and Economic Aspects

Each year snow and ice storms in the snow belt states disrupt daily activities and create emergency conditions in both rural and urban areas. Public officials are forced to determine how much of their resources should be devoted to highway snow and ice removal and what techniques should be used.

Deicing Salts

Deicing salts began to be used extensively for highway snow and ice removal in the early 1960s. Sodium chloride (NaCl) and calcium chloride (CaCl) are the most widely used salts. When applied to snow and ice, NaCl and CaCl bore and penetrate the snow and ice surface, lower the freezing point of water, allowing the resulting brine solution to spread out over the highway, and weaken the bond between the ice and the road.

[a]The first paragraph "transmits" the information contained in the rest of the letter. It performs essentially the same function as does the letter of transmittal in a long formal report.

[b]This is an informational report only. It does not provide interpretation, conclusions, or recommendations.

(continued)

Exhibit 6.12 (*continued*)

Mr. Craig Ackerson
July 1, 19xx
Page 2

Environmental Impacts

The environmental impacts of highway deicing salts include
destruction of roadside soils and vegetation, contamination of
surface and groundwater supplies, and the disruption of aquatic
ecosystems.

Economic Impacts

Adverse economic impacts of highway deicing salts include the
cost co improve or replace contaminated water supplies, damaged
vegetation, corroded automobiles and highway structures, and
damaged underground utilities.

Sincerely,

Scott Olson

Scott Olson
Information Clearinghouse

r

CLASSIFICATION BY PRESENTATION

Reports may be presented in either written or oral form, or the reports may require both kinds of presentation.

Written Reports

Written reports generally require more careful preparation than oral reports. Because written reports are permanent records, report writers and readers tend to pay closer attention to them. Written reports tend to be more formal than oral reports. It is especially important that written reports be accurate, clear, complete, impartial, and objective. They should be written for a particular audience and serve a definite purpose.

Oral Reports

When are reports presented orally?

Most oral reports in business are impromptu and require little or no specific preparation. Others, however, are more formal and require every bit as much preparation as a written report. In fact, many situations in business call for an oral report supplemented by written information or for a written report supplemented by an oral presentation. You might, for example, be asked to present your written report orally to your colleagues, to higher management, to the board of trustees, to the community, or to a professional association. In some ways, presenting the information orally is easier than presenting it in written form because you need not be concerned with spelling, punctuation, and the mechanics of writing. On the other hand, the oral presentation requires careful attention to body language—facial expressions, body posture, hand movements, eye movements, and breathing. Oral presentations will be discussed further in Chapter 18.

SUMMARY

Every business and organization prepares a report of one kind or another. These reports will vary from organization to organization depending on the purpose of the report and the practices of the organization. Reports can be classified according to function, time intervals, length, importance, subject, reader-writer relationship, and presentation. The basic classification of reports is by function. As such, reports are informational, interpretative, or analytical. Reports classified by time intervals are periodic, progress, and special. Periodic reports are prepared regularly—daily, weekly, monthly, quarterly, or annually. Progress reports explain what has happened in the past on a project during a particular period of time and what can be expected in the future. Special reports are generally prepared on a one-time only basis. Reports can also be classified by length—long or short. Generally, reports ten pages or fewer are short.

When classified by importance, reports can be routine, important, or critical. Routine reports are those written on a regular basis to provide information that may become useful but is not of immediate importance. Important reports are those that need to be considered or acted upon within a short time. Critical reports are those that need to be acted upon immediately, generally within 24 to 48 hours.

Another common method for classifying reports is through major divisions and subdivisions of subject matter. Still another means of classifying reports is by reader-writer relationship—either internal or external. Finally, reports may be presented in written or oral form, or the reports may require both written and oral presentations.

EXERCISES

Review and Discussion Questions

1. Why do report classifications vary from one operation to another?
2. Explain the differences among the reports classified according to function.
3. Which reports are classified by time intervals?
4. What is a progress report?
5. What are special reports?
6. Explain the differences between internal reports and external reports.
7. What is the difference between short reports and long reports?
8. What kinds of reports are classified by importance?
9. State the reason(s) each of the reports included as exhibits in this chapter has been classified in a particular way.
10. Why is it helpful to be familiar with the various systems of classification?

Problems and Applications

1. Visit three local businesses and request sample reports. In a memo to your instructor, classify the reports on the basis of each of the classifications presented in this chapter.
2. Prepare a daily report for one week on how you spent your time (school, work, study, recreation). Make recommendations to yourself.
3. Write a progress report on your assignments in a particular class.

4. What kinds of reports are most appropriate for a person working in your career area? Using the professional journals for your career area, skim a number of issues for references to specific reports. Categorize these reports according to their classifications.

5. What would you consider an ideal system of classifying reports? Why? Prepare your recommendation for an ideal system in memo format.

C H A P T E R   7

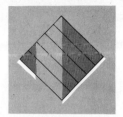

Report Forms and Appearance

Just as you wear different clothes depending on the activity you are engaged in and whom you are with, reports have different forms depending on the job they must perform and the relationship between the reader and writer. This chapter covers the physical appearance of reports. Subsequent chapters will provide information about how these forms are applied in specific instances.

Topics

Communication Conventions
Letters and Letter Reports
Informal Reports
Formal Reports
Parts of the Formal Report
Pagination

Most business reports are requested by the receiver. For that reason, they are designed to meet the needs of the reader. Some of these needs have been created by communication conventions (those things readers have come to expect over the years), some by the demands of the specific situation, and some by the special techniques developed to make reports more readable. The purpose of each of these needs is to help readers make the best decision in the shortest time possible.

COMMUNICATION CONVENTIONS

Routine patterns or conventions help people understand the actions of others. Communication is no exception. The handshake of Western culture, the bow of Oriental culture, and the "hello" of American telephone usage are all examples of communication conventions. Business letters and reports, although more complex, are also conventions.

Letters and reports, for example, are the expected communication in certain situations. Further, when readers receive letters and reports, they expect the writer to have followed some fairly specific rules in writing and presenting the information. Some of these conventions are arbitrary. They have developed over time, and readers expect writers to follow them. Standard spelling and grammar are such conventions. Your readers will expect your letters and reports to be written in standard English. The appearance of letters and reports is also governed by convention. Readers expect letters and reports to look a certain way.

Special Techniques

Other conventions include such special techniques as headings to indicate the major divisions and subdivisions of the report, itemized lists to clarify important points, and graphic aids to help illustrate and explain quantitative information. Headings and lists are covered in Chapter 16, and graphic aids are discussed in Chapter 15.

Formality

What is the most common type of report in business? What factors determine the formality of a report?

Reports may be prepared for audiences either within or outside the writer's organization. As a rule, reports remaining in the organization are less formal than those prepared for outside agencies. The informal memo report, for example, is the single most common report in business today. The least formal report prepared for an outside agency is the letter report.

Internal reports tend to increase in formality as they increase in length and importance, ranging from the casual memo to the bound volume. A short report going up only one or two levels in the organizational hierarchy would probably be written as a memo. A report of more than ten pages designed for a reader several managerial levels above the writer would be prepared as a formal report.

Moreover, the length and formality of reports generally increase as the information becomes more complex. Because the main function of a report is to help the reader make a decision, reports containing complex statistical or technological information require extra attention to organization and clarity of presentation.

LETTERS AND LETTER REPORTS

Why should report writers be familiar with letter formats?

Letters are the most common form of written communication between an organization and outside agencies and individuals. Letters are also used in formal situations between members of the same organization. Most business letters are not reports in the strict sense of the word, but many of them convey the same kind of information found in reports. For these reasons, report writers need to be aware of the common letter formats. Exhibits 7.1, 7.2, and 7.3 illustrate the most widely accepted letter formats and contain explanations of the parts of letters.

How do letter reports differ from other letters?

The letter report is an external means of conveying information between organizations. Letter reports generally are more carefully organized and longer than typical business letters; they are formal, factual, and use basic report-writing techniques, such as headings, itemizations, tables, and figures. The primary objective of letter reports is to provide reliable, objective information. Common letter reports are used for personnel references, letters of recommendation, credit evaluations, and auditor recommendations.

Although letter reports are generally longer (three or four pages) than regular letters, they use the same basic formats. Exhibit 7.4 illustrates a typical letter report.

INFORMAL REPORTS

Informal reports generally convey routine information and do not contain the prefatory parts (letter of acceptance, letter of transmittal, table of contents, abstract) or supplemental parts (bibliography, appendix, and index) found in formal reports. Because these prefatory and supplemental parts are not used and the information is routine, the writing style is also informal. Informal reports can be presented in memorandum or letter form.

Memorandum Reports

A memorandum report is used to convey routine information from one employee to another in the same organization. Because businesses and industries use memorandums for messages to workers within their orga-

Exhibit 7.1   **Modified Block, Mixed Punctuation**

letterhead

CALVIN FRAME COMPANY
1492 Columbus Avenue
Cleveland, OH 44109

date

February 23, 19xx

inside address

Mr. Michael G. Rooney, President
Rooney Overhead Door Company
1066 Hastings Drive
Akron, OH 44302

salutation (colon)

Dear Mr. Rooney:

body

Your new business should prove a tremendous success, Mr. Rooney, and
the 24' frame and shelf sets you ordered will help you store and organize
your inventory.

You will receive your order Tuesday or Wednesday of next week. I shipped
the complete order by Red Ball Express this morning. The driver will call
you before delivery.

The enclosed invoice shows your down payment of $600, the balance of $632,
and shipping charges of $127.50. You have 90 days from the date of delivery
to pay the $759.50.

Assembly instructions are packed with the frames and shelves, Mr. Rooney.
I enclosed an extra package of nuts, lock washers, and bolts to make sure
that you'll have everything you'll need to assemble the units. While it is
possible for one person to complete assembly without assistance, you'll find
that the work will be faster and easier if you have at least one person help.

Please call me if you have questions about assembly.

signature block

complimentary
close (comma)

Sincerely,

John Calvin

typed name
title

John Calvin
President

reference initial

s

enclosure notation

enc

Exhibit 7.2   **Block Format, Mixed Punctuation**

letterhead

A-1 Forms

19 Century Avenue
Victoria, MO 63123

date

January 23, 19xx

inside address

Mrs. Joyce James
Assistant to the President
Issuant Computers Inc.
Siliconville, CA 94040

salutation (no
punctuation)

Dear Mrs. James

body

Here are the sample sales contract and personnel evaluation forms you
requested. As you can see, each was designed to meet the specific needs
of a particular company.

The sales contract forms we designed for CALC Company, for example,
contain more options and a more complex service agreement than you will
require. Their general appearance, however, would be suitable for Issuant
Computers. The other contract forms may give you additional ideas.

The kind of personnel evaluation form you need depends on a variety of
factors, including how often each employee is to be evaluated, the purpose
of the evaluation, and how long the form itself is to be kept. As you
suggested in your letter, you'll probably wish to have a form that lends
itself to computer entry and storage of data.

The enclosed brochure describes the general requirements of forms design
and the papers and quantities available. Use the graph paper provided to
sketch the forms, and use the key on p. 17 of the brochure to indicate
typefaces and size.

As soon as I receive your sketch, I'll prepare samples and have one of our
technicians test them for readability and ease of use. Call me collect if you
have questions.

Sincerely

signature block

Samuel Perelman

complimentary
close (no comma)

Samuel Perelman, Chief
Forms Design

name, title
department

t

reference initial[a]

enc

enclosure initial

c Joseph Sidney
      Forms Technician

copy notation[b]

[a]Use the initial of the typist's last name. First and last initials are required only when more than one
typist in an office has the same last initial. One change that has taken place in recent years is the
elimination of the dictator's initials. Because the dictator's name is already typed in full in the
signature line, it is not necessary to repeat the initials.

[b]Older letter forms used "CC" for "carbon copy," but now that most copies are made
photomechanically, only the "c" (lowercase, no colon) is required to show that a copy of the letter
is being sent to someone else.

Exhibit 7.3   Simplified Letter Form

personal return
address
date

inside address

subject line

body[a]

> 735 Bede Drive
> Fairview, CO 80229
> February 23, 19xx
>
>
> Mr. Joseph Sidney
> Forms Technician
> A-1 Forms
> 19 Century Avenue
> Victoria, MO 63123
>
> LETTER FORMATS
>
> You're right about letter formats, Joe. Modified block and block
> formats are both used widely. Open punctuation (which omits the
> colon after the salutation and the comma after the complimentary
> close), however, has never caught on. Almost everybody uses
> mixed punctuation.
>
> Block format is a bit more economical than modified block because
> it begins each line on the left margin, whereas modified block indents
> both the date line and the signature block. In block format, paragraphs
> are blocked on the left margin, but modified block permits both blocked
> and indented format.
>
> The format used for this letter, Joe, is known as the Simplified Letter
> Form (SLF). It is more economical than block format because it omits
> the salutation and the complimentary close. Most companies still use
> modified block or block formats because they feel that the SLF violates
> too many of the expected conventions of letter writing. Many business
> people feel that readers will be offended by the omission of the usual
> salutation and complimentary close. Companies that have switched to
> SLF for reasons of economy report that most readers don't notice the
> difference.

[a]Try to use reader's name in the first line.

Exhibit 7.3 (*continued*)

second (and
following) page
heading[b]

last line[c]

name, title
reference initial
enclosure notation[d]
copy notation
postscript[e]

> Mr. Joseph Sidney   February 23, 19xx   2
>
> At the end of this letter, I've indicated the common notations that
> are used regardless of the letter format you select.
>
> Let me know when I can help again.
>
> *Karen Stone*
> KAREN STONE, CPS
>
> s
>
> enc
>
> c
>
> PS

[b]Heading is the same for all formats: modified block, simplified block, and simplified.

[c]A short last line helps retain a traditional appearance. Leave five lines for the signature.

[d]Use the enclosure notation to indicate the presence of one or more enclosures. When enclosures are especially important, list them by document title and specify the number; for example:

3 enc
  1. Invoice
  2. Contract
  3. Sample brochure

[e]A postscript is always the last entry in a letter, and because it comes last the notation isn't necessary to indicate that it is a PS. In general, avoid postscripts in formal correspondence. It's better to rewrite a letter than to reveal a lack of planning. The main purpose of a postscript is to add a personal note to a business letter.

nization, they are called interoffice memorandums or memos, for short. Memo reports are the company's major medium for internal written communication. Although a rare memo might require several pages, memorandum reports are usually neither so formal nor so long as letter reports. They can, in fact, be only one line long.

October 8, 19XX

TO: Jean Burke

FROM: Jack Plano

SUBJECT: February Sales

Great job, Jean. You earned your bonus this month.

Exhibit 7.4 A Letter Report

May 9, 19xx

Bass Credit Data
1776 Avenue of the Americas
Cleveland, Ohio
44140

Ms. Alice Mitchell
Assistant Vice President
Business Credit Incorporated
220 South Michigan Avenue
Columbus, OH 43215

Dear Ms. Mitchell:

Thank you and Mr. Denando for meeting with me on March 24 when we discussed
the programming specifications for Business Credit Incorporated (BCI) to
report consumer credit information to Bass Credit Data.

While discussing some of the specifications we agreed upon with some of BCI's
user banks, several problems and questions were raised. I believe that the
following concerns require further discussion and must be resolved before I
can provide you with definitive program specifications. I am hoping that a
meeting between BCI, Bass, and representatives from the major banks on the
BCI system can be arranged within the next few weeks to discuss these items.

Account Number

Some banks have expressed concern over the type of account number that would
be reported to and maintained by Bass. These banks know that a certain level
of security would be provided if Bass were to display an account number of
the credit report that is different from the customer's true account number.
Because such "scrambled" account numbers would not present a problem to the
banks or BCI when verifying account information or when making purchase
authorizations, Bass's security department would allow "scrambled" account
numbers in Bass's file. Our understanding is that these numbers will remain
the same from month to month instead of being "rescrambled" each month.
Bass's security department also conducts fraud seminars which would enable
BCI's users to further curtail fraud.

One of my concerns is about the account number changes planned for BCI for
some time this year. As we discussed, Bass would like to begin receiving
update tapes from BCI before the fourth quarter of 1980. The account number
change should be accomplished before reporting to Bass is initiated to prevent
account number changes within Bass's system.

If your account number change is not accomplished before the fourth quarter
of 19xx, however, the banks' accounts should still be reported to Bass with
the old account numbers. Then, when the new account number is assigned, it
can be reported to Bass's E1 segment, which is specifically designed to effect
account number changes within Bass's file. The format and use of the E1 segment will be discussed if it becomes necessary.

Status Code

We decided to report Bass status code 97 (charge off) for all accounts with
a BCI status of "0." Since then I have learned from the banks that this
would be improper because an "0" account might have previously had a rating

[a]Any letter using headings, tables, charts, or other report writing techniques is technically a letter
report.

Exhibit 7.4   *(continued)*

Ms. Alice Mitchell   May 9, 19xx   2

of "F" (fraud). If such accounts were reported as charge off, we in effect
would be penalizing the customer who might merely be the victim of the fraud.
Therefore, some consideration should be given to preventing fraud charge offs
from being reported as charge offs. Perhaps this could be accomplished by
using a BCI status other than "O" to denote fraud charge offs.

The automated reporting of charged off accounts should be pursued even though
most banks would agree to report their charge offs manually. The reason is
that Bass's central file actually consists of two independent files. One
contains account balance information reported by balance contributors such
as BCI. The other file contains exception information reported by exception
and manually reporting subscribers. Therefore, if a bank manually reports a
charged off account, the balance information previously reported by BCI for
that same account could not be updated, but a separate transaction
would be established on the file. The account would then appear in Bass's
file twice, once as a charge off and again with whatever status was last
reported by BCI for that account.

Another status code I am concerned about is 03 (lost or stolen card). We
thought that status code 03 should be reported for all accounts with a BCI
status of "L" (lost), "S" (stolen), "C" (counterfeit), or "F" (fraud). This
is unsatisfactory to the banks because a new account number is not always
assigned to such an account, in which case the status 03 would simply overlay
any status code previously reported for the account. This would make it
possible for a delinquent customer with some knowledge of credit reporting
to report a lost or stolen card and have his or her delinquent history erased
from Bass's file. Keep in mind that since the customer is delinquent, the
bank would usually not issue a new account number to this customer, and no
further reporting of that customer would occur.

As was mentioned earlier, manually reported information will not update the
automated information reported by BCI. So again, we should try to eliminate
the need for the banks to report status code 03 manually.

One possibility that some banks agreed to was the automated reporting of
status code 03 for all accounts with status "L," "S," "C," or "F" when the
balance of the account is zero. We thought that this would be safe because
the customer would probably not be trying to subterfuge the intent of the
reporting system if he or she had a zero balance. Most of these accounts
would then be issued a new account number which would be reported to Bass.

On the other hand, those accounts with a status of "L," "S," "C," or "F" and
with a balance greater than zero could be reported with a special comment
code "S" which will result in the message "Special Handling--Contact Subscriber If Additional Information Required" on the credit report. Of course,
this special comment code could be reported along with the appropriate status
code (current or delinquent). The accounts should be reported in the above
manner each month until the accounts reach a zero balance, at which time they
could be reported with status code 03.

(continued)

Exhibit 7.4   *(continued)*

Ms. Alice Mitchell   May 9, 19xx   3

Transaction Type Code

The most important transaction code that will be used by the BCI credit
reporting program will be transaction type code 1. This code indicates a
new account and is required for Bass to establish a new account in our files.

We tentatively thought that transaction type code 1 would be determined for
all new accounts on each monthly update tape by the date opened. This method,
however, will not work for accounts issued new account numbers due to a lost
or stolen card because the original date opened of the account is retained.

Therefore, some consideration should be given to the ability to distinguish
these replacement accounts from new accounts so that they can be properly
reported and established by Bass.

Amount

One major bank on the BCI system has expressed reluctance to report the
credit limits of its accounts. In the interest of keeping the program specifications as straightforward as possible and to establish a meaningful information exchange between all credit grantors, this information should be
reported to Bass. Currently no Bass subscribers withhold this information.

Special Comment Code

Currently, your system is not capable of detecting disputed accounts. Again,
in the interest of avoiding manual reporting by the banks, we should establish
a disputed account indicator to enable BCI to report special comment code "X"
or "Y" to produce the "Account in Dispute--Reported by Subscriber" message on
the credit report. These special comment codes can be reported manually as a
last resort.

Originally, we thought that Bass's special comment code "L" could be reported
for all accounts with a BCI status of "B" (blocked), "W" (wild), and possibly
"H" (hold). When a special comment code "L" is reported, the message "Credit
Line Closed--Reported by Subscriber" will appear on the credit report. We
thought the use of this code would provide additional information about the
account but would still allow the appropriate status code (current or delinquent) to be reported as opposed to Bass status code 20 (credit line closed,
reason unknown or by customer request) or 90 (credit line closed, not paying
as agreed) which would not indicate whether the account is current or delinquent.

I later learned that BCI status codes "B," "W," and "H" are not used uniformly
by all BCI banks. This voids the above conclusions. I hope that we can agree
on how and when to use which codes at our next meeting.

Exhibit 7.4   *(continued)*

Ms. Alice Mitchell   May 9, 19xx   4

I am looking forward to meeting with you and the banks' representatives at
2:00 p.m. on May 19.

Sincerely,

Donald L. Moorman

Donald L. Moorman
Senior Analyst
Bass Credit Data

e

c Adam Borcher--First National Bank in Columbus
   Leslie Hall--Ohio National Bank
   Richard Reddy--First National Bank of Cincinnati
   Zeke Zelner--Mercantile Trust Company N.A.

Why do memos not
require a
letterhead?

Because memo reports remain within your own organization, they use a standardized, informal format. Instead of a letterhead, printed across the top of the memo stationery, and usually in all capital letters, are the words: OFFICE MEMORANDUM, INTEROFFICE MEMORANDUM, or INTEROFFICE CORRESPONDENCE.

What are the four
headings used?

Unlike letters—which use the formal inside address, salutation, complimentary close, and typed signature—memos provide four informal, printed headings: DATE, TO, FROM, and SUBJECT. While the arrangement and design may vary among companies, these four headings appear on most forms. Printing of the heading lines is either vertical or horizontal, depending on your company's preferences.

Printed headings in the horizontal placement form two columns:

TO: DATE

FROM: SUBJECT:

In the vertical placement they are a single column:

DATE:

TO:

FROM:

SUBJECT:

What other
headings may be
added for the
convenience of
readers and
writers?

You may want to include other printed headings, such as department, branch, location, or room number. Even the words *message* or *body* may be printed on the memo form to indicate where the memo message is to begin. Optional parts of the memo are the signature, reference initials, and enclosure and copy notations.

The current date appears after the "Date" line. Even though the memo report is informal, do *not* use all figures (10/14/xx). Spell out or abbreviate the name of the month.

October 14, 19xx

Oct. 14, 19xx

14 October 19xx

14 Oct. 19xx

19xx 10 14 (Computer date form)

When no printed date line is provided, type the date (omitting the word *date*) a double space after the memo heading, INTEROFFICE MEMORANDUM, or type it several spaces above the "To" line.

The name of the addressee appears after the "To" line. You may use courtesy titles (Mr., Mrs., Miss, Ms.) or professional titles (Dr.) or omit them depending on your company's preferences. A good rule to follow is this: If you use a title when talking with that individual, use a title in the memo. If you are writing to an executive of the company or to a person of a higher rank than you, you might want to use his or her title even if you are on a first-name basis when talking informally.

When an organization is large enough to warrant further identification or clarification, use department names or job titles after the name in the "To" line. If you address the memo to several people within the organization, then "See Below" appears after the "To" line. List the names of the individuals at the end of the message in alphabetical order or in rank order—president, vice president, and so forth.

If you want to send the memo report to a particular group of people and the group is so large that it would be impossible to list all the names, then the "To" is followed by the group's identifying classification, such as "Department Heads," "Employees," or "Faculty and Staff."

When writing the memo report, place your own name after the "From" line. Do not use a courtesy title unless you are a woman and particularly concerned about how others address you: Ms., Miss, or Mrs. If you feel, however, that the reader would not know you, use your job title or department name after your name. For example:

> From: Linda Lindauer, Controller

> From: Gregg Houfly, Accounting Department

Although the writer's name on the "From" line makes a typed or written signature unnecessary, you may prefer to personalize your memo report or show that you have read the typed message. You may sign memos requiring authentication. If you wish to sign your name, place your handwritten initials above, below, or to the right of your typed name on the "From" line.

What is the subject line?
The "Subject" line is a brief and concise statement telling the reader at a glance what the memo is about. For example:

> Subject: A Survey of Employee Qualifications

> Subject: Third-Quarter Report

Because the "Subject" line immediately tells what the memo report is about, it also aids in filing the report.

After the text of the report has been presented, the typist places the initial of her or his last name a double space below the last line of the report. If several typists in the office have the same last initial, the typist should use the initials of her or his full name.

How are enclosures noted?
If enclosures or attachments are included with the memo report, reference is made to them by typing the words, *Enclosure, enc,* or *att* a double space below the reference initial. When several enclosures or attachments are included with the report, provide a specific list of them.

att List of employees who participated in the survey

Line chart showing the salary increases over a 5-year span

How are names listed in copy notations?

Names of persons receiving copies of the memo report are typed below the enclosure notation. If several persons are to receive copies of the report, place their names in alphabetical order or in rank order after the copy notation. For example:

c   Tom Bieterman
    Vic Donahue
    Carrie Henderson

c   Malcolm McLean, President
    Ray Thoma, Vice President
    Shannon Coyle, Treasurer

What is included in second-page headings?

When a memo report contains more than one page, the heading for the second and succeeding pages begins 1 inch from the top edge of the paper. The memo headings are the same as those used for business letters; namely, addressee's name, date, and page number. Use either the horizontal or vertical (block) style.

Horizontal: Addressee's Name   Date   2
Vertical: Addressee's Name
            Date
            Page 2

Triple space below the heading and continue with the memo report. Exhibits 7.5 and 7.6 illustrate memorandum reports.

Caption-Style Reports

The caption-style format may be used for letter reports or memos. Note that the format, illustrated in Exhibit 7.7, is highly readable. Its narrow column of type, however, makes it unsuitable for longer reports.

FORMAL REPORTS

Formal reports can be either short or long. Generally, short reports (ten pages or fewer) are informal and long reports (11 pages or more) are formal, although short reports may be presented formally. As a rule, short reports, whether informal or formal, are single-spaced. Long reports are always double-spaced. Because long reports may be bound on the top or on the left, the top margin or the left margin may need to be increased to accommodate the binding.

Short Formal Reports

A short formal report uses some—but generally not all—of the major divisions of a long report, such as prefatory parts, report proper, and

Exhibit 7.5   ## A Memorandum Report

INTEROFFICE CORRESPONDENCE

November 24, 19xx

TO: R. T. Bloom

FROM: D. J. Baseler

SUBJECT: SLIDE FILE

Here's the report you requested on the costs involved in putting your slides in the existing file.

1. <u>Software Development</u>
    The file will have to be reprogrammed to enable use of an interactive terminal to search for a slide number. By knowing at least two parameters (such as requestor, date, division, etc.), you can use the terminal to determine specific slide numbers, no matter whether they are yours or ours. Estimated programming cost is $5,000, and we propose that we split this cost.

2. <u>Terminal Lease</u>
    If you don't have access to a terminal, lease cost would be about $125 a month.

3. <u>Slide Insertion</u>
    The cost of keypunching, verifying and inserting slides into the file is about $50 for each 500 slides.

4. <u>Storage and Use</u>
    Storage costs are about $2.00 a month. Each time you do a search in the file, the cost is about $2.50.

Assuming you have about 5,000 slides, the initial cost to put them in the file would be about $3,000. Then annual upkeep would be about $2,200, including terminal lease, storage, and one search a day.

This does not include your labor costs to sort and catalog the slides. I'd suggest you consider using temporary help to do the initial job (5,000 slides will probably take about two to three months), then train someone on your staff to maintain the file.

We're all ready to start on the software development, so we would appreciate your reactions as soon as possible.

Exhibit 7.6   A Memorandum Report

December 21, 19xx

TO: A. Hamilton

FROM: B. Kramer *βK*

MONTHLY REPORT

Here's the monthly report that you requested.

    I.   Advertising
       A. Print schedule for January 19xx:

Commercial Car Journal	Fleet Owner
Heavy Duty Trucking	Refrigerated Transporter
Diesel Equip. Supt.	Fleet Maintenance & Spec.
Construction Equipment	Highway & Heavy Const.
Construction	Dixie Contractor
Bus & Truck Transport	Motor Truck
Fleet Specialist	Heavy Duty Distribution

       B. Radio schedule of January 19xx:
          Weeks of January 7 and 21.
       C. Specific projects:
          1. Negotiated to share all 19xx covers in Commercial Car Journal
            and Heavy Duty Distribution with Freightliner and IHC, respec-
            tively.
          2. Product, Parts, and Business ads are in copy approval or pro-
            duction stage. Construction ad is in planning stage.
   II. Direct Mail
       A. First scheduled mailing is construction brochure in March.
       B. JWT is developing direct mail brochures for Construction and Fuel
          Economy. Brochure on RT-6610/6613 is in planning stage.
  III. Sales Promotion
       A. Literature
          1. Shipments included 132 paid orders and 135 miscellaneous orders.
            We are two months behind on answering ad inquiries (approximately
            1000 inquiries).
          2. Ford/China Engineering sheets and Engineering Reference Book
            sheets have been printed.
          3. Mack/Fuller dealer brochure is being revised for the third time.
          4. Revision of 1157 sales sheets is in production.
       B. Audio Visual
          1. Slide production--252 original slides produced (this includes
            storyboards, art work, photography, processing, mounting, and
            filing).
          2. Other production included parts shots for Research, prints for
            Ford PRC Program, scripts for IHC Peru presentation by TCM, and
            publicity shots of visiting disc jockeys.

routine heading[a]

outline form[b]

[a]The reader of this report obviously expects it and is familiar with its contents. Either the subject line or the first sentence normally clarifies the purpose of the report.

[b]Note that this report consists primarily of lists of things. Many business reports—especially routine, periodic reports—follow this practice.

Exhibit 7.6   *(continued)*

A. Hamilton   December 21, 19xx   2

    3. Productions in progress:
      a. In-house productions include White Motor Installation
        program, Nissan Diesel slides for L. Matsuura, GMC presen-
        tation for J. Way, and Engineering Presentations for R. Denes.
        These are scheduled for completion in January.
      b. RT-9508--Jaqua Company--rough script is completed, will be
        reviewed January 8. Completion date--March 19xx.
      c. Drive Instruction programs--script revision in progress.
        Completion date--February 19xx.
      d. RTO-1157--Bradshaw Advertising--initial concept and budget
        being developed--ready for review by January 10. Completion
        date--March 19xx.
      e. GMC Movie--initial outline approved and scripting in progress.
        Completion date--May 19xx.
      f. RT-9509--all material complete except binders. Will be
        shipped first week of January.
      g. New model slides--being revised to add latest information.
        Ready in January.
    4. NOTE: Since June 1, 19xx, original slides have been produced
       in-house--an average of almost 200 a month.

IV. Trade Shows
    A. First trade show of 19xx is ConAG in Houston, January 27-31. Hugh
       Sprague plans to attend.
    B. All displays are being coordinated with TCM. Specifically, the
       Fuller Parts panel is being redone.

V. Miscellaneous
    A. Personnel--transition of Product Literature and Marketing Communi-
       cations people is progressing satisfactorily.
    B. TCM Coordination--objectives have been established for slides,
       flipcharts, and direct mail. A task force (Shedden from TCM,
       Johnson from Axle, Passage from Brake, and Baseler from Trans-
       mission) has been formed to establish specific guidelines and
       formats. First meeting is January 9 in Southfield.
    C. New Building--Serge Caillet hopes to have time in January to work
       on design of conference rooms and A-V facilities. A consultant
       has been recommended and has had an initial meeting with us.

VI. Next Month (in addition to what's listed above)
    A. Establish guidelines for specialty program and begin search for
       specific items.
    B. Work closely with JWT to improve its service.
    C. Reorganize handling of purchase orders and invoices.
    D. Catch up on all literature requests.
    E. Begin cataloging of all slides for computer entry.
    F. Review copier requirements for cost savings, quality, and efficiency.

Exhibit 7.7   Short Informational Report in Caption-Style Format

computer date form[a]

Harwick Word Processing Consultants Ltd.
12302A Jasper Avenue, Edmonton, Alberta T5N 3K5
(403) 488—0752

harwick
Word Processing

19xx 11 18

Joel P. Bowman
College of Business
Dept. of Bus. Ed. and Admin. Svcs.
Western Michigan University
Kalamazoo, Michigan 49008

Subject: Caption-Style Report Format

PURPOSE   This is in response to the queries in your 3
                           November 19xx letter concerning the "report
                           format" used in my letter to the committee.

NOT AN ORIGINAL IDEA   My first task at Syncrude was to develop the
                           standards for technical manuals.

                           One of our owners, Esso--the Canadian Exxon
                           affiliate--used a layout similar to this for
                           its manuals.

                           After researching readability and legibility--
                           boy! can Journal of Applied Psychology articles
                           be boring--I modified the format somewhat and
                           adopted it for use in Syncrude.

GOOD POINTS   For manuals--and reports--captions allow for
                           creation of an index and table of contents.
                           The writing of captions is much more rigorous
                           when they have to be used in this manner.

                           We teach people that the captions function like
                           headlines in a newspaper. As such, they must
                           be descriptive of the material that follows.

                           Captions really help when you're trying to find
                           specific information--especially when you're
                           referring to a previously read document. (One
                           accounting firm using the style cites the
                           biggest advantage as being able to find infor-
                           mation fast--like the "note to file" on the
                           conversation with a given client on a given
                           topic.)

[a]Note the computer date form. Many companies use this date form for internal messages and on company forms. It is not used much in correspondence or in business reports.

Source: Report courtesy of Raymond W. Beswick, Partner, Harwick Word Processing Consultants.

Exhibit 7.7   *(continued)*

Joel P. Bowman   19xx 11 18   2

GOOD POINTS   We teach people to read the subject titles and
(continued)   then the captions. This gives them a good
                                  idea of what is being covered and in what
                                  order. (Reading speed is increased if these
                                  are known.) It also allows readers to pick
                                  and choose what to read--for example, why
                                  would a subject matter expert want to read
                                  something captioned "basic technical descrip-
                                  tion"?

                                  The layout allows the text to be in about 4-
                                  inch lines. This is an ideal length for speed-
                                  reading. (Look at the line length of a pocket
                                  book sometime.) The layout is psychologically
                                  good because the page is not intimidating to
                                  look at--compare it with a page of "wall-to-
                                  wall" words.

BAD POINTS   Using the layout does take more paper--but we
                                  consider this to be more than offset by the
                                  benefits.

                                  Also, "conservatives" rebel at the sight of this
                                  unconventional page layout. (One of our clients
                                  used it for a very conservative client and re-
                                  ceived a call stating that the report was
                                  unacceptable in this format!)

MEMOS AND REPORT, TOO   As I was charged with developing spoken and
                                  written communication courses as well as the
                                  manuals program at Syncrude, it was "a natural"
                                  to consider using the layout for letters,
                                  memos, and reports.

                                  Letters can use it <u>but</u> you really have to know
                                  your audience. Often, we'll use a conven-
                                  tionally set-up covering letter and attach a
                                  "report" in caption style.

                                  The format is not universally used in Syncrude
                                  memos and reports. However, anything that is
                                  typeset automatically goes into the format.

OTHER USES   I've alluded to several other users. We've
                                  installed caption style in several government
                                  departments, accounting firms, oil companies,
                                  and a firm of insurance adjusters.

(continued)

Exhibit 7.7   *(continued)*

Joel P. Bowman   19xx 11 18   3

OTHER USES   (There's an interesting anecdote associated
(continued)   with the insurance adjusters. We asked them
                                 if we could use them as a reference. They
                                 said, basically, "hell, no. We've got a com-
                                 petitive edge using this writing style and
                                 layout and we don't want to lose it!")

If you want any more information, just let me know.

Ray

Raymond W. Beswick
Partner

How do you like the new letterhead?

supplementary parts. These divisions are explained below. Exhibit 7.8 illustrates a short formal report with a title page and letter of transmittal.

Long Formal Reports

A long formal report is similar to the short formal report except in length. Long reports usually deal with more complex problems than short reports and, therefore, require greater attention to organization and logical presentation so that the reader can assimilate the material easily. Chapter 17 illustrates a long, formal report.

PARTS OF THE FORMAL REPORT

Although the organization of long formal reports may vary from one company to another, the formal report parts presented in this chapter are considered acceptable and desirable by most readers and organizations.

In what order do report parts normally appear?

The following report parts, listed in the order in which they normally appear, are generally found in long formal, analytical reports. Depending on the requirements, complexity, and formality of the report, some of these parts may be omitted.

When your company does not provide specific guidelines, choose those parts that will best communicate the information you want to convey. Physical presentation is discussed in Chapter 17.

Major Divisions

Formal reports contain three major divisions: prefatory parts, report body, and supplementary parts. Each of these divisions contains several subdivisions.

Prefatory Parts

Cover

Title Fly

Title Page

Letter of Authorization

Letter of Acceptance

Letter of Transmittal

Table of Contents

Table (or List) of Illustrations

Exhibit 7.8   A Sample Short Report

title page

A PRACTICAL GUIDE FOR SELECTING VISUAL AIDS

Prepared for

Ms. Opal Klammer
Director of Corporate Communication
Fine Arts Company
2030 Wallace Street
Johnson City, TX 37601

Prepared by

Mr. Pat Lemanski
Research Director
Eaton Corporation

January 26, 19xx

Exhibit 7.8   *(continued)*

letter of transmittal

EATON CORPORATION
Public Relations Department
0002 Karl Avenue
Rochester, NY 14610

January 26, 19xx

Ms. Opal Klammer
Director of Corporate Communication
Fine Arts Company
2030 Wallace Street
Johnson City, TX 37601

Dear Ms. Klammer:

Here's the report on the visual aids that you requested on January 15, 19xx.

The report covers 35mm carousel projects, poster boards, flipcharts, overhead projectors, display boards, chalkboards, and opaque projectors.

The information on these items should help you make a decision about which would be best for your needs.

Let us know when we can help again.

Cordially,

Pat Lemanski

Pat Lemanski
Research Director

enc

opening[a]

summary[b]

closing[c]

[a]The first paragraph "transmits" the report.

[b]In short reports, the letter of transmittal almost always contains a brief summary of the report contents.

[c]Letters of transmittal usually conclude with an offer to help again in the future.

Source: Courtesy of Eaton Corporation.

(continued)

Exhibit 7.8   (*continued*)

ECONOMICAL GUIDELINES FOR THE USE OF VISUAL AIDS

To use audio visuals economically and yet effectively to make presentations to internal or external audiences, several primary factors should first be determined:

What is the message to be conveyed?
What is the composition of the audience?
What part of the message lends itself to visualization?
What equipment lends itself best to the message and the audience?
How can the appropriate equipment be procured and used?

Deliberately excluded in this list that follows are the more expensive techniques such as video, motion pictures, and multimedia efforts, which presently can be justified only under circumstances that clearly call for their use. Techniques are listed generally in order of total expense--the costliest equipment-plus-material first.

This presentation is necessarily limited in scope, but, particularly in Eaton locations away from World Headquarters, it can serve as a useful guide in the absence of on-the-spot professional counsel.

To seek further information, guidance, or advice as to techniques, vendors, and the like, feel free to call Thomas R. Tucker, manager of visual media services. With his associates, he will be happy to provide any additional counsel desired--by phone, letter, or personally.

Exhibit 7.8   *(continued)*

illustrated format[d]

VISUAL AIDS: DESCRIPTIONS

<u>35mm Carousel Projectors</u>

A 35mm carousel projector is probably the
most effective method (within these guidelines) to present material, particularly
to a large audience. It is a highly flexible technique and offers the widest range
for both graphic design and ease of projection.

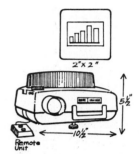

To present the most readable on-screen
image, 35mm slides should be prepared in
a 2" x 3" (horizontal) format. Vertical
slides should be avoided, if possible,
because they diminish the appearance of
uniformity and continuity. They will also
bleed off the top and bottom of the projection screen when the screen is set for
horizontal slides, thus losing considera-
ble detail.

For better readability and retention, the
<u>less</u> information placed on each slide the
better. If a substantial amount of information (especially financial data) is
required, it is best to separate it into
units so that the material can be shown
as a series, each part on a single slide
containing one section of the total data.

Projection is generally accomplished by throwing the image forward from the
center or rear of the room. If space permits, however, the image can be made
more effective and unobtrusive by using rear-screen projection. Using this
method, the path of projection is from behind the screen, which separates and
hides the projector from the audience.

Costs can be minimized by (1) providing sufficient time for examining data to
be used, (2) keeping the material on each slide simple and at a minimum, and
(3) allowing enough time for preparation (several days at least).

The average cost of producing a quality 35mm slide is $20, but, depending on
its complexity, it can reach $35 or $40. Duplicate slides can be produced
for about 65¢ each.

[d]Note the specialized format, which permits the parallel presentation of the text and the
accompanying illustrations.

(continued)

Exhibit 7.8   *(continued)*

3

Poster Boards

Poster boards are almost identical in design
to flipcharts. But instead of paper pads,
cardboard posters are used (such as those
used in COMM/PRO presentations). These can
be prepared in advance, mounted on easels
or even attached to walls with push pins or
tape.

For more complex presentations, large
acetate sheets can be hinged to the front
of a board, dropped behind it, then brought
forward and placed on top of the basic design
as an overlay to add another step or more
information to these basic data on the first
sheet. China marking pencils can also be
used to emphasize points--or even to make
last minute changes.

Posters are available in a range of colors and textures. Standard sizes
(20" x 24") cost approximately 65¢ a sheet. Simple sketches or drawings
can be added for approximately $8 a sheet.

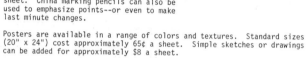

Flipcharts

A flipchart is simply a large pad of paper
mounted on a movable easel.

Ideally, information or illustrations to be
used should be sketched lightly with pencil
on the paper prior to the presentation.
Then, during the program, a felt tip marker
can be used to trace the penciled lines.
This technique can also serve as a personal
reminder for the speaker.

If simple art sketches or drawings are
required rather than freehand sketches,
they can be professionally done directly
on the pad for approximately $8 a page.

Overhead Projectors

An overhead projector is approximately twice
the size of 35mm projectors. It uses 10" x
10" acetate transparencies projected upward
from a flat glass surface above the light
source. The transparencies are then reflected onto a screen from an obliquely
positioned mirror held on a metal arm
extending upward from the equipment.

Exhibit 7.8   (*continued*)

4

Key points can be discussed by using a pointer on the transparency itself without interfering with the path of projection.

The machinery is light in weight, operates quietly, and offers a bright image for easy viewing even in a fully lighted room. It also has great flexibility and can readily project line drawings, standard typewriter copy, and a variety of graphic designs, all of which can be produced on Xerox equipment.

Display Boards

Display boards, similar to blackboards, can be obtained with flannel or magnetic surfaces. Hooks, in place or added later, can also be used to hold and display materials such as three-dimensional objects.

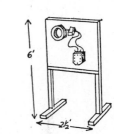

Posters of varying sizes can be sketched or drawn in advance on a variety of colored stock.

Illustration costs are similar to that of displays such as flipcharts and poster boards.

Chalkboards

Standard fixed chalkboards are generally green in tone, which aids visibility. Portable roll-around chalkboards provide additional opportunities for flexibility-- and the imaginative use of multicolor chalks, stencils, chalk compasses, and the like can result in very informal and effective presentations.

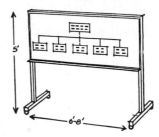

The cost for these materials is minimal.

Opaque Projectors

Opaque projectors project any opaque material (as distinct from transparencies): book pages, line drawings, blueprints, drawings, typewritten copy, and the like. This projector is much larger and more cumbersome than overhead projectors, although some newer models are slightly more compact.

This equipment's light source is bounced downward onto the flat-surface material,

(*continued*)

Exhibit 7.8 *(continued)*

5

reflected upward at an angle onto an obliquely positioned mirror, then projected onto the screen. Its image quality is not so sharp as the other
equipment. Consequently, it requires (1) the size of the audience be
relatively small, (2) the meeting room be darkened, and (3) the distance
to the screen be minimal (7-10 feet). Points to be made to the audience
can also be indicated by the built-in illuminated arrow directly on the
material as it is being projected.

Abstract

Body of the Report

Introduction

Text—usually divided into sections by major heads, subheads, and subsubheads

Conclusions—listed separately or combined with Recommendations

Recommendations

Supplementary Parts

Appendix (or Appendixes)

Bibliography

Index

Prefatory Parts

The prefatory parts of a report include the cover, title fly, title page, letter of authorization, letter of acceptance, letter of transmittal, table of contents, table of illustrations, and abstract.

Cover The purpose of the cover sheet is to identify and protect the report. The cover contains the title of the report and the author's name. When a title is more than one line long, it should be typed in inverted pyramid style:

The Feasibility of the Restoration
of the Water Tower on
Clemson University's
East Campus

What are the requirements for a good title? What words should not be included?

The report title should be accurate, clear, concise, complete, and descriptive. Whenever possible, it should answer who, what, when, where, why, and how. The title should not include such words or phrases as "a study of," "a report of," or "a survey of."

Title Fly The title fly merely carries the title of the report. It is generally considered unnecessary and omitted in typewritten reports.

Title Page The title page carries (1) the name or title of the report; (2) the name, title, and address of the person, group, or organization of the intended reader of the report; (3) the name, title, and address of the person, group, or organization writing the report; and (4) the date of presentation. The words "prepared for" or "submitted for," and "prepared by" or "submitted by" often precede the names. The generally accepted format is described and illustrated in Chapter 17.

Letter of Authorization   The letter or memorandum of authorization is written by the person who requests or authorizes the report. It states the problem, the scope, and limitations of the report. The letter of authorization also serves as a notice that the report writer prepared and presented the report as directed. Most companies prefer to omit the letter of authorization from all but the most formal reports.

When is the letter of authorization omitted?

Letter of Acceptance   The letter of acceptance is the reply to the letter of authorization. It accepts the request to conduct the study and prepare the report. It restates the problem, the scope, and limitations of the report as presented in the letter of authorization. It may confirm time limitations, fees, expenses, and other contractual agreements. The letter of acceptance is usually omitted from the report.

When is the letter of acceptance omitted?

Letter of Transmittal   The letter of transmittal, or covering letter, accompanies the finished report to the reader and is prepared after the report is completed. The letter begins with an appropriate reference to the transmission of the report and to the letter of authorization. For example:

Formal: As you requested in your letter of May 5, here is the report on . . .

Informal: Here's the report you asked me to prepare on . . .

The letter of transmittal may also include the title of the report, the scope, the limitations, the procedure or methodology used, and acknowledgments of assistance given by others. If the report does not contain a separate abstract, the letter of transmittal should include major findings, conclusions, and recommendations.

What should the letter of transmittal include?

The letter should end on a positive note—usually an expression of appreciation for the opportunity to do the report (an opportunity to learn or appreciation for the business, if an outside consultant), and an offer to do a similar assignment in the future.

Table of Contents   Prepare the contents page after the report has been typed and page numbers are known. The table of contents shows the organization of the report. It is the report outline and, as such, it lists the report headings exactly as they appear in the report. The table of contents serves as a guide to the reader because it lists the beginning page numbers of the major headings and subheadings of the report. It helps the reader locate information.

What is the purpose of the table of contents?

Because the prefatory parts precede the table of contents, they should not be included. List the abstract first, if one is prepared separately, because it follows immediately after the contents page. The supplemental parts of the report—appendix, bibliography, and index—are listed without outline symbols because they are not part of the report proper.

The generally accepted format is described and illustrated in Chapter 17.

Table (or List) of Illustrations When a report contains graphic aids (Table 1, Table 2, Figure 1, Figure 2, Exhibit 1, Exhibit 2, and so forth) a table of illustrations will help the reader locate them. When a sufficient number of each type of graphic aid is presented in the report, list each type separately (list of tables and a list of figures). When the list of illustrations is short, type it on the table of contents page if space is available. Otherwise, type it on a separate page immediately following the contents page.

Abstract The abstract (or synopsis or summary) is a brief overview of the entire report, as discussed in Chapter 5.

Body of the Report

The body of the report consists of the introduction, the text, the conclusions, and the recommendations.

Introduction The introduction *introduces* the reader to the text of the report. It should answer the questions **who**, **what**, **when**, **where**, and **why**. You answer these questions by giving the background of the problem, stating the problem clearly, defining the scope, and detailing the limitations of the study.

How does the introduction answer the *how* question?

The introduction also answers the **how** question. How did you conduct the investigation? You answer this question by explaining the method of research and the sources and procedures used to gather the data for your report. When a review of the related literature will help the reader understand the problem, it should also be included in the introduction.

Presentation of data in the introduction and the report as a whole can be either deductive or inductive. The deductive—direct—plan introduces the report by presenting the conclusions and recommendations first and then presents the findings. The inductive—indirect—method of presentation gives the background information first, followed by the findings and finally the conclusions and recommendations.

Text The text of the report follows the introduction. It is the heart and bulk of the report. It includes the findings section, the part of the report that presents, analyzes, and interprets the information the investigator has gathered. Whenever possible, the report writer discusses the important facts and findings of the report and shows their relationships with each other.

Headings, subheadings, itemizations, and graphic aids are used to aid the report writer in presenting the data.

Conclusions and Recommendations   The conclusions and recommendations follow the findings section of the report when the indirect pattern of organization is used. With the direct approach, the conclusions and recommendations follow immediately after the introduction. This latter method is being used more frequently today so that the busy executive who receives many reports daily may quickly read through the conclusions and recommendations and make a decision or decide to read the entire report for complete details.

Some report writers prefer to use separate sections for conclusions and recommendations to avoid confusion about which were the conclusions and which were the recommendations. Also, some writers prefer separate sections because conclusions are objective (factual statements) whereas recommendations are personal opinions (value judgments) based on the conclusions.

Whether they appear in one section or two, the conclusions and recommendations provide the answers to the problem statement in the introduction. While all analytical reports will have conclusions, not all will have recommendations. Conclusions are drawn and recommendations are made on the basis of the findings of the report. No new material should be presented in the conclusions and recommendations section of the report.

To help you present the conclusions and recommendations and so that you can refer to them by number, itemize and number the items in each category and follow the rules for parallel construction. Also, as an aid to the reader, provide reference page numbers after each item. Then, if your readers wish to refer to the discussion in the text, they have an immediate page reference.

Supplemental Parts

The supplemental parts of the report are the appendix, the bibliography, and the index.

Appendix (or Appendixes)   The appendix is the place for supplemental information which the reader would consider either too detailed or not important for understanding the report. The appendix supports the body of the report. It usually contains copies of the cover letter and questionnaire used in a survey, elaborate formulas, a glossary of terms, interview schedules, sample forms, statistical computations, computer printouts, and any additional information that would be of interest to the reader.

Where do conclusions and recommendations appear when the indirect pattern of organization is used? When the direct pattern is used?

When are graphic aids placed in an appendix?

Although tables and figures should be placed in the text to aid the reader, some graphic aids may be too extensive and not necessary for understanding the report. These aids then should be placed in an appendix. The guideline to follow for deciding whether the information should be included in an appendix is, if the reader needs the material to understand the report, place it in the appropriate section; otherwise, place it in the appendix. Governmental and military reports use the term "Tab" to refer to an appendix.

Bibliography   The bibliography or reference section is an alphabetized list of secondary sources used in preparing the report. Chapter 11 describes and illustrates bibliographic entries.

How is an index prepared without the use of a word processor or computer?

The Index   The index is an alphabetic listing of names, places, and subjects mentioned in the report. It provides the page reference for each item. Although most business reports do not contain an index, you may on occasion be asked to provide one. Should you need to prepare an index, try to use a word processor that has a built-in indexing function to prepare the report. Or you may use an outlining program with a "sort" or alphabetize function to arrange index entries and subentries. If a computer program is not available, underscore the main words on each page. Then prepare a 3″ x 5″ card for each underscored word, indicating the page references. Arrange all the 3″ x 5″ cards in alphabetic order. Use "See" references and "See also" references, which refer the reader to different entries, sparingly.[1]

PAGINATION

Because it is possible for pages to become separated from a report and because page numbers serve as a point of reference, pages in informal reports and formal reports should be numbered.

Informal Reports   When an informal report exceeds one page, the second page and all succeeding pages should be numbered in unadorned Arabic numbers in the upper-right corner. Positioning should be uniform from the top of the paper—either 1 inch or 4 lines.

Formal Reports   Although page counting begins with the title fly page, it is not actually numbered; neither is the title page. Each of the other prefatory parts begins a new page and is numbered with lowercase Roman numerals. Number the first page of the report proper using Arabic number 1. Number consecutively the succeeding pages. Positioning of the numbers is described and illustrated in Chapter 17.

---

[1] For more information about preparing an index, refer to Harold Borko and Charles L. Bernier, *Indexing Concepts and Methods* (New York: Academic Press, 1978).

SUMMARY

Reports can be either informal or formal depending on how the information is expressed (writing style) and presented (format). Informal reports generally convey routine information and are presented in memorandum or letter form.

A memorandum report is used to convey routine information from one employee to another in the same organization. The letter report is an external means of conveying information between organizations.

Formal reports can be either short or long. A short formal report uses some—but generally not all—of the major divisions of a long formal report, such as prefatory parts, report proper, and supplementary parts. A long formal report is similar to the short formal report except in length. Although the organization of long formal reports may vary from one organization to another, formal reports have three major divisions: prefatory parts, report body, and supplementary parts. Each of these divisions contains several subdivisions.

Because it is possible for pages to become separated from a report and because page numbers serve as a point of reference, pages in informal reports and formal reports should be numbered.

EXERCISES

Review and Discussion Questions

1. What is the difference between informal and formal reports?
2. What is a memorandum report? Letter report?
3. What are the printed headings of memorandum reports?
4. The second-page heading of memorandum reports and letter reports should contain what information?
5. How does a letter report differ from a typical business letter?
6. What is the primary objective of a letter report?
7. What is the difference between short and long formal reports?
8. What are the three major divisions of formal reports?
9. What are the subdivisions of the prefatory parts? Body? Supplementary parts?
10. What is an abstract?

Problems and Applications

1. Obtain three reports from local businesses (or use the ones you obtained for Problem 1, Chapter 6) and analyze them. Are they informal or formal reports? Short or long? Why? Are they memo reports? Letter reports? Do the reports use headings? Are there

other significant features of the report? Submit the information in a memo report to your instructor.

2. In teams of two, interview a high ranking official of a local business. Call for an appointment and prepare a list of questions that you would like answered. Ask about the company's communication process, the importance of reports, kinds of reports written by the company employees. Are most of the reports written? Oral? Who writes the reports? How often? Does the company have a special format for reports? Headings? Ask other questions that you think would be of interest to the class. Prepare a written report to your instructor.

3. Solicit memorandum forms from local businesses and prepare a bulletin board display of them. As a class, discuss the differences and similarities.

4. From your school's business library, obtain a copy of a master's thesis or doctoral dissertation on a topic of your choice. Analyze the document. Does it have the three major divisions of a report? Do these divisions have subdivisions? Bring the document to class and share your findings with the class.

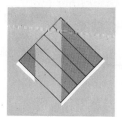

Common Types of
Reports

Although no two reports will be identical, some types of reports have become common because they have demonstrated their usefulness in solving certain kinds of recurring problems. These reports have more in common than they have differences. Regardless of type, a report should convey information quickly and clearly to a reader who needs the information to make a decision.

It would be virtually impossible to list all the types of reports used on a regular basis in business, industry, and the professions. In this chapter, we present a wide variety of the most common types. You will quickly see that these types are the logical result of applying the general considerations we've been discussing in the previous chapters to specific situations.

Topics

Proposals
Progress Reports
Justification Reports
Staff Reports
Feasibility Reports
Short Informational and Analytical Reports
Evaluations
Accident Reports
Annual Reports
Library Research Reports
Reports of Experimental Results
Audit Reports
Special Applications

How can you be
sure that you know
what your boss
expects?

When you begin working and writing reports for an organization, you
will need to discover exactly what your supervisor and others in the
organization expect to be included in specific reports. Even when your
boss uses the same descriptive word that we use here, she or he may
expect a report that either includes additional components or excludes
some of those we suggest. The only way to be sure that you are providing the right type of report is to ask. Nevertheless, you will undoubtedly
encounter the report types we present here, and in most cases they will
include the components we suggest.

PROPOSALS

Why do proposals
contain a
persuasive
element? Where is
it usually included?

Proposals are an increasingly common report form. In a proposal, the
writer offers to solve a problem for the reader in exchange for something. Because the writer will benefit if the reader accepts the proposal,
proposals—or more appropriately, cover letters accompanying them—
usually contain a persuasive element not found in other reports. Proposals, however, are legitimate reports; the information they contain
must be accurate, impartial, and complete.

Proposals may be requested by an organization with a problem, or
the writer may assume that an organization has a problem that he or she
is uniquely qualified to solve. A proposal and subsequent letter of
acceptance constitute a contract to perform certain work in a specified
way.

Solicited Proposals

Solicited proposals, those requested by an organization, are usually
widespread invitations to bid. In some cases, the organization will
expect the proposal to contain complete and accurate specifications on
the work to be done. In others, the organization wishes to receive a
possible solution or solutions to a problem and will wish to discuss spe-
cifics later. The request for proposals (RFP) may appear in business
journals or, for government work, in government publications. An organization might also request proposals from specific companies or individuals by mail. Typically, organizations or individuals wishing to submit a proposal in response to an ad in a journal will need to write for a
specific RFP. Many companies, especially those offering grant money,
and foundations have developed specific formats and procedures for
proposals, which you will need to follow exactly.

Occasionally, you may be asked to submit a proposal as a result of a
conversation you have had with an officer or agent of an organization.
More often, however, you will need to compete with others—perhaps a
great many others—who will also be submitting proposals. When you
receive a request to submit a proposal, you will need to study the invi-

tation carefully to determine whether you can solve the problem or meet the specifications as required. You will also need to determine whether you or your organization is better qualified to solve the problem than others who will probably be submitting proposals.

Solicited proposals often provide specific guidelines for completion, including requests for details about methodology, techniques, funding, and personnel. When an invitation to bid does not contain specific guidelines, use the pattern presented for unsolicited proposals.

Unsolicited Proposals

When you perceive a problem in an organization or industry that you are qualified to solve, you may send a letter of inquiry to determine interest or send your proposal and a letter of transmittal. When you do not have specific guidelines for preparing the proposal, include the following components:

Why should the introduction stress the benefit?

A Summarizing Introduction   The initial section may be the only part of your proposal your audience reads. For this reason it will need to demonstrate that you understand the problem, have a method to solve it, and have the ability to complete the necessary work. Give the reader an overview of the entire proposal, focusing on your objective and approach, your proposed solution, the benefit the audience would receive if you do the work, and the main reason you or your organization should do the work. Unless the problem and proposed solution are specifically technical, omit technical details from this section.

What is the reader's problem?

A Detailed Problem Statement   What is the problem? Both solicited and unsolicited proposals need to demonstrate that the writer understands the reader's problem. Your problem statement should include an accurate description of the problem itself and a description of the problems associated with solving that difficulty. What will you and the reader have to do to solve the problem, and what difficulties will you encounter as you work to solve the problem?

How will you solve the problem?

A Statement of Methodology   What will you do to solve the problem? How do you know it will work? Your reader will want to see proof that you know how to solve the problem. Have you conducted a preliminary investigation? Have you solved a similar problem previously? Place the results of research and descriptions of techniques in this section, and place documentation (questionnaires, computer printouts, calculations, or other statistical evidence) and other supporting details in an appendix.

Who will do the work?

A Project Management Statement   What will you do, when will you do it, how will you go about it, and how much will it cost? The reader will want you to be as specific as possible. If you and the reader are simply exploring possibilities, be specific about how you will conduct the preliminary investigation. Remember that your proposal is an offer to perform work, and once accepted, it will be legally binding. Give the reader specific dates and lists of materials and other resources. Clarify who will report to whom, and let the reader know how you will measure your progress and at what intervals you will report on your progress to your reader.

How will you measure progress?

Are you qualified to do the work?

A Statement of Your Qualifications   What makes you or your organization uniquely qualified to solve the reader's problem? When your qualifications are not already well-known to your audience, you will need to prove your credibility. What training and experience do you and the others involved have? What are your resources? What proof can you offer that you can perform the necessary work? Your reader will probably want to see the resumes of key personnel, so consider placing them in an appendix. Exhibit 8.1 illustrates a typical proposal.

PROGRESS REPORTS

What do progress reports describe?

A progress report is an informational report designed to inform the reader of the progress on a particular project over a particular time. Some projects may require only one or two progress reports. Others may call for a series of reports, the final one to be submitted upon completion of the project. Many periodic reports are essentially progress reports because they include information about the status of a project or activity. In some organizations, progress reports are referred to as status reports.

A progress report usually includes the following components:

1. Identification of the project and the time period covered
2. A summary of previous progress
3. A description of the progress during the time covered by this report, including
   a. Problems encountered and solved
   b. Problems not solved
   c. Explanations for any delays
4. A summary of the plans for completing the project, including significant dates

Progress reports vary in length from one-page summaries to book-length studies with many pages of statistical or technical information. The physical presentation of progress reports will naturally be influenced by the length, formality, and content of the report. See Exhibit 8.2 for a sample progress report.

Exhibit 8.1 **Proposal**

cover sheet form[a]

THE BIG BYTE EDUCATION FOUNDATION

20525 MaryAnn Avenue, Cupertino, CA 95014

GRANT PROPOSAL RECORD

Organization: Midwestern Business College	**Date:** May 15, 19xx
Address: Chicago, IL	

Responsible Officer for Contact: **Principal Investigator:** Robert Farentino, Ph.D.
     Dr. Albert Smith   **Address:** Department of Management
                                             Information Systems.
Address: Division of Sponsored Research   MBC, Chicago, IL
         Midwestern Business College

Phone:	**Value of Hardware Requests**	**Estimated Project Time (months):**
517-383-1907	$18,190	12 months

Programs and/or materials that would result from this project:

1. A unique set of algorithms for evaluating student writing, initially applied to business communication course content.

2. A workbook and series of diskettes comprising a CAI package for college-level instruction in business communication.

Project Abstract:

This project will create CAI materials to help teach concepts of business communication to undergraduate college and university students. The materials will benefit students by allowing them to develop required skills at their own rate in a nonthreatening atmosphere. They will benefit teachers by reducing the time required to evaluate student writing and by providing a logical, uniform basis for evaluating business letters and reports. The materials should also prove beneficial to those in business who wish to improve written communication skills.

Within each unit, the materials will proceed from simple (quizzes requiring recall only) to complex (message assembly from given components and message creation). A student may need to repeat material or may be rewarded for superior performance. Tutorials will be incorporated in a game structure to enhance motivation.

A unique set of algorithms for evaluating student writing will be developed and applied to business communication course content. The product will consist of (1) a student workbook containing instructions and problems, (2) a set of diskettes containing simulations and evaluative programming, (3) a user orientation and record keeping diskette, (4) an instructor's manual orienting teachers to the material, and (5) an instructor's diskette for profiling the class and evaluating student performance.

Dissemination of the materials will be through a commercial publishing house. The approximate market size is 500,000 business communication students a year.

[a]Many proposals must be completed on forms designed by the company requesting them. Note that the cover sheet for this proposal requests specific information and provides space for only an extremely brief summary. The letters used with the headings throughout the proposal refer to questions in the original request for proposal (RFP).

Exhibit 8.1   (*continued*)

A. HARDWARE BUDGET REQUEST

Qty.	Manufacturer's Name and Product Number	Product Name/Description	Item Cost	Total Cost
	All items manufactured by Big Byte.			
2	BB 2S1048	Super Big Byte Micro-Computers	$6,900	$13,900
2	BB 2M0044	40MB Internal Hard Drives	1,295	2,500
2	BB 2M0003	Developer's Tool Kits	895	1,790

Total Cost _____ $18,190 _____
Transfer Total Cost to Cover Sheet

Exhibit 8.1   *(continued)*

GRANT PROPOSAL

COMPUTER-ASSISTED INSTRUCTION IN BUSINESS COMMUNICATION

B. Project Objectives

1. College courses in business communication currently require instructors to spend excessive amounts of time grading papers, but also suffer from
a lack of uniformity in grading standards from instructor to instructor. A
CAI program in business communication would benefit students by allowing them
to develop required skills at their own rate in a nonthreatening atmosphere
and by providing consistent and predictable objectives. The program would be
adaptable to freshman composition, report writing, and technical writing
courses as well as to education and training programs in business and industry. The materials would also benefit teachers by allowing them to spend
less time evaluating written work and more time developing creative teaching
strategies and by helping establish uniform grading standards for written
business messages. We anticipate improving student performance and reducing
teacher-evaluated papers by 50% at the same time.

Current CAI materials in business communication and related areas are of
two types: simple drill and practice/tutorial programs (Atari) or sophisticated writing analysis programs (GMI's "star"). The first type is not well
suited to teaching the complex concepts of college-level writing. The second
does not include an instructional component and is not well suited to the
hardware available at most colleges and universities.

Our project will be the first to provide both instruction and evaluation
for written material in a form suitable for use on microcomputers.

The CAI package will use computer assisted testing, tutorials, and simulations (with the emphasis on simulations) to teach the concepts. The major
simulation used throughout the seven-unit package will be the student's
development from an entry-level employee to one of the senior officers of
a company. At each stage, the "employee" will be asked to write certain
types of business communication (e.g., positive, neutral, and negative
messages). Depending on how well the student does, the student could be
dropped back to a previous unit, given a PERK (e.g., car, salary increase),
or moved to a higher level position (the next unit). Point totals will be
kept so that some elements of a game are introduced into the package.

The tutorials will be written as simulations. For example, in preparing
a negative response letter, the student will be asked to assemble a message
from a numbered set of sentences. The computer will then evaluate content
and structure of the letter based on variance from an optimal letter.

A special algorithm will evaluate letters composed by students in response
to problems posed in the manual. This algorithm will evaluate for writing
style, correctness, and message structure. It will offer many of the features
included in more complex programs without requiring an extensive internal
memory.

(continued)

Exhibit 8.1   *(continued)*

2. The product will consist of a workbook (containing instructions, information needed to understand the simulations, and problems) and a set of diskettes (containing quiz materials, PERK information, and evaluations). The package will also contain a diskette for user orientation and record keeping and a teacher's diskette, which will provide a profile of class progress.

The initial program will be designed especially for the nearly 500,000 college students who take a business communication course each year. Subsequent programs will address the needs of education and training programs in business, report writing, and English composition.

3. The workbook and diskettes will be published and marketed by a commercial publisher of college textbooks.

C. The Development Plan

1. The development of this package will follow a standard systems approach as espoused by W. J. Dick (see Bibliography). A set of goals and objectives has been written and mockups of standards are being constructed to enable the content experts to visualize a completed unit. When a microcomputer becomes available, a prototype unit (or prototype sections of units) will be developed. This prototype will be evaluated for its ability to teach, for its ease of use, and for its ability to motivate students. Results of this evaluation will be incorporated into a fully developed pilot version of the package. Again, a formative evaluation will be performed on this version, measuring the same characteristics as for the prototype. Additional evaluation will compare the CAI exercises with "standard" exercises used in classes at MBC. Finally, a production version of this package will be developed incorporating the results of the pilot version evaluation and a final evaluation will be performed.

2. Robert Farentino, Ph.D.   10 hours a week
   Caroline Phillips, Ed.D   10 hours a week
   Melanie Schlosser, Ph.D.   10 hours a week
   Scott Steele, Ph.D.   10 hours a week
   Brenda Winter (Ph.D. candidate)   10 hours a week

3. Assuming we receive equipment in time, we anticipate presenting a complete pilot version at the International Convention of the American Business Communication Association in October 19xx in New York City. Our time table is as follows:

Times (in months)

	1	2	3	4	5	6	7	8	9	10	11	12
Mockup	⊢—⊣											
Prototype	⊢——⊣											
Evaluation		⊢——⊣										
Pilot		⊢———⊣									
Evaluation				⊢——⊣							
Product				⊢————⊣					
Evaluation						⊢—⊣		

Exhibit 8.1   *(continued)*

4. Developmental Flow Chart

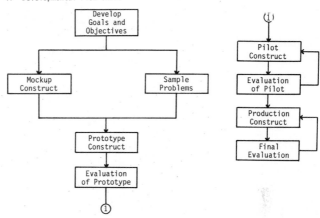

D. Equipment Justification

The equipment listed in A is the minimum necessary for creating and evaluating the materials. Because evaluation at prototype and pilot stages is essential to the software development, two systems are necessary to permit a sufficient number of students to complete testing procedures.

E. Available Facilities

The Department of Management Information Systems, Midwestern Business College, Chicago, IL 60055, will make office space available for the equipment.

The Department will provide access to appropriate utilities for operation of the equipment, and maintenance is available locally through The Computer Room, 455 N. Michigan, Chicago, IL 60657.

F. Evaluation Procedures

As stated in C1, the development plan includes several evaluative components. In addition, The Dryden Press will conduct a market survey and arrange for outside agencies to test and evaluate the program at prototype and pilot stages.

(continued)

Exhibit 8.1   (*continued*)

```
        G.  Background Information

            1.  Resumes of key personnel are attached.
            2.  A bibliography of key articles is attached.
            3.  A description of Midwestern Business College is attached.
            4.  The required letter of approval is attached.
            _____
            Attachments omitted to save space.
```

JUSTIFICATION REPORTS

Why are
justification reports
also called
unsolicited
recommendation
reports?

Justification reports, a special form of recommendation report, are another report form that contains a persuasive element. Unlike proposals, which are written from one individual or organization to another, justification reports remain within the writer's organization.

Typical recommendation reports are written when management has observed a problem (perhaps one previously mentioned in an informational report) and has requested a recommendation. Justification reports are unsolicited recommendation reports.

The writer initiates a justification report when she or he observes a problem and wishes to recommend a solution. Many companies have established specific formats and guidelines for unsolicited recommendation reports. In the absence of such guidelines, be sure to cover the following topics:

1. **Purpose.** What are you recommending? What problem will your recommendation solve?

2. **Advantages.** What will your organization gain if your recommendation is accepted? Be specific about costs (initial and continuing) and savings.

3. **Method.** How will you implement your recommendation? What procedures will you use?

4. **Conclusions.** How do you know that your recommendations will result in the anticipated savings? The conclusions should *justify* the recommendation.

5. **Discussion.** Amplify the preceding sections by including information about the history of the problem, previous attempts to

Exhibit 8.2   **Progress Report**

Brown and Bacon Construction
1591 Duxbury Boulevard
Charleston, WV 25306

June 23, 19xx

TO: Arnold Eisenberg, Project Manager

FROM: Anne Houck, Supervisor *ah*

SUBJECT: Restoration of Heritage Hall

time period
covered[a]

This report covers the period from June 7, when the restoration of Heritage
Hall began, to June 21.

Crew Hired

Hideyoshi Musashi, Robert Wallechinsky, and I arrived in Richmond, VA, on
June 6. We spent June 7, 8, and 9 hiring the carpenters, plumbers, and
electricians needed to begin the process of restoration.

Work Completed

Exterior work is proceeding on schedule. The eaves have all been replaced,
and the carpenters have begun replacing the rotten wood on the north side.
Three (of 27) windows have been replaced with double-glazed replicas.

All of the plumbing will need to be replaced. New fixtures have been
installed in the upstairs bath, and the main drainage pipes are in place.

The electricians have installed the new panel and have completed rewiring
the kitchen.

Problems Encountered

I have not been able to hire someone qualified to restore the marble stairway. Your original suggestion to use Leonardo Di Salvo from Milan, Italy,
may prove the most economical solution.

As usual with restorations of buildings as old as Heritage Hall, most walls
are out of plumb. We are restoring plumb where possible and custom fitting
when necessary.

Work Scheduled

The plumbers are working on installing the supply lines and water heater.
Tomorrow they will install the new fixtures in the downstairs bath.

[a]If the subject line or a special "period covered" line does not specify the time covered by the
report, the first sentence should do so.

(*continued*)

Exhibit 8.2   (*continued*)

Arnold Eisenberg   June 23, 19xx   2

None of the old wiring (installed between 1927 and 1934) is reusable. In
most cases, we will be able to pull the new wire through the existing conduit.
Several rooms will require additional wiring.

Except for the construction required for the new marble stairway, we expect
to be through with the rough work by August 1, two weeks ahead of schedule.
If we encounter no additional difficulties, I will begin hiring painters the
first week in August. We should begin the process of stripping and refin-
ishing by the tenth.

directive for
further action[b]

Please check once more on the availability of craftsmen qualified to restore
the stairway. If we are to remain on schedule, we will need to begin work
on the stairway by August 20.

[b]In addition to reporting on what was accomplished, problems encountered, and plans for
completing the project, a progress report should let the reader know if he or she needs to take any
action.

solve it, alternative solutions, and secondary benefits that might
result.

Exhibit 8.3 illustrates a justification report.

STAFF REPORTS

Although the term staff report may be applied to almost any report a
supervisor's staff produces for him or her, it is most often used to indicate a recommendation report requested by a supervisor or manager.
Length, format, and components of staff reports will vary widely
depending on the situation. Exhibit 8.4 illustrates one possibility.

FEASIBILITY REPORTS

What types of
questions do
feasibility reports
usually answer?

A feasibility report is designed to answer questions about the possibility
and desirability of undertaking a particular course of action. It may be
simply interpretive (presenting and explaining the data) or analytical
(including conclusions and recommendations).

Feasibility reports are usually preliminary investigations designed to

Exhibit 8.3   **Justification Report**

PC Form 30–30
Rev 4–80

Parker Corporation
Interoffice Correspondence

TO: Alice Ferrick   **Copies To:**

FROM: Donald Persing

DATE: October 14, 19xx

SUBJECT: Purchase of a Comp 600 Phototypesetter

recommension[a]

I recommend that we purchase a Comp 600 phototypesetter for use in the
Communications Department. A Comp 600 will save Parker approximately $2,500
a month in fees to outside suppliers. The initial investment of $32,500
would be recovered in less than 15 months.

Cost and Savings

The purchase cost of a Comp 600 is $32,500. The annual service contract is
$1,200, and typical costs for supplies will amount to $2,300 a month. The
Comp 600 will allow us to do in-house all the artwork currently being sent
to outside suppliers. Appendix A* lists the art projects completed over the
past quarter and shows fees paid and estimated labor and supplies costs for the
Comp 600. The mean figures are as follows:

		Comp 600	
Supplier Fee (Paid)	Labor		Supplies
	1 1/2 hours ($32)		$145
$630		$177	

As we have between four and seven projects each month requiring art, the Comp
600 should easily be able to save us $2,500 a month. That saving, plus the
investment tax credit and standard depreciation, should make the Comp 600 a
good investment.

Procedure

Because the Comp 600 does represent a substantial investment, I recommend
that we initially lease with the option of buying. A three-month lease will
cost $2,700, all of which will be applicable to the purchase price if we
decide to purchase before 90 days expire.

The lease period would allow us to obtain a more accurate fix on costs and
would also permit us to evaluate the versatility and quality of work of the
Comp 600.

---
*Appendixes omitted to save space.

[a]Whenever your recommendation is the most important part of your report, consider putting it in the
first sentence. Delay making your recommendation only when the reader would react negatively to it
unless you provide good reasons to support it first.

(*continued*)

Exhibit 8.3   *(continued)*

Alice Ferrick   October 14, 19xx   2

<u>Conclusions</u>

Should the Comp 600 perform as expected, Parker could save $30,000 a year and have better control over the production of artwork .

<u>Discussion</u>

The Comp 600 phototypesetter is a quality piece of equipment manufactured by Redkey Printing and Electronics. Appendix B contains Redkey's descriptive brochure, and Appendix C is a letter I received about the Comp 600 from Terry McDonald, Vice President of Corporate Communications, Beta-Naught, Inc.

Installation of the equipment could take place three weeks after we sign the lease-to-buy agreement. Redkey will provide 15 hours of instruction covering operation and routine maintenance for three employees. I suggested that David Winesoup be placed in charge of the Comp 600, with Sally Meyers and Roger Bently also being trained to use it.

---

answer questions about *whether* an action would be possible or desirable rather than about *how* an objective should be accomplished. A feasibility report will provide the direction for continued exploration of the problem or experimentation with possible solutions. Exhibit 8.5 shows an example of a feasibility report.

SHORT INFORMATIONAL AND ANALYTICAL REPORTS

How may short, informal reports differ from long reports?

Short reports are far more common in business than long reports. In general, the length of a report is directly related to the complexity of the problem. As the problem becomes more complex, the coverage of it necessarily becomes more complex and detailed. Short reports, whether informational or analytical, are usually (though not always) less formal than long reports.

Because they are shorter and less formal, they often omit many of the preliminary and supplemental parts included in formal reports. They will also require fewer levels of headings and may eliminate introductions and summaries. Although each short report will have different requirements depending on the situation and context, consider making the following changes in presentation form as the report becomes shorter and less formal.

Exhibit 8.4 | **Staff Report**

specialized format[a]

DATE: August 2, 19xx

SUBJECT: P.C. #12-79-22, Park-Emerson Rezoning

APPLICANT: Stanley G. Hagarty

OWNERS: James S. Gilley, Jr. & Hoyt L. Pitrim

LOCATION: East side of South Park Street, generally between Emerson
                   and Maple Streets

CURRENT ZONING: Zone 6 (Apartment-Hotel District) and
                   Zone 7 (Dwelling-Apartment District)

PETITIONED
ZONING: Zone 5A (Professional Office District)

ACREAGE: 1.9+ acres

SURROUNDING
ZONING: North--Zone 6
                   South--Zone 6 and 7
                   East --Zone 7
                   West --Zone 4

SURROUNDING
LAND USE: North--Single-Family Homes & Vacant Land
                   South--Vacant Land
                   East --Single-Family Homes & Vacant Land
                   West --Commercial Uses

CURRENT LAND
USE OF SUBJECT
PARCEL: Vacant Land

LAND USE PLAN
RECOMMENDATION: Residential Low Density

ZONING HISTORY: The Subject Parcels have been Zone 6 and 7 since 1954.

INTENT OF
APPLICANT: To construct offices on the subject site.

STAFF RECOM-
MENDATIONS: The Planning Division recommends approval of the request from
                   Zone 6 to Zone 5A, excepting the parcel located in Zone 7
                   fronting Park Street for the following reasons:

                   1. Low Density Residential Land Use as recommended in the
                       Land Use Plan would not be reasonable for this site in
                       terms of traffic noise generated by South Park Street.
                       It is not likely that single-family or low density resi-
                       dential development would locate on this particular site
                       due to the size of the site.

[a]Note the specialized format. The readers of this report would be familiar with the format and would appreciate being able to find essential information quickly and easily. Note also that the discussion follows the recommendations so that only those readers who are concerned about the rationale for the recommendations need to read the supporting reasons.

(*continued*)

Exhibit 8.4   *(continued)*

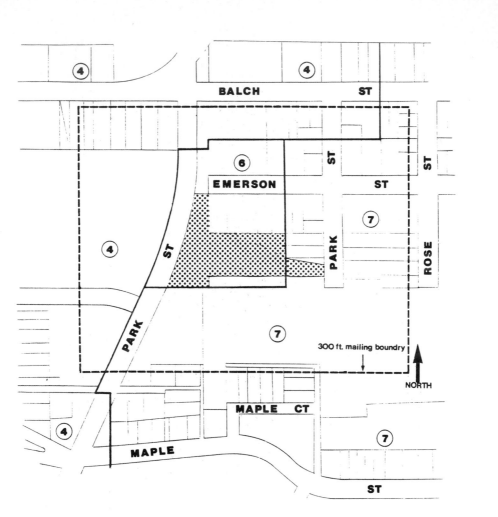

AREA REQUESTED FROM ZONE 6 & 7 to ZONE 5A

Park Street Rezoning

12-79-22

Exhibit 8.4   (*continued*)

2

2. Conditions have changed in the area since 1954 when Zones
    6 and 7 were designated as the appropriate zoning dis-
    tricts. In terms of change, Park Street was widened from
    2 to 4 lanes and the Jewel-Osco shopping center was con-
    structed directly west of the subject parcel. Little or
    no residential housing has developed in this area since
    1954.

3. The uses permitted in Zone 5A would be reasonable for
    this particular site and would not adversely affect the
    area or existing neighborhood. Zone 5A uses are low
    intensity type uses and would not have an impact on
    the adjacent area.

4. Zone 5A would provide a transition between Park Street
    and the neighborhood to the east and north.

5. The City of Randolph currently has a very low vacancy
    rate for existing office space. The Randolph Gazette
    reported in an article on July 15, 19xx, that the current
    vacancy rate is between 1 and 2 percent.

6. The subject site is adjacent to the Crosstown Commercial
    node. The Comprehensive Plan indicates that this node
    should be maintained as a community shopping center/office
    park area; however, Limited Commercial (office use) is the
    most reasonable use for this particular site.

7. We further recommend that the existing Zone 7 parcel
    fronting on Park Street remain in Zone 7.

Step 1: Omit the title fly.
Omit the letter of authorization.
Include the synopsis within the letter of transmittal.

Step 2: Omit the table of contents.
Omit the letter of transmittal, and provide the synopsis in the
introductory paragraph.

Step 3: Use letter or memo format (which eliminates the title page).

Exhibit 8.6 illustrates a short analytical report.

EVALUATIONS

Procedures, products, projects, and people all must undergo occasional
evaluations. Someone with expertise in a given area will be asked to
report on the adequacy of something or somebody to perform a given
job.

Exhibit 8.5   Feasibility Report in Personalized Letter Format

Pro-Ease Communications

19 Kalona Avenue
Des Moines, IA 50312
344-5555

January 27, 19xx

Mr. Scott Perrin, President
Perrin and Associates
2020 Johnston Road
Des Moines, IA 50324

personalized
opening[a]

Yes, Mr. Perrin,

It would be possible to install a satellite antenna system on top of the Perrin Bank Building.

The installation, however, would not be easy. Because both installation and maintenance of any of our satellite antenna systems require easy access, the current stairwell would need to be remodeled, and the 8-foot vertical ladder should be eliminated and replaced with conventional stairs. Further, access to the stairway should not be through the vice presidents' office complex.

I believe these alterations are necessary if you are to obtain full use of and satisfaction from your own satellite antenna.

Should you decide to pursue installation, I will be glad to work with the contractor of your choice in preparing your building for the antenna.

personalized
closing[b]

Give me a call.

Howard Severson, Jr.

Howard Severson, Jr.
President

[a]Personalized letter format omits the salutation but uses the reader's name in a brief opening phrase that simulates the appearance of the salutation. Some people consider this style friendlier than the traditional, ''Dear Mr. Perrin.''

[b]The personalized format also omits the complimentary close, substituting a brief, appropriate phrase.

Exhibit 8.6   **Short Analytical Report**

title page

ADDING LIGHT-GAUGE PREFINISHED
FRAMES TO CURRENT LINE

Prepared for

Norman R. Menning, President
Sanders Steel Company
Fairview, New Jersey 08606

Prepared by

Andrea Brody
Central Marketing Group
Detroit, Michigan 48014

September 12, 19xx

(*continued*)

Exhibit 8.6   (*continued*)

letter of transmittal

Central Marketing Group
1904 Gasoline Alley
Detroit, MI 48014
313/555-1000

September 12, 19xx

Mr. Norman R. Menning, President
Sanders Steel Company
4000 Manhattan Road
Fairview, NJ 08606

Dear Mr. Menning:

Here is the report you requested on June 22 assessing the potential of a light-gauge (18-22) prefinished steel door frame to supplement your current line of heavy-duty frames.

I recommend that Sanders either begin producing the light-gauge steel frames or acquire a manufacturing facility currently producing them.

Our study reveals that light-gauge prefinished frames are gaining market share, especially on the West Coast and in Florida and Georgia. The market for the lighter frames is already extensive, and it seems to be growing as well, as prefinished steel frames are replacing conventional door frames in many construction markets.

The light-gauge prefinished steel door frames are as functional and long lasting as conventional frames; plus they offer lower price, ease of installation, a variety of colors, and years of maintenance-free operation.

I have enjoyed preparing this report, Mr. Menning. Please let me know when I can help again.

Sincerely,

Andrea Brody

Andrea Brody
Market Researcher

enc

Exhibit 8.6   *(continued)*

recommendation

ADDING LIGHT-GAUGE PREFINISHED
FRAMES TO CURRENT LINE

    I recommend that the Sanders Steel Company either begin manu-
facturing light-gauge (18-22) prefinished steel door frames or
acquire a manufacturing facility currently producing them.

    This report is the result of a study authorized on June 22,
19xx, by Norman R. Menning, President of Sanders Steel Company.

Purpose and Scope

    As a result of loss of market share, especially on the West
Coast, Sanders Steel Company hired Central Marketing Group to
study the current and future impact of light-gauge prefinished
steel door frames on several construction markets. The objectives of the study were to identify and define:

    ◆ Market size.
    ◆ Product features desired.
    ◆ Principal producers.
    ◆ Major end-use markets.
    ◆ Representative prices.
    ◆ Future trends in product use.

    The scope of the study did not include a detailed explanation
of market size and trends for conventional, heavy-gauge (14, 16,
and 18) unfinished steel door frames.

Methodology

    A sample of 600 door frame distributors was selected to
include an equal number of dealers handling Sanders conventional
frames and those handling the light-gauge prefinished frames only.
State populations and predicted growth rates were used to determine the number of dealers selected from each state. Table 1,
Appendix A,* shows the breakdown by geographic area.

    I mailed questionnaires to the dealers on July 15 and began
phoning those who had not responded on August 15. By September 1,
I had received complete information from 372 dealers, an ample
number on which to base predictions.

----
*Appendix material omitted to save space.

(continued)

Exhibit 8.6   *(continued)*

brief summary

2

    I tabulated each question by geographic region, distributor status, frame types handled, and dollar volume of sales of prefinished light-gauge and conventional frames. The questionnaire and tabulations are presented in Appendix B.

<u>Findings</u>

    The questionnaire revealed the following facts about the dealers and the market for light-gauge steel prefinished door frames:

1. The survey revealed that 87.2 percent of the dealers stock both conventional and light-gauge steel door frames. Only those dealers who do not stock wood doors carry the conventional frames only.

2. The average dealer has a sales volume of $182,000 a year, with approximately 17 percent accounted for by steel door frames of all types.

3. Those dealers handling both types of door frames reported that the light frames accounted for 23 percent of their door frame sales.

4. A majority (67 percent) of the dealers prefer handling the light-gauge prefinished steel frames. The features most often cited were price, ease of installation, absence of maintenance, colors, and availability.

5. The average cost of a prefinished frame to a dealer is $23.47. The selling price to contractors is $33.39, which provides a markup of 42 percent. The cost to dealers for prefinished steel with a high quality door is 5 percent less than the cost of a prehung wood unit.

6. Office buildings and high-rise apartment buildings are the most common end-use application.

7. Residential use has increased by 12 percent each year since 1979 in spite of the housing slump caused by the recession.

8. Increased urbanization and the continual increasing costs of wood and the labor associated with wood products will ensure a growth market for light-gauge steel prefinished doors.

<u>Producers</u>

    The two largest producers of light-gauge prefinished steel doors are Barnes (Sunnyvale, CA) and Advance (Dallas, TX), with 38.6 percent and 29.5 percent of the market, respectively.

Exhibit 8.6   *(continued)*

positive closing

```
                                                                    3

                              Conclusions

          Based on the sample, I conclude that total sales of conven-
     tional and prefinished frames will amount to $5.6 million.  Of
     this, prefinished frames will account for close to $2 million.

          Dealers uniformly predicted that increased urban construc-
     tion consisting of high density housing and office complexes
     would increase the demand for light-gauge prefinished steel
     door frames.  Statistics compiled by the Federal Government
     and such publications as Predicasts support dealer predictions
     (see Appendix C).

          Dealers currently carrying Sanders conventional steel frames
     indicated that they would prefer stocking prefinished frames
     manufactured by Sanders rather than the brand they now carry.

                            Recommendations

          Sanders should begin producing light-gauge prefinished steel
     frames or acquire a facility currently manufacturing such frames.
```

complete title repeated

Procedures, Products, and Projects

Evaluations of procedures, products, and projects are almost always analytical reports in which the writer, because of her or his experience in an area, examines the procedure or item in question and renders an opinion about its adequacy. Recommendations for changes or improvements are usually included as well.

A company might, for example, hire a consultant to evaluate its computer system to determine whether a new system would be a good investment. Or an organization might hire a time-and-motion specialist to evaluate work flow within a plant. The length and formality of evaluation reports will vary according to the situation and people involved. Exhibit 8.7 illustrates an evaluation of a product.

Personnel

Nearly everyone who works in an organization is evaluated on a regular basis. Most organizations provide forms to help managers be complete and objective. While the topics covered by the form will vary from organization to organization and from occupation to occupation, most cover the following areas:

- Knowledge of job duties/responsibilities
- Quality of work

Exhibit 8.7   **Evaluation of a Product**

February 11, 19xx

TO: Mort Wetherspoon
            Bill Warren
            Lee Rauch
            Duane Kohr

FROM: Mark Schadlein

ARTIC BONE REMOVER/GRINDER EVALUATION

On February 6, 19xx, testing of the Artic bone remover/grinder
was concluded. The decision was made to return the unit to
Artic. Its bone removing capabilities were inferior to the
Weiler system currently in use.

Testing included evaluation of product quality, grinding rates,
and bone removing capabilities. Tests were conducted at Toledo
on January 22, 23, and February 6.

Results

On January 22, approximately 500 pounds of meat were ground
through the Artic. Grinding rate and finished product were
determined acceptable by Toledo Quality Control personnel and
me.

On January 23 and February 6, comparisons were made between the
Artic bone remover/grinder and the Weiler bone remover/ grinder.
On each testing date 6,000 pounds of meat were ground through
both the Artic and Weiler grinders. "Like" preblends were used
in each test situation. On January 23, ejected material flow
rates were set at 8#/1000# on each system. This was done in an
effort to minimize processing variables and obtain a comparison
strictly on bone removing capabilities. Results from this
testing showed that the Weiler system removed more bone than
the Artic.

On February 6, a similar test was conducted. For this test,
however, the Weiler ejected material flow rate was set at
8#/1000# and the Artic flow rate was set at 2#/1000#, the
recommended setting for the Artic. Again, the Weiler system
proved superior in bone removal. The following table summarizes
the Artic evaluation.

Exhibit 8.7   (*continued*)

```
ARTIC BONE REMOVER/GRINDER EVALUATION
Page 2
February 11, 19xx
```

Date	Grinder	Preblends	Grinding Rate (lbs./minute)	Ejected Material Flowchart	Avg. Bone Removed (grams/1000# ground)
1/23	Weiler	3YL 0018 03 3XF 0021 04	350*	8#/1000#	4.8
	Artic	3YL 0018 03 3XF 0021 04	480	8#/1000#	0.5
2/6	Weiler	3YL 0032 07 3XF 0032 05	350*	8#/1000#	9.4
	Artic	3YL 0032 07 3XF 0032 05	495	2#/1000#	0.5

*Typical grinding rate for Weiler grinders at Toledo.

Conclusions

The Artic bone remover/grinder is an impressive piece of machinery. It can produce a quality product (from an appearance standpoint) at a high grinding rate. Within Eckrich processing parameters, however, its bone removing capabilities are inferior to those of the Weiler system.

Further testing in bone and gristle reduction will concentrate on the 1/2-inch grind size of the 3YL lean preblend.

If you have any questions, please let me know.

bme

- Quantity of work
- Reliability
- Ability to follow instructions
- Initiative
- Attitude toward work, others, and the organization
- Promotability

If you ever need to evaluate a subordinate without a form, use the categories above as headings and provide objective and specific comments for each area. Examples showing strengths and weaknesses in each area are helpful. Memo format would be appropriate in most organizations. Exhibit 8.8 illustrates a form for evaluating an employee.

Exhibit 8.8   Report Form for Evaluating an Employee

BORROUGHS
A DIVISION OF LEAR SIEGLER, INC.
3002 N. BURDICK STREET · KALAMAZOO, MICHIGAN 49007

PERFORMANCE
APPRAISAL
INTERVIEW

MANAGEMENT
PERSONNEL

Employee Name: _____

Position: _____

Date: _____   Review Period: _____

Date of Interview: _____

Appraiser: _____

Employee Signature: _____

Source: Form courtesy of Borroughs Manufacturing Co.

Exhibit 8.8   *(continued)*

INSTRUCTIONS TO APPRAISER
AND APPRAISEE:

The appraisal you are about to record and discuss is intended to be a summarization of supervisory judgments about performance - that is, about how work is achieved rather than about quantitative results as such. The appraisal process is intended to result in: (1) a clear understanding of how performance is judged, and (2) mutually understood goals and plans about any changes in future work performance and/or change in duties.

The appraisal is a result of judgments, not of measurements. Therefore, the appraisal judgments should be viewed as approximations rather than as precise numbers even though numbers are used in the scales for convenience in locating or representing judgments made.

RATING LEVELS

OUTSTANDING (9 - 10):   Exceptional, superior, near perfect.

EXCELLENT (7 - 8):   Considerably above average.

SATISFACTORY (5 - 6):   Meeting acceptable standards.

LESS THAN SATISFACTORY (3 - 4):   Not quite meeting acceptable standards.

NOT ACCEPTABLE (1 - 2):   Serious deficiency.

N. A.:   Not applicable.

(continued)

Exhibit 8.8   *(continued)*

PERFORMANCE FACTORS

	RATING LEVELS
COMMUNICATION: Expressing points of view and information clearly and concisely in written and oral forms.	0 .. / .. / .. / .. / .. / .. / . . / . . / . . / . . 10
CONTROL: Effective use of assigned people, equipment and staff while meeting cost and quality standards.	0 .. / .. / .. / .. / .. / .. / . . / . . / . . / . . 10
DECISION-MAKING: Screening facts and making sound, timely decisions.	0 .. / .. / .. / .. / .. / .. / . . / . . / . . / . . 10
DELEGATION: Assigning work and authority appropriately to others with appropriate follow-up.	0 .. / .. / .. / .. / .. / .. / . . / . . / . . / . . 10
DEVELOPMENT OF PERSONNEL: Effectively selecting, counseling and training subordinates, collaborating in plans for their professional and personal growth.	0 .. / .. / .. / .. / .. / .. / . . / . . / . . / . . 10
PLANNING: Arranging work systematically and in practical ways, establishing priorities for efficiency.	0 .. / .. / .. / .. / .. / .. / . . / . . / . . / . . 10
PROBLEM ANALYSIS: Breaking problem tasks or situations into essential components logically and system- atically, gathering facts and evaluating them accurately.	0 .. / .. / .. / .. / .. / .. / . . / . . / . . / . . 10
QUALITY OF WORK: Thoroughness, accuracy and overall caliber of completed work.	0 .. / .. / .. / .. / .. / .. / . . / . . / . . / . . 10
QUANTITY OF WORK: Accomplishments in relation to requirements; results in relation to objectives and timeliness.	0 .. / .. / .. / .. / .. / .. / . . / . . / . . / . . 10

Exhibit 8.8   (*continued*)

PERSONAL FACTORS

ABILITY TO WORK WITH OTHERS: RATING LEVELS
Establishing and maintaining productive
working relationships with others.   0 . . / . . / . . / . . / . . / . . / . . / . . / . . / . . / . . 10

ADAPTABILITY:
Reaction to change while working
towards desired results.   0 . . / . . / . . / . . / . . / . . / . . / . . / . . / . . / . . 10

ATTITUDE:
Commitment to and concern about
company doing well.   0 . . / . . / . . / . . / . . / . . / . . / . . / . . / . . / . . 10

CREATIVITY:
Ability to devise improved or new
procedures or applications in pursuit
of new results.   0 . . / . . / . . / . . / . . / . . / . . / . . / . . / . . / . . 10

INITIATIVE:
Self-starting in dealing with work tasks
or problems.   0 . . / . . / . . / . . / . . / . . / . . / . . / . . / . . / . . 10

JUDGMENT:
Identification and evaluation of alternative courses of action towards desired
results.   0 . . / . . / . . / . . / . . / . . / . . / . . / . . / . . / . . 10

LEADERSHIP:
Influencing subordinates and associates
toward accomplishment of desired results.   0 . . / . . / . . / . . / . . / . . / . . / . . / . . / . . / . . 10

PERSISTENCE:
Pursuit of progress towards results even when
encountering lack of interest and/or
opposition.   0 . . / . , / . . / . . / . . / . . / . . / . . / . . / . . / . . 10

PERSUASIVENESS:
Influencing behavior changes on the part
of other people.   0 . . / . . / . . / . . / . . / . . / . . / . . / . . / . . / . . 10

SELF-CONFIDENCE:
Self-assuredness, including under pressure;
sense of personal competence.   0 . . / . . / . . / . . / . . / . . / . . / . . / . . / . . / . . 10

SELF-DEVELOPMENT:
Accomplishing self-improvement with goals.   0 . . / . . / . . / . . / . . / . . / . . / . . / . . / . . / . . 10

(*continued*)

Exhibit 8.8   (*continued*)

CONCLUSIONS: This section is intended as a vehicle for summarizing the results of the appraisal process overall.

SIGNIFICANT MAJOR ACCOMPLISHMENTS is intended as an opportunity for the supervisor to highlight particular accomplishments by the employee which may not be visible on the Factor ratings. Here there might be elaboration of the accomplishments referred to in any given Factor rating so as to amplify the meaning of the rating given.

DEVELOPMENTS OR IMPROVEMENTS SINCE LAST REVIEW should be used to call attention to Factor ratings which reflect particularly noteworthy changes in performance since the last review. Comments about the extent to which the individual may have (or has not) achieved developmental goals and objectives set previously may also be included here.

DEVELOPMENT GOALS AND PLANS is where statements of what the employee is going to try to do more or less of, in some particular behavior, as referred to in any of the Factor ratings. Please try to be specific about what behavior is being focused on for change.

CAREER ADVANCEMENT POTENTIAL should include any comments about this aspect of the employee's future career as viewed by either employee and/or supervisor. This is a very sensitive topic and should be addressed with appropriate care to be realistic yet try to avoid encouraging or discouraging an employee to excess.

LIKELY REPLACEMENTS is intended to contain a list of other specific positions within the company from which the employee's position could realistically be filled, as viewed by both supervisor and employee.

OVERALL PERFORMANCE RATING should contain reference to the employee's performance as generally being classified as Outstanding, Excellent, Satisfactory, Less Than Satisfactory, or Not Acceptable, along with any appropriate elaborative remarks deemed relevant by the supervisor.

Exhibit 8.8   *(continued)*

<u>CONCLUSIONS</u>

SIGNIFICANT MAJOR ACCOMPLISHMENTS:

_____

_____

_____

_____

DEVELOPMENTS OR IMPROVEMENTS SINCE LAST REVIEW:

_____

_____

_____

_____

DEVELOPMENT GOALS AND PLANS:

_____

_____

_____

_____

CAREER ADVANCEMENT POTENTIAL:

Employee Views: _____

_____

_____

Supervisor Views: _____

_____

_____

(continued)

Exhibit 8.8   *(continued)*

LIKELY REPLACEMENTS:

_____

_____

_____

_____

OVERALL PERFORMANCE RATING:

_____

_____

_____

_____

OVERALL COMMENTS:

Supervisor:_____

_____

_____

_____

Employee:_____

_____

_____

_____

ACCIDENT REPORTS

What are the two basic requirements for an accident report?

Most organizations have specific forms for use in reporting accidents. Because accidents, especially those involving serious injury, are traumatic, the forms can be an important aid to objectivity. Accuracy and objectivity are the two critical requirements for accident reports.

When you must report an accident and you do not have a form, be sure to cover the reporter's six "serving men":

Who: Who was involved? Who else might have observed the accident? Who might have had difficulties with any equipment involved previously? Who was notified first?

What: What actually happened? What equipment was involved? What events immediately preceded the accident?

Where: Where did the accident happen? Where were the people involved immediately before the accident occurred? Where were they afterward?

When: At what time did the accident occur? In what order did events take place? How long did it take for help to arrive?

Why: Why did the accident happen? What seemed to be the cause of the accident?

How: How did one thing lead to another? How could similar accidents be avoided?

Exhibit 8.9 illustrates a typical accident report.

ANNUAL REPORTS

Individuals, departments (and other divisions), and organizations are usually required to prepare annual reports. Annual reports are essentially informational progress reports that provide a record of activities over a given time. They may include budget or other financial statements, and they may include plans for the next reporting period.

Why are annual reports said to serve a public relations function?

Individuals and departments usually report according to objectives set and met, including explanations for those objectives not met and statements of progress on long-term objectives. Both individuals and departments may need to account for expenditures; departments also would need to account for changes in personnel, equipment, or operating procedures.

Most organizations also prepare annual reports that present information about the status of the organization to interested parties. Personnel, equipment, procedures, financial data (assets, liabilities, income, expenditures, projected income, and projected.expenditures), and other details influencing the organization should all be included. Length and format vary greatly from organization to organization. Churches, for example, might provide parishioners with an inexpensively reproduced report only a few pages long containing news of members, donations to charities, work on the church, and the like. A Fortune 500 company, on the other hand, would prepare an impressive package of accomplishments, plans, and financial status.

Exhibit 8.9   Accident Report

SANDERS STEEL COMPANY
Fairview, New Jersey 08606

ACCIDENT REPORT

1. Type of Accident: Personal injury. Hand caught in metal press.

2. Date and Time Accident Occurred: December 15, 19xx, at 2:00 p.m.

3. Personnel Involved: Charles Marczynski

4. Witnesses: None

5. Details: Marczynski was cleaning the press when the brake slipped, and his hand was caught between the ram and the table.

6. Cause of Accident: Human error caused the accident even if the brake is defective. The operation manual specified that the press must be turned off for cleaning.

7. Medical Disposition: Marczynski is in the hospital. He will lose at least three fingers and will be unable to work for at least six months.

8. Recommendations: New warning labels should be installed on all presses to remind operators to turn presses off before cleaning.

LIBRARY RESEARCH REPORTS

All complete analytical reports begin with a review of secondary sources. If the procedure required to gather primary data is either expensive or time consuming, the results of library research may be presented first. Management can then base its decision on whether to proceed with primary research on the materials gathered from secondary sources.

Library research reports may be informational (presenting only that information gathered from secondary sources), interpretive (explaining the relevance of the information to the writer's organization), or analytical (drawing conclusions and making recommendations). The format may vary from informal (memo) to formal depending on the length and importance of the topic. Because documentation plays such an important role in these reports, make sure that you use the most reliable sources available, that you report on them accurately, and that you cite them correctly.

REPORTS OF EXPERIMENTAL RESULTS

Different subjects will have different requirements for reporting experimental results, and if you are involved in experimental research, you will need to have copies of appropriate laboratory, publication, and style manuals. We will focus here on those factors common to reports of experimental results.

The objective of these reports is to convey enough information to enable a reader to replicate (duplicate) the experiment and obtain the results. For this reason, absolute accuracy in reporting the following topics is essential:

Method: *What* did you do, and *how* did you do it? Who were your subjects? How many were there? How did you select them? What were their demographic characteristics?

What materials did you use? Be specific about even seemingly ordinary details (not *a chair,* but *a typical classroom chair with attached right-hand table*). For special equipment, state the manufacturer's name and the model number. What procedure did you follow? What were your variables? What changes did you introduce? What measurements did you apply?

Results: What were the results of the experiment? Present the data without interpretation. Include appropriate tests for significance.

Discussion: Do the results support your original hypothesis? Interpret and evaluate the results, clarify any limitations in the study, and explain the significance of the results.

Documentation: Provide complete citations for all references. Use the method of citation common in your field of research.

AUDIT REPORTS

Short- and long-term audit reports are an accountant's method of verifying an inspection of a firm's financial records. The short-form report appears as a standard part in the financial section of corporate annual reports, and over the years accountants have agreed to the language illustrated in Exhibit 6.10. The long-form audit report contains more information about the audit, including tests performed and exceptions to standard accounting principles.

~~~IAL APPLICATIONS

In addition to reports, people working in business, industry, and the professions may be responsible for a wide variety of writing that calls for many of the same skills required for writing reports. Some of the more common writing tasks are journal articles, procedure manuals, job descriptions, employee publications, public relations brochures, and corporate annual reports.

Journal Articles

Each journal has its own requirements for submitting articles. These requirements are usually specified on one of the first pages of each issue of the journal. Most journals will specify a style sheet for use as a guide in manuscript preparation.

When should you query a journal editor?

In writing for publication in a journal, your purpose and audience remain the most important considerations. The editors of the journal will have a good idea of what their audience will want and expect in an article, so pay particular attention to what the editors have to say about appropriate material. If you are uncertain about the suitability of an article for a particular journal, send a letter of inquiry to the editor. If you want the journal to return your manuscript, include a postage-paid reply envelope large enough to accommodate the materials.

Procedure Manuals

What must the writer of a procedure manual keep in mind?

A procedure manual provides a description of the process to be followed in performing a particular act. The writer needs to remember that the reader will not be familiar with the process and that each step must be explained in its proper order. Do not give in to the natural tendency to make assumptions. A new computer user, for example, needs to be told how to turn the machine on.

Job Descriptions

Job descriptions delineate areas of responsibility. They are necessary for two reasons: first, they clarify who is to be responsible for what work; and second, they indicate what qualifications a person must have to perform the work. Job descriptions usually include the following information:

1. Job title
2. Description of primary duties
3. Description of secondary duties
4. List of required equipment and materials

5. Descriptions of special requirements
6. Job functions
   a. Supervisor
   b. Subordinates
   c. Work flow
   d. Promotional route
7. Qualifications
   a. Education
   b. Experience
   c. Required exams or licenses
   d. Special (when appropriate)
      (1) Height
      (2) Weight
      (3) Sex
      (4) Vision (color and/or acuity)
      (5) Hearing
      (6) Strength
      (7) Reflexes

Employee Publications

Large organizations almost always have a variety of employee publications to help communicate matters of importance to employees: company newsletters; special brochures about insurance, new products, retirement benefits, and other items of interest; and a wide variety of announcements. All help keep organizational members working together to meet common objectives.

Most of this material is informational. It conveys accurate and reliable information to an audience that will base decisions on the information. Suppose your company provided several options for health insurance—a group program with different coverages and rates, and membership in two different health maintenance organizations. You would need to explain all the options, including their advantages and disadvantages, so that each employee could make a logical selection of health insurance.

Public Relations Materials

Nearly every decision made in a modern organization is subject to public scrutiny. For this reason, organizations must work constantly to provide the public with accurate information about personnel, policies, procedures, projects, and plans. Large organizations usually hire public relations specialists to manage the PR function. Nevertheless, every employee will have an impact on the public's perception of the organization.

Managers especially need to ensure that the public hears about the good as well as the bad, about the achievements as well as the accidents. When a report contains information about an accomplishment or deals with an issue of importance to the community, cooperate with the PR staff in making the information available to the appropriate media.

The corporate annual report is probably the best known use of a report to convey a public relations message. Corporate annual reports are designed to provide stockholders, potential investors, employees, and interested others with an understanding of (and a favorable view of) the organization's activities and financial status.

How should negative information be treated in a public report?

One of the most difficult communication skills to master is the art of maintaining accuracy and reliability while presenting things in a favorable light. This can usually be accomplished by emphasizing positive factors while subordinating the negative. The use of positive language (describing a cup as half full rather than half empty) also helps. When you are tempted to omit negative information from a public report, remember that nothing is more important than your credibility. The public will never forgive being lied to. Your reports to the public should follow the same standards for accuracy and reliability that you follow in reporting to management.

SUMMARY

No two reports are identical, but some types of reports have become common because they have demonstrated their usefulness in solving certain kinds of recurring problems. Each of these types is a logical result of applying the general techniques of report writing to a specific situation.

Each organization and individual has different expectations about what a report should include. The only way to be sure that you are providing the right information is to ask.

Proposals, whether solicited or unsolicited, are offers to solve a problem, usually in exchange for a fee. A proposal and letter of acceptance constitute a contract.

Progress reports provide information about the progress on a project over a particular time. They vary in length from one-page summaries to book-length studies.

Justification reports, also known as recommendation reports, are writer-initiated efforts to convince management to solve a problem in a specific way.

A feasibility report answers questions about the possibility and desirability of undertaking a particular course of action. It may be interpretive or analytical.

Short informational and analytical reports follow all of the rules for longer reports except that, as the length decreases, they omit some of the parts included in longer reports. They also tend to be less formal.

Evaluation reports discuss the adequacy of something or someone to perform a given job. Procedures, products, projects, and personnel require evaluation from time to time to see whether improvements are necessary or possible.

Accident reports are another common type. Most organizations use a form to help report accidents accurately. When no form is available, be sure to clarify who, what, when, where, why, and how.

Annual reports are prepared by individuals, departments, and organizations. They include a record of progress as measured against objectives, financial data, and plans for the future.

Library research reports are reports on secondary resources. They may be informational, interpretive, or analytical. They are useful to determine whether the time and experience of primary research would be a good investment.

Reports of experimental results may be necessary to justify a decision. Absolute accuracy is essential in reporting the method, results, and implications of the study.

Audit reports are an accountant's method for verifying an inspection of a firm's financial records. The short-form report is a standardized statement that appears in most corporate annual reports. The long-form report varies according to tests performed and to exceptions in standard accounting principles.

Those responsible for writing reports may also be responsible for journal articles, procedure manuals, job descriptions, employee publications, and public relations materials. In each of these special applications, the writer should be accurate, reliable, and complete.

EXERCISES

Review and Discussion Questions

1. Why do you need to ask your supervisor for specific information about the kind of report you are to write?
2. What is a progress report, and what should it include?
3. What are the differences between solicited and unsolicited proposals?
4. What is the basic organizational pattern for a proposal?
5. Why does a writer need to be especially accurate when typing proposals?
6. In what way are justification reports recommendation reports? What makes them different?
7. What should a justification report contain?
8. What is a staff report?
9. What is a feasibility study?

10. Aside from length, what are the differences between short and long informational and analytical reports?

11. What is the function of an evaluation?

12. What are the differences in report content between evaluations of products and those of personnel?

13. What should an accident report contain?

14. What are the differences among individual, departmental, and corporate annual reports?

15. What is the main use for library research reports in business, industry, and the professions?

16. What should be included in reports of experimental results?

17. What is the function of an audit report?

18. In what way does the other writing you will be required to do on the job resemble report writing?

19. What should be included in a job description?

20. Describe and explain the public relations function of corporate annual reports and other business publications.

Problems and Applications

Many of the problems appropriate for this section are included in Appendix B, Report Problems. In addition to those problems presented explicitly, other problems are implied. In writing one of the complete analytical reports, for example, you might be required to prepare

- A proposal
- An outline
- One or more progress reports
- A library research report
- A report of experimental results
- A paper prepared for publication in a professional journal
- The complete analytical report itself

Proposals

1. Select a problem with which you are familiar and propose a solution. Use an appropriate format based on length, content, and audience.

2. National Discounts, a major retailer, is interested in hiring your management consulting firm to solve its morale problem. Nick Yamana, Vice President of Personnel, has asked you to submit a proposal.

3. You believe that the hospital in your community should allow your

catering service to assume the responsibility for all hospital meals. You believe that you can provide meals, including those for patients with dietary restrictions, at a lower cost than the hospital currently charges.

4. You have been invited to bid on the design and construction of a new building (be specific about size, function, and other details). Submit a proposal, preliminary drawings, and estimates of costs.

5. National Computer Brokers, a national chain of computer outlets specializing in micro- and minicomputers for personal and business use, is looking for a new advertising agency. You have been asked to submit a proposal.

6. As governor, you would like to attract more firms to your state. Select a business you believe would make a good contribution to your state's economy, and send a proposal.

7. You believe that a new "super train" running at high speed on a special track (that eliminates grade crossings) between New York City and Washington could be profitable. Propose that the government finance the construction of the train and the preparation of the railbed for the new train.

8. Propose that your company institute a quality circle program.

Progress Reports

1. Select a project you are currently working on, and prepare a progress report on your efforts and plans for completing it. Use memo format.

2. You are in charge of one of the projects listed below. Prepare a progress report for the appropriate person. In each case, assume that the project is about half complete.
   a. Installing a new main frame computer for your company
   b. Conducting the annual United Way campaign for your community
   c. Preparing a Boy/Girl Scout camp for summer occupancy
   d. Remodeling a bank
   e. Preparing a weekend managerial seminar on report writing
   f. Preparing the marketing strategy for a new product
   g. Preparing the prototype of a new, fuel-efficient car
   h. Conducting an audit of a multinational corporation
   i. Investigating a case of embezzlement in your company
   j. Preparing an advertising campaign for the product of your choice
   k. Converting an apartment complex into condominiums
   l. Making a multimillion-dollar movie
   m. Conducting a tour of the United States for a popular performer or group

Justification Reports

1. Your company has had a hiring freeze for over a year now, and your department is currently three people short. The work is beginning to pile up. Justify hiring a new person, being specific about job duties, benefits to the company, costs, and savings.

2. Your department handles a lot of repetitive typing. Justify the purchase of a new word processor.

3. You do a lot of traveling for your company. The company's current practice is to give you a travel advance (in cash) for airfare and hotel expenses. Other expenses must be charged to your own credit card, and you apply for reimbursement after you return from your trip. Write a justification report demonstrating your need for a company credit card.

4. Justify the installation of a cafeteria offering subsidized meals to the members of your organization.

5. Justify the elimination of your company's cafeteria, which offers subsidized meals to company employees.

6. As Vice President of Public Relations for a large chemical company, justify an increased public relations program, including media training for all high-ranking company officers (in addition to traditional PR functions).

7. Your company is considering dropping sponsorship of a series of high-quality TV dramas because the ratings have been low (be specific about Gross Rating Points—GRPs). You believe that even if the audience is small, it represents the population you wish to reach. Justify continuing to sponsor the show.

8. Justify the adoption or elimination of a policy or procedure with which you are familiar. Provide specific information about the organization.

Evaluation Reports

1. Evaluate a product with which you are familiar.

2. Evaluate a procedure with which you are familiar.

3. Using the form presented in this chapter as a sample, evaluate hypothetical individuals who have been working for you for one year.

Accident Reports

Locate newspaper accounts of one or more accidents that occurred in your community. Assume that you were the investigator for a concerned organization (company involved, insurance agency) and write the accident report(s). Change the names of the people and organizations involved, and make up any additional details required for completeness.

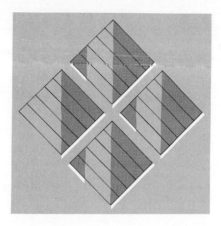

Research and
Presentation of Data

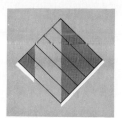

Planning

"An ounce of prevention is worth a pound of cure" applies to report writing every bit as much as it does to the practice of medicine. Planning is the "prevention" necessary to avoid serious problems as the report nears completion. The few hours it takes to plan can save countless hours of reinvestigating, restructuring, and rewriting.

Topics

The Nature of Planning
Problem Identification and Definition
Preliminary Investigation
Tentative Report Plan

Military commanders are especially fond of three sayings:

1. When the going gets tough, the tough get going.
2. If you fail to plan, you are planning to fail.
3. Take the time to do it right—there is always time to do it over.

While the relationship between the first of those sayings and report writing is accidental only, the other two are germane. Report writers frequently spend too little time planning, and, as a result, too much time writing—and rewriting.

THE NATURE OF PLANNING

In some ways, planning simply means thinking ahead. If you are driving across town to visit a friend, for example, you might not need to do much planning. If you are already familiar with the place your friend is living and you are familiar with the town, you might just get in your car and go. On the other hand, if you are going to drive from Boston to San Francisco, you would want to make sure that your car is in good working order, check a map to select the best route, and perhaps make hotel/motel reservations at appropriate places along the way. The same is true of report preparation.

On what does the *amount* of planning required depend?

The amount and kind of planning necessary will naturally vary from report to report. In some cases, you may be able to carry out the entire planning process in your head before you write a brief report. In other cases, developing an acceptable plan will prove one of the more time-consuming parts of the report writing process. The discussion that follows presents all the steps necessary for planning the most complex reports. Short reports dealing with simple issues will obviously not require all the steps. We suggest that you use the planning checklist in Exhibit 9.4 (presented at the end of the chapter) until you are thoroughly familiar with the procedures involved.

Just as a drive across the country may present unforeseen problems and possibilities, a report writer cannot anticipate all the eventualities of a report investigation. For this reason, the best plans are both complete and flexible, providing the researcher with guidelines but allowing for changes in direction or scope as required by circumstances.

Scientific Method

The procedure by which investigators achieve accuracy and objectivity is known as the scientific method. Business report writers search for facts, truth, and verifiable results every bit as much as scientists working in laboratories. The scientific method consists of the following steps:

1. Define the problem and formulate it in specific terms for investigation.

2. Define the audience.

3. Select an appropriate research methodology.

4. Collect data, usually through observation or experiment.

5. Organize data.

6. Interpret and evaluate data.

7. Generate solutions.

8. Draw conclusions and make recommendations based on the data.

If the problem is not solved, go back to defining the problem or to trying or generating other solutions. The scientific method is the most efficient procedure for investigating and solving problems yet devised. Its chief advantage is that, when properly used, its results are accurate and verifiable. **Facts** (observable, measurable data), **inferences** (assumptions based on fact), and **value judgments** (opinions not based on fact) are explicitly identified in the interests of objectivity.

The steps in the scientific method are recursive. At each stage, the investigator may need to reevaluate decisions made at earlier stages. The first definition of the problem, for example, may need modification once some initial data are collected.

On what does the *kind* of planning required depend?

In general, the kind of planning required corresponds with the complexity of the problem and formality and length of the expected report. Planning may be informal, semiformal, or formal.

Informal Planning

Informal planning may consist of individual or group brainstorming (see Chapter 5) and a series of quick generalizations about the problem and its possible solutions. If the problem is simple and the solution fairly obvious, informal planning may be sufficient to produce a report. The problem and solution may be presented in a brief, informal memo.

Semiformal Planning

More complex problems require more extensive planning and more thorough analysis. The initial stage of planning remains the same—some form of individual or group brainstorming. When the problem is complex, however, the initial planning stage may produce more questions than answers, which leads to a new round of planning. The report writer may need to conduct some preliminary research before deciding on the actual report problem or determining the appropriate research methodology.

Formal Planning

Semiformal planning is usually sufficient for most business reports. Some problems, however, are sufficiently complex that the researcher will need to conduct a full-scale preliminary investigation before beginning work on the report. At the most formal level, a researcher may be required to submit a formal proposal containing a complete description of the problem, intended research methodology, equipment and facility needs, budgetary requirements, expected outcomes, and qualifications of the researchers.

Even under these circumstances, the beginning point for the investigation is the series of ideas created by the individual or group responsible for the research. Formal planning simply makes more extensive use of the scientific method, confirming previous decisions on the basis of new information on a regular basis.

PROBLEM IDENTIFICATION AND DEFINITION

A report is a product designed to meet specific needs. Obviously the needs that may require reports are too numerous and varied to detail here. Recognizing problems requires a thorough knowledge of the subject involved. As a rule, those with more experience identify the problem for the writer and assign the report, either as a regular part of the job (periodic reports) or as a special assignment (task reports). Specialists may also perceive a problem related to their specialty and submit a writer-initiated report (a proposal, for example).

When the report is a regular part of the job, the problem—or the organizational need—will remain essentially the same from report to report. In many companies, production records rarely change much from week to week or month to month. If they did, someone would insist on receiving a special report to explain the change. Task reports and writer-initiated reports require special attention to defining and limiting the problem.

What, exactly, have you been told to do? Or what, exactly, have you decided needs to be done? Before you can develop an adequate plan, you need a clear and exact point from which to begin. You can begin to define the problem by clearly stating either the problem itself or the desired outcome.

What is the first step in defining the problem?

In either case, begin by stating the problem or the outcome in specific, descriptive terms. Whenever possible use words that lead to acts of observing, counting, or measuring. If you are defining a problem, you may use an infinitive phrase, a question, or a declarative sentence. Whichever of these forms you select, your problem statement should be both limited and focused because the problem statement essentially defines the contents of the planned report. When your problem statement is too broad or poorly focused, you might include a number of irrelevant factors in your investigation and report. Compare the following:

To Examine Public Relations Practices

To Examine XYZ's Public Relations Practices

To Examine Sources of Customer Dissatisfaction with XYZ's Products and Services

To Evaluate XYZ's Responses to Customer Complaints

To Evaluate XYZ's Responses to Customer Complaint Letters

Note that each of these problem statements defines a different problem. The first is the broadest, with each subsequent statement narrowing the focus of the investigation. An adequate discussion of the first would require a book-length document. The last could probably be covered in a 30-page report. Which of these is best? That depends on what you have been asked to do.

As an example, your boss may tell you that absenteeism in your division is too high, that she wants to know why, and that she wants something done about it. Possible problem statements would include the following:

Infinitive Phrase: To Discover the Causes of High Absenteeism in the Production Division

To Reduce the High Absenteeism in the Production Division

Question: What Are the Causes of High Absenteeism in the Production Division?

How Can We Reduce the Rate of Absenteeism in the Production Division?

Statement: We will examine the causes of high absenteeism in the Production Division.

The rate of absenteeism in the Production Division needs to be reduced.

Why is an infinitive phrase generally preferable for the problem statement?

As you read these possibilities, you can quickly see that some are better than others because they result in a clearer, more forceful conception of the problem. In general, we prefer the infinitive phrase because it results in a concise, goal-directed problem statement. When using this form of goal statement in any written presentation, however, you will need to remember to put it in the form of a complete sentence:

The purpose of my investigation will be *to discover the cause of high absenteeism in the Production Division.*

I propose *to reduce the rate of absenteeism in the Production Division.*

You will also note that we have divided the problem into two main parts, one that focuses on the causes of absenteeism and one that focuses on reducing absenteeism. The same logical division would occur if you were to focus on the desired outcome of your investigation. In this case, however, you would need to determine what you wanted to result from your investigation. Results should be stated in terms of goals or specific objectives:

To ensure a rate of absenteeism of less than 4 percent in the Production Division.

Note that, to accomplish this result, you would need to discover the current rate of absenteeism, the causes of the absenteeism, and the most logical methods for reducing absenteeism—*if* it really does need to be reduced.

Whether you use a problem statement or a long-range goal or short-term, specific objective as a starting point, a clear and measurable outcome *must* result from your research and reporting procedure. Consider the following:

How do you know absenteeism really is high in your division?

What is the rate of absenteeism in your division?

What is the rate of absenteeism in other divisions of the company?

How does the rate of absenteeism in your division compare with that in the production divisions of other companies in similar industries?

If the rate of absenteeism is high, is the cause something over which you have control?

If you can control the cause, what is the best method for reducing the rate of absenteeism?

Obviously, what began as a simple directive from your boss—to find out why your division has a high rate of absenteeism and to do something about it—has turned into a complex report-writing situation. Is it worth it? That depends. How high is the absenteeism? How much is it costing your company? How much would corrective action cost?

PRELIMINARY INVESTIGATION

When should the writer be concerned about the cost effectiveness of a report?

Your boss will naturally not want you to spend more time and money solving the problem than the problem is worth. Before conducting a full-scale investigation, answer those questions you can answer quickly and easily. In the case of high absenteeism, you could check your division's records for the past several years, the records of other divisions within your own company, and the records of production divisions in similar companies. You might also want to speak informally with several people in your division. By then you will have a good idea of the extent of the problem, which will enable you to decide whether to pursue the issue, and—if you need to pursue—how to go about it.

Consensus on Whether and How to Proceed

Unless you are very sure of yourself and of your boss's attitudes and managerial style, you should take the results of your preliminary investigation back to your boss to make sure that he or she agrees with your assessment of the problem and the need for further study. Until you have that approval, you cannot be sure that you and your boss are actually concerned about the same issues.

Unlike most term papers you have written for instructors in school, reports are not usually specific assignments that you complete as best you can. Rather, reports are likely to be a step-by-step process of investigation and evaluation. The report writer, supervisor, and others concerned about the outcome work together to define the problem and determine the best method for investigating it.

With the problem of absenteeism, for example, your boss made the statement that the rate of absenteeism was "too high." Some of the possible problem statements presented for investigating this problem in effect challenged that statement. Before you begin an investigation that might prove your boss wrong, you would obviously want to discuss the possibilities and approaches. See the problem from his or her point of view before you begin.

What is an important difference between business research and scientific research?

This is one of the critical differences between business research and scientific research. Business researchers use the scientific method when it is essential to achieve absolutely accurate results regardless of cost. In many cases, however, accuracy less than absolute will prove more cost effective. Business research should be impartial and objective, but sometimes the speed of a decision will be more important than the completeness of the research. Determine before you begin a project what kind of research will be appropriate.

Once you and your boss agree, restate the problem in writing, using specific language once again. An accurate and impartial investigation of the problem requires language that leads to measurements of one sort or another. We cannot, for example, know whether absenteeism is "high" until we know what constitutes "high"—is it 5 percent, 10 percent, or 25 percent? Similarly, we cannot effectively reduce absenteeism until we set a specific objective.

Even in those cases that do not lend themselves to exact measurements, the more precise you can be in defining the problem or the desired outcome, the better off you will be. Many business decisions must, of course, ultimately rest on a manager's intuition about a course of action. Guesswork, however, is most successful when it is based on a solid foundation of knowledge established by the accumulation of facts.

Problem Scope and Limits

When are scope and limit usually defined?

In addition to defining the problem, you will be responsible for defining both what the problem is and what it is not. **Scope** refers to what will be covered in the report. **Limits** refer to the boundary of the scope. The two are usually defined together in one or two sentences early in the report. In the case of the Production Division's absenteeism, for example, absenteeism caused by on-the-job accidents may be beyond

Exhibit 9.1   Report with Subtopics

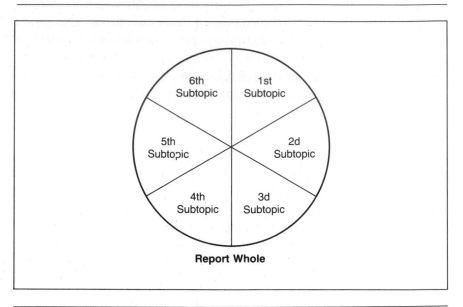

Report Whole

Exhibit 9.2   Vertical Chart

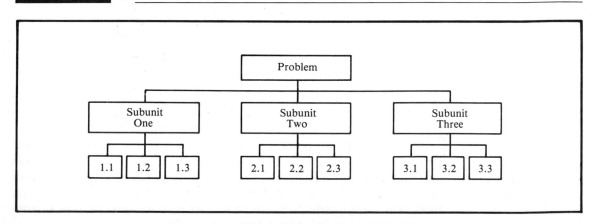

Exhibit 9.3   **Horizontal Chart**

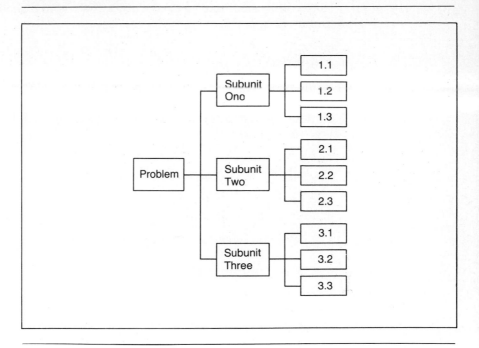

What is the value
of factoring? What
is the logical
result?

The advantage of factoring or charting the problem is that it allows you to anticipate many of the problems you will encounter in investigating and reporting the problem. In determining possible subtopics, be sure to consider the reporter's "serving men": who, what, when, where, why, and how.

The logical result of factoring is a **tentative outline** that can be used to guide the investigation.

Problem Statement
I. Subunit One
   A. Subsubunit
   B. Subsubunit
II. Subunit Two
   A. Subsubunit
   B. Subsubunit

A tentative outline helps the investigator place data in the appropriate division and to see the relationships of the parts to the whole as the evidence is collected and evaluated. Chapter 16 contains more information about outlining.

Not all report writing situations will require a formal, scientific methodology with a hypothesis or null hypothesis for investigation. When the problem is complex, however, a formal approach is essential. And even when the problem is simple and easily solved, familiarity with the basics of the scientific method will enable you to discover the best solution more quickly.

Audience

While most of your planning time will be spent determining what you are going to investigate and how you will go about it, analyzing your audience is also important. For more information about audience analysis, see Chapter 2.

Probable Problems and Questions

What problems might you encounter in gathering and analyzing data?

The final phase of planning is to list problems you think you may encounter in conducting your investigation or in analyzing the data.

Will you have sufficient time to do the job right?

Will you have enough money?

Do you have access to the appropriate resources (people, materials, facilities, etc.)?

Will your investigation require the cooperation of others?

Will your investigation require specialized knowledge that you do not have?

In the case of high absenteeism, for example, you might need to find out from those employees who are absent most often why they miss work. How will you persuade them to tell you their *real* reasons? Or perhaps you might anticipate that an accurate analysis of the problem will require the assistance of a statistician. By anticipating problems of this variety, you will be in a better position to solve them when they occur.

Likewise, you should anticipate questions your audience may have about the problem, your research, and possible solutions. Because readers will be using your report to make a decision, many questions will center on those aspects of the situation that lead to a possible action, including costs, options, advantages, disadvantages, benefits, and timing.

What questions might readers have?

Keep in mind that technical and nontechnical audiences tend to ask different sorts of questions. Technical readers will have fewer questions about how technical processes work and more questions about costs, options, and possible benefits. Nontechnical audiences will naturally have more questions about technical processes and their advantages and disadvantages. A report planning checklist is given in Exhibit 9.4.

After you have completed your initial planning, you will need to

Exhibit 9.4   Report Planning Checklist

Report Planning Checklist

The following checklist shows you the steps to take in planning
to solve typical report problems.

    1. Define the problem or objective.
        1.1 Use specific language.
        1.2 Set limits.
    2. Conduct an informal, preliminary investigation.
        2.1 Check easily obtainable sources.
        2.2 Reevaluate problem.
    3. Confirm problem statement with the primary reader of
        the proposed report.
        3.1 Cite results of preliminary investigation.
        3.2 Estimate the cost effectiveness of the report and
             any changes that may occur as a result.
    4. Develop a tentative report plan.
        4.1 State the general purpose of the report.
             4.1.1 To inform
             4.1.2 To analyze
             4.1.3 To recommend
        4.2 State the specific purpose of the report, using
             language that leads to quantifiable data or to
             verifiable observations.
        4.3 Develop a research methodology.
             4.3.1 Use a hypothesis or null hypothesis when
                    appropriate.
             4.3.2 Divide report whole into possible component
                    parts by factoring or charting.
             4.3.3 Analyze the audience--How will the
                    reader's(s') background, personality,
                    and vested interests influence the
                    reception of the report?
             4.3.4 Anticipate problems and questions.
                    4.3.4.1 How much time will your study
                             require?
                    4.3.4.2 How much will your study cost?
                    4.3.4.3 What resources will you require
                             to conduct your study?
                    4.3.4.4 What questions--technical or
                             nontechnical--will readers have
                             about the study?

begin appropriate research. When the problem is complex, you will conduct both secondary research (discussed in Chapter 10) and primary research (discussed in Chapter 12) before you begin the process of organizing and interpreting the data (Chapter 14).

SUMMARY

The amount and kind of planning will vary from report to report, but every report requires planning if it is to be effective. Because reports are expected to be accurate, impartial, and complete, most reports at least informally follow the guidelines of the scientific method.

Report writers should first define the problem in specific terms for investigation. A hypothesis or null hypothesis or other statement that can be proved or disproved is useful in many cases. Sometimes a desired objective can form the starting point for a report. In any case, the problem statement should be both limited and focused.

Second, the investigator should divide or factor the problem into its probable component parts. Pie charts, vertical charts, and horizontal charts help a report writer visualize the component parts of a report problem. The logical result of charting or factoring is a tentative outline.

Finally, after conducting some preliminary research, the writer should develop a tentative report plan that includes statements of purpose, research methodology, problem subtopics, audience needs, and probable problems and questions. When appropriate, the writer should present the tentative report plan to the person who authorized the report to ensure that the final product will meet the readers' expectations.

EXERCISES

Review and Discussion Questions

1. What is planning?
2. What is the scientific method?
3. What is a problem statement? What three forms may a problem statement take?
4. What are the purposes of a preliminary investigation?
5. What should a tentative report plan include?
6. Explain the functions of and differences between a hypothesis and a null hypothesis.
7. Why is specific language important in report formulation?
8. How can factoring or charting help a report writer?

9. How will a reader's background, personality, and vested interests influence an investigation of a problem?

10. What categories of problems and questions should a writer anticipate?

Problems and Applications

For each of the following report writing situations (or for one or more of the report problems in Appendix B) provide

- **Statement of the problem(s)**
  Using an infinitive phrase
  Using a question
  Using a declarative sentence
- **Possible hypotheses and null hypotheses**
- **Possible problem subtopics**
- **Procedures for preliminary investigation**
- **A tentative report plan,** stating logical assumptions about your purpose, research methodology, audience, and probable problems and questions.

1. As national marketing manager, you must report on the impact of caffeine-free cola sales on the sale of your Quench Cola, which contains caffeine.

2. You have been asked to prepare a report on recent management-union negotiations in anticipation of your own company's upcoming negotiations.

3. The owner/manager of a major department store in your area wants to know
   a. What kind of service the store's sales clerks are providing
   b. Why sales in the Toy Department have dropped by 22 percent over the past 14 months
   c. Whether he/she should begin validating parking tickets for customers who park in the city lot adjacent to the store
   d. Whether he/she should add a new line of microcomputers to the store's TV-stereo department

   Treat each of these as a separate problem.

4. The president of the savings and loan association for which you work has requested a report analyzing the effects recent changes in interest rates will have on your organization.

5. You have been asked to report to the manager of Public Works for the city of Kingsport, TN, on the costs of replacing a 75-year-old, one-lane, 28-foot bridge spanning Coopers Creek on the edge of town. The new bridge will be two lanes wide.

6. The laboratory in which you work needs a new piece of research equipment. Be specific about the kind of laboratory and the piece

of equipment, and write the report to your vice president of research and development.

7. Your local Chamber of Commerce has asked you how it can increase its membership.

8. Your company—a manufacturer of petrochemicals—has asked you how it can improve its image in the community. Local ecological groups have been picketing your main plant because your manufacturing process produces a noticeable odor and discharges effluents (filtered to meet federal and state requirements) into the river that passes close to town.

9. The senator for whom you work has asked you to prepare a report on the relative effectiveness of free and controlled market systems.

10. The president of your company wants to know what the impact would be of replacing 200 of your organization's 1,200 hourly employees with computer-controlled robot devices.

11. A hardware store in Cedar City, UT, is using your company name, Fair Deal. Although you do not currently have an outlet in the Cedar City area, you do not want the local store confused with your national chain of hardware stores. What action should your company take?

12. Your company recently negotiated a new, tough contract with the union, forcing the union members to make many concessions in wages and benefits because of the current economic difficulties in your industry. Now, less than two months after the new contract went into effect, the company's board of directors has awarded many managerial personnel huge bonuses, and the furious union members are talking about going on strike. As the Director of Public Relations, you've been asked to recommend the best course of action.

13. Over the past six months, you have received 15 reports from doctors that people taking your new medication, Tachinol, to control mood fluctuations in manic-depressives have developed high fevers and convulsions, with one death attributed to the drug. As the person responsible for supervising the field tests of the drug, you are required to submit a report to the company president.

14. You have discovered that a simple change in your organization's security system could reduce by half the losses resulting from employee theft of the small computer components your firm manufactures. The losses over the past two years have amounted to nearly $800,000.

15. Should the publishing company for which you work publish a new magazine in your field? Consider the audience (size, distribution, etc.) and circulation, potential advertisers, content, and costs and problems of production.

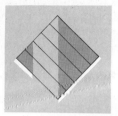

Secondary Research

What was the annual salary of petroleum engineers in Texas last year?
What was it in 1980? What marketing method resulted in highest sales
of powdered milk in Central Africa from 1975 to 1985? Answers to
these questions—and to many others—are available in secondary
sources. Many business reports can be based entirely on secondary
research: someone else will have already solved a similar problem and
published details about it. Secondary research is also the beginning
point for reports that will eventually require primary research. This
chapter covers secondary sources, and Chapter 12 discusses the
process of collecting primary data.

Topics

Secondary Sources
Guides to Secondary Sources
Computerized Databases
Note Taking

After you have determined the purpose of your report and defined the problem, you will need to conduct research to arrive at a solution to the problem. Your preliminary investigation will have uncovered several possible sources of information. You will probably have already taken a quick look through your company records, for example, to see whether a similar problem has occurred in your company before.

During the preliminary investigation, your search may have been informal and incomplete. You may have called two or three "old hands" to see if they remembered anything similar and had anything in their files. At this point, however, you will have to be formal and thorough in your investigation of the problem and use secondary or primary sources and perhaps both.

SECONDARY SOURCES

Secondary sources are just that: secondhand. They contain information that others have collected and reported. Secondary sources may be published—printed for public distribution and sale—or unpublished. Secondary research allows the report writer to benefit from the work already performed by others or, in other words, to avoid reinventing the wheel. Although some business problems may be unique, most are not. Even when the problem is unique, secondary research can save the report writer hours of effort by helping define and limit the problem and by narrowing the focus of the investigation.

Where do you begin to look for information? In many cases, your first step should be a search of company records and company libraries.

Company Records and Libraries

What types of company files may be useful in secondary research?

Company records can provide useful secondary information; in fact, they may provide information that you cannot obtain elsewhere. Use company records for historical, financial, or operational information. You might also find useful information for your report from other company records, such as sales reports, audit and tax reports, and annual reports. Prepared speeches given by company personnel may also help you in your investigation.

The company library may house specialized collections of reports, books, magazines, journals, newspapers, and other publications that might prove useful in your investigation.

In addition to the company library, check with key personnel of the company. They may give you information you need or else direct you to information and materials that may be stored in the company's (1) inactive files, (2) centralized files, or (3) decentralized files of executives or departments.

Research in Other Libraries

Why is secondary research also called library research?

After you have thoroughly investigated your company's materials, your next step is to locate information in libraries—public, college or university, and private. Because most secondary information can be found in libraries, secondary research is frequently referred to as library research. Someone may have already researched and recorded a solution to a similar problem, so examining that material may save you hours of collecting new information. Although you may find both published materials (books, periodicals, newspapers) and unpublished materials (dissertations, manuals, brochures, booklets) in public libraries, you can also check special libraries, such as those maintained by businesses, trade, professional, and technical groups.

How are books cataloged?

The first place to check to determine whether the library has the documents you need is the card catalog, which is arranged alphabetically by author, subject, and title. The card catalog will give you the call number—the location of the document on the shelves in the library. Different libraries, of course, use different methods of cataloging and shelving books. Some libraries use the Dewey decimal system, while others use the Library of Congress system. Some provide online computer access to the catalog, while others make the catalog available on microform. In most cases, the differences from library to library will not affect your research methodology. If you have a problem understanding or using the system in your library, check with the librarian, who will be glad to explain the system to you and to help you with your search.

The card catalog is only a beginning. Materials listed in the card catalog may be unavailable or outdated. By the time research information appears in a book, for example, it may be as much as 4 years old. For this reason, you will also need to check current periodicals and the materials in the reference section of the library.

Why should periodicals, newspapers, and dissertations be checked?

Remember, too, that many materials that may be important to your search may be available only on microform—microfilm or microfiche. Doctoral dissertations, back issues of newspapers, back issues of some journals, and perhaps back issues of some newspaper indexes are typically available on microfilm or microfiche and will require a special reader.

Because of the continual increase in the number of published materials and because of limited budgets, libraries cannot possibly afford to purchase as many works as they would like; they need to be selective in their acquisitions. When it happens that your library does not have a particular source that you need for your report, it may be possible to obtain a copy of that work through a system called **interlibrary loan.** The interlibrary loan system is a process by which a library will lend materials to another library. After you have determined that your library does not have the source you need, ask the librarian if another library has it and if it is possible to obtain it through interlibrary loan. You will

When should you request an interlibrary loan?

probably need to submit a request form with complete and accurate information about the author, title, year, and where you found the source listed. The librarian will locate the lending library, which will forward the document to your library, which will then notify you.

Selection

A word of caution about using secondary resources: be discriminating. From the abundance of information available, select only that information that relates specifically to your problem. Remember that business reports are *not* term papers. Your objective is not to read everything that has been written about the problem under study but rather to read enough to be able to recommend a specific course of action with confidence or to otherwise present accurate, reliable, and objective data. Secondary sources that may prove useful to your investigation include the following:

Almanacs	Documents
Annual Reports	Encyclopedias
Articles	Government Publications
Books	Newspapers
Brochures	Pamphlets
Dictionaries	Periodicals (magazines, journals)
Directories	Yearbooks

Most of these secondary sources are available in typical public and college libraries. But of all sources available, your reference librarian is the one who can help you the most. Be sure to check with him or her when you need assistance. The expertise of the reference librarian can save you hours of searching and frustration.

GUIDES TO SECONDARY SOURCES

When you do not know where to begin searching for the information you need, begin with one of the many guides to secondary sources. Again, ask a librarian for help. With the information explosion that has taken place over the past 30 years, the number of sources of information has increased so greatly that no one source can be complete. You may find helpful materials in sources that you would initially dismiss as unrelated to your topic.

Suppose, for example, you had to prepare a report on computer graphics for your company. Your initial thought might be to search computer publications only, but you might well find something more related to your needs in one of the following publications: *Administra-*

tive Management, Business Week, Journal of Accountancy, The Journal of Business Communication, Journal of Systems Management, or *Management World.* All have published articles discussing computer graphics.

Fortunately, most publications are **indexed,** which means that a record of their content is listed in separate publications so that users can find information they need. Guides to secondary sources tell you where to find material about specific topics. Although hundreds of reference sources are available, the following ones should prove helpful—especially to the beginning researcher.

Almanacs and Atlases

When are almanacs useful?

Almanacs are excellent tools for locating quick answers to a variety of questions on nations, states, people, education, sports statistics, and lists of colleges and universities. The *Dow Jones-Irwin Business Almanac* in particular provides data on business, finance, and economics; it includes tables, graphs, rankings, and contacts for business information.

Dow Jones-Irwin Business Almanac. Homewood, IL: Dow Jones-Irwin, 1977 to date.

Information Please Almanac, Atlas and Yearbook. New York: Simon & Schuster, 1947 to date.

Reader's Digest Almanac and Yearbook. New York: N. W. Norton, 1966 to present.

The World Almanac and Book of Facts. New York: Doubleday, 1868 to present.

Bibliographies

What is the definition of bibliography?

A bibliography is a listing of publications often focusing on one particular topic. A general source for bibliographies, the *Bibliographic Index,* provides a listing of books and other published sources that contain a bibliography.

Bibliographic Index: A Cumulative Bibliography of Bibliographies. New York: H. W. Wilson, 1937 to date.

Bibliographic indexes can be specialized. For example

Walsh, Ruth M., and Stanley J. Birkin. *Business Communications: An Annotated Bibliography.* Westpoint, CT: Greenwood Press, 1973.

Falcione, Raymond L., and Howard H. Greenbaum and Associates. *Organizational Communication.* Beverly Hills, CA: Sage Publications, 1980.

Thompson, Marilyn Taylor. *Management Information: Where to Find It.* Metuchen, NJ: Scarecrow Press, 1981.

Biographical References

What kinds of
specialized
biographical
references are
available?

Biographical references contain information on well-known people, living or dead. Specialized references are available for sections of the United States—*Who's Who in the East, Midwest, South and Southwest,* and *West*. Also, many fields have specialized biographical directories. Check with your librarian for specific titles.

Biography Index. Bronx, New York: H. W. Wilson, 1946 to date.

Current Biography. Bronx, New York: H. W. Wilson, 1940 to date.

Who's Who in America. Chicago: Marquis Who's Who. Similar biographical references include *Who's Who in Finance and Industry, Who's Who in Education,* and *Who's Who in Insurance*.

Books

What is the
quickest way to
determine the
books available on
a topic?

Not all books that have been published are in your library. The following references list books currently in print. Entries generally include author, title, subject, price, and publisher. *Books in Print* is probably the best source for quickly determining what books are currently available on a given topic:

Books in Print. New York: R. R. Bowker, 1948 to date.

Subject Guide to Books in Print. New York: R. R. Bowker, 1957 to date.

Business and Economics Books and Serials in Print. New York: R. R. Bowker, 1981 to date.

Cumulative Book Index. New York: H. W. Wilson, 1928 to date.

Business, Financial, and Credit References

What kind of
information do
business references
provide?

The following references provide information on companies, including their subsidiaries, financial statements, properties, products, corporate histories, and the like. In addition, the *Value Line Investment Survey* offers trend analysis and gives summary information on selected industries.

Moody's manuals. New York: Moody's Investors Service. *Bank and Finance, Industrial, International, Municipal and Governmental, OTC Industrial, Public and Utility, and Transportation* manuals.

Standard Corporation Records. New York: Standard & Poor's, 1940 to date.

Value Line Investment Survey. New York: Arnold Bernhard & Co., 1969 to date.

Directories

What information is
given in business
directories?

Directories furnish information about businesses and organizations, their operations, products, and other facts. Many of them provide names and addresses of the companies and identify their officers or directors.

Business Organizations and Agencies Directory. Detroit: Gale Research, 1980.

Directory of Directories. Detroit: Gale Research, 1980 to date.

Guide to American Directories. 10th ed. New York: B. Klein Publications, 1978.

Million Dollar Directory. New York: Dun & Bradstreet, 1959 to date.

National Trade & Professional Associations of the U.S. and Canada. Washington: Columbia Books, 1966 to date.

Standard & Poor's Register of Corporations, Directories and Executives. New York: Standard & Poor's, 1928 to date.

Thomas Register of American Manufacturers. New York: Thomas Publishing, 1905 to date.

Trade Directories of the World. Queens Village, NY: Croner Publications, 1952 to date.

World Guide to Trade Associations. 2nd ed. Detroit: Distributed by Gale Research, 1980.

Encyclopedias

Encyclopedias are best used as sources of general background information.

Encyclopedia Americana. International ed. Danbury, CT: Grolier Educational, 1829 to date.

The New Encyclopaedia Britannica, 15th ed. Chicago: Encyclopaedia Britannica Education, 1981.

What specialized
encyclopedias are
useful to business
report writers?

In addition, several specialized encyclopedias are available, such as the *Accountant's Encyclopedia, Encyclopedia of Associations, Encyclopedia of Banking and Finance, Encyclopedia of Information Systems and Services,* and *International Encyclopedia of the Social Sciences.*

Guides

A wide variety of guides is available to help researchers locate business information.

Brownstone, David M., and Gorton Curruth. *Where to Find Business Information: A Worldwide Guide for Everyone Who Needs the Answers to Business Questions*. 2nd ed. New York: John Wiley, 1982.

Daniells, Lorna M. *Business Information Sources*. Berkeley: University of California Press, 1976.

Fiqueroa, Oscar, and Charles Winkler. *A Business Information Guidebook*. New York: AMACOM, 1980.

Grant, Mary, and Norma Cote. *Directory of Business and Finance Services*. 7th ed. New York: Special Libraries Assn., 1976.

Johnson, H. Webster. *How to Use the Business Library: With Sources of Business Information*. 4th ed. Cincinnati: South-Western Publishing, 1972.

Piele, Linda J., John C. Tyson, and Michael B. Sheffey. *Materials and Methods for Business Research*. New York: Neal-Schuman, 1980.

Wasserman, Paul, Charlotte Georgi, and James Way. *Encyclopedia of Business Information Sources*. 4th ed. Detroit: Gale Research, 1980.

Government Publications

Which government publications are readily available?

The U.S. government provides thousands of publications each year. The various departments, bureaus, divisions, and agencies release information that is vital to business.

American Statistics Index. Washington: Congressional Information Service, 1973 to date.

Guide to U.S. Government Publications. McLean, VA: Documents Index, 1981 (microfiche only).

Federal Index. Cleveland, OH: Predicasts, 1977 to date.

Monthly Checklist of State Publications. U.S. Library of Congress, Processing Department. Washington: Government Printing Office, 1910 to date.

Monthly Catalog of United States Government Publications. U.S. Superintendent of Documents. Washington: Government Printing Office, 1895 to date.

Statistical Abstract of the United States. Washington: Government Printing Office, 1878 to present.

U.S. Bureau of Census Publications: *Census of Manufacturers, Census of Retail Trade, Census of Service and Industries, Census of Wholesale Trade*.

Newspaper Indexes

Newspaper indexes summarize news by subject, person, and frequently by company. They obtain a variety of information on topics covered in today's newspapers—political, technical, medical, educational, and business.

> *Bell & Howell Newspaper Index.* Wooster, OH: Bell & Howell, 1972 to date. (indexes for *Chicago Sun Times, Chicago Tribune, Christian Science Monitor, Denver Post, Detroit News, Houston Post, Los Angeles Times, New Orleans Times Picayune, St. Louis Post Dispatch, San Francisco Chronicle,* and *Washington Post*)

> *The New York Times Index.* New York: The New York Times, 1913 to date.

> *The Wall Street Journal Index.* New York: Dow Jones, 1958 to date.

Periodical Indexes

Which publisher pioneered in establishing indexes to periodicals?

Periodical indexes give references to articles (and occasionally to books) arranged by subject or topic. They provide excellent coverage of the business, social, and political fields. Each of the indexes will tell you which periodicals are included.

> *Accountants' Index Supplement.* New York: AICOA, 1921 to date.

> *American Statistics Index.* Washington: Congressional Information Service, 1973 to date.

> *Applied Science and Technology Index.* New York: H. W. Wilson, 1958 to date.

> *Business Periodicals Index.* New York: H. W. Wilson, 1958 to date.

> *Education Index.* New York: H. W. Wilson, 1929 to date.

> *Engineering Index.* New York: Engineering Index, 1928 to date.

> *F & S Index.* Cleveland, OH: Predicasts, 1960 to date.

> *Index to Legal Periodicals.* New York: H. W. Wilson, 1908 to date.

> *P.A.I.S. (Public Affairs Information Service Bulletin).* New York: P.A.I.S., 1915 to date.

> *Reader's Guide to Periodical Literature.* New York: H. W. Wilson, 1900 to date.

> *Social Sciences Index.* New York: H. W. Wilson, 1974 to date.

COMPUTERIZED DATABASES

The competitiveness of business today makes timely information essential. As a direct result of the increased use of computers in all phases of business, researchers now have the ability to acquire all kinds of information on virtually any topic— whether business, educational, governmental, legal, medical, or technical—in virtually a matter of minutes. The method that allows them to do this is known as an **online search.**

What is an online
information search?

An online information search is an interactive method of requesting citations and perhaps complete abstracts on specific topics from vast quantities of data stored in a wide variety of electronic databases. A database is simply computer-stored information from a given source. Database producers lease or sell their databases to online vendors (or search services), who sell access to the databases through their computer systems.

Just a few years ago, one had to be an expert to conduct an economical online search. This is no longer true. CompuServe (IQuest), SearchLink (through *InfoWorld*), the DIALOG Business Connection, and a variety of other online services now provide easy access to more than 800 electronic databases containing information about everything from new products and services to financial data, to market facts, to business law. These services guide the user through the process of selecting and searching the appropriate databases. Although these services charge a fee (usually based on the time spent online plus the number of titles found and the number of abstracts requested), the time they save by eliminating hours—and perhaps days or even weeks—of manual searching make them not just economical but a real bargain.

Classifications

What are the three
classifications of
databases?

Databases are classified as bibliographic, factual, and numeric. A **bibliographic** database contains the title, author, source, and summary of published information found in sources, such as articles and books. A **factual** database contains organization names and addresses, licenses available, transportation routes, and the like. A **numeric** database contains manipulable data, such as economic and labor statistics, prices, and demographic data.

What are
descriptors?

Regardless of the type of databases selected, the procedure for conducting the search is the same. As the report writer, you—or perhaps a librarian experienced with online search procedures—select the appropriate database or databases and enter the key words or phrases—**descriptors**—to be searched. Most computer databases use **Boolean logic** to limit the key terms you wish to search. Boolean logic relies on *and, or, not,* and *adjacent* to tell the computer how the search should be performed. The following would all be possible:

- **Teleconferencing *and* productivity.**   Would result in a listing of all articles in which both teleconferencing and productivity were discussed.
- **Teleconferencing *or* productivity.**   Would result in a listing of all articles in which either teleconferencing or productivity was mentioned.

- **Teleconferencing *not* productivity.** Would result in a listing of all articles in which teleconferencing was mentioned but productivity was not; articles mentioning productivity would be excluded.
- **Teleconferencing *adjacent* productivity.** Would result in a listing of all articles in which teleconferencing productivity was discussed, with the terms adjacent to one another.

To obtain useful information, you would, of course, need to use the right descriptors. Many corporate, university, and public librarians have had special training in electronic data retrieval. Until you are familiar with the search procedures, you would do well to obtain the assistance of a professional.

What is the most economical method of obtaining abstracts?

The computer performs the search and provides the list of citations. If you so desire, you may request complete abstracts of any or all of the cited articles. Depending on the kind of computer and software used, you may record the list of citations and abstracts that appear on your computer screen and print them later, print them while online, or request an offline printout from the vendor. The most economical of these methods is simply to record or **download** the information to disk and then print it later.

Electronic (Online) Databases

ABI/INFORM contains more than 230,000 citations with abstracts of periodicals in the business and management area. Database topics range from economics to information science. The information can be searched by key word or topic and is designed for the novice user. It is accessed through BRS, DATA-STAR, DIALOG, ITT Dialsom, ESA-IRA, or SCD Information Service.

The Accountants' Index is the electronic version of the printed Accountants' Index directory. The service provides an index of literature about business and financial topics with an emphasis on accounting. The index does not abstract the cited material. It is accessed through SDC Information Services.

Which databases contain full-text articles of interest to business writers?

Bibliographic Retrieval Service (BRS) contains more than 80 databases covering physical and social sciences, business, education, and medicine. It is accessed through BRS.

BRS After Dark contains more than 30 databases of its parent BRS. It is run during nonprime hours, allowing lower cost. It is accessed through BRS.

Dow Jones News and Dow Jones Free-Text Search are online databases containing full-text and edited news stories from *The Wall Street Journal,* Dow Jones News Service, and *Barron's.* The News service allows searching by company stock symbol, industry, and government codes. The Free-Text service allows searching by key words on the full text. Both databases are accessed through Dow Jones and Company Inc.

HBR/Online (Harvard Business Review) contains the full-text version of the *Harvard Business Review*. It includes articles appearing in the magazine since 1976. Citations and abstracts of articles appearing between 1971 and 1976 and 700 classic articles published between 1925 and 1971 are also included. It is accessed through BRS and DIALOG.

Management Contents contains citations and abstracts from more than 725 business and management publications. More than 100 of these publications deal with business law and taxation. The service is designed as an industry analysis and prediction tool. It is accessed through DIALOG, BRS, and The Source.

Exhibit 10.1 illustrates the range of databases available through just one of the popular information services.

What are two disadvantages of online searches?

Online searches have just two disadvantages. First, electronic databases are in many cases simply the electronic version of information already available in printed form. For this reason, the information in the database may lag behind that available in printed form. Even though you have completed an online search, you should still check the most recent editions of the appropriate periodicals to make sure that you have not overlooked an important source of information.

Second, the computer search will find only those articles to which the key terms apply. Unless you select the descriptors very carefully, important related material might be missed. For this reason, it may be advisable to conduct a quick check to see whether a manual search will result in additional useful information and perhaps even suggest additional descriptors for a second online search.

NOTE TAKING

Regardless of the method you use to locate your sources, you will need a well-organized plan for recording the essential information obtained from secondary sources. Your goal in taking notes is to simplify the writing process by making important information easy to find, and—even more important—useful when you find it.

Photocopies

What are the advantages of photocopying?

Perhaps the easiest method of keeping track of secondary information is simply to photocopy the pertinent information. That way you know exactly what you have and can use it appropriately in your report. One of the principal advantages of photocopying is that you have the information in its original context so that, if necessary, you can reread the original document in its entirety to obtain a better understanding of a critical passage. The cost of photocopying is usually offset by the time saved because information need not be copied onto note cards or full sheets.

Exhibit 10.1   Sample Listing of a Computer Information Service

This unparalleled range of databases is supplied to DIALOG from a variety of widely recognized publishers, government agencies, corporations, and associations who are responsible for database content and editorial control. Complete database supplier information is provided in the DIALOG user's manual. Brief descriptions and typical applications summarize each database.

Source: DIALOG Information Services, Inc., Palo Alto, CA 94304

ABI/INFORM. Extensive summaries of articles from top business and management journals—business practices, corporate strategies, and trends.

ADTRACK. Descriptions of advertisements from 150 U.S. consumer magazines—competitive tracking and product announcements.

ARTHUR D. LITTLE/ONLINE. Management summaries from A. D. Little's market research reports—planning and industry research.

BI/DATA FORECASTS. Briefings on the economies, social, and political outlook for 35 major countries—economic and industry forecasting.

BI/DATA TIME SERIES. Over 300 economic indicator time series for over 130 countries—international business and banking.

BLS CONSUMER PRICE INDEX. Time series of consumer price indexes calculated by the U.S. Bureau of Labor Statistics—economic analysis.

BLS EMPLOYMENT, HOURS, AND EARNINGS. Time series on employment, hours of work, and earnings for the U.S. by industry—economic trends and analysis.

BLS PRODUCER PRICE INDEX. Time series of producer price indexes, formerly Wholesale Price Indexes, for over 2,800 commodities—economic analysis.

CENDATA. News Releases from the U.S. Bureau of the Census with textual and tabular information covering Census surveys in business, agriculture, population, and more—tracking current economic and demographic trends.

CHEMICAL INDUSTRY NOTES. Extracts from articles in worldwide business-oriented periodicals for chemical-processing industries—chemical industry news and tracking.

COFFEELINE. Summaries of articles and data from over 5,000 publications covering all aspects of the coffee and production trade—industry research.

COMMERCE BUSINESS DAILY. Definitive source of notices from U.S. Department of Commerce for government procurement invitations, contract awards, surplus sales, R&D requests—competitive tracking, purchasing, and sales leads.

D & B—DUN'S MARKET IDENTIFIERS®. Directory of over 1,000,000 public and private companies with ten or more employees, listing address, products, sales executives—corporate organization, subsidiaries, industry information, sales prospects.

D & B—MILLION DOLLAR DIRECTORY®. Privately held and public companies with net worths over $500,000, includes data on sales, type of organization, address, employees, key executives—corporate analysis and information.

D & B—PRINCIPAL INTERNATIONAL BUSINESSES®. Directory listings, sales volume, corporate data, and references to companies for non-U.S. private and public companies from 133 countries—international trade and industry prospects.

DISCLOSURE® II. Detailed financials for over 9,000 publicly held companies, based on reports filed with the U.S. S.E.C.—sales, profit, corporate organization, key personnel.

DISCLOSURE®/SPECTRUM OWNERSHIP. Detailed ownership information for thousands of U.S. public companies—investment analysis.

DONNELLEY DEMOGRAPHICS. U.S. demographic information including 1980 Census, current year estimates, and five-year projections, from zip code level to the U.S. summary—demographic and market analysis.

ECONOMIC LITERATURE INDEX. Index to articles from economic journals and books—economic research and teaching.

ECONOMICS ABSTRACTS INTERNATIONAL. Summaries of literature in all areas of international economic sciences—determining industries, distribution channels.

ELECTRONIC YELLOW PAGES. Unparalleled number of listings of U.S. businesses; retail, services, manufacturers, wholesalers, etc. Over 9 million listings with name, location, line of business—sales prospecting and location tool.

FIND/SVP REPORTS AND STUDIES INDEX. Summaries of industry and market research reports, surveys from U.S. and international sources—market, industry, and company analyses.

FOODS ADLIBRA. Concise summaries of articles and reports on current developments in the food industry and technologies—market and food sciences research.

FOREIGN TRADERS INDEX. Directory of manufacturers, services, representatives, wholesalers, etc. in 130 non-U.S. countries—direct marketing and sales outside the United States (available in United States only).

HARFAX INDUSTRY DATA SOURCES. Descriptions of sources for financial and marketing data in major industries worldwide,

(continued)

Exhibit 10.1   (*continued*)

including market research, investment banking studies, forecasts, etc.—industry tracking and analysis.

HARVARD BUSINESS REVIEW. Text of Harvard Business Review, covering the range of strategic management subjects—management practices and strategies.

ICC BRITISH COMPANY DIRECTORY
ICC BRITISH COMPANY FINANCIAL DATABASE
Listing of detailed financial information and ratios for nearly one million British companies as filed with the Companies Registry of Companies House—identification of U.K. companies and financial analysis.

INSURANCE ABSTRACTS. Brief summaries of articles from life, property, and liability insurance journals—tracking insurance industry trends and practices.

INTERNATIONAL LISTING SERVICE. Directory of worldwide public and private business opportunities—buying, selling, and obtaining financing for businesses.

INVESTEXT®. The complete text of prestigious Wall Street and selected European analysts' financial and research reports on over 3,000 companies and industries—corporate and industry analysis plus financial and market research.

MANAGEMENT CONTENTS®. Informative briefs on a variety of business and management related topics from business journals, proceedings, transactions, etc.—management, finance, operations decision making.

MEDIA GENERAL DATABANK. Trading information with detailed financial information on 400 publicly held companies over a seven-year period—charting market and financial performance.

MOODY'S CORPORATE PROFILES. Equity database with financial data and business descriptions of publicly held U.S. companies, with five-year histories, ratios and analyses on companies with high investor interest—assess investment opportunities.

PHARMACEUTICAL NEWS INDEX. References to major report publications, covering drugs, cosmetics, health regulations, research, financial news—drug and cosmetic industry developments and regulation.

PTS ANNUAL REPORTS ABSTRACTS. Detailed statistical, financial, product, and corporate summaries from annual and 10 K reports for publicly held U.S. corporations and selected international companies—product, industry, company identification, and strategic planning.

PTS DEFENSE MARKETS AND TECHNOLOGY. Summaries of major articles and reports from defense sources, includes contracts, the industry, and more—defense industry contracting and tracking.

PTS F & S INDEXES (Funk & Scott). Brief descriptive annotations of articles and publications covering U.S. and international company, product, and industry information—company and industry tracking.

PTS INTERNATIONAL FORECASTS. Summaries of published forecasts with historical data for the world, excluding the United States, covering general economics, all industries, products, end use data—strategic planning for international development.

PTS INTERNATIONAL TIME SERIES. Forecast time series containing 50 key series for each of 50 major countries, excluding United States, and projected to 1990, as well as annual data from 1957 to date—international economic analysis.

PTS PROMT. Primary source of information on product introductions, market share, corporate directions and ventures, and companies in every industry, containing detailed summaries of articles from trade and industry sources—market and strategic planning, tracking new technologies and products.

PTS U.S. FORECASTS. Summaries of published forecasts for United States from trade journals, businesses and financial publications, key newspapers, government reports, and special studies—short- and long-term forecasting.

PTS U.S. TIME SERIES. 500 time series for United States from 1957 and projected to 1990 and annual data from 1957 to date on production, consumption, prices, foreign trade, manufacturing, etc.—tracking economic and industry trends.

STANDARD & POOR'S CORPORATE DESCRIPTIONS. In-depth corporate descriptions of over 7,800 publicly held U.S. companies with background, income account and balance sheet figures, and stock and bond data—competitive and financial analysis of companies and products.

STANDARD & POOR'S NEWS. Late-breaking financial news on U.S. public companies, including earnings, mergers and acquisitions, joint ventures, management, and corporate changes and structure—current awareness of corporate activities.

TRADE & INDUSTRY ASAP®. Indexing and complete text of articles from 85 industry trade journals and general business publications—current awareness and industry tracking.

TRADE AND INDUSTRY INDEX®. Index with selected summaries of major trade and industry journals and the complete text of press releases

Exhibit 10.1   (*continued*)

from PR Newswire—industry and company information and news.

TRADE OPPORTUNITIES. Purchase requests by the international market for U.S. goods and services, describing specific products or services in demand by over 120 countries—leads to export opportunities, sales, and representation opportunities.

TRINET COMPANY DATABASE. Directory information on U.S. and non-U.S. company headquarters with aggregate data from

establishments, including sales by SIC code—headquarter analysis and industry sales.

TRINET ESTABLISHMENT DATABASE. Directory of U.S. corporate establishments with address, sales, market share, employees, and headquarters information—corporate and market analysis.

U.S. EXPORTS. Time series of U.S. Bureau of the Census statistics on exports of merchandise from the United States to other countries—tracking U.S. and international economies and industry-specific trends.

We recommend photocopying when possible. In some cases, however, you will have no choice but to take notes on your secondary sources.

Note Cards

What information is noted on the 3″ × 5″ card? On the 5″ × 7″ card?

One system of note taking that has proved both efficient and effective is the use of 3″ × 5″ note cards for bibliographic data and 5″ × 7″ note cards for content data. Use the 3″ × 5″ cards to record the bibliographic data—author, title of book or magazine, title of article, edition number, volume number, page numbers, date of publication, publisher, and location of publisher—of the reference. It is a good practice to record the library call number on the card in case you need to relocate a reference quickly. Because the cards will be used to prepare the bibliography, record the information in proper bibliographic format (as described in Chapter 11). Use a separate card for each reference. Also, number the cards consecutively so that they can be keyed with the 5″ × 7″ content cards.

The 5″ × 7″ content cards are used for recording information. Use a separate card for recording information on one topic from each reference source. When possible, place a subject heading (topic or subtopic) at the top of the card. Subject headings can be useful when you are ready to organize your data. Be sure to record the corresponding number of the bibliography card and the page number on which you found the data. Exhibits 10.2 and 10.3 illustrate the 3″ × 5″ bibliographic note card and the 5″ × 7″ content note card.

Note Sheets

Another method of taking notes is simply to use full sheets to record information on a source-by-source basis. This method will save time in taking notes but may require more time when you need to organize and use the information in your report. The main objective of any recording system is to help you relocate and use the information in writing your report. Use the system that works the best for you.

Exhibit 10.2   A 3″ x 5″ Bibliographic Note Card

5

Feinberg, Lilian O. <u>Applied Business Communication.</u>

Sherman Oaks, CA: Alfred Publishing, 1982.

Exhibit 10.3   A 5″ x 7″ Content Note Card

MBO   5

"Management by objective (M.B.O.) was conceived as a technique that managers could use to make employees aware of the organization's objectives and to motivate employees to achieve those objectives." p. 33

Codes

Why should direct
quotations be
coded on note
cards or sheets?

After you have determined the system you will use for note taking, you need to decide how to record the information you select from the various secondary sources. Three common ways of reporting information are to copy it verbatim, to paraphrase it, or to summarize it. To help you identify your notes, code them by (1) using quotation marks for material copied verbatim, (2) writing *p* or *par* for paraphrased material, and (3) writing *s* or *sum* for summarized material. This is important so that you do not inadvertently present someone else's ideas as your own. (See Chapter 11 for more information about documentation and plagiarism.)

A passage from Jean Wyrick's *Steps to Writing Well* (New York: Holt, Rinehart and Winston, 1987, 72) is used to illustrate the three kinds of note taking.

Verbatim: The absolute necessity of revision cannot be overemphasized. All good writers rethink, rearrange, and rewrite large portions of their prose. The French novelist Colette, for instance, wrote everything over and over. In fact, she often spent an entire morning working on a single page. Hemingway, to cite another example, rewrote the end to *A Farewell to Arms* thirty-nine times. While no one expects you to make thirty-nine drafts of each essay, the point is clear: revision is an essential part of good writing. It is part of your commitment to your reader. Therefore, plan to spend at least a third to a half of your overall writing time revising and polishing your essay.

Paraphrase: Revision is essential to good writing. Good writers rethink and rewrite their material many times. Two writers, Colette and Hemingway, for example, are known to have written materials over and over again. Colette is said to have spent an entire morning rewriting one page; Hemingway is said to have written an ending to one of his novels 39 times. At least a third to a half of your overall writing should be spent in revising and polishing your essay.

Summary: The need for revision cannot be overemphasized. Good writers rethink, rearrange, and rewrite much of their prose. The French novelist Colette, for example, often spent an entire morning working on a single page. Hemingway rewrote the ending to *A Farewell to Arms* 39 times. The point is clear: revision is essential to good writing. Spend at least a third to a half of your writing time revising and polishing your material.

SUMMARY

After determining the purpose and defining the problem of your report, you will need to research all the resources available. Secondary sources contain information that others have collected and reported. Company records can provide useful secondary information; use them for historical, financial, or operational information.

After you have investigated your company's materials, then locate information in public libraries, college and university libraries, and private libraries. Card catalogs, reference books, and reference librarians can help you locate the information you need.

When you have located information you want to include in your report, you need to take accurate notes. Note taking requires a careful analysis and evaluation of the reference source. Not all information must be copied verbatim. You will definitely need bibliographic data for documentation.

The bibliography is an orderly listing of source materials. Bibliographic entries refer to entire works, not just parts or pages as do the footnotes, and they come at the end of the report or paper. Bibliographic entries are arranged in alphabetical order; by classifications, such as books, periodicals, government publications; by subject; and by chronological order.

With the availability of computers, researchers now have the ability to acquire—worldwide—all kinds of information on any topics of interest within minutes. An online information search is an interactive method of requesting citations on specific topics from vast quantities of data stored in approximately 800 databases. A database is simply computer-stored information—bibliographic, factual, and numeric.

EXERCISES

Review and Discussion Questions

1. What are secondary sources? Give five examples.
2. What is library research?
3. What is the interlibrary loan system?
4. What is an online information search?
5. What are the two disadvantages of online research?
6. Why should direct questions be coded on note cards or sheets?
7. What are the three classifications of databases?
8. What are descriptors, and why must they be carefully selected?
9. What are the advantages of each type of note taking?
10. What are three common ways of reporting information?

Problems and Applications

1. Write a brief memo report to a student who is interested in pursuing a career in your major. Check your local library and make a list of available resources, such as abstracts, biographical references, bibliographies, dictionaries, directories, periodical guides, indexes, and government reports. Be extra helpful by providing the call numbers.
2. Write a letter report to an English-speaking foreign student who plans to enroll in your college next term. The student plans to major in accounting and would like you to check the school library and provide him/her with a list of five accounting

periodicals to which the library subscribes. Briefly tell the student why those periodicals are important and what their strengths are.

3. In a memo to your boss, describe a problem situation and the sources you would use to solve the problem.

4. Write a letter report to a student from a foreign country who plans to enroll in your college and wants to know more about the city.

5. In the *Business Education Index,* locate three articles on report writing

6. From the *Monthly Catalog of United States Government Publications,* list the names and prices of five publications that interest you.

7. Ask a librarian at your school which computerized databases are available through your school. Prepare a memo report for your instructor.

8. Select a passage from last week's issue of *Time* or *Newsweek* and quote it verbatim, paraphrase it, and summarize it.

9. What special libraries are in your city? What general libraries? Prepare a list of the libraries, stating whether the library is special or general and the purpose of the library. Also, provide the address, phone number, and name of the head librarian.

10. On a topic of your choice, prepare a list of possible Boolean descriptors and state which electronic databases you would search to obtain information.

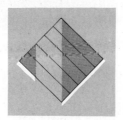

Documentation

Documentation will allow readers to check your sources to see if they agree with your interpretation of the data and will help establish your credibility by showing the nature and extent of your research. Readers who wish to further investigate the topic will appreciate the references you provide. Documentation of reference sources is also essential under copyright laws and common law. Ideas, words, statements, or passages not originated by the writer must be acknowledged and identified.

Topics

Plagiarism and Copyright Laws
Style Manuals
Placement of References and Notes
MLA Style for Footnotes and Bibliographic Entries
APA Style for References
Bibliography and Annotated Bibliography

Whenever you use a secondary source, whether directly (verbatim) or indirectly (paraphrased or summarized), you must document it; that is, give credit to the originator by providing a reference number *and*, if the material is quoted verbatim, enclosing it in quotation marks. Documentation not only gives credit where credit is due, but also adds credibility to the report. Not to give credit, which leads the reader to believe that you originated the information, is unethical and, in most cases, illegal.

PLAGIARISM AND COPYRIGHT LAWS

What is plagiarism?

To present the ideas or material—condensed or abstracted—of others as your own is plagiarism and is punishable by law. In other words, if you were to use material from another source—books, periodicals, newspapers, dictionaries, television, radio, lectures, other students' papers, speeches, letters, interviews—and did not give proper credit to that source, you would be guilty of plagiarism.

Only when information is considered general knowledge and cannot be attributed to one particular source are you not obligated to cite the source. For example, if you say that two methods of collecting primary or original data are experimentation and observation, you would not need to give credit for that statement because it is general knowledge. If you quote information verbatim, however, you must give credit to that particular source even when material is considered general knowledge. The reference to a source of information is called a **citation.**

When does copyrighted material enter the public domain?

Copyright laws protect published materials from being copied without permission. Whenever you wish to use published or copyrighted materials, you need to obtain permission from the author or the holder of the copyright to reproduce that material. The copyright holder may legally charge you a fee. Fifty years after the death of the author or copyright holder, the material enters the public domain. You need not have permission to quote the material, but you do need to acknowledge the source.

STYLE MANUALS

A style manual provides a reference on how to prepare term papers, reports, manuscripts, and scholarly research papers. Style manuals give explicit directions on the form—margins, spacing, indentions, typing, footnoting, table and figure illustrations, documentation, and pagination. When you are not directed to follow a particular format or style manual, you have a wide choice. Some of the more widely used style manuals are

Campbell, William Giles, and Stephen Vaughan Ballou. *Form and Style: Theses, Reports, Term Papers.* 7th ed. Boston: Houghton Mifflin, 1986.

The Chicago Manual of Style. 13th ed. Chicago: The University of Chicago Press, 1982.

Gibaldi, Joseph, and Walter S. Achtert. *MLA Handbook for Writers of Research Papers.* 2nd ed. New York: The Modern Language Association, 1984.

Publication Manual of the American Psychological Association. 3rd ed. Washington: American Psychological Association, 1983.

Turabian, Kate L. *A Manual for Writers of Term Papers, Theses, and Dissertations.* 4th ed. Chicago: University of Chicago Press, 1973.

Is the report writer usually free to choose a style manual? Why or why not?

When preparing manuscripts for publication, theses or dissertations for requirements for a degree, or reports for class or companies, determine whether you are to follow a particular style manual. Many professional journals require that you follow the *MLA Handbook;* other journals require that you follow the *APA Manual.*

Because the *MLA Handbook* is one of the most widely used by professional journals and universities, we have used it for our entries here. The Association for Business Communication, however, requires that articles submitted for publication follow the *APA Manual,* so we have provided entry samples for that style as well.

PLACEMENT OF REFERENCES AND NOTES

Two commonly used methods of documentation in business are parenthetical references and footnotes. A third method—endnotes—is used infrequently in business.

Parenthetical References

What are the three formats for placement of parenthetical references in the text?

Citations within the text of the report are popular because of the ease in reporting them for the writer and the ease in referring to them by the reader. Three formats for parenthetical references are (1) the complete citation, (2) the author and year of publication, and (3) the number.

Complete Citation   When you will have only a few reference notes in your report, give the complete citation within the text itself. For example:

> According to Elwood N. Chapman (*Your Attitude Is Showing.* 4th ed. [Chicago: Science Research Associates, 1983] 51), "Greater productivity must be the goal of American business organizations if they are to survive and compete with other world markets where labor costs are much lower."

Author and Year of Publication   In the author and year of publication format, the complete citation is given in a bibliography and only the author's last name and the year of publication of the work appear in parentheses in the appropriate place in the text.

A recent study of job interviews (Fisher 1987)

When necessary to refer to a particular page rather than to an entire study or work, present the citation as follows:

(Fisher 1987, 25–26)

When two or three authors are cited, list the last names of the authors:

(Dvorak, Tallman, and Verser 1987, 202)

When is et al. used in MLA style?

When more than three authors are cited, list the last name of the first author and then "et al." or "and others."

(VanHoeven et al. 1987)

(LaForge and others 1987)

When two works of the same author are cited, add the title of the publication:

(Haynes, *Personal Time Management* 2)

To avoid duplication when referring to the author by name in the text, place just the page number in parentheses:

Haynes notes that "disorganization is a key culprit for wasted time" (2).

Number   In the number format, the bibliography lists the references serially or alphabetically, and then numbered sequentially. This number identifies the citation in the text of the report. When a citation is identified by number, place the number in parentheses after the reference. In the following example, 2 refers to the second item in the bibliography and 40 refers to the page number.

"Disorganization is a key culprit for wasted time" (2, 40).

Footnotes

What three purposes may footnotes serve?

Footnotes are placed at the foot, or bottom, of the page. They identify the source of information, provide explanations or additional comments, or refer the reader to other sections of the text.

Footnotes appear at the bottom of the page on which references are made to them. They are separated from the last line of the text by a 1½ inch horizontal line beginning at the left margin. Use the underscore key on the typewriter to make the line. Type it a single-space below the last line of the text and double-space after it. Even if the page contains only a few lines of typewritten material, place the footnote at the bottom of the page. Indent the first line of each footnote five spaces (or the same number of spaces as for paragraph indentions within the text).

Type the reference number a half line space above the footnote. Space once after the raised number. Single-space succeeding lines of the same footnote beginning at the left margin. The next footnote begins a double-space after the preceding one. Whenever possible, footnotes should be complete on one page. Footnotes are keyed to the text by superscripts (raised Arabic numbers). These numbers are typed a half space above the typewritten line in the text immediately after the last typed character in the words cited. Number footnotes consecutively throughout the report or begin anew for each chapter.

MLA STYLE FOR FOOTNOTES AND BIBLIOGRAPHIC ENTRIES

Acoording to *The MLA Handbook,* references to secondary sources should include the following information for books and periodicals.

Books

1. Author's name
2. Title of the part of the book
3. Title of book
4. Name of the editor, translator, or compiler
5. Edition
6. The number of volumes
7. Name of the series
8. Place of publication, name of the publisher, and date of publication
9. Page numbers

Periodicals

1. Author's name
2. Title of article
3. Name of periodical
4. Series number or name
5. Volume number
6. Date of publication
7. Page numbers

Although many bibliographic entries or footnotes will contain all the items, some will not. For example, one entry may not have a series or volume number.

Form for Entries

What are the obvious differences in punctuation for footnotes and bibliographic entries?

Bibliographic entries and footnotes are similar, with some minor differences. Compare the following examples based on the *MLA Handbook.* In each instance, the footnote is given first and then the bibliographical entry.

Book with One Author

[1]Bernadine P. Branchaw, *English Made Easy,* 2nd ed. (New York: Gregg Division/McGraw-Hill, 1986) 23.

Branchaw, Bernadine P. *English Made Easy.* 2nd ed. New York: Gregg Division/McGraw-Hill, 1986.

Book by Two or Three Authors

[2]Joel P. Bowman and Bernadine P. Branchaw, *Business Communication: From Process to Product* (Chicago: The Dryden Press, 1987) 124–27.

Bowman, Joel P., and Bernadine P. Branchaw. *Business Communication: From Process to Product.* Chicago: The Dryden Press, 1987.

Book with More Than Three Authors

[3]Bernadine P. Branchaw et al., *Office Procedures for the Professional Secretary* (Chicago: Science Research Associates, 1984) 49.

Branchaw, Bernadine P., et al. *Office Procedures for the Professional Secretary.* Chicago: Science Research Associates, 1984.

When should the author's name be omitted in footnotes and bibliographic entries?

Books by the Same Author or Authors   When citing two or more works by the same author or authors, list the names of the author or authors in the first entry only. After the first entry, type three hyphens instead of the name followed by a period. Space twice and then provide the rest of the entry.

[4]Joel P. Bowman and Bernadine P. Branchaw, *Business Communication: From Process to Product* (Chicago: The Dryden Press, 1987) 124–27.

[5]---.*Business Report Writing* (Chicago: The Dryden Press, 1988) 25–29.

Bowman, Joel P., and Bernadine P. Branchaw. *Business Commu-*

nication: From Process to Product. Chicago: The Dryden Pr
1987.

---. *Business Report Writing.* Chicago: The Dryden Press, 1988.

Book with No Author Given or an Anonymous Book

[6] *The MLA Style Sheet,* 2nd ed. (New York: The Modern Language
Association of America, 1970) 26.

The MLA Style Sheet. 2nd ed. New York: The Modern Language
Association of America, 1970.

Edited Book

[7] John Stewart, ed., *Bridges Not Walls: A Book about Interpersonal Communication,* 4th ed. (New York: Random House, 1986)
12.

Stewart, John, ed. *Bridges Not Walls: A Book about Interpersonal
Communication.* 4th ed. New York: Random House, 1986.

Unpublished Dissertation

[8] Lowell E. Crow, "An Information Processing Approach to
Industrial Buying: The Search and Choice Process," diss., Indiana
U, 1974, 24.

Crow, Lowell E. "An Information Processing Approach to Industrial Buying: The Search and Choice Process." Diss. Indiana U,
1974.

Book without Place of Publication, Publisher, Date, or Pagination

n.p.—no place of publication given

n.p.—no publisher given

n.d.—no date of publication given

n.pag.—no pagination given

The abbreviations are given where the full information would be cited
if available. For example:

(New York: Harper & Row, 1986) 25

(n.p.: n.p., n.d.) n.pag.

do entries
for journals
n continuous
gination? From
ournals that begin
each issue on page
1? From
magazines?

Article in a Journal with Continuous Pagination

[9]Larry R. Smeltzer, "An Analysis of Receivers' Reactions to Electronically Mediated Communication," *The Journal of Business Communication* 23 (1986): 38.

Smeltzer, Larry R. "An Analysis of Receivers' Reactions to Electronically Mediated Communication." *The Journal of Business Communication* 23 (1986): 38–54.

Article in a Journal for Which Pagination Is Not Continuous

For a journal that begins each issue on page 1, add a period and the issue number directly after the volume number.

[10]Ronald D. Michman, "Linking Futuristics with Marketing Planning, Forecasting, and Strategy," *Journal of Consumer Marketing* 1.3 (1984): 21.

Michman, Ronald D. "Linking Futuristics with Marketing Planning, Forecasting, and Strategy." *Journal of Consumer Marketing* 1.3 (1984): 17–23.

Article in a Magazine

[11]Jo-Anne Harman, "Royal Holiday," *Michigan Living* Feb. 1987: 24.

Harman, Jo-Anne. "Royal Holiday." *Michigan Living* Feb. 1987: 24–28.

What is MLA style
for dates of
newspapers?

Article from a Daily Newspaper

[12]Paul Keep, "Hobby Develops into Growing Company," *Kalamazoo Gazette* 15 Feb. 1987: El.

Keep, Paul. "Hobby Develops into Growing Company." *Kalamazoo Gazette* 15 Feb. 1987: El.

Editorial

[13]"State a Good Spot for Super Collider," editorial, *Kalamazoo Gazette* 15 Feb. 1987: A22.

"State a Good Spot for Super Collider." Editorial. *Kalamazoo Gazette* 15 Feb. 1987: A22.

Anonymous Article

[14]"Troubled Conscience," *Time* 16 Feb. 1987: 43.

"Troubled Conscience." *Time* 16 Feb. 1987: 43.

Government Publications   Because of the thousands of materials published by the government, it would be impossible to give examples of footnotes to cover all situations. Briefly, when citing a government publication, give the author's name (if known) first, then the agency, such as:

U.S. Congress, Senate

U.S. Congress, House

Michigan Department of Transportation

Why is GPO often abbreviated?

then the title of publication (underscored), followed by the place, publisher (Government Printing Office [GPO]), date, and page numbers.

[15]United States, Dept. of Commerce, Bureau of the Census, *Population Estimates and Projections* (Washington: GPO, 1980) 3.

United States. Dept. of Commerce. Bureau of the Census. *Population Estimates and Projections.* Washington: GPO, 1980.

The Complete Guide to Citing Government Documents by Diane Garner and Diane H. Smith (Bethesda, MD: Congressional Information Services, 1984) provides an excellent source for documenting government publications.

Personal Letters

[16]Edward C. Blake, letter to Doris M. Milligan, 18 Mar. 1987.

Blake, Edward C. Letter to Doris M. Milligan. 18 Mar. 1987.

Personal or Telephone Interview

[17]Ian Vanderhorst, personal interview, 1 Mar. 1987.

Vanderhorst, Ian. Personal interview. 1 Mar. 1987.

Computer Software

[18]*Word Juggler,* computer software, Quark, 1982.

Word Juggler. Computer software. Quark, 1982.

Radio and Television Programs

[19]*Today,* NBC, New York, 12 May 1986.

Today. NBC. New York. 12 May 1986.

Speeches and Lectures

[20]Harriet Folz, "Community Involvement," monthly meeting of the Zonta Club, Kalamazoo, MI, 20 Jan. 1987.

Folz, Harriet. "Community Involvement." Monthly meeting of the Zonta Club. Kalamazoo, MI. 20 Jan. 1987.

APA STYLE FOR REFERENCES

Does APA style permit all three MLA formats for parenthetical references?

According to the *Publication Manual of the American Psychological Association,* references within the text briefly identify the source so that readers may refer to the alphabetical reference list at the end of the article for complete bibliographic information. For reference citations in the text, the *APA Manual* recommends the author-date method of citation—inserting the surname of the author and the year of publication at the appropriate place.

Elements

All elements in the citation should be arranged in the following sequence.

Books

1. Book authors or editors
2. Date of publication
3. Book title
4. Publication information

Periodicals

1. Article authors
2. Date of publication
3. Article title
4. Journal title and publication information

Examples of Text Citations

The following examples illustrate citations within the text.

One Author

Jones (1986) designed . . .

In a recent experiment (Jones, 1986) . . .

In 1986, Jones designed . . .

Two Authors

Sloan and Meijers (1985) learned . . .

As shown by Sloan and Meijers (1985) . . .

When is *et al.* used in APA style?

More Than Two Authors

Hay, Haines, and Barton (1986) learned [first occurrence] . . .

Hay et al. (1986) learned [subsequent citations] . . .

No Author   Cite the first two or three words of the reference list entry, which is usually the title, and the year.

the article "Survey in Chicago," 1986

on child care ("Survey in Chicago," 1986)

(Anonymous, 1983)

Corporate Author   The first text citation gives the full corporate name.

(Association for Mental Health [AMH], 1986)

Subsequent text citations may be abbreviated if the abbreviation is familiar or readily understandable.

(AMH, 1981)

Authors with Same Surname   Include the authors' initials in all text citations.

G. H. Daley (1986) and F. A. Daley (1985)

Multiple Citations

Studies (Arnold, 1965, 1970, 1980a, 1980b)

Studies (Bates, 1965; Collins, 1970; Walters, 1980)

Examples of References in Bibliography

The following examples illustrate how references would be presented in the bibliography.

Does APA style permit the spelling out of authors' first names? Does MLA style?

Book with One Author

Branchaw, B. P. (1986). *English made easy* (2nd ed.). New York: Gregg Divison/McGraw-Hill.

Book with No Author

The MLA style sheet. (2nd ed.). (1970) New York: The Modern Language Association of America.

Edited Book

Stewart, J. (Ed.). (1986). *Bridges not walls: A book about interpersonal communication.* (4th ed.). New York: Random House.

Unpublished Doctoral Dissertation

Brown, S. W. (1984). *Mental health clinics.* Unpublished doctoral dissertation. St. Mary's University, Halifax, Nova Scotia.

Journal Article with One Author, Journal Paginated by Issue

Smeltzer, L. R. (1986). An analysis of receivers' reactions to electronically mediated communication. *The Journal of Business Communication, 23*(4), 38–54.

Does APA style use the ampersand when listing multiple authors? Does MLA style use the ampersand?

Journal Article with More Than Two Authors, Journal Paginated by Issue

Brown, S. C., Roen, D. H., & Ingham, Z. (1986). The reader as entity. *The Journal of Business Communication, 23*(2), 13–21.

Magazine Article

Harman, J. A. (1987, February). Royal holiday. *Michigan Living,* pp. 24–28.

Newspaper Article

Keep, P. (1987, February 15). Hobby develops into growing company. *Kalamazoo Gazette.* p. E1.

Computer Software

Word juggler. (1982). [Computer program manual]. Denver: Quark.

BIBLIOGRAPHY AND ANNOTATED BIBLIOGRAPHY

The bibliography is an orderly listing of source materials. The bibliographic entries refer to entire works, not just parts or pages as do the footnotes, and they come at the end of the report or paper.

Because the prefix *biblio* is the Greek word for book, some people prefer the heading *References* or *List of Works Cited.* Bibliography, however, is appropriate for all source materials, whether books, periodicals, interviews, letters, speeches, films, or other secondary sources.

The bibliography includes all works referred to in the text or in the footnotes. Do not include works that you have consulted and did not use.

What is an
annotated
bibliography?

Bibliographic entries are usually arranged in alphabetical order by the author's last name. When no author is given or when a work is anonymous, use the first word in the title other than a definite or indefinite article (*A Map of Maps* would be alphabetized under *M*). See Exhibit 11.1. When you have a number of diverse sources, you may further arrange your bibliography by classifications, such as books, periodicals, government publications, and others. You may also arrange your bibliography by primary and secondary sources, by chronological order, or by subject. When you use separate categories, alphabetize the entries within them.

As Exhibit 11.2 illustrates, when the bibliography entry gives a brief description of the value and content of the source, it is called an annotated bibliography.

SUMMARY

Documentation of reference sources is essential under copyright laws and common law. Ideas, words, statements, or passages not originated by the writer must be acknowledged and identified.

Plagiarism is presenting ideas or materials of others as your own and is punishable by law. Copyright laws protect published materials from being copied without permission.

A style manual provides a reference on how to prepare term papers, reports, manuscripts, and other scholarly research papers. Style manuals give explicit directions on how to prepare the final report. The *MLA Handbook* is widely used; however, the Association for Business Communication specifies use of the *APA Manual*.

Two commonly used methods of documentation in business are parenthetical references and footnotes. A third method—endnotes—is used infrequently in business.

The bibliography is an orderly listing of source materials. Bibliographic entries refer to entire works, not just parts or pages as do the footnotes, and they come at the end of the report or paper. Bibliographic entries are arranged in alphabetical order; by classifications, such as books, periodicals, government publications; by subject; and by chronological order.

EXERCISES

Review and Discussion Questions

1. What is documentation?
2. Why is documentation necessary?
3. What is plagiarism?
4. What is a citation?

Exhibit 11.1   **Sample Bibliography in MLA Style**

BIBLIOGRAPHY

Blyth, W. John and Mary M. Blyth. <u>Telecommunications</u>. Indianapolis: Bobbs-Merrill, 1985.

Chapman, Elwood N. <u>Your Attitude Is Showing</u>. 5th ed. Palo Alto, CA: Science Research Associates, 1987.

Katzan, Harry, Jr. <u>Office Automation: A Manager's Guide</u>. New York: AMACOM, 1983.

Kirszner, Laurie G. and Stephen R. Mandell. <u>The Holt Handbook</u>. New York: Holt, Rinehart and Winston, 1986.

Larson, Steven B. "Microcomputer Activities Can Enhance Your Office Procedures Class." <u>Business Education Forum</u> 41.5 (1987): 14-16.

O'Connor, Bridget N. "Telelearning: Teleconferencing and the Business Educator." <u>Journal of Business Education</u> May 1985: 317-320.

Quible, Zane K. and Margaret H. Johnson. <u>Introduction to Word Processing</u>. Cambridge, MA: Winthrop, 1980.

Exhibit 11.2   **Sample Annotated Bibliography in MLA Style**

BIBLIOGRAPHY

Blanchard, Kenneth and Spencer Johnson. <u>The One Minute Manager</u>. New York:
Berkley Books, 1981. An easy-to-read text on one-minute goal settings,
one-minute praisings, and one-minute reprimands.

Fisher, Roger and William Ury. <u>Getting to Yes: Negotiating Agreement Without
Giving In</u>. New York: Penguin Books, 1983. A thorough and interesting
treatment of the techniques of principled negotiations.

Kriegel, Robert and Marilyn Harris Kriegel. <u>The C Zone: Peak Performance
Under Pressure</u>. Garden City, NY: Anchor Books, 1984. A practical
approach to dealing with stress in productive ways.

Maltz, Maxwell, <u>Psycho-Cybernetics</u>. Englewood Cliffs, NJ: Prentice-Hall,
1960. A classic treatment of the influence of attitude on performance.

Peters, Thomas J. and Robert H. Waterman, Jr. <u>In Search of Excellence</u>. New
York: Harper & Row, 1982. Covers business success in general, but contains many ideas about how interpersonal communication can contribute to
organization success.

5. When does material enter the public domain?

6. What are style manuals? Name two of them.

7. Where can documentation of reference sources be placed?

8. Why are footnotes so called?

9. What is the difference between endnotes and footnotes?

10. What is the difference between a bibliography and an annotated bibliography?

Problems and Applications

1. Prepare a bibliography for five books on a topic of your choice.

2. Prepare a bibliography for five magazines on a topic of your choice.

3. Prepare a bibliography containing at least three books and three periodicals on report writing.

4. Prepare the following:
   a. Footnote (No. 4) referring to page 185
   b. Bibliography
   Using this information:

   - Book title—*A Passion for Excellence*
   - Authors—Tom Peters and Nancy Austin
   - Publisher—Random House
   - Place of publication—New York
   - Date of publication—1985
   - Total pages—437

5. Prepare footnotes from the following information:
   a. Sage Publications, "The Interpretive Perspective: An Alternative to Functionalism," *Communication and Organizations: An Interpretive Approach* by Linda Putnam. Editors—Linda Putnam and Pacanowsky, Michael. Beverly Hills, California, 1983. Pages 31–54.
   b. Ede, Lisa and Andrea Lunsford. "Audience Addressed/Audience Invoked: The Role of Audience in Composition Theory and Pedagogy." *College Composition and Communication.* May 1984. pp. 155–171. 35, No. 2.
   c. Reading, MA. Addison-Wesley Publishing Company. Jay Galbraith. *Organization Design.* pp. 36–37. 1977.

6. Prepare a bibliography from the information in Problem 5.

7. Prepare a ten-item bibliography on one aspect of your major. The bibliography should include books, periodicals, newspapers, interviews, a reference book, and a dissertation.

8. Prepare two footnotes each from *The Wall Street Journal* and *The New York Times.*

9. Prepare four footnotes and a bibliography for a telephone interview and a personal interview.

10. Check your library's subject card catalog and select a topic on which you have little information. Prepare a bibliography of between five and ten sources giving call numbers after each bibliographic entry.

11. Prepare footnotes (assume page numbers) and the corresponding bibliographic entries for the following items. Use the MLA style.
    a. A book with one author
    b. A book with three authors
    c. An edited work
    d. An article in a magazine
    e. An article in a reference work
    f. An unpublished dissertation
    g. A government publication
    h. An article from a newspaper
    i. A lecture
    j. A telephone interview

12. Using a convenient library, locate, record, and document information on the following:
    a. The origin of the word bibliography
    b. The names and addresses of the executive officers of IBM
    c. Titles and sources of information of three articles on computerized databases
    d. *The New York Times'* headline on the day you were born. Provide the information in a memo report to your instructor.

13. In any one of *Moody's* manuals that your school's library possesses, locate information on a business of your choice. In a memo report, provide that information along with complete bibliographical data to your instructor.

14. Check your library's bound periodicals and locate issues of *Time* and *Newsweek* for the day you were born. Prepare a short report on the happenings covered in that issue. What were the cover stories? What films were being reviewed? What books were being reviewed? What was reported on education? national news? medicine? Give complete bibliographic data.

C H A P T E R   1 2

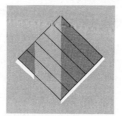

Primary Research

Information gathered by experimenting, asking questions, or watching others is called primary research because *you* are the first to obtain it. Secondary sources may not provide the information you need to make a decision. When you cannot find the data you need in an existing source, you will have to collect it yourself.

Topics

Observation
Experimentation
Survey

After you have thoroughly checked the secondary sources available to solve the problem you are investigating, you may need to conduct some original research. In other words, you may need to obtain the information firsthand.

Information you obtain by asking and analyzing questions, watching and interpreting the behavior of others, and testing and evaluating, is called primary research because you are the first to find and interpret that information. Because primary research is more time consuming and more expensive than secondary research, primary research is conducted only when necessary to understand a situation or solve a problem. When secondary research provides the information you need, use it. Do not duplicate someone else's research unless you need to verify the accuracy or applicability of that research. As a researcher, you need to decide what kind of information to gather and where and how you will gather it. This will require extensive and careful planning on your part. The overall plan or strategy for investigating a problem is called a **research design.** It includes a procedure for collecting, measuring, analyzing, and interpreting data. Three main methods of collecting primary data are observation, experimentation, and surveys.

OBSERVATION

Collecting raw data by watching or seeing what is happening to people, objects, or events and noting that information is called **observation.** Observation is used when you need to obtain data through the use of the five senses—seeing, hearing, touching, tasting, or smelling. For example, you use observation when you need to (1) count the number of women wearing slacks in an office; (2) listen to sounds of music; (3) touch various samples of cloth; (4) taste food and drink; or (5) smell such items as flowers, perfumes, spices, or wines.

What is the harm in controlling or manipulating the people, objects, or events being observed?

You examine phenomena under existing conditions. You merely observe what is taking place; no attempt is made to control or manipulate conditions. Observation requires a systematic procedure for observing the phenomena and for recording that information.

In a supermarket, you can determine brand preferences by observing shoppers as they make their selections; in an office, you can determine the number of women wearing slacks or dresses; or standing on a corner at a busy intersection, you can determine the number of people who pass by.

Observation can also include a search of a company's records for such items as production figures, advertising costs, volume of sales, and amount of sales. These figures will provide you with primary data. In Chapter 10, we discussed using company records as secondary data. The difference depends on whether you will use material or information already recorded by someone else or are searching company records to collect new data. For example, if you were to use a salesperson's call report for a customer's profile, that would be secondary research. (The salesperson recorded the description first in the call report.) On the other hand, if you were using that call report and other call reports from that same company to record the total sales for each call and then using that raw data for a report, that would be primary investigation. You would be taking raw data—sales figures—from company records to prepare an original report on total sales in a particular region. When accountants examine or observe and analyze the company's financial records to prepare their audit reports, they are conducting primary research—using raw data—to draw new conclusions.

Procedure

Before you attempt to make your observations of certain phenomena, you should have a clear understanding of the purpose of your investigation. Do you want to know the exact number of minutes that a secretary spends typing in one hour? two hours? in the morning? afternoon? When the purpose is clear, then you can design a form for recording and tabulating your observations. The form should be arranged so that it allows for quick and easy recording of observations that you make. In addition to the form, you also need to decide who, what, when, where, and how.

Who: Whom will you observe? typists? secretaries? administrative assistants? anyone who types?

What: What job classification will you use? What is to be observed? What companies should you investigate? financial institutions? medical? educational? government agencies?

When: When will you conduct the investigation? morning? afternoon? what day? week? month? year?

Where: Which section of the city should be included? east? west? north? south? some from each? all?

How: How many observations should be made? How long will you observe? How will you record the observations? stopwatch? counter? tally sheet?

Why must the observer's plan of action be specific?

Your plan of action should be specific so that, when several people are doing the observing, each will be following the same procedure.

Exhibit 12.1 illustrates an observational tally sheet.

Advantages

The advantages of using observation as a research technique are the following:

1. Observation may be the only method for recording the particular phenomena that can be seen, such as physical activities, company records, processes, environment, and human behavior.

2. The accuracy of observation is high. Trained observers record only what they see—not what others tell them. They attempt to report accurately what they see in spite of any prejudices or biases they may have.

independent variable and a dependent variable. Two common experimental designs are the one-group and the two-group methods.

One-Group Method

In the one-group method of experimentation, the experimenter adds to or subtracts a single experimental factor from a group (or an individual) and then measures the resulting change. In other words, one group is evaluated (or tested), then subjected to the influence of a variable, and then evaluated a second time. For example, an office manager wants to increase office productivity and believes the purchase of a word processor would help. First, the office manager would select an experimental group of typists and then measure the number of pages typed before introducing a word processor. After the installation of the word processor and a reasonable length of "learning" time, the office manager would again measure production. The differences in measurements could be the result of the use of the word processor.

Step 1: Select Experimental Group (Typists)

Step 2: Measure Variable (Pages Typed)

Step 3: Add Experimental Factor (Word Processor)

Step 4: Measure Variable (Pages Typed)

The difference between the measurement of Step 2 and that of Step 4 *could* be the result of the experimental factor.

In an experiment of this kind, however, serious errors can be made. For example, the office manager would need to make certain that no other factor—the enthusiasm of the office manager or typists toward the experiment, the willingness of the typists to increase productivity, the arrival of new equipment in the office, the motivation of the typists to do well, or the kinds of material typed—affected the results of the experiment.

Two-Group Method

What is the purpose of using a control group when conducting an experiment?

Often the experiment may involve two or more groups. In the two-group method of experimentation, the experimenter uses two or more groups—a **control group** and an **experimental group** (or groups). The two groups must be essentially alike (age, sex, intelligence, background, familiarity with subject matter, and the like) before a variable or experimental factor is added to (or subtracted from) the experimental group. Groups are measured before and after the added or subtracted variable; the differences between the two groups can be attributed to the effect of the added or subtracted variable.

For example, suppose that the office manager wanted to test two groups of typists—a control group and an experimental group. Both groups are selected according to predetermined criteria so that they are essentially alike. At the start of the experiment, the production of both groups is measured using electric typewriters. The subjects in the experimental group are given word processors; no change is made in the control group. The production of the two groups is measured over a set period of time to determine the differences that occurred since the first production measurement. Differences between the first and last measurement within the control group could be attributed to other influences; differences between the control group and the experimental group could be attributed to the added variable—the word processor—and other influences. The word processor may or may not have been an influence on the second group of typists. Other influences may have been at work in either of the groups. See Exhibit 12.2.

Procedure

What are some questions the experimenter must consider when designing an experiment?

As is true in observation, the experimenter must have a clear understanding of the problem under investigation. In addition, the researcher needs to carefully design the experiment. Will one group be used or two? How will subjects be selected? Under what conditions and setting? Because of the uniqueness of each situation, we cannot provide exact procedures for all experiments. Each experimenter must design a procedure for his or her individual study. The following guidelines will help you design your study.

One-Group Method When the experimenter elects to use the one-group method, he or she needs to select the subject or subjects. Then the experimenter measures the variable, introduces the experimental factor, and after a reasonable and predetermined length of time, again measures the variable. Differences in measurements can be attributed to the experimental factor. See Exhibit 12.2.

Assume that a company wants to determine the effectiveness of television advertising for Product A as measured by sales. The procedure for the experimenter would be

1. Select the experimental group—in this case, Product A.
2. Record sales (the variable) of Product A for one month.
3. Introduce experimental factor—television advertising.
4. Record sales of Product A during the month of television advertising.
5. Find differences between the two measurements (record of sales).
6. Analyze the results, draw conclusions, and make recommendations.

Exhibit 12.2   Experimental Group and Control Group

Step 1:	Select Experimental Group	Select Control Group
Step 2:	Measure Variable	Measure Variable
Step 3:	Add Variable	
Step 4:	Measure Variable	Measure Variable

Differences in measurement at Steps 2 and 4 in the Experimental Group could be the result of the added variable and other factors. Differences in measurement between Steps 2 and 4 for the Control Group are the result of other factors only. Comparing the differences between the Experimental Group and the Control Group shows the influence of the variable.

Differences in sales—before and after television advertising—could be attributed to the experimental factor—television advertising. For example, if 10,000 Product As were sold before and 100,000 after television advertising, the experimenter could assume that the increase in sales was due to television advertising. Other factors that could have influenced sales—such as time of year, holidays, or economy—should be considered as well.

Two-Group Method When the experimenter elects to use two groups—control and experimental—he or she needs to select subjects who are essentially alike. The experimenter measures the variable, introduces the experimental factor into the experimental group only, and then again measures the variable in both groups. The differences between the two measurements in the control group may be the result of other influences; and in the experimental group, differences may be the result of the experimental factor plus other influences. See Exhibit 12.2.

Assume that a company wants to determine the effectiveness of a motivational seminar for its salespeople. The procedure for the experimenter would be

1. Select subjects—salespeople—according to predetermined criteria, such as sex, age, and number of sales so that they are essentially alike.
2. Randomly place all salespeople in either the control group or the experimental group.

3. Record the sales of both groups for one month.

4. Have the experimental group attend a 5-day motivational seminar. (The control group does not attend the seminar.)

5 Record the sales of both groups for 1 month after the seminar.

6. Find differences between the two measurements of the control group and of the experimental group.

7. Analyze the results, draw conclusions, and make recommendations.

Differences in sales between the two groups could be attributed to the experimental factor—the motivational seminar. For example, suppose that the total sales for both groups were relatively equal—about $100,000—before the motivational seminar. If after the seminar the experimental group had total sales of $250,000 and the control group had only $150,000, the experimenter could assume that the increase in sales for the experimental group was the result of the motivational seminar. Other influences (time of year, advertising) could also have affected the differences in both groups.

Advantages

How can the computer be used in experimentation?

Some of the advantages of using experimentation as a research technique are

1. Experimental research yields extremely precise results when conducted in the laboratory. It is especially useful in the sciences—physics, chemistry, biology, medicine.

2. Experimentation using the one-group or the two-group method can be highly reliable and accurate outside the laboratory when all variables can be controlled or held constant.

3. Computer research can create simulated environments so that variables can be manipulated and analyzed quickly and easily.

Disadvantages

The disadvantages of experimentation are

1. Many business problems do not lend themselves to experimental research.

2. Experimentation using the one-group method is not as reliable as using the two-group—control and experimental.

3. It is almost impossible to have two groups exactly alike.

4. It is difficult to control and identify all factors that may effect the experiment, such as the enthusiasm of the experimenter or the effort of subjects to do well when they know they are part of an experiment.

SURVEYS

Because not all elements can be observed or examined experimentally, you need to obtain much information by asking questions or surveying people. The survey (also called the interview technique) is a method of research used to gather information about existing situations. It is concerned with finding out who, what, when, where, and how much. (Experimental researchers, on the other hand, are concerned with the why, the cause and effect relationship.) The survey is the main procedure for investigating attitudes, opinions, and motives. It is a highly structured interview that does not need to be done face-to-face. Generally, a list of questions (questionnaire) is prepared first and then the survey is conducted by personal, telephone, or mail interviews. (See Chapter 13 for a discussion on questionnaires.) People surveyed or questioned are selected by statistical procedures called **sampling.**

Sampling

When is sampling necessary?

When an entire population—called the **universe**—cannot be surveyed (because the population is too large or a complete survey is not economically feasible), the researcher needs to select a representative sampling of the universe. A sample is a part of a larger group. A population may be people, but it may consist of other items, too (see Chapter 14). Coffee-bean buyers, for example, determine the quality of the beans by examining a sample of the whole. The belief is that the sample will be representative—a cross-section of the whole. Three principles of sampling are representativeness, reliability, and validity.

What must be determined before sample size?

Representativeness The representativeness of the sample must be determined before its size; if the sample is unrepresentative, increasing the size will not make it representative. A sample selected from a population of all students living in dorms at one university, for example, would not be representative of the entire school population regardless of sample size, because not all students live on campus. The characteristics of the sample must be the same as the characteristics of the entire population.

Suppose you want to investigate the attitudes of the students at a local college or university. If 35 percent of your universe are freshmen; 30 percent, sophomores; 20 percent, juniors; and 15 percent, seniors; then your sample should reflect the same proportions. The sample should also take into consideration other differences, such as sex, age, and grade point average. This process of making sure that each part of the population (universe) appears in the sample in the same percentage as in the population is called **stratification.** The population is divided into strata (subgroups) and then samples are taken proportionately from each stratum.

What is stratification?

Reliability   Reliability refers to accuracy or dependability of results. A general law of sampling says that the larger the sample, the higher the degree of reliability. In other words, when a larger number of units is taken randomly (each unit in the population has an equal chance of being in the sample) from a large population, they will have a greater chance of having the same characteristics as the larger population. If the sample is reliable, no matter how many times the survey is conducted, the results would be the same—they would be consistent.

Too large a sample, however, is a waste of time and effort, and too small a sample contains chance of errors. You would probably have unreliable results if you survey only five units from an entire population of 500. As you increase your sample size, however, your findings would tend to stabilize. In other words, as the sample size increases, less fluctuation in the findings occurs. See Appendix A.

How do researchers decide on a sample size to assure reliability?

To determine how many survey returns will produce reliability, the researchers arbitrarily select a sample size. They randomly arrange the total number of surveys and divide them into equal groups (10, 50, 100, or whatever number is best) and then select one or more questions that require the most reliability.

The researchers tally the responses for the selected question for the first group and compute the percentage (or average). They then tally the responses for the second group, combine the number with the count for the first group, and compute the percentage (or average) for the cumulative total. After they do the same for all remaining groups, they plot the cumulative percentages (or averages) on a grid. At first the percentages (or averages) will have an erratic pattern, but as the totals are accumulated, they will tend to stabilize. When any additional group's percentage (or average) does not affect the cumulative total, the researchers can assume that they have found the correct number of returns to produce reliability.

In a survey of 1,000 students, for example, the researchers first select a significant question that they want to test for reliability—whether Class A or Class B was more beneficial to the student. Although the researchers could tally either response—Class A or Class B—they decide to tally the Class A responses. They then randomly divide the 1,000 surveys into 10 groups of 100. In the first group of 100 surveys, the researchers find 80 Class A responses, or 80 percent. They plot the 80 percent on the grid. In the second group of 100, they find 70 Class A responses. They add the 70 percent to the first group's total of 80 for a cumulative total of 150 Class A responses. The cumulative percentage of Class A responses (150 ÷ 2) is 75. They plot the 75 percent on the grid.

For the third group, the researchers find 65 Class A responses. They add the 65 to the total of group 1 and 2 (150) and a new cumulative percentage of 71 (215 ÷ 3), which is plotted on the grid. The researchers continue to plot the percentage of each new group combined with

Exhibit 12.3   Cumulative Frequency Test to Determine Reliability

Group Number	Class A Responses in Group	Cumulative Class A Responses	Cumulative Percentages of Class A Responses
1	80	80	80%
2	70	150	75
3	65	215	71
4	48	263	65
5	59	322	64
6	74	396	66
7	76	472	67
8	67	539	67
9	72	611	67
10	61	672	67

those of the preceding groups. Exhibits 12.3 and 12.4 show the erratic pattern in the Cumulative Percentage of Class A Responses column at the beginning. Later, as each new group's responses are cumulated, the findings become more stabilized. At the point where the findings are stable, it is not necessary to analyze additional surveys; you would have a reliable finding for that one question. Although researchers need not test every question in the survey, they should test several of the significant questions to ensure reliability of the entire survey. (See Appendix A for statistical inferences.)

What is meant by a valid survey instrument?

Validity   Your survey instrument must be valid; that is, the survey instrument or technique must measure what it is supposed to measure.

When your survey instrument is ineffective in returning accurate and reliable data, your time and money have been wasted. Survey instruments require trial runs to reveal questionable items—items that are unclear, ambiguous, catchy, subjective, and the like. (Pilot tests are discussed in Chapter 13.)

What may result from asking biased questions in a survey? of using words unfamiliar to the people questioned?

Researchers want to develop as objective a test as possible to have a valid instrument. Although researchers should *never* seek to prove a hypothesis true, some may wish to do so by asking biased questions. This would invalidate the results of the questionnaire.

Another factor that would yield a low validity is using words unfamiliar to the reader. Consider using similar questions—questions that ask for the same information but in a different wording—to check the accuracy of the respondent.

Sampling Techniques

The four major sampling techniques are random, stratified random, systematic, and quota. Other sampling techniques exist and may be described in statistical textbooks.

Exhibit 12.4   **Plotted Cumulative Frequencies**

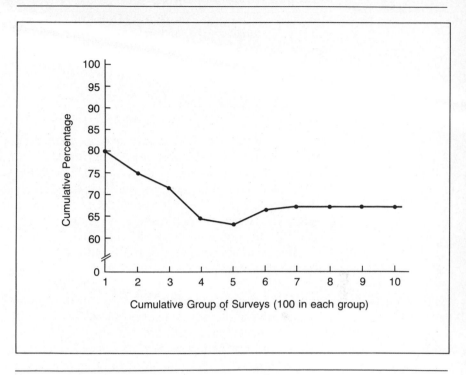

Cumulative Percentage

Cumulative Group of Surveys (100 in each group)

What is a random
sample?

Random Sampling Perhaps the most important, most common, and easiest method of sampling is random sampling. A random sample means that every element in the population has an equal chance to be selected for the sample. Suppose you wanted to draw a random sample from the seniors at the local college. First, place each senior's name on a slip of paper. Next, place all the slips into a container, mix thoroughly, and draw the desired number of names. This method is ideal if you have a hundred or so in the class, but when you have a population of several thousand you might want to consider using a table of random numbers (usually generated by a computer). Books of random numbers are available in most libraries, and most statistics textbooks also carry sample random number tables to which you can refer.

If you want a random sample of 50 students from a senior class of 4,408, make an alphabetic list of all seniors and assign them numbers starting with 0001 consecutively to 4,408. Then, using a four- or five-digit random number book, turn to any page and blindly select a starting point. Numbers can be read in any order—across the rows (forward and backward), up and down the columns, or diagonally. When you come to a number higher than the population total, such as 4,506, simply ignore it because the population only goes to 4,408. Also ignore any

Exhibit 12.5   Stratified Random Sampling

	Total	Percentage of Total	Number Selected
East	648	32	64
West	542	27	54
South	303	16	30
North	507	26	52
	2,000	100	200

repeat numbers—those that appear more than once. Continue the process until you select 50 numbers. Match those numbers with the numbers on your original list. You now have your random sample of 50.

To ensure a random sample, your original list of names must be complete and current. If your list of students contained names of some students who were juniors instead of seniors—or graduates—then all items in the population would not have an equal chance of being selected. Also, if the names of some seniors had been omitted from the list, the resulting sample would not be truly random.

What is a stratified random sample?

Stratified Random Sampling The stratified random sampling method divides the population into subgroups (strata) and then randomly takes a sample from each subgroup (stratum). A sample size of 5 from each of 10 subgroups would give you a sample size of 50. Each subgroup is represented in the sampling according to its proportion of the universe. If you wished, for example, to obtain information as it applies to voters, and your district contains three times as many Republicans as Democrats, your sample should include three times as many Republicans as Democrats.

Or, perhaps you want to divide a population of 2,000 people according to the sections of the United States—East, West, North, or South. If 32 percent (648 ÷ 2,000) of the population comes from the East, then 32 percent of the sample—64 (.32 × 200)—would also come from the East. See Exhibit 12.5.

How is systematic sampling conducted?

Systematic Sampling Systematic sampling is the method of taking selections at regular intervals from a list of the entire population. You select a starting point and then select every *nth* item. For example, if by chance you choose 12 as your first number and use 20 as the *n*, you would select the 32nd (12 + 20), 52nd (32 + 20), 72nd, 92nd, etc. item on the list.

What is the advantage of quota sampling?

Quota Sampling Quota sampling is a nonrandom technique that ensures a sample with the same characteristics as the entire population. Researchers would use this technique whenever they have several factors that they believe would be important considerations in solving the problem. For example, market researchers may want to survey a population of 1,000 and need a sample of 100 to determine factors that influ-

Exhibit 12.6   Quota Sampling

		Population	Percentage	Sample Number
Total				
		1,000	100	100
Sex				
	Female	570	57	57
	Male	430	43	43
Marital Status				
	Single	250	25	25
	Married	750	75	75
Income				
	less than $10,000	50	5	5
	$10,000–$19,999	250	25	25
	$20,000–$29,999	320	32	32
	$30,000–$39,999	260	26	26
	$40,000–$49,999	40	4	4
	$50,000–$59,999	30	3	3
	$60,000–$69,999	30	3	3
	$70,000 or more	20	2	2
Family Size				
	1	350	35	35
	2–3	330	33	33
	4–5	270	27	27
	6–7	20	2	2
	8 or more	30	3	3
Age				
	Less than 1 year	10	1	1
	1–10	10	1	1
	11–20	240	24	24
	21–30	360	36	36
	31–40	200	20	20
	41–50	110	11	11
	51–60	30	3	3
	61–70	30	3	3
	71 and over	10	1	1

ence buying a particular product. They may assume that sex, marital status, income, family size, and age are important characteristics to consider. The researchers would have quotas to fill for each factor. For example, if the total population were 1,000 and of that population 570 were female and 430 male, then the researchers would have a quota of 57 females and 43 males because 57 percent of the total are female and 43 percent are male. Exhibit 12.6 illustrates the number to be surveyed for each characteristic.

Advantages and Disadvantages

The advantage of the survey method is that you can obtain desired information by asking specific questions. Through the survey method you can ask who, what, when, where, and how questions. For example, you can ask a person about his or her age, income, attitudes, opinions, motives, desires, goals, values, or fears.

The disadvantage of the survey method is that the research must generalize from the sample of the population. Because the entire population is too large or a complete survey is not economically feasible, the researcher selects a representative sample, which reflects the composition of the population.

Chapter 13 discusses the advantages and disadvantages of mail questionnaires, personal interviews, and telephone interviews.

SUMMARY

Information obtained by asking and analyzing questions, watching and interpreting the behavior of others, and testing and evaluating is called primary research because you are the first to find the information and interpret it. Three main methods of primary research are observation, experimentation, and surveys.

Collecting raw data by watching or seeing what is happening to people, objects, or events and recording that information is called observation.

In the experimental method of research, controlled conditions are established for an orderly form of testing that is highly reliable and accurate. Experimentation is a form of research that manipulates one variable while holding all others constant.

Because not all elements can be observed or experimentally examined, you may need to obtain your information by asking questions or surveying people. The survey is a method of research used to gather information about an existing situation. It is concerned with finding out who, what, when, where, and how much. People surveyed or questioned are selected by a statistical procedure called sampling. The major sampling techniques are random, stratified random, systematic, and quota.

EXERCISES

Review and Discussion Questions

1. Define primary research. How does it differ from secondary research?
2. What are the three main methods of primary research? Define each.
3. What are the advantages and disadvantages of the observation method of research?
4. Company records can be used for both primary and secondary research. Explain.
5. Describe the differences between the one-group method and the two-group method of experimentation.

6. What are the advantages and disadvantages of the experimental method of research?

7. What is sampling? What is random sampling, stratified random sampling, systematic sampling, and quota sampling?

8. What is meant by representativeness?

9. What is the difference between reliability and validity?

10. What are the advantages and disadvantages of the survey method of research?

Problems and Applications

1. Go to a supermarket on a Saturday between 1 and 4 p.m., and observe 25 customers as they leave the checkout lanes. Observe their appearance, sex, approximate age, and number of grocery bags. Prepare an observation sheet for ease in recording the observations. Write a memo report to your instructor giving the results of your supermarket survey.

2. Conduct an experimental study on a topic of your choice for a 2-week period. Use a one-group method or the two-group method. Prepare a short report.

3. Using a random number table, prepare a random sampling of a group of 25 people. The group can be people in a particular class, people in your dorm, people at work, etc. Choose a sample size of five. Submit a memo to your instructor telling what you did and how you did it. Submit with the memo the list of the entire population, the list of selected names, and the random number table that you used.

4. Prepare a stratified random sampling of a particular population from the classified section of the telephone directory. For example, take the population for surgeons and physicians. The strata might be types of practice—allergy, cardiology, dermatology, etc. Write a memo report to your instructor saying how you arrived at your stratified random sampling. Photocopy pages of the directory, if necessary.

5. For each of the following kinds of primary research, give five examples of the kinds of problems you could solve. Explain your choice.
   a. Experimentation
   b. Observation
   c. Survey

6. For each of the following kinds of sampling techniques, cite three examples that could use each effectively.
   a. Random sampling
   b. Stratified random sampling
   c. Systematic sampling

d. Quota sampling (State at least four important characteristics to consider.)

7. Prepare an observational tally sheet on a topic of your choice.

8. Prepare an observational tally sheet on a parking problem.

9. You are asked to determine—by observation—the effectiveness of the new packaging of a product of your choice. In a memo to your instructor, state what you would do.

10. Because students frequently complain about inadequate parking facilities on your campus, you are asked to prepare a short report identifying the problem and an observational tally sheet.

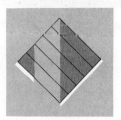

Surveys

Because you will not always be able to obtain information through observation or experimentation, you may need to conduct a survey by developing a series of questions and asking them of a specific audience. This chapter presents the basic considerations for conducting reliable and objective surveys.

Topics

Questionnaires
Interviews
The Delphi Technique
Ethics

The most widely used method for asking questions to obtain primary data is the questionnaire. How do your employees feel about the flextime policy soon to be introduced in your company? What changes could your company make in a product to increase its attractiveness to consumers? These are questions that you can answer only by asking appropriate people about their attitudes, opinions, and ideas through mail surveys, personal interviews, or telephone interviews.

QUESTIONNAIRES

What is the purpose of a questionnaire?

A questionnaire is an orderly list of questions used to obtain primary data—facts, opinions, attitudes, behavior characteristics, and preferences—from people. It provides answers to questions about what people think and why they think in a certain way. In addition, questionnaires can help answer questions about how people will react. The answers from questionnaires provide information for making decisions, improving products, recommending policies and procedures, and suggesting changes.

Advantages

Using questionnaires for obtaining information has many advantages. Some are

1. Mail questionnaires can be distributed at low cost.
2. They can be distributed quickly and easily.
3. They can reach large numbers of people scattered over a large geographic area.
4. Respondents can remain anonymous.
5. Prejudices and biases of the interviewer can be eliminated.
6. Respondents can complete questionnaires at a time convenient for them.
7. Time can be saved by both interviewer and interviewee.

Disadvantages

Questionnaires also have disadvantages.

1. Mail questionnaires may be sent to a representative sample of the population, but the returns may not be representative.
2. Questions may be misinterpreted, answered inadequately, changed, overlooked, or omitted.
3. Convincing people to respond and to respond by a specific time is difficult.

4. Questionnaires may be invalid and unreliable if not prepared properly.

5. Questions that seem clear to the researcher may be ambiguous to the respondent.

6. It takes time to design, test, evaluate, and refine a questionnaire.

Guidelines

What are some ways to make questions clear? easy to answer? (These may be found throughout the list of 30 guidelines.)

When you have a carefully prepared questionnaire, you can expect good results. The following guidelines can help you design a questionnaire that will eliminate many of the disadvantages.

1. Identify the questionnaire by giving it a title, stating its purpose, and identifying yourself and the organization with which you are affiliated.

2. Provide clear instructions. What do you want your respondent to do? Circle? Check one? Check all that apply? Select the best answer? Rank in order of preference? Adequate instructions tend to increase reliability and validity of the questionnaire.

3. Make questions clear, easy to understand, and concerned with only one topic. Avoid ambiguous or unfamiliar words, technical jargon, vague expressions, and relative terms, such as often, regular, and the like.
   a. Do you regularly drive to work?
      (What is regular? daily? weekly? monthly?)
   b. How do you drive to work?
      (In a car? by Main Street? alone? fast?)
   c. Have you ever had amoebiasis?
      (What is it?)
   d. Why did you sell your condominium?
      (Money? neighbors? location? construction? taxes?)

4. Make questions easy to answer so that respondents can complete the questionnaire quickly and easily.

5. Design questionnaires so that respondents can mark them easily and you can tabulate them easily. Use mark sense answer sheets for machine scoring when appropriate.

6. Write questions for your particular audience. Use vocabulary appropriate for your group.

How can respondents be encouraged to answer personal questions?

7. Avoid personal questions unless they are essential to your study. When it is necessary to know the respondent's age or income, provide ranges. Because people may be offended by personal questions, place them toward the end of the questionnaire rather than at the beginning. If the questions were at the beginning, respondents might not complete the questionnaire. If respondents encounter them at the end, they are more likely to provide the

information because they have already spent the time answering the previous questions. They are also more likely to answer personal questions if you tell them how the information will be used and explain its importance to the study. Assure respondents that information will be kept confidential. Guarantee anonymity. Consider the following questions:

What is your age? Check one.

_____ 20 or under

_____ 21–30

_____ 31–40

_____ 41–50

_____ 51–60

_____ 61–70

_____ 71 or over

What is your yearly income? Check one.

_____ under $10,000

_____ $10,000–19,999

_____ $20,000–29,999

_____ $30,000–39,999

_____ $40,000–49,999

_____ $50,000–59,999

_____ $60,000–69,999

_____ $70,000 or over

What are leading questions?

8. Avoid leading questions—those that strongly suggest a biased answer. Leading questions do not elicit accurate answers. Instead of asking, "Do you prefer Apple computers?" ask "What brand of computer do you prefer?" It is better to ask, "What is your favorite television program?" than "Is 'Dallas' your favorite television program?" Many respondents would answer "yes" even if they did not watch it.

9. Ask questions for which answers are easy to provide. How many respondents, for example, would make computations for the question, "How much money do you spend each year on gas for your car?"

10. Avoid negative phrasing of questions—especially double negatives. Negative phrasing is confusing. State questions in positive terms.

Poor: Would it not be uncommon to. . . .

Did you not hear about . . .

You subscribe to *The Wall Street Journal,* don't you?

Better: Would it be common to. . . .

What have you heard. . . .

To what daily newspaper do you subscribe?

11. Begin questions with "Who," "What," "When," "Where," "Why," or "How," and you will probably receive specific answers.

12. Limit each question to one item. When respondents are asked a question that suggests two answers, they will not know which answer to give. Consider the question: "Would you like to receive a copy of *The Wall Street Journal* at your home? If the respondent answers "no," does it mean that he or she does not want *The Wall Street Journal* or that he or she does not want it at home?

13. Avoid questions that make your respondents look from one question to another, such as "If you answered "a" in Question 8, go to Question 12; if you answered "b" go to Question 15; and if you answered "c" go to. . . .

What are contingency questions? When should they be used?

14. Use contingency questions when a question depends on a previous question. Contingency questions permit respondents to disregard questions that do not apply to them. For example:

Were you ever a committee member? Yes _____ No _____
If yes, how many hours a week were devoted to attending committee meetings?

_____ **0–4**

_____ **5–8**

_____ **9–12**

_____ **13 or more**

15. Include a "don't know" choice (or something similar) when you have questions that ask for a "yes" or "no" response.

16. Provide a space for "other (please specify)" answers when using a checklist. For example:

What is your classification? Check one.

_____ **Freshman**

_____ **Sophomore**

_____ **Junior**

_____ **Senior**

_____ **Other (please specify)**_____

"Other" would include any other possibility, from a graduate student to a senior citizen who has permission to attend class.

17. Arrange questions in a neat and logical order. Progress from the simple to the complex. Questions should flow smoothly from one to the other.

18. Categorize questions when possible. Grouping not only presents an organized questionnaire but also encourages respondents to complete the categories and simplifies the process of organizing the results. For example, use such categories as "Personal," "General," "Education," or "Employment."

What is the purpose of a pilot test?

19. Test the questionnaire with people who are similar to your intended audience. A pilot test can quickly identify weaknesses. Make corrections and improvements as necessary.

20. Keep the questionnaire short—one to two pages when possible. People do not want to take time to answer long questionnaires. The questionnaire should not take more than 10 to 15 minutes to complete.

21. Avoid using both sides of the paper. People generally overlook the back side.

22. Be concise. Avoid adjectives, or limit them to a few. Also avoid wordy expressions (in order to) and expletives (there is, there are, it is).

23. Be precise. Such words as lovely, fantastic, evening, early, frequently, soon, often, and regularly may have different meanings to different poeple.

24. Ask only those questions that you need. Phrase them so that the answers will provide the exact information you want.

25. Mail questionnaires at appropriate times. Avoid mailing, for example, at Christmas time, February 14, April 15, Mother's Day, and other heavy mail times.

What are ways to encourage return of a questionnaire?

26. Offer a financial reward or other incentives for completing the questionnaire by a certain date. Because many respondents would be interested in seeing your results, offer to send them a copy as an incentive.

27. Use quality paper and printing for the questionnaire. They create a good first impression. Returns are greater than for those questionnaires prepared on low-quality paper.

28. Supply space for respondents' names and addresses if you say you will send them a copy of the report or a summary of the findings.

29. Provide a stamped, addressed envelope for returning the questionnaire—as a courtesy and to encourage the return of the questionnaire. Or the questionnaire can be designed so that, when folded and stapled, it can be returned without an envelope or stamp. See Exhibit 13.1.

Exhibit 13.1   ## Postpaid Questionnaire That Needs No Envelope

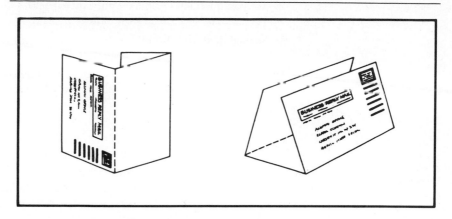

30. Provide a cover letter that clearly states the purpose and importance of the study and provides a reader benefit.

Forms of Questions

After you have compiled a list of all the conceivable items of information that you wish to obtain from the survey, you need to compose questions that will provide you with the information you desire to prepare your report.

Select the *type* of question that will best solicit the information. Also, consider the time it will take a reader to answer a question and the time it will take you to tabulate the answer. Seven types of questions most frequently used on questionnaires are as follows:

Either-Or An either-or question offers the respondent a choice between two answers, such as:

yes/no	for/against
true/false	favor/oppose
agree/disagree	approve/disapprove
like/dislike	before/after

May either-or questions offer a third choice?

Sometimes a question needs a third choice. For example, the question, "Will you run for governor?" can be answered "Yes," "No," or "Not sure." Other third-choice selections could be "Don't know," "No opinion," or "Undecided." Either-or questions are the best questions to use because they can be answered quickly and easily by the respondents, and the replies can be accurately and easily tabulated. The disadvantage of the either-or question is that most questions cannot be answered simply by "Yes," "No," or "Don't know," as when you ask people for their opinions or motives. Consider the following either-or questions.

1. Are you currently employed? Yes _____ No _____

2. Are you qualified to operate a forklife truck?
   Yes _____ No _____ Don't know _____

3. Manual dexterity should be a requirement for the job.
   True _____ False _____ Not sure _____

4. Only people with doctorates should be promoted.
   Agree _____ Disagree _____ No opinion _____

Why are checklists popular with researchers? with respondents?

Checklist In a checklist, the respondent is given a statement (or question) and a list of possible answers to be checked. More than one item may be checked. A good checklist contains *all* possible options, which may include "None of the above" or "Other (please specify)." Checklists are popular with researchers because responses can be tabulated easily. They are also popular with respondents because checklists permit a quick and easy means of indicating choices. For example:

In which team sports have you participated within the past ten years? Check as many as apply.

_____ Baseball   _____ Rugby

_____ Basketball   _____ Soccer

_____ Field hockey   _____ Softball

_____ Football   _____ Volleyball

_____ Hockey   _____ Other (please specify)

_____

How are multiple-choice questions different from checklists?

Multiple Choice Multiple-choice questions are similar to the checklist (they provide several choices), but they require the respondent to choose only one answer. Again, all possible choices must be included. Include a blanket category, such as "None of the above," or "Other (please specify)" to avoid a forced answer that could reduce the reliability of the study. For example:

Which make of U.S. automobile do you prefer? Check one.

_____ American Motors

_____ Chrysler

_____ Ford

_____ General Motors

_____ None of the above

_____ Other (please specify) _____

Fill-in-the-Blank   Fill-in-the-blank questions permit the respondent to provide a short answer. They are also used to elicit factual answers or opinions. For example:

How many years have you lived at your current address? _____
How many brothers and sisters do you have? _____

Ranking   A ranking question asks the respondents to rank items in a list in order of their preferences. Lists should be kept short—not more than five items. However, if it is necessary to have longer lists, ask respondents to rank only the five most important. To avoid confusion, specify that tie rankings are not permitted. For example:

What would be your order of preference (one is high) if your company required you to travel?
_____ South _____ North _____ East _____ West

Which types of questions ask about preferences, opinions, and attitudes?

Scaling   Scaling questions measure intensity of feeling. Respondents are asked to mark responses on a continuum that is closest to their feelings.

A three-point scale might read:
above average, average, below average.

A four-point scale might read:
excellent, very good, good, fair.

A five-point scale might read:
strongly approve, approve, undecided or neutral, disagree, strongly disagree.

How would you rate your superior?

Excellent	Very Good	Good	Average	Fair	Poor	Bad
+3	+2	+1	0	−1	−2	−3

Semantic Differential   The semantic differential, a scaling technique, has the respondent rate an attitude toward an object, person, or event on a number of five- or seven-point bipolar adjectives or phrases. For example:

Please rate yourself on each of the following:
Consistent _____: _____: _____: _____: _____: _____: Inconsistent
Direct   _____: _____: _____: _____: _____: _____: Indirect
Happy   _____: _____: _____: _____: _____: _____: Unhappy
Rigid   _____: _____: _____: _____: _____: _____: Flexible

Open-Ended   Open-ended questions permit respondents to express their exact feelings and opinions. They do not limit the range of possible answers as do other forms of questions. Although these questions are difficult to tabulate, they can provide valuable information.

I enjoy my time most when . . .

I would enjoy my work more if . . .

I suggest that in the future we . . .

Exhibits 13.2, 13.3, and 13.4 provide good examples of questionnaires.

Machine-Scored Questionnaires

What is the advantage of using sense sheets?

If equipment is available, you may wish to have the questionnaires scored by machine. Some organizations and many colleges have equipment that will permit the direct tabulation of data from specially prepared **sense sheets.** If you plan to have your questionnaire machine scored, ask the respondents to mark their answers on a mark sense sheet. The main advantage of using mark sense sheets is that no data transfer occurs (as with punched cards); therefore, no data transfer errors are possible. Because of these advantages, you should check with the appropriate department in your organization or with your college testing center to see what is available. Follow the instructions provided by the testing center. Exhibit 13.5 shows an example of a mark sense sheet.

Testing

After you have drafted, edited, and polished your questionnaire so that you believe it is an exceptionally good one, give it a trial or pilot test to debug it (eliminate errors). Testing will save you time, effort, and money in the long run. A faulty questionnaire can cause you to conduct the entire survey over again. Make several photocopies of it and distribute them to individuals who are similar to people on your selected mailing list. They can tell you if a question is not clear. Also, their answers to the questions may reveal ambiguities that they were not aware of while completing the questionnaire. Ask these people for constructive criticism and then heed their advice. Make the necessary corrections to improve the instrument. Eliminating poorly phrased questions will result in more usable questionnaires.

Data Tally Sheet

When is a data tally sheet not needed?

After you have received the desired number of returns, you will need to develop a system for tallying each question on the questionnaire. An effective system for tallying data is to prepare a data tally sheet. A data tally sheet can be a blank questionnaire with ample space for recording tallies or a sheet of paper specifically designed so that all responses can be tallied in one place for summarization. The data tally sheet displays all response options for each item. See Exhibit 13.6.

Exhibit 13.2   Questionnaire

BUSINESS LIAISON COMMITTEE
The Association for Business Communication

Please return this questionnaire with your answer sheet.

1. I would be interested in subscribing to a publication that applies communication principles to solving the practical problems of business: productivity,
employee cooperation, job satisfaction, issuing directives, information
exchange, customer relations, public relations, government regulation,
employee motivation, etc.

   (1) Yes

   (2) No

2. I would prefer receiving the business communication publication

   (1) Once a month

   (2) Once a quarter

   (3) Twice a year

   (4) Other (please specify) _____

Please rank items 3-20 according to the following scale:

   (1) Extremely important

   (2) Very important

   (3) Important

   (4) Relatively unimportant

   (5) Of no importance

3. Improving my writing to make it clear, concise, coherent, and courteous

4. Issuing directives

5. Improving customer relations

6. Improving public relations

7. Writing for government agencies

(continued)

Exhibit 13.2   (*continued*)

8. Dictation aids

9. Good listening practices

10. Group communication techniques

11. Hints for writing evaluations

12. Letter writing hints

13. Management of training programs

14. Proposal writing tips

15. Report writing techniques

16. Speech making hints

17. Techniques for interviewing

18. Theoretical articles

19. Tips about conducting meetings

20. Other (please specify) _____

    _____

What business publications do you read? Use the following scale for marking.

(1) Read regularly

(2) Read sometimes

(3) Read rarely

(4) Never read

21. ABC BULLETIN

22. ABC JOURNAL

23. BUSINESS AMERICA

24. BUSINESS WEEK

25. COMPUTER WORLD

26. DATA MANAGEMENT

27. DATAMATION

28. FORBES MAGAZINE

Exhibit 13.2   *(continued)*

---

29. FORTUNE

30. INFOSYSTEMS

31. JOURNAL OF MACROMARKETING

32. JOURNAL OF MANAGEMENT STUDIES

33. JOURNAL OF MARKETING

34. JOURNAL OF MARKETING RESEARCH

35. MARKETING COMMUNICATIONS

36. MERGERS AND ACQUISITIONS

37. NEWSWEEK

38. SALES AND MARKETING MANAGEMENT

39. TIME

40. Other (please specify) _____

     _____

41. I am willing to submit articles for publication.

     (1) Yes

     (2) No

42. I am interested in learning more about the Association for
     Business Communication.

     (1) Yes

     (2) No

     If yes, use space below to provide name and address.

43. I would like to receive the results of this questionnaire.

     (1) Yes

     (2) No

Name _____ Company _____

Address _____

City _____ State _____ Zip _____

Exhibit 13.3 Questionnaire

PLEASE CIRCLE THE NUMBER CORRESPONDING TO THE APPROPRIATE RESPONSE

Do you have a savings account?

1. NO ──────────────▶ (IF NO) INASMUCH AS OUR SURVEY FOCUSES
2. YES   ON THE SERVICES PROVIDED BY FINANCIAL
                 INSTITUTIONS AS SEEN BY PEOPLE WHO HAVE
                 SAVINGS ACCOUNTS, WE DO NOT NEED YOUR
                 ANSWER TO SECTIONS I, II, III, IV.
                 HOWEVER, YOU MAY HELP US GAIN A BETTER
                 UNDERSTANDING OF THE NON-DEPOSITOR BY
                 ANSWERING THE QUESTIONS IN SECTION V.
                 ABOVE ALL, PLEASE RETURN THE QUESTIONNAIRE
                 IN THE SELF ADDRESSED ENVELOPE

SECTION I

Q-1. Do you have more than one savings account?

1. NO ──────────────▶ (IF NO) PLEASE SKIP TO QUESTION-4.
2. YES

Q-2. Are your savings accounts in the same financial institution: bank, savings/loan, or credit union?

1. NO
2. YES ──────────────▶ (IF YES) PLEASE SKIP TO QUESTION-4.

Q-3. Which of the following describes where you have your savings accounts?

1. IN BOTH A BANK AND SAVINGS AND LOAN
2. IN BOTH A SAVINGS AND LOAN AND CREDIT UNION
3. IN BOTH A CREDIT UNION AND A BANK
4. IN BANKS, CREDIT UNIONS, AND SAVINGS AND LOANS
5. OTHER COMBINATION (PLEASE SPECIFY) _____

Q-4. Where do you keep your largest savings account, including CD's?
(Do not consider stocks and bonds as savings accounts)

BANKS	SAVINGS/LOAN	CREDIT UNION
1. AMERICAN NATIONAL BANK	6. FIDELITY FEDERAL	10. EMPLOYEE TYPE
2. INDUSTRIAL STATE BANK	7. FIRST FEDERAL	11. NEIGHBORHOOD TYPE
3. FIRST NATIONAL BANK	8. KALAMAZOO SAVINGS AND LOAN	12. OTHER TYPE
4. MICHIGAN NATIONAL BANK	9. OTHER SAVINGS & LOAN	
5. OTHER BANK		

13. OTHER THAN ABOVE (PLEASE SPECIFY) _____

Q-5. How many years have you saved at the financial institution that has your largest savings account?

1. LESS THAN 1 YEAR
2. 1 TO 5 YEARS
3. 6 TO 10 YEARS
4. OVER 10 YEARS

Q-6. When dealing with the institution that has your largest savings account, how do you handle your savings transactions a majority of the time?

1. IN PERSON AT A BRANCH OFFICE
2. IN PERSON AT THE MAIN OFFICE
3. BY MAIL
4. AUTOMATIC PAYROLL DEDUCTION
5. OTHER (PLEASE SPECIFY)

Q-7. Please try to recall the source(s) of information you used in selecting the financial institution that has your largest savings account. (You may circle more than one answer).

1. FAMILY/RELATIVES
2. FRIENDS
3. CO-WORKERS
4. NEWSPAPER ADVERTISING
5. RADIO, T.V.
6. PERSONAL VISITS TO FINANCIAL INSTITUTION
7. OTHERS (PLEASE SPECIFY) _____

Q-8. Before choosing a place to open your largest savings account, which of the following types of financial institutions did you consider.

1. I ONLY CONSIDER BANKS
2. I ONLY CONSIDER SAVINGS AND LOANS
3. I ONLY CONSIDER CREDIT UNIONS
4. I CONSIDERED BOTH BANKS AND SAVINGS AND LOANS
5. I CONSIDERED BOTH SAVINGS AND LOANS AND CREDIT UNIONS
6. I CONSIDERED BOTH CREDIT UNIONS AND BANKS
7. I CONSIDERED BANKS, SAVINGS AND LOANS AND CREDIT UNIONS
8. OTHER (PLEASE SPECIFY) _____

PLEASE CONTINUE TO SECTION II

Source: Courtesy of Dr. Lowell E. Crow, Department of Marketing, Western Michigan University.

Exhibit 13.3 *(continued)*

SECTION II

When choosing a place to keep your largest savings, how important are the following factors in making your decisions? Please circle the number on the right hand page which indicates how important each factor is to you when choosing a place to keep your largest savings account. Read the examples on the top of the next page before answering.

EXAMPLES: When choosing a place to keep your largest savings account, on the first scale below, a circle around a 7 indicates that to you, "HOURS OF OPERATION" is an EXTREMELY IMPORTANT factor to consider; whereas a circle around a 1 indicates that to you, "HOURS OF OPERATION" is NOT an important factor to consider.

LIST OF FACTORS	NOT IMPORTANT	SLIGHTLY IMPORTANT	REASONABLY IMPORTANT	MODERATELY IMPORTANT	VERY IMPORTANT	UNUSUALLY IMPORTANT	EXTREMELY IMPORTANT
				IMPORTANCE			
1. HOURS OF OPERATION	1	2	3	4	5	6	7
2. LOCATION/CONVENIENCE	1	2	3	4	5	6	7
3. REPUTATION IN COMMUNITY	1	2	3	4	5	6	7
4. OBTAINABILITY OF MORTGAGE LOAN	1	2	3	4	5	6	7
5. OBTAINABILITY OF OTHER LOANS (AUTO, FURNITURE, ETC.)	1	2	3	4	5	6	7
6. PHYSICAL FACILITIES	1	2	3	4	5	6	7
7. PERSONAL RECOGNITION BY EMPLOYEES	1	2	3	4	5	6	7
8. FREE CHECKING WITH MINIMUM BALANCE IN SAVINGS ACCOUNT	1	2	3	4	5	6	7
9. OVER-DRAFT PRIVILEGES	1	2	3	4	5	6	7
10. SERVICE CHARGE ON CHECKING ACCOUNT	1	2	3	4	5	6	7
11. RECOMMENDATION BY OTHERS (FRIENDS, RELATIVES, CO-WORKERS)	1	2	3	4	5	6	7
12. INTEREST CHARGES & TERMS OF OTHER LOANS (AUTO, FURNITURE, ETC.)	1	2	3	4	5	6	7
13. INTEREST CHARGES & TERMS OF MORTGAGE LOANS	1	2	3	4	5	6	7
14. INTEREST RATES ON SAVINGS ACCOUNTS	1	2	3	4	5	6	7
15. FULL SERVICE OFFERING (CREDIT CARDS, TRUST SERVICES, SAFETY DEPOSIT BOXES)	1	2	3	4	5	6	7
16. EASE OF FINANCIAL TRANSACTIONS (WALK-UP & DRIVE-IN WINDOWS, MAIL DEPOSIT, PARKING, 24-HOUR AUTOMATED TELLER)	1	2	3	4	5	6	7
17. DIRECT DEPOSITS OF CHECKS (SOCIAL SECURITY, PAYROLL)	1	2	3	4	5	6	7
18. COMPETENT & EFFICIENT SERVICE	1	2	3	4	5	6	7

PLEASE CONTINUE TO SECTION III

(continued)

Exhibit 13.3 (continued)

SECTION III

The following list of factors is identical to those in the previous section II; however, this time the task is different. When choosing a place to keep your largest savings, you may feel that in some ways financial institutions are similar and in other ways these institutions are different. Please circle the number on the right hand page which indicates how different you feel the institutions you considered are on each factor. Once again, read the examples on the top of the next page before answering.

EXAMPLES: When choosing a place to keep your largest savings account, on the first scale below, a circle around a 7 indicates that the institutions have EXTREMELY DIFFERENT, "HOURS OF OPERATION"; a circle around a 1 indicates that you feel there is NO DIFFERENCE between the institutions in "HOURS OF OPERATION"; a circle around an x indicates that you are NOT AWARE of any differences between the institutions in "HOURS OF OPERATION".

LIST OF FACTORS

	NOT AWARE	NO DIFFERENCES	SLIGHTLY DIFFERENT	SOMEWHAT DIFFERENT	MODERATELY DIFFERENT	VERY DIFFERENT	REMARKABLY DIFFERENT	EXTREMELY DIFFERENT
1. HOURS OF OPERATION	X	1	2	3	4	5	6	7
2. LOCATION/CONVENIENCE	X	1	2	3	4	5	6	7
3. REPUTATION IN COMMUNITY	X	1	2	3	4	5	6	7
4. OBTAINABILITY OF MORTGAGE LOAN	X	1	2	3	4	5	6	7
5. OBTAINABILITY OF OTHER LOANS (AUTO, FURNITURE, ETC.)	X	1	2	3	4	5	6	7
6. PHYSICAL FACILITIES	X	1	2	3	4	5	6	7
7. PERSONAL RECOGNITION BY EMPLOYEES	X	1	2	3	4	5	6	7
8. FREE CHECKING WITH MINIMUM BALANCE IN SAVINGS ACCOUNT	X	1	2	3	4	5	6	7
9. OVER-DRAFT PRIVILEGES	X	1	2	3	4	5	6	7
10. SERVICE CHARGE ON CHECKING ACCOUNT	X	1	2	3	4	5	6	7
11. RECOMMENDATION BY OTHERS (FRIENDS, RELATIVES, CO-WORKERS)	X	1	2	3	4	5	6	7
12. INTEREST CHARGES & TERMS OF OTHER LOANS (AUTO, FURNITURE, ETC.)	X	1	2	3	4	5	6	7
13. INTEREST CHARGES & TERMS OF MORTGAGE LOANS	X	1	2	3	4	5	6	7
14. INTEREST RATES ON SAVINGS ACCOUNTS	X	1	2	3	4	5	6	7
15. FULL SERVICE OFFERING (CREDIT CARDS, TRUST SERVICES, SAFETY DEPOSIT BOX)	X	1	2	3	4	5	6	7
16. EASE OF FINANCIAL TRANSACTIONS (WALK-UP & DRIVE-IN WINDOWS, MAIL DEPOSIT, PARKING, 24-HOUR AUTOMATED TELLER)	X	1	2	3	4	5	6	7
17. DIRECT DEPOSITS OF CHECKS (SOCIAL SECURITY, PAYROLL)	X	1	2	3	4	5	6	7
18. COMPETENT & EFFICIENT SERVICE	X	1	2	3	4	5	6	7

DIFFERENCES

PLEASE CONTINUE TO SECTION IV

Exhibit 13.3 (continued)

SECTION IV

Please rate the institution where you have your largest savings account on the following pairs of characteristics. Circle the number on each scale which describes how you view this place of savings (For example: on the first scale below, a circle around a "1" indicates a very progressive institution; a circle around a "7" indicates a very conservative institution; a circle around a "4" indicates an institution that is neither progressive nor conservative.

THE PLACE WHERE I HAVE MY LARGEST SAVINGS ACCOUNT IS:

1.	PROGRESSIVE	1 2 3 4 5 6 7	CONSERVATIVE
2.	IMPERSONAL	1 2 3 4 5 6 7	PERSONAL
3.	MODERN	1 2 3 4 5 6 7	OLD-FASHIONED
4.	AGGRESSIVE	1 2 3 4 5 6 7	RESERVE
5.	A LEADER	1 2 3 4 5 6 7	A FOLLOWER
6.	DYNAMIC	1 2 3 4 5 6 7	STATIC
7.	COMFORTABLE	1 2 3 4 5 6 7	UNCOMFORTABLE
8.	INTERESTED IN HELPING PEOPLE	1 2 3 4 5 6 7	INTERESTED IN MAKING MONEY
9.	CONCERNED WITH SELF	1 2 3 4 5 6 7	CONCERNED WITH COMMUNITY
10.	WELL KNOWN	1 2 3 4 5 6 7	NOT WELL KNOWN
11.	SMALL	1 2 3 4 5 6 7	LARGE
12.	FORMAL	1 2 3 4 5 6 7	INFORMAL
13.	UNRELIABLE	1 2 3 4 5 6 7	RELIABLE
14.	COMPETITIVE	1 2 3 4 5 6 7	NOT COMPETITIVE
15.	COOPERATIVE	1 2 3 4 5 6 7	UNCOOPERATIVE
16.	ORGANIZED	1 2 3 4 5 6 7	DISORGANIZED
17.	COMPLEX	1 2 3 4 5 6 7	SIMPLE

Once again, please rate the place where you have your largest savings account on the following pair of characteristics. Circle the number or each scale which describes how you view your place of savings. Follow the same method of circling response as before.

THE PLACE WHERE I HAVE MY LARGEST SAVINGS ACCOUNT HAS:

18.	STRICT PROCEDURES	1 2 3 4 5 6 7	FLEXIBLE PROCEDURES
19.	INEFFICIENT SERVICE	1 2 3 4 5 6 7	EFFICIENT SERVICE
20.	FRIENDLY EMPLOYEES	1 2 3 4 5 6 7	UNFRIENDLY EMPLOYEES
21.	LOW INTEREST ON SAVINGS	1 2 3 4 5 6 7	HIGH INTEREST ON SAVINGS
22.	FULL SERVICE	1 2 3 4 5 6 7	LIMITED SERVICE
23.	TENSE ATMOSPHERE	1 2 3 4 5 6 7	RELAXED ATMOSPHERE
24.	CLEAN FACILITIES	1 2 3 4 5 6 7	DIRTY FACILITIES

Please circle the number that reflects your overall evaluation of the financial institution that has your largest savings account.

EXTREMELY POOR	VERY POOR	POOR	AVERAGE	GOOD	VERY GOOD	EXTREMELY GOOD
1	2	3	4	5	6	7

PLEASE CONTINUE TO SECTION V

(continued)

Exhibit 13.3   *(continued)*

SECTION V

In order to better understand your responses, we need to ask you a few final questions. Again, any information supplied in the questionnaire will not be associated with your name in any way. Please circle the correct response.

Q-1. What is your sex?

1. MALE
2. FEMALE

Q-2. Which of the following categories includes your age?

1. UNDER 18
2. 18 - 34 YEARS
3. 35 - 49 YEARS
4. 50 - 64 YEARS
5. 65 & OVER

Q-3. What is your marital status?

1. SINGLE
2. MARRIED
3. DIVORCED/SEPARATED
4. WIDOW/WIDOWER

Q-4. How many dependent children do you have?

1. NONE
2. 1 OR 2 CHILDREN
3. 3 OR 4 CHILDREN
4. OVER 4 CHILDREN

Q-5. What is the occupation of the primary income earner?

1. PROFESSIONAL
2. WHITE-COLLAR
3. BLUE-COLLAR
4. RETIRED
5. FARMING
6. SELF-EMPLOYED
7. OTHER (PLEASE SPECIFY) _____

Q-6. How long have you lived in Southwest Michigan?

1. 0 - 3 YEARS
2. 4 - 10 YEARS
3. 10 - 20 YEARS
4. OVER 20 YEARS

Q-7. Which of the following describes your housing situation?

1. I OWN MY HOME
2. I AM BUYING MY HOME
3. I AM RENTING MY HOME
4. I AM RENTING AN APARTMENT
5. OTHER (PLEASE SPECIFY) _____

Q-8. What is the level of education of the primary income earner?

1. 0 - 8 YEARS
2. 9 - 12 YEARS
3. 13 - 16 YEARS
4. OVER 16 YEARS

Q-9. Which of the following categories includes your total household income for 1979 (before taxes)?

1. UNDER $5,000
2. $5,000 to $9,999
3. $10,000 to $14,999
4. $15,000 to $19,999
5. $20,000 to $24,999
6. $25,000 to $29,999
7. $30,000 to $49,999
8. $50,000 & OVER

Q-10. Which of the following categories reflect your total savings level?

1. NONE
2. LESS THAN $3,000
3. $3,000 to $6,999
4. $7,000 to $9,999
5. OVER $10,000

THANK YOU FOR YOUR COOPERATION, PLEASE RETURN THE QUESTIONNAIRE IN THE ADDRESSED, STAMPED ENVELOPE

Exhibit 13.4   Sample Questionnaire

WESTERN MICHIGAN UNIVERSITY
ANNUAL FACULTY – STAFF HEALTH SURVEY

Please circle the appropriate category for each question. Do NOT include your name. This survey is anonymous, and your answers will be kept in strictest confidence.

1. Your age
   - (1) 18-28
   - (2) 29-38
   - (3) 39-48
   - (4) 49-58
   - (5) 59 or older

2. Your sex
   - (1) Male
   - (2) Female

3. Your ethnic origin
   - (1) Black
   - (2) White
   - (3) Hispanic
   - (4) Asian American
   - (5) American Indian
   - (6) Other

4. Your employee group
   - (1) Faculty
   - (2) Administrative/ Professional
   - (3) Clerical/Technical/Police
   - (4) Maintenance/Food Service

HEALTH AND LIFESTYLE

The following questions relate to your personal health habits. Please respond as specifically as possible by circling the most appropriate answer.

5. How often do you drink milk or eat other dairy products such as yogurt and cheese?
   - (1) 3 or fewer times/week
   - (2) 4-5 times a week
   - (3) Daily

6. How often do you eat foods containing saturated fats such as beef, pork, butter, or **whole** milk products?
   - (1) 3 or fewer times/week
   - (2) 4-5 times a week
   - (3) Daily

7. How often do you eat high sodium foods, like cured meats or potato chips, or add salt to your food?
   - (1) 3 or fewer times/week
   - (2) 4-5 times a week
   - (3) Daily

8. (Women only) How often do you examine your breasts for abnormal lumps?
   - (1) Never
   - (2) Less than once a month
   - (3) Once a month

9. (Women only) When was the last time you had a pap smear?
   - (1) 3 or more years ago
   - (2) 2 years ago
   - (3) Within past year

10. When was the last time you had your blood pressure checked?
    - (1) 3 or more years ago
    - (2) 2 years ago
    - (3) Within past year

11. When was the last time you had your blood cholesterol checked?
    - (1) Never
    - (2) 1 or more years ago
    - (3) Within past year

12. How would you describe your weight?
    - (1) Very underweight
    - (2) Slightly underweight
    - (3) Ideal body weight
    - (4) Slightly overweight
    - (5) 20 pounds or more overweight

13. On the average, how much alcohol do you consume a week?
    - (1) None/abstain totally
    - (2) Less than one drink/beer/glass of wine
    - (3) 1-2 drinks/beers/glasses of wine
    - (4) 3-7 drinks/beers/glasses of wine
    - (5) 8-20 drinks/beers/glasses of wine
    - (6) 21 or more drinks/beers/glasses of wine

14. How many times during the past month did you have 5 or more drinks on an occasion?
    - (1) Never
    - (2) 1-4 times
    - (3) More than 4 times

15. How often within the past year have you driven when you've had perhaps too much to drink?
    - (1) Never
    - (2) Less than 3 times
    - (3) 4 or more times

16. How often does stress interfere with your health, personal happiness, or productivity at work?
    - (1) Rarely
    - (2) Weekly
    - (3) Daily

17. Do you use tobacco?
    - (1) Yes
    - (2) No (If no, skip to question 20)

18. If you use tobacco, do you
    - (1) Smoke cigarettes
    - (2) Smoke pipe or cigar
    - (3) Chew tobacco/dip snuff
    - (4) Use tobacco in more than one form

(over)

Source: Reprinted with permission from the University Wellness Programs, Western Michigan University.

(*continued*)

Exhibit 13.4   (*continued*)

19. If you currently smoke cigarettes, on the average, how many cigarettes do you smoke per day?   (1) Less than ½ pack   (2) ½-1 pack   (3) 1½-2 packs   (4) More than 2 packs

20. Are you a former smoker?   (1) Yes   (2) No

21. How often during your workday are you exposed to the second-hand smoke of others?   (1) Rarely   (2) Sometimes   (3) Often

22. How physically fit are you?   (1) Unfit   (2) Average   (3) Very fit

23. How often do you engage in moderately intense exercise for at least 20 consecutive minutes per session using aerobic activities such as swimming, jogging, brisk walking, bicycling, playing racquetball, etc.?   (1) Almost never   (2) 1-2 times a week   (3) 3-5 times a week   (4) 6-7 times a week

24. Do you participate in recreational activities or sports? i.e., golf, bowling, baseball, etc.?   (1) Yes   (2) No

25. If yes, how often?   (1) 1-2 times a week during the season   (2) 3-4 times a week during the season   (3) 1-2 times a week through the year   (4) 3-4 times a week through the year

If you currently participate in fitness activities, please indicate the type of activity, the frequency of your activity, and the facility used. Please check all that apply.

	Facility/Program Used			Number of Times a Week			
	Zest for Life	Self-Initiated Program	Community Program/ Facility	Less than one time per week	1-2 times per week	3-5 times per week	6-7 times per week
26. Group fitness classes							
27. Walking/jogging/swimming/ cross-country skiing							
28. Cycling (indoor/outdoor)							
29. Racquet and court sports							
30. Strength/weight training							
31. Other							

If you have not taken advantage of Western's Zest for Life programs as yet, please provide us with suggestions that would increase the likelihood you would participate: _____

The following questions relate to your present level of interest in developing and maintaining healthful skills. Would you be willing to participate in programs on the following health topics? If interested, please indicate your preferred time period by checking the most appropriate box. If not interested, please leave blank.

	High Interest	12:00-1:00 p.m.	2:30-3:30 p.m.	3:45-4:45 p.m.	5:00-6:00 p.m.	7:00-8:00 p.m.
32. Cancer risk reduction						
33. Stop smoking program						
34. Stress management						
35. Nutrition/cholesterol education						
36. Weight management						
37. Back care program						
38. Arthritis exercise program						

Please list any additional programs/topics of interest to you and times most convenient to your schedule: _____

Exhibit 13.4   (*continued*)

PERSONAL MEDICAL HISTORY

Please indicate which health problems you have experienced that have been diagnosed or treated by a health-care professional.

		Yes	No
39.	Alcohol/drug problem		
40.	Back pain/back strain		
41.	Cancer		
42.	Diabetes		
43.	Emphysema/chronic bronchitis		
44.	Heart problem/heart disease		
45.	Elevated cholesterol/triglycerides		
46.	High blood pressure (over 138/88)		
47.	If yes to question 46, is it controlled under 138/88?		

FREQUENCY EXPERIENCED

		Rarely	Weekly	Daily
48.	Gastrointestinal problems (nausea, cramping, diarrhea, constipation)			
49.	Headaches			
50.	Anxiety that interferes with daily activities			
51.	Periods of prolonged depression (more than 2-3 weeks)			

52. How would you describe your overall health?   (1) Poor   (2) Fair   (3) Good   (4) Excellent

How many days during the past year have you used your sick leave for the following:

		1-2 days	3-4 days	5 or more days
53.	Personal health checkups			
54.	Personal illness/injury/disability			
55.	Illness of spouse/parent			
56.	Illness of child			
57.	Other (please describe)			

58. How often have you used your health insurance benefits for **yourself** for illness or injury within the past year?
(1) None   (2) 1-2 times   (3) 3-4 times   (4) 5 or more times

Thank you for the time and thought given to the completion of this survey. Please return your completed form to
Christine Zimmer
University Wellness Programs
Sindecuse Health Center
no later than February 6, 19XX

Exhibit 13.5   Mark Sense Sheet

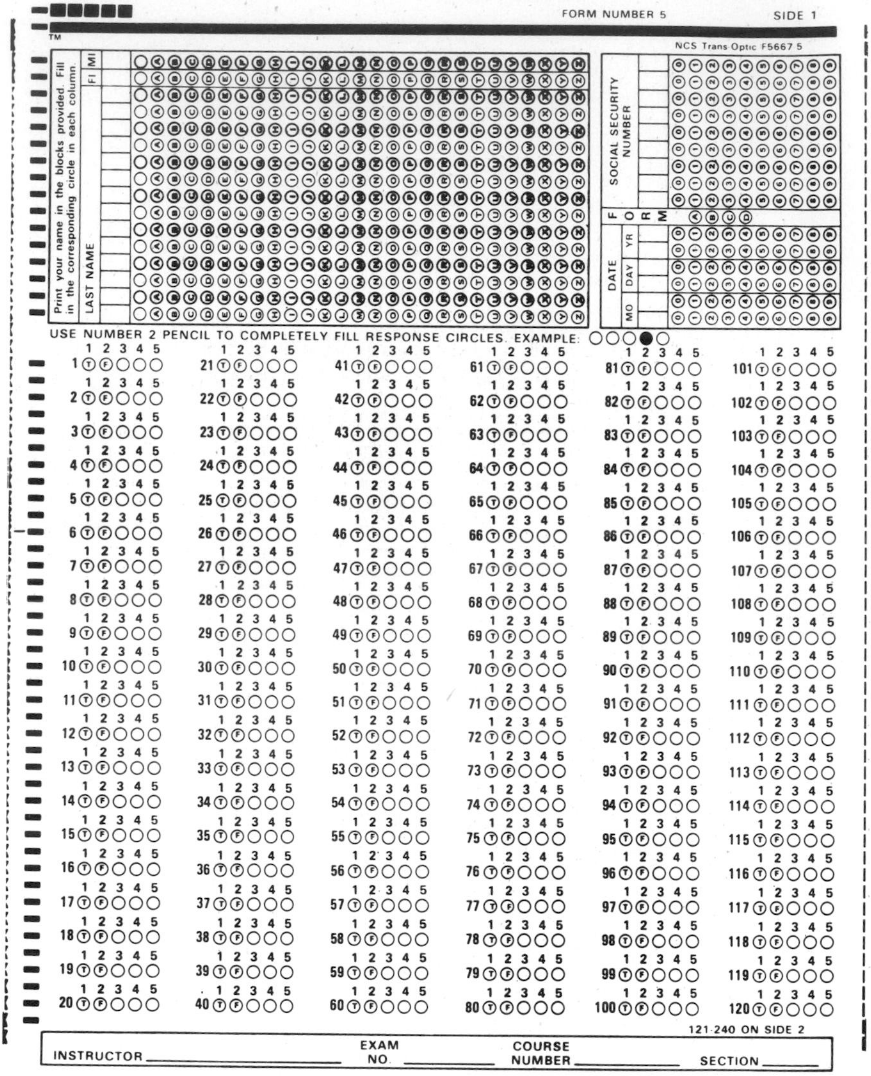

Exhibit 13.6   Format for a Data Tally Sheet

1. <u>Example</u>:   <u>Either-Or</u>:   Would you volunteer to serve as a host/hostess?

Question #	Yes	No	Not sure
1	ⅢⅢ ⅢⅢ	Ⅲ	Ⅱ

2. <u>Example</u>:   <u>Checklist</u>:   In which of the following sports have you participated?

Question #	Baseball	Basketball	Football	Volleyball
2	ⅢⅢ ⅢⅢ Ⅲ	Ⅲ	ⅢⅢ ⅢⅢ	Ⅲ

3. <u>Example</u>:   <u>Multiple Choice</u>:   Which card game do you prefer?

Question #	Bridge	Hearts	Pinochle	Uno
3	ⅢⅠ	Ⅲ	ⅢⅢ Ⅲ	ⅢⅢ Ⅲ

4. <u>Example</u>:   <u>Fill-in-the-Blank</u>:   How many years have you attended the Indy 500?

Question #	
4	5-1-2-4-7-10-2-1-3-4

5. <u>Example</u>:   <u>Ranking</u>:   What is your order or preference (one is high) if you had your choice of location?

Question #	South	North	East	West
5	1-4-2-2-2	2-3-4-3-3	3-2-3-4-4	4-1-1-2-1

6. <u>Example</u>:   <u>Scaling</u>:   How would you rate your supervisor using the following scale?

Question #	Unsatisfactory	Poor	Satisfactory	Good	Outstanding
6	Ⅰ	Ⅰ	ⅢⅢ	ⅢⅢ	Ⅲ

7. <u>Example</u>:   <u>Open-Ended</u>:   What is your opinion of the new vacation policy?

Question #	
7	*I like it. It provides a week in summer for all, etc.*

Because of the increasing popularity and accessibility of computers, you may be able to save yourself hours of computations. Investigate all possibilities open to you for machine scoring and computer analysis of data. In any case, prepare your data tally sheet so that it will be convenient for you to transfer figures into the computer. You may not need a data tally sheet; you might be able to transfer figures directly from the questionnaire answer sheet to the computer. Again, you will need to check with the specialists in your organization.

Some suggestions for tallying the results of your questionnaire are

1. Select a quiet spot where you will not be interrupted by phone or friends.
2. Record tallies on a data tally sheet.
3. Use stick figures in groups of four with the fifth stick crossing the fourth when you tally. This is simple and easy. For example:

$$\text{卌 卌 卌 卌} = 20.$$

4. Arrange all questionnaires in one stack and tally one complete questionnaire—item by item—before going on to the next questionnaire. To double check your work, use another data tally sheet and tally the first item for each questionnaire. Next, tally the second item for each questionnaire. After you have tallied all the questionnaires, compare the two data tally sheets. Where there is a difference in tallies, you will need to recheck them.

Computations

After the questionnaires have been tallied, you will want to summarize the responses for the individual questions for your written report. In some cases, computations will mean simply adding tallies.

What type of computation is used for ranking questions?

Example   When you have a ranking question, you merely add the tallies. The total for each item ranked provides the ranking order. For example

If we were to purchase word processors, what is your order of preference (use "1" to indicate your first choice) of brands?

	Total
_____ Apple	300
_____ IBM	100
_____ Radio Shack	400
_____ Wang	500
_____ Xerox	200

Because "1" would indicate the respondents' first choice, the *lowest* total score would indicate the first-ranked response.

When reporting the data in your report, you might write something like this:

> When asked their order of preference for an office word processor, the respondents selected IBM as their first choice, Xerox as their second choice, Apple as their third, Radio Shack as their fourth, and Wang as their fifth.

Or you could refer your readers to a table:

> Table 15 shows the order of preference of brand names for an office word processor.
>
> 1. IBM
> 2. Xerox
> 3. Apple
> 4. Radio Shack
> 5. Wang

Example The responses to multiple-choice questions might be reported as follows:

> Of the 50 respondents, 22 were female and 28 were male. They reported having participated in the following activities:

	Females	Males	Total
Drama	15	23	38
Music	12	7	19
Art	25	18	43
Dance	32	5	37

Example Sometimes you may want to convert numbers into percentages.

> When asked how they learned about the Office of Management Development, the 50 respondents replied as follows:
>
> 13 Newspaper
> 23 Newsletter
> 6 Director
> 8 Colleague
> 50

To compute the percentage in the above example, divide the number of responses for each item by the total number of responses, and then multiply by 100. For example:

$$\frac{\text{Number of responses to item 1}}{\text{Total number of responses}} = \frac{13}{50} = 0.26 \times 100 = 26\%$$

The result could be reported as follows:

Newspaper	Newsletter	Director	Colleague	
13	23	6	8	= 50
26%	46%	12%	16%	= 100%

What must the total percentage be when numbers are rounded off?

Example   When you round off numbers, the total will always equal 100 percent:

87.5% rounded off =   88% (rounded *up* to even whole)

12.5% rounded off =   12% (rounded *down* to even whole)

100%   100%

Example   Percentages may be calculated for responses to either-or questions.

When asked whether they planned to get a bachelor's degree, 70 percent of the respondents said yes, and 20 percent said no. Ten percent were uncertain.

Question	Yes	No	Uncertain	
1	35	10	5	= 50
	70%	20%	10%	= 100%

The percentages in this example were calculated as follows:

$$\frac{\text{Number of yes responses}}{\text{Total number of responses}} = \frac{35}{50} = 0.7 \times 100 = 70\%.$$

$$\frac{\text{Number of no responses}}{\text{Total number of responses}} = \frac{10}{50} = 0.2 \times 100 = 20\%.$$

$$\frac{\text{Number of uncertain responses}}{\text{Total number of responses}} = \frac{5}{50} = 0.1 \times 100 = 10\%.$$

When is a group average appropriate?

Example   When respondents are asked to mark responses on a continuum, you may want to report a group average.

What is your opinion about the new vacation policy?

Extemely Dislike	Dislike	OK	Like	Extremely Like
1	2	3	4	5

For computation count the number of responses for each point.

Point	Number of Responses
1	5
2	10
3	21
4	8
5	6
	Total 50

Multiply the number of responses times the value of the responses and total the results.

$$2 \times 10 = 20$$

$$3 \times 21 = 63$$

$$4 \times 8 = 32$$

$$5 \times 6 = \underline{30}$$

$$150$$

Divide the value total by the total number of responses.

$$150 \div 50 = 3$$

Three is the average (mean) response. It shows an average response. If the average were 2.3, the responses would be to the "Dislike" side of the neutral point. If the average were 4.02, the responses would be to the "Like" side of the middle.

What should be done if group averages polarize?

Example   When a group average can be misleading, it would be better to report the responses individually. Suppose, for example, that the responses in the preceding example fell at the two ends of the continuum making the opinions polarized—two conflicting or contrasting positions:

	Extremely Dislike	Dislike	OK	Like	Extremely Like	
Scale	1	2	3	4	5	
Responses	20	4	2	4	20	
Value × Response	20	8	6	16	100	= 150

The average would be 3 (150 ÷ 50), but to report that result as an average would mislead your readers. Because 20 responded "Extremely dislike" and 20 responded "Extremely like," you could not report that the group response was average. You would need to report the bimodal—two frequency values—character of the responses.

In Appendix A, we discuss the ways researchers can use averages and differences among data to display, summarize, and interpret results.

How are open-ended questions reported?

Example When reporting open-ended questions, display them in table form or in an enumerated list. Whenever possible, categorize them. For each category, list the responses reported:

> When asked their positive self-verbalizations, respondents' replies fell into four categories—appearance, health, accomplishments, and attitudes.

Appearance:
1. I'm beautiful.
2. I like the way I look.
3. I'm happy with my physical looks.

Health:
1. I feel great.
2. I like exercising.
3. I eat well.

Accomplishments:
1. I can do it.
2. I enjoy working.
3. I'm glad I can type (swim, teach, supervise, manage).

Attitude:
1. I like myself.
2. I feel good about my friends.
3. I'm happy.

How should computations be presented in the report?

After all the computations have been made for each question, record them on a blank questionnaire. This serves two purposes: (1) your data are summarized for you, so it should be easier for you to write the report, and (2) your readers can see an item-by-item display of the results if you place a complete copy of the questionnaire—with the typed-in results—in the appendix of the report.

Letter of Transmittal

Questionnaires sent by mail must have an accompanying letter, usually called a letter of transmittal or cover letter. The quality and tone of the transmittal letter will directly affect the rate of returns.

What are ways to improve the rate of return for one questionnaire?

Generally the rate of return for mail questionnaires is less than 15 percent. With a well-organized cover letter stressing a reader benefit, a well-prepared questionnaire, and a selected mailing list, however, the rate of return can be 50 to 75 percent. When returns reach 80 percent, you know your findings will be reliable and no additional returns, therefore, are required. If you receive too few responses to guarantee reliability, you can use statistical methods to determine the probability of reliability based on the returns you do receive. See Appendix A.

Here are some recommendations for writing a good letter of transmittal:

1. Consider using a simulated inside address when you are sending a form letter to many people. The simulated inside address will

help maintain a traditional letter appearance while avoiding a general "Dear Friend" salutation.

2. Start the letter with a reader benefit. What will the reader gain by completing your questionnaire? Will a report improve the reader's environment? Is there a monetary or reward incentive (book, coupon)? Appeal to the writer's goodwill or sense of responsibility. These benefits can be classed as direct or indirect. Direct benefits are those that will contribute directly to the reader's well-being. Indirect benefits are those that contribute indirectly. The same benefit might be direct for one reader and indirect for another. If you are asked to complete a report on the working conditions for secretarial personnel in your company, the improved working conditions that could result would be a direct benefit for the secretaries and an indirect benefit for management personnel.

3. Provide an explanation of the study. What is the purpose of the study, and what do you hope to accomplish? Why is the study important? Who will benefit?

4. Tell the reader how the information will be used.

5. Tell the reader how long it should take to complete the questionnaire.

What information lends credibility to the study?

6. Mention the particular person or organization who is authorizing, supporting, or directing your study. This fact not only gives credibility to your study, but will probably increase the number of responses.

7. Use you-attitude throughout the letter and make the letter personal. Use personal pronouns, such as "I," "you," and "your." Seek the reader's contribution and cooperation in completing the questionnaire and study.

8. Assure the reader of confidentiality and anonymity. You are interested only in the answers from people who have the expertise to make the study a good one.

When might respondents wish to identify themselves?

9. Offer to send the respondent a copy of the report, a summary of your findings, or an abstract of the report. Respondents could complete the form on the bottom of the questionnaire that solicits their names and addresses. If the respondent wishes to remain anonymous, he or she may return an enclosed postage-paid reply envelope separate from the questionnaire or may write you for a copy of the report after a certain date.

10. End date and justify the letter of transmittal. Ask the respondent to return the completed questionnaire by a specific date—usually 10 days or, for those far away, about 3 weeks. Encourage a prompt return by giving a reason. For example

Because the results of the study will be presented at the Tenth Annual National Convention of Office Managers on June 1, we would appreciate your returning the completed questionnaire in the enclosed postage-paid envelope by May 1.

Exhibits 13.7, 13.8, and 13.9 illustrate letters of transmittal.

Follow-up Correspondence

Because mailed questionnaires often have a low rate of returns, plan a follow-up procedure. After waiting 3 or 4 weeks for the return of the questionnaire or after the end date specified in your transmittal letter, you may wish to follow up on the returns so that you will have your predetermined percentage of returns or a reliable rate of return. See Exhibit 13.10.

How can the researcher follow up questionnaires that are signed or coded? questionnaires that are anonymous?

If the questionnaires are signed, marked, or coded so that you know which individuals did not return the questionnaire, you may telephone them and ask for a quick return. Or, you may send them a follow-up note or card asking them to do so. When you make a follow-up phone call, you might say:

> I'm calling to ask if you have received the questionnaire that I mailed to you on (date).

If the person says he or she did not receive the questionnaire, offer to send another. If the person says "Yes," mention a deadline:

> Because we need your input, we would appreciate your completing the questionnaire by (date).

On the other hand, if you are unable to determine which individuals on your mailing list have not responded because of confidentiality or anonymity, send a follow-up card to everyone (providing you can handle the cost) reminding him or her to return the completed questionnaire by a certain date. When you follow up with a note or card, call attention to the fact that the input from the respondent is needed for reliable results and for a high rate of return. Because some of the people may have already returned the questionnaire, add a qualifying statement, such as:

> If you have already returned the questionnaire, please disregard this notice.

INTERVIEWS

Another source for primary data is the interview. Interviews can be done face-to-face, or they can be done over the telephone.

Personal Interviews

When are personal interviews best used? Why?

In the personal interview, information is obtained through face-to-face conversation with another person or a group. In addition to obtaining information through discussion, the interviewer can obtain information

Exhibit 13.7   Letter of Transmittal

**simulated inside
address**

reader benefit

purposes

instructions

end date and justify

offer of response

May 1, 19xx

Are the memos and
Reports in your company
As clear and concise
As they should be?

If your company is like most, ineffective communication could be costing you
thousands of dollars a year.

Perhaps written instructions are misunderstood, or perhaps some of your
personnel have difficulty with sales presentations or media appearances.

We'd like to know whether you and your company are concerned about the
quality of communication. Will you spend a few minutes now to help the
Association for Business Communication determine whether a special
publication for business people could help solve this problem? Your answers
to the questions on the attached questionnaire will help us determine how
important you consider communication skills and how much of a problem you
have found ineffective communication to be.

Please use a No. 2 pencil to record your answers on the enclosed computer
scoring sheet. (Estimated completion time: 5 minutes.)

Because we would like to prepare your answers for the Business Liaison
Committee by July 1, please complete and return the questionnaire to us by
June 15.

To receive a copy of the results of the questionnaire, simply mark "yes" for
item No. 43 and give us your name and address in the space provided.

Sincerely,

Gerald D. Rieselman

Gerald D. Rieselman

enc

Exhibit 13.8   Letter of Transmittal

Dear Student:

Are rising college costs getting you down? Attending City College gets more expensive each year and coping with these increases is often a major concern of students. Because I believe many CC students are having difficulty making ends meet, I am conducting a survey to find out how students like you are meeting their financial obligations.

The information you provide will help me to complete a research project for my report writing class. The results of this survey will also be shared with the financial aid office to improve the quality of future financial aid programs.

Your name was chosen randomly from City College's student population. It is important that each questionnaire be completed and returned to ensure statistical validity. Your answers, therefore, are critical. The survey form takes only 20 minutes to complete. Your time and assistance are much appreciated.

You are assured complete confidentiality. The questionnaire is numbered for mailing purposes only. Your name will remain anonymous. Should you have any questions about the survey, please call me after 9 p.m. at 555-7274.

Because the report is due December 1, may I please have your completed questionnaire by November 15?

Sincerely,

Robin Mobley

Robin Mobley

enc

Source: Courtesy of Robin Mobley.

Figure 13.9   **Letter of Transmittal**

Western Michigan University
Kalamazoo, Michigan 49008-3899

January 26, 19xx

[Inside Address]

Dear Colleague:

The health of each of us at Western lies in the connection between individual
health practices and a healthy work environment. To help the University
address these needs more effectively, we have designed a questionnaire to
evaluate those needs.

Because you have been chosen as a part of a small random sample to represent
your employee group, your response is extremely important to us. It takes less
than 15 minutes to complete the questionnaire. The Committee is interested
only in the data from your employee group, so the survey is designed to be
anonymous.

Because we plan to publish the findings of our report by April 1, please
complete the enclosed survey and return it by February 6 in the envelope
provided for privacy.

Sincerely,

Christine G. Zimmer

Christine G. Zimmer, Chairperson
University Wellness Committee

enc

Source: Christine Zimmer, University Wellness Programs, Western Michigan University, Kalamazoo,
MI.

Exhibit 13.10   Follow-up Letter

Western Michigan University
Kalamazoo, Michigan 49008-3899

February 6, 19xx

[Inside Address]

Dear Colleague:

About a week ago you were sent a WMU Faculty/Staff Health Survey from the
University Wellness Committee. Because this survey is being returned
anonymously, we have no way of knowing whether you received your copy or if you
have responded.

If you have already completed and returned your questionnaire, thank you for
your prompt response. If you have not yet had time to return the questionnaire, we would appreciate your doing so.

Because you have been chosen as a part of a small random sample to represent
your employee group, your response is extremely important to us. The Committee
is interested only in the data from your employee group, so the survey is
designed to be anonymous.

If you did not receive the questionnaire, please call me at 555-3838, and I
will send you one.

Your response will assist us in making recommendations for policies and
programs that support healthful choices at WMU.

Sincerely,

Christine G. Zimmer

Christine G. Zimmer, Chairperson
University Wellness Committee

Source: Christine Zimmer, University Wellness Programs, Western Michigan University, Kalamazoo,
MI.

through observation of the interviewee or respondent. The interviewee's voice, facial expression, gestures, behavior, posture, and surroundings can sometimes reveal more than the spoken word.

Because of the expense and time involved, personal interviews are best used for a small sample size in one relatively small and compact geographic area. Personal interviews are also best for soliciting information that might not be available from mailed questionnaires, such as motives and reasons, or when the information is too complex to be gathered by any other method.

Why should the interviewer pay attention to the interviewee's behavior? his or her own behavior?

Procedure　Well-organized interviews can provide valuable information for the report and can be relaxing and rewarding as well. To ensure a carefully prepared interview, here are some suggestions for you to follow.

1. Select interviewees carefully. Ask only those people who can provide the information you need.

2. Call for an appointment at least one week ahead of time. Introduce yourself and explain the purpose of the interview. Let the person know that his or her responses are important for your study, and if necessary, let the person know that the information will be kept confidential.

3. Prepare a specific list of appropriate questions for your selected audience and then organize them so that they follow a logical pattern. Do not jump from one topic to another. Ask the easy questions first, and then go on to the complex ones. Go from the general to specific questions. Ask the same questions in the same way for each interviewee.

4. Once prepared, rehearse. Go over the questions several times so that you are familiar with them and can ask them fluently. Remember not to interrupt the respondent. Also, learn to avoid disagreeing and showing emotional responses, such as frowning, which may inhibit the respondent. *Remain neutral.*

5. Good manners should dictate your appearance and behavior at the interview. Be well dressed, pleasant, and poised. Watch your mannerisms, posture, and other nonverbal behaviors.

6. Arrive for the appointment on time. Although you introduced yourself over the phone when you made the appointment, you should introduce yourself again. Explain the purpose of the interview, and why you selected him or her (because of his or her knowledge of the subject, for example).

7. Pay careful attention to what is being said in the interview. Listen not only to *what* is being said but also to *how* it is being said. When necessary, ask for a clarification or for an explanation.

8. Choose a method of recording that makes you and the respondent comfortable. A tape recorder may make some people uncomfortable. When this is so, do not use one in the session. Although notes can be taken during the interview, take them sparingly and unobtrusively. Record key phrases and important data, such as names, dates, and figures. When necessary, though, record responses verbatim.

9. Be sure to thank the respondent for granting you the interview. Promise him or her a copy of the report, a summary of the findings, or an abstract. Send a thank-you letter, thanking the interviewee for his or her time and information.

10. Write or record a complete summary of the interview shortly after the interview so that you will not forget important details.

Advantages and Disadvantages   The advantages of personal interviews are

1. They provide immediate feedback and evaluation.
2. They provide an opportunity for the interviewer to ask for further explanations when something is not clear and to rephrase a question for the respondent when he or she does not understand the question.
3. They provide an opportunity to gather complex information.

The disadvantages of personal interviews are

1. They can be time consuming and expensive.
2. They can be an invasion of privacy.
3. They can report inaccurate information. Respondents may distort their answers and interviewers may incorrectly interpret responses.

Telephone Interviews

How do questions asked in telephone interviews differ from questions in personal interviews? Why?

Still another source for collecting primary data is the telephone interview. It is the fastest of the survey methods. Telephone interviews are similar to personal interviews except that instead of face-to-face conversation, you have communication over the telephone. Because people can be antagonistic and reluctant to answer questions over the phone, you should keep your questions brief and limited in number.

Procedure   The procedure for conducting telephone interviews is as follows:

1. Determine the number of calls needed to have a reliable representation.
2. Select your population randomly.

3. Choose a time of day for making the telephone calls when you know your respondents will be home. Do not call before 8 a.m. or after 8 p.m. unless you know your audience will accept earlier or later calls.

4. Follow the same procedure for preparing and rehearsing questions as for the personal interview

5. Introduce yourself after your party has answered the phone. Explain the purpose of the call and the reason the person should be a part of the survey.

6. Listen carefully to what is being said and how it is said. When necessary, ask for a clarification or explanation. Rephrase a question when it is not clear.

7. Be sure to have prepared an interview sheet for recording your notes after each question.

8. Thank the respondent for taking the time to answer your questions.

Advantages and Disadvantages   The advantages of telephone interviews are

1. They are fast; they can quickly reach large groups of people.

2. They are inexpensive and can save time.

3. They can provide a random sample when the entire population has a listed telephone.

4. They are more economical and convenient than travel.

The disadvantages of the telephone interview are that

1. Many people object to telephone interviews.

2. People are reluctant to answer more than a few brief questions.

3. Some people do not have a telephone; therefore, a random sample may not be possible.

4. Observation is not possible.

THE DELPHI TECHNIQUE

Sometimes the use of expert judgment is necessary for developing criteria used in certain research studies. For example, a researcher may wish to develop a rating scale to evaluate the secretarial skills of office workers.

What is the Delphi Technique? Why was it developed?

Avoiding conflicts that may develop between individuals of different rank and personality and getting the experts together can prove difficult and often impossible. For these reasons, the Delphi Technique was developed. The Delphi Technique is a method whereby a consensus of experts is achieved, not through direct discussion but through a series of questionnaires interspersed with comments or feedback from the other responding experts. These anonymous opinions are evaluated by the other respondents.

In other words, one expert's views are examined and evaluated by other experts. A respondent has an opportunity to reconsider or revise his or her original comments based on the critique of the other experts. A respondent may change his or her opinion because of an idea brought out by another participant's response. As a result of the Delphi Technique, the researcher is able to have the consensus of the experts for his or her research study without a direct confrontation.

The Delphi Technique method consists of these steps:

What are panel members asked in the first round?

1. At the request of the researcher, a panel of experts (external and internal) make individual comments, opinions, suggestions, estimates, dates, forecasts, or the like, anonymously.

2. An independent researcher or analyst summarizes the responses.

3. The researcher sends each panelist a summary of the views of the other panelists and asks each to make a second round of judgments based on the information provided by the first round. Panelists are given an opportunity to revise their statements.

4. The process is repeated three or four times, until it appears that further rounds would not result in significant changes among the panelists.

5. The researcher prepares a final summary.

You might, for example, need to determine the likely impact of technology on organizational communication practices in the next 10 years. After selecting a number of experts willing to participate in your study, you would begin with an initial round of questions to determine the experts' predictions of the ways in which technology will influence communication within organizations. One of the questions in such a study might ask experts to express an opinion of the importance of desktop publishing, ranking their responses on a scale of 1 to 5, with 1 being "of critical importance" and 5 being "of no importance." This question, as would be true for all your questions, would provide space for the respondents to comment on their answers. During the initial round, the experts may be asked to provide additional questions and alternate phrasings to clarify existing questions.

What are panel members told in the second round?

On the second round, you would show each expert how his or her opinion compared with those of the other experts and provide a summary of the rationale. Suppose, for example, one respondent said that desktop publishing was "of no importance" because it was "simply a gimmick," whereas another respondent said that it was "very important" because it "sets new standards for the physical appearance of written communication." Your second-round questionnaire would include both those comments (plus other comments by other respondents) and show each of the respondents how his or her answer compared with the average of all the responses. On the second round, the respondents would be able to consider the opinions and comments of others in responding to the questions again.

What do panelists do in the second round?

On the second round, the respondents might simply defend their original opinions, with the one saying that desktop publishing is of no importance because it does not influence the content or quality of messages themselves and another saying that desktop publishing will influence people's expectations of what business messages should look like. As the process continues, respondents are free to comment on the comments of others and to clarify their own comments. Each time the questionnaires come back, you would prepare a summary of responses and comments so that each respondent would be able to see his or her own responses in comparison with those of the others.

How many rounds are needed?

You would continue this process until the experts reached consensus, until their opinions remained consistent, or until a predetermined number of rounds was reached. If the majority of respondents in our hypothetical example felt that desktop publishing were going to become very important because people will come to expect letters, memos, and reports to look printed, the expert who originally felt that desktop publishing was "simply a gimmick" might change his or her mind about the impact it is likely to have on organizational communication.

Given willing respondents and sufficient time, the Delphi Technique may be applied to virtually any topic requiring the opinions of experts. Because the respondents are usually required to comment on the reasons for their responses, the questionnaires require more time to complete and to tabulate than other questionnaire types. For this reason, the Delphi Technique is most often applied when major changes requiring substantial investment are contemplated.

ETHICS

Laws protect the rights of individuals in research. When gathering data for your research project, you need to consider the ethics involved.

1. Individuals have a right to choose whether to participate in your study. Therefore they must be told the purpose of the study and how the data will be used.
2. Individuals may not be deceived or coerced into participating.
3. Individuals need to be assured that their responses will remain anonymous.

As dictated by governmental regulations, most universities have established policies and procedures protecting human subjects.

SUMMARY

A questionnaire is a list of questions used to obtain primary data. The questions provide answers to what people think and why they think a certain way. Eight types of questions most frequently used on questionnaires are either-or, checklist, multiple choice, fill-in-the-blank, open-ended, ranking, scaling, and semantic differential. Questionnaires sent by mail must have an accompanying letter, called a letter of transmittal.

Another source for primary data is the interview—the personal interview and the telephone interview. In the personal interview, information is obtained through face-to-face conversation with another person or a group of persons. In the telephone interview, information is obtained, as the name implies, over the telephone.

The Delphi Technique is a method whereby a consensus of experts is achieved through a series of questionnaires interspersed with feedback from the other responding experts.

Research ethics require that individuals have the right to choose to participate in a study based on accurate knowledge of the nature and purpose of the study. Respondents also have the right to remain anonymous.

EXERCISES

Review and Discussion Questions

1. What is a questionnaire?
2. State the advantages and disadvantages of questionnaires.
3. Give ten guidelines for preparing a questionnaire.
4. Define the eight types of questions used on questionnaires. Give an example of each.
5. Why is it a good idea to give your questionnaire a trial run?
6. What is a data tally sheet?
7. How do you compute an average? a percentage?
8. How do you compute a scaling question?
9. What is a letter of transmittal? What should it contain?
10. Why do you write a follow-up letter? When?
11. What are personal interviews?
12. What are telephone interviews?
13. What are the advantages and disadvantages of telephone interviews?
14. What is the Delphi Technique?

15. What ethical considerations are necessary in gathering data for your research project?

Problems and Applications

1. Write three questionnaire items for each of the eight kinds of questions.

2. Prepare a 20-item mail questionnaire on a topic of your choice, using at least one example of each of the eight types of questions discussed in this chapter.

3. Give five examples of leading questions, and tell why they are leading.

4. Give five examples of ambiguous questions, and tell why they are ambiguous.

5. Prepare a question for each of the following:
   a. A person's age
   b. A person's religious affiliation
   c. A person's political party
   d. A person's morals

6. Give five examples of questions that respondents cannot recall easily. Convert the questions into ones that they can easily recall.

7. Give three examples of negative questions. Restate them using positive language.

8. Give three examples of questions that have two answers. Convert the questions into two separate parts.

9. Give two examples of contingency questions.

10. Prepare a ten-item questionnaire, and have ten people test it. In a memo to your instructor, say what you learned from the trial run. Submit the original questionnaire, the ten tested questionnaires with the comments and corrections, and the revised questionnaire incorporating the recommendations from the ten people.

11. Design a tally sheet for an observation survey and for a questionnaire survey.

12. What are the percentages for each of the following items?

	a.		b.		c.	
	5	grapefruit	205	tomatoes	Yes	37
	20	strawberries	168	green beans	No	63
	16	melons	349	potatoes		100%
	25	oranges	108	corn		
	10	bananas	92	peas		
	24	apples	78	carrots		
		100%		100%		

13. How would you report the group average for a and b?

    a.

	Excellent	Very Good	Good	Fair	Poor
Value	1	2	3	4	5
Numbers	40	75	50	25	10
			Total responses		200

    b.

	Excellent	Very Good	Good	Fair	Poor
Value	1	2	3	4	5
Numbers	48	52	0	54	46
			Total responses		200

14. Prepare a cover letter and questionnaire for each of the following. Supply whatever additional information is necessary.
    a. Your state representative wants to conduct a citizens' survey for input on such key matters as tax relief, governmental reform, educational reform, health care services, and other important proposals.
    b. The Energy Administration of the State Department of Commerce wants to conduct a survey about energy conservation in homes.
    c. Your company wants to conduct a survey of all employees to learn which tasks are performed by each employee so that the company can make an evaluation of how the office is functioning.

15. Prepare five statements along with illustrations that could be mailed on a postcard to remind people to return their questionnaires.

16. Interview five people on a topic of your choice. Prepare a list of questions that you wish to ask. Call for an appointment. Write a summary of your findings, and present them in a memo report to your instructor.

17. Interview five people over the telephone. Prepare a list of questions that you intend to ask.

18. Arrange for an interview of a person who has achieved success in your major. Prepare the questions and conduct the interview. Prepare a report of your findings, and submit it to your instructor.

19. Interview 25 business people in various areas, such as banking, education, government, manufacturing, insurance, etc., and ask what professional associations they belong to and what professional magazines they subscribe to.

20. Treat the following as a class project:
    a. Brainstorm for a problem (or check with administration).
    b. Design a questionnaire to solve that problem.
    c. Conduct a trial run.
    d. Select a sample technique.
    e. Prepare a cover letter.
    f. Prepare a follow-up notice.
    g. Conduct the survey.
    h. Conduct a personal survey—prepare questions, etc.
    i. Conduct a telephone survey—prepare questions, etc.
    j. Prepare the written report.

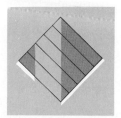

Organization and Interpretation of Data

"Two cyclists begin to pedal toward each other at the same moment. They are thirty miles apart and their rates are equal, fifteen miles per hour. Simultaneously a fly takes off from *A*'s handlebar to *B*'s handlebar, and back to *A*'s, in an ever-decreasing round trip. The fly's rate is forty miles an hour—with no allowance for stops and starts. When the cyclists meet, the hard-working fly is crushed between the handlebars. How far has the fly flown?"[1]
How do we determine how far the fly in Stuart Chase's story has flown?

In this case, we can find the answer logically, by separating the significant details from the insignificant. It takes the cyclists one hour to cover the 30 miles, and the fly is traveling at 40 miles an hour. Thus, the fly has flown 40 miles.

Topics
Beginning the Process
Classifying Data
Maintaining Objectivity
Interpreting Data
Analyzing Statistical Information
Drawing Conclusions
Making Recommendations

---

[1]Stuart Chase, *Guide to Straight Thinking* (New York: Harper & Brothers, 1956), 8.

Each of the steps listed in the chapter topics can be complex, and we can present only general considerations here. We will present the basic rules for classification, the common logical fallacies, the most often used techniques of qualitative and quantitative analysis, and the basic guidelines for drawing conclusions.

BEGINNING THE PROCESS

Which individuals or groups may challenge the report writer's interpretation of data?

Making sense of data[2] is one of a report writer's most important tasks. Especially today, when many are suspicious of all statistical information presented by business, report writers need to ensure that they have focused on the significant, presented data accurately, and drawn logical conclusions. The continued well-being of your organization may depend on your ability to organize and interpret information. The chances that your interpretation of data will be challenged—by your boss or someone else in your organization, by a regulatory agency, or by a consumer group—increase every day.

To be meaningful, the information you have collected needs to be organized and interpreted. These tasks are not always easy. Our daily lives do not as a rule require the kind of logic and precision that a business or technical report must have. The same wishful thinking that is acceptable when we predict victory for our team in the absence of evidence is inexcusable if we predict success for a new product without the necessary supporting evidence.

The tasks of collecting and organizing data are obviously not as distinct as our chapter divisions imply. You begin the process of organizing with your first decision to include or exclude a particular topic in your search for information. And, as you proceed with your search, you will be forming ideas about where each item of information belongs, what significance it has, and how to use it in your report. Nevertheless, the serious task of organizing and interpreting data begins once all the data have been collected.

CLASSIFYING DATA

In planning the report, you developed a list of possible topics and subtopics that you thought would form useful categories of information. This was the beginning of your effort to classify your materials, or arrange them according to topic or category.

---

[2]*Data* is a plural form of *datum* and usually requires a plural verb. Some writers use *data* as a collective noun with a singular verb. "The *data,* as a group, *indicates* a slight increase in product awareness." See Carter A. Daniel and Charles C. Smith, "An Argument for *Data* as a Collective Singular," *The ABCA Bulletin* 44.3 (1981), 31.

Report as Whole

The information for most reports will fall into one or more of the following categories.

What has been
tried before?

History   The history of the problem includes not only the discussion of the background of the problem under study, but also an examination of similar problems in your own organization and throughout the industry. If others have encountered the problem previously, what did they do about it, and with what results? The information you discover as a result of secondary research belongs in this category as a "review of literature" when you are using those sources to explain previous efforts to solve a related problem.

What standards
have you set for
your decision?

Criteria   Whenever you are faced with having to make a choice, carefully define the criteria on which you will base your decision. Then, classify information according to the criteria established rather than according to the items or subjects being compared. If you are trying to decide which word processing equipment to install, for example, you would organize the information by such factors as cost, ease of use, flexibility, repair record, and features rather than by brand name.

How do you know
what you know?

Descriptions and Explanations   What research methodology did you use and why? At some point in your report, you will need to tell your reader how you know what you know. Describing your efforts to remain objective and explaining the procedures you used to ensure valid results are your best means of convincing your reader to accept your results, conclusions, and recommendations. A description of scope, explanations for limitations, and definitions fall in this category.

What do the data
show?

Results   What did you learn as a result of your research? Results are usually presented in the form of raw data. Your reader may want to see your results to evaluate your conclusions or recommendations. For this reason, you should keep the results and your discussion and analysis of the results in separate categories.

Trends   Changes over time will probably require special attention. Trends may be worthy of separate consideration, or they may influence other aspects of your report.

What do the data
mean?

Discussion of Results   What do your results mean? Are some aspects more significant than others? Analytical reports require you to interpret and analyze your results for your reader. Further classification may be necessary to show significant relationships among the topics examined.

What courses of
action are possible?

Alternatives   What possible courses of action are available? What are the advantages and disadvantages of each?

Conclusions and Recommendations   Because conclusions and recommendations are not data but are based on data, you will need to remember that your conclusions and recommendations are separate categories of information. Be sure to note that difference for yourself as you organize your material for presentation.

Findings

Why may it be useful to classify research results?

In addition to placing information in general categories according to the function it will play in the report, you may need to classify the results of research to ensure a clear, systematic presentation of facts. Classification is, in fact, an important technique for demonstrating points of similarity and difference among things. In classifying data, use the following rules.

Clarify What Is Being Classified   Whenever you are dividing a whole into its component parts, you need to clarify (definition, scope, limits) the whole so that the relationship among parts will be meaningful to the reader.

Select a Significant Basis for the Classification   The basis for your system of classification may be suggested by your topic or purpose, reasons, factors, methods, properties, or qualities. A quality that is significant in one circumstance, however, may not be significant in another. Whether a book is hardbound or paperback may be significant in discussing cost or durability, for example, but irrelevant in discussing content.

Why should the whole equal the sum of its parts?

Make Sure That the Division Is Complete   Just as in geometry the whole must equal the sum of its parts, the subtopics in your division must total the entire category. When you omit one or more subtopics from a category in your discussion, change the title of the division to clarify what you will discuss. If you are discussing natural resources important to your industry, and you need to cover iron, zinc, and copper, your division would be "Three Key Minerals" rather than "Metals."

Why are overlapping categories sometimes impossible to avoid?

Complete One Basis of Classification Before Beginning the Next   When possible, make your divisions mutually exclusive. Ideally, subdivisions should not overlap. Each category by its nature should exclude all other categories. Clearly, in the previous examples, "timber" would not belong in the same category as iron, zinc, and copper. Some topics, however, cannot be divided so absolutely—where do you draw the line between a short report and a long report? Because the bases for classifying reports overlap, a complete coverage of report preparation requires some overlap of categories. A memo report may also be a short analytical report. When categories do overlap, be sure to clarify the nature of the overlap and explain the difference between the categories for your reader.

Be Consistent and Logical   In developing your system of classification, use parallel grammatical structure in listing the categories, and make sure that you have no single subdivisions. Arrange the categories of data in an order that will aid your readers' understanding.

MAINTAINING OBJECTIVITY

In what two ways may biases interfere with objectivity?

If you had the responsibility for recommending new company cars for your organization, what brands and models would you consider and why? Would you include foreign cars in your list of those to be considered? If you automatically excluded foreign cars from your list because you believe that the domestic automobile industry needs support, you were guilty of biased thinking.

Biased—or prejudiced—thinking, however, is not always bad. Wanting the local team to win is normal and justifiable. The managers of a particular organization may decide that they will consider only domestic automobiles for use in the company fleet. Biased thinking, however, can result in problems in two ways. First, we may not be aware of our biases and overlook or distort evidence as a result. Second, if we are aware of our bias, we may still be tempted to persuade our audience to share our prejudice, and we may deliberately distort or suppress evidence.

Fairness

Objectivity in report writing (or any other facet of life, for that matter) requires that we recognize our biases and acknowledge the role they might play in the reporting process. In the case of the decision about the new automobiles for your organization, for example, you could be fair in spite of a bias in favor of domestic cars in a variety of ways.

How can you achieve objectivity in spite of biases?

Fair: Obtain approval for considering domestic cars only.

Fair: Establish performance criteria, obtain approval for those criteria, weigh all cars against those criteria, and recommend the car (foreign or domestic) meeting the most criteria.

Fair: Same as above, but—should a foreign car be best—recommend the domestic car meeting the most criteria and explain your reasons for selecting a domestic car in spite of a foreign car's better performance.

You could also manipulate the data in a number of ways.

Unfair: Eliminate foreign cars without providing an explanation.

Unfair: Manipulate data to ensure that a domestic car would appear superior.

Unfair: Omit data tending to show that a foreign car might be superior.

To ensure fairness, ask yourself the following questions.

1. Do you have any preconceived notions of what the results should be? Have you selected a particular hypothesis because you already believe that is what you will discover? If you have, check your results by also attempting to prove the problem's null hypothesis. If you are a nonsmoker, for example, you may have a preconceived idea of what a study on the relationship between smoking and health ought to be. Report writers need to recognize that their perceptions may not be the only legitimate view of reality and work to ensure that other viewpoints are afforded fair treatment.

2. Do you have any vested interests? Will you profit (emotionally, or monetarily, or in some other way) if your results turn out a certain way? If you own stock in a particular automobile company, for example, you may find it difficult to avoid manipulating the facts in favor of the cars produced by that company.

3. Do you have a special need to impress your readers? Do you believe that your readers desire a certain outcome? If you have either a desire to impress or a need to please your readers, you may be tempted to amplify the importance of small differences or to minimize the importance of significant differences. You might, for example, claim that a 54 percent majority constituted "most respondents" or that 54 percent was a "significant majority" instead of simply reporting "54 percent." Or if 75 percent of the respondents opposed an action you know your readers to support, you might be tempted to say that "although most respondents were opposed, a substantial minority approved."

Until you are well versed in rigorous, objective thinking, it will be worth your while to put these questions and their answers in writing. As you collect the data, you can refer to your notes occasionally to see whether your preconceptions, vested interests, or other biases are influencing your ability to be fair.

Logic

In addition to a desire to be fair, to be truly objective, a report writer must have a basic working knowledge of the principles of logic and semantics.

What is a syllogism?

The study of logic is traditionally divided into **formal** and **informal** branches. Formal logic deals with **syllogisms** and mathematical logic. Informal logic deals with the common logical fallacies that distort our everyday thinking. Informal logic is based on and is a natural result of the syllogism of formal logic, as is illustrated in Exhibit 14.1.

What constitutes a valid proof?

The starting point for every **proof** or **argument** is a premise. The proof consists of an orderly sequence of **propositions,** or statements,

EXHIBIT 14.1   Typical Syllogism

Major Premise All men are mortal.

Minor Premise Socrates is a man.

Conclusion   Socrates is mortal.

that can be proved or disproved. The beginning proposition, the major premise, must have been proved already. The remaining propositions must be logical consequences or also have been proved previously. The last proposition is the conclusion. To be **valid,** the propositions used in the proof must all be true.

Valid Arguments

Most of the arguments or logical proofs we encounter on a daily basis are not, of course, set up as formal syllogisms. Even though the syllogism may not be explicit, every argument is based on a syllogism. Our usual practice is to omit propositions we assume everyone will agree to. Exhibit 14.2 illustrates the syllogism behind an informal argument.

Logical Fallacies

A **logical fallacy,** or error in reasoning, can result from using premises that are not true or that are not logical consequences of previous propositions. Most day-to-day efforts to persuade are based on fallacious reasoning, in that they attempt to convince or persuade without using the steps required by logic to establish a true conclusion. Advertisers, for example, often base their attempts to persuade on a fallacious argument.

One manufacturer of electric razors, for example, stated: "If two blades are better than one . . . try 18 of them." We can more easily examine the logic of this statement if we set it up as a syllogism, as Exhibit 14.3 illustrates.

Is a report writer allowed to be right for the wrong reasons?

The advertiser's argument is fallacious, but the product may still do everything claimed for it. You can use fallacious reasoning and still be right. Those responsible for writing reports, however, cannot afford to use fallacious reasoning, which more often than not leads to erroneous conclusions. The logical fallacies may influence not only the interpretation of data but also the later presentation of that data in the report. If a researcher is not aware that information on which he or she will base decisions contains logical fallacies, the faulty information may be presented as fact in the final document. Even when the data collected have been presented fairly, a report writer may inadvertently introduce one or more logical fallacies into his or her final document.

EXHIBIT 14.2   ## Informal and Formal Arguments

Syllogism:
Major Premise Our office productivity needs improving.
Minor Premise Word processing equipment increases office productivity.
Conclusion   We should buy word processing equipment.

The logical fallacies are divided into three principal categories: the fallacies of ambiguity, the fallacies of presumption, and the fallacies of relevance.

Fallacies of Ambiguity

As the term implies, the fallacies of ambiguity are based on the confusing use of language. If a statement is ambiguous, it may be misinterpreted. Fallacies of ambiguity may be used occasionally for humorous purpose, but they may lead a reader to an erroneous conclusion. The most common fallacies of ambiguity include double-talk, personification, and faulty extension.

What is double-talk?

Double-Talk Double-talk results when a statement can mean more than one thing or when the message conveyed is obviously not what was intended. The effect may be intentionally or unintentionally humorous.

Example: Clothes 50 percent off.

Example: Several good speeches will be given in the morning. Yours will be given in the afternoon.

Double-talk may also simply confuse. In the following example, does *most* include *managers* and *workers,* or does it include *workers only?*

Example: Managers and workers were polled on the matter of compensation. Most believed that the base pay should be raised by $5 an hour.

Sometimes the context in which the statement occurs may influence its meaning.

Example: You never looked better. (But you still look awful.)

Example: Do not speak ill of the dead. (You may speak ill of the living.)

Double-talk may also result if the meaning of a key term changes in the course of a discussion.

Example: Your argument is sound, all sound. (*Sound* changes meaning from *logical* to *noise.*)

Example: He is discriminating in his choice of clothes and in his hiring practices. (*Discriminating* changes in meaning from *good taste* to *prejudiced.*)

EXHIBIT 14.3   Fallacious Argument

Implicit Premise Two safety razor blades are better than one.

Implicit Premise More blades would be better yet.

Implicit Premise What is true of safety razors must also be true of electric shavers.

Conclusion   An electric shaver with 18 blades must be better than a safety razor
                   with two blades.

Which writers may
use personification
as a technique?
Which ones may
not?

Personification When we ascribe human characteristics to abstract concepts, we are guilty of the fallacy of personification. While personification is a legitimate technique for writers of poetry and fiction, its use is not acceptable in report writing.

Example: The company decided to fire Howard Lannon. (Companies cannot make decisions; only people can.)

Example: Management desires to increase profits 10 percent next quarter. (Management is a concept, and concepts cannot desire, only people—managers—can desire.)

Example: Technology will have to work harder if it is to satisfy all our wants. (Only people can work harder.)

Example: My old car likes to warm up for about 10 minutes before being driven. (Cars do not have likes or dislikes.)

What is the
definition of faulty
extension?

Faulty Extension   If we assume that what is true of the whole is also true of its parts, or that what is true of a part is also true of the whole or of other related parts, we are guilty of faulty extension.

Example: IBM is a great company, and we will have the best computers at the best price if we buy IBM. (Just because IBM is a great company does not mean that all its computers provide the best value.)

Example: The bridge is made of first-rate steel, so it must be safe. (Even if the steel is first-rate, the design or construction may be faulty.)

Example: The left front brake is okay, so the right one must still be good too. (The right front brake may have been defective from the beginning.)

Fallacies of Presumption

Fallacies of presumption are a result of misrepresentation of fact. Facts can be overlooked, evaded, or distorted. Fallacies of presumption are among the most common kind, and report writers should take special care to avoid them. They include sweeping generalization, hasty generalization, two-valued thinking, begging the question, loaded question, magic mirror, false analogy, false cause, and irrelevant thesis.

How are sweeping
generalizations
different from
faulty extensions?

Sweeping Generalization   When we assume that what is true under certain circumstances or conditions must be true under all circumstances or conditions, we are commiting the fallacy of sweeping generalization.

Example: More than 200 people died in that airplane crash. Flying is obviously dangerous. (Even with one bad accident, flying may be safer than other forms of travel.)

Example: The MacDougals Restaurant in my hometown is terrible, so I always avoid MacDougals when I travel. (Just because one MacDougals is bad does not mean that others will also be bad.)

Hasty Generalization   The fallacy of hasty generalization results from examining too few specific cases before stating a general conclusion. For this reason, it is often referred to as "jumping to conclusions." Small sample size, short trial runs, and too little experience can all lead to erroneous, hasty generalizations.

Example: My grandfather smoked more than a pack of cigarettes a day from the time he was 12, and lived to be 90. Therefore, smoking does not cause cancer or heart disease. (One healthy smoker does not prove that smoking would not cause health problems for some people.)

Example: The MacDougals in East Lansing does well, and the MacDougals in Ann Arbor does well, so we should consider opening a MacDougals in Jackson. (East Lansing and Ann Arbor both have major universities, which may contribute to the success of MacDougals in those towns. Jackson does not have a major university, so the general conclusion may be false.)

What may happen when contraries are mistaken for contradictories?

Two-Valued Thinking   When we assume that two categories are mutually exclusive, we may be guilty of the fallacy of two-valued thinking. Some conditions really are **contradictories** (on/off, pregnant/not pregnant), but most so-called opposites are simply **contraries**, which indicate degrees of difference (rich/poor, smart/stupid, tall/short). In some cases, the either-or distinction is justified. In most cases, however, it is not, and a variety of possibilities between the two extremes may be overlooked.

Example: We must either divest ourselves of our small-appliance line or sink into financial ruin. (There may be alternatives.)

Example: Although neither Atlanta nor Macon offers an ideal location, I recommend Macon because it is better than Atlanta. (Perhaps a more suitable location could be found.)

Begging the Question   Begging the question is assuming, rather than proving, that the point at issue is true. Begging the question can take the form of a circular argument (in which the conclusion proves the premise that proves the conclusion) or a single word that implies a conclusion without proving the premise.

Example: Johnson's proposal cannot possibly succeed because it is unworkable. (The proposal may not succeed, but the statement does not provide a reason. *Unworkable* merely repeats the concept of not succeeding.)

Example: Any intelligent reader can see that Johnson's proposal cannot succeed. (The word *intelligent* begs the question of why Johnson's proposal would not succeed.)

Loaded Question   The fallacy of loaded question results when a question cannot be answered without implying an answer to a question at issue.

Example: Have you stopped beating your wife? (A person confesses to wife beating with either *yes* or *no*.)

Example: Has Hamblin finally written a report worth reading? (A *yes* implies all previous reports were bad).

Example: Would you prefer the carpeting in tan or beige? (The question implies that the customer has decided to buy the carpet and is now concerned with color only.)

Magic Mirror   We are guilty of the fallacy of magic mirror if we apply different standards to ourselves than we do to others.

Example: I am clever. You are manipulative. He's sneaky.

Example: You really cannot trust the employees who work for this company. When I was checking to see how much I could get away with putting on my expense account, I discovered that some people are really padding their accounts.

When is an analogy false?

False Analogy   An analogy, which compares two things, is said to be false when the things compared are similar in insignificant ways only. To be useful, an analogy must be based on a comparison of things similar in key ways.

Example: You have come a long way, baby. (A popular advertisement implies that the right to smoke is as important as the rights to vote and to equal pay for equal work.)

Example: Our marketing plan for the calculators was successful using TV personalities and their kids; we should use the same plan to sell our new business computers. (The analogy falsely implies that calculators and business computers are sufficiently alike so that the same marketing strategy would work with both.)

False Cause   The fallacy of false cause results when we assume that one event has caused another when a causal relationship has not been established. Both events may have been caused by a third, unidentified, event, or the two events may simply be coincidental.

Example: Breaking a mirror means seven years' bad luck. (Breaking a mirror does not *cause* bad luck, even if some bad luck follows the breaking.)

Example: Our new advertising campaign has resulted in a 43 percent increase in sales. (The campaign may be the cause of the sales increase, but other factors— changes in product, seasonal fluctuations, etc.—would also need to be considered.)

Irrelevant Thesis   We are guilty of the fallacy of irrelevant thesis when we attempt to prove a premise or conclusion other than the one at issue.

Example: We should acquire Tanaka Radio because its main offices are in Tokyo, and we would be able to hold our annual meetings there. (Tokyo's good location for company meetings is an irrelevant issue.)

Example: That job requires a lot of technical skill and the ability to make quick decisions. I do not think that we should hire a woman. (A person's sex is irrelevant. How well an applicant meets the job requirements is the key issue.)

Falacies of Relevance

To what emotions do fallacies of relevance appeal?

These are confusing because they substitute emotion for reason. Fallacies of relevance appeal to prejudice, envy, sympathy, vanity, pride, or fear rather than offer a logical argument. The common fallacies in this category are personal attack; mob appeal; and appeals to pity, authority, ignorance, or fear.

Personal Attack
The fallacy of personal attack results from an attempt to discredit the source of an idea. The source is often, but not always, a person.

Example: Ronald Reagan (or Edward Kennedy) could not possibly design a program to help the poor because he is rich. (The program, not the person, should be evaluated.)

Example: Businesses naturally want reduced worker compensation because they stand to profit from the reduction. (While business may profit from reduced worker compensation, the reasons for the reduction may be logical and not the result of vested interest.)

Mob Appeal
The mob appeal fallacy is based on our natural tendencies to group identification and to going along with the crowd. This fallacy appeals to our emotional need to fit in rather than to our ability to decide logically.

Example: Every other major corporation is acquiring a high-tech business, and we should too. (Perhaps the company should acquire a high-tech business, but the fact that others are doing so is not necessarily a good reason for doing so.)

When should an appeal to pity receive consideration?

Appeal to Pity
The fallacy of appeal to pity is based on our natural desire to help those in need regardless of the logic of the situation.

Example: If I do not get a B in this class, I will flunk out of school. (Sad as flunking out might be, it has nothing to do with the grade earned.)

Example: If we close the Flint plant, hundreds will be out of work. (Unlike the first example, this appeal to pity is worth consideration. The Flint plant may have to be closed anyway, but the legitimate needs of others should receive consideration.)

Appeal to Authority
The fallacy of appeal to authority is the result of ascribing expertise to a source that has not earned or demonstrated expertise in the area at issue.

Example: My doctor invested in Capriotti vineyards, so it must be a good investment. (What does the doctor know about the stock market, and how does he or she know it?)

Appeal to Ignorance
When we attempt to prove that our conclusion must be true because others cannot disprove it, we are guilty of the fallacy of appeal to ignorance.

Example: Smoking must not cause cancer because they have not proved it yet. (The cause-effect relationship may be proved in the future.)

Example: Do not object to my proposal until you have a better alternative. (Just because no one has come up with a better alternate does not mean that the plan under discussion is without flaw.)

Appeal to Fear We are guilty of the fallacy of appeal to fear if we use the threat of harm to persuade someone to accept a conclusion

Example: We have to hire a woman for this position, or we will be in trouble with EEOC. (Whether a woman is hired should depend on the qualification of the candidates, not on the possible reaction of a regulatory agency.)

Example: You cannot afford not to have insurance. What would your family do if you were to die? (This is an attempt to scare somebody into buying insurance.)

The presence of logical fallacy does not necessarily prove that the conclusion is incorrect. A logical fallacy shows an invalid argument rather than a false conclusion. Because an invalid argument may lead to a false conclusion, however, report writers and readers need to examine their arguments for the presence of fallacies.

Semantics

What do general semanticists hope to accomplish?

Semantics is the study of meaning as expressed in words. General semantics is the attempt to improve communication and understanding by analyzing the use of language. Alfred Korzybski, author of *Science and Sanity* (first published in 1933), developed the principles of general semantics to help people use words in a way that more accurately reflects the reality they represent.

Many of the principles of general semantics are related to the common logical fallacies. Both logic and general semantics are attempts to develop a systematic process of observing reality accurately in spite of the metaphorical nature of language. In a standard **metaphor,** one thing symbolizes—or stands for—something else:

The ship of state requires a strong hand at the helm.

This metaphor establishes analogy comparing the captain of a ship with the leader of a government. Both logicians and semanticists are concerned with the accuracy of analogies contained in metaphors, whether the metaphor is explicit (as in the "ship of state" example) or implicit (as in much daily language).

"The map is not the territory" is the phrase general semanticists use to remind us that language is a symbol system that stands for reality but is not reality itself. A map—if it is accurate—gives us a picture of the territory; language—when properly used—gives us a description of reality. Inaccurate maps and faulty language can both get us into trouble, especially when we forget that both maps and language can contain errors.

The most important principles of general semantics are the six that follow.

No Statement Tells the Whole Story   Because we cannot perceive totally or with complete accuracy, we need to recognize that we cannot make absolutely complete or accurate statements.

What is the allness fallacy? How do semanticists try to avoid it?

Each of us abstracts from reality those things seen as most important. No two people will select the same aspect of reality as the most important. When we think we know or have said everything, we are guilty of the **allness fallacy.** General semanticists try to avoid the allness fallacy by mentally adding *etc.* to the ends of sentences as a reminder that more remains to be said.

No Two Things Are Identical   The human mind works by a process of generalization and differentiation. When things are similar, we tend to class them together and treat them alike. Some things that seem similar, however, have significant differences. When we overlook these differences, we are guilty of the semantic fallacy, **failure to discriminate**. Because we are used to looking for similarities so that we can classify things and make generalizations about them, we need to remind ourselves to look for and evaluate differences as well.

What is an inference? A value judgment?

Facts, Inferences and Value Judgments Are Not the Same   A **fact** is something that has been verified by direct observation. We know, for example, that it is 2,054 miles between Chicago and Los Angeles. That distance has been measured several times by independent observers. Because both Chicago and Los Angeles are large cities, we could infer that several airlines would offer direct flights between them. An **inference** is an assumption, which—like a hypothesis—needs to be tested before we can be sure whether it is correct or incorrect. You might prefer Los Angeles to Chicago (or vice versa), and that preference would be a **value judgment**. A value judgment is simply an opinion, which may be based on facts and inferences but is not itself a fact. You might hold the opinion that large cities are "unfit for human habitation," but that value judgment, contradicted as it is by the numbers of people who choose to live and work in large cities, says more about you than it does large cities.

Few Things Are Either-Or   (See the logical fallacy *two-valued thinking*.) Like the logicians, general semanticists are concerned about our failure to recognize the middle ground between extremes. We tend to think in terms of **abstract absolutes**: best, worst; tallest, shortest; most expensive, cheapest; fastest, slowest; and so on. We need to remind ourselves that a middle ground almost always exists, and that the abstract terms are relative to something specific. Something can be "best" only in relation to other things and only in specific ways.

Time Changes All Things   More than 2,000 years ago, a Greek named Heraclitus observed that a person cannot step in the same river twice.[3] Heraclitus recognized that, between steps, the river changed. The water that was there is gone. "New" water had arrived by the time of the second step. When we fail to recognize that things and people change over time, we are guilty of the fallacy, **frozen evaluation**. Semanticists recommend that we date observations to remind ourselves that things change and need periodic reevaluation. Judith Holcombe (1985) refused a promotion because she did not want to relocate. Judith Holcombe (1988) may desire the promotion and relocation.

What is the harm in a frozen evaluation?

Time Sequence Alone Does Not Establish a Cause and Effect Relationship   (See the logical fallacy, *false cause*.) When one event closely follows another, we tend to assume that the first caused the second. We need to remind ourselves that the events may be unrelated, coincidental, or effects of a third event not yet identified. Because we also have the tendency to think of causes of events as immediately preceding the event in question, we tend to ignore causes that may be remote in time. It may take years, for example, to know the long-term health effects of certain modern chemicals, especially insecticides, herbicides, and even medicines. For this reason, report writers need to be aware that the cause of an event may be fairly far removed in time or place from the event itself.

INTERPRETING DATA

Even though your data have been properly classified and you have been careful to maintain objectivity in evaluating that data, you may still make errors in interpretation. The most common errors of interpretation are emphasizing the unimportant, comparing the noncomparable, forcing a conclusion, oversimplifying, reasoning in circles, and assuming the obvious.

Emphasizing the Unimportant

In your desire to be objective, you may feel that you need to include everything and may thus bog your reader down with a mass of detail, failing to distinguish between the important and the unimportant. In any study, the chances are that not all data will be of equal significance. As a report writer, you will need to present the most important data in a way that helps the reader grasp their significance. Do not allow your major points to get lost in a multitude of insignificant details.

---

[3]Wendell Johnson, *People in Quandaries: The Semantics of Personal Adjustment* (New York: Harper & Row, 1946) 23–34.

Comparing the Noncomparable

Some comparisons are legitimate, but some are not.

Legitimate: Apples are like oranges in that both are fruit, both contain fiber, and both contain vitamin C.

Not legitimate: Apples cost only $2 a dozen, so it is unreasonable to pay $3 a dozen for oranges.

How can you avoid the mistake of comparing the noncomparable?

To avoid comparing data that really cannot be compared, you need to know how the data were derived. In comparing the costs of apples and oranges, for example, you would need to know their relative costs of production and distribution as well as a number of market factors, such as supply and demand.

In comparing data based on studies conducted in different countries, you might need to have a thorough knowledge of the different cultures to avoid comparing data that should not really be compared. Would it be valid, for example, to compare data based on the decision-making process in Japanese organizations and that used by American organizations? Because the Japanese and American cultures have such different conceptions about how decisions should be made in organizations, one would need to be very careful to ensure that cultural differences did not render the comparison invalid.

Forcing a Conclusion

In some cases, a conclusion may simply not be possible. Your data may be contradictory (50 percent are in favor, and 50 percent are against), you may not have had sufficient time to collect enough data, or perhaps circumstances changed since you began your study and rendered your data obsolete. Naturally, no report writer likes to end a report after weeks and perhaps months of study by saying that no conclusions were possible, but honesty and objectivity may require it on occasion. Perhaps your only conclusion will be that further study is required (or that further study would prove useless).

Oversimplifying

Do most things fall into mutually exclusive categories? How does this affect report writing?

Sometimes, in a desire to be decisive, a report writer may forget that many problems are complex and require complex solutions. Few things fall neatly into mutually exclusive categories of right or wrong, good or bad. Most things fall somewhere in between; a solution may be better than another in some ways but not in others. One computer system may offer certain advantages over another, but at a higher cost. Be sure to weigh all the relevant factors before reaching a conclusion, and be sure to clarify those factors for your reader.

Reasoning in Circles

When a writer uses a restatement of the premise for the conclusion, he or she is guilty of reasoning in circles. When the statement is short, it is easy to see that circular reasoning is based on a redundancy

> More people preferred Brand A because more people selected Brand A as their first choice.

In some cases, however, the original premise and the conclusion may be separated by pages of "evidence." When you are examining the data you intend to include in your report, check to see if any of your sources have been guilty of reasoning in cricles by finding explicit and implicit premises and their related conclusions. If the conclusion merely repeats the premise using different words, reevaluate the data. Also, watch your own writing to ensure that you are not guilty of circular reasoning.

Assuming the Obvious

Report writers may forget that what is obvious to them may not be obvious to the reader. As you evaluate your sources of information, beware of statements that begin

> Everyone knows . . .

> It is obvious that . . .

> It goes without saying . . .

> It is clear that . . .

> You will agree that . . .

What should writers do about sources that assume the obvious?

The statement that follows may or may not be true, but "everyone knows" does not prove that it is. You will need to determine that for yourself.

You also need to be careful to avoid assuming the obvious when you are preparing your own report. When you have been working with data for weeks, you may think that certain conclusions based on the data are self-evident. The reader, however, will not have had the opportunity to study the data long enough to have reached the conclusions that seem so obvious to you.

ANALYZING STATISTICAL INFORMATION

Statistics are inescapable. Very few decisions in business, industry, or government are made without some consideration of statistical data.

Financial data, population demographics, attitudes of important publics, and a wide variety of other factors are best understood in terms of
quantities. Wherever you work, whatever your job, you will need to use
statistics to solve many of the problems you will encounter.

Depending on the kind of research with which you are involved, you
may be examining either **qualitative data** or **quantitative data.** In
many cases, you will need to consider both.

What are
qualitative data?
quantitative data?

Qualitative Data

The term qualitative data refers to the qualities or **attributes** of the
items being investigated: colors, sizes, shapes, or behavioral characteristics. Stereo tape recorders, for example, come in a variety of formats:
reel-to-reel, cassette, and eight-track cartridge. They are available with
and without Dolby noise reduction circuits, with and without automatic
reverse features, and so on. These are all qualities that would be significant in decisions about stereo tape recorders.

Qualitative data are especially important when you are trying to solve
"human" problems. Attitudes, opinions, and belief systems are not
always easy to measure quantitatively. Nevertheless, to be meaningful,
qualitative data usually must be converted to numerical values before
they can be analyzed. First, attributes can be assigned to categories. By
counting the number of items in each category, we establish **nominal
data.** Second, by assigning relative values to each attribute and ranking
them by order of preference, we establish **ranked order.**

Suppose you have been authorized to evaluate the restaurants in your
area to determine the best place for your company to entertain clients
at business lunches and dinners. You could establish a variety of
categories

Location

Kind of food (French, Mexican, American, Chinese, etc.)

Quality of food

Quality of service

Atmosphere

What are nominal
data? ranked data?

The number of restaurants in a given area and the number of restaurants
of a particular kind would be nominal data. The quality of food and the
quality of service would be ranked data. Atmosphere could be either
nominal (number of restaurants with a particular kind of atmosphere)
or ranked (the quality of atmosphere).

Much qualitative data tend to be subjective. What constitutes a
French restaurant? In some cases, a restaurant is obviously French: it has

a French name, French service personnel, and nothing but French cu,ᵢᵣ sine and wines. But what about the restaurant that has a French name and only one or two authentically French meals? Placing such a restaurant in a category calls for a subjective decision. Ranking, too, calls for a subjective evaluation. How good must food and service be before you would call them "excellent"?

Quantitative Data

Suppose that you are working for a manufacturer of personal computers and you are assigned the task of forecasting the number of units your company should sell next year. A number of the questions you would need to answer to solve this problem call for an understanding of statistics

How many people are likely to buy personal computers next year?

What is your market share likely to be?

How will the general economic situation affect sales of personal computers?

In Chapter 12 you learned that because it is impractical to interview everybody throughout the area where you market your computers you will need statistics to help determine the kind of sample that will result in accurate data. Sampling is one of the most important statistical concepts for report writers. Some occupations rely heavily on statistical information as a tool for decision making. Others may not require knowledge of statistics on a regular basis, but regardless of your occupational specialty, statistics will play a sufficiently important role to justify your spending some time becoming familiar with the most common techniques of qualitative and quantitative data analysis.

Our discussion here is intended primarily for those who have a limited background in statistics, and our primary focus is on basic sampling techniques and the accurate presentation of statistical information. Those of you who will be working in market research, financial forecasting, any of the technical fields, or other occupations requiring regular use of statistics should invest in a course in statistics.

We will begin here with definitions of basic terms.

How is population defined by statisticians? What is a subset of a population?

Population   The collection, or set, of individuals or objects whose properties will be analyzed is a population (see Chapter 12.) In the example cited above, the population would probably be defined according to age, income level, and education based on what was already known about buyers of personal computers. The population must be well-defined to obtain useful information. In statistics, a population can be a collection of animals, measurements, or inanimate objects.

- **Tests for Use of Logical Fallacies.** Because reports should be objective and rely on logic to convince, you should check your report materials for the unintentional use of the common logical fallacies. Substitute propositions and logical proof for any fallacies you discover.
- **Tests for Statistical Accuracy.** Ensure that the data you have collected justify your conclusions. If in doubt, increase your sample size, attempt to replicate your results with another population, or increase your number of observations.

What is the writer's most basic obligation to readers when presenting conclusions?

The most important, rule, however, is simply to be fair and to let the reader know exactly how you reached each of your conclusions.

While many business and technical decisions can be made on the basis of clear-cut, "hard" evidence, many cannot. Often, the decision must be made on somebody's intuitive feeling about the right course of action. All the evidence—including extensive market surveys—indicated that Ford Motor Company's Edsel would be a huge success. It flopped. Yet products like the Hula Hoop and the Pet Rock have proved successful in the absence of evidence to predict success.

The same is true in areas other than market research. What the evidence says *should* work does not always prove successful, and what the evidence says will not work, often does. Aeronautical engineers have "proved" that, on the basis of body weight and wing area, it is impossible for a bumble bee to fly.

Because you cannot draw the correct conclusions every time, you need to be especially careful to be explicit about what you are concluding and why. No one will expect more of you than an honest experiment or other collection of data and an objective presentation of the evidence. Use hard—quantitative—evidence when possible, but avoid using statistical analysis unless the data are truly amenable. Heavy use of statistics can intimidate and manipulate some readers, so include any explanations and interpretations of quantitative data your reader may require or appreciate.

When you present your conclusions in the report, do so in an orderly manner. Show how each is based on certain supporting data, and—in general—present your conclusions in hierarchical fashion, with your most important conclusions presented first and the least important last. Use a numbered list.

When, if ever, may new data be presented in the conclusions? Why?

Do not introduce new data as part of or in support of any of your conclusions. If you discover new data when you are preparing your conclusions, you will need to revise your presentation and interpretation of the data so that your conclusions can be based on the data actually presented in the report. Also, check to make sure that your conclusions actually pertain to the subject under study.

If a conclusion is based on certain assumptions, say so:

> Assuming a continuing rate of growth at 3 percent, ABC Corporation will require a new mainframe within the next 3 years.

If a personal preference has influenced one of your recommendations, say so:

> Although Computer A and Computer B operate with equal efficiency and their costs are identical, I preferred the "feel" of Computer B, which gives the impression of being sturdier than Computer A.

Your conclusions should follow the same style of writing as that used in the rest of the report. If you have been using the personal style (with pronouns), then continue to use them. If you have been using the impersonal style, do not introduce pronouns at this point. Try to avoid simply substituting "the writer" for "I." It is, after all, your report, so the conclusions are obviously yours.

Not this: The writer concludes that. . . .

But this: The most important conclusion is that. . . .

Or this: The data indicate that. . . .

When are conclusions written if they are presented at the beginning of the report?

Remember that, in many reports, the conclusions (along with the recommendations) may be presented at the beginning of the report, but these sections should not be prepared until the interpretation of the data is complete.

MAKING RECOMMENDATIONS

On what are recommendations based?

How should the problem under investigation be solved? Your recommendations for solving the problem *must* be based on your conclusions, just as the conclusions were based on the data. The conclusions are the logical result of the interpretation of the facts, and the recommendations state what should be done as a result of that interpretation. Two or more conclusions may result in one recommendation:

Conclusion: The high rate of turnover is caused by poor morale.

Conclusion: The poor morale is the result of employees' belief that the company makes too many changes in work procedures without consulting or informing them.

Conclusion: The workers feel that they have too little control over their work life.

Recommendation: The company should institute a system of quality circles to solicit suggestions from employees and to keep them informed of necessary changes in work procedures.

As was true with the conclusions, recommendations should usually be arranged in hierarchical fashion, with the most important first. Use a numbered list so that each recommendation will stand out. Recommendations should be explicit and straightforward.

Not this: Perhaps we should consider purchasing a new computer system.

Not this: A new computer system might solve our problem.

But this: I recommend that we purchase a new computer system.

In short reports and in long reports with few separate conclusions and recommendations, the conclusions and recommendations may be presented together in one combined section. For most readers, these two elements are the most important parts of the report. They may, in fact, be the only elements your readers actually read, so prepare them with care.

SUMMARY

To be meaningful, data must be organized and interpreted. While this task begins at the inception of the report writing process, most organizing and interpreting occurs once all the data have been collected. The overlapping phases of organizing and interpreting data include (1) classifying data, (2) maintaining objectivity, (3) interpreting the data, (4) analyzing statistical information, (5) drawing conclusions, and (6) making recommendations.

Data can be classified according to how each item or category fits into the report as a whole. Possible categories for this method of classification are history of the problem, criteria leading to a choice, descriptions and explanations, results, trends, discussion of results, alternatives, conclusions, and recommendations.

Data can also be classified to ensure a clear, systematic presentation of facts. To ensure an adequate demonstration of facts, (1) clarify what is being classified; (2) select a significant basis for the classification; (3) make sure that the division is complete; (4) complete one basis for classification before beginning the next, and make divisions mutually exclusive; and (5) be consistent and logical in developing your system of classification.

Maintaining objectivity requires a sense of fairness, which allows the researcher to be objective in spite of preconceived notions and vested interest. In addition to a willingness to be fair, objectivity requires an understanding of logic and semantics.

Formal logic is based on the concept of the syllogism, in which a series of true propositions lead to a valid conclusion. Informal logic consists of implicit applications of a syllogism, in which some propositions may be assumed.

Logical fallacies, or errors in reasoning, can result from using premises that are not true or are not logical consequences of previous propositions. Fallacies of ambiguity result from the use of confusing language. Fallacies of presumption result from misrepresentation of facts by overlooking, evading, or distorting them. Fallacies of relevance result from the substitution of emotion for reason.

Semantics is the study of meaning as expressed in words. General semantics is the attempt to improve understanding by analyzing the use of language and attempting to use it accurately. The following are the most important semantic principles: (1) no statement tells the whole story; (2) no two things are identical; (3) facts, inferences, and value judgments are not the same; (4) few things are either-or; (5) time changes all things, and (6) time sequence alone does not establish a cause and effect relationship.

Most decisions in business, industry, and government are based at least in part on consideration of statistical data. Data are classed as qualitative or quantitative. Qualitative data include the qualities or attributes of the items being investigated. Quantitative data include the numerical factors that influence the items being investigated. Qualitative data can be quantified for analysis by counting, which results in nominal data, or by ranking, which results in ranked order.

In obtaining quantitative data, a population (of people or objects) or a sample of the population is examined with respect to one or more variables. A variable that applies to the whole population is known as a parameter of the population. Quantitative data are discrete when the variables are counted item by item and continuous when the variables can assume virtually any value.

Probability theory is concerned with the chance that an event will occur when all possibilities are known, and statistics is concerned with inferring the possibilities based on the results of a sample.

SUGGESTED READINGS

Capaldi, Nicholas. *The Art of Deception.* New York: Donald W. Brown, 1971.

Covers the use of informal logic for both presenting evidence and examining evidence presented by others. More difficult to read than Chase's Guide, but more thorough.

Chase, Stuart. *Guide to Straight Thinking.* New York: Harper & Brothers, 1956.

An excellent, simplified introduction to logical fallacies. Rightly considered a classic.

Cohen, Morris R. *A Preface to Logic.* New York: Dover Publications, 1972.

A thorough introduction to modern, formal logic. Coverage is more technical than many would prefer.

Engel, S. Morris. *Analyzing Informal Fallacies.* Englewood Cliffs, NJ: Prentice-Hall, 1980.

An entertaining presentation and analysis of common logical fallacies.

Hayakawa, S. I. *Language in Thought and Action.* New York: Harcourt, Brace, 1978.

A classic, simplified introduction to semantics. Good coverage of the ways in which inferences and value judgments interfere with objectivity.

Huff, Darrell. *How to Lie with Statistics*. New York: W. W. Norton & Company, 1954.

The classic treatment of using statistics to manipulate an audience. Covers the common ways statistics can be used to mislead.

Kahane, Howard. *Logic and Contemporary Rhetoric: The Use of Reason in Everyday Life*. 2nd ed. Belmont, CA: Wadsworth Publishing Company, 1976.

A popular and thorough examination of logical fallacies, with many examples taken from business, industry, and the media. Includes both formal and informal logic.

EXERCISES

Review and Discussion Questions

1. What materials should be included in each of the following categories?
   a. History of the problem
   b. Criteria
   c. Description and explanations
   d. Results
   e. Trends
   f. Discussion of results
   g. Alternatives
   h. Conclusions
   i. Recommendations

2. Name and explain the five rules for classifying data.

3. How does the concept of *fairness* contribute to objectivity in report writing?

4. What is a syllogism? What is required for a syllogism to be valid?

5. What is a logical fallacy?

6. Name and explain the fallacies of ambiguity.

7. Name and explain the fallacies of presumption.

8. Name and explain the fallacies of relevance.

9. How would a writer's study of general semantics contribute to the accuracy of his or her reports?

10. Name and explain six principles of general semantics.

11. Is *data* singular or plural?

12. Define and explain the concepts of qualitative data and quantitative data.

13. What are the differences between discrete and continuous data?

14. Define the following terms: population, sample, variable, parameter, and probability.

15. Define and explain the terms mean, median, and mode (see Appendix A).

16. Define and explain the terms range, average deviation, variance, and standard deviation (see Appendix A).

Problems and Applications

1. What evidence is there that language is metaphorical? Using at least three sources, explain the metaphorical nature of language in a paper of no more than five pages. Include a brief discussion of the ways in which your findings should influence report writers.

2. Select between five and ten advertisements from a recent magazine and analyze them for logical fallacies. If your instructor directs, organize your results and draw appropriate conclusions.

3. Select a recent editorial from your local newspaper. Analyze the editorial, looking for implied syllogisms and logical fallacies. Submit your findings in whatever form your instructor directs.

4. Under what circumstances should professional athletes be allowed to bet on games in their own sport? Should referees be allowed to bet on contests even when they are not refereeing? Explain your reasoning in a paper three to five pages long.

5. What constitutes a *vested interest?* What is the difference between vested interests and conflicts of interest? Why does the Securities Exchange Commission (SEC) prohibit those with inside knowledge of business transactions that will influence stock values from taking advantage of that knowledge? Describe and discuss a recent example of unfair behavior reported in a recent business publication. Why was the activity involved unfair? What should the people involved have done? Submit a photocopy of the article you have used as a source along with a paper of no more than five pages.

6. For one of the problems in Appendix B, make the following calculations for all significant variables:
   a. Mean
   b. Median
   c. Mode
   d. Range
   e. Average deviation
   f. Variance
   g. Standard deviation
   h. Linear correlations between at least two related data

i. Linear regression predicting the value of one variable when the value of another variable is known or assumed
j. Student's *t*-test
k. Test for proportion
l. Chi-square test

Be sure to label each item and to show all the steps in your work.

7. Perform the computations listed in the preceding problem on the data you have collected for your own report.

8. Perform the computations listed in Problem 6 above for the following data:

Respondent	Age	Highest Level of Education	Annual Income
1	47	H.S.	$115,000
2	52	B.A.	42,000
3	29	B.A.	37,000
4	31	M.A.	41,000
5	23	H.S.	12,000
6	62	B.A.	47,000
7	59	Ph.D.	32,000
8	47	Ph.D.	250,000
9	42	M.A.	26,000
10	46	H.S.	23,000
11	32	B.A.	33,000
12	31	Ph.D.	31,000
13	40	H.S.	17,000
14	52	H.S.	21,000
15	29	M.A.	41,000
16	47	B.A.	48,000
17	38	H.S.	30,000
18	55	B.A.	52,000
19	60	B.A.	46,000
20	60	B.A.	29,000
21	58	Ph.D.	75,000
22	49	B.A.	92,000
23	24	H.S.	13,000
24	65	M.A:	88,000
25	60	B.A.	81,000
26	47	B.A.	52,000
27	44	Ph.D.	73,000
28	30	B.A.	18,000
29	38	M.A.	48,000
30	42	H.S.	28,000

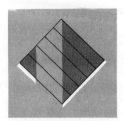

Graphic Aids

"A picture is worth a thousand words."

Topics

Fundamentals
Identification and Mechanics
Tables
Figures
Computer Graphics

In previous chapters we talked about presenting data clearly and concisely, quantitatively and qualitatively. Now we will discuss techniques for presenting data graphically so that your reader can have a complete picture of what you want to say.

FUNDAMENTALS

What are graphic aids?

Although some people refer to graphic aids as visual aids, most people make a distinction between the two terms. Graphic aids are tables and figures presented in written material to clarify a discussion, whereas visual aids refer to such materials as models, chalkboards, flipcharts, and slides used in oral presentations.

Which should appear first—the text or the related graphic aid?

Graphic aids are used to clarify and help present complex information. First we need the words to explain, and then we use the graphic aids—the pictures—to assist the words. Words are the primary means of presentation; graphic aids are secondary supports. Graphic aids are just that—aids and supplements—not substitutes; they do not take precedence over or substitute for words. Graphic aids are placed *after*—not *before*—the text that mentions them. In other words, we first describe or explain, and then we present the material graphically.

Never include a table or figure without a reference to it. As we will discuss later in the chapter, just as the text must be independent of the graphic aid, so, too, the graphic aid must tell the entire story without the text. If the table or figure were removed, the text should be complete without it, and the graphic aid should be complete without the text.

Because of the increase in the number of reports—possibly as a result of computers and word processors—busy executives do not have time to read through long reports. They want facts and figures that can be read quickly and easily. And so report writers are providing a second report—a summary report supported by graphic aids. This trend makes the self-sufficiency of graphic aids even more important.

Graphic aids are used when they are needed to clarify a discussion; they are not used for adornment. When the information is clear and the reader will not have difficulty interpreting it, a graphic aid would be superfluous.

The quality of a graphic aid is measured by the clarity with which it

1. Shows the data.

2. Helps the reader focus on the data rather than on the graph itself.

3. Avoids misleading the reader or distorting the data.

4. Simplifies the reader's comprehension of the data.

5. Is consistent with the verbal description of the data.[1]

---

[1]For more information about achieving graphical excellence, see Edward R. Tufte, *The Visual Display of Quantitative Information* (Cheshire, CT: Graphics Press, 1983).

Purposes

Why are graphic
aids used?

The primary purpose of graphic aids is to present a picture of what the
text says. The picture can be in the form of a table or figure. Graphic
aids convert and condense complex information into pictorial form,
helping the reader visualize relationships. Graphic aids also emphasize
material that needs extra attention or coverage. Because they present a
vivid image, graphic aids are easy to read, remember, follow, and interpret. And finally, graphic aids enhance the appearance and readability
of the report, making it more attractive to readers.

Placement

Ideally, graphic aids are placed as close as possible to the text they illustrate. Do not, however, insert one within a paragraph. When a graphic
aid is small, it can be placed on the same page as the text, following the
paragraph that refers to it. Do not divide an illustration that can be
placed on one page: place it on the following page. When a graphic aid
takes a full page, place it on a page facing the explanation or on the
next page available following the explanation. When the explanation
itself occupies several pages, however, place the graphic aid on the first
full page that follows the first mention of it. Illustrations too wide for
regular placement may be placed sideways on a single page or on continuing pages, with the top of the page at the left.

Avoid long tables. When it is necessary to continue a table onto a
second page, write "continued" at the bottom of the page and begin
the second page with the number and title of the table plus the word
"continued." Also, repeat column headings on the second and following pages of the table.

When are graphic
aids placed in an
appendix?

When graphic aids are not essential but can be useful to the reader,
place them in an appendix along with other long and complex graphic
aids.

Subordination

When it is necessary to refer the reader to a table or figure, the emphasis
should be on the statements or comments made about the illustration
and not on the table number or location. The significant fact is that you
want the reader to see a relationship or make a comparison in a particular table, so you would refer to the table or figure number subordi-
nately by placing it in a dependent clause. Here are a few examples:

As shown in Exhibit 4, . . . (main clause)

As Table 3 indicates, . . .

As Chart 1 illustrates, . . .

. . . , while Figure 5 shows . . .

. . . , as is shown in Exhibit 4.

. . . (see Map 2).

IDENTIFICATION AND MECHANICS

Identify tables and figures by their numbers rather than by "the table above," "the figure below," "the following table," or the "preceding map."

All graphic aids should be self-explanatory. This means that they need complete identification—title, number, key or legend, and documentation of sources. In addition, graphic aids need to be presented so that they are attractive and inviting to the reader.

Size

What criteria are used in deciding the size of a graphic aid?

How large should your graphic aid be? It depends. How complex is the information it presents? How important is the information? How much data does it contain? What size graphic aid will look best with the other material you must present? What size is necessary for readability? The size of a graphic aid is best determined by the importance, the amount, and the nature of data contained in it. Does the aid need to be enlarged? Can the print be reduced? Could a photograph, for example, be reduced from 8½" by 11" to a 5" by 7" without losing important detail?

When the illustration is simple, a quarter or a third of the page might be sufficient. When the illustration is complex or important, use a half or full page. Sometimes, when an illustration is much larger than the page size, (1) you can have it photographically reduced, or (2) you can fold the wider paper into thirds, quarters, or whatever is best to match the size of the other pages. To make it easy for your reader to open and read folded pages, fold from the outside in and from the bottom up. Also, illustrations that cannot be folded, stapled, or punched can be inserted into a "pocket" on a page. See Exhibit 15.1.

Rules and Frames

To help display information attractively, use internal rules and frames. Vertical and horizontal rules within a complex table separate columns and rows neatly and make data easier for the reader to grasp. Omit them, however, when tables are simple and the columns are far enough apart. Enhance and emphasize tables and figures by framing them with rules above and below or all around them. When a frame is used, leave three blank spaces above and below the graphic aid. Leave at least 1 inch of space above and below graphic aids when no frames are used. Rules that cannot be made on the typewriter should be made with a ruler and pen using India ink.

Exhibit 15.1   **Folded Sheets**

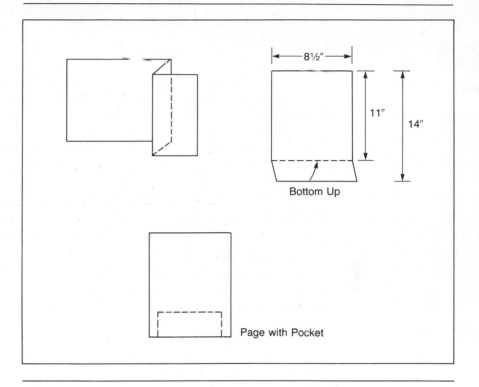

Bottom Up

Page with Pocket

Color

Color can make graphic aids more interesting. Color attracts attention and produces a positive image. It is especially useful to emphasize differences. For example, in a pie chart sectioned in thirds, you might want to use a different color for each third. In a line chart using three plot lines, you could use a separate color for each line. Bars and columns can also be made attractive with the use of color, especially when cross-hatching or shading is desirable. If you use color, remember that not all copiers will reproduce colors. Design your report so that it will reproduce attractively in black and white.

Check with local office supply or art stores for materials and advice. Clerks at these stores can recommend products that will help you prepare professional graphic aids.

Labels and Numbers

All graphic aids (except informal tables) in the report are labeled (Table, Figure, Chart) and numbered so that they can be identified and

Which is preferable
for identifying
illustrations—
Roman numerals or
Arabic numbers?

located. Generally tables are assigned Arabic numerals and numbered consecutively and separately from other graphic aids. Tables can also be numbered in capital Roman numerals (I, II, III, and so on), but this practice is declining.

When a report contains several different types of graphic aids—such as 1 chart, 2 diagrams, 3 maps, and 1 model—you can group them into tables and figures. For example, you might have Table 1, Table 2, Figure 1, Figure 2, Figure 3, and so on.

When a report, however, contains numerous examples of different types, each type could be numbered consecutively. For example, you might have Table 1, Table 2, . . . Table 15; Model 1, Model 2, . . . Model 10; Diagram 1, Diagram 2, . . . Diagram 8; Chart 1, Chart 2, . . . Chart 20; and so on.

Illustrations are listed at the end of the Table of Contents or in a separate list, as discussed in Chapter 7.

Titles

Each graphic aid is titled (or captioned) appropriately for its contents. The title should be not only concise but also descriptive. Whenever possible, include the five *Ws* of information—who, what, when, where, and why.

What trend is
developing in the
treatment of figure
and table titles?

In traditional practice, table titles, typed in all capitals, began on the second line *after* the table number and above the tabular illustration. Figure titles, typed in capital and lowercase letters or all capitals, began on the second line *below* the illustration, preceded by the figure number. Increasing in popularity, however, is the practice of placing titles above the illustrations, preceded by their numbers and labels and using capital and lowercase letters for both tables and figures. For example:

Table 1. Job Qualifications for a Secretary

Figure 1. Map of Will County

The title may be centered, or as is more common now, typed at the left margin of the illustration. When a title requires more than one line, single space the additional lines. If a title is a complete sentence, it ends with a period (or question mark); otherwise, no end punctuation is used.

Footnotes

The information gathered from primary research and presented in tables and other graphic aids by the report writer is considered primary data and does not need to be footnoted. If documentation is necessary, you would write in the footnote position, "Source: Primary."

Footnotes for graphic aids are required when

1. A secondary source is used

Exhibit 15.2   Table Consisting of Words Only

Table 2. Principal Parts of Verbs		
Present	**Past**	**Past Participle**
am	was	been
begin	began	begun
break	broke	broken
choose	chose	chosen
do	did	done
eat	ate	eaten

2. A reference is needed to explain or clarify an item

3. Directions, keys, legends, or scales are necessary for reading or interpreting. (Generally, keys and legends are typed on the graphic aid itself rather than below it.)

A table or figure may require all three references. The footnote for a secondary source is always the first one, and does not begin with an Arabic number as do other footnotes in the report. It begins at the left margin with the word *Source* followed by a colon, two spaces, and then the documentation (see Chapter 11).

For a footnote referring to any part of the graphic aid, you may use lowercase letters (a, b, c, etc.), asterisks (*, **, ***), degree symbol (°), or daggers and double daggers (†, ††) followed by the notation. When using symbols, be sure that the symbol also appears at the end of the word (or item) to which reference is being made. Sometimes you may wish just to type the word *Note* followed by a colon, two spaces, and then the notation.

Footnotes are typed on the second line below the graphic aid. They are single-spaced with double-spacing between footnotes. The lowercase letters or symbols used to designate footnotes may be placed either as a superior or online. Follow the same format throughout the report.

TABLES

What is tabular form?

Graphic aids can be broadly classified as tables and figures. Tables can be further classified as informal or formal and general or special.

A table consists of data—qualitative, quantitative, geographic, time series—arranged systematically in rows and columns. This is called tabular form. Tables may also consist entirely of words as shown in Exhibit 15.2. Technically, tables are not truly graphic, but because they do provide information in a nonnarrative manner, they are appropriately classified as graphic aids.

Exhibit 15.3   Table Consisting of Numerical Data

Table 5 Work Stoppage: 1985–1988			
Year	Number of Stoppages	Number of Workers Involved	Number of Idle Worker Days
1985	3,205	1,410,000	32,300,000
1986	3,105	1,300,000	30,146,000
1987	3,010	1,004,385	29,430,976
1988	4,581	1,989,786	38,000,456
Source: Primary			

When data are presented in paragraph form, the reader has difficulty seeing details and relationships. Tables are used, therefore, to present data so that the reader can readily see relationships and make comparisons.

Compare, for example, the information in the following paragraph and the information in Exhibit 15.3.

> In 1985 there were 3,205 work stoppages, 1,410,000 workers involved, and 32,300,000 idle worker days. In 1986 there were 3,105 work stoppages, 1,300,000 workers involved, and 30,146,000 idle worker days. In 1987 there were 3,010 work stoppages, 1,004,385 workers involved, and 29,430,976 idle worker days. In 1988 there were 4,581 work stoppages, 1,989,786 workers involved, and 38,000,456 idle worker days.

Although both contain the same information, it is easier to read and interpret the data in the table than in the narrative. Also, the table is more physically attractive than the solid block of figures and prose.

Types of Tables

Tables can be classified as informal and formal, or general and special.

Do informal tables have titles? vertical or horizontal rules?

Informal Tables   Informal tables present a single group of data, usually in columns with white space around them to emphasize the data—numerical or verbal. Informal tables

1. Are short and simple
2. Are not numbered or titled
3. Are not included in the List of Illustrations
4. Are not framed
5. Do not use vertical or horizontal rules
6. Break up a page of prose

Here is an example of an informal table:

The Five Candidates for the School Board

Name	Age
Donald Fordyce	41
Mary Litten	32
Lyndon Medema	46
Shirley Stryker	52
Justine Vicol	44

Do formal tables
have titles? vertical
or horizontal rules?

Formal Tables   Formal tables present complex data in rows and columns that interact with each other to show comparisons and relationships. Formal tables are

1. Made up of several columns and rows of data

2. Ruled internally

3. Numbered and titled

4. Framed

5. Included in the List of Illustrations

Why are general
tables called
repository tables?

General Tables   General tables present detailed and descriptive data collected by the researcher for general information but not used for analytical purposes. An example of a general table would be a copy of a questionnaire with the total number (percentages or averages) of responses recorded for each item. Also, most federal government tables (e.g., census) are general tables containing original information for the public's use. General tables are also called **repository** tables because they store information. General tables usually appear in the appendix.

Special Tables   Special tables (also called analytical tables) provide information that resulted from an analysis of the raw data collected by the researchers. An example of a special table would be specific questions taken from the questionnaire and presented in table form for an analysis in the report. Only desired data, then, will be presented for emphasis and for comparison. These tables appear in the report near the section where they are discussed.

Parts of a Table

A table consists of several parts. Different names may be applied to these parts, but generally they are referred to by the names that follow. The layout and identification of parts of a formal table are illustrated in Exhibit 15.4

   I. Heading
      A. Table Number

Exhibit 15.4   Format for Typical Formal Tables

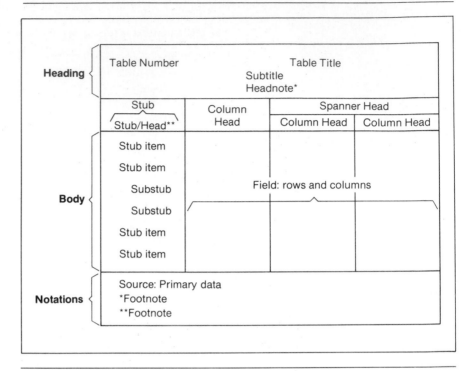

B. Table Title
   1. Subtitle, if any
   2. Headnote

II. Body
   A. Stub
     1. Stub Head
     2. Stub Item
       a. Substub I
       b. Substub II
   B. Spanner Head
     1. Column Head
     2. Column Head
   C. Field
     1. Rows
     2. Columns

III. Notations
   A. Source
   B. Footnotes

What are stub heads? column heads? spanner heads?

Every column and every row must have a heading that identifies the data, and these headings must be parallel. Table number, title, source, and footnotes have already been discussed.

The first column on the left is the stub column. Above it is the stub head. A stub is a title to the horizontal row of data. Within the stub column, substubs are indented two or three spaces to show subordination. A spanner head extends over several column heads. Column heads are titles of vertical columns, and the field or body is the actual data found in the rows and columns.

Construction Guidelines

Although the construction of tables will vary according to the data they present and the creativity of the report writer, here are some general construction guidelines for all tables.

1. Number and title each formal table.
2. Tables should be self-explanatory. When taken out of context, they must be clear to the reader.
3. Mention the table in the text before presenting it.
4. Give page number and table number when referring to earlier or later tables.
5. Identify every column and row. Use subtitles when necessary.
6. Align digits from the right. Use decimals rather than fractions and align decimal points. For example

3	.002
15	3.1
232	2.25
1,691	43.170
15,284	162.1498

7. Use footnotes for clarification. Source footnotes appear immediately below the table.
8. Do not use ditto marks; they can be confusing.
9. Use three hyphens (---), alternating periods and spaces (. . .), or "N.A." for a blank space or to indicate that information is not available.
10. Symbols—such as #, %, °—may be used in column heads to conserve space.
11. Place dollar signs and other symbols before the first entry at the top of the column and with the totals.
12. Indent total and mean lines (and other lines) that summarize preceding data. Total lines appearing at the beginning of the table for emphasis are not indented.
13. Make tables attractive, inviting, readable, and clear.
    a. Use plenty of white space within and around them.
    b. Use horizontal and vertical rules sparingly and carefully.

What are ways of indicating that information is not available?

Exhibit 15.5   Table Consisting of Data Arranged by Year

Table 15
Expenditures on Major Programs
(Millions of Dollars)

	1980	1985	1990
Dental Program	—	—	7.2
Disability	2.1	2.6	3.8
Education and Training	—	1.0	1.1
Food Service	0.6	3.6	16.2
Health Insurance	2.4	4.4	13.7
Retirement	1.8	4.5	17.5
Social Security	26.8	48.3	138.0
Workers' Compensation	1.5	2.4	5.3
Totals	4.2	13.5	202.8

Exhibit 15.6   Table Consisting of Dollar Amounts and Total

Table 16
Major Equipment Purchases for
Fiscal Year 19XX

Automobiles	$138,095
Computer Hardware	224,100
Computer Software	49,500
Duplicators	119,000
Ovens	67,000
Trucks	390,000
Total	$987,695

    c. Frame the table with rules above and below or all around it.
    d. Do not extend the table beyond the margins of the page.

14. Round off figures when appropriate. Do not round off numbers that require exact calculations.

15. Arrange data in a logical order—chronologically, alphabetically, geographically, descending, ascending, or by cost, quantity, or other important facts. Exhibits 15.2 to 15.6 illustrate various kinds of tables.

Exhibit 15.7   ## Grid Showing Four Quadrants

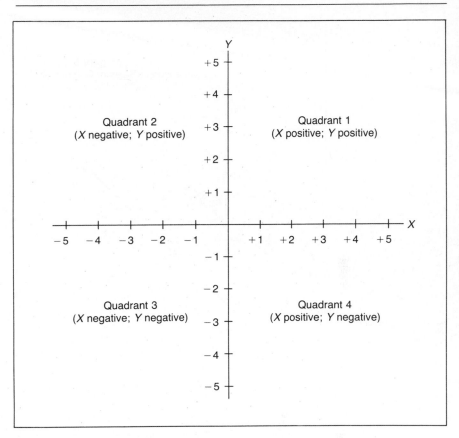

FIGURES

Figures are all graphic aids except tables. They are not substitutes for tables; tables give exact values, and figures give approximate values. Data presented in pictorial form are easier to comprehend than that presented in tables.

Three main types of graphs (also called charts) are the line, bar, and pie.

Line Graphs

When are line graphs used?

Line graphs (or curve charts) are best used to depict trends or changes over time, such as price changes, or relationships between two or more variables.

These variables are shown along two axes, commonly referred to as the *Y* axis (vertical) and the *X* axis (horizontal). These axes divide data into four quadrants, as shown in Exhibit 15.7.

Exhibit 15.8   Line Graph

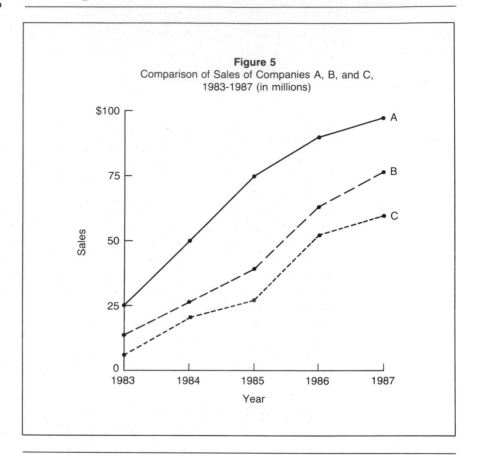

Figure 5
Comparison of Sales of Companies A, B, and C,
1983-1987 (in millions)

Most business applications involve positive values in both axes. For this reason, most business graphs show only the first quadrant of the grid in Exhibit 15.7.

Why do most business graphs show only the first quadrant of the grid?

The line graph has

1. Two scales with specified values
    a. A vertical scale is used for the amount (dollars, sales).
    b. A horizontal scale is used for time (years, months).
2. Two axes, one for each scale
    a. A vertical axis (or *Y* axis) called the ordinate represents the dependent variable.
    b. A horizontal axis (or *X* axis) called the abscissa represents the independent variable.
3. A plot line or curve, which represents the data
    a. Plot lines should be kept to a minimum.

Exhibit 15.9   Line Graph Showing Grid

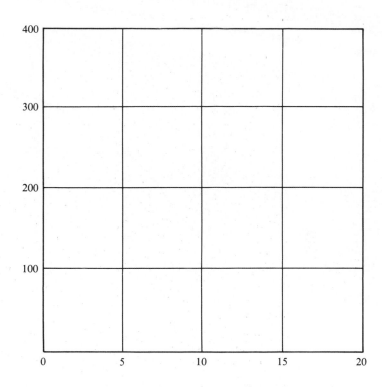

b. When more than one plot line is used, the lines can be made clearly distinguishable from each other by the use of color or by variations in the lines: solid lines (——), dots (. . . .), dashes (----), or the like. See Exhibit 15.8.
c. The greater the number of lines, the more difficult the graph will be to read. The maximum number of lines is five.
d. To identify for the reader the different lines used, a legend should be included within the line chart.

4. A complete grid when accuracy is essential to construction and interpretation
a. A grid is the pattern of horizontal and vertical lines that form squares when the scale marks are extended horizontally and vertically across the graph. See Exhibit 15.9.
b. In most graphs, the grid can be omitted.

Exhibit 15.10   Simple Line Graph with One Plot Line

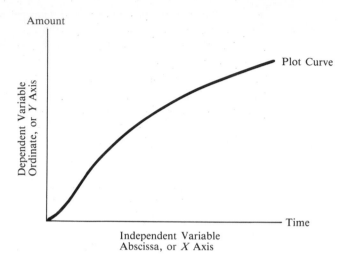

Amount

Dependent Variable
Ordinate, or *Y* Axis

Plot Curve

Time

Independent Variable
Abscissa, or *X* Axis

Exhibit 15.10 illustrates a simple line graph with one plot line. Follow these guidelines when designing line graphs.

Must the vertical
line of a line graph
begin at zero? the
horizontal line?

1. Begin the vertical line (*Y* axis) at zero to show the entire graph in proportion and to avoid misrepresentation, as shown in Exhibit 15.8. The horizontal line (*X* axis) does not have to begin with zero because it represents time, an independent variable.

What are three
ways of breaking
the vertical line?

2. As shown in Exhibit 15.11, break the vertical line between zero and the lowest value when the height becomes too unwieldy. This may be done in any one of the three ways illustrated in Exhibit 15.12.

3. Keep all vertical gradations equal and all the horizontal gradations equal; otherwise, you can distort the graph and deceive the reader. In other words, use equal spaces for equal amounts. See Exhibit 15.13.

4. Select appropriate values for use on the *X* axis and the *Y* axis. The values you select will alter the appearance of your graph and influence the reader's impression of your data. See Exhibit 15.14.
   In Exhibit 15.14, for example, either graph could be valid and accurate under certain circumstances. They do, however, give decidedly different visual impressions.

Exhibit 15.11   Two Versions of a Line Graph Showing Lowest Usage Value

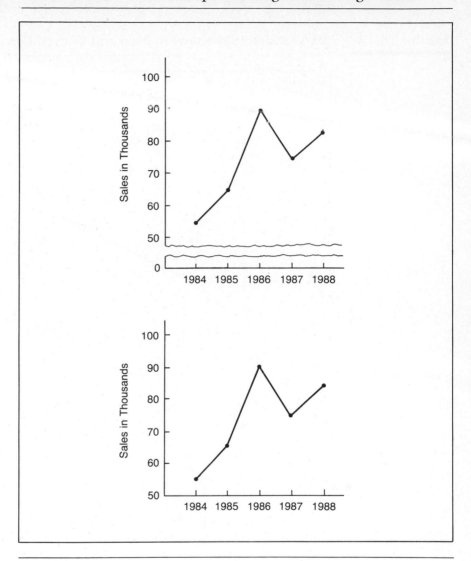

Exhibit 15.12   Ways to Break Vertical Scale of Line Graph

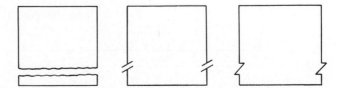

Exhibit 15.13   Two Line Graphs Showing Even and Uneven Gradation

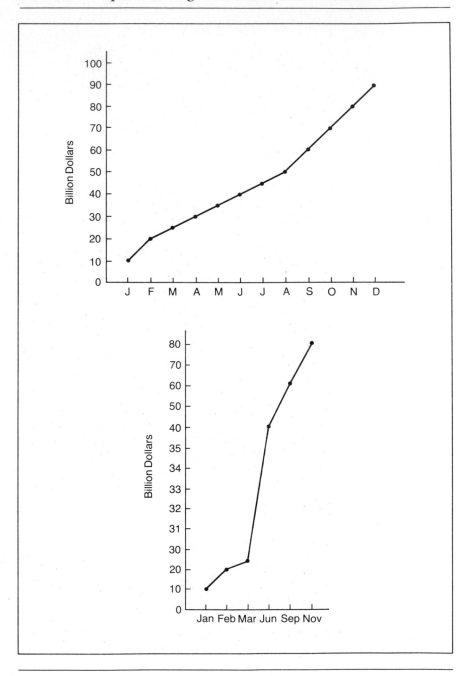

Exhibit 15.14   Two Different Graphs Presenting the Same Information

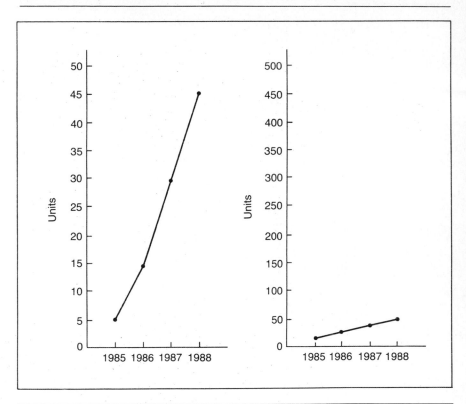

5. Draw vertical lines from equidistant points on the horizontal base line, and draw horizontal lines from equidistant points on the vertical axis. The spaces formed by the lines should be square or nearly so. Make the height approximately the same as the width. Expanding the distance between scale marks on one axis while contracting the distance between scale marks on the other axis creates a distortion. See Exhibit 15.15.

6. Label items on the horizontal and vertical lines.

7. Plot your numbers as a set of points where the horizontal and vertical lines intersect. Plotting is easily done on graph paper. A point on a graph plots a combination of two variables. Connect points by drawing a line from one point to another. The line of the graph is a series of connecting points. See Exhibit 15.16.

8. Include a legend to identify each line for a multiple line graph.

Exhibit 15.15   Three Comparable Line Graphs with Different Vertical Scales

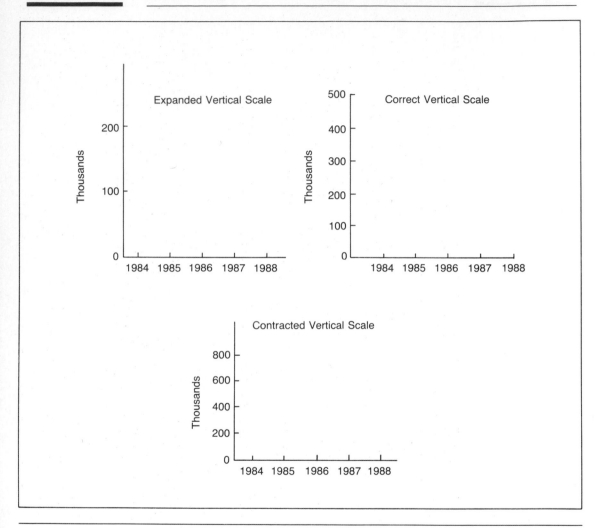

Bar Charts

When are bar
charts used?

The bar chart is the best choice for showing simple comparisons, especially changes in quantity. Bar charts can be presented either vertically or horizontally.

What type of bar
chart has its base at
the horizontal axis?
at the vertical axis?

Vertical Bar Chart   Vertical bar charts have their bases at the horizontal (X) axis. They are charts with the value of the bars on the vertical (Y) axis and the time variables on the horizontal (X) axis because time is an independent variable and independent variables are always on the X axis. See Exhibit 15.17 for an illustration of a vertical bar chart.

Exhibit 15.16   Plotting and Connecting Points

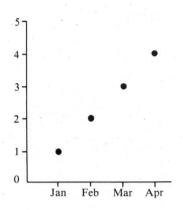
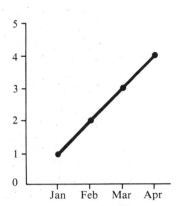

Exhibit 15.17   Vertical Bar Chart

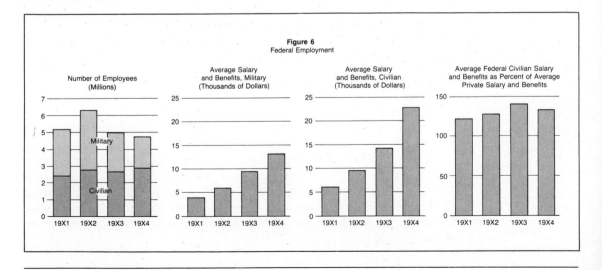

Exhibit 15.18   Histogram

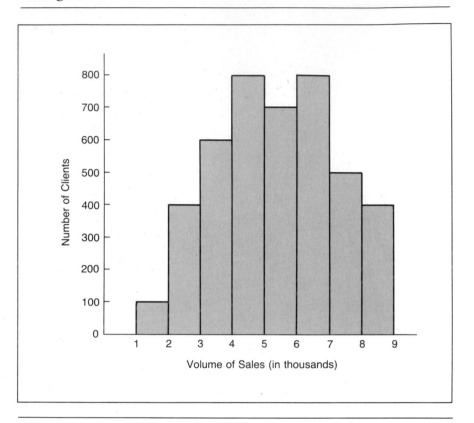

Use vertical bars (1) for comparing data over a certain time so that the time scale would be on the *X* axis and (2) for representing height.

What is a
histogram?

Histogram   A vertical bar chart illustrating a frequency distribution is a histogram, as shown in Exhibit 15.18.

Because a histogram has no spaces between columns, leave a space of at least one half the width of the bar at each end of the *X* axis. In the histogram, columns are adjacent or contiguous to each other because the intervals of distribution are continuous, as might be the case with income, age, height, or weight. See Appendix A for a description of continuous data.

Horizontal Bar Chart   A horizontal bar chart has its base at the vertical (*Y*) axis. Use horizontal bar charts (1) for comparing data for a particular point in time and (2) for representing distance. Exhibits 15.19 and 15.20 illustrate horizontal bar charts.

Exhibit 15.19   Horizontal Bar Chart

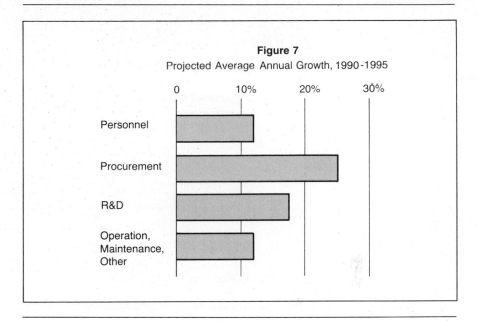

Figure 7
Projected Average Annual Growth, 1990-1995

Variations of the simple bar chart are the multiple bar chart, the bilateral bar chart, and the segmented bar chart.

When is a multiple bar chart used?

Multiple Bar Chart   When you want to compare two or three variables within a single bar chart, use a multiple bar chart, as shown in Exhibit 15.21.

The multiple bars are distinguished one from the other by color, shading, or crosshatching. Avoid comparing more than three variables for a single item on one chart. For example, you could compare five sections of the United States but only three or fewer variables for each of the five sections.

Bilateral Bar Chart   A bilateral bar chart (also called the plus and minus or positive and negative chart) shows increases on one side of a zero line and decreases on the other side of the zero line, as illustrated in Exhibit 15.22.

What kind of bar chart is used to present both positive and negative values? to show percentage change?

The zero line is at or near the middle of the graph so that space is provided for both the positive and negative bars. Bilateral charts use either vertical or horizontal bars and are used for showing percentage change and whenever data to be presented have both positive and negative values.

Exhibit 15.20   Horizontal Bar Chart

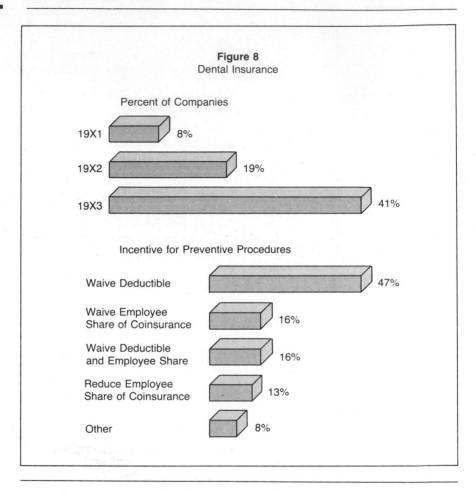

Figure 8
Dental Insurance

Percent of Companies

19X1	8%
19X2	19%
19X3	41%

Incentive for Preventive Procedures

Waive Deductible — 47%

Waive Employee
Share of Coinsurance — 16%

Waive Deductible
and Employee Share — 16%

Reduce Employee
Share of Coinsurance — 13%

Other — 8%

Exhibit 15.21   A Multiple Bar Chart

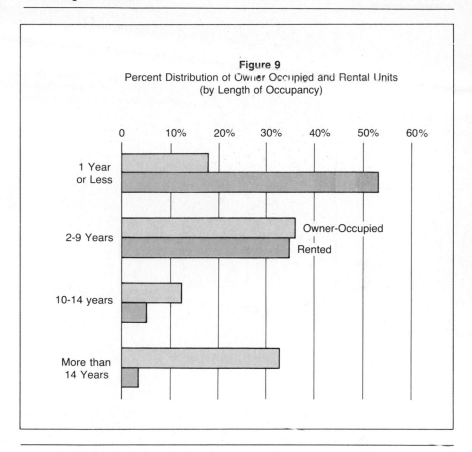

Figure 9
Percent Distribution of Owner Occupied and Rental Units
(by Length of Occupancy)

Exhibit 15.22   **Bilateral Bar Chart**

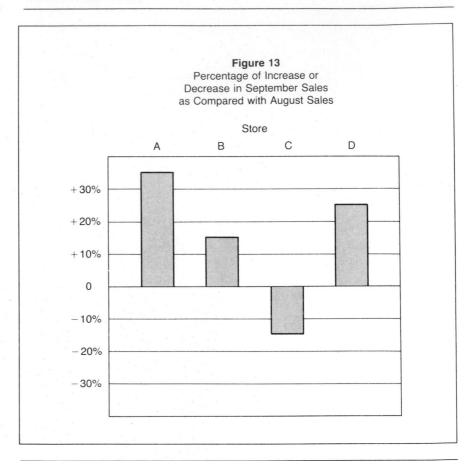

Figure 13
Percentage of Increase or
Decrease in September Sales
as Compared with August Sales

Exhibit 15.23   Segmented Bar Chart

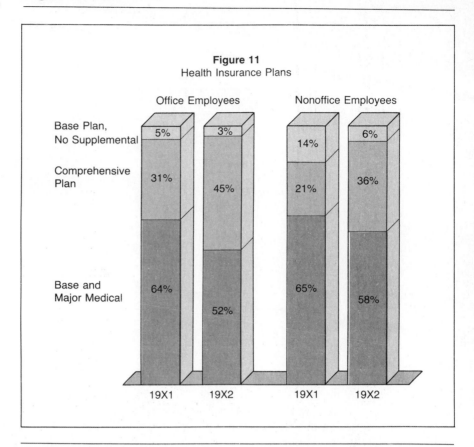

Figure 11
Health Insurance Plans

Office Employees   Nonoffice Employees

Base Plan, No Supplemental: 5%, 3%, 14%, 6%

Comprehensive Plan: 31%, 45%, 21%, 36%

Base and Major Medical: 64%, 52%, 65%, 58%

19X1   19X2   19X1   19X2

What is a
segmented bar
chart used to show?

Segmented Bar Chart The segmented bar chart (also called compo-
nent-part or subdivided bar chart) is used to show the composition of
the variables being compared, as shown in Exhibits 15.23 and 15.24.

Bars can be both horizontal and vertical. When crosshatching, shad-
ings, or colors are used to distinguish each segment, a legend should
be included on the chart. When using color, start with the dark colors
at the base and move up to lighter colors.

When a segmented bar chart is used to indicate percentages, each
bar in the chart equals 100 percent. Because each bar represents 100
percent, each is the same length or height, but the sizes of the segments
vary according to their percentages. For example:

| 50% | 50% | = 100 percent |

| 25% | 25% | 25% | 25% | = 100 percent |

Exhibit 15.24   ## Segmented Bar Chart

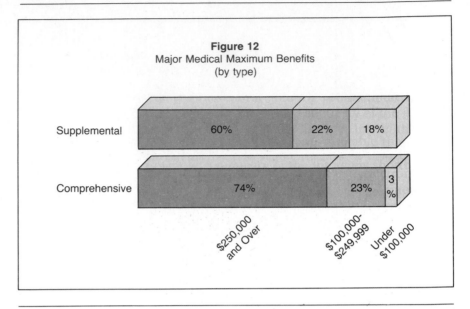

Figure 12
Major Medical Maximum Benefits
(by type)

A single segmented bar may be used to show percentages of a whole, as shown in Exhibit 15.25. It is a variation of a pie chart, or a bar chart used horizontally or vertically, or it can be in the shape of a company's product.

Guidelines   The following guidelines will help you prepare bar charts.

1. Begin the vertical (Y) axis at zero.
2. Break the vertical line with a wavy line or slash marks between zero and the lowest value when the height becomes too great.
3. Use grid lines only when necessary to help the reader compare lengths. If bars are horizontal, then the grid lines are vertical and vice versa.
4. Keep all the vertical gradations equal and all the horizontal gradations equal.

Why must all bars in a graph be equal in width?

5. Keep the width of all bars equal to avoid distortion of the data. Keep the width of the space between bars equal. For emphasis, make the bars wider than the space between the bars.
6. Arrange bars alphabetically, chronologically, numerically, or in

Exhibit 15.25   Segmented Bar Chart

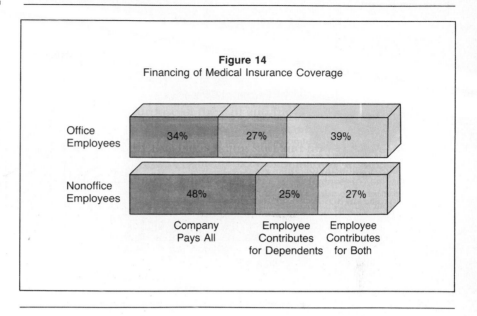

Figure 14
Financing of Medical Insurance Coverage

Office Employees: 34% | 27% | 39%

Nonoffice Employees: 48% | 25% | 27%

Company Pays All — Employee Contributes for Dependents — Employee Contributes for Both

descending (generally preferred) or ascending order. See Appendix A for various ways to present data.

7. Use color, shading, or crosshatching for emphasizing, contrasting, and distinguishing bars from one another.

8. Include a legend to identify various bars on a multiple-bar chart.

9. Label items on the horizontal and vertical lines and the bars. Place figures within bars or at the top of each bar to give the exact amount. Additional bar charts are presented in Exhibits 15.26 and 15.27.

Pie Charts

Pie charts (also called circle graphs) are used to depict parts of a whole. The pie or circle is the whole; the slices or segments are the parts. These parts must add up to 100 percent, as shown in Exhibit 15.28.

Why are percentage figures shown on a pie chart?

To avoid misrepresentation in a pie chart, include not only the description of each segment, but also the percentage figures, which are the most important information for making quick and easy comparisons.

Exhibit 15.26   Bar Chart

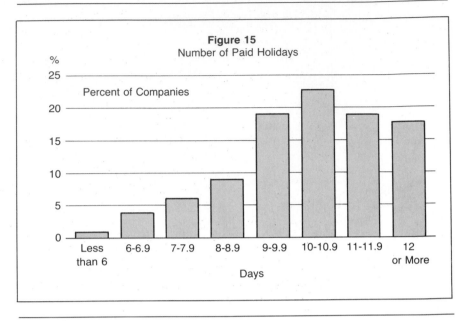

Figure 15
Number of Paid Holidays

Exhibit 15.27   Bar Chart

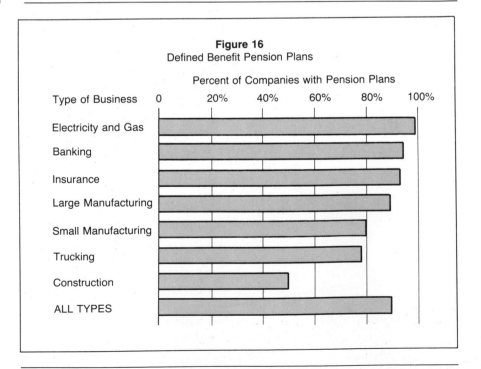

Figure 16
Defined Benefit Pension Plans

Exhibit 15.28   Pie Chart

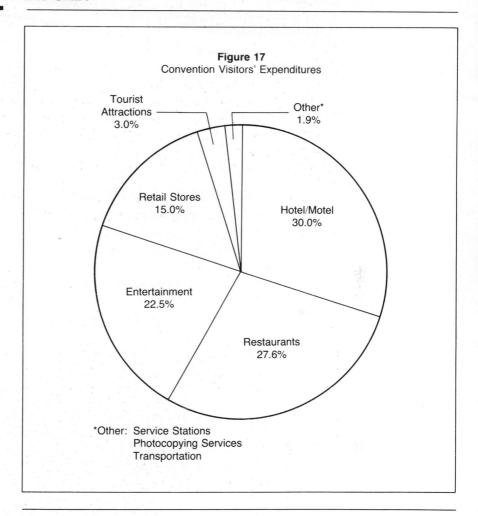

Figure 17
Convention Visitors' Expenditures

Tourist
Attractions
3.0%

Other*
1.9%

Retail Stores
15.0%

Hotel/Motel
30.0%

Entertainment
22.5%

Restaurants
27.6%

*Other: Service Stations
Photocopying Services
Transportation

The following guidelines will help you prepare pie charts.

1. Convert raw figures into percentages whenever possible. For example:

Raw Data	Percent
115 ÷ 1,000 = 0.115 × 100 = 11.5	
202	20.2
294	29.4
389	38.9
1,000 total	100

2. Start segmenting your pie chart by making the first radial line at the 12 o'clock position, continuing clockwise in descending order, from the largest to the smallest percentage: 38.9, 29.4, 20.2, 11.5.

3. Convert percentages to degrees.

Percent		Degrees
11.5 × 360 (degrees in a circle) = 41.40 rounded off to 41		
20.2	= 72.7	73
29.4	= 105.84	106
38.9	= 140.04	140
100		360

4. Use a compass to draw a circle and locate its center.

5. Use a protractor for exact segmentation.

What is the minimum number of segments in a pie chart? the recommended maximum?

6. Have at least three segments; otherwise the chart is not necessary. Avoid having more than seven segments. Combine several small categories in a single segment labeled "Miscellaneous" or "Other," which is always the last segment, even though it may be larger than the preceding segment. When appropriate, include a description of "Other." For example:

$$\text{Other} \left\{ \begin{array}{l} \text{Paper} \\ \text{Pens} \\ \text{Pencils} \end{array} \right.$$

7. Identify each segment (description and figure) horizontally within the circle if space permits; otherwise, use guidelines with the identification placed outside.

8. Coloring, shading, or crosshatching can be used for emphasis.

9. Make the size of the pie chart appropriate for the page.

Pictograms

A pictogram (pictograph or pictorial chart), a variation of the bar chart, uses pictures or symbols rather than lines or bars to represent data. For example, coins, books, houses, ships, people, animals, or barrels can be used to depict appropriate data. See Exhibit 15.29.

Pictograms should

1. Present simple information

2. Use representative pictures and symbols that are easily recognized by the reader

3. Show quantities by number of units rather than by differences in sizes

4. Present units that are identical and of equal size

Exhibit 15.29   Pictogram

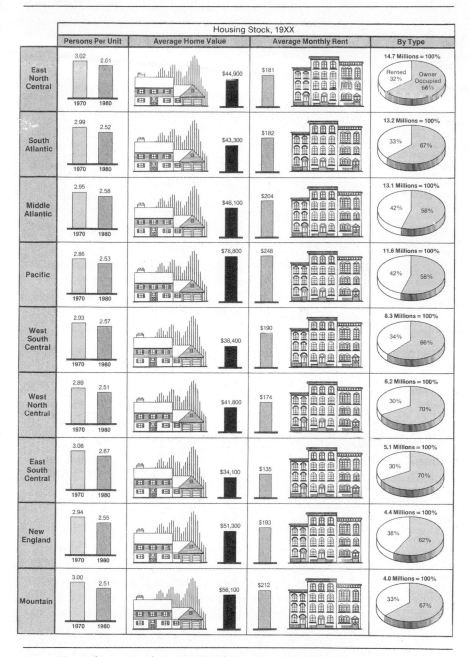

Housing Stock, 19XX			
Persons Per Unit	Average Home Value	Average Monthly Rent	By Type

East North Central — 3.02 (1970), 2.61 (1980); $44,900; $181; 14.7 Millions = 100%; Rented 32%, Owner Occupied 68%

South Atlantic — 2.99 (1970), 2.52 (1980); $43,300; $182; 13.2 Millions = 100%; 33%, 67%

Middle Atlantic — 2.95 (1970), 2.58 (1980); $46,100; $204; 13.1 Millions = 100%; 42%, 58%

Pacific — 2.86 (1970), 2.53 (1980); $78,800; $248; 11.6 Millions = 100%; 42%, 58%

West South Central — 2.93 (1970), 2.57 (1980); $38,400; $190; 8.3 Millions = 100%; 34%, 66%

West North Central — 2.89 (1970), 2.51 (1980); $41,800; $174; 6.2 Millions = 100%; 30%, 70%

East South Central — 3.06 (1970), 2.67 (1980); $34,100; $135; 5.1 Millions = 100%; 30%, 70%

New England — 2.94 (1970), 2.55 (1980); $51,300; $193; 4.4 Millions = 100%; 38%, 62%

Mountain — 3.00 (1970), 2.51 (1980); $56,100; $212; 4.0 Millions = 100%; 33%, 67%

Source: The Conference Board, Economic Road Maps, Nos. 1918–1919, January 1982.

What risk is
involved in using
pictograms?

Although pictograms attract attention because of their novelty and eye appeal, they can easily mislead readers and distort data. Consider the following example. Suppose, for example, that you want to compare the average monthly oil production of Company A (10,000 barrels) and Company B (20,000 barrels). You could use a vertical bar chart as follows:

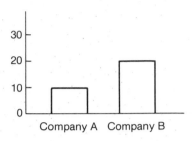

The chart is clear. Company B produces twice as much as Company A. But because you want to attract the reader's attention with a more appealing and pertinent picture, you decide to use a pictogram. A common approach is to use one barrel to show the production capacity of Company A and a barrel twice as big to indicate the production capacity of Company B.

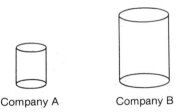

How can
distortion or
misrepresentation
be avoided in
pictograms?

The problem with this is that the visual representation misleads the reader because barrel B is twice as high as barrel A. It is also twice as wide, which gives it the appearance of having four times the volume. Worse, because readers tend to supply the implied third dimension, barrel B may appear to have eight times the volume of barrel A. To prevent misrepresentation and distortion, keep the barrels uniform in size, adding barrels to show increased production.

Photographs

Photographs can be very useful in business reports because they

1. Have visual appeal
2. Provide accurate representations
3. Are persuasive as evidence or proof
4. Can clearly identify elements of complex layouts, machinery, etc.
5. Can provide aerial views of large geographic areas
6. Can show comparisons with before and after pictures
7. Can give good overall views or focus on one detail

Companies use photographs in their annual reports to show new buildings, plants, or products. Insurance companies especially use photographs to show the extent of damages. One example of the persuasive power of a photograph was offered by an irate motorist who submitted a photograph of the chuck hole in the road that damaged his radial tire and rim with his claim to the road commissioner. As a result of the photographic proof, he was reimbursed for repairs.

What advantages do photographs have in illustrating complex layouts, machinery, etc.? What disadvantage?

Photographs not only can be taken quickly and easily but also can be reproduced in seconds, especially with the latest models of cameras. Builders, contractors, and designers can take photographs and pencil in notations rather than laboriously prepare sketches or diagrams.

Photographs, however, provide only a surface print and cannot give a dimensional picture. A good photograph is well focused and concentrates on one aspect; it does not look cluttered.

Diagrams

What is the advantage in using a diagram? an exploded diagram?

A diagram is a sketch or drawing designed to demonstrate or explain the relationship of parts. It has an advantage over a photograph because it can include as much detail as is needed for the reader. Diagrams are used for illustrating

1. How to assemble a product
2. How to repair an item
3. How to operate a piece of equipment
4. How one item interacts with another
5. How to get from one point to another
6. The internal structure of an item

Exploded diagrams are excellent for showing the reader the component parts of a piece of equipment, as shown in Exhibit 15.30.

Cutaway and exploded diagrams are prepared by artists who have the necessary skill to draw them accurately.

Exhibit 15.30 Diagram

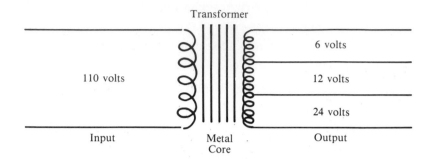

Organizational Charts

An organizational chart indicates the flow of authority, responsibility, and chain of command within an organization and the relationship among positions.

Because organizational charts show graphically who reports to whom, new employees especially appreciate them for viewing the various levels and divisions within a company.

Organizational charts will vary from one organization to another. They can be vertical, starting at the top and branching downward; or they can be horizontal, starting at the left and branching to the right. Some organizational charts may be circular, showing authority coming from the center and branching outward. Exhibit 15.31 illustrates an organizational chart.

Flow Charts

When are flow charts used?

A flow chart is a schematic representation of a sequence of steps; it traces the movement of a product, process, or procedure from beginning to end. Steps in the procedure are described in boxes, with arrows indicating the flow of direction.

Because flow charts outline specific steps, they are valuable for visualizing the sequence of activities involved in a particular process. Flow charts are frequently used in production; sales; accounting; and various

Exhibit 15.31   Organization Chart

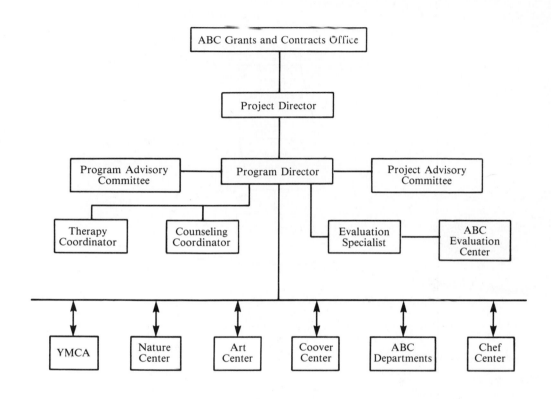

office systems, such as work flow, mail handling, and filing. Exhibit 15.32 illustrates a flow chart.

Maps

When are maps used in business reports?

When you wish to show representation that is dependent on geographical or spatial relationships, maps (or cartograms) are your best choice. They can be specific geographic areas, such as counties, cities, states, regions or countries. Color, shading, crosshatching, charts, pictures, numeric figures, dots, and other symbols are used to indicate the characteristics in each of the various geographic segments. When using dots, each dot must be the same size and represent a given quantity.

Exhibit 15.32   Flowchart

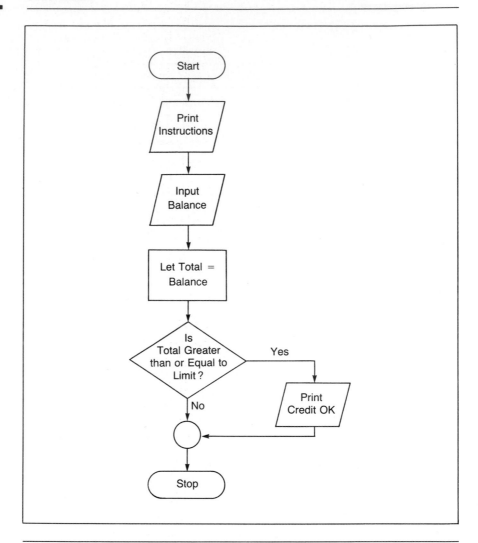

Maps are useful for comparing quantitative data by geographic loca-tions. Companies use maps in annual reports to show distribution of dealers, stockholders, products, sales, resources, and so forth. Exhibits 15.33 and 15.34 illustrate maps.

Other Graphic Aids

What are
scattergrams?

Although we have discussed several of the frequently used graphic aids, you may select still other designs that would best present your data graphically. For example, blueprints, scattergrams (see Appendix A)

Exhibit 15.33   Area Code Map

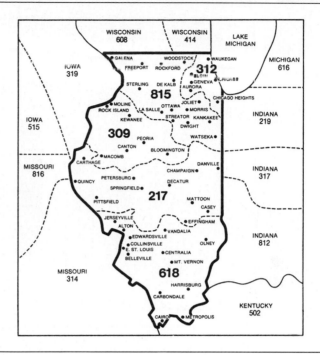

Source: Illinois Bell Telephone Company

Exhibit 15.34   Zip Code Map

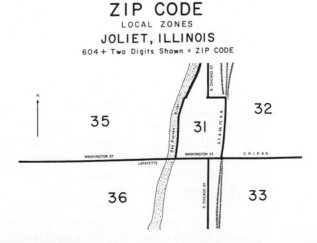

Source: United States Postal Service

Exhibit 15.35   **Computer-Generated Bar Chart**

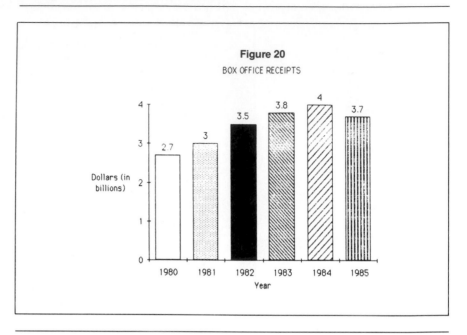

and samples of fabrics or other materials (paper, paints) all can help you communicate your data. Your imagination will help you present the best picture for your audience—use it!

COMPUTER GRAPHICS

What kinds of graphic aids can be prepared on a computer?

Computers have revolutionized report writing through their capabilities for presenting complicated data in dramatic forms. What was done traditionally with pen, pencil, protractors, and compasses can be done quickly, easily, and accurately using a computer. Instead of having artists or skilled technicians laboriously design graphics, the report writer can employ a computer to prepare easy-to-comprehend charts and graphs: line graphs, bar charts, pie charts, diagrams, flow charts, organizational charts, and maps. The report writer selects the design that will best display the data, and then instructs the computer to create the appropriate business graphic. See Exhibits 15.35, 15.36, and 15.37 for graphics prepared on the computer.

When using the computer to generate graphics, follow the guidelines for preparing graphic aids. When selecting the appropriate graphic on the computer, be sure that pie charts begin at the noon posi-

Exhibit 15.36   **Computer-Generated Pie Chart**

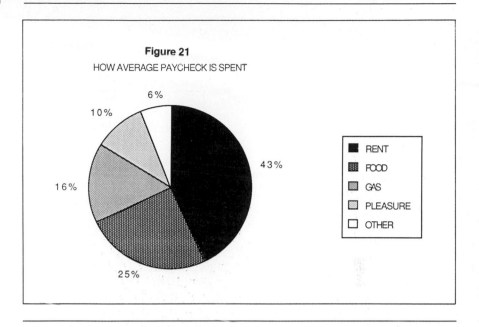

Figure 21

HOW AVERAGE PAYCHECK IS SPENT

- RENT
- FOOD
- GAS
- PLEASURE
- OTHER

6%
10%
43%
16%
25%

tion and that the vertical gradations and the horizontal gradations are equal on line charts. Not all computer graphics programs are capable of producing accurate and correct charts, so you may have to try two or three programs before you find one that produces the desired results.

Computer graphics convert endless columns of data into charts and figures. They can

1. Schedule projects and production
2. Project worker hours and costs
3. Estimate costs
4. Record sales and stock activities
5. Keep schedules of costs current

Computer graphics, in fact, can take any numerical information and convert it into easy-to-comprehend charts and graphs.

Applications

Computer graphics can be used to

1. Monitor performance in such areas as marketing, production, and finance

Exhibit 15.37   **Computer-Generated Line Chart**

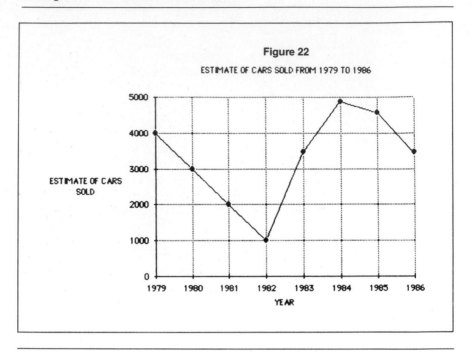

2. Compare expenditures with the budget
3. Market products by convincing prospects or clients that a purchase should be made
4. Compare sales and earnings with past performances and company projections
5. Serve as a presentation tool in the boardroom
6. Alert personnel to potential problems
7. Help in the decision-making process
8. Analyze and test designs

Advantages and Disadvantages

Computer graphics have many advantages and few disadvantages.

Advantages   The major advantages of computer graphics are that they

1. Make information more visible
2. Combine and plot information stored in the computer without having to reenter data

3. Create charts from data not already in the computer when computer production costs would be lower than manual production costs

4. Achieve a high degree of accuracy

5. Create designs on short notice and thereby permit the presentation of up-to-date data rather than artists' designs that take weeks to execute and may become obsolete

6. Create, modify, and print charts and graphs easily

7. Permit production in a variety of colors

8. Allow you to load, plot, and analyze data

9. Draw almost any kind of design, which can then be changed repeatedly

10. Speed production

What are two disadvantages of computer graphics?

Disadvantages   Computer graphics have two disadvantages:

1. The high cost of computers to produce them

2. The need for qualified personnel to operate the computers

SUMMARY

Graphic aids are tables and figures presented in written material to clarify a discussion. Graphic aids are not substitutes for words, and they are placed after the text that explains them. The primary purpose of graphic aids is to present a picture of what the text describes. The picture can be in the form of tables or figures. Graphic aids also emphasize material that needs extra attention or coverage, convert and condense complex information into a pictorial form, and enhance the appearance of the report.

All graphic aids should be self-explanatory, and their sizes should be determined by the importance and the amount of data they contain. Rules help to separate data, and frames attractively display the graphic aid. Color is used to emphasize differences and to create an inviting picture.

All graphic aids (except informal tables) in the report are labeled and numbered so that they can be identified and located in a report that has a list of illustrations. When necessary, give documentation.

A table consists of data arranged systematically in rows and columns. Tables can be classified as informal and formal, special and general. Figures are all other graphic aids except tables. The three main types of graphs are the line, bar, and pie. Line graphs are best used to depict trends over a time period; bar charts are best for showing simple comparisons; and pie charts are used to depict parts of a whole.

Other graphic aids include pictograms, photographs, diagrams, organizational charts, flow charts, maps, scattergrams, and samples.

Computer graphics convert endless columns of data into charts and figures.

EXERCISES

Review and Discussion Questions

1. What are graphic aids? Give five examples.
2. What are the purposes of graphic aids?
3. Where are graphic aids placed in the report?
4. How should you refer to graphic aids in the report? Why?
5. What does it mean to say that graphic aids should be self-explanatory?
6. How large should a graphic aid be?
7. When do you use rules or frames in graphic aids?
8. When do you use color in graphic aids?
9. Why are graphic aids labeled and numbered?
10. When are footnotes for graphic aids required?
11. How can tables be classified? Explain each.
12. Define the three main types of graphs, and tell when you would use each of them.
13. What is the difference between a vertical bar chart and a horizontal bar chart?
14. What is a histogram? multiple bar chart? bilateral bar chart? segmented bar chart?
15. What is a pie chart?
16. What are computer graphics?
17. Why is it important to begin the vertical axis at zero?
18. In a pictogram, why is it important to keep symbols a uniform size?
19. Illustrate three ways to show a break in the vertical line.
20. Why are photographs important in business reports?

Problems and Applications

1. Select the most effective graphic aid for illustrating each of the following:
   a. A breakdown of how you spend your time for a typical week

   b. A comparison of three brands of typewriter according to price, weight, and special features

   c. How Company X spent its revenue

   d. The number of units of Product Y produced during four quarters

   e. A comparison of the percentage of decrease or increase in sales for September as compared with August sales

   f. Net profits over a 5-year span

   g. Number of tasks completed for each month for one year by three employees

   h. Gross sales for a 10-year period

   i. Population of the United States by geographic divisions

   j. System for handling mail in Company Y

   k. Position of authority and responsibility and the relationship of each position to the others for Company A

   l. Components of a bicycle

   m. Changing prices of Product A and Product B over the past year

   n. An illustration of a broken carton

   o. An illustration of a damaged ship

   p. A comparison of five fruits on the basis of calories, nutritional value, and cost

   q. Census information from the government

   r. Profits and losses for five stores of one chain for five years

   s. Net income for five organizations

   t. Percentage changes (negative and positive) in sales

   u. How a company's income dollar was earned

   v. How dollars were spent for five items over a five-year span

   w. Percentage breakdown of company's product

   x. Allocation of the time spent on a project

   y. Daily high and low temperatures for one week

2. Prepare a flow chart for a process or procedure with which you are familiar. Include a full title and provide a prose discussion.

3. Prepare a poster that illustrates five different kinds of graphic aids found in magazines, current newspapers, or brochures. Include a line graph, a bar chart, and a pie chart. You may photocopy graphic aids that appear in books or other library materials.

4. Prepare an organizational chart for an organization where you work or go to school.

5. Construct a pie chart to illustrate your monthly expenditures. Include a full title and provide a prose discussion.

6. Draw a diagram showing the layout of

   a. An office

   b. Your home or apartment

   c. Library

   d. Store

   e. A recreational center

7. Gather statistics—age, height, weight—on the members of your class, family, or club and arrange the information in a table.

8. Gather statistics of your choice from a group of ten people and present the data in a table.

9. Give a specific example of data that each of the following graphic aids could illustrate effectively:

   a. Formal table
   b. Line chart—one item
   c. Line chart—two items
   d. Vertical bar chart
   e. Histogram
   f. Horizontal bar chart
   g. Multiple bar chart
   h. Bilateral bar chart
   i. Segmented bar chart
   j. Pie chart
   k. Pictogram
   l. Photograph
   m. Diagram
   n. Organizational chart
   o. Flow chart
   p. Map
   q. Samples

10. From reference books, such as:

    ▪ *Business Statistics*
    ▪ *Demographic Yearbook*
    ▪ *Federal Reserve Bulletin*
    ▪ *Information Please Almanac*
    ▪ *Statistical Abstract of the United States*
    ▪ *Statistical Yearbook*
    ▪ *Statistical Yearbook of the United Nations*
    ▪ *World Almanac and Book of Facts*

    select the necessary data and construct the following:

    a. A formal table
    b. A line chart—one item
    c. A line chart—two items
    d. A vertical bar chart
    e. A horizontal bar chart
    f. A multiple bar chart
    g. A bilateral bar chart
    h. A segmented bar chart
    i. A pie chart with at least five divisions
    j. A pictogram

Number graphic aids consecutively and give each a title. Label parts when necessary. Use a separate sheet of paper for each graphic aid. Use at least five different sources and provide documentation. Use a ruler and India ink for drawing lines. Type all information. Provide a text discussion for each.

11. Prepare and submit all the graphic aids that you will use in the major report(s) you are writing this semester or term.

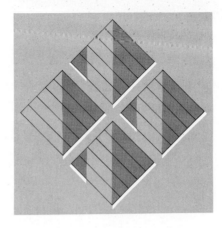

Formal Reports

C H A P T E R   1 6

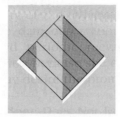

Report Organization

Organization is an aid to clarity and understanding. A logical, well-balanced presentation of information helps readers grasp and remember important points. How you organize the material in your report will be one of the critical factors in determining how well your report is received.

Topics

Basic Considerations
Common Structural Patterns
Methods of Outlining
Headings

Some of your report structure will be determined by the material itself. You might, for example, need to explain a new procedure according to the steps required for completion, or you might need to explain a problem before you can propose a solution. Regardless of the particulars, however, report organization is based on three overriding principles.

1. Every report (and every other piece of communication) must have a beginning, middle, and end.
2. Your readers will tend to be predisposed either to accept or to reject your conclusions and recommendations.
3. Central—or most important—ideas should receive emphasis.

By this point, of course, you would have analyzed your audience (see Chapter 2) and developed a good understanding of your readers' interest in, knowledge of, and prejudices about the topic. Remember that you are writing the report as a benefit for your readers and not as a means of self-expression. In organizing the report, your objective should be to present the information in a way that will facilitate acceptance and understanding of the material.

BASIC CONSIDERATIONS

You have to start somewhere; the question is how to begin in a way that will both orient your readers to the topic of the report and be interesting as well. In general, your opening will accomplish both purposes if you begin with a statement telling what the report is about (your *purpose* or *thesis*) and explaining the need for the report. Both should be expressed in terms of the benefit readers will gain as a result of the report.

The middle of the report is used to present and interpret data or the application of criteria. The concluding section may contain conclusions and recommendations and, when the report is long, a summary of important points. The ending should also be decision and action oriented (when the writer has been authorized to propose specific courses of action).

Organize for Reader Acceptance

Even though a report *must* be an objective presentation of facts, report writers do not always prepare their presentations for objective people. In most cases, the recipient of a report will be either inclined to accept the writer's conclusions and recommendations, or neutral—willing to examine the data with an open mind. Every now and then, however, a reader will be predisposed to reject a particular solution that the writer may have determined is the best possible one.

When should
deductive order be
used? When is
inductive order
usually preferable?

When the reader is willing to accept the writer's conclusions, or when the reader has a neutral, unbiased attitude, some form of direct or immediate beginning is best. A major conclusion, a major recommendation, or a major benefit should be presented first. The rest of the report provides the support and explanation the opening requires. This is known as **deductive** order.

When the writer has reason to suspect that the reader will resent or resist the conclusions and recommendations in a report, a slower, more methodical approach will increase the chances that the report will receive a fair hearing. With this approach, the supporting details are presented first, and the conclusions and recommendations are withheld until all the evidence has been explained. This is known as **inductive** order. We will discuss deductive and inductive order at greater length later in this chapter.

Organize for Emphasis

What do you want your readers to remember? Those ideas should receive emphasis. Obviously, not all ideas in a report will be of equal importance. You will need to select the ones most important for your readers to remember and present them in ways that will increase readers' ability to retain them.

How many key
points are most
readers able to
remember?

Because people tend to remember best whatever they read first or last, important points belong at the beginning or end—of the report as a whole, of units within the report, or of paragraphs. Readers are also more inclined to remember generalizations than they are to remember specific facts. Your readers' ability to remember your key points will depend as well on how many points you present, how well those points are related to material readers already know, and how well the points are related to each other. Readers remember about seven items of new information fairly well, but remembering more than seven items is difficult for most people. Your readers will also tend to remember items associated with other items with which they are already familiar. For this reason, analogies can be an aid to memory as well as a means of explaining or illustrating.

Finally, the way in which you write about something can help readers focus on the items you consider most important. Stylistic means of controlling emphasis include placement, proportion, language, and mechanics.

Placement   Put key points first or last in the report. Major subtopics should receive similar emphasis within report divisions. As a rule, the first sentence in a paragraph should introduce the topic or main idea of the paragraph. The rest of the paragraph usually contains supporting or explanatory details.

Proportion   How much time you spend on one topic in relation to other topics is an indication of its importance. In general, when an idea is important, you should allocate it a greater amount of space and explain it more thoroughly. When this is not possible, use one (or more) of the other means of providing emphasis to draw extra attention to the idea.

Language   Readers pay closer attention to sentences about people doing things than to sentences about ideas. Make sentences specific and people oriented:

Strong: Closing line 3 will put 57 people out of work and save the company only $1,350 a year.

Weak: The minimal savings that would result from closing line 3 will not justify the poor morale that would result from the concomitant layoffs.

Also, you can use language to emphasize an idea simply by telling your reader that it is important:

> The most significant result was . . .

> The important factor for our company is . . .

What are some mechanical means for emphasizing ideas?

Mechanics   You can emphasize ideas through mechanical means. Underscoring, color, solid capital letters, main points in a numbered list, and graphic aids to help the reader visualize important ideas are all ways to stress things you want readers to remember.

COMMON STRUCTURAL PATTERNS

While the basic considerations just described apply in nearly every report writing situation, specialized patterns have developed because they are effective for presenting certain kinds of data. The structured patterns used most often include deductive, inductive, order of importance, chronological, step by step, spatial, topical, problem to solution, criteria to application, and cause and effect. In addition, some situations require the use of more than one pattern.

Reports as a whole are usually arranged either deductively or inductively, with various components employing the structural patterns most appropriate for their purposes. Entire reports, however, may make use of any of the structural patterns.

Deductive Order

The basic organizational pattern for most business reports is deductive. In deductive order, the main point, general conclusion, or most important recommendation is presented first. Supporting details and explanations are presented second. Exhibit 16.1 illustrates deductive order. The advantage of deductive order is that it tells readers instantly every-

Exhibit 16.1   **Deductive Order**

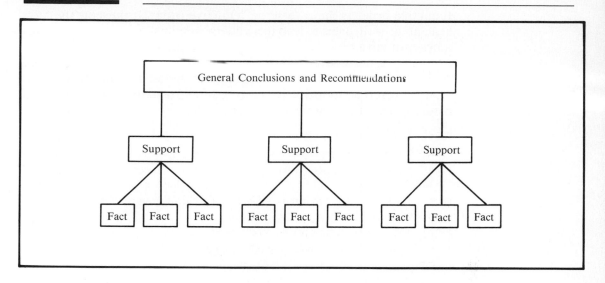

thing they need to know to make a decision. Unless readers are particularly interested in the subject or in how you reached your decision, they may not need to read the entire report. With deductive structure, the reader sees the *result* of the reasoning before the reasons themselves are presented.

Conclusions: The company needs to reduce operating expenses by at least $10,000, and the only possible source of this saving is a reduction in personnel.

Recommendation: Morris L. Burner, the company's least productive employee, should be fired.

Fact: Last year the company lost $9,500.

Fact: This year the company will lose about $9,750.

Fact: Manufacturing costs have risen; production levels cannot be increased because sales have peaked.

Fact: Personnel reduction is the only means of reducing costs until retooling takes place.

Fact: The least productive person should be fired.

Why may deductive order be best even when the reader is biased?

The disadvantage of this organizational pattern is that it enables a biased reader to develop arguments against your conclusions before reviewing the facts that lead to the conclusion. As we mentioned previously, if your reader has a preconception or a bias that you may need to overcome, deductive order may not prove successful. You should also consider your reader's time. A reader may be more biased against the slower inductive order of presentation than he or she is biased against your idea; thus you would gain nothing by using inductive order. For most business reports, deductive order is the better organizational pattern.

Inductive Order

Inductive order is the reverse of deductive order. It presents the facts first and uses the facts to lead to a general conclusion. Exhibit 16.2 illustrates inductive order.

Inductive order is a slower order of presentation. Readers must consider a series of facts before learning the writer's point. As a result, reports presented inductively may be a little frustrating for readers, who naturally want to know what the facts mean.

Fact: Last year the company lost $9,500.

Fact: This year the company will lose about $9,750.

Fact: Manufacturing costs have risen; production levels cannot be increased because sales have peaked.

Fact: Personnel reduction is the only means of reducing costs until retooling takes place.

Fact: The least productive person should be fired.

Fact: Morris L. Burner is the least productive person.

Conclusions: The company needs to reduce operating expenses by at least $10,000, and the only possible source of this saving is a reduction in personnel.

Recommendation: Morris L. Burner (the president's son-in-law) should be fired.

The inductive approach may be best when the reader will need to be persuaded to give your ideas a fair hearing. If you know the reader has a preconception or a bias that is contrary to your findings, you may still be able to convince your reader by showing how the facts lead to only one conclusion.

Order of Importance

When you organize according to order of importance, you can use either the most important item or the least important item as a starting point. Suppose you were submitting a report on the actions your company could take to save money. You might organize these steps in decreasing order of importance, from greatest savings to least savings, because that order would probably be an order of priority as well. The advantage of this order of presentation is, as with deductive order, that it begins with the item of greatest interest to your readers. The disadvantage is that, once the main point has been stated, the remainder of the report is less interesting.

What is climax order of presentation?

The organizational pattern leading from the least important item to the most important is also known as the **climax** order of presentation. As with inductive order, its chief use is to gain acceptance for a controversial idea. In the money-saving report, for example, if the idea that would result in the greatest savings were also something controversial, you might begin with the change that would result in the least savings. You would then work up to the more controversial idea that would result in the greatest savings.

Exhibit 16.2   **Inductive Order**

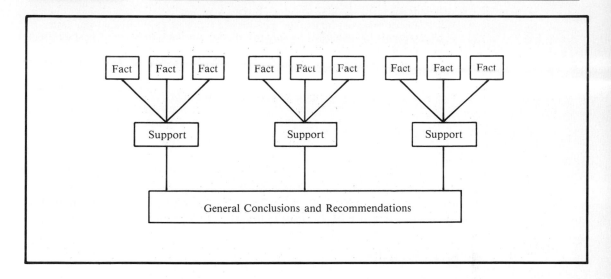

This order of presentation is also useful in oral presentations because it places the most important point last, so the reader will be likely to remember it until he or she has an opportunity to act on it.

Chronological Order

What types of reports call for chronological presentation?

In reporting events or procedures that happen according to a specific time sequence, chronological order is the logical choice. Police and fire reports, work schedules, minutes of meetings, trip and call reports, and accident reports are among those that call for a chronological presentation at some point within the report.

In chronological order, the items or events are arranged in the order in which they occurred or should occur. They may be designated simply as *first, second, third,* and so forth, or they may be identified as having occurred at a specific time:

The meeting was called to order at 8:05.

The meeting was adjourned at 9:20.

Step-by-Step Order

Step-by-step order is an adaptation of chronological order for those events or procedures that should occur in a particular sequence but for which the time is not an important factor. Descriptions of mechanisms, explanations of processes, and instructions are usually written in step-by-step order. Exhibit 16.3 illustrates a step-by-step sequence.

Exhibit 16.3   **Step-by-Step Sequence**

Step 1: Insert key in ignition switch on steering column.
Step 2: Check to make sure that the transmission is in Park (P) or Neutral (N). If the transmission is in N, make sure that the hand brake is in the "set" position (see p. 7).
Step 3: Set the automatic choke by depressing the accelerator pedal to the floor *once*. Depressing the pedal more than once may flood the engine and prevent starting.
Step 4: Take your foot off the accelerator pedal and turn the key to "start" position.
Step 5: Release key when engine starts or after 10 seconds.
Step 6: If engine does not catch, wait 5 seconds and repeat steps 4 and 5.
Step 7: If engine does not catch after three repetitions of Step 6, repeat procedure beginning at Step 3.

The biggest difficulty with step-by-step sequence is that the writer is almost always more familiar with the process or procedure than the readers, and it is easy to omit some of the steps required.

Spatial Order

What are the key elements in spatial ordering?

When the spatial arrangement of physical features is an important factor in a report, the arrangement should be described in spatial order. Dimensions (height, width, length, depth), directions (north, south, up, down), shape (circular, rectangular, square), relationships (higher, lower, above, below), and proportions (larger, smaller, one-half, two-thirds) are the key elements in spatial ordering.

Spatial order may be used alone in describing the physical features of a construction site, a laboratory, or an office layout. It may be combined with a chronological or step-by-step pattern to show movement or progress of an item through space and time, as would be the case of components moving along an assembly line.

Spatial order is also useful for discussing factors that vary according to geographical divisions. A company might divide its marketing responsibilities according to geographical areas: Northwest Region, Southwest Region, Midwest Region, and so on. The results of market research or sales would probably be presented using that same spatial organization.

Topical Order

A topical organizational pattern presents information according to categories or topics. A company annual report, for example, might be arranged according to topic:

Letter to Shareholders

Operations Review

Sales and Income

Products and Services

Social Responsibilities

Financial Data

Topical order is most useful when the categories to be discussed are separate and distinct. The writer can cover one topic before beginning the next.

Problem-to-Solution Order

Should you let the reader know the solution in advance of the facts?

Problem-to-solution order is an application of the inductive order of presentation. The problem can be any unsatisfactory condition, and the solution would be the recommended method of correcting the difficulty. Proposals are a common use of this organization pattern. The writer perceives and defines a problem, explores possible solutions, and selects and recommends the solution with the most advantages and/or the fewest disadvantages.

Suppose, for example, you were working for a manufacturer of packaging materials that had begun as a small, midwestern company, serving essentially a local clientele. Company sales reps have always traveled by car, and they still do, even though many of the company's clients are now located hundreds of miles from the plant. One day while driving nearly 800 miles between calls, you did some calculating and determined that the automobile travel—considering cost of cars, gas, hotels, and sales time lost—exceeded that of travel by air. In proposing a change to management, you would use a problem-to-solution order. You could do this in one of two ways. You could present your solution and the resultant benefit first, and then review the problem and the alternatives you considered. Or you could begin (more convincingly) with the problem and the costs associated with it, explain the alternatives, and offer the solution last.

The *basic* order in either case is inductive. The first case, which presents the solution first, appears at first glance to be deductive. The basic structural pattern, however, is inductive because it retains the inductive method of beginning with specific facts and working to a general conclusion (with the exception of letting the reader know the solution in advance). Straight deductive order would present the solution and offer those facts in support of the solution rather than provide an examination of the problem.

Criteria-to-Application Order

What is the primary use for criteria-to-application order?

Criteria (plural of *criterion*) are the standards by which something is measured or evaluated. Criteria-to-application structure is primarily used to compare products or ideas in relation to their use. A company purchasing new equipment, for example, would want to know which brand or model would best serve its needs. By using the criteria-to-application order, the writer could evaluate costs, useful life, flexibility, and other criteria deemed significant. This pattern is also useful for evaluating the proposed solutions in the problem-to-solution organizational pattern.

When using this system, use the criteria as the major divisions and the items being evaluated as the minor divisions.

I. First Criterion
   A. Product 1
   B. Product 2
   C. Product 3

II. Second Criterion
   A. Product 1
   B. Product 2
   C. Product 3

Organizing by criteria helps the reader to focus on and emphasizes the points that will determine the conclusions and recommendations, rather than the features of individual products or ideas. Of course, the criteria might need to be subordinated for complete analysis, or the applications may need further subdivision for complete coverage.

Cause-and-Effect Order

When would you use cause-and-effect order? effect-to-cause order?

The cause-and-effect order is useful for analyzing the possible consequences of a particular action. Its opposite, the effect-to-cause order, is useful for tracing an effect back to its cause. Either of these schemes is likely to include elements of chronological or spatial order. Cause-and-effect order moves from a known factor or event to a probable result. It is a form of forecasting: What will happen to profits if we increase prices by 12 percent?

Effect-to-cause order attempts to discover the cause of a particular event or situation. Because causes must precede effects, using a reverse chronological order is basic. This pattern may prove complex because an effect may have more than one cause, and the factor that seems to be the cause may be only a related effect.

The effect-to-cause pattern is often used to investigate problems:

What is causing the low morale in the Tennessee plant?

Why has production declined over the past 90 days?

Mixed Patterns

Patterns may be combined. In fact, the longer the report, the greater is the likelihood that it will contain more than one organizational pattern.

Each of the patterns will help you achieve a specific objective, and when you have more than one objective, you will naturally use more than one system of organization. In criteria-to-application order, for example, you might wish to list your criteria in decreasing order of importance so that your reader could see at a glance how the criteria were weighted.

Although you do not need to be specific in telling readers what organizational pattern you are using, the pattern itself needs to be sufficiently clear so that readers will know what you are doing at each step of the way. If you are combining chronological and spatial orders, for example, be explicit about references to time and place so that readers will be able to tell which is which.

Also, do not confuse systems of classification—which *must* be the same throughout—with patterns of organization. A discussion of office layout, for example, would have to stick to the factors that influence layout: furniture, equipment, traffic patterns, and so forth. The discussion could include elements of spatial order, chronological order, cause-and-effect order, effect-to-cause order, criteria-to-application order, and others. The overall structure for the discussion could be either deductive or inductive.

METHODS OF OUTLINING

At what stages of report writing is an outline useful?

An outline is the skeleton of your report. It reveals the structure on which the substance will hang. Outlines will prove useful three times in the writing process. First, a tentative outline developed in the planning stage (see Chapter 9) will enable you to explore the possible sequencing of and relationships among the areas to be covered. Second, a working outline, prepared after the data have been collected and analyzed, provides the structure for the final report. The working outline is the guide you intend to follow. It is not, however, immutable. The writing process may reveal weaknesses in the outline that should be corrected. Third, once the report is complete, a final outline can serve as a table of contents and as a guide to headings within the report.

Regardless of its purpose, the principle behind any outline is the division of a whole into its component parts. Although what you consider the "whole" of your topic may change from the time of initial planning to the writing of the final report, the same rules apply to dividing the whole in a logical and appropriate way. Select a system for your outline, and follow the basic rules.

Systems of Outlining

Which system of outlining is gaining popularity?

Whatever the purpose of the outline, it will use one of three symbol systems to indicate the divisions and sequence of ideas. The most common symbol system remains the Roman numeral system, which uses Roman numerals to designate the main topics (Exhibit 16.4). The other

Exhibit 16.4   Roman Numeral System of Outlining

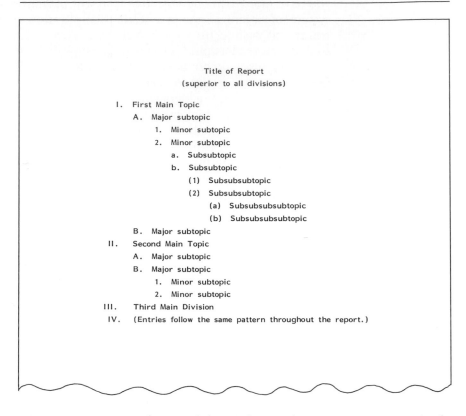

```
                        Title of Report
                   (superior to all divisions)

        I.   First Main Topic
             A.  Major subtopic
                 1.  Minor subtopic
                 2.  Minor subtopic
                     a.  Subsubtopic
                     b.  Subsubtopic
                         (1)  Subsubsubtopic
                         (2)  Subsubsubtopic
                              (a)  Subsubsubsubtopic
                              (b)  Subsubsubsubtopic
             B.  Major subtopic
        II.  Second Main Topic
             A.  Major subtopic
             B.  Major subtopic
                 1.  Minor subtopic
                 2.  Minor subtopic
        III. Third Main Division
        IV.  (Entries follow the same pattern throughout the report.)
```

two systems use numbers and decimals to indicate main topics and subtopics, with one system indenting to show subordination (Exhibit 16.5) and the other beginning all entries on the left margin (Exhibit 16.6). The decimal systems have been gaining popularity in recent years.

Rules for Outlining

Whichever system of outlining you use, the same five basic rules apply:

1. **The Whole Must Equal the Sum of Its Parts.** The main divisions must add up to or equal the whole expressed by the title. That is, the title should neither state nor imply more or less than the report will actually cover. The same rule applies to each of the topics and its subtopics.

2. **Divisions Should Be Organized for Relative Balance.** No one division should be very much larger or smaller than the other divisions.

3. **Single Subdivisions Should Not Occur.** Because a whole cannot be divided unless at least two parts result, no topic can be divided unless at least two subtopics result.

Exhibit 16.5   Decimal System with Indentation

```
                              Title of Report

            1.  First Major Topic
                1.1  Major subtopic
                    1.1.1  Minor subtopic
                    1.1.2  Minor subtopic
                        1.1.2.1  subsubtopic
                        1.1.2.2  subsubtopic
                            1.1.2.2.1  subsubsubtopic
                            1.1.2.2.2  subsubsubtopic
                1.2  Major subtopic
            2.  Second Major Topic
                2.1  Major subtopic
                    2.1.1  Minor subtopic
                    2.1.2  Minor subtopic
                2.2  Major subtopic
            3.  (Entries follow the same pattern throughout the report.)
```

Exhibit 16.6   Decimal System without Indentation

```
                              Title of Report

            1.          First Main Topic
            1.1         Major subtopic
            1.1.1       Minor subtopic
            1.1.1.1     subsubtopic
            1.1.1.2     subsubtopic
            1.1.2       Minor subtopic
            1.2         Major subtopic
            2.          (Entries follow the same form throughout the report.)
```

4. **Main Divisions Should Be Expressed in Parallel Grammatical Form.** Subdivisions within each division must use parallel grammatical structure, but subdivisions of one topic need not be parallel with subdivisions of a separate topic.

5. **Divisions and Subdivisions Should Be Selected to Help the Reader Focus Quickly on the Significant Ideas.** When possible, the number of parts within any division should not be fewer than three nor more than seven.

Depending on the kind of report you are preparing, your most logical basis for dividing your topic may be time, place (geographic area), quantities, or qualities. Time periods are commonly used divisions for progress reports. Reports based on geographic location would be useful for site selections and some sales reports. Divisions based on quantities would be useful for evaluations based on statistical information (age, income, production amounts, and so on). Reports with qualities as the major divisions would be useful for comparing items against certain criteria (cost, performance factors, and the like).

Informal Outlines

Tentative outlines and sometimes working outlines as well are usually *informal,* or *topical,* outlines. Such outlines use one or two words to indicate the topic covered in each division and subdivision. Exhibit 16.7 illustrates an informal outline.

What is the purpose of an informal outline?

The main use of an informal outline is to help the writer organize the material in the planning or writing stage. While it allows the writer to work quickly in deciding what element belongs in which position, a topical outline does not provide enough information to be useful to a reader. Any outline that will be seen by a reader should be a formal outline.

Formal Outlines

Formal outlines are designed to communicate some essential information to the reader. To do so, they use phrases or complete sentences to describe the divisions more fully than the one or two words used in information outlines. Exhibit 16.8 illustrates a formal outline using phrases.

The formal outline may use complete sentences in the place of phrases. In place of the first phrase in Exhibit 16.8, for example, the writer could use a complete sentence:

Phrase: The Cause of the Accident on 23 May
Sentence: Brake failure caused the accident on 23 May.

Exhibit 16.7   ## Informal Outline

```
                        Truck Accidents

            I.   The Accident on May 23
                 A.  Police Report
                 B.  Driver's Report
                 C.  Mechanic's Investigation
           II.   Vehicle Repair Records
                 A.  Every Six Months
                 B.  Accidents
          III.   Safety Record
                 A.  Vehicle Breakdowns
                 B.  Accidents
           IV.   Inspections Required
                 A.  Procedure
                 B.  Costs
                 C.  Savings
```

Are full sentence outlines useful to readers? to the writer?

The use of full sentence outlines is limited because they supply more information than readers expect or want in an outline. A sentence outline, however, may help a writer develop *topic sentences* for the paragraphs of the report. Without the outline designations (numbers and letters), a sentence outline may serve as an abstract or summary of the entire report.

HEADINGS

Just as the writer uses the title of the entire report to tell readers what the report is about, he or she can help readers follow the report by using titles for each section of the report. Titles for the divisions and subdivisions are called **headings,** or **heads,** because they are placed at the "head" of sections.

A Good Heading

What information does a good heading convey?

A good heading is both brief and specific, letting readers see what topic the following material will cover and providing some information about that topic. A good heading also lets readers know the relative importance of the material that follows. Is the material a main division, a subdivision, or a subsubdivision? What is its relationship to the material preceding and following it?

Exhibit 16.8   Formal Outline Using Phrases

Reducing the Number of Truck Accidents

I. The Cause of the Accident of May 23

    A. The Police Report Cites Brake Failure

    B. The Driver's Report Blames the Brakes

    C. The Mechanic's Investigation Confirms Brake Failure

II. Problems Revealed by Vehicle Repair Records

    A. Vehicles Examined Only Twice a Year

    B. Potential Hazard on Most Vehicles

III. Projected Savings Resulting from Improved Safety Records

    A. The Costs of Vehicle Breakdowns

    B. The Costs of Accidents

IV. The Value of More Frequent Inspections

    A. Quarterly Schedule for Inspections

    B. Some Increase in Costs

        1. Three Additional Trucks Required

        2. One Additional Mechanic Required

    C. Savings to Exceed Costs

        1. Reduced Vehicle Downtime

        2. Fewer Breakdowns on Road

        3. Fewer Accidents Caused by Mechanical Failures

        4. Reduced Risk of Potentially Serious Accidents
            in Future

As a rule, the phrases developed for the formal outline may be used as the headings in the report, and the same rules apply to the use of headings as to outlining. The formal outline prepared for the final report will also provide the topic entries for the table of contents. For this reason, the outline needs to be checked carefully to see whether it adequately represents the material covered by the report. In addition, the physical form of headings must make their relative importance clear at a glance. This requires that the system used be consistent throughout the report and that the form used for major headings appear superior to that used for minor headings.

In general, the relative importance of a heading is indicated by the size of type used in the heading (printed reports), its position on the page, and the amount of space allowed for it. Take a look through the pages of this book, for example, and note the type size, position, and space allocation for chapter titles and for major and minor divisions within the chapters. Note that you can easily determine which sections are main divisions and which are subdivisions by the physical appearance of the heading.

Basic Rules

The same differentiation should occur in typewritten material. Although different organizations may require different systems of headings in their reports, the following rules apply in most typewritten systems:

1. Headings in solid capital letters are superior to headings that include lowercase letters.
2. Centered headings are superior to headings on the margin.
3. Headings that stand on a line alone are superior to those that run into the line of text.
4. Headings in solid caps are not underscored, but headings using caps and lowercase letters are underscored to increase their visibility.
5. No two headings should appear without intervening text. Because no subdivision can be the equal of the main division of which it is a part, the main division must include information about all the subdivisions included within the division.
6. The report title must be in a form clearly superior to all the headings used in the report.
7. The text of the report must be coherent with all headings removed. The headings should not be used as antecedents for pronouns nor should the paragraph that follows assume that the heading has communicated specific facts.
8. Whatever forms are used, the same system must be used consistently throughout the report.

Why are sentences
seldom used as
headings?

In general, headings should *not* be complete sentences; sentences are usually too wordy to focus readers' attention on the topic. The exception to this rule is a series of questions. Short questions may serve as effective headings:

I. What Will Be Covered?

II. Who Should Attend?

III. How Will ABC Benefit?

Questions as headings are most effective in short reports. You can imagine how predictable and tiresome this technique would become after the tenth question.

More often, the wording for headings should be infinitive phrases, noun phrases, participial phrases, or verbal or noun clauses (containing a subject and a verb but not expressing a complete thought). Whichever form of wording you select, remember to retain that style for other equal headings in that division.

Infinitive phrases: To Study Current Costs of Document Design
  To Evaluate New Desktop Publishing Equipment
  To Compare Desktop Publishing Software
  To Compare Costs of Document Production Using New Technologies

Noun phrases: Current Costs of Document Design
  New Desktop Publishing Equipment
  Desktop Publishing Software
  Cost of Document Production with New Technologies

Participial phrases: Studying Current Costs of Document Design
  Evaluating New Desktop Publishing Equipment
  Comparing Desktop Publishing Software
  Comparing Costs of Document Production Using New Technologies

Noun clauses: Current Costs of Document Design Studied
  New Desktop Publishing Equipment Evaluated
  Desktop Publishing Software Compared
  Costs of Document Production Using New Technologies Compared

Typewritten Forms

As mentioned previously, heading use corresponds with that of outlining:

Title

I. (or 1.) First-degree or first-level heading
   A. (or 1.1) Second-degree or second-level heading
      1. (or 1.1.1) Third-degree (level) heading
         a. (or 1.1.1.1) Fourth-degree (level) heading
            (1) (or 1.1.1.1.1) Fifth-degree (level) heading

When might five
levels of headings
be necessary?

The term **degree** or **level** is used to indicate the division designation, beginning with first-degree to indicate the main divisions, and second- through fifth-degree to indicate major and minor subdivisions. Only the

longest, most formal reports are sufficiently complex to require five levels of headings. Exhibit 16.9 illustrates typewritten forms for five levels of headings with double-spaced text. Many reports require only one level of heading, and most reports require three or fewer levels.

What style of
heading is most
commonly used
when only one
level is required?
two levels? three
levels?

When one level only is required, the form shown in Exhibit 16.9 as a third-degree heading is most common. When two levels of headings are required, the forms for second and third degrees are most common. When three levels are required, main divisions can be indicated by centered heads, using caps and lowercase letters. Major subdivisions can be indicated by marginal heads, using caps and lowercase letters. Minor subdivisions in this system can be indicated by a run-in head, separated from the text by a period or a period and a dash.

When typing headings that consist of caps and lowercase letters, remember to use lowercase letters for articles (a, an, the), conjunctions (and, but, or, for, nor, yet, and so), and prepositions of fewer than four letters (for, on, by, to, of). The first and last word in a heading is always capitalized.

Modern word processing equipment provides greater flexibility in the appearance of headings than is possible with a typewriter. Boldface print may replace the underscore. Different levels of heading may be indicated by type size, typeface, or a combination of the two. Regardless of how you choose to present your headings, the basic rules apply. Also, keep in mind that the main functions of a heading are to alert the reader to the contents of the material that follows and to indicate its relative importance.

Report examples throughout this text illustrate many of the possibilities. (See especially Exhibits in Chapters 8 and 17.)

SUMMARY

Report structure is influenced by the material itself, the fact that the report must begin and end somewhere, readers' predisposition to accept or reject the report, and the need to emphasize central ideas. The opening—or introduction—should orient readers to the problem and be interesting from the readers' point of view. The middle—or body—of the report presents and interprets data. The ending of the report may contain conclusions and recommendations or a summary.

When a reader is predisposed to accept the contents of a report, deductive structure, which places the important conclusions first, is best. Inductive structure, which begins with facts and ends with the conclusions, is often best for readers who are biased against the conclusions in the report. Whichever structure is used, the writer needs to use placement, proportion, language, and mechanics to emphasize the most important ideas.

Common structural patterns include deductive, inductive, order of importance (most to least and least to most), chronological, step-by-

2. For each of the five reports, reconstruct the appropriate formal outline and compare the outline with the headings used. Evaluate the reports based on that comparison.

3. For each of the common structural patterns, list three possible applications. Explain why the structural patterns are appropriate for the applications.

4. For one of the problems listed in Appendix B or for a report problem of your own choosing, prepare complete informal and formal outlines.

5. The hospital for which you work has asked you to investigate the feasibility of establishing a special burn unit. One of the things you have been asked to investigate is the efficacy of water beds in burn-care units. Prepare a formal outline showing your basic structural pattern. Along with your outline, submit an explanation of other structural patterns that might be appropriate for use within sections. If the hospital should install a burn-care unit, for example, what step-by-step procedure should be followed in establishing it? Where should the unit be located? Use as many common structural patterns as possible.

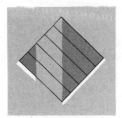

Report Presentation

After you have researched, gathered, analyzed, and organized the information for your business report, you are ready to present the data clearly and objectively. Getting the report read is one of your primary objectives and will depend on how attractively you present the results of your research.

Topics

Title Page
Letter of Transmittal
Table of Contents
Table of Illustrations
Abstract
Body of the Report
References
Appendix

Chapter 7 discussed the parts of the formal report. This chapter illustrates how these parts are presented in the long, formal report.

TITLE PAGE

The title page contains four main elements—the title, the "prepared for" line, the "prepared by" line, and the date. Center each line on the title page, and keep the spacing between sections equal or well-balanced. When a report is to be bound on the left, allow an extra half inch at the left margin. When a report is to be bound at the top, allow an extra half inch at the top margin.

What is inverted
pyramid style?

Title   The title of the report is typed in capital letters and underscored. When the title occupies two or more lines, double-space and follow the inverted pyramid style of presentation: break the lines between thought units, with the longest line first followed by shorter lines.

"Prepared for" Line   Follow the title of the report with the phrase "prepared for" ("submitted to") using capital and lowercase letters. Because a colon must not separate a preposition from its object, do not place a colon after "for." Double-space after the "prepared for" line. Use single-spacing, and type the name, title, organization, and address of the recipient.

"Prepared by" Line   Follow the "prepared for" line with the phrase "prepared by" (or "submitted by") using capital and lowercase letters. Double-space after the "prepared by" line. Single-space the name, title, organization, and address of the writer.

Date Line   Include the date on which you present the report to your reader.
    Exhibit 17.1 illustrates a title page.

LETTER OF TRANSMITTAL

The letter of transmittal, which submits the report to the reader, is typed on letterhead stationery in the traditional business letter format. It includes the return address, date, inside address, salutation, body, complimentary close, signature block, and reference and enclosure notations. Exhibit 17.2 illustrates the letter of transmittal.

TABLE OF CONTENTS

The table of contents should begin 1 inch from the top of the paper with the title CONTENTS typed in capitals. Triple-space after the title. Type the word "Page" flush with the right margin and double-space.

Exhibit 17.1   Title Page

SHOULD IBM PCs REPLACE THE XEROX WORD PROCESSING EQUIPMENT

USED BY THE UNIT 7293 SECRETARIAL STAFF?

Prepared for

Richard Dawson
Director, Biostatistics
Hamilton Products Inc.
4000 Milwaukee Avenue
Chicago, IL 60606

Prepared by

Lynn A. Searles
Administrative Support Technician
Mercantile Supplies
8614 Dolphin Street
Chicago, IL 60608

December 10, 19xx

Exhibit 17.2   Letter of Transmittal

**Mercantile Supplies
8614 Dolphin Street
Chicago, Illinois
60608**

December 10, 19xx

Dr. Richard Dawson
Director, Biostatistics
Hamilton Products Inc.
4000 Milwaukee Road
Chicago, IL 60606

Dear Dr. Dawson:

Here is the report you requested on replacing the Xerox word processing
equipment with IBM PCs.

I recommend that we continue to study the problem for at least another year.
Unit 7293 needs more data before the best system for document preparation can
be determined.

The study showed that the unit needs a more efficient document preparation
system because turnaround time is slow, reformatting documents from the
computer is cumbersome, and integration is needed between the secretaries who
type the documents and the professionals who write them.

Let me know when I can help again, Dr. Dawson.

Sincerely,

Lynn A. Searles

Lynn A. Searles
Administrative Support Technician

enc

What is the
purpose of leaders
on the contents
page?

Beginning at the right margin, type the major headings and subheadings, preferably as they appear in the report. Generally, major headings are typed in all capital letters and subheadings are typed in capital and lowercase letters. You are also correct when you use capital and lowercase letters for all entries on the contents page.

Unless the page is short, use leaders (spaced or solid periods) to guide the reader to the page numbers, which are aligned on the right. Provide the page number on which the heading appears in the report. Double-space above and below the major headings (I, II, III). Single-space subheadings. Some authorities recommend double-spacing the contents page when the report is double-spaced. Number the page with a lowercase Roman numeral in the center of the page 1 inch from the bottom.

Exhibit 17.3 illustrates a contents page.

TABLE OF ILLUSTRATIONS

When is a list of
illustrations used?

Prepare a table (or list) of illustrations when the report contains four or more illustrations or when you wish to emphasize the illustrations. The list of illustrations may be a continuation of the contents page or a separate entry. When the list of illustrations is a continuation of the contents page, triple-space after the last contents entry. When the list of illustrations is a separate entry, type the title 1 inch from the top of the paper.

Center and title the page appropriately. For example, use LIST OF ILLUSTRATIONS when you have both tables and figures. Alternately, type separate lists—LIST OF TABLES and LIST OF FIGURES—when you have a sufficient number of each. You may also have pages with titles such as LIST OF MAPS or LIST OF PHOTOGRAPHS. On a single page titled LIST OF ILLUSTRATIONS, all of the various types—tables, figures, maps, and the like—can be listed in groups by using subheadings.

Follow the title with a triple-space and the word "Page" aligned at the right margin. Double-space and type at the left margin the number and title of the illustrations as they appear in the report. Like the contents page, the list of illustrations may use leaders to guide the reader from the illustration number and title to the page number on which the illustration appears. Number the page with a lowercase Roman numeral in the center of the page 1 inch from the bottom. See Exhibit 17.4.

ABSTRACT

How long should
the abstract be? In
what order should
the information be
presented?

The abstract (executive summary or synopsis) is an overview of the report. It summarizes the problem statement, purpose, scope, limitations, methodology, significant findings, and major conclusions and recommendations. The abstract is about 10 percent of the length of the

Exhibit 17.3   Contents Page

CONTENTS

iii

Exhibit 17.4 List of Illustrations

ILLUSTRATIONS

iv

report but no longer than one single-spaced page. Present the information in the abstract in the order that it appears in the report.

Center and type the word ABSTRACT in all capitals 1 inch from the top of the paper. Triple-space and begin the text. Indent paragraphs five spaces when the text is doubled-spaced; use blocked paragraphs with double spacing between paragraphs for single-spaced material. Do not use headings in the abstract. Number the abstract page with a lowercase Roman numeral in the center of the page 1 inch from the bottom. See Exhibit 17.5 for an illustration of an abstract.

BODY OF THE REPORT

As discussed in Chapter 7, the body of the report consists of the introduction, the text, the conclusions, and the recommendations. The introduction presents the problem statement, the purpose, the scope, the limitations, and the methodology. Include in the introduction the material that your readers will need for a clear understanding of the report.

Two inches from the top of the paper type in capitals the report title, which is centered and underlined. Triple-space after the title and begin typing the report. Because two headings should not appear without intervening text and because the reader will know that the first part of your report is the introduction, you need not use an introduction heading. Use descriptive headings in the introduction for the problem statement, purpose, scope, limitations, and methodology.

What is a widow?

Widows   A widow is a single line of a paragraph at the bottom or top of the page. Widows should be avoided. Be sure that at least two lines of a paragraph appear at the bottom of a page, and at least two lines of a paragraph appear at the top of the next page. A heading near the bottom of a page should have at least two lines of text material below it.

Indentation   Reports may be double-spaced or singled-spaced. When you double-space the text, use a five-space indention for paragraphs. When you single-space the text, use block paragraphs and double-space between paragraphs. Keep at least a 1-inch margin on the sides and bottom. Allow an extra half inch at the left margin for reports that are to be bound at the left or an extra half inch at the top for reports that are to be bound at the top.

What is on page 1 in a long report?

Pagination   The pages in the body of the report may be numbered at the top center, top right, top left (especially for two-sided pages) for the even-numbered pages, or bottom center. Number the first page of the introduction with an unadorned Arabic number in the center of the page 1 inch from the bottom. Number consecutively the subsequent pages of the report 1 inch from the top of the paper at the center, at the right margin, or at the left margin for reports that will be printed on

Exhibit 17.5   Abstract

ABSTRACT

Unit 7293 needs a more efficient document preparation system because turn-around time is slow, reformatting documents from the computer is cumbersome, and better integration is needed between the secretaries who type the documents and the professionals who write them.

No personnel from other units participated in this study except two individuals who were interviewed and contributed information about the systems implemented in those units within the past two years. Time was limited and budgetary constraints inhibit any major changes until we are satisfied with T^3 or some other software.

I designed a questionnaire and distributed it to 45 people, but only 20 individuals responded. Most individuals do not mind inputting their own documents or making corrections and changes. Many believe we need a more efficient system and better integration between the equipment used by professionals and that used by the secretarial staff.

We received no significant data from the responses on the questionnaires that would justify any major changes at this time. Of those individuals who responded, several suggested that the current system is lacking in efficiency. The document cleanup procedure needed when transferring documents from the mainframe computer to the Xerox word processor by TTY is cumbersome and time consuming.

Unit 7293 needs to address this issue and study the efficiency of using T^3 or some other software on the PCs, and perhaps determine if the current system used in the Pathology-Toxicology unit would fit our needs.

v

both sides of the paper. It is also correct to type the page number on line 4. Triple-space after the page number and begin typing the text material.

Exhibit 17.6 illustrates the first page of the body of the report. Succeeding pages of the report appear in Exhibit 17.7.

APPENDIXES

What is an appendix?

The appendix is a collection of supplementary information that supports the text of the report. Information that would be helpful but is not essential to the understanding of the report is placed in the appendix. A copy of the cover letter, questionnaire, interview questions, forms, names of companies or individuals who participated in the survey or study, statistical formulas, or computer printouts are examples of what might be included in the appendix.

Place each type of example in a separate appendix. Identify the appendixes by an appropriate title, as follows:

Appendix A: Cover Letter

Appendix B: Questionnaire

Appendix C: Computer Printouts

All appendixes should be referred to in the text of the report and be listed in the table of contents. Exhibit 17.8 illustrates an appendix to a long report.

REFERENCES

References are listed in alphabetical order according to the author's last name, as explained in Chapter 11. When the author's name is unknown or the work is anonymous, list the reference alphabetically according to the title of the book or article.

What is hanging format?

Type the page number 1 inch from the top of the paper. Triple-space and center in capital letters the title REFERENCES. Triple-space after the title and type the reference entries in hanging format; that is, indent five spaces from the left margin all lines but the first. Single-space the entries but double-space between them. Exhibit 17.9 illustrates a reference page.

SUMMARY

Getting the report read is one of your primary objectives and will depend on how attractively you present the results of your research. The

Exhibit 17.6   Body of the Report—First Page

<u>SHOULD IBM PCs REPLACE THE XEROX WORD PROCESSING EQUIPMENT</u>

<u>USED BY THE UNIT 7293 SECRETARIAL STAFF?</u>

The document preparation procedure for Unit 7293 is outdated, and the unit needs a more efficient procedure. The unit uses three ways of preparing documents. The first procedure involves typing documents from handwritten material. The second procedure begins with a professional typing documents into the mainframe computer; the secretary then transfers the document to a Xerox word processor using TTY and cleans up the document. The third procedure starts with a professional inputting a document into the computer using a Memo-text file and printing the document using Memogen; the secretary does only the distribution. Cleaning up or reformatting computer-generated documents takes almost more time than typing a document from handwritten material and causes delays in distribution. All three methods include computer generation of most tables using SAS.

<u>Problem Statement</u>

The primary problem of Unit 7293 is the need to develop a more efficient document preparation system and determine if the present Xerox word processing equipment should be replaced by IBM PC/XTs or IBM PC/ATs.

<u>Purpose</u>

The purpose of this report is to show whether replacing the current equipment used in Unit 7293, the Xerox word processor, with IBM PC/XTs or PC/ATs would improve the document preparation procedure.

1

Exhibit 17.7   Body of the Report

2

<u>Scope and Limitations</u>

   The research data obtained for this survey came primarily from Unit 7293 personnel; however, interviews with persons from units now using Local Area Networks (LANs) or similar systems were held to obtain expertise and determine the feasibility of changing our system. Members of the Research Computer Center were also asked to give input in comparing the Xerox word processors and IBM PCs. Time and budgetary constraints do prohibit any major change at this time, but a two- to five-year time frame for any major changes appears feasible.

<u>Methodology</u>

   I developed a questionnaire on October 6, 19xx, and distributed it to 45 people in Unit 7293 on October 29. Forty-four percent (20) responded by November 4. The unit director, John S., charged Tom V. with the job of locating a good software package for word processing with scientific equations for the IBM PC/XT or PC/AT. We ordered a copy of T^3 on October 21 for the professional walk-up PC in Room 225. I then researched magazine articles, newspaper articles, and books in the Chicago Public Library and obtained copies of those that were most helpful. I spoke with Jan G. of the Computer Center and obtained a schematic from her comparing the qualities of the Xerox word processor with those of the IBM PC. I then developed a list of questions that would be useful when interviewing two individuals about LANs used in the Patent Law and the Pathology-Toxicology units. I interviewed Nancy H. and C. Lara M. about their current document preparation systems, which have both been developed within the past two years.

Exhibit 17.7   (*continued*)

3

FINDINGS

As a result of the survey conducted on Unit 7293 document preparation, I obtained the following information.

Document Input

When asked if they would mind inputting their own documents, 20 percent (4) of the professionals responded that they would mind and 80 percent (16) indicated they would not mind. Four notes were added by the respondents indicating they do input their own documents now, and one respondent only wanted to do parts of a document (edit scientific equations) rather than type in whole documents.

Equipment Used

Three types of equipment were listed, with a fourth category for fill-in. Eighty percent (16) of the respondents use computer terminals, 35 percent (7) use IBM PC/XTs or PC/ATs, 20 percent (4) use the Xerox word processor, and no one filled in any additional equipment in the "other" category. Also, 30 percent checked more than one category, indicating they use more than one kind of equipment: 15 percent (3) use either a PC or the Xerox, 10 percent (2) use either a terminal or a PC, and 5 percent (1) use either a terminal or the Xerox word processor. As Table 1 shows, of those unit individuals who responded to the questionnaire survey, most use computer terminals, very few have PCs, and only the secretarial staff uses the Xerox word processors (one professional walk-up station is in the Computer Room).

(*continued*)

Exhibit 17.7   (*continued*)

4

Table 1. Equipment Used in Unit 7293

Equipment	Number	Percent
Computer Terminals	16	80
IBM PC/XTs or PC/ATs	7	35
Xerox Word Processors	4	20
Other	0	0

Equipment Preferred

Twenty-five percent (5) of those who responded to the questionnaire did not answer this question. When asked what equipment they prefer, 45 percent (9) indicated they prefer using an IBM PC/XT or PC/AT, 25 percent (5) prefer using a computer terminal, 10 percent (2) prefer using the Xerox, and no one preferred using the Wordstream computer terminal. Replying in the "other" category, 5 percent (1) indicated a preference for an IBM 3179-G terminal.

Figure 1 shows the comparison between equipment used and equipment preferred.

Documents Prepared a Month

Twenty-five percent (5) of the respondents did not answer this question. When asked how many documents each individual prepared a month, 20 percent (4) indicated they prepare 5 documents a month, 15 percent (3) prepare 2 documents a month, and 10 percent (2) prepare 3 documents a month. As Figure 2 shows, 5 percent (1) of the respondents prepare 1, 1 to 2, 3 to 4, 4, 5 to 10, and 8 documents a month respectively.

Exhibit 17.7   *(continued)*

5

Figure 1. Comparison between Equipment Used
And Equipment Preferred

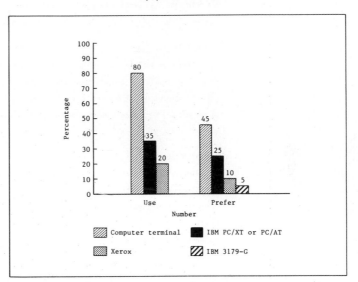

Document Type

When asked to rank the type of document they prepare in order of
importance, 65 percent (13) of the respondents gave a rank of 1 to memos with
tables, 20 percent (4) to manuscripts with equations, 10 percent (2) to
technical reports with tables, and 5 percent (1) to program documentation. A
rank of 2 was given by 30 percent (6) to memos with equations, 20 percent (4)
to memos with tables, 10 percent (2) to 1-page memos, 10 percent (2) to manuscripts with tables, 5 percent (1) to time accounting, and 5 percent (1) to

(continued)

Exhibit 17.7   *(continued)*

6

technical reports with tables. Fifty percent (10) of the respondents ranked the documents they prepare beyond 2; however, these rankings do not change the outcome of the study and are too varied to mention.

Document Reformatting

Fifteen percent (3) of the respondents did not answer this question. When asked if professionals should input documents and have the secretaries reformat them, 24 percent (4) of the respondents strongly agreed, 47 percent (8) agreed, 18 percent (3) were undecided, 6 percent (1) disagreed, and 6 percent (1) strongly disagreed.

Current System Problems

Twenty-five percent (5) of respondents did not answer this question. When asked what was wrong with the current system, 20 percent (4) said that typing statistical equations was too difficult, especially when there was a lack of communication between the secretaries and the professional who writes the document; 30 percent (6) believed that turnaround time was hampered because of document reformatting problems between machines; 10 percent (2) of the professionals felt that there should be a mechanism to transmit documents back and forth between machines; 5 percent (1) felt there were too few secretaries; 5 percent (1) thought there were too few machines and proper software; and 5 percent (1) of the respondents thought the system worked okay.

Document Completion

When asked how often documents take longer than three days for completion because of errors or misunderstandings, 55 percent (11) of the respondents to the survey did not answer the question. Of those who did answer, 11 percent (1) indicated problems with every document, 11 percent (1) indicated problems

Exhibit 17.7   *(continued)*

7

with every document that includes tables, 33 percent (3) indicated problems
with every document that includes equations, and 44 percent (4) have problems
with only every other document.

Document Procedures

When asked if the professionals generated any of their own documents now,
90 percent (18) of the respondents said they do generate their own documents;
10 percent (2) indicated they do not.

Ten percent (2) of the respondents did not respond to the question about
the Memogen procedure. Of the respondents who answered yes to generating their
own documents, 61 percent (11) indicated they did use the Memogen procedure in
XEDIT on the mainframe computer, and 39 percent (7) do not use Memogen.

The respondents who do not use Memogen were asked to indicate what method
they do use. Thirty-five percent (7) of the respondents do not use Memogen,
but 14 percent (1) of those neglected to indicate what method they do use. Of
the others, 15 percent (3) use SCRIPT or SCRIPT2 on the mainframe com-puter, 15
percent (3) use the Xerox word processor, 10 percent (2) use the Word Perfect
word processing package on the IBM PC, 10 percent (2) use KEDIT on the IBM PC,
5 percent (1) use a blank memo already prepared and fill in what they need (no
elaboration was provided which would explain this method more clearly), and 5
percent (1) use XEDIT on the mainframe computer.

Summary

The results of the questionnaire survey indicate that most of those surveyed do not mind typing the documents they prepare, that 80 percent of those
who prepare documents still use computer terminals rather than IBM PCs, and
that 45 percent prefer using an IBM PC for preparing documents. The data also
show that 30 percent of the respondents use more than one type of equipment.

(continued)

Exhibit 17.7   *(continued)*

8

The unit's personnel included in the questionnaire survey generate an average of 5 documents a month, and 65 percent prepare memos with tables. The survey also showed that 71 percent of those participating in the study either strongly agreed or agreed that professionals should input their own documents, and the secretaries should be responsible for the corrections or reformatting as well as the distribution. The consensus of most of the participants was that the current system used for unit document preparation was inefficient and that turnaround time was too slow. As Figure 2 indicates, the equipment used and the equipment preferred are not very different. The equipment used most of the time by those participating in the survey is the computer terminal, primarily because the unit is dependent upon the mainframe computer, and we still have few PCs.

INTERVIEWS

I interviewed Nancy H. of the Patent Law unit and C. Lara M. of the Pathology-Toxicology unit on November 2 about the document preparation systems used by each unit. The Path-Tox unit does not have a local area network (LAN), but was the first unit in the Pharmaceutical Research Division to do a pilot study for improving document preparation, especially for technical reports. The Patent Law unit implemented a LAN in 19xx.

Nancy H.

Nancy H. works in the Patent Law unit as an Office Supervisor. Nancy indicated the Patent Law unit currently uses IBM PCs, PC/XTs, a Laserjet printer, a Diablo printer, and an Epson printer. Each lawyer and each secretary has an electronic work station, and one work station is dedicated to connecting to the COUSIN data base and for communication (telexes). The

Exhibit 17.7   *(continued)*

9

Figure 2. Documents Prepared a Month

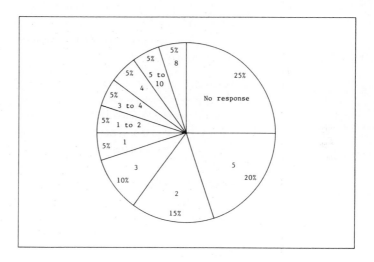

lawyers input their own documents, and the secretaries do any editing required
by retrieving each document from a shared space on the network.

From the planning phase to implementation the whole LAN took approximately
6 to 8 months. During training there was little problem with continued
productivity. The Patent Law unit has not replaced any of the three secretaries who retired during the last few months, but productivity is greater than
when the staff was larger.

(continued)

Exhibit 17.7   (*continued*)

Nancy said there were no disadvantages with the new system; system maintenance is planned in advance and failures have been minimal. The advantages,
though, have been many: E-mail allows mail to be distributed to the whole unit
with one keystroke; all forms, labels, and letterheads are set up in macros and
pro-grams allowing easy printing and less wasted paper. The Patent Law unit is
functioning very well with their new system.

C. Lara M.

Lara works in the Pathology-Toxicology unit as a Lead Secretary. Lara
indicated that Path-Tox uses IBM PCs and Xerox word processing equipment. In
one method of generating documents, the professionals input a document on an
IBM PC that is linked directly to the Xerox laser printer with software called
XNS, and the document is distributed as is. A second method also involves professional input of documents; the secretary then links to the professional's
computer id, transfers the document to the Xerox word processor, and prints the
document with no cleanup at all. Some professionals, however, have trained on
the Xerox equipment and do their own documents with no secretarial involvement
except in the duplication and distribution process.

The Path-Tox unit began a pilot trial in 19xx and started a second pilot
in 19xx. These trials are finished; and the system is implemented and working
well. Productivity has improved greatly; no data were collected to show this,
but time is no longer spent handwriting documents. The major disadvantage is
the lack of uniformity between documents that results from their being
generated by the professionals according to personal preferences. Another
disadvantage is that the professionals must do all corrections and spend time
inputting documents, work that a secretary would normally do.

Exhibit 17.7   *(continued)*

11

CONCLUSIONS

Based on the findings of my study, I conclude the following:

1. Eighty percent (16) of the professionals indicated that they do not mind typing their own documents.

2. Only 35 percent (7) of the respondents currently use IBM PC/XTs or PC/ATs.

3. Forty-five percent (9) of the professionals prefer using an IBM PC.

4. Of those individuals responding to the survey, 30 percent (6) indicated they prepare at least 5 documents a month.

5. Sixty-five percent (13) of the survey respondents primarily prepare memos with tables; 30 percent (6) prepare memos with equations.

6. Twenty-four percent (4) of the respondents strongly agreed and 47 percent (8) agreed when asked if professionals should input their own documents.

7. Twenty percent (4) of the respondents agreed that a lack of communication or lack of integration between equipment, between the secretarial staff and the professionals did exist and hampered efficient document preparation.

8. Fifteen percent (3) of the respondents indicated that the documents they prepare that include equations take longer than 3 days to finish.

RECOMMENDATIONS

Based on the conclusions, I recommend the following:

1. Because most professionals do not mind typing their own documents, I recommend we test the T^3 word processing package for another few months. If T^3 works well, and the Hewlett Packard laserjet printer prepares high quality documents, the professionals should use this method.

(continued)

Exhibit 17.7   *(continued)*

12

2. We study the possibility of replacing more computer terminals with IBM
    PC/XTs or PC/ATs. The major change in the unit document procedure could
    be accomplished only by changing equipment.

3. We study the feasibility of more individual training on PCs, especially
    for the secretarial staff. If more people are trained on the PC, the use
    of the unit walk-up PC in Room 225 might increase.

4. We keep the level of productivity at least at the current level.

5. Most of the tables generated within Unit 7293 are produced by SAS on the
    mainframe computer, but we need to continue studying the T^3 package for
    producing equations.

6. We do not need an increase in the number of professionals who currently
    input documents, because the level is quite high already. I recommend,
    however, that we encourage more professionals to produce their own
    documents.

7. The current system of document preparation needs enhancing, and we need
    less reformatting of documents from the mainframe computer. I recommend
    we look for another way of producing documents from the computer by using
    the IBM PC instead of the mainframe.

8. The problem of equations remains the primary one for deterring document
    turnaround. If a professional could input equations using T^3 or make
    changes or corrections when proofreading, the time lapse would decrease.

Exhibit 17.8   Appendixes

13

QUESTIONNAIRE AND TALLY
SHOULD IBM PCs REPLACE THE XEROX WORD PROCESSING EQUIPMENT
USED BY THE UNIT 7293 SECRETARIAL STAFF?

As a BIS 343 Report Writing student, I am conducting a study to aid management
in determining the most efficient system for Unit 7293 document preparation.
Please answer the following questions as they pertain to your position and
requirements for document preparation using the Unit 7293 secretarial staff.

1. Would you mind inputting your own documents?

    Yes _4 (20%)_ No _16 (80%)_

2. What type of equipment do you currently use? (Check any that apply.)

    _16 (80%)_ Computer terminal   30% use more than one: 3 (15%) use a PC
                                     or the Xerox, 2 (10%) use a terminal or
    _7(35%)_ IBM PC/XT or PC/AT   a PC, and 1 (5%) use either a terminal
                                     or the Xerox.
    _4 (20%)_ Xerox Word Processor

    _0_____   Other (Please specify) _____

3. Which type of equipment do you prefer to use? (Check only one.)

    _9 (45%)_ IBM PC/XT or PC/AT
                                 3 (15%) did not respond to this question.
    _5 (25%)_ Terminal

    _0 (0%)_ Wordstream

    _2 (10%)_ Xerox Word Processor

    _1 (5%)_ Other (Please specify) ___3179 G_____

4. How many documents do you prepare a month? _____

5. What kind of documents do you prepare most often? (Please rank in order
    of importance with 1 = most important and 7 = least important.)

    _____ Manuscripts (with tables)

    _4 (20%)_ Manuscripts (with equations)   1 Rankings

    _13 (65%)_ Memos (with tables)

    _____ Memos (with equations)

    _2 (10%)_ Technical reports (with tables)

    _____ Technical reports (with equations)

    _1 (5%)_ Other (Please specify) _____

(continued)

Exhibit 17.8   (*continued*)

14

6. Do you think professional inputting of documents with secretarial reformatting would be more efficient than the current system?

Strongly Agree	Agree	Undecided	Disagree	Strongly Disagree
+2	+1	0	-1	-2

<u>4 (24%)</u>   <u>8 (47%)</u> <u>3 (18%)</u> <u>1 (6%)</u>   <u>1 (6%)</u>

17 of 20 (85%) responded; 3 of 20 (15%) did not respond.

7. What is the main problem that you see with our current system?

_____

_____

_____

_____

8. How often do your documents take longer than three days to complete because of errors or misunderstanding the text?

<u>1 (11%)</u> Every document

<u>1 (11%)</u> Every document with tables

  9 of 20 (45%) responded
<u>3 (33%)</u> Every document with equations 11 of 20 (55%) did not respond

<u>4 (44%)</u> Every other document

9. Do you generate any of your own documents now?

Yes <u>18 (90%)</u> No <u>2 (10%)</u>

10. If you generate your own documents, do you use the Memogen procedure for XEDIT?

Yes <u>11 (61%)</u> No <u>7 (39%)</u>   18 of 20 (90%) responded
  2 of 20 (10%) did not respond

If you answered No to this question, what procedure do you use to prepare your documents?

_____

Please return your completed questionnaire to Lynn Searles by November 4.

Exhibit 17.8   *(continued)*

15

INTERVIEW QUESTIONS

1. What kind of equipment does your unit use for preparing documents?

2. Do professionals input any or all parts of documents?

3. How long did it take to implement your new system?

4. Have you any evidence of improved productivity?

5. What advantages or disadvantages do you see with your system?

Exhibit 17.9　References

16

REFERENCES

Bogue, D. T. "Document Processing Can Slow the Paper Explosion." <u>The Office</u>
103 (April 1986): 26+.

Gentile, G. W. "LANS: Some Initial Thoughts." <u>The Office</u> 103 (May 1986):
42+.

Green, James H. <u>Automating Your Office--How to Do It, How to Justify It</u>. New
York: McGraw-Hill, 1984.

Kneale, Dennis. "Sharpening an Edge: A Look Inside IBM's Internal Networks."
<u>The Wall Street Journal</u> Nov. 10, 1986: 38.

Naj, Amal Kuman. "The Human Factor: Returning to the Worker for Help in
Automating." <u>The Wall Street Journal</u> Nov. 10, 1986: 36.

Pava, Calvin H. P. <u>Managing New Office Technology: An Organizational
Strategy</u>. New York: The Free Press, 1983.

title page contains four main elements—the title, the "prepared for" line, the "prepared by" line, and the date. Each of the lines on the title page is centered, and the spacing between elements is equal or well balanced.

The letter of transmittal submits the report to the reader. It is typed on letterhead stationery in the traditional business letter format.

The contents page presents the major headings and subheadings as they appear in the report. Headings are preceded by their outline symbol. Leaders are usually needed to guide the reader to the page numbers, which are aligned on the right.

Type the table (or list) of illustrations as a continuation of the contents page or on a separate page. Like the contents page, the list of illustrations uses leaders to guide the reader from the illustration number and title to the page number on which the illustration appears.

The abstract is the report in miniature. It is about 10 percent of the length of the report but no longer than one single-spaced page.

The body of the report consists of the introduction, the text, the conclusions, and the recommendations. The introduction presents the problem statement, the purpose, the scope, the limitations, and the methodology.

References are listed in alphabetical order according to the author's last name. Type reference entries in hanging format; single-space the entries but double-space between them.

The appendix is a collection of supplementary information that supports the text of the report. Information that would be helpful but not essential to the understanding of the report is placed in the appendix. All appendixes should be referred to in the text of the report and listed in the table of contents.

EXERCISES

Review and Discussion Questions

1. What are the four elements on a title page?
2. What is the purpose of the letter of transmittal?
3. What are leaders and what purpose do they serve?
4. When should a list of illustrations be included in the report?
5. What is an abstract? What does it do?
6. What is included in the introduction of the report?
7. What is a widow?
8. Explain the pagination in reports.
9. What is a hanging format?
10. What is an appendix?

Problems and Applications

1. Prepare a title page using the following information: Title: What procedures would be most effective for marketing products X and Y in the central part of the state?
   Prepared by: Jack DeVries, Sales Representative for Parker-Haines Company, 3978 South Jackson Street, Eau Claire, WI 54701.
   Prepared for: Thomas Siegel, President, Central Purchasing Company, 505 King Boulevard, Lewisville, TX 75067.
   Date: February 21, 19XX.

2. Prepare a table of contents using the following information: abstract, iv; introduction, 1; background, 1; problem statement, 1; scope, 1; limitations, 2; methodology, 3; findings, 4; conclusions, 6; recommendations, 6; appendixes, 7; references, 8.

3. Prepare a list of illustrations using the following information:
   Table 1, Confidence in leaders of ten institutions, 1980–85, page 5.
   Table 2, What should Social Security do? page 8.
   Figure 1, How much should we spend? page 12.
   Figure 2, Voting patterns, page 15.
   Figure 3, Marital status of women 18 to 25, page 18.
   Figure 4, Marital status of men 18 to 25, page 19.

4. Prepare an abstract of the cover story of the current issue of *Time* or *Newsweek*.

5. Using the information in Problem 1, write a letter of transmittal. Say that the report focuses on five effective procedures for marketing products X and Y and that the information presented in the report should help the reader make a decision. Offer to be of help again.

6. Write a paragraph with a third-degree heading of methodology. Explain that primary and secondary sources were used to obtain the data and information for the report. Primary sources included a ten-item questionnaire that you designed and distributed to 100 people selected at random. Secondary sources included library research on marketing procedures.

7. Prepare a table, give it a title and a number, and write a paragraph about it. Use the following information:

   Question: Should government restrict imports of autos made in Japan?

	1982	1983	1984	1985	1986	1987
Yes	61%	59%	62%	63%	63%	65%
No	39%	41%	38%	37%	37%	35%

8. Prepare a pie chart, give it a title and a number, and write a paragraph about it. Use the following information:

   Question: How is your weekly salary of $500 spent?

   Answer: Food 33%, housing 25%, utilities, 15%, entertainment 5%, medical 8%, savings 14%.

9. Prepare a reference page on post-secondary education. Cite two books, two articles, two newspapers, and an educator whom you interviewed.

10. Photocopy a magazine article that uses at least three degrees of headings. Prepare an outline of the article.

Subjects for Business Report Problems

1. What problems face managers who administer performance appraisals?
2. How extensively are graphic aids used in businesses?
3. What is the best method for motivating office employees?
4. How are organizational charts used in organizations?
5. How do businesses conduct meetings?
6. What is the best procedure for starting a small business?
7. What are the advantages and disadvantages of buying on credit?
8. What conflicts arise when dealing with international firms?
9. Which format do personnel directors prefer for résumés?
10. Which letter formats are used predominately in business?
11. What is the average reading level of letters written by a particular firm?
12. What is the average reading level of articles in one of the popular weekly magazines?
13. Can the parking situation on campus be improved?
14. What is the nutritional value of food served in fast-food restaurants?
15. How can a youth organization raise funds?
16. How can time be used most effectively?
17. What is the absentee rate for a company, school, or organization?
18. What scholarships are available for students?
19. What student organizations are available on campus?
20. What community organizations are listed with the local chamber of commerce, and what are their purposes?
21. What is the composition of the work force at a particular firm?

22. Who/what/which should be recommended?
    a. Which person to hire for the job
    b. Which building site to select
    c. Which computer to purchase
    d. Which computer program to purchase
    e. Which car to purchase
    f. Where to live: on campus, off campus
    g. Whether to buy or to rent
    h. Which company to chemically treat your lawn
    i. Which insurance company to select
    j. Which furnance to buy

23. What do beginning jobs in accounting, finance, law, management, or marketing offer?

24. What is the image of women in advertising?

25. How has cigarette advertising changed over the past five years?

26. What is the history of company day-care centers?

27. What are companies proposing for in-house physical fitness centers?

28. How are company cafeteria foods selected?

29. What makes a successful businessperson?

30. How does one begin an international business?

31. What should an office manual for clerical employees contain?

32. What new office equipment should be purchased for a particular company?

33. What is the Gunning Fog index for a particular magazine article or textbook?

34. How would you invest $10,000 wisely?

35. How do international trade agreements affect the small businessperson?

36. What is the history of robotics?

37. What should be done for nontraditional students on campus?

38. How can the community help the unemployed?

39. What is the effect of training on the job?

40. Should the company sponsor an in-house seminar?

41. How do people (male and female) dress for success?

42. What are the advantages of selling on commission?

43. Which methods are best for attracting customers?

44. Which is the best sales strategy for a new product?

45. What is the history of the following?
    a. Typewriters
    b. Computers

      c. Telephones
      d. Answering machines
      e. Electronic mail

46. What are the advantages of life insurance?

47. What is the best way to develop an investment portfolio?

48. What are the procedures for initiating a grievance?

49. Is ethics a problem in businesses?

50. Who should conduct feasibility studies?

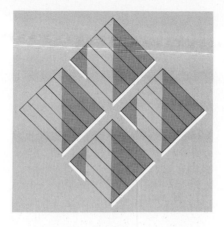

Special Applications

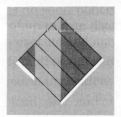

Oral Reports and Presentations

Your ability to express yourself orally can be an asset that will help make you a success in life no matter what career you choose. Every managerial position requires regular oral reports, and the better your skills at presenting material orally, the more knowledgeable you will appear. A successful oral presentation to the right audience can make a significant contribution to your career.

Topics

Preparation
Visual Aids
Delivery
Audience Participation
Feedback
Television and Videotape Presentations
Team Presentations

Most important business reports are written, but many of these written reports will have to be presented orally as well. In addition, routine business life will require many less formal oral reports. The short, informal talks are those given when a supervisor calls you in the office and asks for the sales figures for the week or when the manager stops by your desk and asks for your recommendation on a particular policy or procedure. Longer, more formal speeches include those given to groups at sales conventions, board of directors' meetings, dinner meetings, conventions, seminars, and civic gatherings, such as the Chamber of Commerce or City Commission meeting.

Oral reports have one advantage over written reports: message transmission and feedback are immediate. Oral communication provides speaker and listener with the opportunity to discuss and exchange information until the message is clearly understood.

Oral communication is important, too, because it provides you with an opportunity to express your convictions and beliefs as well as your ideas. If you are a dynamic speaker, you can impress others not only with your knowledge but also with your personality. For this reason, oral reports can be more persuasive than their written counterparts.

Your ability to communicate orally is especially important when you apply for a job. When you can express yourself well, you have an edge. Also, once you have the job, an ability to communicate orally will separate you from those who are ineffective communicators. Your oral skills can be the reason for your advancement on the job and your success in life.

Effective oral communication calls for all of the same skills that contribute to effective written communication. See especially those techniques outlined in Chapter 16. In addition, oral reports call for special skills of preparation, delivery, use of visual aids, audience participation, and feedback. This chapter will emphasize the techniques required for formal oral reports. If you master them, the shorter, informal presentations will be easy.

PREPARATION

Two general aspects of oral reporting are preparation and delivery. Preparation includes determination of the purpose, audience analysis, and organization.

Purpose

The three purposes of oral presentations are (1) to inform, (2) to persuade, and (3) to entertain. Technically, oral reports fall into the first category, even though they also perform the other report functions of interpreting and analyzing data, drawing conclusions, and making recommendations.

What are some
types of
informational
reports?

Inform   When you are asked to report on a study you conducted, conduct a training seminar, explain a procedure or policy, describe a new product or service, or convey information to an audience, your general purpose is to inform.

Informational talks present objective data, such as facts and figures, explanations, or descriptions. So that your audience will understand the information you present, concentrate on clarity. A clear and well-organized message helps your audience remember the content. Select words that convey your exact meaning, and when you are describing an item that is unfamiliar to your audience, use analogies. Analogies compare the known with the unknown (see Chapter 14).

The organizational pattern of an informational presentation is similar to the pattern used for written messages. When your audience will accept your message, use the immediate presentation, beginning with your main point first and then concluding with supporting details.

When your audience may reject your message, use the delayed presentation by beginning with supporting details and summarizing with conclusions and recommendations.

How do persuasive
talks differ from
informational ones?

Persuade   When you want your audience to accept or reject a proposal, buy or sell a product or service, change a behavior or attitude, vote on an amendment, or support a cause, your general purpose is to persuade.

Persuasive talks require logical and psychological appeals in addition to facts and figures. As in written communication, persuasive presentations use the following pattern of organization:

1. **Attract Attention.** Begin by asking rhetorical questions, giving startling statistics, telling amusing anecdotes, or showing how the audience will benefit from the presentation, product, or proposal.

2. **Arouse and Maintain Interest.** Provide explanations and definitions. Provide physical and psychological descriptions. How will the audience benefit?

3. **Convince and Prove.** Deliver the facts. Demonstrate the product. Supply samples. Tell how others have benefited (give names). Provide testimonials. Give the results of performance tests.

4. **Ask for Action.** Having described the product, service, or concept and having convinced your audience, you end your persuasive presentation by encouraging them to act as you requested.

Entertain   Oral presentations meant to be entertaining include humorous speeches, drama, suspense stories, and dramatic readings. Entertaining an audience requires enthusiasm, colorful and descriptive language, body movement, vitality, creativity, and genuine love for people and attention.

How is humor used
in business
presentations?

Although the purpose of some oral presentations is pure entertainment, most business presentations use entertainment within an informative or persuasive context to provide a release from tension, stress, boredom, or fatigue. Humor can be effective in changing the pace, proving a point, relating to an audience, and attracting and holding an audience's attention.

Here are a few guidelines for including some entertainment in your presentations:

1. Know your audience. Will they appreciate humor?
2. Avoid ethnic, religious, and other jokes that belittle, ridicule, insult, offend, or embarrass others.
3. Make your humorous material relevant to your topic.
4. Practice telling jokes to your friends first. If they laugh, use the jokes on your audience.
5. Keep humorous stories short and to the point.

Audience Analysis

The most important step in developing an oral presentation is to analyze your audience. In addition to those questions applicable to all reports you should also consider:

1. What is the size of your audience? 5? 25? 50? 500? 5,000?
2. What is their educational background? high school? college? Do they hold degrees? bachelor's? master's? doctorate? In what areas? educational? technical? medical?
3. What are their occupations? educators? government employees? business people? technical people? medical personnel?
4. What is the background of your audience? age? income? social? cultural? religious? political?
5. Is your audience male? female? mixed?
6. What is the audience's relationship to you? personal? professional?
7. What does the audience know about your subject? What do they not know about it?
8. Why does the audience want to hear you?
9. What is your purpose in addressing the audience?
10. What is the attitude of the audience toward you? your topic? What are your audience's biases?
11. Does the audience expect a speech that will inform? convince? persuade? entertain?

Other questions you should consider when preparing your oral presentation are

1. How much time do you have or need? 20 minutes? 45 minutes? one hour?

2. Will you allow for questions and answers? If so, how much time?

Why must you
know in advance if
you are the
keynoter?

3. Are you the keynoter? luncheon or banquet speaker?

4. Where will your presentation be held? classroom? conference room? meeting room? auditorium?

5. Which visual aids will best communicate your message? boards? charts or graphs? projectors? videotapes?

You may not be able to obtain answers to all your questions. But the more answers you have, the better the relationship will be between you and your audience and the more appropriate your presentation. Many presenters make the mistake of assuming that their audience has the same background, interests, and attitudes as they do. A speaker with a technical background in a subject addressing a nontechnical audience faces the same difficulties as a writer attempting to explain a technical subject in a report to a reader without technical expertise.

How do you analyze an audience? The best way, of course, is to talk directly with the individuals who will comprise your audience. Obviously, this method is impractical, and in most cases, impossible. So, your next step is to ask the person who invites you to give the presentation. That person is usually familiar with the group members and the group's goals and objectives.

Once you have the information about your audience, how does it influence you? When you know, for example, that the size of your audience will be large, you would select visual aids appropriate for that size group. You would want to be sure that everyone could hear and see you. Also, you know that with a large audience the chance is greater for having a heterogeneous group—a group that will have variation in attitudes, education, and knowledge about the subject.

Whom should you
address in a large,
diverse group?

A large, diverse group presents a difficult challenge; if you attempt to meet everyone's needs, your presentation will lose focus and you will please no one as a result. Attempt instead to meet the needs of a representative member of the audience. You will not please everyone equally, but at least you will be addressing the needs of most members of the audience.

Regardless of its size, you should attempt to discover the attitude your audience has toward you and your topics. When you know, for example, that your audience has a positive attitude toward you and your topic, you can begin immediately with your subject matter. On the other hand, if you know that your audience has a negative attitude toward you, you may wish to have someone else give the presentation. If that is impossible, try to find out why the audience has those negative thoughts. If you know the audience has a positive attitude toward you but a negative attitude toward your subject, you can plan your presentation to allay those negative feelings. Begin your presentation with something positive and try to explain why you have taken your particular position.

When you know, for example, the educational level of your audience and how much they know about the subject, you can adapt your vocabulary for your audience, explain terms they will not understand, and use visual aids that will clarify and emphasize major points.

Remember that, unless you are reporting to one person only, no audience is uniform or completely homogeneous. You analyze the audience as best you can so that you know what to emphasize and what to avoid. Understanding the audience's makeup enables you to select your topic, to tailor your presentation, and to adapt your material to their needs and interests. The more you know about your audience in advance, the better you can predict how they will respond to you and your message, and the more effective you will be as a speaker.

Organization

After you have determined the general and specific purposes of your oral presentation and have analyzed your audience, your next step is to collect all the information, materials, examples, statistics, and visual aids that you will be using and arrange them in an orderly manner.

The order of arrangement will depend on the purpose of your presentation, the audience, the setting (physical environment), and the circumstances (psychological environment). Several methods of arrangement are available—deductive, inductive, chronological—and are discussed in Chapter 16.

Regardless of what arrangement you select, all oral presentations will have three main parts—opening, body, and closing.

Opening

What purposes are served by the opening remarks?

The purpose of the opening (or introduction) is to (1) establish rapport with the audience, (2) attract the audience's attention, (3) create interest in your subject, and (4) orient the audience to the purpose and plan of your presentation.

Your opening is critical because the way you begin will usually determine the audience's attitude toward you and your message. The following techniques have been used effectively by professionals:

1. Unusual, suspenseful, or startling statement; arresting fact
2. Reference to the audience or to familiar event
3. Rhetorical question
4. Quote
5. Joke
6. Humorous story
7. Anecdote
8. Background information

9. Preview or plan of your presentation

10. Benefit or promise to solve a problem

11. Goodwill statement

What are four opening techniques you should avoid?

Techniques that you should avoid are

1. Apologizing to your audience

2. Criticizing the circumstances, setting, competitor, or opponent

3. Condemning or complaining

4. Using profanity

These techniques could alienate you from your audience. No matter what technique you select to begin your oral presentation, it must be relevant to your topic; otherwise, you are wasting not only your time but also your audience's. A successful opening is one that has the audience anticipating the heart of your presentation.

Before you actually begin your presentation, mingle and talk with members of your audience whenever possible. Doing so will help you establish rapport. Also, be alert for any information that you could use within your talk. Information gleaned from the audience beforehand will help you identify with the group.

What are ways to involve the audience?

After you have been introduced, be sure to thank the person who introduced you and the person who invited you to speak. Also, it is a good idea to get the audience involved at the beginning of the presentation. With large groups, you can do this by having them applaud someone in the group, perhaps the chairperson who organized a successful program. Another way to involve a large audience is to have them raise their hands in response to questions about their interests. Small groups may answer questions directly, or introductions may be used to relax the group.

Body

Just as the body of the written report is its heart, the body is also the heart of the oral report. The opening is the introduction that tells your audience what you are going to say, the body is where you tell them, and the closing is the conclusion that summarizes what you have told them.

Like the written report, the oral report contains a central thesis (theme) with main ideas and supporting details. The central thesis, which gives the purpose of the presentation and summarizes the main idea, is usually stated immediately after the introduction.

How many main ideas are acceptable in an oral report?

Following the thesis are the main ideas with their supporting details, which in turn support the central theme. A good oral presentation will not have more than five main ideas because it is difficult for an audience to retain more than that.

Supporting statements include definitions, descriptions, examples, illustrations, visual aids, statistics, testimonials, and quotations. They all help convince and prove that what you are saying has credibility. In outline form, you would have

Central Theme
I. Main Idea 1
  A. Supporting Details
  B. Supporting Details

II. Main Idea 2
  A. Supporting Details
  B. Supporting Details

III. Main Idea 3
  A. Supporting Details
  B. Supporting Details
    1. Subsupporting Material
    2. Subsupporting Material

See Chapter 16 for a discussion of the various ways to arrange the content of the body of the oral report.

Closing

Why is the conclusion called the action ending?

The closing or conclusion is the clincher of the oral presentation and, some authorities say, the most important part because it is the last impression the audience will have of you.

The conclusion recaps, restates, or summarizes the central theme—it tells the audience what you have told them. The conclusion is the action ending. It can propose a solution, quote an authority, challenge the audience, recommend a course of action, or visualize the main ideas of your presentation.

The *worst* way to conclude is by saying "That's it" or "That's all," as if you did not know how to end or what else to say. You should also avoid saying "thank you," as though you are grateful the audience members have not left yet. When you indeed are thankful for an audience's participation or attention, be specific about what you are thanking them for: "Thank you for your warm response."

VISUAL AIDS

In written reports, graphic aids clarify complex information. In oral reports, visual aids are effective in helping the audience understand the oral message.

Visual aids are used in oral presentations to

1. Clarify concepts
2. Attract attention
3. Add interest

4. Support statements

5. Convince the audience

6. Emphasize facts

7. Simplify ideas

8. Increase retention

9. Prove points

10. Enliven presentations

11. Reinforce verbal messages

12. Supplement speech

13. Minimize misunderstandings

14. Explain statistics or relationships

15. Add variety

16. Help the speaker remember the material

What percentage
do we remember of
what we hear? see?
hear *and* see?

Like graphic aids, visual aids supplement the text; they are not substitutes for it. They are planned and prepared to aid the speaker get the message across to the audience. Visual aids are important because they help the audience remember. Studies have shown that we remember only about 25 percent of what we hear, but we remember approximately 40 percent of what we see, and nearly 60 percent of what we hear and see.

Although the most important visual aid is the speaker (as discussed later in this chapter), the frequently used visual aids are boards, charts and graphs, handouts, samples, models, projectors, and videotapes.

Boards

Chalkboards, display boards, poster boards, and flip charts are the main types of boards used to present visual material. Boards may be used to present outlines, key terms, formulas, flow charts, or graphs.

Line graphs, bar charts, pie charts (see Chapter 15) and other miscellaneous charts, such as diagrams and layouts, can be prepared ahead of time and displayed on just about every medium—boards, flip charts, transparencies, and slides. Charts and graphs are used effectively when statistical data need to be presented to show percentages, trends, and relationships. The main advantage of using charts and graphs as visual aids are that they are portable, easy to prepare, easy to handle, recalled easily, and can be prepared ahead of time. Their disadvantages are that they are difficult to prepare in sizes appropriate for large groups and generally require professionals to prepare them attractively.

What is the main
advantage of
chalkboards? the
main disadvantage?

Chalkboards   Chalkboards are familiar to all of us. Most conference rooms and meeting rooms have them installed permanently. Portable chalkboards are also readily available. The main advantage of chalkboards is that they are one of the easiest to use and least expensive visual aids. Their main disadvantage is that space is limited, and messages must be continually written and erased, which is an inconvenience to the speaker and sometimes a distraction to the audience.

Boards can be prepared ahead of time. For example, you can place an outline of your speech on the board before the talk, and then refer to it during the presentation. When you decide to use a chalkboard, remember the following guidelines:

1. **Write legibly.** Make characters (words and symbols) large enough so that everyone can see and read what you have written on the board. Stand to the left and write until you get to the middle of the board. Then switch sides and, standing at the right, start writing at the middle of the board.

2. **Keep messages simple.** Use key words or phrases rather than complete sentences.

3. **Stand to the side of the board.** After you have written your message on the board, stand to one side to make your comments.

4. **Use a pointer.** When it is necessary to single out a fact, use a pointer rather than your finger.

5. **Keep the board clean.** After you have made comments on what you have written on the board, erase the board and go on to another topic. Boards filled with writing can distract the audience.

Display Boards   Felt, flannel, peg, and magnetic display boards are used when the information will be displayed throughout the presentation or when the speaker wishes to add to the display as the speech progresses. The felt or flannel board has a rectangular surface covered with flannel or felt. Display items are backed with material that adheres to the boards. The speaker can add on to the display or rearrange items already displayed. Pegboards have small holes to receive hooks for holding items. Pegboards are especially useful for displaying three-dimensional objects. Magnetic boards require magnetized letters, figures, and objects that adhere to the surface of the board. The main advantage of using felt, flannel, peg, and magnetic display boards is that the speaker can relocate items and create new messages without too much difficulty. Their disadvantage is that they are not flexible and not always available. Display boards can be mounted on the wall, can be placed on an easel or tripod, or can stand by themselves.

What is the main advantage of display boards? the main disadvantage?

Poster Boards   Many speakers prefer poster boards for presentations for several reasons:

1. They are readily available.
2. They can be prepared ahead of time.
3. They are portable.
4. They are inexpensive.

5. They can be used on both sides.

6. They can be mounted most anywhere—wall, easel, tripod, table, podium.

7. They come in a variety of colors and textures.

8. They come in standard sizes of 20″ by 24″.

The main disadvantage of poster boards is that they are inappropriate for large groups. Posters are most effective when they are prepared professionally, which can be expensive. Remember these guidelines when preparing posters:

1. Use a separate poster for each idea.

2. Keep the message simple. Use as few words as possible. Avoid clutter.

3. Use broad, bold lettering so all can see the message.

4. Use color for emphasis.

5. Make the posters attractive by providing plenty of white space.

Flip Charts   Flip charts consist of a pad of paper—usually 28″ by 34″ —mounted on an easel or tripod. They, too, are easy to prepare and inexpensive. Sheets can be prepared ahead of time or during the presentation. When the speaker is finished with one sheet, he or she merely flips it over and goes on to the next sheet. Should the sheet be needed later, the speaker can flip the sheets back. Although black markers are best for flip charts because they show up best, color markers are good for highlighting points. The main disadvantage of flip charts is that they are small and not effective for large audiences.

Handouts

When should handouts be distributed?

Handouts are written materials distributed to the audience either before or after the oral presentation. If handouts serve as worksheets, for example, they should be distributed ahead of time; otherwise, distribute them at the end to avoid having people looking at them during your presentation. Handouts can be color coded for easy reference. They can be single sheets of information; packets or folders of many sheets; or copies of pamphlets, brochures, books, or magazines. Handouts are useful for

1. Providing statistical or complex data

2. Providing material you do not have time to cover

3. Serving as an agenda

4. Evaluating your presentation

The main advantage of handouts is that each person has an individual copy of the material that may be kept. People like handouts. The disadvantage of handouts is that they can be expensive to distribute to large groups, especially if they consist of several pages.

Samples

Samples are used to show audiences the actual object. The main advantage of using samples in an oral presentation is that they are authentic; they are not models or replicas. When objects are small, they can actually be passed around in small groups. When objects are large, they can be displayed on a table or platform for all to examine. The disadvantage of using samples is that they may be too small or too large to display conveniently, in which case models would have to be used.

Models

When an object cannot be displayed for one reason or another (too small, too large, or unavailable), a model, usually built to scale, represents the object. Models may be used by architects to show the plans or design for a new building, by salespeople to demonstrate a new product, or by engineers to illustrate a particular system. The advantage of using models is that sometimes they can be more effective than the actual sample. A model of an engine, for example, can be disassembled so that the audience can see the internal workings. Also, an enlarged model of a small object can be viewed by the audience better than the actual sample. In some cases models may be a good deal less expensive than a sample; in other cases a model may be costly or unavailable for showing.

When are models used?

Projectors

The four main projectors are overhead, opaque, slide, and movie.

Overhead Projectors The overhead projector projects images on a screen. Material to be projected is placed on a transparency—a thin sheet of thermoplastic especially designed to accept images, usually by a process of heat transfer.

The speaker, facing the audience, can stand next to the overhead projector and point out important areas on the transparency using a pointer or pencil. The speaker can also highlight material on or add material to a transparency by using a special felt-tip marker.

Transparencies are available in several colors. Material may also be added to a transparency by means of overlays. An overlay begins with a single transparency. Additional transparencies are attached and exposed one at a time. Place the second transparency over the first one, the third over the second, and so on until you achieve your composite picture.

Overhead projectors are probably the most popular and most widely

What is a transparency?

How is material added to a transparency?

used visual aids in oral presentations because of their many advantages over other visual aids. The advantages of the overhead projector are that it

1. Is easy and simple to use.
2. Can be used in a fully lighted room.
3. Can be used for any size group—large or small.
4. Lets you face the audience and maintain eye contact.
5. Permits you to cover material point by point.
6. Puts you in control. By turning off the projector, you direct the audience's attention to you and away from the screen.
7. Can be operated by the speaker or another person.
8. Permits the speaker to mark on a transparency as it is being shown on the screen.
9. Is portable.
10. Is silent and does not distract the audience.
11. Permits the speaker to point directly on a transparency rather than on the screen.

Another advantage is that transparencies can be easily, quickly, and inexpensively made on many copy machines. One disadvantage of the overhead projector is the initial expense, although overhead projectors can be rented for nominal fees at most convention sites. Another disadvantage of the overhead projector is that it is subject to breakdowns. Lamps burn out frequently, so it is a good idea to have a spare one on hand.

Although a separate screen is best for showing images, a wall would suffice. Practice your presentation before you deliver it to an audience. You will need to find the best place for stacking the transparencies you are about to use and those you have used already. You will also need to coordinate transparencies with the relevant material in your presentation so that you use each transparency at the proper time.

The following guidelines will help you prepare transparencies:

1. Write large and legibly.
2. Title and label all information on a transparency.
3. Use colored markers (available at office supply stores) on clear transparencies for emphasis.
4. Use colored transparencies for eye appeal.
5. Limit each transparency to a key idea. Avoid solid blocks of material.
6. Provide plenty of white space.
7. Prepare neat, well-planned, and well-balanced transparencies.
8. Frame transparencies you plan to reuse for easy handling and storage.

What is the main
advantage of the
opaque projector?
the major
disadvantage?

Opaque Projectors   Like the overhead projector, the opaque projector also projects images on a screen. Unlike the overhead projector, though, it projects images from materials typed or printed on opaque paper. That is the main advantage of the opaque projector. You do not need to prepare transparencies. You can use any available printed material appropriate for your presentation—pages from a book or magazine, pictures and photographs, business forms, and other similar items.

The major disadvantage is that an opaque projector requires a dark room, which puts the speaker at a disadvantage. The speaker in effect loses control of the audience. Other disadvantages are that opaque projectors are expensive, awkward, generally unavailable, and noisy.

What is the
advantage of using
slides as visual
aids? the
disadvantage?

Slide Projectors   Slide projectors are popular for showing photographs or pictures of people, places, and things. The main advantages of a slide projector are the realism of the color and the accuracy of the photographs. In other words, slide projectors provide for true and accurate reproductions. Slide projectors also have remote controls that allow the speaker to operate the projector from the front of the room. The disadvantage of slide projectors is that the room must be dark, which again puts speakers at a disadvantage because they no longer have eye contact with the audience.

Audiotapes   When a special message must be delivered with word-for-word accuracy, a tape recorder may be used in conjunction with a slide presentation to present material in a prearranged order. When using audiotapes, be sure that they are clear and audible. When the tape is garbled and the audience must strain to make out the words, everyone becomes frustrated.

Movie   Because movies provide both motion and sound, they give a more realistic and, hence, believable presentation of information. Movies, however, are substitutes for the oral presentation and not supplements. They replace the speaker. The main advantage is that they provide the movement and sound needed in certain situations. When the same information must be delivered in the same way to different audiences in different locations or at different times, a movie may be the most economical means of conveying the message. Salespeople, for example, use movies to show their products or services; engineers use them to show how their mechanisms or systems operate. The disadvantages of movies are that they are expensive and require a projector, screen, and a dark room.

Video Presentations

Closed-circuit television, videotape recorders, and monitors have been effective instructional devices and are being used increasingly in oral presentations for many reasons.

1. They allow for filming interviews, demonstrations, events, working operations, on-the-spot activities, and other scenes and situations that lend themselves to being taped.

2. They provide for immediate feedback. After rewinding, the tape can be played again for a complete critique.

3. They provide an opportunity for the speaker to rehearse the presentation on tape, play it back so it can be analyzed or critiqued by another person, and rehearse it again.

4. Videotapes can be used repeatedly. When you no longer wish to use a particular tape, erase it and use it again.

5. Because videotapes do not require film processing and developing, you do not have to wait to see the recorder message.

6. They eliminate handling of all other visual aids that are to be used in the oral presentation and free the speaker to concentrate on other elements of the presentation. By videotaping charts, graphs, diagrams, and other visuals ahead of time the speaker does not have to worry about working with them during the actual presentation. The speaker merely plays the videotape and can observe the audience's reactions.

7. Videotapes can be edited. Sections of unwanted or unnecessary tape can be removed. Once the desired segments have been joined, the viewers will be unable to detect the splice. Tapes can also be shortened or lengthened to fit a specific time requirement.

What are the disadvantages of closed-circuit television and videotapes?

The disadvantages of using television and videotapes are that, although camera and recorder are portable, the equipment necessary for play-back—television or monitors, carts and stands, and electrical cords and outlets—can be bulky and cumbersome. Also, monitors are inappropriate for large audiences unless several can be placed throughout the room or large wall-sized screens are available so that everyone can see.

Guidelines

People expect visual aids in oral presentations, and effective speakers use them. Visual aids not only help the speaker control the meeting but also keep the audience alert and attentive to what the speaker is saying. Your success as an oral presenter will depend to some extent on the visual aids you select and how skillfully you use them. The following guidelines apply to the various aids in general:

1. Prepare visual aids in advance.

2. Keep them organized.

3. Keep them clear, uncluttered, and brief.

4. Keep them simple and understandable.

5. Make them legible. Print. Use bold, black lettering or bright colors. Use only large capital letters.

6. Make them realistic.
7. Keep them manageable.
8. Check them for accuracy.
9. Use only relevant information.
10. Place them where everyone can see them.
11. Use only visual aids appropriate for your presentation.
12. Stand to the left or right of the visual aid; do not block the audience's view.
13. Remove visual aids after they have served their purposes.
14. Adjust the projected images by focusing, raising, or lowering them.
15. Use the projector's on/off switch to control the audience's attention.
16. Use a pointer for directing the audience's attention to particular points.
17. Have them prepared by a professional.
18. Check to see that you have all the necessary equipment, such as extension cords, spare lamp, empty reel, pointer, markers, chalk, eraser, pen and pencils, hooks and pins, stands and charts. Also check for electrical outlets in the room when you will be using electrical equipment.
19. Check visual aids before the audience arrives. Sit in a far corner to test visibility. Focus a transparency (or film) ahead of time.
20. Face the audience at all times, and maintain eye contact. Avoid talking to visual aids or turning your back to the audience.
21. Test all equipment and make sure everything is in operating order.
22. Be creative when preparing visual aids.

DELIVERY

Once you have done your homework—selected and researched your topic, determined your purpose, analyzed your audience, and organized your material for presentation—you are ready for the delivery of your message.

You have seen and heard good speakers—in the classroom, on stage, or on television. You know a good speaker when you hear one. Just what are the physical characteristics of good speakers? In addition to preparing quality materials, good speakers know how to overcome stage fright and how to make a good appearance. They also know how to use their body movements and how to use their voices.

Stage Fright

What are some
techniques for
reducing anxiety?

For many people, giving a speech can be a traumatic experience. Before they go on stage, their pulse rate increases, perspiration drips, hands tremble, and the body quivers. Butterflies are in the stomach, and breathing is difficult.

According to *The Book of Lists*,[1] speaking before a group is first on the list of the 14 most common human fears.

Feelings of nervousness and tension are normal even for professional speakers and generally are more noticeable to the individual than they are to the audience. Some of the world's greatest orators—Demosthenes, Lincoln, Churchill—had speech impediments, which they were able to overcome with practice and persistence. And so can you.

The following guidelines can help you reduce your anxieties about giving an oral presentation:

1. Select a familiar topic, one in which you are sincerely interested and about which you have strong convictions.

2. Prepare for your presentation. Research your topic and know it thoroughly. Prepare more material than time will permit you to present.

3. Practice your speech repeatedly until you are confident in what you say and how you say it. Do not, however, memorize your speech.

4. Use gestures and movements to help channel your nervous energy.

5. Have a positive mental attitude toward yourself and your audience. Tell yourself that you are competent and confident, and that is what you will be.

6. Remember that some nervousness is normal and can actually work for you rather than against you. Your audience probably will not notice that you are nervous unless you tell them. Use the extra energy to gain enthusiasm.

7. Be enthusiastic and excited about what you have to say. Be lively, and so will your audience.

Appearance

To create a successful image, speakers should consider carefully their overall appearance. Remember the sayings: (1) you do not have a second chance to make a first impression and (2) you give two speeches at the same time—the one heard and the one seen.

What is appropriate
attire for a speaker
in a formal setting?
an informal setting?

Your audience will form its first impression of you by your appearance. And speakers show an interest in their audience by dressing neatly and appropriately. Inappropriate dress detracts from your mes-

---

[1]David Wallechinsky, Irving Wallace, and Amy Wallace, *The Book of Lists* (New York: Bantam Books, 1977) 469.

sage. In a formal setting, formal attire is a must—in cooler months, a three-piece suit for men and a suit or dress with jacket for women. In less formal situations, men may wear a sports jacket and slacks, and women wear dresses. Wear comfortable clothing and choose colors that complement you. Avoid extremes in dress, flashy colors, and trendy fashions. Be conservative rather than flamboyant.

Speakers should also concentrate on other factors that contribute to their total grooming—hair, fingernails, shoes, jewelry, and cologne. Neatness counts: hair should be trim and clean, clothes pressed, shoes polished and well maintained, jewelry and cologne used sparingly, and fingernails manicured. Men may wish to shave right before a presentation to avoid "five o'clock shadow." Women may wish to touch up their makeup before stepping on stage.

Avoid chewing gum and smoking. Nothing is more distasteful than to see a speaker chewing gum and trying to speak at the same time. Words come out garbled, and, of course, the sight of the jaws going up and down and the sound of cracking gum are offensive to an audience. Smoking is another nervous habit that speakers should avoid when giving a presentation. In addition to being distracting and distasteful, smoking can actually be a health hazard for some people in the audience.

When you are on the platform giving an oral presentation, keep in mind that you are on display. All eyes are on you, and you want to look your best and be your best.

Body Movements

Body movements are significant and speak more loudly than words. As a speaker, you should know what they are and how to use them effectively. The three main body movements are posture, facial expressions, and gestures.

Posture   Your posture communicates a powerful message to your audience whether you are sitting, standing, or moving. A slovenly or slouching posture portrays disrespect, laziness, indifferent attitude, a lack of interest, and careless physical habits. And when you display careless physical habits, your audience will assume you also have careless mental habits.

Standing or sitting erect, on the other hand, shows vitality, respect, interest, alertness, and a positive mental attitude. Strong, definite movements—especially when walking—project confidence; weak, hesitating movements reflect insecurity.

To present the perfect posture, speakers should stand firmly on both feet. Shifting weight from one foot to another indicates a speaker who is uncomfortable, ill at ease, or nervous. The speaker who has good posture—head erect, shoulders back, and stomach in—commands the audience's attention. Poor posture—head down, shoulders rounded, and stomach out—portrays a lack of confidence, enthusiasm, and forcefulness.

Facial Expressions   The face is a potent source of information; it can form over twenty thousand expressions. Facial expressions—including smiles, frowns, scowls, and grimaces—reveal emotions such as happiness, sadness, anger, delight, love, and hate. When you are feeling good about yourself, your facial expressions will show your confidence. When you are uncomfortable and nervous, your facial expression will reveal your anxiety. Develop a positive mental attitude so that you can face an audience with a smile, an expression that shows interest, warmth, and good will.

What are two reasons eye contact is important?

Eye contact can also reveal your feelings. People who avoid direct eye contact seem to say, "I feel inferior," "I'm guilty," "I'm unprepared," "I'm not interested," or "I'm afraid." When you avoid eye contact with your audience, you cannot see how they are reacting to your message.

A good speaker, one who has control and confidence, looks the audience in the eyes and not over their heads. The speaker is saying "I'm interested in you," "I respect you," or "I'm attentive to your needs." A good speaker does not stare at one person but scans the entire audience looking directly into their eyes, observing their behavior, and nonverbally asking for their approval. When a speaker observes that the audience is bored or lost, he or she can change the pace, ask questions, or call for a stretch break.

Gestures   Gestures are motions made by our bodies to help express our thoughts. Gestures are normal reactions in communication with others. For example, we nod our heads in agreement, and we shake our heads when we disagree. Some people use gestures more than others. Some seasoned speakers use gestures intuitively; some beginning speakers are inhibited and are unable to move, let alone gesture.

Gesturing can be very effective in speaking. Gestures can contradict, complement, or substitute for words. A clenched fist, for example, can signify conviction, a bang on the lectern can call attention to the audience, and a frown can indicate anger.

Speakers also use gestures to emphasize and enumerate. For example, a speaker points the index finger for emphasizing a fact, or raises the fingers one at a time to enumerate 1, 2, 3 . . . .

Too much gesturing, however, can be distracting. Learn to use gestures spontaneously and sparingly. As a speaker, observe also the gestures of your audience. When you see their heads nodding and their bodies fidgeting and twisting in the chairs, adjust your presentation—announce a 10-minute break.

Voice

Vocal qualities and elements, such as volume, rate, pitch, diction, and paralanguage, are other primary sources of information in communication. They communicate our attitudes and emotions to the audience.

Why must speakers adjust voice volume? Why should they vary it?

Volume   Volume—or loudness of sound—is a quality that all speakers need to develop to get their messages across to an audience. Obviously, if your message is to be heard, you need to project your voice; that is, increase its volume and power so that everyone can hear you. Speakers also need to adjust the volume of their voices to the size of the audience, the size of the room, and to other noises surrounding them while they are giving an oral presentation.

Variations in volume—loud to soft—are effective in controlling an audience's attention. For example, speakers who do not vary the volume of their voices lack interest and expressiveness. Variation in volume is needed to alert the audience to what is important and to emphasize key ideas. Speaking loudly for the entire presentation not only wears out the speaker but also the audience.

Rate   The rate (or pace) of speaking—fast or slow—will depend to some extent on the material being presented. When material is uncomplicated or less important, you can increase your pace; when material is complex, essential, and important, decrease your pace so that the audience has time to digest the information.

Beginning speakers usually speak too fast because they are nervous. And when speakers are nervous, they cannot breathe properly; they're gasping for breath, which makes them uncomfortable and the audience uncomfortable, as well. Also, audiences find it difficult and tiring to follow a speech that is delivered rapidly.

Experienced and professional speakers possess the art of increasing or decreasing their rate of delivery at appropriate times to achieve their desired effect. They adjust their rate according to their audiences and their material.

What do pauses accomplish?

Pauses help to slow a speaker's rate of delivery and are effective in gaining the audience's attention. When you practice your oral presentation, deliberately plan pauses to emphasize particular points.

Why should you avoid a monotone? How can you do so?

Pitch   Pitch refers to the highs and lows in our voices. When speakers do not vary their pitch, the result is a monotone. Speakers who speak in a monotone lull their audiences to sleep and come across as being lazy and lifeless. Being enthusiastic and excited about your message, however, can eliminate sameness of pitch. When you are excited, your voice automatically changes pitch, which dispels monotone.

Because everyone is capable of achieving a variety of ranges in pitch, you can improve your pitch by practicing. Record your presentation on a tape recorder, listen to yourself, and have someone else listen and evaluate your voice. Where do you need to improve? Practice repeatedly, and your voice will improve.

Diction Speakers who do not enunciate their words, who garble or mumble, who swallow or mispronounce their words, are violators of good diction—speaking clearly and distinctly. Pronounce every syllable in a word:

Say: *interest,* rather than *intrest*
            going to, rather than gonna

and pronounce words correctly

Say: *get,* rather than *git*
            for, rather than *fir*
            want to, rather than *wanna*
            yes, rather than *yeah*

When you are not sure of the correct pronunciation of a word, check the dictionary. To improve poor diction, open your mouth wide and pronounce words correctly, clearly, and distinctly.

What is
paralanguage?

Paralanguage Paralanguage refers to the nonverbal voice qualities (pitch, volume, rate) and to vocalizations (throat clearing, coughing, laughing, crying). Similar to paralanguage are meaningless words, habitual expressions, and mindless repetitions, a few of which are *um, uh, okay, you know, and what not, you see,* and *see what I mean.*

Paralanguage communicates our attitudes and emotions. By paralanguage, we tell our audience whether we are nervous or relaxed or comfortable or uncomfortable. The audience, for example, can detect variations in our pitch and sense our nervousness.

Effective speakers learn to control nervous mannerisms by practicing their presentation on audio and video recorders.

AUDIENCE PARTICIPATION

Because people learn by doing and because people learn from each other, have the audience participate in your oral presentation. You can do this in several ways.

Introduction You can get the audience involved by having them introduce themselves to each other when the group size permits such an activity. Participants enjoy exchanging demographic information—name, company name, occupation, and reason for attending the session. As mentioned earlier, have the audience applaud someone for something (chairperson for organizing) early in your presentation. Getting the audience involved from the beginning helps you establish rapport with them.

How can an
audience
participate in
brainstorming?

Body   You can involve the audience by having them respond to a question by a show of hands or by calling out their responses. Another effective technique is brainstorming. You give the audience about five or ten minutes to write down their ideas, suggestions, or solutions to a problem that you have posed, and then record their responses on a chalkboard, flip chart, or transparency. You can also involve the audience by having them engage in games, role playing, and written exercises. When the group size permits it, break the audience into groups or teams of four to six people to discuss a problem or situation. After an audience has been sitting for about an hour, give them the opportunity to stand and stretch.

Conclusion   Questions and answers always provide an excellent opportunity for the audience to express themselves. Audience participation is especially helpful when your presentation is for an hour or more. Shorter talks require less participation.

FEEDBACK

Feedback is an important ingredient in oral presentations. When you want to know whether the audience has heard and understood your message, you need some kind of feedback. Feedback also helps you to improve your future presentations.

Nonverbal

One form of feedback is the audience's nonverbal behavior: puzzled looks, shaking and nodding heads, smiles, frowns, looks of approval or disapproval. When you observe this nonverbal behavior in an audience, you can adapt your speech in several ways: ask questions, restate the information, give illustrations, use visual aids, draw diagrams, or give a stretch break.

Verbal

At what point in a
formal presentation
are questions
usually asked?

Verbal feedback includes oral commentaries and written evaluations. Oral feedback is obtained through questions and answers. In informal presentations, the speaker may invite questions at any time during the presentation; in more formal situations, the speaker may call for questions only at the end of the presentation.

Observe the following suggestions when conducting the question-and-answer period after a presentation.

1. Repeat the question for the entire audience when it is necessary.
2. Keep your answers and explanations brief.

3. Give your undivided attention to the questioner when the question is being asked, but observe the entire audience as you give your response.

4. Do not spend too much time with one questioner. Acknowledge another questioner in another section of the room.

5. Answer one question at a time even if two are asked at the same time.

6. Admit it when you do not know the answer to a question. The audience will appreciate your honesty.

7. Give everyone an opportunity to ask questions. Take questions from all sections of the room—front and back, sides, and middle.

8. Invite people for a further discussion after the time period has elapsed. Or, when the room will not be used by another group, allow the audience to leave and continue to discuss an issue with those most interested.

9. Do not argue with a heckler. Answer the questions and be friendly.

10. Do not spend too much time with a hostile questioner. Answer the person courteously and quickly and move on to someone else.

So that you can improve your future presentations and identify your strengths and weaknesses, obtain feedback from your audience. Your audience will make comments informally to you and to others, and formally on an evaluation sheet, when one is provided. Because people can remain anonymous, written evaluations are more reliable than oral evaluations.

When evaluation sheets are not provided by the organization or individuals who invited you to give the presentation, prepare your own. Exhibit 18.1 illustrates an evaluation sheet.

TELEVISION AND VIDEOTAPE PRESENTATIONS

The chances are that someday you will be asked to give an oral report on television or on videotape. What will you do? How can you prepare? Here are some pointers that may help:

1. You are the visual aid so your image is important. Even though a makeup artist may do touch-ups on you, you should pay particular attention to your total grooming.

2. Most of what has been said about preparation and delivery of oral presentations also applies to television and videotaped presentations. Note especially what has been said about nonverbal communication—posture, gestures, voice.

Exhibit 18.1   Sample Evaluation Sheet of an Oral Presentation

Speaker _____

Topic _____

	Good	Acceptable	Poor
I. Organization			
A. Introduction			
1. Attracts attention	____	____	____
2. Creates interest	____	____	____
3. States purpose	____	____	____
B. Body			
1. Clarifies central theme	____	____	____
2. Emphasizes main ideas	____	____	____
3. Provides examples, explanations, descriptions, and definitions	____	____	____
C. Conclusion			
1. Summarizes	____	____	____
2. Restates theme	____	____	____
3. Has action ending	____	____	____
II. Content			
A. Clear	____	____	____
B. Easy to follow; logical	____	____	____
C. Well organized	____	____	____
III. A. Delivery			
1. Appearance	____	____	____
2. Audience involvement	____	____	____
3. Creativity	____	____	____
4. Enthusiasm	____	____	____
5. Eye contact	____	____	____
6. Facial expression	____	____	____
7. Gestures	____	____	____
8. Mannerisms	____	____	____
9. Poise	____	____	____
10. Posture	____	____	____
11. Preparation	____	____	____
12. Timing	____	____	____

Exhibit 18.1   *(continued)*

	Good	Acceptable	Poor
IV. Voice			
A. Volume (loud-soft)	___	___	___
B. Rate (fast-slow)	___	___	___
C. Pitch (high-low)	___	___	___
D. Diction			
1. Clear and distinct speech	___	___	___
2. Correct pronunciation	___	___	___
3. Correct grammar	___	___	___
E. Paralanguage			
1. Throat clearing, coughing, nervous laughter	___	___	___
2. Meaningless words ("um," "ah," "you know," "okay," "and whatnot," "you see")	___	___	___
V. Visual Aids			
A. Accurate and attractive	___	___	___
B. Readable	___	___	___
C. Simple and clear	___	___	___
D. Relevant	___	___	___

Additional Comments:

_____

_____

_____

_____

_____

_____

3. Timing is most important; be sure to practice your speech so it can be given in the allotted time.

4. Limit your topic to one central idea. Select only those words that will best convey your message. Use concrete and specific words rather than abstract and general words.

5. Watch the television show you will be appearing on at least three times to see how the host interviews the guests and how the questions are handled.

6. Ask whether the show will be videotaped or aired live. When the show is taped, editing can distort your message.

7. When possible, have the film crew avoid the "talking head" presentation. Film from a variety of distances and angles. Obtain professional help with filming and editing.

TEAM PRESENTATIONS

How is time divided in a team presentation? What are the moderator's responsibilities?

Sometimes individuals who have expertise in various areas are asked to give a presentation as a group. For example, group presentations have been effective in persuading businesspeople to invest in a certain project, in informing a company how a system will operate, or in explaining why a company should build a plant at a particular location.

When planning a group presentation, observe the following guidelines:

1. Divide the time more or less equally for each speaker.

2. Plan the presentation so that continuity prevails. You want a unified presentation and not a series of isolated individual speakers. Each speaker should tie in with what the preceding speaker has said and should make reference to the succeeding speaker.

3. Avoid repetition and overlap. Each speaker should have a specific topic not covered by any of the other speakers.

4. Direct the presentation to the audience and not to the other team members.

5. Have one member of the team serve as moderator or coordinator for the group. The moderator would be responsible for
   a. Introducing each member of the team.
   b. Making sure that each speaker observes the time limit.
   c. Handling the question-and-answer period.

SUMMARY

Oral reports are spoken messages given to two or more people. They are used every day in business at all levels of management. Oral communication is important because message transmission and feedback are immediate. Oral communication is important, too, because it provides you with the opportunity to express your ideas and beliefs, and to impress others with your knowledge and your personality. Your oral skills are important when you apply for a job or when you are considered for promotion.

Two general aspects of oral reporting are presentation and delivery. Preparation includes determination of your purpose, audience analysis, and organization. The three purposes of oral presentations are to inform, to persuade, and to entertain. The most important step in developing and planning an oral presentation is to analyze your audience. Understanding the audience's makeup enables you to select your topic, tailor your presentation, and adapt your materials to their needs and interests. All oral presentations are organized into three main parts—opening, body, and closing.

Visual aids are effective in helping the audience understand the oral message. The most frequently used visual aids are boards, charts and graphs, handouts, samples, models, projectors, and television and videotapes.

Delivering the oral presentation involves overcoming stage fright, knowing how to dress, knowing how to use body movements effectively, and using the voice to its best advantage.

Because people learn by doing and because people learn from each other, have the audience participate in your oral presentation. Feedback is important. When you want to know whether the audience has heard and understood your message, you need feedback—oral and written.

When asked to give a television or videotape presentation, practice your speech so that it can be delivered in the allotted time. Also, limit your topic to one central idea and select only those words that will best convey your message.

When planning a group presentation, divide the time equally for each speaker, plan the presentation so that continuity prevails, avoid repetition and overlap, and have one member of the team serve as a moderator.

EXERCISES

Review and Discussion Questions

1. Define oral reports. Give two examples of oral reports.
2. Why is oral communication important?
3. What are the three purposes of oral presentations?
4. What is the organizational pattern when your purpose is to inform? persuade?
5. How do you analyze an audience?
6. What are the three main parts of an oral presentation?

7. What is the purpose of the opening of an oral presentation?

8. What is the purpose of the conclusion of an oral presentation?

9. What are the three main body movements?

10. What are gestures?

11. Define volume, rate, and pitch.

12. Define paralanguage. Give three examples.

13. Name three ways an audience can participate in your oral presentation.

14. Why is feedback important?

15. Give five reasons for using visual aids in oral presentations.

Presentation Problems

1. You have been asked to give a 15-minute after-dinner speech to 500 accountants, who have had a taxing day attending meetings. Select a topic that would be interesting and entertaining to accountants.

2. One of your responsibilites as president of an organization (club, fraternity, sorority, professional group) is to give the welcome at the organization's annual conference. Prepare and present a 5-minute welcoming speech to about 200 members of your organization.

3. Prepare and present a 5-minute oral presentation that illustrates how to do something (repair a leaky faucet, install a garage door opener, change a spark plug, landscape the lawn, change a tire). Specify your audience.

Oral Report Problems

1. Prepare a 5-minute oral report for any written report you have been working on during the term. Specify your audience.

2. Make a 3-minute persuasive oral presentation to your wealthy aunt and uncle. Ask them to lend you $10,000 to complete your college education.

3. As chairperson for a site selection committee (city and hotel) for the annual convention of the National Association of (your choice), present the committee's recommendations to the association's board of directors.

4. As public relations director for a company of your choice, you have been asked to present a 5-minute oral report to your board of directors on how to improve company morale among the employees.

5. You are a representative from the Southern Power Company. Prepare a 5-minute oral presentation to the Home Owner's

Association's monthly meeting of approximately 100 members on how to conserve energy in the home.

6. Prepare and present a 5-minute oral presentation on a topic of your choice. Use appropriate visual aids.

7. You are the spokesperson for a team of engineers (carpenters, technicians, analysts) who have perfected a new process (procedure, system, mechanism). Persuade the president and vice president of the company to accept and adapt your process.

8. As a student or employee, select a problem that your school or office is trying to solve. Present your solution in a 5-minute oral report to the office manager and supervisors or to the Student Government Association.

9. Prepare and present a 5-minute oral presentation to incoming freshmen during orientation week about your college's professional and social organizations that they may wish to join.

10. Prepare and present a 5-minute oral presentation to parents who will be attending Parent Orientation Day. You will want to tell the parents something about housing and food services, financial aid and scholarships, health care services, and extracurricular activities.

11. As a student, prepare and present a 10-minute oral presentation to the dean of your college on why the college should offer a particular course in your area of interest.

12. Interview a top executive in a local business on the importance of oral presentations. Present your findings in a 5-minute oral report to the class.

13. You would like to see a change in parking regulations (registration procedures, vacation scheduling, or promotion policies). Prepare and present a 5-minute oral presentation to supervisors, managers, faculty, board of directors, or any group that will accept or reject your suggestion.

C H A P T E R 1 9

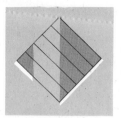

Computer-Based Reports

The amount of information available to report writers has been increasing exponentially. Approximately 90 percent of all the scientists who have ever lived are living now—and they are producing almost 10,000 scientific articles each day. The amount of associated professional material is even more overwhelming. No manager can hope to read everything he or she should to remain current in his or her occupational area. Computers, especially the microcomputer, are at least partially responsible for the information explosion. They also may prove the cure. This chapter discusses the common ways managers use comptuers and related technology to collect and process the information used in reports.

Topics

The Manager's Changing Role
Telephone and Dictation Equipment
Computer Hardware and Software
Common Computer Applications
The Computer in Your Future

As John Naisbitt and Patricia Aburdene have rightly said, we are in the process of "reinventing" the corporation.[1] The role of management is changing, and the equipment managers use to accomplish their tasks is changing as well. Regardless of the kind of organization for which you plan to work, you will be using this new technology in ways undreamed of only a few years ago.

THE MANAGER'S CHANGING ROLE

Technology is changing the way organizations do business. In fact, technology is changing the very shape of organizations. Most people are aware that the computer—through **robotics**—has eliminated many blue collar jobs by replacing people with robots. Robots now lift, carry, weld, paint, and even assemble parts in a wide variety of manufacturing industries. What is less well-known is that technology, primarily the microcomputer, has eliminated numerous middle management jobs as well.

How have the information needs of an organization traditionally been served? Why is this changing?

Middle managers have traditionally served the information needs of an organization. They were responsible for gathering, analyzing, and transmitting information to the upper level managers who made the decisions and for passing those decisions and related instructions down to the employees performing the tasks. Computers are now performing this function, allowing those doing the work to communicate directly with those who make the decisions. In general, this combination of changes means that fewer managers are responsible for supervising more employees and that each of those employees is responsible for more—and more sophisticated—equipment. This also means that the managers who remain are expected to keep track of much more information than was ever expected of managers in the past.

The offices in which managers typically work have also been changing. In the nineteenth century, clerks (the middle managers of the time) used quill pens to prepare correspondence and keep all records in massive ledger books. In the early twentieth century, typewriters made handwritten correspondence obsolete, and managers adopted the process of dictating correspondence to secretaries. By the 1960s, most offices were using electric typewriters and had installed dictation equipment to reduce the time required for dictation and transcription of correspondence: managers dictated to machines, and their words were transcribed by secretaries working in typing pools or newly formed word processing centers.

Today, managers and their administrative assistants share computer files, with managers increasingly assuming the responsibility of prepar-

---

[1]John Naisbitt and Patricia Aburdene, *Re-inventing the Corporation,* New York: Warner Books, 1985.

ing the first draft of a document before the administrative assistant puts it in final form. Each year, new technology makes increased productivity possible; it also requires, however, that business people master an increasingly complex array of equipment. From the office telephone to desktop publishing, virtually all the equipment managers use to collect and process information for presentation in reports has changed. Further, while the general concepts we provide here will remain true, virtually any specific we provide will be obsolete in a few years. The technological revolution is just beginning.

TELEPHONE AND DICTATION EQUIPMENT

What are the advantages and disadvantages of communicating by telephone?

The telephone is an extremely versatile, effective tool for business communication. Telephone communication is often the fastest, most effective way to reach an agreement with someone. Virtually every office in both the public and private sectors has at least one telephone, and the chances are excellent that it will be used several times every day. In fact, it is difficult to conceive of what life would be like today without telephones.

The telephone is also an economical means of communicating. Even long-distance phone calls can be inexpensive when they save the cost of writing a letter, prevent a misunderstanding, or help establish (or reestablish) goodwill.

Furthermore, modern telephone equipment offers expanded services such as teleconferencing, videoconferencing, and voice store-and-forward capabilities in addition to traditional one-to-one conversation.

Telephone Services

What are common telephone services, and how are they used?

The following services increase the usefulness of the telphone to businesses and many individuals.

- **WATS.**   Wide-area telephone service reduces the cost of long-distance telephone service to companies that make many calls.
- **INWATS (800 service).**   Incoming long-distance calls can be made without charge to the caller, which helps businesses establish and maintain customer goodwill.
- **Mobile phone service.**   Both local and long-distance calls can be made to and/or from automobiles, trucks, boats, and—more recently—aircraft.
- **FAX (facsimile transmission).**   Special equipment is available to transmit drawings, graphs, pictures, and written messages over the telephone lines.
- **Pagers.**   A wide variety of equipment is available to let users know when they have a call waiting. Pagers use a radio signal to "beep" the user, and, as a result they have earned the nickname, "beepers."

- **Intercom service.**   Most businesses' telephone systems provide an intercom service so that members of the organization can have direct telephone connections with each other simply by dialing a short code number.
- **Speaker phones.**   Speaker phones enable more than one person to participate in a telephone conversation.
- **Automatic sending and receiving equipment.**   Special equipment is available to automate the process of dialing phone numbers and delivering a recorded message. Other automated equipment is available to answer the telephone and record incoming messages.

Teleconferencing and Videoconferencing

What is an audio teleconference? What techniques will help ensure the success of an audio teleconference?

Audio teleconferencing is simply a telephone conversation involving several people, perhaps at several locations. A teleconference may be arranged either through the appropriate telephone company or through an organization's private communication network. Standard telephones may be used, or speaker phones may be more appropriate if several people at each location will be participating.

As a rule, a telecommunications specialist (an operator with the phone company, for example) will assist in placing the conference call at a prearranged time. Successful communication during a teleconference is a little more difficult to achieve than during a typical phone call because several people may speak at once, and more information is exchanged. The following procedure will help ensure the success of an audio teleconference:

1. **Make arrangements in advance.**   Each participant should know when he or she needs to call the designated operator. Allow enough time for equipment difficulties to be overcome.
2. **Prepare for the conference.**   Know the names of the others who will be participating. Study the issues. As much as possible, know what questions you wish to ask and what answers you wish to provide to the questions you may be asked. Organize your notes.
3. **Begin with introductions.**   Have each participant introduce himself or herself so that participants can begin to recognize each other's voices. Appoint one person the moderator, who will have the responsibility of determining whose turn it will be to speak.
4. **Let each person have a turn.**   Allow each participant a set amount of time (equal to the time allowed the others) for making an initial statement. Questions and answers should follow a predetermined order so that each participant has an equal opportunity.
5. **Summarize the conference and follow through.**   Before the teleconference is concluded, the moderator should summarize

Exhibit 19.1   Videoconference Room

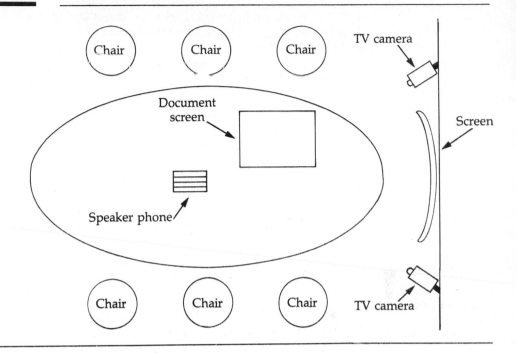

points of agreement, required actions, and the responsibilities of each of the participants. Follow through by preparing and distributing a written summary of the points of agreement and necessary actions.

What is a videoconference?

The procedures for videoconferencing, which allows participants at two or more locations to see as well as hear each other, are essentially the same as those for audio teleconferencing. The obvious difference is that appearance is more important as a result of the visual component. Because the participants can see each other, their nonverbal communication plays an important role in how their message is perceived by the others.

Videoconferencing is not yet as common in business as audio teleconferencing because the equipment is both expensive and complex, often requiring the use of satellite transmissions. The use of videoconferencing, however, is sure to increase because it is such a powerful communication tool for a wide variety of presentations and decision-making activities.

If you have ever had one of your presentations videotaped, you have some idea of how you will appear to others on a television screen. Were you happy with the image you presented? If not, you may wish to improve your areas of weakness and try again. Exhibit 19.1 illustrates a typical videoconference room so that you can approximate the conditions under which your future videoconferences may well take place.

Voice Store-and-Forward Equipment

As useful as they are, telephones have three problems: (1) they ring when you do not want them to; (2) it is often difficult to think of exactly the right thing to say on the spur of the moment, which is required in telephone conversations; and (3) the other person may not be available to answer your telephone call, and when she or he returns the call, you may not be available to answer it. The answer to these problems is voice store-and-forward equipment.

How can voice store-and-forward equipment solve common problems of communicating by mail?

Voice store-and-forward equipment provides the equivalent of an audio mail system. It is, in fact, similar to a wide-area dictation service, allowing the sender of a message to dictate the message, listen to it, and edit it before sending it to the receiver. Unlike the regular telephone system, voice store-and-forward systems are *closed;* that is, you must know a special phone number and the identification number of your receiver to be able to use the system to send or receive messages.

Each person with access to the system can check his or her "mailbox" for messages when convenient to do so. A message may be listened to several times if necessary, and a reply may be dictated at any time.

What is telephone tag?

Voice store-and-forward equipment is both practical and economical. It eliminates much of the unnecessary chit-chat included in regular telephone conversations, and it eliminates the time wasted through **telephone tag,** in which the parties keep missing each other and leaving "call back" messages. By reducing the time spent on each phone conversation, voice store-and-forward equipment may also reduce the cost of telephone service.

Dictation Equipment and Skills

Under what circumstances might dictating correspondence be more efficient than preparing it directly on a microcomputer?

Although executive use of personal and portable computers has reduced the importance of dictation in recent years, many executives still prefer to dictate letters, memos, instructions, and other short messages. Many executives, for example, use a cassette tape recorder to dictate material while commuting to and from work. Others use dictation equipment while traveling, and some dictate material for later preparation in a word processing center.

Regardless of its type, dictation equipment allows the user to stop and start the recording medium (magnetic belt or tape) quickly and easily, to edit specific portions of the recorded message, and to transmit the recorded message (either physically or electronically) to the place it will be transcribed. In some companies the telephone equipment has a special number for dictation. Other companies prefer to use standard or microcassette recorders. The following procedures apply regardless of the type of equipment you are using.

1. **Prepare before you begin.**   Write an outline for your message according to the principles presented in Chapter 16. Your notes should include all the major points you wish to make.

What techniques will help ensure that dictated material is transcribed correctly?

2. **Provide all necessary instructions for message preparation at the *beginning* of the message.**   Will it be a memo or a letter? Should it be a final copy or only a rough draft? Should it be double spaced or single spaced? Will you be sending copies to anyone? Will you need envelopes?

3. **Speak up and enunciate clearly.**   Listen to what you have dictated before sending it to be transcribed. Would you be able to understand the message if you were not already familiar with it? Do not smoke, chew gum, or eat while dictating. Repeat or spell difficult words. Distinguish clearly between singular and plural forms of words. Repeat monetary amounts and other figures (but tell the typist to omit the repetition). If you have many figures, submit them separately and in writing.

4. **Spell names, unusual words, and homonyms.**   Let the transcriber know whether you mean *there* or *their; who's* or *whose; site, sight,* or *cite.* Although a good secretary will often be able to determine what you mean from the context, it only takes one mistake for both of you to look foolish. Do not take the chance.

5. **Dictate unusual punctuation.**   If you want a semicolon instead of a comma, or instead of a period and a new sentence, say so. Indicate quotation marks, new paragraphs, parentheses (open and close).

6. **Avoid irrelevant comments.**   Irrelevant comments have a way of turning up on the typed document. Letters have been mailed including such comments as, "Who does this SOB think we are, anyway." Editorialize *before* you begin to dictate.

7. **Let the secretary make appropriate changes in grammar and punctuation.**   Your message may sound acceptable when you play it back, but some grammatical errors, such as lack of parallel construction and mismodification, may become noticeable in the printed document. Delegate responsibility for correcting errors in grammar and mechanics to the secretary.

8. **Read documents before signing or sending them.**   Because you *think* you know what the document says, it is easy to overlook mistakes. Something as small as a misplaced decimal point could cause you very big trouble.

COMPUTER HARDWARE AND SOFTWARE

How is technology changing communication, records management, and other office activities?

Most modern office equipment is based on computer technology. Modern duplicating equipment reduces, enlarges, prints on both sides, and collates materials; modern word processing equipment greatly facilitates the production of written materials. Electronic storage media reduce both the cost and space required for storing large amounts of information.

The equipment, regardless of function, is known as **hardware.** The term **software** refers to a special set of instructions—a computer program—required to make some hardware function. Complicated duplicating machines, for example, may contain a computer chip known as a **microprocessor** to control their various operations. All the possible functions are encoded into the microprocessor. A personal computer, on the other hand, is capable of performing a wide variety of functions, depending on the software the user selects.

What is a microprocessor?

The same computer may be used for word processing, financial calculations, mail list management, or telecommunications, depending on the software selected by the user. You should be familiar with the following types of hardware, software, and related terms frequently used in business:

Why are technical terms frequently used in discussing computer hardware and software?

- **ASCII.** The American Standard Code for Information Interchange allows information to be exchanged between different kinds of computers.
- **Baud.** Computers transmit data at high rates of speed measured in baud, a figure equal to the number of characters being transmitted each second times 10. Common rates are 300 baud (30 cps); 1200 baud (120 cps); 2400 baud (240 cps); and 9600 baud (960 cps). Most telecommunications programs using public telephone lines operate at either 300 baud or 1200 baud.
- **Communications programs.** Communications programs enable one computer to communicate with another (by a modem—explained later in this list). Computers that are otherwise incompatible may exchange information by using communications software. Communications software may allow two microcomputers to talk to one another or a micro to talk to a mainframe (explained later in this list). Communications software also allows individual users to access national information sources, such as CompuServe, The Source, or Dialog.
- **Configuration.** Computers and their peripheral devices must be *configured* to work with each other. The user must tell the computer which device is connected in which place and what kind of signals that device expects to send and receive. Special cables may be required to connect a computer with its peripheral devices.
- **CRT or video display.** A CRT is simply a television-like screen for viewing certain computer operations. CRTs have higher resolution than standard television screens so that they will be easier to read. CRTs are also referred to as **monitors.**
- **Database management programs.** Information that must be compared with other information is usually stored in some kind of database. A list of a company's customers showing where they live, what they have bought, and when they made their last purchase may be accessed in a variety of ways: by the name of the customer, by zip code, by purchase date, or by the amount of the purchase.

Relational database programs, which allow the user to check for multiple relationships, are extremely useful in business.

- **Disk drive.** A disk drive is the device that enables the computer to record and read the information on a disk.
- **File server.** A file server is a particular set of instructions that controls access to the files on a hard disk. A file server prevents two people from attempting to change the same information (file) at the same time.
- **Floppy disk.** Information for microcomputers and minicomputers is stored on a record-shaped sheet of specially coated mylar with a cardboard cover. A disk is able to record magnetic impulses from the computer. The computer may also read the impulses that have been stored on (**saved to**) the disk. Floppy disks may be commercially prepared with programs (program or turnkey disks), or they may be used to store user-generated data (data disks).
- **Graphics programs.** A graphics program can turn information from a spreadsheet into a neat bar graph or pie chart and print the result.
- **Hard disk.** A hard disk serves the same purpose as a floppy disk, but it holds more information and is able to access it faster. Hard disks may hold millions of bytes of data (typically 10 to 40 *mega*bytes), and they are capable of accessing the information so quickly that they can support many users simultaneously.
- **Integrated programs.** Several programs are available that combine two or more of the common functions. The most complex of the programs contain word processing, database management, spreadsheet, graphics, and communications. At least one program adds project management to the more common functions. Integrated programs have the advantage of allowing the user to move quickly and easily from one application to another, moving data as necessary. Sometimes, however, the integrated packages do not perform any of the applications as well as separate programs would.
- **Interface.** The connection between a computer and its peripheral devices is known as an interface. One of the curent problems with computer equipment is that special interfaces may be required to make one device compatible with another.
- **Keyboard.** The keyboard is the typewriter-like input device for a computer. It allows the user to communicate with the computer.
- **LAN.** LANS, or local-area networks, are means of connecting microcomputers so that they can share the same peripheral devices. Computers on a LAN, for example, may share the same hard disk, allowing many people to use the same programs and files and allowing them to send and receive electronic mail.
- **Macro.** A mainframe computer or a single-key command that initiates a preset sequence of other commands or characters. Macros

(single-key commands) are useful for entering complex data required on a regular basis.

- **Mainframe.**   The largest computers are known as mainframes or *macros*. They are large multi-user, mulit-tasking computers designed for organizational or research applications requiring either greater storage or greater computing power than is available in minicomputers.
- **Microcomputer.**   Computers are available in three basic sizes: small, medium, and large. Microcomputers, the smallest, are designed primarily for individual use. The smallest microcomputers are severely limited in their applications, while the largest of them rival minicomputers in power and versatility. Microcomputers are also known as personal computers or home computers.
- **Minicomputer.**   Minicomputers are designed primarily for business use and can usually accommodate several users and perform more than one operation at a time.
- **Modem.**   A modem (MOdulator-DEModulator) is a device that converts computer signals into a form that can be transmitted over telephone lines and converts incoming signals back into a form readable by the computer. Most modems are designed to operate at either 300 or 1200 baud. Newer modems may operate at 2400 baud.
- **Photocopiers.**   Photocopiers have all but replaced ditto and mimeograph machines for reproducing documents. Photocopiers duplicate an original by transferring the image electrostatically to a blank piece of paper. The better machines can duplicate on both sides, copy colors, copy multiple sheets automatically, collate pages in their correct order, and staple them.
- **Phototypesetters.**   Phototypesetters automatically prepare material entered on a computer keyboard for printing.
- **Printer.**   A printer converts computer signals into images on paper. Letter-quality, or correspondence-quality, printers use a daisy wheel or print thimble to transfer ink from a ribbon in the same way that typewriters put characters on paper. Dot matrix printers form their characters with a configuration of pins, which transfer the ink to the paper in corresponding dots. Laser printers use beams of light to transfer the ink to the paper.
- **Programming language.**   A special language designed to give instructions to computers is called a programming language. The most common programming languages used in business include BASIC, COBOL, FORTRAN, Pascal, and APL. Each language has certain advantages and disadvantages.
- **RAM.**   RAM, or Random Access Memory, is the storage area of the computer. When people speak of a 128 K computer, they are referring to the amount of RAM it contains. A 128 K machine contains roughly 128 *thousand* bytes of RAM. A computer stores both the application software and any documents produced with the

software in its RAM. In general, the larger the RAM, the more powerful the computer is. RAM is **volatile memory**: everything in it disappears when the computer is turned off.

- **ROM.**   ROM, or Read Only Memory, refers to the instructions built into a computer. ROM is **fixed memory.** It is "there" when the computer is turned on, and changing computer operations does not affect it.
- **Spreadsheets.**   Financial spreadsheets allow the user to perform a wide variety of financial (and other mathematical) functions quickly and easily. Rows and columns of figures can be calculated, recalculated, and printed in numerous ways to demonstrate the possible consequences of specific business decisions.
- **Video recorders.**   Video recorders are large-size tape recorders designed to record a video (television) signal. They are widely used in business in training programs.
- **Word processing programs.**   Word processing or **text editing** software is especially designed to allow the user to create, alter, store, and print written documents.

COMMON COMPUTER APPLICATIONS

We have already discussed three of the most common computer applications: word processing (Chapter 5), online database retrieval (Chapter 10), and computer-generated graphic aids (Chapter 15). In addition to these functions, report writers also use computers to keep track of financial and other numerical data and for storing, organizing, and retrieving a wide variety of text-based data as well. The programs used to accomplish these tasks are spreadsheets and databases. Exhibit 19.2 illustrates a typical spreadsheet.

Spreadsheets

What is a spreadsheet cell?

Regardless of brand, a spreadsheet arranges information by *rows* (horizontal) and *columns* (vertical). The intersection of a row and a column is a *cell.* Information entered in the cells of a spreadsheet may be either alphabetical or numeric, with alphabetical entries functioning as labels. Some numerical data (Social Security numbers, parts numbers, invoice numbers, and the like) may also be entered as labels. The main function of a spreadsheet, however, is to perform mathematical computations on the numerical data entered as numbers.

What kinds of calculations can spreadsheets make?

For either rows or columns, spreadsheets can calculate totals and averages, find the largest or smallest entry, determine percentages, or simply count the number of entries. Most spreadsheets can also determine absolute values and square roots and perform calculations based

Exhibit 19.2　　　**Typical Spreadsheet**

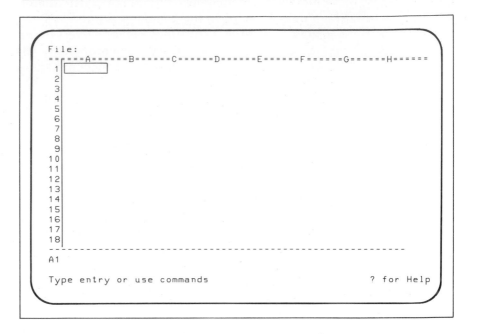

on logical functions. If, for example, you wanted to flag all accounts that had exceeded their credit limit, you could instruct the spreadsheet to compare the cells in the column (or row) containing the account total with the cells in the column (or row) containing the amount of credit authorized. Exhibit 19.3 illustrates the result of such a comparison.

How can writers use spreadsheet files that are not compatible with their word processors?

Managers frequently use spreadsheets to maintain departmental budgets, records of employee expense accounts, and specific project expenditures. Much of this information will naturally be included in a variety of reports. Currently, however, many spreadsheet files are not directly compatible with word processing programs, so moving the information from the spreadsheet into the word processing file for inclusion in a report may require an intermediate step of printing the selected portion of the spreadsheet to disk (instead of to the printer). When a spreadsheet file is printed to disk, it is converted to ASCII format and can then be loaded by most word processors.

Some spreadsheets contain graphics capabilities that enable them to convert the numerical data in either columns or rows into pie charts, line charts, bar graphs, or scattergrams. Some spreadsheets also permit sorting or arranging the data in rows or columns based on numerical value (from highest to lowest or from lowest to highest). The sort feature would be useful for determining such things as which customers purchased the most (or the least) from your organization during a particular month.

Exhibit 19.3   ## Spreadsheet Application

```
File: Credit Accounts
=======A========B========C========D========E========F========
 1 NAME     CR LIMIT  AMT OWED  CR AVAIL OVER LIMIT
 2 ==============================================================
 3 Adams       3000      1765     1235      OK
 4 Carmona     5000      2400     2600      OK
 5 Davis       2500      3200     -700    ERROR
 6 Engles     10000      6652     3348      OK
 7
 8
 9
10
```

Databases

As discussed in Chapter 10, some databases contain huge amounts of information and are available on a national basis. Most organizations also find a variety of uses for databases on a local basis. A company might, for example, use an electronic database to keep track of which customers order which products in what amounts at what intervals. This information could be made available to everyone on the organization's LAN or, by using **passwords,** restricted to those who needed access to that data to perform their jobs.

Departments within the organization might also develop and maintain their own databases. A personnel department, for example, could maintain a record of training programs offered throughout the organization, including such information as the title of the program, the names of instructors, the number of hours of instruction, scheduled dates, and lists of participants.

What are database fields? records?

A database consists of individual categories or **fields** of information, which are collected into sets known as **records.** Exhibit 19.4 illustrates two records from a database on the training programs mentioned previously.

One of the principal advantages of electronic databases is their ability to sort through large numbers of records quickly. If you had a database containing your customers' names and addresses and the products they had purchased from you, for example, you would very quickly be

Exhibit 19.4   Database Records

```
        File:    TnG Programs                                Page 1
        Report:  Tng Programs                              29 Mar 87

        Title: Accounting for Managers
        Instructors: G. Morley and R. Wason
        Hours: 14
        Dates: 9 and 10 Mar
        Participants: L. Blakey, R. Charles, B. Dodson, M. Johnson,
        Participants: N. Noonan, L. Smith, R. Smith, T. Taylor,
        Participants: N. Wilson


        Title: Office Procedures
        Instructors: M. Marconi and C. Freemyer
        Hours: 21
        Dates: 15, 16, and 17 Sep
        Participants: S. Adams, M. Buckley, E. Gasta, S. Kosnik,
        Participants: L. Oehler, R. Pabis, R. Prough, K. Pluard,
        Participants: S. Shaw, M. Singer, S. Stanley, D. Szpiech,
        Participants: M. Tyler, J. Ureel
```

able to determine which of your products sold best in which part of the country. If you had additional demographic information about your customers (age, income, and the like), you would also be able to correlate product sales with that information. If you needed to know how many women living in South Dakota had purchased a particular product, a database could quickly locate all the records meeting those criteria.

Outline and Index Generators

Spreadsheets and database programs are the two most useful programs serving as research aids. Outline and index generators are useful writing aids. Some word processing programs contain built-in outline and index generators, and separate programs of this variety are compatible with most word processing programs.

What is the principal advantage of an outline generator?

With an outline generator, a report writer can organize his or her ideas in much the same way people used to use 3″ by 5″ index cards. Outline generators can show major divisions, minor divisions, and content included in the divisions. The principal advantage of an outline generator is its ability to rearrange sections. When you are planning your report, you may discover that Section IV would serve better as Section III. With an outline generator, it is a simple procedure to rearrange the outline so that all the material under IV is moved to Section III.

Those who prepare long, formal reports requiring indexes will appreciate index generators. Index generators may work directly with the document file, in which case the writer simply marks words to be included in the index throughout the file, and the program essentially does the rest, including calculating the pages on which the terms will fall when the document is printed. Other indexing programs require the author to enter the page references and to indicate which subentries belong with which main entry. In this case, the document is printed first, and the author uses the printed file to develop the index.

Spelling and Grammar Checkers

Why are human proofreaders needed even when spelling and grammar checkers are available for word processors?

Spelling checkers are available for most word processing programs, and grammar checkers are available for some. These supplemental programs can be valuable in helping a writer discover errors in a report document. They cannot, however, find all the mistakes that may work their way into a document. Spelling checkers, for example, match words in the document against words in a dictionary; so as long as the words are spelled correctly, the spelling checker thinks that everything is fine. Today's spelling checkers would find the following sentences perfectly acceptable:

The manager *red* the report.

I went *their* to *sea* a friend.

Similar problems exist with current grammar checkers. While grammar checkers can find certain errors, they cannot find them all. Further, they are usually slow. Although future developments in spelling and grammar checkers will undoubtedly increase the speed, accuracy, and thoroughness with which they check documents, reports will still require human proofreading for many years to come, and this responsibility will continue to rest primarily with the report writer.

Project Planning Programs

For what types of reports are project planning programs most useful?

Programs are available to help report writers produce Gantt charts, PERT charts, critical-path charts, and combinations of these. These programs are especially helpful in producing proposals and progress reports.

While these charts can be produced using more common word processing and graphics programs, the project planning programs allow the user to ask a variety of *what if* questions about a project: What if we finish Step A by March 15? The program would automatically calculate the changes in scheduling, costs, and other factors entered in the program. Finishing Step A by March 15, for example, might require the rescheduling of deliveries of a variety of goods and services and ultimately save the organization thousands of dollars. Project planning programs allow the report writer to model a variety of possibilities and to plan for a number of contingencies.

Desktop Publishing Programs

What is the quality of reports produced on laser printers?

Desktop publishing is one of the most significant advances in technology in recent years. With the right combination of computer, software, and laser printer, a report writer can produce a document that looks as though it were typeset. Although the resolution produced by laser printers is less than that produced by an offset press (300 dots per inch—DPI—as compared to 2450 DPI), for most documents prepared in an office this difference is insignificant.

The basic procedure for producing a report using a desktop publishing program and laser printer remains the same. The writer still needs to define the purpose, collect and analyze the data, and—when appropriate—draw conclusions and make recommendations. The text of the report is still entered in the computer in the same way. When the report is complete, the writer uses the desktop publishing program to select the typeface and size of type for the headings and the text and to position the graphic aids on the page. When printed by the laster printer, the final document will appear to have been printed.

A variety of recent studies have indicated that readers show a definite preference for documents produced with desktop publishing programs and printed on laser printers. Proposals prepared in such a way, for example, have a much higher acceptance rate than those produced by standard letter-quality printers. Documents produced in this way, in fact, are so much better in appearance than documents produced with more traditional equipment that they will doubtless become the expected standard within the next few years.

THE COMPUTER IN YOUR FUTURE

The computer age has just begun. Microcomputers are already more powerful than all but the largest mainframe computers of a few years ago. Their power will enable these machines to do more things and to simplify the process for the user at the same time.

Although no one can predict the future with any certainty, we anticipate that computer usage at all phases of report preparation will continue to increase over the next several years. In fact, computers may begin preparing certain kinds of reports by themselves. Progress reports, sales reports, reports on inventory status, and other informational reports might well be generated automatically at certain intervals. That would, of course, eliminate the need for many managers who have traditionally spent time keeping track of and reporting on such details. It also means that the managers who remain would spend more of their time working on more complex problems and writing more complex reports to help solve those problems.

SUMMARY

The amount of information available to report writers has been increasing exponentially. The role of management is changing, and the equipment managers use to keep track of the increased amounts of information is changing as well. Much manual labor is now being performed by robots, and much information processing is handled by computers and other technological innovations.

New telephone and dictation equipment provides a range of communication services not possible until a few years ago. Managers may also use audio or video teleconferencing to communicate with other managers about important projects. Voice store-and-forward equipment provides the equivalent of a voice mail system, making "telephone tag" virtually obsolete. Although many managers are responsible for their own data entry, some executives still prefer to dictate correspondence and other short documents. Specific techniques are required for effective dictation.

Most modern office equipment is based on computer technology. Computer equipment, or hardware, requires software—programs—to perform its operations. Managers need to be familiar with computer terminology and with the more common computer applications. Managers may use spreadsheets to keep track of and report on financial and other numerically based information. They may also use departmental, organizational, and national databases to store and access information required for the successful completion of the assignments.

Outline and index generators, spelling and grammar checkers, and project planning programs may help with planning projects and preparing reports. Desktop publishing programs may assist with final document preparation. Computers and software will undoubtedly be more powerful and yet easier to use.

EXERCISES

Review and Discussion Questions

1. What is robotics?
2. How have offices changed since the nineteenth century?
3. What does the term technological revolution mean?
4. Name and describe eight modern telephone services.
5. List and explain the five steps required for a successful teleconference.
6. Define videoconferencing. Explain its advantages and disadvantages.
7. What is voice store-and-forward equipment? How does it help overcome common telephone problems?

8. List and explain the eight procedures required for effective dictation.

9. In what way are microcomputers, minicomputers, and mainframe computers different?

10. How do spreadsheets organize information, and how can they manipulate it?

11. What kind of information may be stored in a database?

12. What programs might a manager find helpful in preparing departmental reports?

Problems and Applications

1. Your supervisor has asked you to prepare a report on the changing role of management, covering both changes in the recent past and anticipated changes in the future. She has asked you to draw conclusions and to suggest ways your organization can plan for the changes likely to occur in the next ten years.

2. Arrange to visit your local telephone company (or a local business with the required equipment) for a demonstration of a teleconference (or videoconference, if available). Write a brief report of your experience, reporting both your observations and your analysis of events.

3. Your department manager has always dictated his correspondence directly to his secretary. Yesterday he learned that his secretary has been promoted and will not be replaced. Your manager has been given the choice of learning to use the dictation equipment or the personal computer already in the office. He has asked you to prepare a brief report outlining the advantages and disadvantages of each course of action.

4. How is technology influencing the career area in which you plan to work following your graduation? What percentage of people working in the area use computers? What hardware is being used? What software? What are new college graduates expected to know about computer applications? Prepare a report for your instructor informing him or her of the important facts and providing recommendations if he or she so desires.

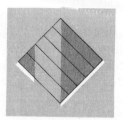

The Cultural Context
of Reports

Reports are, of course, written within a larger cultural context that influences both their form and their content. This cultural context is comprised of a variety of factors, some external to the organization and some internal. This chapter discusses those factors and shows how report writers may be influenced by them.

Topics

International Communication

Ethics

Organizational Values, Objectives, and Public Relations

Until now the discussion of report writing has focused on the preparation of specific reports without much regard to the larger context in which all organizational communication takes place. Every organization is influenced by the outside world with which it interacts, and every organization creates its own internal culture of shared values. In the past few years, we have become increasingly aware of external and internal cultural belief systems and the ways in which they influence the communication process.

The technological advances mentioned in the previous chapter have indeed made the world smaller. Most organizations have been influenced, for example, by the relative ease with which we can travel to other countries, exchange goods and services with them, and relay information from country to country. While these international relationships greatly expand our horizons, they also complicate the communication process. Further, modern technology, especially television and satellite transmission of information, have made every organization—regardless of size—highly visible. If we make a mistake in word or deed, everyone is likely to know. For this reason, report writers need to develop an appreciation of the cultural context in which reports are written.

INTERNATIONAL COMMUNICATION

What do many people in foreign countries dislike North Americans?

When Edward T. Hall wrote *The Silent Language*,[1] few North Americans engaged in international communication. North Americans abroad, in fact, were usually considered self-centered and boorish for their lack of understanding of other cultures. As a result of increased world trade, most businesspeople can now expect to be involved in intercultural communication at some point in their careers. Both large and small businesses export and import goods. Nonprofit organizations, too, have international branches and only rare individuals will not need to communicate with their counterparts from other cultures.

Why is it important to know the language of a country with which you want to do business?

Communicating with someone from a different culture is more difficult than communicating with someone from your own for two reasons. First, even if you speak the other language or—which is more likely—the other person speaks English, no one thinks in a foreign language in quite the same way as does a native. Obviously, the better you know the language of the country you are visiting, the better off you will be—even if all your conversations are in English. The French, Germans, Spanish, Italians, Japanese, Chinese, and every other cultural group with whom you may do business in the future have distinct perspectives of the environment, unique ways of looking at things. Their use of language will reflect that unique perspective, even when they speak in English.

---

[1]Edward T. Hall, *The Silent Language* (New York: Fawcett, 1959).

In addition to the increased difficulty of communicating with someone whose native language is different from your own, intercultural communication presents problems because cultural expectations may be significantly different. Attitudes toward time, space, food, appearance, religion, and manners will all be different from what Americans accept as normal.

North Americans may be considered rude because of the way they treat time. Why?

Time   North Americans value punctuality and like to reach business decisions quickly. In general, people from Latin America or the Middle East are casual about time; they frequently arrive at social and business meetings late by North American standards and are slow to make business decisions, preferring to get acquainted with somebody socially before discussing business matters. The Japanese, although extremely punctual, also prefer to spend time socializing before discussing business matters. North Americans who expect to have one lunch, one dinner, and then conclude a multimillion dollar deal when abroad are bound to be disappointed.

North Americans may be considered rude because of the way they treat personal space. Why?

Space   How much space do you require to feel comfortable? Most Americans prefer to keep at least 18 inches between themselves and another person with whom they are conversing. We are uncomfortable when we cannot avoid closer contact, such as in a crowded elevator. In many countries, however, much closer contact is the norm. Conversational distance in much of the Middle East allows for very little distance between people. In Japan, India, and much of the Far East, the people are accustomed to and comfortable with being in what Americans would consider crowded, confined conditions.

In what parts of the world would drinking alcoholic beverages be considered unacceptable behavior? In what parts would *not* drinking alcoholic beverages be considered unacceptable?

Food   Although McDonald's has demonstrated the international popularity of the hamburger, the rest of the world eats many types of food that North Americans find unpalatable or lacks food that many North Americans expect to have regularly. In the Far East you might have to drink tea rather than coffee. In much of the Middle East you would have to go without your morning bacon or sausage because pork is forbidden. Also, in Moslem countries the possession and use of alcoholic beverages would be a serious crime. Be sure to study the food preferences and prohibitions of countries you will visit, and be prepared to accept the standards of the host country.

How can your reactions to the traditional clothing of a country influence communication?

Appearance   The Western business suit (whether for males or females) is usually considered acceptable dress for business, regardless of where you may be. Blue jeans, too, have become an acceptable international uniform for young people. Business people may be invited to social functions, however, where natives will wear traditional clothing, such as the Japanese kimono or a Scottish kilt. When you are scheduled to travel abroad, study the clothing style of the countries you will be visiting so that you will know what to expect. Your business negotiations will not go well if you communicate the attitude that Western dress is somehow superior to the traditional clothing of your host country.

Religion History is replete with wars fought over religious beliefs, and in spite of the fact that the United States was founded on the principle of religious freedom, too many Americans forget that most of the peoples of the world are neither Christians nor Jews. Buddhism, Hinduism, and the Moslem religion have all profoundly influenced the cultures in large parts of the world. Beware of communicating the attitude that the religion and values of your host country are inferior to your own, regardless of how different they may be.

What should you learn about the manners and customs of a country before you attempt to conduct business there?

Manners Americans tend to be casual and open in their relationships, often calling each other by first names only a few minutes after first meeting. Many other cultures are more formal. In Japan, for example, only a Japanese man's mother has the right to use his first name; others would be considered impolite for using it.

In many cultures, including the Japanese, the bow rather than (or in addition to) a handshake is the traditional greeting. In some cultures, eye contact is considered impolite; in others, the *lack* of eye contact is considered impolite. In some cultures, you are expected to bring a gift to your host or hostess. In other cultures, such gifts would be considered attempted bribes. Some cultures expect the young to defer to their elders, while others allow for a free exchange of ideas regardless of age. Not all cultures regard women the equal of men, nor do all cultures regard men the equal of women.

If you are selected to serve in an international division of an organization, you may well have the responsibility of evaluating reports written in the language of the country where you are serving, translating them to English, and preparing summaries of those reports to send back to headquarters. You may also have the responsibility of preparing official correspondence and reports for the foreign government in the language of that country. The penalty for errors in these documents may be severe.

How might a European read 7/4/90?

Remember, too, that successful international communication will require you to abandon certain communication conventions to which you may be accustomed. A date written with all figures, for example, will have different meanings depending on who is reading it. In the United States, 3/4/88 usually signifies March 4, 1988, but to a European, it would signify April 3, 1988 (Europeans would normally use periods instead of slashes: 3.4.88).

If you are doing business with an organization in Japan, China, South Korea, or other Far Eastern countries, you will need to remember that the International Date Line separates the United States from the Far East. When it is January 1 in California, it is already January 2 in Japan. Correspondence, contracts, and business reports all need to take that difference into account.

Obviously, the more you know about the culture of the country you will be visiting, or of the people with whom you will be dealing, the better off you will be. When people do not understand each other because of cultural differences, feelings are bound to be hurt. Even when people have great differences, however, they can communicate successfully if they are willing to accept each other's world view and work at the process of mutual understanding.

ETHICS

What is ethics?

As our world shrinks, ethics—the study of moral behavior—has become a more critical issue. Many North Americans believe that what they consider ethical behavior is the universal standard. But just as conceptions of time, space, food, and appearance vary from culture to culture, ethical norms also differ.

Most cultures share certain values: that murder and theft are wrong, that keeping one's word in important, and that telling the truth is better than lying. Not all cultures, however, would interpret even these fundamental ethical concepts in the same way, and cultures may have radically differing views of some behaviors. In North America, for example, gifts of money or other valuables to governmental officials to encourage awarding of licenses or contracts are considered bribes. In many other parts of the world, such gifts are thought of as a normal part of doing business. Such conflicting ethical conceptions of a particular action clearly complicate matters for businesspeople.

Advances in technology have also created new ethical concerns. Ask yourself the following questions:

- When should a terminally ill person be taken off life support systems?
- Should women be allowed to become surrogate mothers?
- Should businesses be allowed to manufacture and sell radar detectors and thereby help people break speed limit laws?
- Should people be allowed to install satellite antenna dishes and signal descramblers so that they can receive pay TV channels without paying?

A person's response to any of these issues would be influenced by his or her religious values, culture, and personal beliefs. From a practical standpoint, however, ethical belief systems constitute the ways in which people are taught to weigh their self-interests against the interests of others. A student, for example, might decide to cheat on an exam to improve his or her own score but at the same time be opposed to cheating by other students because that would "ruin the curve." Because many individuals have a difficult time choosing between their own self-interests and those of others, the legal systems in most countries include provisions for punishing those who violate the principal norms of ethical behavior.

In addition to being familiar with the basic legal structure of the country in which you are doing business, you should also be familiar with the laws that apply directly to the kind of business you are conducting. In the United States, for example, many laws apply directly to communication practices in business. An exchange of letters, for example, may establish a legally binding contract. In some cases letters, memos, personnel documents, and other written communications may constitute an **implied contract.** In our increasing litigious society, in which people often take their differences to court, writers need to ensure that the words they choose do not suggest more (or less) than is intended. If a personnel manual, for example, says that a person may be fired only "for cause," that may constitute a contract that takes precedence over other employment documents. If a brochure says that a special clutch makes your company's chain saw "completely safe to use," your company may be liable for *any* accident that occurs with the saw.

When should you solicit the advice of an attorney before mailing a letter?

Honesty is usually sufficient protection from prosecution under the law or civil action, and an overview of some of the legalities of business communication will alert you to some of the more common legal considerations. For some of the situations you encounter in business, however, you may need the advice of an attorney because the legal system is so complex. Laws may have their source in a state or federal constitution, a statute (local, state, or federal), a regulation (based on a governmental agency's interpretation of a law), or a court decision. What seems logical to a lay person may not be what a court would decide. For example, although the law allows a person to keep unordered merchandise, it is not clear whether the law applies to truly accidental mailings or only to deliberate mismailings that attempt to force recipients to pay for merchandise they do not want. Cases must be examined and decided on individually.

When the Law Is Clear

Some guidelines are available to help keep business writers out of trouble. Laws concerning the following areas are of greatest concern to business communicators: defamation, fraud, discrimination, coercion, unmailable and unordered items, and use of copyrighted materials.

What is *malicious intent,* and why should business writers avoid it?

Defamation   Defamation is the false or unjustified injury to the reputation or character of another by **slander** (oral defamation) or **libel** (written defamation). If a statement can be proven true, it is usually not considered grounds for legal action. Even if it is true, however, you may be sued if you made your statements with malicious intent. Also, remember that what you know to be true and what can be proven true in court may not be the same.

Be especially careful to ensure that you avoid making potentially damaging statements (either orally or in writing) about someone to a third party. You can tell a person that she or he is incompetent or dishonest to her or his face, but if you publish that statement by making it known to a third party (whether by a written or an oral statement), you may be sued.

Credit and employment references pose the greatest damage for most business writers. When you answer inquiries about people, make sure that the information you supply is as accurate as possible.

Fraud   The term fraud covers a broad range of situations in which deceit is used to gain an unfair advantage over others. If you were to misrepresent your product or service to a customer, and the customer were damaged (physically, emotionally, or financially) as a result, you would be guilty of fraud. The so-called truth-in-advertising and truth-in-lending laws cover specific kinds of fraud that pertain to business communication. Special laws also cover the fraudulent use of the U.S. postal system.

Under what circumstances might a failure to reveal a defect constitute fraud?

Because business communication, especially persuasive communication (advertising) relies so heavily on emphasizing the positive, you should remember that the failure to reveal a defect may constitute fraud even in the absence of a deliberate misstatement. The critical tests from a legal point are whether injury may result from the deception and whether the other party would have agreed to your terms if he or she had known the truth. In the example of the "absolutely safe" chain saw mentioned previously, almost any accident would indicate fraud.

Discrimination   Discrimination on the basis of race, color, religion, sex, national origin, and—in many cases—age is illegal. Title VII of the Civil Rights Act of 1964, as amended in 1972 and 1978, prohibits discrimination in a wide variety of employment matters. To avoid the possibility of legal action and the virtual certainty of poor public relations, most organizations have established specific guidelines to help employees avoid even the appearance of discrimination.

Coercion   It is illegal to unreasonably oppress, harass, abuse, or intentionally cause mental distress to anyone. As a business communicator, you may attempt to persuade someone to act in a particular way. If the person does not respond to reasonable persuasion, however, the only force you may take is legal action through the courts. In attempting to collect on an overdue bill, for example, you can use persuasion (appeal to the reader's sense of fair play), but you cannot threaten (tell the reader that people who do not pay get their legs broken).

Would you have the right to keep an expensive and unordered fur coat sent to you through the mail? Why or why not?

Unmailable and Unordered Items   Certain items (firearms, alcoholic beverages, and a variety of printed matter) cannot be mailed. A complete list of unmailable items is available from your local postmaster. Sending unordered merchandise through the mail is not illegal, but it may be unwise, because the recipient of unordered merchandise may consider it a gift and simply keep it. In that event, you will probably have no legal recourse to recover the cost of the merchandise.

Use of Copyrighted Materials The U.S. Copyright Law (effective January 1, 1978) protects copyrighted materials—including books, articles, poems, essays, cartoons, photographs, graphic aids, and computer software—from being copied without the prior permission of the copyright owner. Single copies made for personal (noncommercial) use and brief quotations (primarily for educational purposes) are exempt.

Businesspersons are likely to have trouble in this area by using previously published materials in reports or other documents that are eventually published. When such materials are used without providing adequate documentation, such borrowing is called plagiarism (see Chapter 11). Even with documentation, however, using copyrighted material without permission may be illegal.

When Expediency Is a Factor

As a businessperson, you may face ethical decisions on a regular basis. In a report-writing situation, the facts may not "speak for themselves." The right facts must be presented in the right way if the reader is to know how to interpret them. Further, the political climate in your department or organization as a whole may influence the advisability of a particular decision or what you choose to report. What would you do, for example, in the following situations?

- A building inspector requests a kickback for approving construction of a building for which you are responsible.
- You have the opportunity to pass used merchandise off as new on an unsuspecting client.
- You have been asked to approve a TV advertisement that promises more than your product can deliver.
- You have the opportunity to provide a glowing recommendation for an inadequate employee who will be hired by a competitor based on your recommendation.
- You have been asked to falsify the results of tests on the purity of water you use in your manufacturing process.
- You have the opportunity to visit with an old friend whom you have not seen in years and can either take a day of vacation or call in sick.

How frequently do report writers make decisions that involve ethical considerations?

Unlike the ethical questions posed earlier, in each of these cases we know what the ethical decision should be, but depending on the potential gain for ourselves and the risk of harm to others, we may choose the profitable course of action rather than the right course of action. Virtually every report you write will entail ethical decisions—perhaps not on the same scale as those presented earlier in the chapter, but you will still need to choose between something you know to be right and something that may be more expedient. The words you select to describe a person, event, or product; the facts you decide to include or to exclude; and even your organizational structure may be ethical or unethical. Some decisions may not be easy. The words you select to describe a 55 percent majority or a $1 million profit may rightly vary depending on circumstances. In one case, 55 percent may be a "bare majority," while in another it could legitimately be a "significant achievement."

In your effort to make ethical decisions and to report them in an ethical way, consider the following factors:

What are the three key factors in making ethical decisions?

1. **Who benefits and who may be hurt?** In general, ethical decisions benefit more people than they harm. If your company develops a new, simplified procedure for manufacturing a product that will greatly reduce its cost, for example, it would be ethical to change to the new method even though a few people might lose their jobs. On the other hand, if the new, economical procedure were also dangerous, possibly resulting in death or serious injury to some workers, it would be unethical to change. Decision makers need to weigh potential gains against possible losses.

2. **What rights are involved?** Virtually every country affords its citizens certain rights, which are guaranteed by law. Perhaps the best known rights are those specified in the Bill of Rights included as the first ten amendments to the Constitution of the United States. Even these rights, however, may be abridged depending on the circumstances. The right of free speech, for example, does not apply to someone who would yell "fire" in a crowded theater. Likewise, laws against defamation (libel and slander) limit freedom of speech so that one person's right does not deprive another of his or her rights.

3. **What is fair?** Throughout this text we have stressed the need for accuracy, impartiality, and reliability in reports. An unbiased examination of the evidence should result in an ethical decision, and certainly those who receive reports deserve to receive accurate and objective information. Suppose, however, that you have good reason to believe that the manager to whom you report would make an unethical and illegal decision if you submitted a complete, objective report about an upcoming merger? Would it be ethical to report everything and hope for the best, or should you omit those details that might cause your reader to commit an unethical act?

Who is ultimately responsible for the ethics of a report writer's decisions?

Behaving in an ethical way is not always easy. In some cases, it may be difficult to determine the ethical course of action, and reasonable people may disagree about such cases. Abortion is such an issue: is a woman's "right to choose" more important than the fetus' "right to life"? Even when the ethical course of action is clear, choosing that course may be difficult because it would endanger one's vested interests. Ultimately, you are responsible for the ethics of the decisions you make. If you are honest with yourself about your own motivations and the possible consequences of your decisions, you should be able to make ethical choices most of the time.

ORGANIZATIONAL VALUES, OBJECTIVES, AND PUBLIC RELATIONS

Organizations are human institutions—designed by people and for people. As such, they are more ideas in the minds of the people who compose them than they are the land, buildings, and equipment owned by them. The most important of these ideas are the values by which the organization wishes to be known. Whether the value is "Keep the Quality Up" (The Upjohn Company), "Quality is Job 1" (Ford Motor Company), "Progress Is our Most Important Product" (General Electric), or "Better Things for Better Living through Chemistry" (DuPont), the central values of an organization provide it with meaning and direction.

What is a mission statement? corporate creed?

These core values are usually expressed in a mission statement. Every organization has a mission, or reason for being. In the best organizations, the mission is clear and well-known. Virtually everyone working for the organization understands its purpose and shares the vision of the goal the organization is trying to achieve. In some organizations, however, the mission may not be clear or stated explicitly, and organizations may lose track of their missions as they and the world around them change. Nevertheless, report writers need to recognize how particular reports contribute to the missions of the organizations for which they work. Based on its mission, an organization will develop a corporate creed—or system of beliefs—to define the values by which it expects its members to be governed. Based on those values, it develops specific policies and procedures it believes will help implement that creed and accomplish its mission.

Problems arise when the creed and policies conflict. The corporate creed may stress "First Quality, Then Profit," yet in daily practice the policy may be "ship the product and let the dealer fix the problems." Conflicts of this variety are more common than they should be for reasons presented earlier in the discussion of ethics: the corporate creed is the ideal, and the policy is the practical as influenced by self-interest.

An organization is clearly better off if its creed is supported by its policies and if its methods, procedures, and daily practices are designed to implement its policies. In the best organizations, each employee knows the mission of the organization, understands its policies, and knows how his or her daily activities support that creed and help the organization achieve its objectives.

What are good public relations?

As a rule, organizations try to earn the good will of their employees and their external publics—clients, customers, suppliers, dealers or distributors, neighborhood residents, government agencies, and the media. Also as a rule, an organization's actions will have greater impact on its relationships than will its communications: actions speak louder than words. While many still think of public relations as putting Band-Aids on organizational mistakes, today's employees and external publics are too well informed for that approach to be effective.

To create and maintain good will with its internal and external audiences, an organization needs to establish credibility: its deeds must match its words. Good public relations requires both right actions and effective communication about those actions. Employees want to believe that they are appreciated for the work they do and that their rewards are commensurate with their accomplishments. External audiences want to believe that the organization provides a good value in products or services and that organizational decisions are made with the general good in mind. To achieve these ends, communication needs to be based on a foundation of right actions.

Because virtually any report you prepare may eventually be made public and have lasting impact on your organization, you should be especially careful to ensure that your reports are both accurate and fair. As a report writer, you will be helping the organization define its relationship with its internal and external audiences with each report you prepare. You and your organization will be more successful in the long run if you take that responsibility seriously.

SUMMARY

Technological advances have made the world smaller. The amount of international communication increases every year. As a result of increased world trade, nearly everyone in business must eventually communicate with people from other cultures. Most of these cultures have different communication conventions, which greatly complicates the communication process. People who will be responsible for intercultural communication should study the language and culture of the other country before they communicate, even if all the actual communicating will be in English. People who are able to accept cultural differences and accept others as they are can become effective intercultural communicators.

As our world shrinks, ethics—the study of moral behavior—has become a more critical issue. Most cultures share certain fundamental conceptions of right and wrong, but interpretations may vary. Some ethical questions are difficult to answer, and reasonable people may have differing opinions about what is ethical. In other cases, we may know what is ethical and yet not choose the ethical course of action because of self-interests. Because desire to promote self-interest may result in unethical behavior, the legal systems of most countries include provisions for punishing those who violate the principal norms of ethical behavior. Laws against defamation, fraud, discrimination, coercion, inappropriate use of the postal system, and unauthorized use of copyrighted materials are the most important for report writers. In your effort to make ethical decisions and to report them in an ethical way, consider who benefits and who may be hurt, what rights are involved, and what is fair.

Organizations are human institutions—designed by people and for people. As such, the organization has a culture based on the shared values of those who work for it. The culture of an organization is expressed by its mission statement and corporate creed. These beliefs are put into practice by policies and procedures. Problems will arise when the creed and policies conflict. When an organization's stated creed and its daily actions conflict, the actions will be believed. A history of right actions communicated effectively will result in credibility and good internal and external public relations for the organization.

EXERCISES

Review and Discussion Questions

1. In what way is technology responsible for the increasing importance of international communication?

2. If English is the "international language," why should North Americans bother to learn the languages of other countries with which they may do business?

3. Describe the ways in which differing cultural attitudes toward time, space, food, appearance, religion, and manners may influence the communication process.

4. What is the International Date Line, and how might it influence business relationships?

5. Why might cultures have differing views of ethical behavior?

6. How has technology influenced our conception of ethical behavior?

7. What is an implied contract?

8. What is defamation? fraud? plagiarism?

9. Do the facts always speak for themselves? What kind of "help" might they need?

10. What kinds of situations may cause a person to behave in unethical ways?

11. What are the three major guidelines for determining ethical behavior?

12. In what way are organizations human institutions?

13. What is a "corporate creed"?

14. Why should an organization or its employees be concerned about internal and external public relations?

Problems and Applications

1. Your company is about to open a new office in Tokyo (or London, Paris, Bonn, Lisbon, Madrid, Rome, Mexico City, Rio de Janeiro,

Seoul, Moscow, or other foreign city of your choice), and your boss has asked you to prepare a short analytical report on the culture and business climate she should expect when she arrives to open the office and begin dealing with contractors and suppliers.

2. Which of the following behaviors are ethical? Which would you be willing to do? How many of your classmates share your views? Develop a questionnaire based on the following behaviors, have at least 20 of your classmates complete it anonymously, and submit your findings to your instructor in an informal report.

   a. Having someone proofread a paper to help you catch typographical and other mechanical errors before you turn it in for a grade.

   b. Having someone proofread a paper and make suggestions about improving its content before you turn it in for a grade.

   c. Having someone help you revise portions of a paper before you turn it in for a grade.

   d. Having someone write portions of a paper for you before you turn it in for a grade.

   e. Using portions of articles without documenting them in a paper you submit for a grade.

   f. Using a paper you submitted for a grade in a previous class in a second class after making corrections suggested by the professor in the first class.

   g. Copying a paper written by a classmate and submitting it for a grade in one of your classes.

   h. Purchasing a paper from a term paper service and submitting it for a grade.

3. Analyze the Code of Professional Standards adopted by the Public Relations Society of America. How do the precepts presented in it apply to those who write business reports?

4. Why is the mission statement of central importance to an organization? Compare the mission statements of at least five campus organizations and determine whether the policies, procedures, and daily practices within the organizations support or conflict with their mission statements.

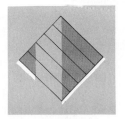

Statistics and the Decision-Making Process

The brief coverage of statistics presented here is not meant to substitute for a thorough introduction to the subject. Its main purposes are to remind those who have had such an introduction of how to apply common statistical measures and to show those unfamiliar with statistics how those measures may be applied. We cover both descriptive and inferential statistics and provide the most common statistical tables.

DESCRIPTIVE STATISTICS

Descriptive statistics are the methods used to describe aspects of a collection of numbers. The most useful methods of describing a set of numbers are measures of central tendency and measures of dispersion. These measures tell researchers where the center of a set of numbers is and how the other numbers are grouped in relation to the center.

Measures of Central Tendency

One of the most significant uses of statistics is to provide researchers with an idea of the center of a set of data. Measures of central tendency include the mean, weighted mean, median, mode, and midrange.

Mean   The arithmetic average, or mean, is obtained by adding the values of the variable and dividing by the total number of cases.

The formula for obtaining the mean is:

$$\overline{X} = \frac{\Sigma X}{n}$$

in which $\overline{X}$ (X-bar) is the mean, Σ is the sum of the values of variable X, and n is the number of cases. If you were to take a course with four exams, each weighted equally, you would determine your final grade by adding your scores on each of the exams and dividing by 4.

$$
\begin{array}{ll}
\text{Exam 1:} & 78 \\
\text{Exam 2:} & 94 \\
\text{Exam 3:} & 87 \\
\text{Exam 4:} & \underline{94} \\
\end{array}
$$

$$353 \div 4 = 88.25.$$

Weighted Mean   The weighted mean is the arithmetic average when all variables are not weighted equally. The formula for obtaining the weighted mean is

$$\text{Weighted mean} = \frac{\Sigma w_i x_i}{\Sigma w_i}$$

in which the sum (Σ) of the variables multiplied by their weighted values is divided by the sum of the weighted values. If you were to take a course with two papers, each worth 20 percent of your final grade, a midterm worth 25 percent, and a final worth 35 percent, you could determine your final grade using the following formula:

Grades		(Weight)
Paper 1:	87	(20%)
Paper 2:	96	(20%)
Midterm:	85	(25%)
Final:	94	(35%)

$$
\begin{aligned}
\text{Weighted mean} &= \frac{.20(87) + .20(96) + .25(85) + .35(94)}{+ .20 + .20 + .25 + .35} \\
&= \frac{17.4 + 19.2 + 21.25 + 32.9}{1} \\
&= 90.75.
\end{aligned}
$$

Median   The median divides an ordered set of variables into two equal groups, with half having values less than the median and half having

Exhibit A.1

Hypothetical Company Salaries

President	$600,000 a year
2 vice presidents	$100,000 a year, each
5 sales managers	$50,000 a year, each
1 production manager	$35,000 a year, each
50 hourly employees	$18,000 a year, each
50 hourly employees	$11,000 a year, each

values greater. The median is obtained by counting the pieces of data, adding 1, and dividing by 2.

$$\text{Median} = i = \frac{n + 1}{2}.$$

You might wish, for example, to know the median income of people who have purchased one of your company's products. To do so, you would count the number of responses arranged according to ranked categories, add 1, and divide by 2.

Category	Responses
1. Below $15,000	0
2. $15,000–$19,999	15
3. $20,000–$24,999	25
4. $25,000–$29,999	32
5. $30,000–$34,999	41
6. $35,000–$39,999	26
7. $40,000 or above	12
	Total responses: 151

$$n = \frac{151 + 1}{2} = 76.$$

Beginning at either end, count 76 responses. The *median* occurs in the $30,000–$35,000 category, with 72 responses below that category, and 79 responses in that category and above. The *mean,* however, would fall in category 4, at about $27,450, which shows that the mean and the median are not interchangeable. The mean is influenced by extreme scores much more than the median is.

The difference between these two measures of centrality is even clearer when comparing a smaller number of specific numbers. If you examined the salaries of employees working at a small company, you might find something like those in Exhibit A.1.

The *mean* salary would be determined as follows:

$$\frac{\$2,535,000 \text{ (total salary)}}{109 \text{ (number of employees)}} = \$23,256.88.$$

The *median* would be determined as follows:

$$\frac{109 + 1}{2} = 55.$$

Or, the 55th response, counting from either end is the median salary, or $18,000.

Which "average" would a company be more likely to report?

Mode   The mode is the value that occurs most frequently. In the case of the company salaries, two figures—$18,000 and $11,000—appear with equal frequency, so there is no single mode in this case, which has **bimodal** distribution.

Midrange   The midrange is the number occurring midway between the lowest score and the highest. It is determined by adding the low score (L) and the high score (H) and dividing by two. Again, let's look at the salaries:

$$\frac{\$11,000 \ (L) \ + \ 600,000 \ (H)}{2} = \$305,500.$$

The differences among these figures show how important it is for the report writers to use the most significant measure of centrality for a given situation and to indicate clearly which measure is being used. When more than one measure is useful, provide both and label each clearly.

Measures of Dispersion

In addition to finding out the nature of the middle of a set of data, researchers also need to know the amount of **dispersion,** or **spread.** Measures of dispersion reveal whether the numbers being examined are close together or widely spread out. Values that are relatively close together are said to have **low dispersion,** whereas widely spaced values are said to have **high dispersion.**

The most often used measures for dispersion include range, average deviation, variance, and standard deviation. For each of these measurements, the lower the number, the lower will be the amount of dispersion.

Range   The range is simply the difference between the largest (H) and smallest (L) values in the data collected:

$$\text{Range} = H - L.$$

For the company salaries in Exhibit A.1, for example, the range would be computed as follows:

$$600{,}000 - 11{,}000 = 589{,}000.$$

The range shows the total amount of spread in a set of numbers. The other measurements are used to show the amount of dispersion using the mean as a reference point. The range is easy to compute and understand. It cannot, however, provide information about values other than the extremes. If we want to understand the relationships among all the values in a given set, we will need to use one of the other measurements.

Average Deviation   The average deviation, also known as the **mean absolute deviation (MAD)**, measures the average deviation around the mean. With this measure, we are concerned with the difference between individual values and the mean, as expressed by the formula $X_i - \overline{X}$, in which X_i represents the values, and $\overline{X}$ (X-bar) represents the mean.

Suppose we poll the members of an organization to discover how far they commute to work. We would compute the average deviation according to the steps outlined in Exhibit A.2. (We will use all whole numbers to simplify the illustration.)

The number 2.176 in Exhibit A.2 shows how far the values are—on the average—from the mean.

Variance   Although a bit more difficult to compute, the variance is generally a more useful measure of dispersion. The variance is computed in essentially the same way as the average deviation, except that the deviations are squared before summing, and the average is found using $n - 1$. Exhibit A.3 illustrates the method for obtaining the variance using the data from Exhibit A.2.

The variance of a sample is a measure of the dispersion of the data about the mean. To obtain the variance for a population as a whole (rather than for the sample), simply substitute n for $n - 1$ in the formula.

Standard Deviation   The standard deviation is the positive square root of the variance. Exhibit A.4 illustrates the formula for standard deviation as applied to the variance computed in Exhibit A.3.

The standard deviation is one of the most commonly used measures of distribution because the resulting figure is in the same units as those

1. Gather raw data:

Miles to Work	Responses	Total Miles
1	4	4
2	6	12
3	3	9
4	8	32
5	10	50
6	2	12
7	1	7
10	3	30
22	1	22
Totals	38	178

2. Compute the mean $\left(\overline{X} = \dfrac{\Sigma X}{n} \right)$:

$$\overline{X} = \frac{178}{38} = 4.6842105.$$

For most business purposes, you will not need to figure beyond two decimal places, so round off answers to the nearest hundredth. (When rounding off a five, round to the *even* value: 7.45 to 7.4, but 7.55 to 7.6.)
   The *mean* number of miles commuted would be 4.68

3. Subtract the mean from each of the values and multiply by the number of observations or responses:

Observations or Responses		Values X − Mean $(X_i - \overline{X})$				Absolute Value
4	×	$(1 - 4.68)$	=	4×-3.68	=	-14.72
6	×	$(2 - 4.68)$	=	6×-2.68	=	-16.08
3	×	$(3 - 4.68)$	=	3×-1.68	=	-5.04
8	×	$(4 - 4.68)$	=	$8 \times -\ .68$	=	-5.44
10	×	$(5 - 4.68)$	=	$10 \times\ \ .32$	=	3.20
2	×	$(6 - 4.68)$	=	$2 \times\ \ 1.32$	=	2.64
1	×	$(7 - 4.68)$	=	$1 \times\ \ 2.32$	=	2.32
3	×	$(10 - 4.68)$	=	$3 \times\ \ 5.32$	=	15.96
1	×	$(22 - 4.68)$	=	$1 \times 1\ 7.32$	=	17.32
Totals 38						82.72

4. Ignore the negative signs (that is, use *absolute values*) and compute the average deviation using the following formula:

$$\text{Average Deviation} = \frac{\Sigma(X_i - \overline{X})}{n}$$

or:

$$\frac{82.72}{38} = 2.176.$$

Exhibit A.3   Sample Variance

$$\text{Variance} = S^2 = \frac{\Sigma(X - \overline{X})^2}{n - 1}$$

Values X − Mean =	Deviation	Deviation^2
1×4 = 4 − 4.68	−0.68	0.46
2×6 = 12 − 4.68	7.32	53.58
3×3 = 9 − 4.68	4.32	18.66
4×8 = 32 − 4.68	27.32	746.38
5×10 = 50 − 4.68	45.32	2053.90
6×2 = 12 − 4.68	7.32	53.58
7×1 = 7 − 4.68	2.32	5.38
10×3 = 30 − 4.68	25.32	641.10
22×1 = 22 − 4.68	17.32	299.98
		3873.02

$$S^2 = \frac{\Sigma(X - \overline{X})^2}{n - 1} = \frac{3873.02}{38 - 1} = 104.68$$

in the mean. The standard deviation of 10.23 in Exhibit A.4, for example, is in miles, the same units as the mean established in Exhibit A.2. (The variance is in units *squared.*)

Understanding Centrality and Dispersions

Centrality is easier to visualize and understand than dispersion. The measures for centrality—especially the mean—tell us how to find the center point in a set of data. The measures of dispersion tell us how the data are grouped around that center point.

Exhibits A.5, A.6, and A.7 illustrate possible distributions of data in reference to a mean.

Exhibit A.4   Sample Average Deviation

$$S = \sqrt{\frac{\Sigma(X - X)^2}{n - 1}} \quad \text{or} \quad \sqrt{\frac{3873.02}{38 - 1}} = \sqrt{104.68}$$

$$S = 10.23$$

Note: As was true in computing the variance, substituting n for $n - 1$ will show the standard deviation for the population rather than for the sample.

Bivariate Data

Measures of centrality and dispersion describe single units of information about a population or a sample. Frequently in business, however, information about single units of information is not enough. We may need to study two pieces of data to see if a relationship exists between them.

Is there a relationship between education and income?

Exhibit A.5   ## Symmetrical Distribution

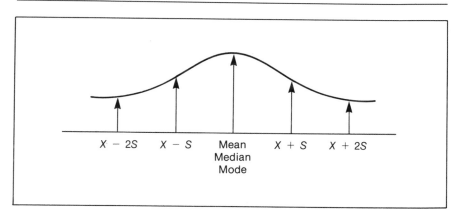

A relationship exists between measures of centrality (the mean = X and standard deviation = S).

Exhibit A.6   ## Skewed Distributions

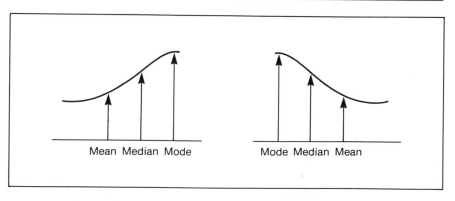

With unequal distribution, the mean and median are pulled toward the extremes.

Exhibit A.7   **Bimodal Distribution**

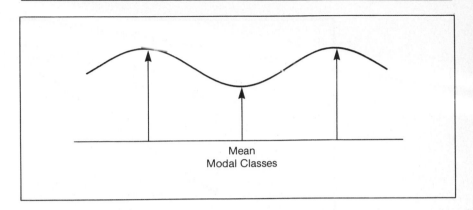

Is there a relationship between consumption of vitamins and health?

Is there a relationship between grades earned in college and occupational success?

Bivariate—or two variables—data are measured in two principal ways. We can examine the data for **linear correlations,** or we can study the data for **linear regression.**

Linear Correlation   The correlation between variables is a measure of the *strength* of the relationship, whereas the *nature* of the relationship is discovered by regression analysis. These measures are useful because they tell us something about the strength of relationships and allow us to make predictions about the values of one variable when we know (or assume) the values of the other.

Bivariate data are expressed mathematically in terms of ordered pairs, where X denotes the first variable and Y denotes the second. In a perfect, positive correlation, for example, the value of X and Y would increase at the same rate, as Exhibit A.8 illustrates.

Linear correlation can be either positive or negative. A positive relationship is one in which the value of Y increases as the value of X increases. In a negative relationship, the value of Y would decrease as the value of X increases. The scattergrams in Exhibit A.9 illustrate the possibilities.

Each of the dots in the scattergrams in Exhibit A.9 represents the combined values of X and Y. Suppose that you wanted to compare annual incomes and the amount of money spent on home purchases.

Exhibit A.8   Perfect Linear Correlation

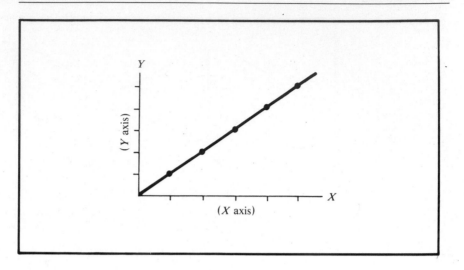

You would collect data as follows:

Buyer	Income	House Value
1	$10,000	$27,000
2	$15,000	$36,000
3	$20,000	$47,000
4	$25,000	$68,000
5	$30,000	$59,000

You would then designate one variable X and the other Y. These would be plotted on a scattergram as shown in Exhibit A.10.

The mathematical formula for determining the **coefficient of linear correlation, r,** is complex.

$$r = \frac{n(\Sigma XY) - (\Sigma X)(\Sigma Y)}{\sqrt{n(\Sigma X^2) - (\Sigma X)^2} \times \sqrt{n(\Sigma Y^2) - (\Sigma Y)^2}}.$$

Applied to our extremely small sample of house buyers in Exhibit A.10, the formula works like this:

$$r = \frac{5(5220) - (100)(237)}{\sqrt{5(2250) - (10,000)} \times \sqrt{5(12,339) - (56,169)}}$$

$$r = \frac{26,100 - 23,700}{\sqrt{1,250} \times \sqrt{5,526}}$$

Exhibit A.9   **Possible Correlation**

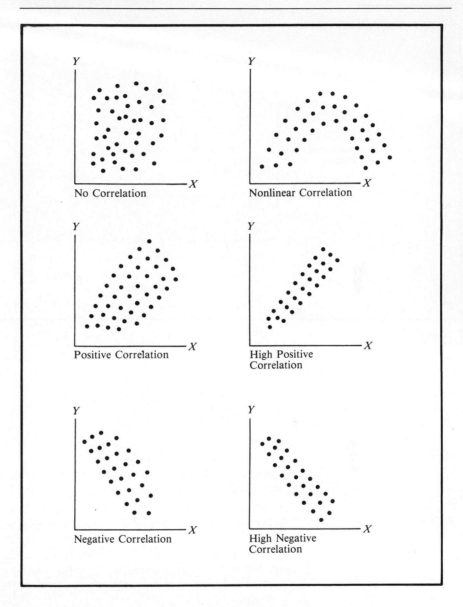

Exhibit A.10   **Scattergram Illustrating X and Y**

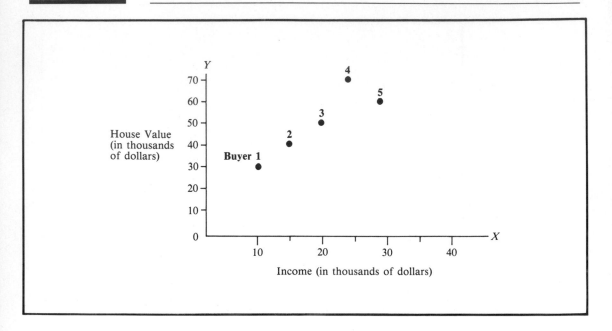

$$r = \frac{2{,}400}{(35.36)(74.34)}$$

$$r = \frac{2{,}400}{2628.66}$$

$$r = +.91.$$

A perfect positive correlation would be $+1$, and a perfect negative correlation would be -1. The $+.91$ indicates that, for our small sample, there is a high positive correlation between income and the amount of money spent on a house. To obtain a percentage, simply square the r. In this case $r^2 = 83$ percent. The 83 percent tells us that income accounts for 83 percent of the variance in the amount of money spent for houses among the cases examined, or that some factor other than income accounts for 17 percent of the variance in the amount of money spent for a house.

Because the complexity of the mathematics increases the possibility of error, researchers often use computer programs to determine linear correlations. You can imagine how difficult it would be to compute figures for thousands of home buyers instead of five.

Linear Regression   Linear regression is the attempt to develop a mathematical equation that describes the relationship between two variables. Simple linear regressions, dealing with two variables only, are the most commonly used, though multiple regressions and curvilinear (other than straight line) regressions are possible.

Linear regressions allow us to make predictions about the value of one variable when we know the value of the other and when we know that the values have a high correlation.

The formula for the linear equation that allows us to make predictions is

$$Y = a + bX.$$

The values a and b are determined by the sample data: a is the value of Y at the point $X = 0$, and b is the slope of the line (the amount of change in Y or one unit of change in $X (\Delta Y/\Delta X)$.

Suppose that there is a high correlation between the assembly time required for products in a company and the number of steps required to assemble the product. The company is about to introduce a new product and would like to predict how long the assembly of the product will take (which will help determine the cost of manufacturing the product). Exhibit A.11 illustrates the application of the linear equation.

If the new product is going to have nine steps in the production process, we would then calculate the time required to manufacture the product as follows:

$$Y = 1.5 + (2 \times 9)$$

$$Y = 1.5 + 18$$

$$Y = 19.5 \text{ (hours required for production)}.$$

Linear correlations and linear regressions both show relationships. Neither can demonstrate a cause and effect relationship. Over the past 25 years, for example, you would find that the number of people attending college has increased. You would also find that the number of movies made each year has increased. Sampling would result in a high positive correlation, but neither increase could be said to be the cause of the other. Both are probably the result of some third factor, such as an expanding economy.

INFERENTIAL STATISTICS

Descriptive statistics describe the characteristics of a single set of data. In many cases, however, it is necessary to make decisions about differences among sets of data. Inferential statistics provide the means for making those decisions by testing hypotheses.

In any testing situation, it is useful to know the possibility of error. In testing our hypothesis, we will need to make inferences about the population mean, about the population proportions, and about the standard deviation.

Exhibit A.11   Linear Equation

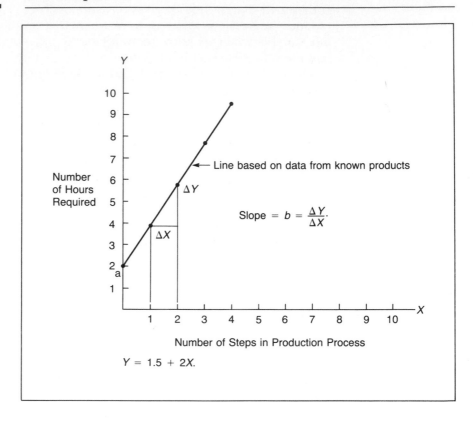

Inferring the Population Mean

When the sample size is larger than 30, the mean of the population will be a close enough approximation of the mean of the sample for most purposes. When the sample is smaller than 30, we can increase the accuracy of our estimate of the population mean by using the *Student's t Distribution* (so called because it was originally published by W. S. Gosset under the pseudonym *student*). The formula is as follows:

$$t = \frac{X - \mu}{\dfrac{S}{\sqrt{n}}}$$

where

X = the sample mean

μ = the population mean

S = sample standard deviation

n = sample size

t = an index of observed differences based on a sample.

Statistical Table 1 provides critical values for t, showing the index number for sample sizes ranging from 2 to 30 and differing rates of error. (Statistical tables are grouped at the end of this appendix.) The following example illustrates the application of the Student's t Distribution formula and table.

You might, for example, want to test for the purity of water used in the process of manufacturing pharmaceuticals. The water must contain no more than 14 parts per million of all impurities combined to meet required federal standards. You can use the Student's t to predict the quality of the water using a relatively small number of samples.

Sample	Impurities (parts per million)	Deviation
1	8	−4.1
2	14	+1.9
3	10	−2.1
4	11	−1.1
5	12	−0.1
6	16	+3.9
7	14	+1.9
8	12	−0.1
9	15	+2.9
10	9	−3.1

Sample mean = $\overline{X}$ = 12.1.

$$\text{Sample standard deviation} = \sqrt{\frac{\Sigma(X_1 - \overline{X})^2}{n - 1}}$$

$$S = \sqrt{\frac{62.9}{9}}$$

$$= 2.64.$$

Now that we know that the sample mean is 12.1 and the sample standard deviation is 2.64, we can use the Student's t test to determine the probability that the water purity of the population (all the water) is the same as that in the sample. We do this in the following way:

1. State our goal as a hypothesis or null hypothesis.

    $\mu \leq 14$ ppm—The water quality is acceptable.
    (Recall that μ is the population mean.)
    $\mu \geq 14$ ppm—The water contains too many impurities.

2. Determine the amount of error acceptable. In this case, we will set the amount of error acceptable at 0.025, which results in 97.5 percent confidence that our hypothesis is correct.

$$\alpha = 0.025.$$

TABLE 1:
Standard Normal Curve

Value in Table is $P(0 \leq z \leq z_0)$

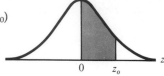

z_0	.00	.01	.02	.03	.04	.05	.06	.07	.08	.09
0.0	.0000	.0040	.0080	.0120	.0160	.0199	.0239	.0279	.0319	.0359
0.1	.0398	.0438	.0478	.0517	.0557	.0596	.0636	.0675	.0714	.0753
0.2	.0793	.0832	.0871	.0910	.0948	.0987	.1026	.1064	.1103	.1141
0.3	.1179	.1217	.1255	.1293	.1331	.1368	.1406	.1443	.1480	.1517
0.4	.1554	.1591	.1628	.1664	.1700	.1736	.1772	.1808	.1844	.1879
0.5	.1915	.1950	.1985	.2019	.2054	.2088	.2123	.2157	.2190	.2224
0.6	.2257	.2291	.2324	.2357	.2389	.2422	.2454	.2486	.2517	.2549
0.7	.2580	.2611	.2642	.2673	.2704	.2734	.2764	.2794	.2823	.2852
0.8	.2881	.2910	.2939	.2967	.2995	.3023	.3051	.3078	.3106	.3133
0.9	.3159	.3186	.3212	.3238	.3264	.3289	.3315	.3340	.3365	.3389
1.0	.3413	.3438	.3461	.3485	.3508	.3531	.3554	.3577	.3599	.3621
1.1	.3643	.3665	.3686	.3708	.3729	.3749	.3770	.3790	.3810	.3830
1.2	.3849	.3869	.3888	.3907	.3925	.3944	.3962	.3980	.3997	.4015
1.3	.4032	.4049	.4066	.4082	.4099	.4115	.4131	.4147	.4162	.4177
1.4	.4192	.4207	.4222	.4236	.4251	.4265	.4279	.4292	.4306	.4319
1.5	.4332	.4345	.4357	.4370	.4382	.4394	.4406	.4418	.4429	.4441
1.6	.4452	.4463	.4474	.4484	.4495	.4505	.4515	.4525	.4535	.4545
1.7	.4554	.4564	.4573	.4582	.4591	.4599	.4608	.4616	.4625	.4633
1.8	.4641	.4649	.4656	.4664	.4671	.4678	.4686	.4693	.4699	.4706
1.9	.4713	.4719	.4726	.4732	.4738	.4744	.4750	.4756	.4761	.4767
2.0	.4772	.4778	.4783	.4788	.4793	.4798	.4803	.4808	.4812	.4817
2.1	.4821	.4826	.4830	.4834	.4838	.4842	.4846	.4850	.4854	.4857
2.2	.4861	.4864	.4868	.4871	.4875	.4878	.4881	.4884	.4887	.4890
2.3	.4893	.4896	.4898	.4901	.4904	.4906	.4909	.4911	.4913	.4916
2.4	.4918	.4920	.4922	.4925	.4927	.4929	.4931	.4932	.4934	.4936
2.5	.4938	.4940	.4941	.4943	.4945	.4946	.4948	.4949	.4951	.4952
2.6	.4953	.4955	.4956	.4957	.4959	.4960	.4961	.4962	.4963	.4964
2.7	.4965	.4966	.4967	.4968	.4969	.4970	.4971	.4972	.4973	.4974
2.8	.4974	.4975	.4976	.4977	.4977	.4978	.4979	.4979	.4980	.4981
2.9	.4981	.4982	.4982	.4983	.4984	.4984	.4985	.4985	.4986	.4986
3.0	.4987	.4987	.4987	.4988	.4988	.4989	.4989	.4989	.4990	.4990

From ELEMENTS OF BUSINESS STATISTICS by R. C. Gulezian. Copyright © 1979 by W. B. Saunders Company. Reprinted by permission of Holt, Rinehart and Winston.

Exhibit A.12   Sample Entries for Student's *t* Distribution

T = 2.262

df	Amount of α in one tail (half the total error).				
	—	—	—	—	.025
—	—	—	—	—	—
—	—	—	—	—	—
—	—	—	—	—	—
9	—	—	—	—	2.262

Note: The *df* number (degree of freedom) is always $n - 1$, or 1 less than the sample size.

3. Using Statistical Table 1, find the critical *t* value for a sample size of 10 and α of 0.025. Exhibit A.12 shows a sample entry for the Student's *t* distribution.

4. Use the formula to compute the observed *t* value:

$$t = \frac{12.1 - 14}{2.64/10}$$

$$t = \frac{-1.9}{.84}$$

$$t = -2.26.$$

5. Compare the critical and observed *t* values: $-2.262 \leq -2.26$.

6. Because the observed *t* value is greater than or equal to the critical *t* value, you have confirmed the hypothesis ($\mu \leq 14$ ppm), with 97.5 percent confidence, that the impurities in the water are less than 14 ppm. While there is still a 2.5 percent chance that the impurities are equal to 14 ppm, you had already determined that this degree of risk would be acceptable. If μ had been larger than 14, you would have needed to take corrective action.

Inferring Proportions

Just as we sometimes need to make estimates of the population mean based on a relatively small sample, we sometimes need to infer proportions—or percentages—based on a small sample.

Suppose that you wanted to select one of two ads for testing in a sample geographical area, and you wanted to test the ad that had the better chance of succeeding. You could infer the proportion of the population that would prefer the one ad to the other by using a small sample and the following procedure:

1. Select a random sample. Show sample members both ads and ask which they prefer. Assume that 18 out of 25 people prefer Ad 1.

2. Determine the proportion (p) according to the formula:

$$p = \frac{X}{n} \text{ where } X \text{ is the number of persons preferring Ad 1.}$$

(Note: The conclusions would be the same if we used $X = 7$, the number preferring Ad 2, but the percentages would differ.)

$$p = \frac{18}{25} = 0.72 \text{ or } 72\%.$$

3. State the hypothesis: At least 60 percent of the population will prefer Ad 1 to Ad 2.

4. Determine a range of acceptance using Statistical Table 2. Exhibit A.13 illustrates the procedure for using the table.

   The figures in this table, as is true of the Student's t Distribution, represent figures for half of the distribution. The figure for both halves is simply twice that for one. On the chart, we look for 30 percent. At a Z of 0.85, we find 0.3023, the figure closest to 30 percent. (Note that for the purposes of this test, any error should be in the direction of a larger percentage to ensure greater accuracy.)

   Exhibit A.14 illustrates the relationship of the numbers in the table to the standard normal distribution.

   By using the table, we see that if Z is 0.85 or greater, we will have confirmed our hypothesis.

5. Use the formula

$$Z = \frac{p^1 - p}{\sqrt{pg/n}}$$

where

$p^1 = X/n,$

$p =$ hypothesized percentage, and

$q = 1 - p.$

Result:

$$Z = \frac{.72 - .60}{\sqrt{(.60)(.40)/25}}$$

$$Z = \frac{.12}{\sqrt{.24/25}}$$

$$Z = \frac{.12}{.098}$$

$$.85 \leq 1.22.$$

TABLE 2:
Student-t Distribution

Table gives t_0 such that $P(t \geq t_0) = \alpha$

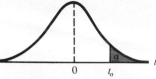

df	$\alpha = .10$	.05	.025	.01	.005
1	3.078	6.314	12.706	31.821	63.657
2	1.886	2.920	4.303	6.965	9.925
3	1.638	2.353	3.182	4.541	5.841
4	1.533	2.132	2.776	3.747	4.604
5	1.476	2.015	2.571	3.365	4.032
6	1.440	1.943	2.447	3.143	3.707
7	1.415	1.895	2.365	2.998	3.499
8	1.397	1.860	2.306	2.896	3.355
9	1.383	1.833	2.262	2.821	3.250
10	1.372	1.812	2.228	2.764	3.169
11	1.363	1.796	2.201	2.718	3.106
12	1.356	1.782	2.179	2.681	3.055
13	1.350	1.771	2.160	2.650	3.012
14	1.345	1.761	2.145	2.624	2.977
15	1.341	1.753	2.131	2.602	2.947
16	1.337	1.746	2.120	2.583	2.921
17	1.333	1.740	2.110	2.567	2.898
18	1.330	1.734	2.101	2.552	2.878
19	1.328	1.729	2.093	2.539	2.861
20	1.325	1.725	2.086	2.528	2.845
21	1.323	1.721	2.080	2.518	2.831
22	1.321	1.717	2.074	2.508	2.819
23	1.319	1.714	2.069	2.500	2.807
24	1.318	1.711	2.064	2.492	2.797
25	1.316	1.708	2.060	2.485	2.787
26	1.315	1.706	2.056	2.479	2.779
27	1.314	1.703	2.052	2.473	2.771
28	1.313	1.701	2.048	2.467	2.763
29	1.311	1.699	2.045	2.462	2.756
∞	1.282	1.645	1.960	2.326	2.576

Exhibit A.13   Sample Standard Normal Distribution

			Second Decimal Place in Z			
Z	.00	.01	.02	.03	.04	.05
.0	—	—	—	—	—	—
.1	—	—	—	—	—	—
.2	—	—	—	—	—	—
.3	—	—	—	—	—	—
.4	—	—	—	—	—	—
.5	—	—	—	—	—	—
.6	—	—	—	—	—	—
.7	—	—	—	—	—	—
.8	—	—	—	—	—	.3023
.9	—	—	—	—	—	—
1.0	—	—	—	—	—	—

Exhibit A.14   Symmetry of the Standard Normal Distribution

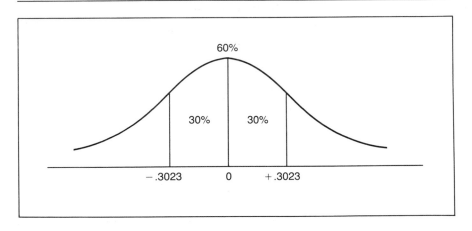

Because the observed Z value is greater than or equal to the critical Z value, we can predict that at least 60 percent of the total population would also prefer Ad 1. Exhibit A.15 illustrates why this is true.

Because Z 1.22 falls outside the hypothesized figure of Z 0.85 (60 percent—or more accurately, ±30 percent), we can infer from our sample that at least 60 percent of the population will prefer Ad 1 to Ad 2. You should note that this test does not *prove* that 60 percent of the population will prefer Ad 1 to Ad 2. It is rather a measure of probability and a predictor of risk. If we wanted to be even more certain that a majority of the population would prefer one ad to the other, we would use a higher percentage in the formula, which would result in a higher critical Z value. In this case, if we had decided on a lower degree of risk,

Exhibit A.15

Standard Normal Distribution Showing Proportions in Reference to Z Numbers

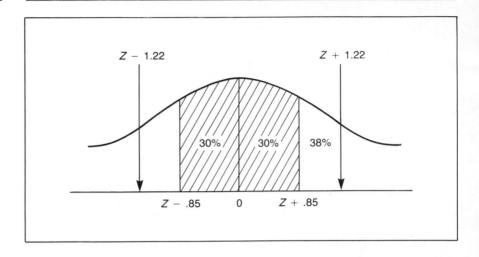

we might not have been able to make the same positive inference the higher degree of risk permitted.

Inferring Variance and Standard Deviation   Another frequently useful test is the chi-square (χ^2) test for variance. The χ^2 test is useful for determining whether a variance is within acceptable limits.

If you worked for a microchip company, for example, you would want to ensure that each microchip was exactly the correct thickness. Let us assume that a variance of 0.005 is acceptable.

Our hypothesis is that the variance is no larger than the specified 0.005. Again, we are going to compare the results of a sample with what we know to be probable. As is true of Student's t and proportions, the chi-square test requires a table. Statistical Table 3 shows the critical values for chi-square.

We would test the hypothesis using the following formula:

$$\chi^2 = \frac{(n-1)S^2}{\sigma^2}$$

where

S^2 = sample variance

n = sample size, and

σ^2 = the value specified in the hypothesis.

Exhibit A.16 illustrates the application of the formula.

To test our hypothesis, we select 14 chips at random. We discover that the variance is 0.0043.

TABLE 3:

Chi-Square Distribution

Table gives k such that $P(\chi^2 \geq k) = \alpha$

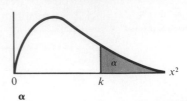

df	.0995	0.990	0.975	0.950	0.900
			α		
1	0.0000393	0.0001571	0.0009821	0.0039321	0.0157908
2	0.0100251	0.0201007	0.0506356	0.102587	0.210720
3	0.0717212	0.114832	0.215795	0.351846	0.584375
4	0.206990	0.297110	0.484419	0.710721	1.063623
5	0.411740	0.554300	0.831211	1.145476	1.61031
6	0.675727	0.872085	1.237347	1.63539	2.20413
7	0.989265	1.239043	1.68987	2.16735	2.83311
8	1.344419	1.646482	2.17973	2.73264	3.48954
9	1.734926	2.087912	2.70039	3.32511	4.16816
10	2.15585	2.55821	3.24697	3.94030	4.86518
11	2.60321	3.05347	3.81575	4.57481	5.57779
12	3.07382	3.57056	4.40379	5.22603	6.30380
13	3.56503	4.10691	5.00874	5.89186	7.04150
14	4.07468	4.66043	5.62872	6.57063	7.78953
15	4.60094	5.22935	6.26214	7.26094	8.54675
16	5.14224	5.81221	6.90766	7.96164	9.31223
17	5.69724	6.40776	7.56418	8.67176	10.0852
18	6.26481	7.01491	8.23075	9.39046	10.8649
19	6.84398	7.63273	8.90655	10.1170	11.6509
20	7.43386	8.26040	9.59083	10.8508	12.4426
21	8.03366	8.89720	10.28293	11.5913	13.2396
22	8.64272	9.54249	10.9823	12.3380	14.0415
23	9.26042	10.19567	11.6885	13.0905	14.8479
24	9.88623	10.8564	12.4011	13.8484	15.6587
25	10.5197	11.5240	13.1197	14.6114	16.4734
26	11.1603	12.1981	13.8439	15.3791	17.2919
27	11.8076	12.8786	14.5733	16.1513	18.1138
28	12.4613	13.5648	15.3079	16.9279	18.9392
29	13.1211	14.2565	16.0471	17.7083	19.7677
30	13.7867	14.9535	16.7908	18.4926	20.5992
40	20.7065	22.1643	24.4331	26.5093	29.0505
50	27.9907	29.7067	32.3574	34.7642	37.6886
60	35.5346	37.4848	40.4817	43.1879	46.4589
70	43.2752	45.4418	48.7576	51.7393	55.3290
80	51.1720	53.5400	57.1532	60.3915	64.2778
90	59.1963	61.7541	65.6466	69.1260	73.2912
100	67.3276	70.0648	74.2219	77.9295	82.3581

TABLE 3:

Chi-Square Distribution (continued)

α					
0.100	0.050	0.025	0.010	0.005	df
2.70554	3.84146	5.02389	6.63490	7.87944	1
4.60517	5.99147	7.37776	9.21034	10.5966	2
6.25139	7.81473	9.34840	11.3449	12.8381	3
7.77944	9.48773	11.1433	13.2767	14.8602	4
9.23635	11.0705	12.8325	15.0863	16.7496	5
10.6446	12.5916	14.4494	16.8119	18.5476	6
12.0170	14.0671	16.0128	18.4753	20.2777	7
13.3616	15.5073	17.5346	20.0902	21.9550	8
14.6837	16.9190	19.0228	21.6660	23.5893	9
15.9871	18.3070	20.4831	23.2093	25.1882	10
17.2750	19.6751	21.9200	24.7250	26.7569	11
18.5494	21.0261	23.3367	26.2170	28.2995	12
19.8119	22.3621	24.7356	27.6883	29.8194	13
21.0642	23.6848	26.1190	29.1413	31.3193	14
22.3072	24.9958	27.4884	30.5779	32.8013	15
23.5418	26.2962	28.8454	31.9999	34.2672	16
24.7690	27.5871	30.1910	33.4087	35.7185	17
25.9894	28.8693	31.5264	34.8053	37.1564	18
27.2036	30.1435	32.8523	36.1908	38.5822	19
28.4120	31.4104	34.1696	37.5662	39.9968	20
29.6151	32.6705	35.4789	38.9321	41.4010	21
30.8133	33.9244	36.7807	40.2894	42.7956	22
32.0069	35.1725	38.0757	41.6384	44.1813	23
33.1963	36.4151	39.3641	42.9798	45.5585	24
34.3816	37.6525	40.6465	44.3141	46.9278	25
35.5631	38.8852	41.9232	45.6417	48.2899	26
36.7412	40.1133	43.1944	46.9630	49.6449	27
37.9159	41.3372	44.4607	48.2782	50.9933	28
39.0875	42.5569	45.7222	49.5879	52.3356	29
40.2560	43.7729	46.9792	50.8922	53.6720	30
51.8050	55.7585	59.3417	63.6907	66.7659	40
63.1671	67.5048	71.4202	76.1539	79.4900	50
74.3970	79.0819	83.2976	88.3794	91.9517	60
85.5271	90.5312	95.0231	100.425	104.215	70
96.5782	101.879	106.629	112.329	116.321	80
107.565	113.145	118.136	124.116	128.299	90
118.498	124.342	129.561	135.807	140.169	100

Exhibit A.16   ## Chi-Square Illustration

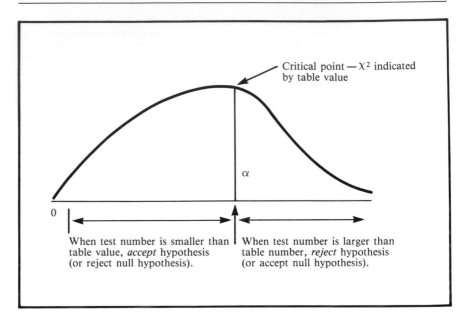

Critical point — X^2 indicated by table value

α

0

When test number is smaller than table value, *accept* hypothesis (or reject null hypothesis).

When test number is larger than table number, *reject* hypothesis (or accept null hypothesis).

Exhibit A.17   ## Critical Point for Accepting the Hypothesis

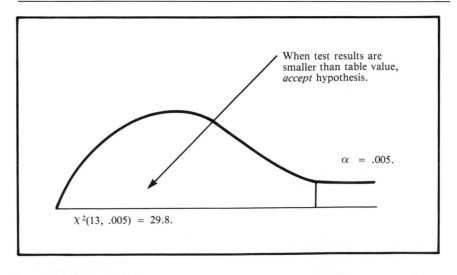

When test results are smaller than table value, *accept* hypothesis.

$\alpha = .005.$

$X^2(13, .005) = 29.8.$

Using Statistical Table 3, we determine the critical point of a sample of 14 with a tolerance of 0.005.

$$df = (n - 1) = 13$$

$$\alpha = .005$$

$$\chi^2 = 29.8$$

Exhibit A.17 illustrates the critical point for accepting the hypothesis.

Does a sample size of 14 with a variance of 0.0043 allow us to conclude that our machinery is working correctly?

$$\chi^2 = \frac{(n - 1)S^2}{\sigma^2}$$

$$\chi^2 = \frac{(13).0043^2}{.005^2}$$

$$\chi^2 = \frac{(13).0000185}{.000025}$$

$$\chi^2 = \frac{.00024}{.000025}$$

$$\chi^2 = 9.6.$$

Because 9.6 is smaller than the table value of 29.8, we accept our hypothesis that the thickness of the microchips falls within acceptable tolerances.

A P P E N D I X   B

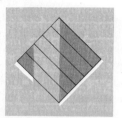

Report Problems

The reports you write as part of your report writing education should be closely related to the kinds of reports you will actually write on the job. Further, you should attempt to write several types of reports that will be common to the kind of work you expect to do after graduation.

MULTIPLE REPORTS

The problems in this section are designed to give you the opportunity to prepare more than one report dealing with the same area of concern. For each of the problems, you might prepare any of the following in addition to a complete analytical report:

1. A feasibility study
2. A proposal
3. A progress report (or series of reports)
4. A report of library research
5. A report of experimental results
6. A synopsis
7. An executive summary
8. A journal publication based on the report
9. Evaluations of personnel, procedures, or products involved in your project
10. Appropriate inserts for employee publications or for individual, departmental, or corporate annual reports
11. One or more oral reports

Each of the cases presented here requires additional information. For some cases, you can assume the data and provide details based on your imagination. For that reason, the cases may be either short or long, depending on the information the writer wishes to convey. In other cases, you will need to conduct at least secondary and perhaps primary research to collect the necessary data. When a case involves a fictional company for which or in which you are to conduct research, you may use a similar local company as a source of information, or you may ask other students to complete appropriate questionnaires. The use of local companies should be coordinated by your instructor so that no one company has too many students requesting permission to conduct research.

Perform any statistical analyses necessary to validate the reliability of your conclusions.

1. What kinds of reports are written by those working in your area of specialization? Do the kinds of reports differ at entry level, middle management levels, and upper-level management positions?

2. Several of the doctors on the staff at the hospital you manage have asked you to purchase a CAT-Scan device. Should the hospital invest in one? Prepare your report for the hospital's board of directors.

3. Your company is a major manufacturer of mainframe computer systems. Should your company attempt to enter the micro and minicomputer business?

4. Evaluate computer scanning devices recently installed in many grocery stores. How well do they work? What do customers think of them? You work for a local grocery store chain, and the president of the company is considering installing them in all your stores.

5. Your company is about to introduce a new product (your choice). As a member of the Marketing Division, you've been asked to plan a marketing strategy for the product. Prepare your recommendations for the Vice President of Marketing.

6. The Dean of the College of Business has asked you, Chairperson of the Department of Accountancy, to prepare a report on the demand for accountants over the next ten years. Be sure to consider the impact of computers and computerized accounting systems.

7. As a member of a management consulting team, you have been assigned the responsibility of evaluating and making suggestions for improvements in the following areas:
   a. Inventory control
   b. Profit planning
   c. Return on equity
   d. Capital investments and depreciations
   e. Bad-debts policy and collection procedures

Select a company with which you are familiar, and prepare your report.

8. Should your company invest in regular motivational seminars? As Director of Education and Training, you have been asked to evaluate the effectiveness of motivational seminars.

9. What form of instruction is most effective for orienting new employees to your company? New employees have to know company objectives; the way departments relate to each other; a wide variety of policies, fringe benefits, and other items of information that will clarify how their jobs fit into the organization as a whole.

10. A contractor has asked you to explain the advantages and disadvantages of buying and leasing capital equipment.

11. The president of your company recently read a report claiming that smokers are less productive than nonsmokers. She has asked you to verify or disprove that report. She also wants to know whether it would be advisable to prohibit smoking except during regularly scheduled break periods. Would smokers feel so resentful about a no-smoking rule that their productivity would be lower still? Should the company hire only nonsmokers in the future?

12. As an investment counselor, you have been asked to advise a client who has $430,000 to invest. What do you recommend and why? How can your client evaluate the trade-off between risk and return?

13. Your state senator has asked you—as a person knowledgeable about business—to evaluate the business climate in your state. What can the state do to encourage business and industry to locate new plants in the state? Should the state work to recruit any particular business or industry?

14. What changes will take place in labor-management relations over the next ten years? How will those changes affect your company? Prepare a formal report for the president of your company, who will be sharing your report with the board of directors.

15. Explain the expression, "Business doesn't pay taxes; it only collects them," to the U.S. Representative from your district.

16. Your supervisor, the Assistant Vice President of Marketing, will be visiting a number of foreign countries to explore the possibility of establishing markets for your products (select a product or products with international potential). Before he leaves, he wants to know more about business customs and the business climate in the following countries: England, France, Germany, Mexico, Japan, and South Korea.

17. Your company has developed a new instant coffee. To produce it, you use a new evaporation process that reduces the caffeine

content by 60 percent and enhances flavor. The result is a better tasting coffee with a low caffeine content. Will people buy the coffee? Which people might buy the coffee? How should the coffee be packaged and presented?

18. Should your company install cassette tape players in company cars so that employees can listen to educational and motivational tapes while driving? Should the company also provide the tapes? The Training Manager has asked for your recommendation.

19. Should your school—or community—install a central parking garage? How should the garage be financed?

20. The department of which you are manager maintains an honor-system coffee pot for the 43 members on your staff. If each person puts in 10 cents for each cup of coffee, the fund should be large enough to pay for the coffee and to save enough to buy a new pot when the current one burns out. Unfortunately, you have been coming up several dollars short each week. What, if anything, should you do about it? Rather than make a decision and force it on your staff, you decide to investigate the problem and share your findings in report form with your staff.

21. As a member of Rotary (substitute any comparable organization), you have been placed in charge of planning the association's national convention, to be held in your town in two years. The president of your local chapter wants to know who should do what and when to make the conference a success. What will the costs of the conference be? How will those costs be financed? How many people will attend? Where will they stay? How long will they stay?

22. Your company is about to repair its offices and conference rooms. What colors should be used? Should all the rooms be painted the same color, or should your company attempt to use color to control the moods of the people in them? Should the employees have a choice? Prepare a report for the Director of Personnel, who is in charge of selecting the paint.

23. Should your company invest in a company gym and jogging track? Would employees use the facilities? If so, when? Also, would the company receive any return for its investment? If so, what?

24. Select three or four similar products appropriate for use in your area of specialization (drafting tables, typewriters, computers, pieces of lab equipment) and evaluate their advantages and disadvantages. Assume that you have been invited to present your findings and recommendation to the president of a company that would use the kind of equipment you have examined.

25. A church group in your community purchased a satellite antenna for the purpose of taping broadcast movies and reshowing them for a fee. Lately, some of the members have begun to worry about

the legality of the taping and reshowing. They have asked you to investigate and to recommend possible alternative methods of raising funds.

26. Your company, Faultless Fabrics, produces three brands of jeans—Sylvia Lannon, expensive designer jeans for women; Brad Barker, expensive designer jeans for men; and Jean-O's, inexpensive but durable jeans for men, women, and children. You have been asked to determine how these products should be marketed in your area. The Vice President of Marketing wants to know whether Faultless Fabrics should open its own store (which could stock additional merchandise) or market through existing outlets.

27. One of the by-products of your manufacturing process is phosphate, which you have been discharging into the local water system. Several of the lakes in the area have recently begun to show signs of eutrophication. Environmentalists in the area are blaming your plant. The president of your company has asked you to prepare a report outlining both a course of action and the best method of communicating that action to the public. She also wants to know how much it will cost to implement your recommendations. Your effluent contains 127–196 ppm of phosphate, 47 ppm of nitrogen, and trace amounts of 12 common minerals.

28. Your company is a major manufacturer of defense-related electronic equipment. You have been asked to investigate and report on state-of-the-art industrial security systems. Prepare an informative report for the president and board of directors.

29. Evaluate the food being served in your company (or school) cafeteria. What changes should the catering company make in the food, the way it is prepared and served, and costs?

30. How can your organization best identify potential leaders? Prepare a report for the Vice President of Personnel.

31. Alvin Toffler's *The Third Wave* suggests that word and data processing equipment will make the present role of secretary obsolete. The Vice President of Corporate Planning has asked you to prepare a study of the electronic office at your organization. How many executives are likely to master the keyboarding skills necessary to make the electronic office function? When is the impact likely to be felt? Who will be affected? What will happen to productivity? How will morale be influenced?

32. As a research assistant for your state governor, prepare a report on the effects of alcohol abuse in the state. How much does it cost? How many people are affected? Can the state take any steps to control it?

33. Your large, multinational corporation has asked you to investigate the problems caused by two-career families. Is there any way your

company can avoid the problems caused by the conflicting needs of the corporation and husbands and wives whose careers are leading in different directions?

34. Over the past 10 years, your company has grown tremendously, and your number of stockholders has grown as well. Your earnings have been high, and your company president thinks that it is time to produce a first-rate annual report. He has asked you to recommend style, format, and content. Give examples of what to include and what to avoid in annual reports.

35. The Vice President of Personnel has asked you to report on what the recent studies of behavior modification have to say about decreasing absenteeism. Are any of the new techniques applicable to your company?

36. How is your company perceived by the community? Use a specific local company and investigate. Does the company need to take any action to improve its image? Prepare the report for the company president or plant manager.

37. What legislation currently pending (local, state, or federal) will influence your company (be specific in selecting a company)? The president of your company wants a concise summary of the legislation and your opinion of the impact it might have on your company.

38. You work for a major American automobile manufacturer, and you have been asked to find out what owners of foreign cars like about them. What can your company do to prevent further erosion of market share to imports?

39. What skills does a person need to be successful in your area of specialization? Your professional association has asked you to research and report on the necessary skills. Your report will be published in an upcoming issue of the professional journal in your discipline. Companies will use the information to help make hiring decisions, so include a section on what recruiters should look for when interviewing.

40. What responsibility should your company assume for staff development? The Director of Personnel has asked you to discover whether the money the company might spend on staff development—including job training, training for new jobs as old jobs become obsolete, and advice about and help with qualifying for promotions—will be worth it.

41. You are a Site Selector for a fast-food chain known for its high quality beef, chicken, cheese, and fish sandwiches for lunch and dinner. You also offer a breakfast menu of pancakes, waffles, French toast, eggs, and all the toast a person can eat. Your prices are a little higher than other better known fast-food restaurants, but your quality is worth it. Should your chain, Sandwich Earl's, open a restaurant in your town? If so, where should it be located?

42. Should your company institute an incentive program for its sales staff? Your sales representatives currently work for a commission, which ought to encourage them to sell as much as possible without additional incentives. Would some form of recognition prove a better incentive than additional money? Be specific in selecting a company and product line.

43. The local Chamber of Commerce has asked you to evaluate your community from the perspective of business climate. What do local businesses like about it? What do they dislike? What can the chamber do to improve the business climate?

44. Should your company institute a quality-circle program? Where did the idea of quality circles come from, and do the circles work?

45. What is likely to happen to interest rates in the next ten years? Should your company borrow the money to build a new facility now, or do a little remodeling now and wait several years before building? Be specific about the company, its current facility, and the costs of new construction.

46. You work for the owner–builder of a luxury apartment complex in your area. You will have 88 two- and three-bedroom units, each with its own laundry facilities. What kind of washer and dryer should be installed in the apartments?

47. You work for a large manufacturing company. Recently, one of your employees fell off scaffolding four stories high and was killed. It was discovered that he was drunk. Now the company president wants to know whether alcoholism is a problem in your company. Should your company attempt to do anything about it? What do other companies do?

48. Your company needs a specific policy on sexual harassment. What is it? What should a woman—or man—do who believes that she or he is the victim of sexual harassment? What evidence is necessary? What kinds of protection should be offered to victims? How do you prevent false accusations?

49. Your boss is in the process of building the world's largest used-car lot. She has asked you to determine what kind of lighting system you should install.

50. Many companies in your industry have recently unionized. Your company does not yet have a union, though some of the employees have been discussing the possibilities. Should your company try to avoid unionization, and what will it need to do to prevent the union from organizing? Prepare your report for the president.

51. Your supervisor, Beth Marks, Manager of Corporate Communication, wants to know which forms of communication are most effective with which employees. You have the following kinds of employees: office workers, maintenance workers, management personnel, lab technicians, and scientists. You have

the following forms of communication: supervisor to subordinate, bulletin boards, PA system, memos to office mailbox, letters to home, company newsletter, and company bulletins. How should important announcements be communicated? Do the different forms of communication serve different functions?

52. A multinational corporation has decided to form a new subsidiary. You have been hired to run the department or laboratory in your area of specialization. (You will need to be specific about the product or service the new company will produce/market.) Submit a report outlining and justifying your needs, including space, equipment, supplies, and personnel.

SHORT REPORTS WITH DATA

53. *Scholarship Recommendation.* Each year the Zonta Club, a classified service organization of executive women, offers a $1,000 scholarship to a full-time college student who is a resident of the community. As Chairperson of the Scholarship Committee, you are to recommend one candidate for the scholarship to the club's membership. You and your committee have evaluated more than 50 applications, interviewed the top five candidates, and have selected two finalists: Brenda Halbert and Cam Fournier. In a memo report to the club membership, present the two finalists and make your recommendation. The following information is a summary of the qualifications provided by the students on their applications:

   Brenda Halbert. A junior at Midwest College with a grade point average of 3.5 (4 = A). Dean's list each semester. Carries 15 semester hours and works 20 hours a week to help finance her education. Activities: member of Alpha Kappa Psi, a business organization, and president of Alpha Lamda Delta, a national honor society. Lives at home with parents and four sisters and two brothers. Letters of reference identified her as an extrovert and a good student.

   Cam Fournier. A sophomore at West Community College with a grade point average of 3.8 (4 = A). Carries 18 semester hours and is a volunteer at the local hospital. Activities: member of Alpha Beta Chi, a business communication society, and president of the French Club. Parents are divorced. Lives with mother, who works outside the home. Letters of reference identified him as a bright student with high moral standards.

54. *Car Colors.* "Any customer can have a car painted any color that he wants, so long as it is black," quipped automobile mogul Henry Ford in 1909. Today people's ideas of colors have changed, and you as Vice President of Production realize that. So that you manufacture the colors preferred by customers, you ask your Vice

President of Marketing to survey the company's dealerships in the state to determine which color is the customer's preferred choice. Here are the results of the survey:

Red	2,856
White	4,123
Blue	3,732
Brown	1,589
Yellow	857
Tan	1,202
Silver	2,298

Prepare a written report of your findings for the Vice President of Production.

55. *Sadie Hawkins Dance.* November 1 is Sadie Hawkins Day, but most men wish it were more often. Men seem to be receptive to the idea, but what do women think? As Chairperson of the Student Activities Committee, you are planning activities for next year and want to know if the student population would support a Sadie Hawkins Dance. Here is what 2,610 students said about women asking men out:

	Approve	Disapprove	Don't Know
Men	950	327	28
Women	658	603	44

Prepare a written report of the findings of your survey for the President of the Student Government Association, who approves student sponsored activities.

56. *Academic Achievement.* As President of the Panhellenic Council, Midwest University, your task is to report on the grade point averages (4 = A) of Greek and non-Greek students as presented in the following table:

	Freshmen	Sophomore	Juniors	Seniors
Men				
Greek	2.40	2.58	2.67	2.75
Non-Greek	2.38	2.53	2.59	2.64
Women				
Greek	2.59	2.78	2.88	3.12
Non-Greek	2.46	2.69	2.76	2.90

Prepare a written report for the Vice President of Student Affairs. In the report, present your interpretation of the grade differences between Greeks and non-Greeks.

57. *Wellness Program.* As the assistant to the Coordinator of the Employee Wellness Programs at United Autoworkers Plant, you are concerned that the programs have been on the decline for the past several months. Employees who initially registered for the various programs no longer attend. You talked about this with the Coordinator, and she suggested that you conduct a survey to determine whether employees were participating in an exercise program outside the company. Here are the resuts of your survey:

> If you are presently participating in a regular exercise program other than through United Autoworkers, what type of program is it?
>
> 230 My own
>
> If your own program, what kinds of activities?

24	Jumping rope
49	Running
55	Swimming
175	Walking
78	Fitness classes
43	Racket sports
18	Weight training
6	Other (4 karate, 2 judo)

Prepare an informational report for the Coordinator of the Plant Wellness Programs.

58. *Slips and Falls.* The Safety Director at the Barrington Packing Plant is concerned about the number of accidents resulting from slips, trips, or falls during the snow season. He directs you to do some research and determine the number of accidents caused by slips, trips, and falls over the past 5 years. Here are the results of your research:

Month	Winter 1	Winter 2	Winter 3	Winter 4	Winter 5[a]
November	2	1	2	0	1
December	12	15	17	11	8
January	22	26	24	23	19
February	20	24	23	20	17
March	5	4	3	3	2

[a]Most recent. For your report, refer to the winters by actual dates.

This year the company wants to reduce employee injuries by another 5 percent and help others avoid a painful accident. Prepare your report and provide recommendations for reducing injuries.

59. *Pets.* During National Adopt-A-Dog Month, the Animal Control Center conducted a survey to determine why people adopt pets. Here is what the survey team uncovered:

Companionship	5,236
Give and receive love	3,298
Safety	2,845
Care for a living thing	1,500
Not sure	845
No answer	75

Prepare a written report of your findings for publication in the center's monthly newsletter.

60. *Who Pays the Nation's Medical Bills?* As the manager of a large insurance firm, prepare a report that you wish to share with your sales staff. Use the data below, which are in billions of dollars.

	Last Year	Five Years Ago
Private insurance	$130	$103
Federal government	122	95
Individual payments	103	76
State and local government	47	20
Other private sources	7	5

LONG REPORTS WITH DATA

61. *Readers' Favorite Comics.* Your local newspaper, the *Gazette Reporter,* printed a questionnaire in its Sunday edition and asked its readership to identify its favorite and least favorite comics. Here are the survey results based on the 5,600 people who responded:

Favorite	Total Votes
Frank and Ernest	487
Family Circus	471
Garfield	431
Bloom County	336
For Better or Worse	287
Doonesbury	232
Rex Morgan	223
Blondie	221
Peanuts	217
Cathy	201

Favorite	Total Votes
Beetle Bailey	200
The Lockhorns	197
Born Loser	184
Gil Thorp	172
U.S. Acres	166
B.C.	156
Marmaduke	145
Mary Worth	144
Apartment 3-G	143
The Neighborhood	142
Ziggy	138
Hagar	130
Wizard of Id	119
Shoe	115
Wee Pals	110
Small Society	100

Least Favorite	Total Votes
The Neighborhood	866
Doonesbury	610
U.S. Acres	336
Wee Pals	328
Rex Morgan	309
Apartment 3-G	302
Mary Worth	289
Gil Thorp	287
Cathy	269
Garfield	156
Bloom County	149
Shoe	146
The Lockhorns	143
Ziggy	138
Wizard of Id	123
Marmaduke	119
Born Loser	115
Small Society	110
Family Circus	98
Blondie	86
B.C.	84
Frank & Ernest	82
Hagar	80
For Better or Worse	77
Peanuts	73
Beetle Bailey	70

Among Men

Favorite	Least Favorite
Bloom County	The Neighborhood
Garfield	Doonesbury
Family Circle	Wee Pals
Doonesbury	U.S. Acres
Beetle Bailey	Mary Worth

Among Women

Favorite	Least Favorite
Frank & Ernest	The Neighborhood
Family Circus	Doonesbury
Garfield	U.S. Acres
Bloom County	Wee Pals
Cathy	Rex Morgan

Requested Comics and Total Votes

Judge Parker, 510

Far Side, 450

Prince Valiant, 390

Hi & Lois, 212

Sally Forth, 210

Andy Capp, 200

Dennis the Menace, 198

Brenda Starr, 145

Nancy, 133

62. *Lifestyle Census.* Where are we? The American Business Clubs (AMBUCS), wanting to improve the quality of life of the citizens in the community, distributed a questionnaire to 500 people. The results of the survey are in, and you have tabulated the data. Now you need to evelute the responses. Analyze the data, and prepare a written report for the president of AMBUCS.

a. What is your age group?

3%	Under 18
12%	18–29
25%	30–39
20%	40–49
25%	50–59
10%	60–69
5%	70 or over

b. Are you married?

81%   Yes   19%   No

c. Do you:

43% Own your own home
57% Rent

d. Length of time at current address:

10% Less than one year
39% One to five years
51% Six years or more

e. Number of children in the family:

28% 0 or 1
34% 2 or 3
22% 4 or 5
16% 6 or more

f. Do you own a car?

88% Yes
12% No

g. Do you own a television set?

96% Yes
4% No

h. Do you own a video recorder?

43% Yes
57% No

i. Do you have a major credit card?

59% Yes
41% No

j. If yes, what credit cards do you have?

65% MasterCard/Visa
35% American Express/Diner

k. Do you currently have

35% Money market certificates
88% Pension palns
72% Stocks/bonds
25% IRAs

l. What is your political party?

49% Republican
30% Democratic
12% Independent
 9% None

63. *Five-Year Study of Graduates with Implications for Curriculum Improvement.* If the business curriculum is to keep pace with the needs of business, it needs periodic evaluation. The purpose of this study is to determine the influence of education on the career patterns of associate degree graduates of the business studies curriculum at State College. As a special project for your research class, you conducted a survey of the business education majors who graduated within the past five years. Here are the results of the survey.
Returns of mail questionnaire:

	Sent	Returned
Male	312	202
Female	231	180

Graduates' current major activity:

Four-year college	202
Work outside the home	102
Looking for work	15
Work in the home	32
Military	23
Other	8

Breakdown of those currently at a four-year college:

Part-time	27
Full-time	175

Breakdown of those currently employed (180 Yes; 50 No):

Part-time	125
Full-time	55

Annual salary of those currently employed:

76	$25,000 or more
45	$20,000–$24,999
37	$15,000–$19,000
22	Less than $15,000

Relationship of present employment to major area of study:

Very related	110
Somewhat related	50
Not related	20

Prepare a written report for the chairperson of the department.

64. *What Do Customers Really Think?* What do customers really think of Davenport's Department Store? An Executive Vice President asked Customer Satisfaction Resources to identify customer attitudes. Here is what the CSR learned after surveying 500 customers (very favorable, somewhat favorable, neutral, somewhat unfavorable and very unfavorable):

	VF	SF	N	SU	VU
Provides reliable service	80%	19%	0%	0%	1%
Meets customers' needs	78	16	1	1	2
Has reasonably priced merchandise	72	20	3	3	2
Treats customers courteously	64	25	5	4	2
Handles complaints satisfactorily	60	28	6	3	1
Has friendly employees	64	26	5	5	0
Is community minded	48	33	19	0	0
Provides clean restrooms	45	28	4	15	8
Provides monthly sales	92	5	1	1	1

Appearance and manner of employees:

Satisfied	98
Unsatisfied	2

Accuracy of monthly statements:

Satisfied	76
Unsatisfied	24

Prepare the CSR report for presentation to the Executive Vice President. Include in your report an overall rating.

Job Application
Materials

This appendix will help you prepare the materials you will need to use when you apply for a job. These consist of a résumé, letter of application, and follow-up correspondence.

Résumé

Every professional person should maintain an up-to-date résumé, or record of achievements, at all times. The résumé lets a reader review a candidate's qualifications for employment quickly and easily. To accomplish this purpose, it must be highly organized and structured to emphasize the person's main qualifications.

Formats for résumés may vary, but regardless of the format used, the résumé should arrange main entries and dates so that they may be read quickly and easily. Printed résumés are generally more successful than typewritten résumés.

A résumé shuld be either one full page or two full pages long. One and a half typewritten pages may be condensed to one printed page, and three typewritten pages may be condensed to two printed pages. Although many personnel directors express a preference for one-page résumés, two-page résumés have proved generally more successful.

Your résumé *should* include the following information:

1. Your *name*.
2. Your complete *address* and *phone number*. You may include two addresses (school and mailing) if you will be moving soon after your résumé is prepared. Be sure to include area codes (phone numbers) and zip codes (addresses).

3. *Job objective* or *qualified by* line. Let your reader see in the first few lines either what you think you can do (job objective) or provide a quick overview of what you have done.

4. *Education.* When and where did you go to school? What degree(s) will you earn by what date? List the schools you have attended in reverse chronological order (most recent first). The degree-granting institution is the school that confers honors and your major and minor. If you are a new college graduate, your education will be an important qualification, so amplify your educational achievements by listing courses or by describing main projects. If you list courses, do so by *title* and not by course number. *Management 404* does not tell a reader what the course was about. *Organizational Behavior* specifies the topic of the class and says something about what you should have learned.

5. *Experience.* What is your work history? List jobs in reverse chronological order. Consider placing career-related experience in a separate category. For each entry, give the dates of employment, your job title, name and complete address of your employer, and your duties and responsibilities. Use language that emphasizes your initiative and special achievements.

6. *Academic and employment references.* Give the titles, names, complete business addresses, and phone numbers for at least three instructors or work supervisors who have agreed to serve as references for you.

7. *Date prepared.* Placing the date of preparation at the end of the résumé assures the reader that the résumé is current.

Your résumé *may* include the following additional entries:

1. *Military experience.* If you have served in any branch of the armed forces, you should include the record of your military achievements. Include dates of service, highest rank, date and type of discharge. Also, include your duties and responsibilities (number of personnel supervised) as with other job entries.

2. *Publications.* If you have published articles, short stories, or poems, provide a list of publications. Use a standard bibliographic entry form.

3. *Extracurricular activities,* hobbies and interests. If these activities show initiative, leadership, or aptitude for the kind of work you plan to do, they may be worth including.

4. *Memberships.* Include memberships in professional associations. Memberships in social and service organizations may be worth including, especially if you have had leadership positions.

Do *not* include

1. *Personal details,* such as height, weight, age, sex, or marital status *unless* the job for which you are applying specifically requires it.

2. A *photograph,* unless the job for which you are applying specifically requires it (modeling, for example).

3. *Personal references.* Relatives, neighbors, doctors, dentists, rabbis, ministers, and priests should not be used as references on your résumé. Employment application forms sometimes ask for names of people who know you well. List personal references there. Use only academic and employment references on the résumé.

Exhibit C.1 illustrates the application of these principles.

Letter of Application

The letter of application is essentially a letter of transmittal that accompanies the résumé. It is prepared *after* the resume is complete and is designed to interpret the résumé in the light of a specific reader's needs.

The letter should begin by applying for a specific job (*not* a "position," "opening," or "anything available"). It should amplify and interpret information on the résumé, rather than merely repeat it. The letter should prove to the reader that you are ready and qualified to perform useful work. Use your education and previous experience to provide evidence of your ability to meet objectives. Mention personal qualities (initiative, perseverance, ability to communicate) that will be an asset on the job. *Show* that you have these qualities by giving illustrations; do not simply *tell* the reader that you have them.

Close the letter by asking for an interview. Do *not* ask for a job in the letter; discuss the job in the interview. The letter of application should not be longer than one page. Exhibit C.2 illustrates a letter of application.

Follow-up Correspondence

If you do not receive a response to your initial application within 4 weeks, send a second application consisting of your letter and résumé. Keep accurate records of to whom you wrote at which company and on which dates you sent your materials.

When your letter and résumé have secured an interview, you will need to send a thank-you letter to the interviewer after you have met with her or him. Use this letter to tell the reader either that you are still interested in the job or that you are no longer interested.

If you are still interested in the job, you may use the letter to supply additional information that will show your qualifications for the job. If the interviewer voiced objections to hiring you (lack of experience, too young or too old, education not ideally suited to the type of work), use the follow-up letter to overcome those objections.

Exhibit C.3 shows an example of a follow-up letter.

Exhibit C.1   Résumé

DENICE D. TROPP

Present Address
530 Locust St., Apt. #1
Kalamazoo, MI 49007
(616) 344-2296

Permanent Address
R#1 Box 911
Buchanan, MI 49107
(616) 695-5325

QUALIFIED BY

A thorough education in all aspects of **management,** including **feasibility studies,** combined with an excellent background in **business communication** and **general business** and more than five years of full- and part-time work experience.

EDUCATION

Sep 19X3 to
Aug 19X5

Bachelor of Business Administration, cum laude (3.77 GPA), August 19X5. College of Business, Western Michigan University, Kalamazoo, MI 49008.

Major **MANAGEMENT:** 8 courses, 24 credit hours. Advanced courses include Management Analysis and Behavior I, II; Management Analysis and Organizational Design I, II; Personnel Management; Administrative Behavior; and Organizational Behavior.

Double
Minor

BUSINESS COMMUNICATION: 7 courses, 21 credit hours. Advanced courses include Organizational Communication, Report Writing, and Publicity and Public Relations.

GENERAL BUSINESS: 7 courses, 21 credit hours. Courses include Statistics, Finance, Accounting, Economics, Business Law, Marketing, and Management.

Sep 19X1 to
Apr 19X3

Associate of Arts Degree, April 19X3. College of Arts and Sciences, Southwestern Michigan College, Dowagiac, MI 49047.

Education financed 100% by scholarships, loans, and part- and full-time employment.

SPECIAL PROJECTS

Sep 19X4 to
Dec 19X4

PUBLIC RELATIONS, Department of Business Information Systems, Western Michigan University. Designed and implemented a promotional campaign for Alpha Beta Chi.

Jan 19X5 to
Apr 19X5

FEASIBILITY STUDIES, Department of Management, Western Michigan University. Managed a task group of 8 people, supervised activities, and conducted a feasibility study integrating relevant variables, analyses, and data into an operating subsidiary company.

WORK EXPERIENCE

Sep 19X4 to
Present

Retail Sales Person, Steketee's Department Store, Kalamazoo, MI 49001. Assist customers, open and close department, and handle routine paperwork. Work 15-22 hours a week during the school year.

Source: Courtesy of Denice D. Tropp.

Exhibit C.1   *(continued)*

Denice D. Tropp

Sep 19X3 to Apr 19X2	**Receptionist,** Britton Hadley Hall, Western Michigan University, Kalamazoo, MI 49008. Greeted guests, helped students with problems, sorted and distributed mail, and handled routine paperwork. Worked 12-20 hours a week during the school year.
Jun to Sep 19X2 & 19X3	**Card Puncher,** Radewald Farms, Niles, MI 49120. Dealt with a group of field workers and was in charge of keeping count of the amount of produce each picked a day; checked the quality of produce picked. Worked 40-60 hours a week during the summers.
Sep 19X2 to May 19X3	**Secretary,** English Department, Southwestern Michigan College, Dowagiac, MI 49047. Worked independently and gained proficiency in typing and editing. Worked 20 hours a week during the school year.
Sep 19X0 to Sep 19X1	**Secretary,** Food Specialties, Buchanan, MI 49107. Calculated daily orders, entered accounts receivable and payable invoices, and typed and edited business letters. In charge of entire office for three weeks while full-time secretary was away. Worked 20 hours a week during the school year and 30-40 hours a week during the summer.

SCHOLARSHIPS, AWARDS, AND MEMBERSHIPS

Sep 19X1 to Aug 19X5	National Standard Competitive Scholarship, Board of Trustees Scholarship at Southwestern Michigan College. Western Michigan University Academic Scholarship. Bowman and Branchaw Business Communication Scholarship. President's List at Southwestern Michigan College. Dean's List at Western Michigan University. Nominee for 1982 Presidential Scholars Convocation. Beta Gamma Sigma membership. Corresponding Secretary for Alpha Beta Chi.

CREDENTIALS

Official transcript and University Placement Service's data sheet are available from Western Michigan University Placement Services, Kalamazoo, MI 49008. (616) 383-1710.

REFERENCES

Dr. Henry Beam, Department of Management, Western Michigan University, Kalamazoo, MI 49008. (616) 383-4081.

Dr. Joel P. Bowman, Department of Business Information Systems, Western Michigan University, Kalamazoo, MI 49008. (616) 383-1703.

Dr. Bernadine P. Branchaw, Department of Business Information Systems, Western Michigan University, Kalamazoo, MI 49008. (616) 383-1908.

Mr. John Prothro, Store Manager, Steketee's Department Store, Kalamazoo, MI 49001. (616) 382-5900, Extension 31.

Prepared March 19X5

Exhibit C.2   Letter of Application

```
530 Locust Street, Apt. #1
Kalamazoo, MI 49007


March 3, 19xx


Ms. Mona Erickson, Personnel Officer
First National Bank and Trust Company of Michigan
108 East Michigan Avenue
Kalamazoo, MI 49007

Dear Ms. Erickson:

Please consider me for the management trainee job you advertised in the
Kalamazoo Gazette on March 2, 19xx.

With my education in management and business communication, I could contribute
to First National Bank's excellent management program.  In one of my manage-
ment courses, I managed a group of eight people and gained experience in both
problem solving and dealing effectively with others.

My education in business communication and management also gives me the
ability to express my ideas clearly and effectively, both orally and in
writing; and, through my various jobs over the last five years, I gained
much experience in dealing with the public.  In my advanced courses, I
established the skills required to develop, edit, and present various busi-
ness reports, which would be especially helpful in organizing statements
and information for your organization.

I am a person who accepts challenges and responsibilities with the enthusiasm
and dedication of a professional.  As a manager, I would have the opportunity
to develop this professional attitude to its fullest and at the same time
make a valuable contribution to your company.

After you read my resume and talk with the people listed as references, I
would welcome the opportunity to discuss my qualifications with you.  I would
be available for an interview on short notice.

Sincerely,


Denice D. Tropp

Denice D. Tropp

enc
```

Source: Courtesy of Denice D. Tropp.

Exhibit C.3   Follow-up Correspondence

530 Locust Street, Apt. #1
Kalamazoo, MI 49007

April 2, 19xx

Ms. Mona Erickson, Personnel Officer
First National Bank and Trust Company of Michigan
108 East Michigan Avenue
Kalamazoo, MI 49007

Dear Ms. Erickson:

Thank you for discussing First American Bank Corporation's trainee program
with me on March 26, 19xx.

As we discussed, I will not be graduated until August, and you are looking
for two trainees to hire in April. After I am graduated, however, I would
be interested in learning more about your company.

Your programs and your organization impress me very much, and I believe
that I can make valuable contributions to your company. Should you decide
to hire another trainee at the end of the summer, please consider me for
that job. I will be available to work at the beginning of September.

Sincerely,

Denice D. Tropp
Denice D. Tropp

Index

Correction Symbols

Ab: Abbreviation. Avoid abbreviations in formal communication. With the exception of commonly used abbreviations (U.S., AFL), spell out the term the first time it is used and place the abbreviation in parentheses.

Ac: Accuracy. Be sure that names, addresses, and other information are correct.

Adapt: Adaptation. Adapt your message to your reader. Use individual names.

Agr: Agreement. Subjects and verbs must agree in number and in person. Pronouns and antecedents must agree in number, person, and in case.

Amb: Ambiguity. Statement is unclear.

Ap: Appearance.

Apos: Apostrophe.

Awk: Awkward.

Cap: Capitalize.

Case: Grammatical case. Use subject, object, and reflexive cases correctly.

Chop: Choppy. Use a variety of sentence structures. Avoid using all simple and short sentences.

Cl: Clarity. Message is unclear.

CM: Confidence in your message.

Coh: Coherence. Writing should flow smoothly from one sentence to another. Watch transitions between sentences and between paragraphs.

Con: Conciseness. Eliminate all unnecessary words and phrases.

Coop: Cooperation of equals. Avoid projecting feelings of either superiority or inferiority.

CR: Confidence in your reader.

CS: Comma splice. Separate two or more independent clauses with a period, a comma and a coordinating conjunction, or a semicolon.

CT: Conversational tone. Use natural language. Avoid jargon, clichés, and trite expressions.

D: Diction. Check dictionary for correct use of word.

Emp: Emphasis. Stress the point or idea.

Enc: Enclosure.

Exp: Expletive. Omit wordy and weak expressions, such as *it is, there are, there is.*

F: Format. Check margins, letter or report parts, and placement.

Fig: Figure. Use figure.

Fl: Flattery. Do not exaggerate.

Frag: Fragment. Sentence must express a complete thought and contain a subject and a verb.

Gob: Gobbledygook. Avoid garbled expressions or excessive use of legalese.

Gr: Grammar fault.